Fodor's The South

MW00398530

Fodor's Travel Publications, Inc.
New York • Toronto • London • Sydney • Auckland

Copyright © 1993
by Fodor's Travel Publications, Inc.

Fodor's is a registered trademark of Fodor's Travel Publications, Inc.

All rights reserved under International and Pan-American Copyright Conventions. Published in the United States by Fodor's Travel Publications, Inc., a subsidiary of Random House, Inc., New York, and simultaneously in Canada by Random House of Canada Limited, Toronto. Distributed by Random House, Inc., New York.

No maps, illustrations, or other portions of this book may be reproduced in any form without written permission from the publishers.

ISBN 0-679-02342-9

Fodor's The South

Editor: Andrew Collins
Contributors: John Branston, John Bowen, Edgar and Patricia Cheatham, Janet Clark, John English, Mitzi Gammon, Wayne Greenhaw, Sylvia Higginbotham, Ann Hughes, Tom Martin, Honey Naylor, Alexander Parsons, Marcy Pritchard, Francis X. Rocca, William Schemmel, Linda K. Schmidt, Carol L. Timblin, Chris Wohlwend
Creative Director: Fabrizio La Rocca
Cartographer: David Lindroth
Illustrator: Karl Tanner
Cover Photograph: Blohm/Masterfile

Design: Vignelli Associates

Special Sales

Fodor's Travel Publications are available at special discounts for bulk purchases (100 copies or more) for sales promotions or premiums. Special editions, including personalized covers, excerpts of existing guides, and corporate imprints, can be created in large quantities for special needs. For more information write to Special Marketing, Fodor's Travel Publications, 201 East 50th St., New York, NY 10022. Inquiries from Canada should be sent to Random House of Canada, Ltd., Marketing Dept., 1265 Aerowood Dr., Mississauga, Ontario L4W 1B9. Inquiries from the United Kingdom should be sent to Fodor's Travel Publications, 20 Vauxhall Bridge Rd., London, England SW1V 2SA.

MANUFACTURED IN THE UNITED STATES OF AMERICA
10 9 8 7 6 5 4 3 2 1

Contents

Maps

Foreword

While every care has been taken to ensure the accuracy of the information in this guide, the passage of time will always bring change and, consequently, the publisher cannot accept responsibility for errors that may occur.

All prices and opening times quoted here are based on information supplied to us at press time. Hours and admission fees may change, however, and the prudent traveler will avoid inconvenience by calling ahead.

Fodor's wants to hear about your travel experiences, both pleasant and unpleasant. When a hotel or restaurant fails to live up to its billing, let us know and we will investigate the complaint and revise our entries where the facts warrant it.

Send your letters to the editors of Fodor's Travel Publications, 201 E. 50th Street, New York, NY 10022.

Highlights'93 and Fodor's Choice

Highlights '93

Alabama The **Birmingham Civil Rights Institute** opened in fall 1992. Located across from Kelly Ingram Park and the 16th Street Baptist Church, the Institute traces the Civil Rights Movement from the end of World War I through the '80s and documents through music, storytelling, and multi-media presentations the on-going progress of race relations in Birmingham.

The **State Capitol** reopened for tours late in 1992 after an extensive renovation. Built in 1852 and the first capitol for the Confederate States of America, the building contains exhibits on Alabama history, Indians, military life, and more.

Five of the eight golf courses planned for the **Robert Trent Jones Golf Trail** around the state are now open: Oxmoor Valley in Birmingham, Magnolia Grove in Mobile, Hampton Cove in Huntsville, Grand National in Opelika-Auburn, and the Highlands in Dothan. Courses in Greenville and Anniston/Gadsden are slated to open in spring 1993.

The **Lake Guntersville Aero Replica Fighter Museum,** at Guntersville Airport, opened in spring 1992 and hosted Aerodome 92, a World War I aviation fly-in, Labor Day weekend.

Georgia The new $3-million **Atlanta Heritage Row,** in the heart of Underground Atlanta, features hands-on learning and fun for every age. Innovative multimedia presentations celebrate Atlanta's past, present, and future.

Also in Atlanta, the **New Georgia Railroad,** a vintage passenger train, offers Saturday trips around the city or to Georgia's Stone Mountain Park. On the Dinner Train you can have an elegant seated-and-served dinner, along with an evening excursion around Atlanta.

The **Georgia Veterans Memorial Golf Course** at Georgia Veterans State Park, Cordele, is a fine new 18-hole championship layout located among lush pine forests and bordering scenic wetlands. There's also a well-stocked pro shop, along with a swimming beach with pool and the 13,000-acre Lake Blackshear for fishing, boating, and waterskiing.

Savannah River Cruise Line now offers a superb dining experience nightly: cruising by Savannah's historic waterfront area on ***The Magnolia,*** a 200-passenger, 82-foot paddle wheeler.

Louisiana **Hurricane Andrew** slammed into the Louisiana coast in late August 1992, wreaking havoc on life and property. At press time, damage estimates are not known, but travelers to South Louisiana are advised to call hotels and visitor centers well before visiting the region. **New Iberia, Morgan City,** and **Franklin** are among the hardest hit areas. One thing *is* known: The storm spared the much-loved **Tabasco-sauce factory** on **Avery Island,** proving that even Mother Nature respects the fiery condiment.

In March 1992 **New Orleans International Airport** unveiled the first phase of its $20 million international concourse, which will be used by **United, Aeromexico, Aviateca, Lacsa, Sasha,** and **Taca.** The final phase of the airport expansion, set for completion in 1995, will add nine more gates, additional restrooms, and more concession and retail areas.

L'Express Airlines, the commuter line that served several Louisiana cities, folded this past year. However, in early 1992, **USAir Express** began service between New Orleans and Shreveport, and there is a possibility that service will be extended to other Louisiana destinations. Meanwhile, **American Eagle, Atlantic Southeast,** and **Continental** connect New Orleans with Lake Charles, Lafayette, and Baton Rouge.

Last year, the Louisiana Legislature passed a bill authorizing **riverboat gambling,** and in early 1992 the New Orleans Steamboat Company announced plans to build a 350-foot sternwheel gambling riverboat called ***America.*** Designed along the lines of a 19th-century floating palace, the four-deck, 3,000-passenger ***America*** will have 1,050 slot machines and 48 gambling tables. She'll make four cruises daily out of New Orleans on the Mississippi River. Other boat-builders are expected to soon follow suit.

The **Hotel New Orleans,** which will be located directly across from the New Orleans Convention Center in the Central Business District, is scheduled to open in spring 1993. The hotel will be part of the Hampton Inn chain. The $10 million project will result in an eight-story, 150-room lodging with 18 suites, two meeting rooms, in-room computer and fax hook-ups, a business center, and a health club.

Mississippi

The **Walter Anderson Museum of Art** in Ocean Springs provides a stunning backdrop for the work of this regional artist, noted for his unique vision of coastal plants, animals, and sea creatures.

The **Mississippi Agriculture & Forestry Museum** in Jackson offers a visit to a 1920s "Small Town," complete with Epiphany Episcopal Church, a general store, and a living-history farm. Also on the site are an **Aviation Museum** and other forays into Mississippi's colorful past.

Jackson's **Smith Robertson Museum and Cultural Center** recently opened the Mississippi Physicians Gallery, featuring Black physicians from throughout the state.

A new museum in Leland honors native **Jim Henson,** creator of the Muppets.

A new national park, **Natchez National Historical Park,** has been established to preserve and interpret the history of Natchez as a significant Southern community. Still in development, the park has acquired two properties, **Melrose,** an 80-acre antebellum estate with its Greek Revival mansion and original furnishings, and the **William Johnson House.** The Johnson House was built by a prominent, free black man in antebellum Natchez. Other historic homes are open for daily tours, too, in belle Natchez.

North Carolina In early 1992 High Point's **Furniture Discovery Center** opened downtown. It shares the history of furniture production and provides the world's only hands-on look at the step-by-step manufacture of home furnishings. Different styles of furniture—from Gothic to 21st-century—are displayed.

At **Carowinds,** located on the North Carolina–South Carolina border near Charlotte, the new attractions for 1992 are the **Rip Tide Reef,** a 6-acre waterpark with 5-foot water swells, and the **VORTEX,** a stand-up rollercoaster. The **Paladium** is attracting large crowds, following its $5 million expansion.

The **Pack Place Education Arts/Science Center** opened on July 4th in Asheville.

Winston-Salem's **Reynolda House,** the former home of R. J. Reynolds and now an art museum, reopened after extensive renovations. The museum's American art collection includes works dating from Colonial times to the present, its most outstanding piece being Frederic E. Church's *The Andes of Ecuador.*

Westglo Spa, the only European-style spa in the state, has opened in Blowing Rock. The facility includes a fully equipped fitness center, indoor pool, restaurant offering spa cuisine, and bed-and-breakfast accommodations.

South Carolina The state opened **Devils Fork State Park** on Lake Jocassee in fall 1991. It offers 20 luxurious lakeside villas, tent and RV camping, hiking and nature trails, fishing, and a boat dock.

Charleston opened its new **Visitor Reception & Transportation Center** in a renovated freight depot built in 1866 and on the National Register of Historic Places. Visitors enjoy displays, maps, paintings, and a film about the city. Parking is provided for cars and buses; carriage rides and trolleys depart from here. The **Anchorage Inn** near Waterfront Park in Charleston has been completely restored as a 17th-century seaside inn. Its 17 guest rooms and two deluxe suites are furnished in antiques and reproductions.

Sidney Park, Columbia's newest downtown park, has been well received.

Tennessee **The Knoxville Museum of Art,** a spectacular new facility faced in Tennessee pink marble, was designed by renowned architect Edward Larrabee of Barnes and Associates in

New York. There are four galleries, a connector gallery, sculpture terrace, Great Hall with a two-story window wall overlooking the World's Fair Park, an auditorium, museum shop/bookstore and indoor/outdoor café.

The new $8.8 million **Civil Rights Museum** opened in Memphis in mid-1991 on the site of the Lorraine Motel on Mulberry Street, where Dr. Martin Luther King, Jr., was shot. The pioneer institution, the first in the United States to honor the Civil Rights movement, has an interpretive education center and civil rights memorabilia.

Delta Ducks, colorfully decorated World War II amphibious carriers, now provide land and water sightseeing tours in Memphis. The Ducks cruise past landmarks in the downtown area, then plunge into the Mississippi River for a quick trip to Mud Island.

The Pyramid, a 320-foot, $62 million arena, is the new signature landmark of Memphis. The Pyramid houses a 20,000-seat arena. Additional space in the building is being developed for other attractions. Tours are available of this unique building located next to the Mississippi River.

Memphis's National Guard Armory complex underwent a $700,000 renovation to house the colorful new **Children's Museum of Memphis,** a hands-on learning adventure. Visitors can learn how a city works by commanding a fire engine, touring a manhole or climbing a skyscraper.

Housed in Nashville's Parthenon, the new ***Athena Parthenos*** is the world's largest indoor statue. *Athena* is made of lightweight gypsum cement with chopped fiberglass reinforcement. The original Athena in the Parthenon in Athens was made of ivory and gold, and plans are under way to gold-leaf Nashville's re-creation of the statue.

Virginia New vineyards continue to pop up in Virginia. Outside Charlottesville, **Oakencroft Vineyard and Winery** is now open for tours seven days a week April through December. A red barn nestled in the farm valley houses the winery and tasting room. At Leesburg, amid gently rolling hills along the Potomac River, **Tarara Vineyard and Winery** showcases award-winning wines aged underground in a cave. It's open for tours and tastings March through December.

There's now a new way to view Colonial Williamsburg Jamestown, Yorktown, and the James River plantations. **Historic Air Tours** offers a bird's-eye view of Revolutionary and Civil War battlefields, Indian village sites, and structures related to the Colonial past.

In Petersburg, **Battersea** has opened to the public. Built in 1770 by John Banister, the structure displays the Palladian influence of Virginia's finest Colonial plantation houses. Petersburg's **Siege Museum,** graphically depicting civilian life during the Civil War, has completed a major addition and is now fully accessible to visitors in wheelchairs.

Fodor's Choice

No two people will agree on what makes a perfect vacation, but it's fun and helpful to know what others think. We hope you'll have a chance to experience some of Fodor's Choices yourself while visiting the American South. For detailed information about each entry, refer to the appropriate chapters within this guidebook.

Alabama

Special Moments A drive through the elegant Birmingham suburb of Mountain Brook

Standing at the pulpit where Dr. Martin Luther King, Jr., first preached, at the Dexter Avenue King Memorial Baptist Church, Montgomery

Festivals Azalea Trail Festival, Mobile

Alabama Shakespeare Festival, Montgomery

Dining Highlands: A Bar and Grill, Birmingham *(Expensive)*

La Louisiana, Mobile *(Expensive)*

Sahara Restaurant, Montgomery *(Expensive)*

Original Oyster House, Gulf Shores *(Moderate)*

Lodging Marriott's Grand Hotel, Point Clear *(Very Expensive)*

Perdido Beach Hilton, Orange Beach *(Very Expensive)*

Original Romar House, Orange Beach *(Expensive)*

Riverfront Inn, Montgomery *(Expensive)*

Wynfrey Hotel, Birmingham *(Expensive)*

The Malaga Inn, Mobile *(Inexpensive–Moderate)*

Museums Mildred Warner House, Tuscaloosa

Oakleigh, Mobile

Montgomery Museum of Fine Arts, Montgomery

Georgia

Special Moments Cold beers and camaraderie at Manuel's Tavern, Atlanta

View from the lounge atop the Westin Peachtree Plaza Hotel, Atlanta

Sights, scents, and sounds of Harry's Farmer's Market, Atlanta

Choir singing at Ebenezer Baptist Church, Atlanta

St. Patrick's Day in Savannah

Scenic Drives Through the Historic District during the Cherry Blossom Festival, Macon

Festivals Peachtree Road Race on July 4th, Atlanta

Piedmont Arts Festival in Piedmont Park, Atlanta

Dining The Dining Room at the Ritz-Carlton, Atlanta *(Very Expensive)*

Abruzzi, Atlanta *(Expensive)*

Elizabeth on 37th, Savannah *(Inexpensive–Expensive)*

Buckhead Diner, Atlanta *(Moderate)*

Mrs. Wilke's Boarding House, Savannah *(Inexpensive)*

Lodging Cloister, Sea Island *(Very Expensive)*

Mulberry, Savannah *(Very Expensive)*

Ritz-Carlton Downtown, Atlanta *(Very Expensive)*

Eliza Thompson House, Savannah *(Expensive)*

Museums High Museum of Art, Atlanta

Coca-Cola Pavilion, Underground Atlanta

Nightlife Blues and beers at Blues Harbor, Atlanta

Early breakfast at the Majestic, Atlanta

Louisiana

Special Moments Pirates Alley in the early morning mists, New Orleans

View of the French Quarter from a riverboat, New Orleans

Waking up in the Madewood plantation house, Napoleonville

Strolling through Longue Vue House and Gardens, New Orleans

Browsing for posters and postcards on Royal Street, New Orleans

Zulu parade on Mardi Gras day, New Orleans

Scenic Drives Creole Nature Trail (LA 27), Sulphur to Lake Charles

Festivals Mardi Gras in Lafayette

Crawfish Festival, Breaux Bridge

A Creole Christmas, French Quarter, New Orleans

Festival International de Louisiane, Lafayette

Dining Commander's Palace, New Orleans *(Very Expensive)*

Arnaud's, New Orleans *(Expensive)*

Cafe Margaux, Lake Charles *(Moderate)*

Palace Cafe, New Orleans *(Moderate)*

Lodging Maison de Ville, New Orleans *(Expensive)*

Olivier House, New Orleans *(Expensive)*

Windsor Court, New Orleans *(Expensive)*

Hotel Acadiana, Lafayette *(Moderate)*

Museums Gallier House, New Orleans

Pitot House, New Orleans

Hermann-Grima House, New Orleans

Nightlife Dancing at Mulate's, Breaux Bridge

Cajun night at the Maple Leaf Bar, New Orleans

Sipping a Pimm's cup on the patio of the Napoleon House, New Orleans

Mississippi

Special Moments Watching the big, colorful balloons rise high above the bluffs, then cross the river into Louisiana, at the Great Mississippi River Balloon Race, Natchez

A drink and the spectacular view at the Delta Point Restaurant, Vicksburg

Feeling William Faulkner's presence in his study at Rowan Oak, Oxford

Standing under the live oaks in the grove at Jefferson Davis's home, Beauvoir, near Gulfport

A visit to Elvis's birthplace in Tupelo

Scenic Drives Natchez Trace (especially between Jackson and Natchez)

Any one of the many "pilgrimages" to antebellum mansions

Festivals Neshoba County Fair, off the Natchez Trace

Jubilee! JAM arts-and-music festival, downtown Jackson

Dining Nick's, Jackson *(Expensive)*

Tuminello's, Vicksburg *(Expensive)*

Lodging Millsaps-Buie House, Jackson *(Expensive–Very Expensive)*

Natchez Eola Hotel, *(Moderate–Expensive)*

Museums Walter Anderson's Home, Ocean Springs

Lauren Rogers Museum of Art, Laurel, east-central Mississippi

North Carolina

Special Moments Standing under the Gothic arches of Duke Chapel

Shooting the rapids on the Nantahala

Recalling the life of Carl Sandburg at Flat Rock

Observing 19th-century living at Old Salem

Festivals Brevard Music Festival

Folkmoot USA–North Carolina International Folk Festival, Waynesville/Maggie Valley

Old Salem Christmas, Winston-Salem

Dining Lamplighter, Charlotte *(Very Expensive)*

Marketplace on Wall Street, Asheville *(Expensive–Very Expensive)*

Angus Barn, Raleigh *(Expensive)*

Old Salem Tavern Dining Room, Winston-Salem *(Moderate–Expensive)*

Lodging Fearrington House, Pittsboro *(Very Expensive)*

Sanderling Inn, Duck *(Very Expensive)*

Green Park Inn, Bowling Rock *(Expensive–Very Expensive)*

Grove Park Inn and Country Club, Asheville *(Expensive)*

Brookstown Inn, Winston-Salem *(Moderate–Expensive)*

Homeplace, Charlotte *(Moderate–Expensive)*

Mast Farm Inn, Valle Crucis *(Moderate–Expensive)*

Museums Discovery Place, Charlotte

Mint Museum of Art, Charlotte

North Carolina Museum of Art, Raleigh

Museum of Early Southern Decorative Arts (MESDA), Winston-Salem

South Carolina

Special Moments Riding a mule-drawn farm wagon at the Plantation Stableyards in Middleton Place

Collecting shells and sand dollars on the beach at Kiawah Island

Boat tour among spring blooms reflecting in the black waters at Cypress Gardens

Relaxing in a rocking chair overlooking luxury yachts in the Harbour Town marina, Sea Pines on Hilton Head

Festivals Historic Charleston Foundation's Festival of Houses

Spoleto Festival USA and Piccolo Spoleto, Charleston

Dining Louis's Charleston Grill, Charleston *(Expensive)*

Robert's of Charleston Dinner Restaurant, Charleston *(Expensive)*

See Captain's House, Myrtle Beach *(Moderate)*

Magnolias–Uptown/Down South, Charleston *(Inexpensive)*

Lodging Mills House Hotel, Charleston *(Very Expensive)*

Omni Hotel at Charleston Place, Charleston *(Very Expensive)*

John Rutledge House Inn, Charleston *(Very Expensive)*

Westin Resort, Hilton Head Island *(Very Expensive)*

Radisson Resort Hotel, Myrtle Beach *(Expensive)*

Museums Charleston Museum, Charleston

Gibbes Art Gallery, Charleston

Patriots Point Naval and Maritime Museum, north of Charleston

Brookgreen Gardens, Murrells Inlet

Rice Museum, Georgetown

Tennessee

Special Moments Ducks on parade in the Peabody Hotel lobby, Memphis

Nashville's Country Christmas: decorations, entertainment, and multicultural events

Viewing the Great Smokies from Lookout Tower at Clingmans Dome, East Tennessee

Rhododendron Gardens in spring atop Roan Mountain, East Tennessee

Festivals Memphis in May International Festival

National Storytelling Festival, Jonesborough

Dining Burning Bush, Gatlinburg *(Moderate–Expensive)*

Miss Mary Bobo's Boarding House, Lynchburg *(Inexpensive)*

Lodging Buckhorn Inn, Gatlinburg *(Very Expensive)*

Opryland Hotel, Nashville *(Very Expensive)*

Peabody, Memphis *(Very Expensive)*

Chattanooga Choo-Choo Holiday Inn, Chattanooga *(Moderate–Expensive)*

Hyatt Regency Knoxville *(Moderate–Expensive)*

Museums Pink Palace Museum, Memphis

Tennessee State Museum, Nashville

Country Music Hall of Fame and Museum, Nashville

Christus Gardens, Gatlinburg

American Museum of Science and Energy, Oak Ridge

Off the Beaten Track Agricenter International, Memphis

Lichterman Nature Center, Memphis

Joe L. Evins Appalachian Center for Crafts, Smithville

Virginia

Special Moments Changing of the guard at the Tomb of the Unknown Soldier, Arlington Cemetery

Running of the ponies at Chincoteague Island

Scenic Drives Blue Ridge Parkway

Skyline Drive

Festivals Spring and fall Foxfield Races, Charlottesville

Virginia Highlands Festival, Abingdon

Dining Eastern Standard, Charlottesville *(Expensive)*

Millie's, Richmond *(Expensive)*

Waterwheel Restaurant, Warm Springs *(Expensive)*

Lodging Jefferson Sheraton Hotel, Richmond *(Very Expensive)*

Mayhurst, Orange *(Expensive)*

Museums Lee Memorial Chapel and Museum, Lexington

Museum of American Frontier Culture, Staunton

Nightlife Whitey's, Arlington

Murphy's Grand Irish Pub, Alexandria

Off the Beaten Track Association for Research and Enlightenment, Virginia Beach

George Washington Masonic National Memorial, Alexandria

The South
ILLINOIS
INDIANA
Springfield
Indianapolis
70
MISSOURI
Jefferson City
St. Louis
64
Louisville
Frankfort
57
55
KENTUCKY
24
40
Nashville
TENNESSEE
24
ARKANSAS
40
45
Chattanooga
Memphis
Huntsville
Little Rock
40
78
55
65
59
Tupelo
278
61
78
65
20
Birmingham
MISSISSIPPI
59
ALABAMA
280
20
20
85
Shreveport
Meridian
20
Montgomery
Jackson
59
LOUISIANA
61
55
84
65
231
Natchitoches
45
84
Natchez
49
Baton Rouge
10
Mobile
49
12
Pensacola
Biloxi
10
10
Lake Charles
Lafayette
New Orleans
N
Gulf of Mexico

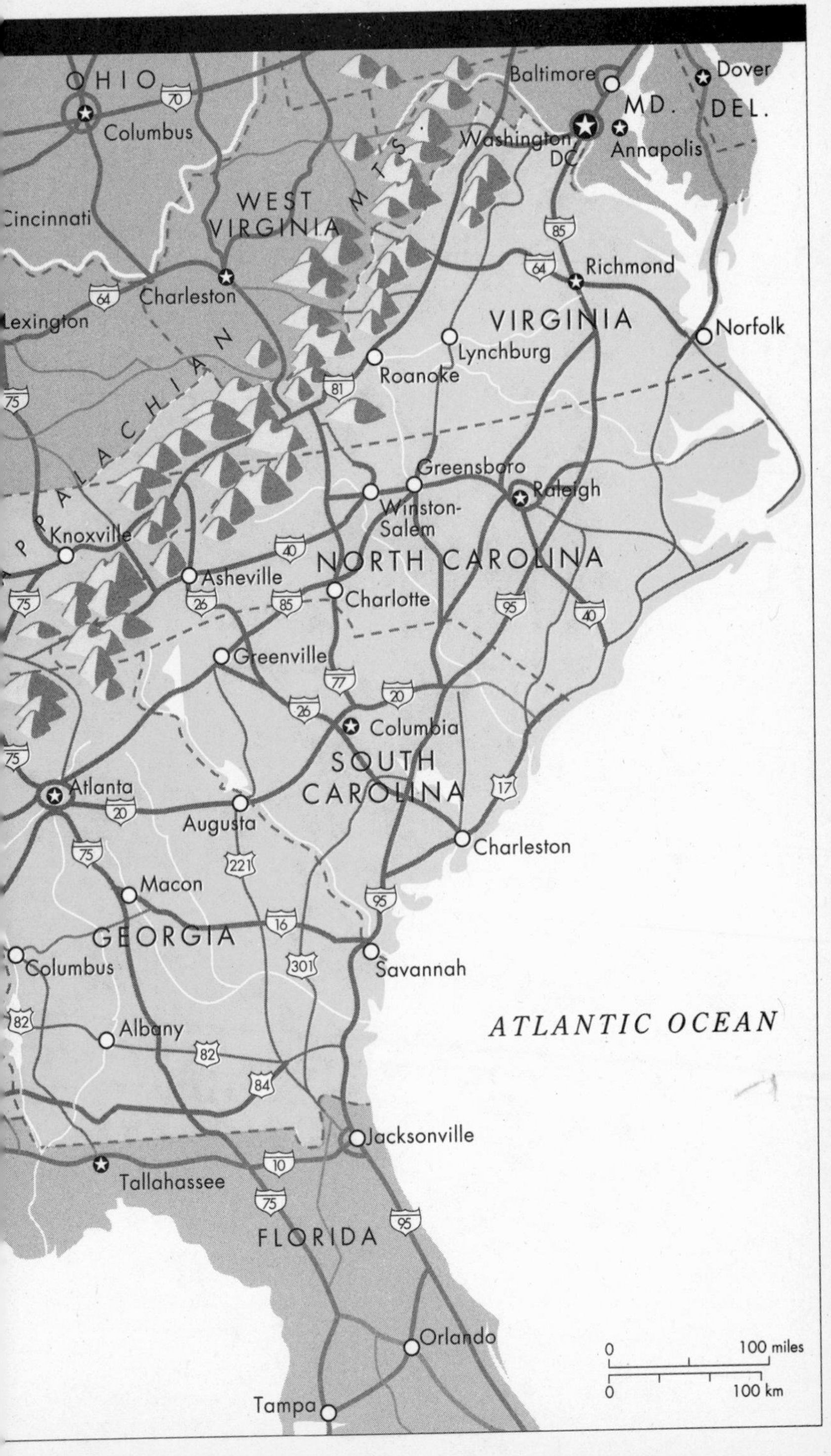
OHIO
Columbus
Cincinnati
Lexington
WEST VIRGINIA
Charleston
APPALACHIAN MTS.
Baltimore
Dover
MD.
DEL.
Washington DC
Annapolis
Richmond
VIRGINIA
Norfolk
Lynchburg
Roanoke
Greensboro
Raleigh
Winston-Salem
Knoxville
Asheville
NORTH CAROLINA
Charlotte
Greenville
Columbia
SOUTH CAROLINA
Atlanta
Augusta
Charleston
Macon
GEORGIA
Savannah
Columbus
Albany
ATLANTIC OCEAN
Jacksonville
Tallahassee
FLORIDA
Orlando
Tampa
0
100 miles
0
100 km
70
64
81
75
40
26
85
95
77
20
17
221
16
301
82
84
10

The United States

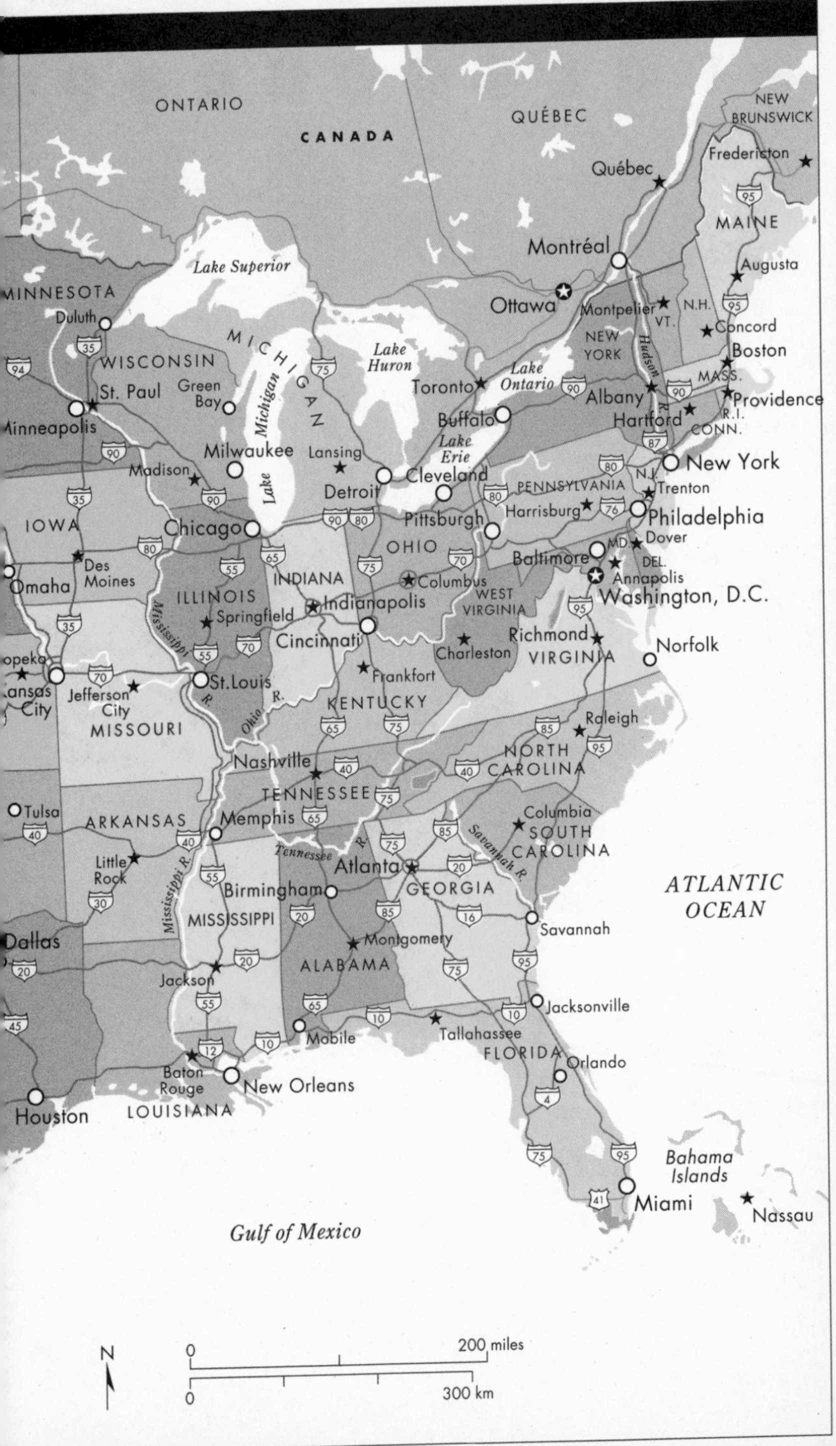
ONTARIO
CANADA
QUÉBEC
NEW BRUNSWICK
Fredericton
Québec
MAINE
Augusta
Montréal
Ottawa
Montpelier
VT.
N.H.
Concord
Boston
MASS.
Providence
R.I.
CONN.
Hartford
Albany
NEW YORK
Hudson R.
Lake Superior
MINNESOTA
Duluth
WISCONSIN
MICHIGAN
Lake Michigan
Lake Huron
Lake Ontario
Lake Erie
St. Paul
Minneapolis
Green Bay
Milwaukee
Madison
Lansing
Detroit
Cleveland
Toronto
Buffalo
New York
N.J.
Trenton
PENNSYLVANIA
Harrisburg
Philadelphia
Pittsburgh
IOWA
Des Moines
Omaha
Chicago
ILLINOIS
Springfield
INDIANA
Indianapolis
OHIO
Columbus
WEST VIRGINIA
Charleston
Baltimore
MD.
DEL.
Dover
Annapolis
Washington, D.C.
Richmond
VIRGINIA
Norfolk
Cincinnati
Frankfort
KENTUCKY
Topeka
Kansas City
Jefferson City
MISSOURI
St. Louis
Mississippi R.
Ohio R.
Nashville
TENNESSEE
Raleigh
NORTH CAROLINA
Tulsa
ARKANSAS
Memphis
Little Rock
Columbia
SOUTH CAROLINA
Savannah R.
Tennessee R.
Atlanta
GEORGIA
Birmingham
MISSISSIPPI
ALABAMA
Montgomery
Savannah
Dallas
Jackson
Mobile
Tallahassee
Jacksonville
FLORIDA
Orlando
Baton Rouge
New Orleans
Houston
LOUISIANA
ATLANTIC OCEAN
Bahama Islands
Miami
Nassau
Gulf of Mexico
N
0
200 miles
0
300 km

World Time Zones

Numbers below vertical bands relate each zone to Greenwich Mean Time (0 hrs.). Local times frequently differ from these general indications, as indicated by light-face numbers on map.

Algiers, **29**
Anchorage, **3**
Athens, **41**
Auckland, **1**
Baghdad, **46**
Bangkok, **50**
Beijing, **54**
Berlin, **34**
Bogotá, **19**
Budapest, **37**
Buenos Aires, **24**
Caracas, **22**
Chicago, **9**
Copenhagen, **33**
Dallas, **10**
Delhi, **48**
Denver, **8**
Djakarta, **53**
Dublin, **26**
Edmonton, **7**
Hong Kong, **56**
Honolulu, **2**
Istanbul, **40**
Jerusalem, **42**
Johannesburg, **44**
Lima, **20**
Lisbon, **28**
London (Greenwich), **27**
Los Angeles, **6**
Madrid, **38**
Manila, **57**

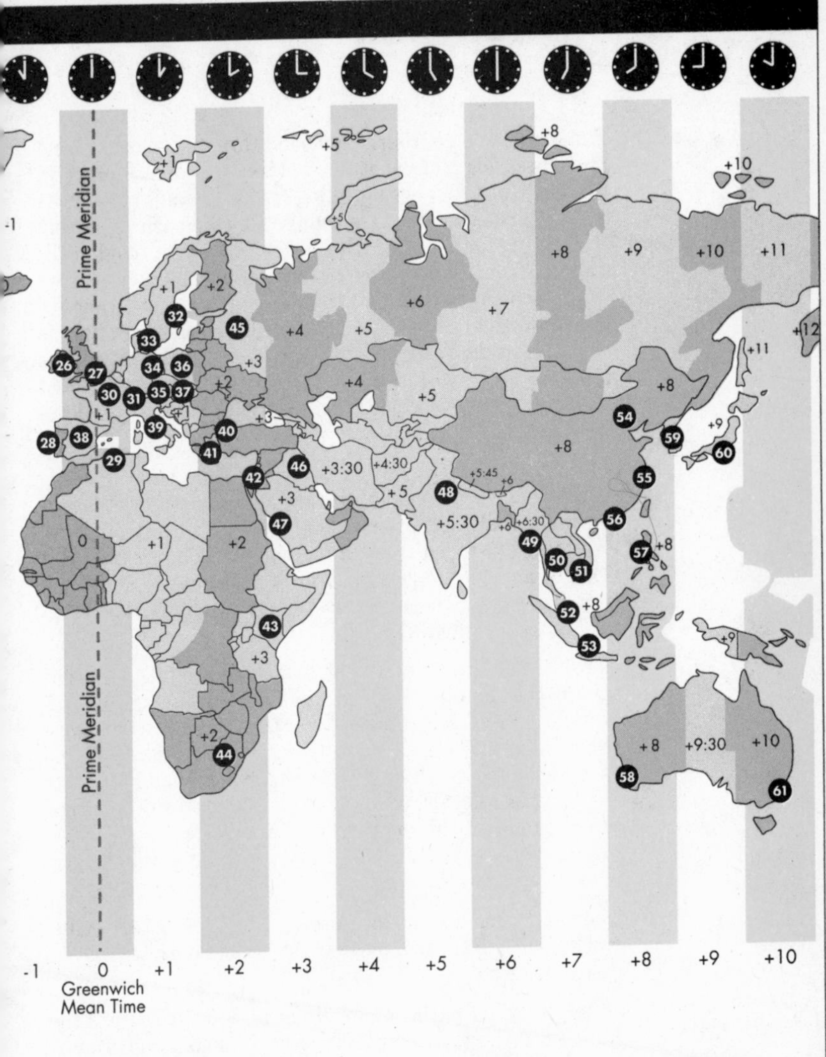

Mecca, **47**
Mexico City, **12**
Miami, **18**
Montréal, **15**
Moscow, **45**
Nairobi, **43**
New Orleans, **11**
New York City, **16**
Ottawa, **14**
Paris, **30**
Perth, **58**
Reykjavík, **25**
Rio de Janeiro, **23**
Rome, **39**
Saigon (Ho Chi Minh City), **51**
San Francisco, **5**
Santiago, **21**
Seoul, **59**
Shanghai, **55**
Singapore, **52**
Stockholm, **32**
Sydney, **61**
Tokyo, **60**
Toronto, **13**
Vancouver, **4**
Vienna, **35**
Warsaw, **36**
Washington, D.C., **17**
Yangon, **49**
Zürich, **31**

Introduction

By Honey Naylor

If you hear a Southern farmhand threaten to cut off one of his arms and eat it, don't scream and call for help. That's just his way of saying that he is hungry—or, as he is also likely to put it, "so hungry my stomach thinks my throat's been cut." A Southern man is not just tired or ill-used. He feels "like I've been rode hard and put up wet" (the reference being to letting a hard-ridden horse unlather before stabling it). A Southern woman in the midst of a tizzy is "running around setting my hair on fire." And if things don't work out right, she may "have to go to bed with a cold rag on my head"; in an extreme case, she may "go completely to pieces."

A proclivity to exaggerate is at the very core of every Southerner's soul, and he will take any opportunity to exercise it—for all Southerners simply *love* to talk. A Southerner setting out to make a transaction, whether it's buying a Coke or a condo, is viscerally aware that in the South the first order of business is almost never business. It's "visiting"—passing the time of day.

Out of these two tendencies—to talk and to talk big—has sprung the age-old Southern tradition of spinning colorfully embroidered stories, which in turn has spawned some great American storytellers. The original version of Thomas Wolfe's novel *Of Time and the River* was about the length of 12 average novels, or twice the length of *War and Peace*. Simply unable to stem the flow of words, he stopped writing only after his editor told him that the novel was finished.

Thomas Wolfe was a Southerner, a native of Asheville, North Carolina, which means that he was born with a bad case of logorrhea.

Other notable Southern storytellers are Mississippi's two Pulitzer Prize winners, Tennessee Williams and Eudora Welty, and its Nobel Prize winner, William Faulkner. All three wrote of eccentric, complex, and occasionally bizarre characters caught up in Byzantine plots, as did Savannah-born Flannery O'Connor, author of *Wise Blood*.

Faulkner wrote his first novel in an apartment overlooking Pirates Alley in New Orleans—a city that gave the world Truman Capote and Lillian Hellman, and which Tennessee Williams called "my spiritual home." A Pulitzer was awarded posthumously to New Orleanian John Kennedy Toole, who wrote the wildly funny *A Confederacy of Dunces*. Frances Parkinson Keyes bought a historic home in the French Quarter of New Orleans, where she wrote *Dinner at Antoine's* and *Steamboat Gothic*. The brilliant Walker Percy, a native of Birmingham, won the National

Book Award for his first novel, *The Moviegoer*, and continued to turn out literary gems from his home in Covington, Louisiana.

In Flat Rock, North Carolina, the home of Pulitzer Prize-winning poet and biographer Carl Sandburg, is a National Historic Site. Tom Wolfe, author of *Bonfire of the Vanities*, was born in Richmond, and Pat Conroy, who write *Prince of Tides*, lives in Atlanta. Margaret Mitchell, also of Atlanta, wrote only one book in her life, but that book was *Gone With the Wind*—the biggest-selling novel of all time.

For other Southerners, the words soar off the page and into the air. The Southland gave birth to the blues, to jazz, and to songwriters and singers of every stripe. The King—Elvis—grew up in Tupelo, Mississippi, and launched his astonishing career in a Memphis recording studio. Each year millions of Presley fans make the pilgrimage to Graceland, his showy home and final resting place in Memphis. Florence, Alabama, gave us W. C. Handy, who first played his "St. Louis Blues" in a Memphis saloon, and Savannah produced Johnny Mercer, a songwriter of considerable notes. The versatile Wynton Marsalis, the late Louis Armstrong, and the lively Pete Fountain are among the scores of great jazzmen from New Orleans, where jazz itself was born. Leontyne Price of Laurel, Mississippi, sang the role of Bess on Broadway in *Porgy and Bess* before giving voice to opera on a grand scale.

Speaking of which, opera lovers the world over flock to the annual Spoleto Festival USA in Charleston and to Wolf Trap Farm in Virginia, both of which also feature theater, ballet, and jazz. In the spring, musicians from as far away as Australia and Finland turn up for the Jazz and Heritage Festival in New Orleans, a city that is not exactly jazzless the rest of the year. Out in the bayous of South Louisiana, contagious Cajun music has virtually the whole world two-stepping; and up in the Blue Ridge Mountains of Virginia and North Carolina, the hills sing with bluegrass music. Tennessee has produced more country-music songwriters, singers, and musicians than you can shake a mike at, and Nashville, the "Country Music Capital of the World," is the foot-stomping ground of the Grand Ole Opry.

"Dixie," incidentally, penned in 1859 by Yankee Dan Emmett, was a marching song originally played by bands of both the North and the South as they paraded into the Recent Unpleasantness—a period of time known to everyone but Southerners as the Civil War.

The Civil War, with a few exceptions, notably Gettysburg, was fought on Southern soil. South Carolina, inflamed by the rhetoric of firebrand John C. Calhoun, was the first state to secede, causing a Union loyalist to snap, "South Carolina is too small for a republic and too big for a lunatic asylum." But the first shots rang out over Charleston Harbor, and the bloody war began. Virtually every Southern city, country crossroad, and sleepy creek was touched by the war, and even now the memories linger on, preserved for all time in yet more colorful stories, passed along from generation to generation in the rooms of antebellum mansions throughout the South.

Today, south of the Mason-Dixon Line (surveyed in the 1700s by British astronomers Charles Mason and Jeremiah Dixon to settle a territorial dispute between Pennsylvania and Maryland), there are almost as many Civil War commemorative plaques as there are black-eyed peas. A slew of the South's most famous sights were once the scenes of hideous battles. Glitzy, modern Atlanta literally grew up out of the ashes Sherman left behind, and Virginia's luxuriant Shenandoah Valley was savaged by Phil Sheridan. Lookout Mountain, Tennessee, with its stunning view, was a vantage point that both sides fought for pretty keenly, and down in Mississippi, Vicksburg held Grant off for 47 days and nights before surrendering. New Orleans fell not long after Farragut shouted, "Damn the torpedoes, full speed ahead!"

The region is also fertile territory for aficionados of earlier American history. Notwithstanding the fame of that piece of rock up in Massachusetts, the first permanent English settlement in the New World was established in Jamestown, Virginia. Pocahontas had saved John Smith's life, married John Rolfe, gone to England to be presented to the king and queen, and died, all before the Pilgrims turned up. Fort Moultrie, South Carolina, is the site of the fledgling nation's first decisive victory over the British during the Revolutionary War, and in Yorktown, Virginia, Cornwallis surrendered to General George Washington after the "victory that made a Nation."

Natchitoches, Louisiana, was the first permanent settlement in the territory comprising the Louisiana Purchase, and the town has a small but beautifully restored historic district. (Holding title to the "oldest" or "first in this country" is dear to the hearts of tradition-cherishing Southerners, and visitors may find themselves deluged with the latter adjectives.) New Orleans's French Quarter, famed for Bourbon Street jazz haunts and exquisite Creole cuisine, is the original colony founded by French Creoles, and there are important historic districts in Savannah, Charleston, and Mobile. At Colonial Williamsburg, capital of Virginia from 1699 to 1779, a whole village has been created with costumed bakers, blacksmiths, and craftsfolk demonstrating various aspects of early Colonial life in authentic surroundings. Adjacent to the Colonial village is the serene green campus of the College of William and Mary, whose illustrious graduates include Thomas Jefferson and James Madison.

But the South is much more than time-honored historic sites. It is a vast sports arena for snow-skiers and water-skiers, scuba divers and horseback riders, spelunkers and hunters, shrimpers and saltwater anglers, hikers, bikers, tennis buffs, golfers, and beachcombers.

Lush carpets of white sand roll down the Atlantic Coast and sweep along the Gulf of Mexico. Seekers of sun and fun head for such resorts as Virginia Beach, Virginia; Sea Island, Georgia; and, in the Carolinas, Cape Hatteras, Hilton Head Island, and Myrtle Beach. Alabama barely sticks its big toe in the Gulf, but Mobile Bay's swank resorts and colorful artists' colonies are among the state's most popular attractions. Twenty-six miles of sun-kissed beaches stretch along the Mississippi coast, dotted with resorts such as Pascagoula, Pass Christian, and Biloxi.

If beaches bore you, there are plenty of hills to head for. The breathtakingly beautiful Blue Ridge Mountains roll through Virginia, the Carolinas, and northern Georgia, and the Great Smokies soar over the North Carolina–Tennessee border. Playgrounds abound in "them thar hills," such as Gatlinburg, Tennessee, and Blowing Rock, North Carolina. From lookout points on Virginia's serpentine Skyline Drive there are soul-stirring views of the mountains and the Shenandoah Valley.

One last note before you go: If you expect to hear the Hollywood version of a Southern accent, you're likely to be surprised. About the only generalization that can be made is that the Southern voice is gentle and soft—except at football games and hog-calling contests. You *will* hear drawls and "y'alls." ("Y'all," incidentally, is a contraction of "you all." It's the equivalent of "you guys," something you will almost never hear a Southerner say.) The Tidewater Virginia accent bears little resemblance to the sounds of south Louisiana, where the language isn't even English—it's Cajun French. And in New Orleans you'll hear an accent that is soft, slightly slurred, but decidedly Brooklynese.

The truth is, the voices of the South are as rich and varied as the land itself. In its shops, restaurants, and homes you can be sure you'll hear those melodic Southern voices say, "Y'all come back."

And that's not just whistling Dixie.

1 Essential Information

Before You Go

Visitor Information

Contact each of the following state travel bureaus for free tourist information. If you wish to speak to a travel representative, you must call the bureau directly; for a free travel information packet, call the toll-free "800" number.

Alabama Bureau of Tourism and Travel (401 Adams Ave., Box 4309, Montgomery, AL 36103–4614, tel. 205/242–4169 or 800/ ALABAMA).
Georgia Department of Industry, Trade and Tourism (Box 1776, Atlanta, GA 30301, tel. 404/656–3950 or 800/VISIT–GA).
Louisiana Office of Tourism (Box 94291, Baton Rouge, LA 70804–9291, tel. 504/342–8100 or 800/334–8626).
Mississippi Division of Tourism (Box 849, Jackson, MS 39205, tel. 601/359–3297 or 800/647–2290).
North Carolina Division of Travel and Tourism (430 N. Salisbury St., Raleigh, NC 27611, tel. 919/733–4171 or 800/VISIT NC).
South Carolina Division of Tourism (1205 Pendleton St., Box 71 Columbia, SC 29202, tel. 803/734–0235).
Tennessee Department of Tourism (Box 23170, Nashville, TN 37202, tel. 615/741–2158).
Tourism Development Group, Virginia Department of Economic Development (1021 E. Cary St., Richmond, VA 23219, tel. 804/ 786–2051 or 800/932–5827).

Tour Groups

If you prefer to have someone else drive while you sit back and enjoy the ride, you might do well to consider a package tour. Although you will have to march to the beat of a tour guide's drum rather than your own, you are likely to save money on airfare, hotels, and ground transportation while covering a lot of territory. For the more experienced or adventurous traveler, there are a variety of special-interest and independent packages available. Listed below is a sample of available options. Check with your travel agent for additional resources.

When considering a tour, be sure to find out exactly what expenses are included (particularly tips, taxes, side trips, additional meals, and entertainment), ratings of all hotels on the itinerary and the facilities they offer, cancellation policies for both you and the tour operator, and if you are traveling alone, what the single supplement is. Most tour operators request that bookings be made through a travel agent; there is no additional charge for doing so.

General-interest Tours

Mayflower Tours (1225 Warren Ave., Downers Grove, IL 60515, tel. 708/960–3430, or outside Illinois, tel. 800/323–7604) offers a six-day tour of New Orleans during the spring and fall.

Bixler Tours (Box 37, Hiram, OH 44234, tel. 216/569–3222 or 800/325–5087) can take you to Atlanta, North Carolina and Cape Hatteras, The Homestead in Virginia, the Grand Ole Opry, and the Smoky Mountains.

Domenico Tours (751 Broadway, Bayonne, NJ 07002, tel. 800/ 554–TOUR or 201/823–8687) offers tours of New Orleans, New

Orleans/Memphis/Nashville, and Atlanta. The Texas/New Orleans/Cajun Country tour traverses Louisiana and Texas, and includes a swamp cruise, while the Smoky Mountains tour takes in Nashville, Gatlinburg, and Great Smoky Mountains National Park.

Gadabout Tours (700 E. Tahquitz Way, Palm Springs, CA 92262, tel. 619/325–5556 or 800/952–5068) offers a "Sentimental South" tour designed for those who yearn for antebellum mansions, Civil War lore, and grits and gravy. The "Spring in the South" tour includes several days in Florida.

Globus Gateway/Cosmos (9525 Queens Blvd., Rego Park, NY 11374, tel. 718/268–7000 or 800/556–5454) offers three colorful Southern tours: "Heritage of the Deep South" concentrates on Louisiana, Mississippi, and Alabama. "Country Western USA" highlights Memphis and Nashville. "The Old South and the Golden Isles" winds its way from Atlanta to Charleston, with a stopover on Jekyll Island, among other spots.

Landmark Tour and Travel (4663 First Ave. N, Birmingham, AL 35222, tel. 205/592–5001 or 800/338–4714) offers tours of New Orleans, Cajun Country, Memphis, Nashville, and other southern destinations, plus more than 30 different tours of Alabama.

Maupintour (Box 807, Lawrence, KS 66044, tel. 913/843–1211 or 800/255–4266) takes a step back in time with "Historic Savannah and Charleston." Tours of the Carolinas are also available during the spring and fall.

Tauck Tours (Box 5027, Westport, CT 06880, tel. 800/468–2825 or 203/226–6911) also features an eight-day trip to Charleston and Savannah, including Jekyll Island and Hilton Head. Other tours include a few days of steamboating on the Mississippi River.

Special-interest Tours

Adventure: *Wilderness Southeast* (711 Sandtown Rd., Savannah, GA 31410, tel. 912/897–5108) runs rugged trips through places such as the Okefenokee Swamp in Georgia and the Everglades in Florida.

African-American History: Groups of 15 to 49 who are interested in exploring America's black heritage may want to check out the Pathways to African-American Heritage tours of 40 different states organized by **Pepper Bird Foundation** (Box 69081, Hampton, VA 23669, tel. 804/723–1106). They will customize a trip to your needs, or you can join in on a set three-day tour including Hampton University, Yorktown, Colonial Williamsburg, Monticello, and more. The **Alabama Bureau of Tourism and Travel** (*see* Visitor Information, *above*) offers a self-guided Black Heritage tour that includes 163 sites and five suggested itineraries. The **Birmingham Convention & Visitors Bureau** (2200 9th Ave. N, Birmingham, AL 35203, tel. 205/252–9825) has a self-guided Black Heritage tour of 11 marked sites that relate to the city's history. **The Beach Institute** (E. Harris and Price Sts., Savannah, GA 31401, tel. 912/234–8000) has ongoing exhibits and programs that focus on the black experience in Georgia. In Atlanta, **Lowder City Tours, Inc.** (tel. 404/874–1349 or 800/354–1961) and **Gray Line** (tel. 404/767–0594) offer black heritage tours. **Old Salem** (600 S. Main St., Winston-Salem, NC 27101, tel. 919/721–7300) includes African-American interpretations at each site in the village.

Olympics: Lowder City Tours, Inc. of Atlanta (tel. 404/874–1349 or 800/354–1961) takes visitors on tours of the Olympics sites. (The company plans to do a Margaret Mitchell tour sometime in the future.)

Package Deals for Independent Travelers

American Fly AAway Vacations (tel. 817/355–1234 or 800/321–2121) offers city packages with discounts on hotels and car rental. Also check with **United Vacations** (tel. 800/328–6877), **Delta Air Lines** (tel. 800/872–7786, and **Continental Airlines** (tel. 800/634–5555) for city packages as well as fly/drive deals.

Tips for British Travelers

Government Tourist Office

The United States Travel and Tourism Administration (Box 1EN, London WIA 1EN, tel. 071/495–4466) will send brochures and advise you on your trip to the American South.

Passports and Visas

You will need a valid 10-year passport (cost £15). You do not need a visa if you are staying for fewer than 91 days, have a return ticket, are flying with a participating airline, and complete a visa waiver form (I–94W), available at the airport or on the plane. There are some exceptions to this, however, so check with your travel agent or with the United States Embassy (Visa and Immigration Dept., 5 Upper Grosvenor St., London W1A 2JB, tel. 071/499–3443). No vaccina-tions are required.

Customs

Visitors 21 or older can take in 200 cigarettes or 50 cigars or 2 kilograms of tobacco; 1 liter of alcohol; duty-free gifts to a value of $100. Do not try to take in meat or meat products, seeds, plants, fruits, etc. Avoid illegal drugs like the plague.

Returning to Britain, you may bring home: (1) 200 cigarettes or 100 cigarillos or 50 cigars or 250 grams of tobacco; (2) two liters of table wine with additional allowances for (a) one liter of alcohol over 22% by volume (most spirits), or (b) two liters of alcohol under 22% by volume (fortified or sparkling wine); or (c) two more liters of table wine; (3) 60 milliliters of perfume and 250 milliliters of toilet water; and (4) other goods worth up to £32 but not more than 50 liters of beer or 25 cigarette lighters.

Insurance

We recommend that you insure yourself to cover health and motoring mishaps. **Europ Assistance** (252 High St., Croydon, Surrey CRO 1NF, tel. 081/680–1234) offers comprehensive policies. It is also wise to take out insurance to cover loss of luggage (though check that this isn't already covered in an existing homeowner's policy). Trip-cancellation insurance is another wise buy. **The Association of British Insurers** (51 Gresham St., London EC2V 7HQ, tel. 071/600–3333) will give advice on all aspects of vacation insurance.

Tour Operators

Jetsave (Sussex House, London Rd., East Grinstead, West Sussex RH19 1LD, tel. 0342/312033) offers a 15-day American Jamboree tour taking in New Orleans and Orlando, as well as New York. **Premier Holidays** (Premier Travel Center, Westbrook, Milton Rd., Cambridge CB4 1YQ, tel. 0223/355977) offers the 16-day Dixieland Discovery tour, including New Orleans, Atlanta, Savannah, Charleston, Nashville, and Memphis. They also have 14-night self-drive packages in Virginia and the Carolinas, and a "Southern Belle" tour of several states.

Airfares If you are traveling independently, your best bets for a low-price air ticket are APEX fares. Check with the major airlines, which fly to most Southern cities: **American Airlines** (tel. 0800/010151), **British Airways** (tel. 081/897–4000), **Continental Airlines** (tel. 0293/776464), **Delta Airlines** (tel. 0800/414767), **TWA** (tel. 071/439–0707), and **Virgin Atlantic Airways** (tel. 0293/562000).

If you can afford to be flexible about when you travel, try the small ads in daily or Sunday newspapers for last-minute flight bargains, but check that all airport taxes are included in the price quoted.

When to Go

Spring is probably the most attractive season in this part of the United States. Cherry blossoms are followed throughout the region by azaleas, dogwood, and camellias from April into May, and by apple blossoms in May.

Seasonal and special events occur throughout the year. Festivals (folk, craft, art, and music) tend to take place in the summer, as do sports events. State and local fairs are held mainly in August and September, though there are a few in early July and into October. Historical commemorations are likely to occur at any time of the year.

Climate In winter, temperatures generally average in the low 40s in inland areas, in the 60s by the shore. Summer temperatures, modified by mountains in some areas, by sea breezes in others, range from the high 70s to the mid-80s, now and then the low 90s.

The following are average daily maximum and minimum temperatures for sample Southern cities.

Birmingham, Alabama

Jan.	56F	13C	**May**	82F	28C	**Sept.**	86F	30C
	35	2		58	14		63	17
Feb.	58F	14C	**June**	89F	32C	**Oct.**	77F	25C
	37	3		66	19		51	11
Mar.	65F	18C	**July**	90F	32C	**Nov.**	64F	18C
	42	6		69	21		40	4
Apr.	74F	23C	**Aug.**	90F	32C	**Dec.**	56F	13C
	50	10		65	20		35	2

Atlanta, Georgia

Jan.	52F	11C	**May**	79F	26C	**Sept.**	83F	28C
	36	2		61	16		65	18
Feb.	54F	12C	**June**	86F	30C	**Oct.**	72F	22C
	38	3		67	19		54	12
Mar.	63F	17C	**July**	88F	31C	**Nov.**	61F	16C
	43	6		70	21		43	6
Apr.	72F	22C	**Aug.**	86F	30C	**Dec.**	52F	11C
	52	11		70	21		38	3

New Orleans, Louisiana	**Jan.**	63F	17C	**May**	83F	28C	**Sept.**	86F	30C
		47	8		68	20		74	23
	Feb.	65F	18C	**June**	88F	31C	**Oct.**	79F	26C
		50	10		74	23		65	18
	Mar.	72F	22C	**July**	90F	32C	**Nov.**	70F	21C
		56	13		76	24		56	13
	Apr.	77F	25C	**Aug.**	90F	32C	**Dec.**	65F	18C
		61	16		76	24		49	9
Jackson, Mississippi	**Jan.**	59F	15C	**May**	85F	29C	**Sept.**	88F	31C
		38	3		63	17		65	18
	Feb.	63F	17C	**June**	92F	33C	**Oct.**	81F	27C
		41	5		70	21		54	12
	Mar.	68F	20C	**July**	94F	34C	**Nov.**	67F	19C
		47	8		72	22		43	6
	Apr.	76F	24C	**Aug.**	94F	34C	**Dec.**	61F	16C
		54	12		70	21		40	4
Raleigh, North Carolina	**Jan.**	50F	10C	**May**	78F	26C	**Sept.**	81F	27C
		29	-2		55	13		60	16
	Feb.	52F	11C	**June**	85F	29C	**Oct.**	71F	22C
		30	-1		62	17		47	8
	Mar.	61F	16C	**July**	88F	31C	**Nov.**	61F	16C
		37	3		67	19		38	3
	Apr.	72F	22C	**Aug.**	87F	31C	**Dec.**	52F	11C
		46	8		66	18		52	11
Charleston, South Carolina	**Jan.**	59F	15C	**May**	81F	27C	**Sept.**	84F	29C
		41	6		64	18		69	21
	Feb.	60F	16C	**June**	86F	30C	**Oct.**	76F	24C
		43	7		71	22		59	15
	Mar.	66F	19C	**July**	88F	31C	**Nov.**	67F	19C
		49	9		74	23		49	9
	Apr.	73F	23C	**Aug.**	88F	31C	**Dec.**	59F	11C
		56	13		73	23		42	6
Nashville, Tennessee	**Jan.**	46F	8C	**May**	79F	26C	**Sept.**	83F	28C
		28	-2		57	14		61	16
	Feb.	51F	11C	**June**	87F	31C	**Oct.**	72F	22C
		30	-1		65	18		48	9
	Mar.	60F	16C	**July**	90F	32C	**Nov.**	59F	15C
		38	3		69	21		32	3
	Apr.	71F	22C	**Aug.**	89F	32C	**Dec.**	50F	10C
		48	9		68	20		31	-1
Norfolk, Virginia	**Jan.**	48F	9C	**May**	76F	24C	**Sept.**	80F	27C
		32	1		57	14		64	18
	Feb.	50F	10C	**June**	83F	28C	**Oct.**	70F	21C
		32	1		65	19		53	13
	Mar.	58F	14C	**July**	87F	31C	**Nov.**	61F	16C
		39	4		70	22		43	7
	Apr.	68F	19C	**Aug.**	86F	29C	**Dec.**	52F	11C
		48	9		70	21		35	2

For current weather conditions in foreign and domestic cities, call the **Weather Channel Connection** (tel. 900/WEATHER) from a touch-tone phone. In addition to the weather report you'll hear the local time; helpful travel tips; and hurricane, foliage, and ski reports. The call costs 95¢ per minute.

Festivals and Seasonal Events

Starting with Mardi Gras in New Orleans and ending with Christmas in Natchez, Mississippi, the Southern states hold a wide variety of festivals and special events throughout the year. The following is a sample. For more complete listings of events, contact the Division of Tourism in each state.

January **Alabama:** *Senior Bowl All-Star Classic* is played in Mobile. *Camillias* are in full splendor at Mobile's Bellingrath Gardens, beginning in early January and lasting through February.

Georgia: A *Rattlesnake Roundup* is held in Whigham. *Savannah Marathon* and *Half Marathon* are run. *Martin Luther King, Jr., Week* is celebrated in Atlanta.

Louisiana: The *Sugar Bowl Classic* is played on New Year's Day in New Orleans. *Louisiana Fur and Wildlife Festival* is held in Cameron. The *New Orleans Classical Music Festival* is traditionally held late in the month.

Mississippi: The *Meridian Bud Light Superbowl—Chili Cookoff* is held in Biloxi.

North Carolina: *The Charlotte Observer Marathon* and *Runner's Expo* take place in Charlotte.

South Carolina: Orangeburg invites the country's finest coon dogs to compete in the *Grand American Coon Hunt.*

Virginia: *Robert E. Lee's Birthday* is celebrated at his boyhood home in Alexandria and in his home in Lexington. *Stonewall Jackson's Birthday* is celebrated at his home in Lexington.

February **Alabama:** *Mardi Gras* is celebrated in Mobile and Gulf Shores. *Farm-City Week* is held annually at Selma's Convention Center. *Black History Month* events are held at Tuskegee University in Tuskegee and the W. C. Handy home in Florence. Mobile holds the *Azalea Trail and Festival* during the peak blooming of azaleas. The annual *Renaissance Festival* is held at Dauphin Island. The Clarke County Wildlife Association hosts the *State Turkey Calling Contest* in Jackson. The *Southeastern Livestock Exposition Rodeo and Livestock Week* is held in Montgomery.

Georgia: *Georgia Day Event* is held in Savannah. A two-day *Arts and Crafts Georgia Festival* is held in Kennesaw. Dublin/Laurens County has a *St. Patrick's Festival,* while Fort Valley stages the *Camillia Festival.*

Louisiana: *Mardi Gras* is New Orleans's—and the South's—biggest annual parade and party. *The International Crawfish Tasting and Trade Show* is held in Lafayette.

Mississippi: Biloxi and Natchez celebrate *Mardi Gras.* In Jackson, the *Dixie National Livestock Show* runs most of the month in conjunction with the *Dixie National Rodeo* and the *Dixie National Western Festival.*

North Carolina: Asheville welcomes visitors to its annual *Winterfest Arts and Crafts Show.* Wilmington stages the *N. C. Jazz Festival.* Waxhaw welcomes visitors to the *Women's Antiques Show and Sale.*

South Carolina: Charleston has the *Tour of Charming Dwellings* and the annual *Southeastern Wildlife Exposition,* showcasing original wildlife art. Rock Hill's Museum of York County hosts *Africa Alive.*

Tennessee: Nashville hosts the *Americana Craft Sampler* show. *Heart of the Country Antiques* is at Opryland.

Virginia: *Mardi Gras* is celebrated in Norfolk. Mount Vernon and other towns in Virginia commemorate *George Washington's Birthday.* Alexandria stages a 200-unit parade in his memory. The Colonial Williamsburg Foundation holds the annual *Antiques Forum.*

March **Alabama:** The *Sea Oats Jamboree* is held in Gulf Shores. *Cherry Festival* is held in Montgomery. The annual *Turkey Calling Class* is held in Bessemer; the *Southeastern Turkey Calling Contest* is in Montgomery. Fairhope hosts its *Arts and Crafts Festival.*

Georgia: *Rattlesnake Roundup* is held in Claxton. Macon hosts its *Cherry Blossom Festival.* And *St. Patrick's Day* is especially colorful in Atlanta and Dublin. Callaway Gardens in Pine Mountain has the *Azalea Festival.*

Louisiana: Ville Platte hosts the *Boggy Bayou Festival.* Iowa celebrates its *Rabbit Festival.* The *Tennessee Williams/New Orleans Literary Festival* is a three-day event in New Orleans.

Mississippi: You can revisit the Old South during pilgrimages to antebellum mansions and gardens in Natchez, Port Gibson, Vicksburg, and Columbus. The *Natchez Pow-Wow* at the Grand Village of the Natchez Indians also takes place.

North Carolina: An 18th-century military encampment and Revolutionary War battle reenactment bring history to life on the *Anniversary of the Battle of Guilford Courthouse* in Greensboro. Mooresville hosts the annual *Old Time Fiddlers' and Bluegrass Convention.* Amateur and professional golfers compete in the *K Mart Greater Greensboro Open.*

South Carolina: *Springfest* lasts all month on Hilton Head Island. Charleston welcomes visitors to its *Festival of Houses and Gardens,* and Beaufort holds its *Spring Tour of Homes.* Myrtle Beach stages *Canadian-American Days.* Aiken is the site of the *Aiken Triple Crown.*

Tennessee: Gatlinburg hosts the *Great Smoky Arts and Crafts Community Spring Show.*

Virginia: Fredericksburg welcomes more than 130 artists to its annual *Fine Arts Festival. St. Patrick's Day* is cause for big celebrations in Norfolk. *National Wildlife Week Celebration* takes place at the Virginia Living Museum in Newport News.

April **Alabama:** *Fort Blakely Battle Festival* takes place in Spanish Fort. Birmingham holds the *Festival of Arts.* The annual *Dauphin Island Sailing Regatta* fills Mobile Bay with hundreds of sailing vessels. A *Civil War re-enactment* draws thousands to Selma in late April. Eufaula stages its annual *Pilgrimage and Antique Show. Heritage Week* is held in Tuscaloosa.

Georgia: *Atlanta Dogwood Festival* is held throughout the capital. *River Days* are celebrated at River Front Park in Albany. The *Masters Golf Tournament* is held in Augusta. Waycross holds the *Okefenokee Spring Fling*. Lake Lanier Islands sponsors an *Easter Egg Hunt*.

Louisiana: The *Louisiana Crawfish Festival* takes place in St. Bernard. In New Orleans, major events include the *French Quarter Festival*, *Spring Fiesta*, and the *New Orleans Jazz and Heritage Festival*. *Festival International de Louisiane* is an extravaganza in Lafayette and the *Strawberry Festival* in Ponchatoula is a must.

Mississippi: Eleven Gulf Coast communities—including Carrollton, Holly Springs, and Aberdeen—hold *Spring Pilgrimages* of historic homes. The *World Catfish Festival* is celebrated in Belzoni. *The Landing of d'Iberville* is reenacted in Ocean Springs.

North Carolina: Fayetteville dresses up for its *Dogwood Festival* and Pope Air Force Base and Fort Brag hold a joint open house. The Biltmore Estate is abloom during the *Festival of Flowers*. Southern Pines and Tryon host prestigious *steeplechases*. Wilkesboro holds the annual *Merle Watson Memorial Festival* featuring Doc Watson, his father and renowned bluegrass picker, and other musicians. Wilmington hosts the *North Carolina Azalea Festival*. Late in the month, Charlotte holds its annual *Springfest* and Chadburn its annual *North Carolina Strawberry Festival*.

South Carolina: Art, gardens, tours, concerts, and more are a part of *Rock Hill's Come-See-Me Festival*. Hilton Head Island hosts the *MCI Heritage Classic* and the *Family Circle Magazine Cup* tennis tournament. *Riverfest* is held in Columbia.

Tennessee: Knoxville holds a *Dogwood Arts Festival*. *The World's Biggest Fish Fry* is held in Paris. The annual *Spring Wildflower Pilgrimage* sets off from Gatlinburg.

Virginia: An annual *Dogwood Festival* is held in Charlottesville. Norfolk holds the *International Azalea Festival*. *Historic Garden Week* is celebrated at more than 200 houses and 50 historical landmarks in the state. The *Virginia Horse Festival* is held at the Virginia Horse Center in Lexington. Fredericksburg stages the *Pear Blossom Festival*.

May **Alabama:** The *Alabama Jubilee Hot Air Balloon Classic* takes place in Decatur and the *Montgomery Jubilee* happens near the month's end. Huntsville hosts *Panoply*, an arts festival.

Georgia: It's *"Stay and See Georgia"* at Underground Atlanta. *Prater Mill Country Fair* is held in Dalton. *Arts-on-the-River Weekend* is held in Savannah. Special events mark *Memorial Day* weekend on Jekyll Island and in Savannah.

Louisiana: May brings the *Rose Festival* in Shreveport, the *Louisiana Praline Festival* in Houma, and the *Breaux Bridge Crawfish Festival* in odd-numbered years.

Mississippi: *Jubilee Jam* in Jackson features music and the arts, as do the *Gum Tree Festival* in Tupelo and the *Atwood Music Festival* in Monticello, and the *Jimmie Rodgers Country Music Festival* in Meridian.

North Carolina: Nags Head is the location for the annual *Hang Gliding Spectacular*. Raleigh stages *Artsplosure;* Winston-Salem, *The Crosby;* and Durham, the *Duke Children's Classic*. Musicians meet in Union Grove for the *Ole Time Fiddlers & Bluegrass Festival*.

South Carolina: *Spoleto Festival USA* in Charleston is one of the world's biggest arts festivals. Running concurrently with Spoleto is *Piccolo Spoleto*, which showcases local and regional talent. *Mayfest* takes place in Columbia. Beaufort's *Gullah Festival* highlights the fine arts, customs, and dress of Lowcountry blacks, and Gullah, the African-Caribbean language they speak.

Tennessee: *Memphis in May International Festival* is celebrated all month. *International Folkfest* is held in Murfreesboro. *Knoxville Water Sports Festival* means canoe, kayak, and rowing competitions.

Virginia: The *Jamestown Landing Celebration* is held in Williamsburg and Jamestown. *Spring wildflowers* are celebrated in Shenandoah National Park and at Wintergreen Resort. *Steeplechases* are held at The Plains and at Morven, and *tours of the Virginia hunt country* are given in Upperville and Middleburg. Yorktown has a *Civil War reenactment*. The *Shenandoah Apple Blossom Festival* is in Winchester.

June **Alabama:** The music group Alabama hosts *June Jam* in Fort Payne. Birmingham celebrates the arts with *City Stages*. The *Gehart Chamber Music Festival* takes place in Guntersville. A *Seafood Festival* is held throughout the summer in Bayou la Batre.

Georgia: Stone Mountain Village holds an annual *Festival of the Arts*. Jekyll Island celebrates *Country by the Sea*.

Louisiana: June is food month, with the *Okra Festival* in Kenner, the *Jambalaya Festival* in Gonzales, the *Great French Market Tomato Festival* and *La Fete* in New Orleans, the *Louisiana Blueberry Festival* in Mansfield, the *Feliciana Peach Festival* in Clinton, and the famed *Louisiana Catfish Festival* in Des Allemands.

Mississippi: Biloxi hosts the colorful *Blessing of the Fleet, Shrimp Festival*, and *Black Heritage and Culture Juneteenth Celebration*. The *Bear Creek Festival* is celebrated at Tishomingo State Park and Natchez celebrates *Steamboat Jubilee* with "flozzie" contests. Greenwood hosts the *Mississippi International Balloon Classic*, and Monticello holds the *Pioneer Pilgrimage of Lawrence County* celebrating pioneer life. The *American Dance Festival* is held at Duke University in Durham. The North Carolina Zoological Park celebrates *Zoo and Aquarium Month*. Beech Mountain holds a storytelling festival featuring masters such as Ray Hicks. The *Brevard Music Festival* begins and continues through early August.

North Carolina: The *Kitty Hawk Triathlon* includes hang gliding, windsurfing, and sailing at Nags Head.

South Carolina: *Sun Fun Festival* is held in the Grand Strand. Hampton hosts the *Hampton County Watermelon Festival*, while Greenwood stages the annual *South Carolina Festival of Flowers*.

Tennessee: The *International Country Music Fan Fair* is held in Nashville, and the *Carnival Music Festival* is held in Memphis. The *Riverbend Festival* is held in Chattanooga.

Virginia: The *June Jubilee* is held in Richmond. Norfolk's *Harborfest* enlivens that city's waterfront. The state's "products of the vine" are appreciated at the *Virginia Wineries Festival* in Great Meadow, The Plains.

July **Alabama:** *Alabama Deep Sea Fishing Rodeo* is held in Mobile and on Dauphin Island.

Georgia: In Atlanta, there's the *Independence Festival* and the popular *Peachtree Road Race*, and the *WSB Salute to America parade*. Rockmart hosts the *Homespun Festival*. Major *July Fourth* celebrations are held in Savannah and Columbus.

Louisiana: Galliano hosts the *Louisiana Oyster Festival*. *Cajun Bastille Day* is celebrated in Baton Rouge for three days and Franklinton hosts the *Washington Parish Watermelon Festival*.

Mississippi: The *Deep Sea Fishing Rodeo* in Gulfport is one of the largest fishing contests in the South. In Philadelphia, a major event is the *Choctaw Indian Fair;* the *Watermelon Festival* is held in Mize. Other events you shouldn't miss include the reenactment of the *Final Days of the Civil War* battle in Vicksburg; the *Chunky Rhythm and Blues Festival* in Meridian; and the *"Slugburger" Festival* in Corinth, recalling Depression times when you could buy slugburger (hamburger mixed with bread) for only 5 cents.

North Carolina: In Asheville, clog and figure dancing are part of the *Shindig-on-the-Green*. The annual *Highland Games & Gathering of the Scottish Clans* is held on Grandfather Mountain near Linville. Sparta throws a *Christmas in July* party. *Folkmoot USA–North Carolina International Festival* begins and continues through early August in various mountain communities. Kill Devil Hills hosts the *Wright Kite Festival*.

South Carolina: *July Fourth* is commemorated in Greenville with *Freedom Weekend Aloft*, the second-largest balloon rally in the country. The *South Carolina Peach Festival* is held in Gaffney.

Tennessee: The *Tennessee Peach Festival* is held in Brownsville. *Kingsport Fun Fest* is in Kingsport and *Sportsfest* is in Morristown.

Virginia: *Independence Day* celebrations are annual traditions around the state, including Yorktown, where America's independence was won. *Shenandoah Valley Music Festival* is held in Orkney Springs. Chincoteague stages the annual *pony swim and auction*.

August **Alabama:** The famed *W.C. Handy Festival* goes on in Florence for a week.

Georgia: A *Beach Music Festival* is held on Jekyll Island. *Sea Island Festival* is centered in St. Simons. Hiwassee hosts the *Georgia Mountain Fair*. The *Madison Theatre Festival* is held in Madison.

Louisiana: Morgan City hosts the *Louisiana Shrimp and Petroleum Festival*.

Mississippi: The *Roscoe Turner Hot Air Balloon Race* takes place in Corinth. Greenwoods hosts *Crop Day*, celebrating the history of cotton.

North Carolina: Asheville holds the annual *Mountain Dance and Folk Festival* and, later in the month, the *Annual Summerfest Art and Craft Show*. Kill Devil Hills celebrates *National Aviation Day*. The *North Carolina Apple Festival* is held in Hendersonville.

South Carolina: The *Waccamaw Riverfest* is a citywide event in Conway.

Tennessee: *Elvis International Tribute Week* is held in Memphis. The *Appalachian Fair* is held in Gray, and Shelbyville hosts the *Tennessee Walking Horse National Celebration*.

Virginia: Norfolk hosts the *Jazz Festival*. In Manassas, the *Prince William County Fair* is a large agricultural and industrial exposition. Abingdon stages the *Virginia Highlands Festival*. *1791 Court Days* are observed in Leesburg. The *Hampton Cup Regatta* is held.

September **Alabama:** Gulf Shores hosts the annual *Orange Beach Fishing Rodeo*. The *Rocking Horse World Celebration* takes place in Decatur. Alabama's *Scottish heritage* is celebrated in Montgomery. Greensboro stages the *Alabama Catfish Festival*.

Georgia: *Oktoberfest* begins in Helen, and the *Hot Air Balloon Festival* is held there also. Atlanta hosts the *Fine Arts and Crafts Festival* in Piedmont Park. Georgia's music industry is celebrated throughout the state during the *Georgia Music Festival*.

Louisiana: Truly a festival month, some of the best are Houma's *Labor Day Pirogue Race Festival;* the Southwest *Zydeco Music Festival* in Plaisance; the *Frog Festival* in Rayne; *Festival Acadiens* in Lafayette, and the *Louisiana Sugar Cane Festival* in New Iberia.

Mississippi: West Point hosts the *Prairie Arts Festival*, Columbus the *Possum Town Pig Fest*, Indianola the *Indian Bayou Arts and Crafts Festival*, and Biloxi the *Seafood Festival*. The *Delta Blues Festival* is held in Greenville.

North Carolina: The annual *Woolly Worm Festival* takes place in Banner Elk. Raleigh hosts the *Artsplosure Jazz & Heritage Music Festival*. Seniors 50 and older congregate at Maggie Valley's *Golden Gathering*. Statesville holds the *National Balloon Rally*. Sixty thousand visitors flock to the *Benson mule days* for music, food, and rodeos.

South Carolina: *South Carolina Apple Festival* is held in Westminster. Spartanburg holds the *International Festival*. From late September to early October, Charleston's ten-day *Moja Arts Festival* celebrates the rich African-American and Caribbean cultures found in the Lowcountry.

Tennessee: Nashville hosts the *Tennessee State Fair*. *Artfest* brings visual and performing arts to Knoxville. The *Mid-South Fair* is held in Memphis.

Virginia: The *Apple Harvest Arts & Crafts Festival* is held in Winchester. The *State Fair of Virginia* and *Civil War Days* are held in Richmond.

October **Alabama:** *National Shrimp Festival* is held in Gulf Shores. Spanish Fort hosts the annual *Blakeley Bluegrass Festival* and the *National Peanut Festival* takes place in Dothan, and the *Chitlin' Jamboree* in Clio. *Riverfront Market* is hosted by Selma.

Georgia: *Cotton Days Festival* begins in Marietta. Dalton stages the second *Praters' Mill Country Fair* of the year. The *Georgia National Fair* in Perry highlights agriculture. Dahlonega celebrates *Goldrush Days*. The annual *Fall Bluegrass Festival* is held in Blue Ridge. *National Pecan Festival* is held in Albany. Savannah celebrates its *Oktoberfest*, and *Heritage Holidays* are commemorated in Rome.

Louisiana: Shreveport hosts the week-long *Red River Revel Arts Festival*. The *Gumbo Festival* is held in Bridge City. The *Louisiana Cotton Festival* is held in Ville Platte. Shreveport hosts the *Louisiana State Fair*. New Orleans hosts the *Festa d'Italia*.

Mississippi: The *Scottish Highland Games* are held in Biloxi. Holly Springs stages a *haunted house and hayride*, while Washington offers *ghost tales* around the campfire. Natchez stages the *Fall Pilgrimage*. Jackson has its *Mistletoe Market* late in the month, and Vaughn has *Hobo Day*.

North Carolina: *Clogging champions* are declared at the Stompin' Ground in Maggie Valley. The annual *Fall Festival* is held at the John C. Campbell Folk School at Brasstown. Barbecue and a parade of pigs guarantee fun at the *Lexington Barbecue Festival*. Wilmington is the scene of the spooky *Halloween Festival*.

South Carolina: Top fishermen vie for prizes at the *Arthur Smith King Mackerel Tournament* in North Myrtle Beach. *Halloween* festivities are especially colorful in Charleston, Greenville, and Georgetown.

Tennessee: *Dollywood National Crafts Festival* is held all month in Pigeon Forge. The *Gatlinburg Fall Craftsmen's Fair* is also month-long. Jonesborough hosts the popular *National Storytelling Festival*. Memphis and Clarksville celebrate *Oktoberfest*.

Virginia: Charlottesville revels during the *Bacchanalian Feast/Monticello Wine Festival*, while special *Halloween celebrations* are held in Norfolk, Petersburg, and Staunton. Danville hosts the *Harvest Jubilee & World Tobacco Auctioneering Championship*. *Railroading* is the theme of festivals in Appottomax and Roanoke.

November **Alabama:** *Creek Indian Thanksgiving Day Homecoming and Pow Wow* is held in Poarch, near Atmore. Theodore has a *Pecan Festival*, and Anniston hosts a *Winter Market* for early Christmas shoppers.

Georgia: *Mistletoe Market* is held in Albany. Savannah holds its *Festival of Trees*. *Cane grinding parties* are thrown in Tifton and Juliette.

Louisiana: *Louisiana Pecan Festival* is held in Colfax. Shreveport's *Christmas in Roseland* begins this month and continues through December.

Mississippi: The *Richland Pumpkin Festival* is held in Richland, the *Coast Dixieland Jazz Festival* in Biloxi, and the *Peter Anderson Art Festival* in Ocean Springs.

North Carolina: The *Seagrove Pottery Festival* showcases the works of Sandhills potters. *"Light Up Your Holidays,"* including Christmas at Biltmore, begins in Asheville and continues through December, while Riverfront Park in Wilmington is illuminated nightly.

South Carolina: *Christmas Connection* enlivens Myrtle Beach, as does *Dickens Christmas Show and Festival.*

Tennessee: *Mid-South Arts and Crafts Show/Sale* is held in Memphis.

Virginia: *Holidays in the City* is celebrated in Norfolk. *Virginia Thanksgiving Festival* at Berkeley Plantation in Charles City County commemorates the first official Thanksgiving in 1619. *Hunt races* are held in Montpelier.

December **Alabama:** *Christmas on the River* is held at Demopolis. The main cave of DeSoto Caverns at Childersburg is illuminated from now through Epiphany. *Christmas at Arlington* takes place in Birmingham, and Wetumpka hosts *Christmas on the Coosa.*

Georgia: *Walhaachtsmorkt* (Christmas market) begins in Helen and continues through December. Atlanta hosts its *Holiday Tour of Homes* and the *Peach Bowl and Parade.* Special Christmas celebrations are held in Savannah, at Callaway Gardens, and on Jekyll Island.

Louisiana: *Creole Christmas* is celebrated in the French Quarter of New Orleans. The *Plaquemines Parish Fair and Orange Festival* is held at Fort Jackson. Natchitoches becomes the *City of Lights* with displays along the Cane River.

Mississippi: Special Christmas events, from boat parades to singing Christmas trees, are held in Jackson, Natchez, Meridian, Greenwood, Leland, Inverness, Vicksburg, Aberdeen, Laurel, and Hattiesburg. Biloxi celebrates with *Christmas on the Water.*

North Carolina: Candlelight tours are staged in towns across the state, including Hillsborough, Wilmington, Raleigh, and New Bern. Winston-Salem re-creates a Moravian Christmas during *Old Salem Christmas.* The *Historic Oakwood Candlelight Tour* is held in Raleigh. *First Night Charlotte* is a New Year's Eve festival on the Town Square.

South Carolina: Christmas is celebrated all over the state, with events lasting the entire month in Charleston. Performed by the Senior Lights, a choir from John's Island, the *African-American Spiritual Concert* is held in Charleston's historic Drayton Hall.

Tennessee: *Christmas in the City* is a month-long Knoxville celebration. *Smoky Mountain Christmas* is held in Gatlinburg. Nashville's *Trees of Christmas* light up all month at Cheekwood.

Virginia: *Grand Illumination* takes place in Colonial Williamsburg, and Christmas is celebrated in the old-fashioned way with hot cider, cookies, and gifts during the *Christmas Special. Christmas at Belle Grove* is a Middletown tradition as is the *Yule Log Lighting* in Norfolk. Norfolk also celebrates a *waterfront New Year's Eve Festival*.

What to Pack

Generally, the South has hot, humid weather during the summer and sunny, mild weather in the winter. For winters in the southernmost tier of states, pack a lightweight coat, slacks, and sweaters. The northern tier of Southern states can be very cold and damp in the winter. Snow is not unusual, so be prepared. For summer visits, keep the high humidity level in mind and pack cotton and natural fabrics that breathe. You'll need an umbrella for sudden summer showers, but leave the plastic raincoats behind because the humidity makes them extremely uncomfortable. Take a jacket or sweater for summer evenings, or for restaurants that have air-conditioning going full blast. Always take insect repellent during the summer because the mosquitoes come out in full force after sunset.

Carry-on Luggage Passengers are allowed one piece of carry-on luggage on international flights from the United States. The bag can't exceed 45 inches (length + width + height) and must fit under the seat or overhead.

Checked Luggage Passengers may check two pieces of luggage; neither can exceed 62 inches (length + width + height) or weigh more than 70 pounds. Allowances vary slightly among airlines, so check before you go.

Getting Money from Home

Cash Machines
Withdrawals It's easy to use automated-teller machines (ATMs) to withdraw money from your checking account with a bank card. Just get the name of affiliated cash-machine networks before your departure. (For locations for two of the larger networks, **Cirrus** and **Plus,** call 800/4–CIRRUS or 800/THE–PLUS in the U.S.) Note that you may be charged a fee for withdrawals away from your home turf. Of course, you need to get a personal identification number (PIN) if you don't already have one.

Cash Advances You can also use ATMs to get cash advances on your credit card, provided you have a PIN number for your card. As with cash advances from tellers, you pay interest from the day of posting, and some banks tack on an additional service charge.

For both withdrawals and cash advances there are usually limits on the amount you can access within a given time period. Check ahead.

Bank Transfers It's easiest to transfer money between like branches; otherwise, the process takes a couple days longer and costs more.

American Express Cardholder Services The company's **Express Cash** system links your checking account to your Amex card. For each transaction there's a 2% fee (minimum $2, maximum $6). Call 800/227–4669 for information. Cardholders can also cash personal or counter checks at any American Express office for up to $1,000, of which $500 may be claimed in cash and the balance in traveler's checks carrying a 1% commission.

Wiring Money To send or receive up to $10,000, you can use an **American Express MoneyGram,** and you don't have to have an American Express card. The sender goes to an American Express

MoneyGram agent, specifies an amount, pays up to $1,000 with a credit card (anything more than that in cash), and telephones the receiver with the reference number he is given. The receiver goes to the nearest MoneyGram agent, presents identification and the reference number, and picks up cash. Fees are 5%–10%, depending on the amount and method of payment (AE, D, MC, V accepted). For agent locations call 800/543–4080.

You can also use **Western Union** (tel. 800/325–6000). A friend at home can bring either cash or a check to the nearest office or pay over the phone with a credit card. Delivery usually takes two business days, and fees are roughly 5%–10%.

Traveling with Film

If your camera is new, shoot and develop a few rolls of film before leaving home. Pack some lens tissue and an extra battery for your built-in light meter. Store film in a cool, dry place—never in a glove compartment or on the shelf under a car's rear window.

On a plane, never pack unprocessed film in checked luggage; an X-ray may ruin it. Carry undeveloped film with you through security and ask to have it inspected by hand. Keep your film in a plastic bag, ready for quick inspection. At American airports, requests for hand inspection are honored.

Car Rentals

Outside of south Florida, New Orleans and Atlanta are the South's biggest car-rental centers. **Hertz** (tel. 800/654–3131), **Avis** (tel. 800/331–1212), **National** (tel. 800/328–4567), **Budget** (tel. 800/527–0700), **Thrifty** (tel. 800/367–2277), **American International** (tel. 800/225–2529), **Sears** (tel. 800/527–0770), and **Dollar** (tel. 800/800–4000) have airport locations in New Orleans, Atlanta, Memphis, Jackson, Birmingham, Nashville, Louisville, Charleston, Columbia, Charlotte, and Raleigh. Mid-size cities like Fayetteville, Baton Rouge, and Augusta have at least three or four of the above companies, plus local and regional firms. Expect to pay $35–$45 daily for a subcompact in larger cities, with 75–100 free miles daily. **Alamo** (tel. 800/327–9633) offers some of the region's lowest rates, though it does not have offices in all cities. Unlimited free mileage these days seems to be the exception rather than the rule. Be careful when renting a car for a multistate Southern trip: Many rental companies tack in-state driving restrictions onto their unlimited-mileage specials.

Local and regional companies sometimes skirt the over-25 age restriction and credit-card requirements of many large companies; sometimes they have lower rates, too. Birmingham has **Agency** (tel. 800/321–1972). Nashville and Memphis also have **Agency.** Jackson has **Just A Ride** (tel. 601/355–7433) and **ATR** (tel. 601/948–3391). Raleigh has **Enterprise** (tel. 800/325–8007) and **Triangle** (tel. 919/851–2555). Charleston has **Alamo** and **Enterprise. Columbia, SC, has Not A Lemon Rent-A-Car** (tel. 803/782–2640), Charlotte has **Enterprise** (tel. 704/535–1550, 704/553–8233, 704/391–0061), **Spirit** (tel. 704/532–0064, 704/553–9191), and **Agency** (tel. 704/553–7616, 704/537–7272).

It's always best to know a few essentials *before* you arrive at the car-rental counter. Find out what the collision damage waiver (usually an $8–$12 daily surcharge) covers and whether your corporate or personal insurance already covers damage to a rental car (if so, bring a photocopy of the benefits section along). More and more companies are now also holding renters responsible for theft and vandalism damages if they don't buy the CDW; in response, some credit-card and insurance companies are extending *their* coverage to rental cars. Check the coverage provided by your credit-card company or your car-insurance carrier. Find out, too, if you must pay for a full tank of gas whether you use it or not; and make sure you get a reservation number.

Traveling with Children

Publications ***Family Travel Times,*** an 8- to 12-page newsletter published 10 times a year by Travel with Your Children (45 W. 18th St., 7th floor Tower, New York, NY 10011, tel. 212/206–0688). Subscription costs $35 and includes access to back issues and twice-weekly opportunities to call in for specific advice.

Great Vacations with Your Kids: The Complete Guide to Family Vacations in the U.S., by Dorothy Ann Jordon and Marjorie Adoff Cohen (E.P. Dutton, 375 Hudson St., New York, NY 10014, tel. 212/366–2000; $12.95), details everything from city vacations to adventure vacations to child-care resources.

Bimonthly and monthly publications filled with events listings, resources, and advice for parents and available free at such places as libraries, supermarkets, and museums include ***Atlanta Parent*** (1135 Sheridan Rd., NE, Atlanta, GA 30324, tel. 404/325–1763), which features "Discover Atlanta," a column especially for visiting families, and ***Youth View*** (1401 W. Paces Ferry Rd., Suite A-217, Atlanta, GA 30327, tel. 404/239–0642). For a small fee you can have an issue sent to you before your trip.

Traveling with Children—And Enjoying it, by Arlene K. Butler, offers tips on how to cut costs, keep kids busy, reduce jet lag, and pack properly when traveling domestically and abroad ($11.95 plus $2 shipping; Globe Pequot Press, Box 833, Old Saybrook, CT 06475, tel. 800/243–0495, in CT 800/962–0973).

Hotels **Guest Quarters Suite Hotels** (tel. 800/424–2900) offer the luxury of two-room suites with kitchen facilities, plus children's menus in the restaurants. The hotels also allow children under 17 to stay free in their parents' suite. Many **Days Inn** hotels (tel. 800/325–2525) allow children under 18 to stay free and sometimes offer free meals to very young children (many offer efficiency-type apartments, too).

The Ritz-Carlton, Buckhead (3434 Peachtree Rd., Atlanta, GA 30326, tel. 404/237–2700 or 800/241–3333) pampers children with everything from stuffed lions in their cribs to coloring-book menus in *The Cafe* to tickets to popular Atlanta attractions. A children's program is scheduled during the summer at both **The Cloister** (Sea Island, GA 31561, tel. 912/638–3611 or 800/732–4752) and **Sea Palms Golf and Tennis Resort** (5445 Frederica Rd., St. Simons Island, GA 31522, tel. 912/638–3351 or 800/841–6268).

In winter and summer, programs for children are offered at **Wintergreen Resort** (Wintergreen, VA 22958, tel. 804/325–2200 or 800/325–2200) and at **The Homestead** (Hot Springs, VA 24445, tel. 703/839–5500).

The islands of South Carolina harbor a number of resorts with elaborate children's programs and facilities: **Kiawah Island Resort** (1 Kiawah Beach Dr., Kiawah Island, SC 29455, or Box 12910, Charleston, SC 29412, tel. 803/768–2121 or 800/654–2924 nationwide, 800/845–2471 SC), **Hyatt Regency Hilton Head** (Box 6167, Hilton Head Island, SC 29938, tel. 803/785–1234 or 800/233–1234), **The Westin Resort** (formerly Inter-Continental) **Hilton Head** (135 S. Port Royal Dr., Hilton Head Island, SC 29928, tel. 803/681–4000 or 800/228–3000), **Marriott's Hilton Head Resort** (130 Shipyard Dr., Hilton Head Island, SC 29928, tel. 803/842–2400 or 800/228–9290), and **Palmetto Dunes Resort** (Box 5606, Hilton Head Island, SC 29938, tel. 803/785–1161 or 800/845–6130).

Condo Rentals See ***The Condo Lux Vacationer's Guide to Condominium Rentals in the Southeast,*** by Jill Little (Vintage Books/Random House, New York; $9.95).

Home Exchange Exchanging homes is a surprisingly low-cost way to enjoy a vacation in another part of the country. **Vacation Exchange Club** (Box 650, Key West, FL 33041, tel. 305/294–3720 outside the U.S. or 800/638–3841, fax 305/294–1448) specializes in domestic home exchanges. The club publishes directories in January, March, July, and September each year and updated listings throughout the year. Annual membership, which includes your listing in one book, a newsletter, and copies of all publications, is $55. **Loan-a-Home** (2 Park La., 6E, Mount Vernon, NY 10552, tel. 914/664–7640) is popular with retirees, academics on sabbatical, and businesspeople on temporary assignment. There's no annual membership fee or charge for listing your home, but the cost of receiving one directory and a supplement is $35; two directories and two supplements are $45.

Getting There On domestic flights, children under two not occupying a seat travel free. Various discounts apply to children 2 to 12 years of age. Regulations governing infant travel on airplanes are in the process of being changed. Until they do, however, if you want to be sure your infant is secured in his/her own safety seat, you must buy a separate ticket and bring your own infant car seat. (Check with the airline in advance; certain seats aren't allowed. Or write for the booklet "Child/Infant Safety Seats Acceptable for Use in Aircraft," from the Federal Aviation Administration, APA–200, 800 Independence Ave. SW, Washington, DC 20591, tel. 202/267–3479.) Some airlines allow babies to travel in their own safety seats at no charge if there's a spare seat available on the plane; otherwise safety seats are stored and the child must be held by a parent. If you opt to hold your baby on your lap, do so with the infant outside the seat belt so he or she isn't crushed in case of a sudden stop.

Also inquire about special children's meals or snacks. See the February 1990 and 1992 issues of *Family Travel Times* for "TWYCH's Airline Guide," which contains a rundown of the children's services offered by 46 airlines.

Baby-sitting Services First check with the hotel concierge about child-care arrangements. **Sitters Unlimited** serves northern Virginia and the Washington, DC, area (tel. 703/250–5250).

Hints for Disabled Travelers

The Information Center for Individuals with Disabilities (Fort Point Pl., 1st fl., 27–43 Wormwood St., Boston, MA 02210, tel. 617/727–5540) offers problem-solving assistance, including lists of travel agents that specialize in tours for the disabled.
Moss Rehabilitation Hospital Travel Information Service (1200 W. Tabor Rd., Philadelphia, PA 19141, tel. 215/456–9603; TDD 215/456–9602) for a small fee provides information on tourist sights, transportation, and accommodations in destinations around the world.
Mobility International USA (Box 3551, Eugene, OR 97403, tel. 503/343–1284) is an internationally affiliated organization with 500 members. For a $20 annual fee, it coordinates exchange programs for disabled people in the United States and around the world and offers information on accommodations and organized study programs.
The Society for the Advancement of Travel for the Handicapped (347 5th Ave., Suite 610, New York, NY 10016, tel. 212/447–7284, fax 212/725–8253) offers information. Annual membership costs $45, $25 for senior travelers and students. Send a stamped, self-addressed envelope.
The Itinerary (Box 2012, Bayonne, NJ 07002, tel. 201/858–3400) is a bimonthly travel magazine for the disabled.
Greyhound-Trailways (tel. 800/752–4841) will carry a disabled person and companion for the price of a single fare. **Amtrak** (tel. 800/USA–RAIL) requests 24-hour notice to provide redcap service and special seats. All handicapped passengers are entitled to a 15% discount on the lowest available fare.

Hints for Older Travelers

The **American Association of Retired Persons** (AARP, 601 E St. NW, Washington, DC 20049, tel. 202/434–2277) has two programs for independent travelers: (1) *The Purchase Privilege Program,* which offers discounts on hotels, airfare, car rentals, and sightseeing; and (2) the *AARP Motoring Plan,* provided by Amoco, which offers emergency aid and trip-routing information for an annual fee of $39.95 per couple. AARP also arranges group tours through **AARP Travel Experience from American Express** (400 Pinnacle Way, Norcross, GA 30071, tel. 800/927–0111). AARP members must be 50 or older. Annual dues are $8 per person or per couple.

When using an AARP or other identification card, ask for a reduced hotel rate at the time you make your reservation, not when you check out. At participating restaurants, show your card to the maître d' before you're seated, since discounts may be limited to certain set menus, days, or hours. When renting a car, be sure to ask about special promotional rates, which may offer greater savings than the available discount.

Elderhostel (75 Federal St., 3rd floor, Boston, MA 02110–1941, tel. 617/426–7788, or 617/426–8056) is an innovative program for people 60 and older. Participants live in dorms on some 1,600 campuses around the world. Mornings are devoted to lectures and seminars, afternoons to sightseeing and field trips. The all-inclusive fee for two- to three-week international trips, including room, board, tuition, and round-trip transportation, ranges from $1,800 to $4,500.

Nautilus Tours (5435 Donna Ave., Tarzana, CA 91356, tel. 818/343–6339) has for nine years operated international trips and cruises for the disabled. **Travel Industry and Disabled Exchange** (TIDE, at the same address, tel. 818/368–5648), an industry-based organization with a $15 annual membership fee, provides a quarterly newsletter and information on travel agencies and tours.

National Council of Senior Citizens (1331 F St. NW, Washington, DC 20004, tel. 202/347–8800) is a nonprofit advocacy group with some 5,000 local clubs across the country. Annual membership is $12 per person or per couple. Members receive a monthly newspaper with travel information and an ID card for reduced-rate hotels and car rentals.

Mature Outlook (6001 N. Clark St., Chicago, IL 60660, tel. 312/764–8210 or 800/336–6330), a subsidiary of Sears Roebuck & Co., is a travel club for people over 50, with hotel and motel discounts and a bimonthly newsletter. Annual membership is $9.95 per couple. Instant membership is available at participating Holiday Inns.

Golden Age Passport is a free lifetime pass to all parks, monuments, and recreation areas run by the federal government. People 62 and over should pick them up in person at any national park that charges admission. A driver's license or other proof of age is required.

Credit Cards

The following credit card abbreviations are used: AE, American Express; D, Discover; DC, Diners Club; MC, MasterCard; V, Visa.

Further Reading

For background on Southern writers, take along Paul Buiding's *A Separate Country: A Literary Journey Through the American South.* Chet Fuller's *I Hear Them Calling My Name* is a narrative of a journalist traveling through the South. The *Encyclopedia of Southern Culture,* edited by Reagan Wilson and William Ferris, with a foreword by Alex Haley, offers an extraordinary portrait of the South. Two volumes edited by Ben Forkner and Patrick Samway—*Modern Southern Reader* and *A New Reader of the Old South*—portray the South through stories, plays, poetry, essays, diaries, interviews, and songs.

Eugenia Price's novels *Savannah* and *The Beloved Invader* provide a keen sense of place in a historical-romance frame. Also look for *Cold Sassy Tree,* by Olive Ann Burns and *Alabama: One Big Front Porch,* by Kathryn Tucker Wilson.

Great Itineraries

The following recommended itineraries, arranged by both theme and area, are offered as a guide to planning individual travel.

Prominent Sites of African-American History

Alabama Tour Alabama's historic Civil Rights sites provide a close look at a 200-year struggle for racial equality, culminating in the volatile changes undergone during the 1960s.

Length of Trip Six or seven days

The Main Route **One day:** In Mobile (at the junction of I–10 and I–64) see the antebellum State Street A.M.E. (African Methodist Episcopal) Zion Church and the St. Louis Street Missionary Baptist Church. You can also visit the Slave Market Site, where the last cargo of slaves to enter the country arrived in 1859 aboard the *Clotilde.*

Two or three days: Take I–65 northeast to Montgomery and visit the Dexter Avenue King Memorial Baptist Church, considered by many the birthplace of the Civil Rights Movement. And take in the World Heritage Museum that showcases Montgomery's Civil Rights Movement. Then take U.S. 80 to Selma and see the Edmund Pettus Bridge, famous during the '60s for clashes between civil-rights marchers and police, and First Baptist Church, the scene of meetings and protests in the 1960s. You can also take I–85 and U.S. 29 east from Montgomery to the Tuskegee Institute National Historic Site, which consists of Booker T. Washington's home The Oaks, the George Washington Carver Museum, and Tuskegee University.

One or two days: From Montgomery, go north 86 miles on I–65 to Birmingham and visit its Civil Rights District—the location of Kelly-Ingram Park, which served as a rallying place in the rights movement, and the Sixteenth Street Baptist Church. Then take in the Alabama Sports Hall of Fame; it pays tribute to many of the state's great African-American athletes.

One day: Take I–65 north to Decatur and visit the Old Courthouse, noted for the 1933 retrial of the Scottsboro Boys. Northwest on U.S. 43 is Florence, where attractions include the W. C. Handy Home and Museum.

Information *See* Chapter 2.

Tennessee/ Mississippi Tour For a glimpse of African-American life in the Deep South, visit the cotton country of the Mississippi Delta.

Length of Trip Six or seven days

One day: Begin in Memphis with a stop at the National Civil Rights Museum, located on the site of Martin Luther King, Jr.'s 1968 assassination. Then walk through the shops and blues clubs in the Beale Street Historic District. About 45 miles northeast on U.S. 51 is Henning, hometown of the late Alex Haley and setting for his novel, *Roots*.

Two days: Take I–55 and Route 6 to Oxford and the Ole Miss campus where an African-American was first graduated in 1963. Here also is the Center for the Study of Southern Culture, which focuses on southern music and folklore. Then take Route 6 southwest for 62 miles to Clarksdale and tour the Delta Blues Museum, which pays tribute to famous blues musicians.

One or two days: Take I–55 to Jackson to get an overview of the Civil Rights Movement's history in Mississippi. See the Old Capitol Historical Museum, Jackson State University (tel. 601/

968–2272), and the outstanding collection of art at Tougaloo College (tel. 601/977–7842).

Two or three days: Drive along the Natchez Trace Parkway 50 miles to Port Gibson to visit the African-American quilters' workshop. In Natchez, 25 miles away, you can shop at the "Mostly African Market," and see the historic churches and houses built by prominent free men of color before the Civil War.

Information *See* Chapters 5 and 8.

Lowcountry Tour Blacks and whites in South Carolina's Lowcountry have always lived side-by-side, though, as evidenced by the 1739 Stono Plantation Rebellion and the 1822 Denmark Vesey plot to take over Charleston not always peaceably. This natural distrust also motivated blacks to develop a lilting dialect called Gullah to communicate exclusively with one another. Historical sites in the Lowcountry recall this unique black experience.

Length of Trip One or two days

The Main Route **One day:** In Charleston, begin with a walking tour of Cabbage Row, home of DuBose Heyward and setting for his novel *Porgy*. Then see the Emmanuel A.M.E. Church—the place of worship of the south's oldest A.M.E. congregation. Also here is the Old Exchange and Provost Dungeon, site of the city's busiest slave market. The Avery Research Center in the historic district has an archives and museum that document the heritage of Lowcountry blacks.

One day: Take U.S. 17 and U.S. 21 for 69 miles to Beaufort, where you'll see the Penn School Historic District and York W. Bailey Cultural Museum on St. Helena Island. This community center consists of 17 buildings on the campus of a school that was established in 1862 for freed slaves. Also in Beaufort County is the self-sufficient Daufuskie Island, until recently inhabited exclusively by descendants of slaves.

Information *See* Chapter 7.

The Old Dominion Tour Historical sites in the Old Dominion reflect the contributions to society of both freed men and slaves.

Length of Trip One to three days

The Main Route **One day:** Take U.S. 29 out of Washington, DC, to Arlington and stop by the Dr. Charles Richard Drew House—the former home of the noted black physician and teacher who discovered blood plasma. Then pick up I–95 off I–495 and head to Alexandria to a museum of African-American history at the Alexandria Black History Resource Center. Continue south on U.S. 1 to Mt. Vernon and visit George Washington's estate to learn of black life on an 18th-century tobacco plantation. Or go north out of Arlington via U.S. 29 and routes 7 and 9 to Harpers Ferry National Historic Park, the site of John Brown's abolitionist raid of 1859.

One to two days: Go south on I–95 and tour on foot the historic district in Fredericksburg, the pre-Revolutionary War home of many free blacks. While here, visit the Spotsylvania County military park and the Civil War battlefields where numerous black troops fought for the union. About an hour's drive south on I–95 is Richmond, where you should stop at the Valentine Museum to see exhibits celebrating Richmond's African-American history. Then tour the Jackson Ward Historic District, the nation's foremost black community at the turn of this century. Here you'll find the Maggie Lena Walker House—a former residence of the country's first female (and black) bank president. Drive 75 miles southeast on I-64 to Hampton and see the Fort Monroe U.S. Army-Casemate Museum that looks back at Civil War times when this site served as a refuge for slaves having fled the South. Founded in 1868 to educate free blacks and American Indians, Hampton University has an outstanding collection of African and Native American art.

Information *See* Chapter 9.

Prominent Sites of the Civil War

The Southeastern Tour South Carolina seceded from the Union on December 20, 1860, and the first shot of the war was fired the following April. The war was fought for the most part on Southern soil, and there are more commemorative plaques in the South than there are black-eyed peas. The following itineraries take in the major sites and sights.

Length of Trip Seven to 10 days

The Main Route **One day:** Begin in Charleston, SC, and visit the Ft. Sumter National Monument. On April 12, 1861, Confederate General P.G.T. Beauregard ordered the first shot fired, and the bloody four-year struggle began.

Two or three days: Drive to Atlanta via I–85 (300 miles). See the Eternal Flame of the Confederacy and visit the Cyclorama, which depicts the 1864 Battle of Atlanta. Visit the 3,200-acre Stone Mountain Park to see the Confederate Memorial—the world's largest monument—and the Kennesaw Mountain National Battlefield.

Two days: From Atlanta, drive southwest on I–85 to Montgomery (160 miles), the Cradle of the Confederacy. Visit the State Capitol, which was the first capitol of the Confederacy, and the First White House of the Confederacy, which was occupied by President Jefferson Davis and his family.

Two or three days: From Montgomery head southwest on I–65 toward Mobile. To reach Fort Morgan, exit the interstate on Route 59 and drive south to Gulf Shores, then west 10 miles on Route 180. A museum in Fort Morgan describes the dramatic 1864 Battle of Mobile Bay, during which Admiral David Farragut shouted, "Damn the torpedoes! Full speed ahead!"

Information *See* Chapters 2, 3, and 7.

The South Central Tour The long, colorful trek through Mississippi, Louisiana, and Tennessee offers Civil War–history buffs a wealth of well-preserved battle sites.

Length of Trip 10 to 14 days

The Main Route **Two or three days:** From Mobile, take I–10 west toward New Orleans (146 miles). Right on the highway, overlooking the Gulf of Mexico between Gulfport and Biloxi, MS, is Beauvoir, the home of Confederate president Jefferson Davis. At the Louisiana-Mississippi border, hook up with I–12 and drive to Baton Rouge (bypassing New Orleans, which fell to the Union in 1862). Connect in Baton Rouge with U.S. 61, and drive 14 miles north to the Port Hudson State Commemorative Area, a 650-

acre area on the site of the lengthiest uninterrupted siege in American military history. In 1863, 6,800 Confederates held off 30,000 to 40,000 Federals from May 23 till July 9. Continue north on U.S. 61 to Vicksburg, an important Mississippi River city that withstood Grant's siege for 47 days and nights before falling. Here, visit the Vicksburg National Military Park.

Three days: From Vicksburg, take I–20 east to Jackson, then I–55 north to Memphis (198 miles). The Shiloh National Military Park and Cemetery is 100 miles east of Memphis (via U.S. 64, then Route 22). This national shrine commemorates those who died in the April 1862 battle, one of the bloodiest of the Civil War.

Three days: From Shiloh, continue on U.S. 64 to I–24 (217 miles); take I–24 north to Murfreesboro (90 miles) and exit on U.S. 231. The Stones River National Battlefield is a 351-acre commemoration of the bloodiest battle west of the Appalachians. It was fought in the winter of 1862–63, and 25,000 men lost their lives.

Three to four days: From Murfreesboro, go south on I–24 to Chattanooga. See the Confederama, touted as the world's largest battlefield display of its kind, and visit the eight locations of the Chickamauga-Chattanooga National Military Park, whose headquarters is 10 miles south of the city on U.S. 27. This is one of the nation's largest and oldest national military parks.

Information *See* Chapters 4, 5, and 8.

The Virginia, Maryland, and Pennsylvania Tour

When Virginia voted on April 17, 1861 to secede from the Union, it doomed itself to become a major battleground. Thus, much of this tour is in Virginia, with brief forays across the Mason-Dixon line into Maryland and Pennsylvania. Richmond is the tour's hub.

Length of Trip Eight to 10 days

The Main Route

One day: Start at Hampton, on the peninsula, where Union general George McClellan in 1861 launched his drive toward Richmond. In Hampton visit the Syms-Eaton Museum to see the destruction that took place in the area during the Civil War. Across the channel is Fort Monroe—a Union stronghold in Confederate territory, where Confederate president Jefferson Davis was imprisoned.

Two days: Drive northwest on I–64 up the peninsula to Richmond to visit the Museum and White House of the Confederacy and Richmond National Battlefield Park. Proceed 20 miles south on I–95 to Petersburg, the city that was under siege for many months by Grant's army. While in Petersburg, visit Petersburg National Battlefield and the Siege Museum.

Two or three days: From Richmond proceed north on I–95 to Fredericksburg, site of the Old Stone Warehouse, which served as an arsenal and morgue during the Battle of Fredericksburg in December 1862. See four Civil War battlefields at Fredericksburg and Spotsylvania National Military Park. Return to I–95, and drive northwest to Manassas National Battlefield (Bull Run), where the Confederates won two important victories. Return to Richmond.

Two or three days: Take I–66 north from Richmond into Arlington and see Arlington National Cemetery and Arlington House (General Lee's house for 30 years, before the Union Army confiscated it and turned the grounds into a national cemetery). Then head north on I–270 into Maryland. North of Frederick catch Route 34 out of Boonsboro, and follow it to the Antietam National Battlefield Site. The battle of Antietam was the most fiercely fought, and bloodiest, single-day battle of the war. From Frederick, U.S. 15 heads north across the Pennsylvania border to Gettysburg National Park, which commemorates the catastrophic three-day battle between Lee's Army of Northern Virginia and General Meade's Army of the Potomac, that resulted in a Union victory and a combined loss of an estimated 50,000 lives.

Information *See* Chapter 9 and *Fodor's USA '93*.

2 Alabama

By Wayne Greenhaw

Updated by Carol Timblin

Alabama is indeed—as Governor Guy Hunt, the first Republican to win that office in Alabama in 112 years, declared it—a state of surprises. Visitors are surprised at the physical beauty: from the dramatic rocky, wooded hills and vast caves of the northeast to the expansive lakes and broad rivers of the interior and the snow-white beaches of the Gulf Coast. At the high-tech world of Huntsville's Space and Rocket Center, near Redstone Arsenal, the Saturn rocket was designed. The state's largest city, Birmingham, is one of the South's major medical centers, with 22 institutions, including the University of Alabama at Birmingham Medical Center, ranked among the nation's highest in quality of health care. In 1992 the institution opened the new $125 million Kirklin Medical Center.

The traveler who ventures off the four-lane interstates will find something surprising at almost every turn—a cascading waterfall or showy stand of wildflowers, an archaeological excavation or a Colonial fort, perhaps one of Alabama's 13 covered bridges. At Florence, in 1873, William Christopher Handy, son of a Methodist minister descended from slaves, was born. A teacher, band leader, and author, the Father of the Blues is best remembered for the "Memphis Blues" and "St. Louis Blues." In nearby Tuscumbia, the tiny frame cottage where Helen Keller overcame the loss of hearing and sight sits as a monument to her inspirational life. A few miles south, tucked away on a wooded hillside, is a cemetery for coon hounds, begun in 1937 by the devoted master of Troop, its first resident. A few more miles south is a sunken park (called The Dismals) where junglelike plants, some of which are found nowhere else in this hemisphere, grow in profusion. Tuskegee Institute, founded in 1881 by the distinguished black educator, Booker T. Washington, was where the young botanist, George Washington Carver, headed the agricultural department and did his seminal work in plant derivatives and crop diversification.

Each spring, several Alabama towns hold "pilgrimages"—tours of historic homes (including many private residences not otherwise open to the public), mansions, plantations, churches, gardens, even cemeteries. Hosts and hostesses in period costume greet visitors and tell tales of life in bygone days. It's a lovely time to visit, with the gardens decked out in dogwood, azalea, magnolia, and many other blossoms. Candlelight tours add a romantic touch. For a calendar of events, contact the Alabama Bureau of Tourism and Travel (*see* Essential Information in Chapter 1).

Birmingham

Birmingham, set in a valley below the foothills of the Appalachians, first blossomed around the coal mines and the iron industry in the latter part of the 19th century. In the 1970s, after plastics became commonplace in auto manufacturing, the steel-making plants that had polluted the valley air virtually vanished. The air cleared of soot and dust, and the University of Alabama at Birmingham, with its fast-growing medical center, became the city's largest employer.

Birmingham's image as a backward civil rights territory was reinforced during the '60s when the notorious Eugene "Bull" Conner served as police commissioner and when Dr. Martin

Alabama

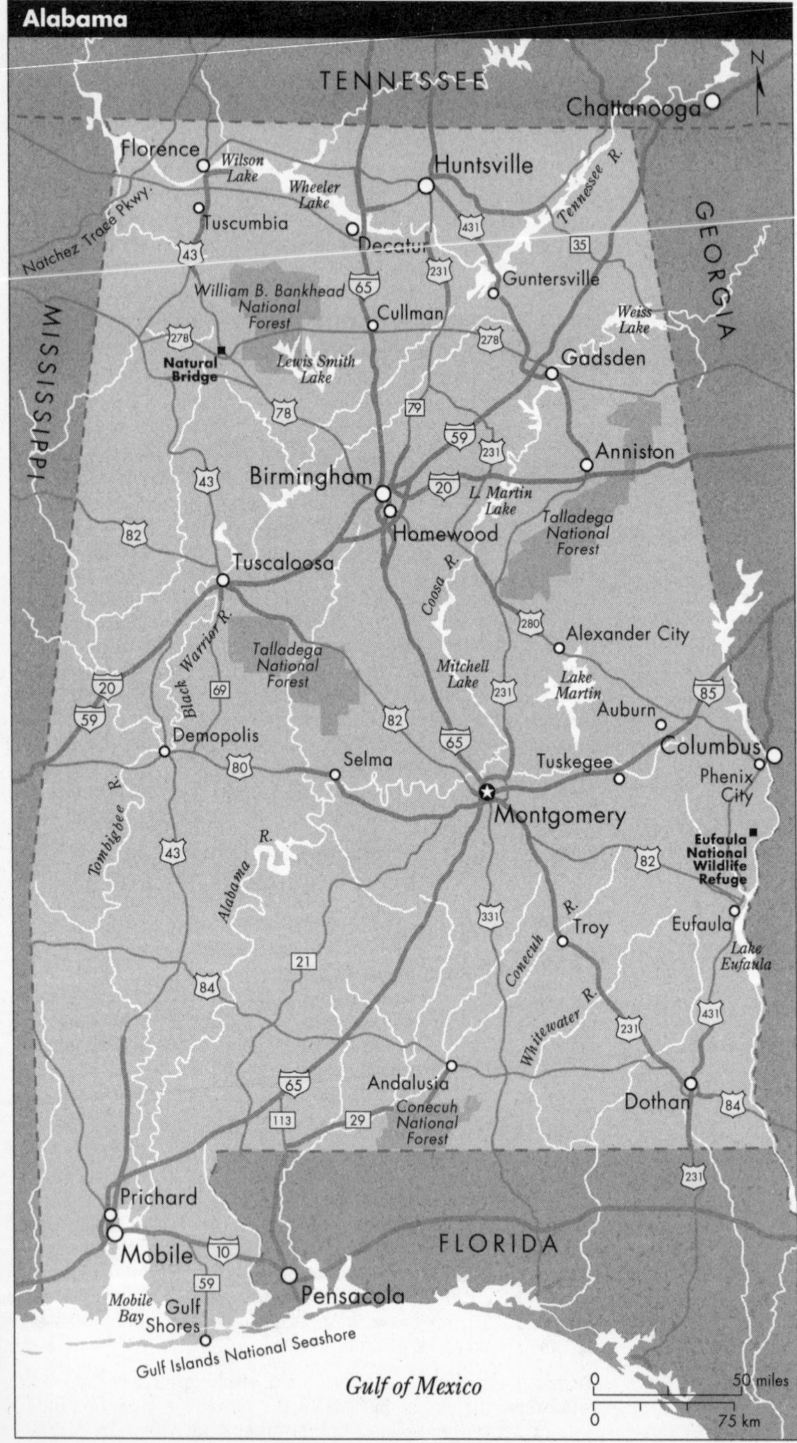
TENNESSEE
Chattanooga
Florence
Wilson Lake
Huntsville
Wheeler Lake
Tennessee R.
Natchez Trace Pkwy.
Tuscumbia
Decatur
GEORGIA
William B. Bankhead National Forest
Guntersville
Cullman
Weiss Lake
MISSISSIPPI
Natural Bridge
Lewis Smith Lake
Gadsden
Anniston
Birmingham
L. Martin Lake
Homewood
Talladega National Forest
Tuscaloosa
Coosa R.
Alexander City
Black Warrior R.
Talladega National Forest
Mitchell Lake
Lake Martin
Auburn
Demopolis
Columbus
Selma
Tuskegee
Phenix City
Tombigbee R.
Montgomery
Eufaula National Wildlife Refuge
Alabama R.
Troy
Eufaula
Conecuh R.
Lake Eufaula
Whitewater R.
Andalusia
Dothan
Conecuh National Forest
Prichard
FLORIDA
Mobile
Pensacola
Mobile Bay
Gulf Shores
Gulf Islands National Seashore
Gulf of Mexico
0 50 miles
0 75 km
N

Luther King, Jr., was put in jail for fighting racial inequality. When the turmoil had finally settled, however, a new city began to emerge. In 1979 Richard Arrington, a successful black businessman, was elected mayor. The racial climate now having improved considerably, the city dedicated the Birmingham Civil Rights Institute in fall, 1992.

Birmingham today is a beautiful, hospitable, thriving metropolis. Several 19th-century houses and commercial buildings have been restored to create a lively shopping and dining area called Five Points South. The city's last remaining antebellum mansion has been restored and functions as a museum. There's also a large zoo and a 67-acre Japanese and botanic garden. Looking down on it all from high atop Red Mountain—so named for the iron ore within it—looms a reminder of the source of an earlier prosperity: a 55-foot-high cast-iron statue of Vulcan, god of the forge.

Arriving and Departing

By Plane
Airports and Airlines The Birmingham Airport (tel. 205/595–0533) is less than three miles from central downtown and is served by **American, Conair, Delta, Northwest Airlink, Southwest, TW Express, United, United Express,** and **USAir.**

Between the Airport and Center City **Taxis** are readily available; the fare to most hotels is about $9. Many hotels provide **limousine service** from the airport by prior arrangement. If you're traveling **by car,** follow the clearly marked signs to the downtown area.

By Train The **Amtrak** station is on Morris Avenue, downtown, tel. 205/324–3033.

By Bus **Greyhound-Trailways Lines** is on 19th Street North, between Fourth and Fifth avenues, tel. 205/252–7171.

By Car I–59 goes northeast from Birmingham to Chattanooga, southwest to Tuscaloosa, and then into Mississippi. I–20 runs east to Anniston and Atlanta. I–65 goes north to Decatur and Nashville and south to Montgomery and Mobile.

Getting Around

This is a city where a car is a necessity—sites are pretty well spread out.

By Taxi Taxis charge $2.95 for the first mile, $1.20 for each additional mile. **Yellow Cab:** tel. 205/252–1131.

By Bus The **Metro Area Express (MAX)** serves the city. Buses require exact change (80¢ fare, 15¢ transfer) and run from 4 AM to 10 PM. For a schedule, call 205/521–0101.

Important Addresses and Numbers

Tourist Information **Greater Birmingham Convention & Visitors Bureau** (2200 9th Ave. N, 35203, tel. 205/252–9825 or 800/962–6453).

Emergencies Dial 911 for **police** and **ambulance** in an emergency.

Doctor The all-night emergency room closest to downtown is at **University Hospital** (1900 Fifth Ave. S, tel. 205/934–5105).

Dentist **Dental Care** offers 24-hour emergency service at Eastwood Mall, tel. 205/956–2999.

Pharmacy **Eckerd Drugs** (Eastwood Shopping Plaza, tel. 205/956–0400; open daily 7 AM–midnight).

Guided Tours

Not much in the way of guided tours exist, except for large groups. Mrs. Virginia Rekoff (tel. 205/324–2757) offers sunset strolls of downtown Birmingham to small groups. **The Greater Birmingham Convention & Visitors Bureau** (*see* Tourist Information, *above*) has free brochures for self-guided tours of the downtown and Five Points South areas.

Exploring Birmingham

Numbers in the margin correspond to points of interest on the Birmingham map.

Alabama has long been noted for its excellence in sports, and
1 the **Alabama Sports Hall of Fame Museum,** in the Civic Center, displays memorabilia of such Alabama heroes as coach Bear Bryant, Jesse Owens, Willie Mays, Billy Williams, and Hank Aaron. *Corner 22nd St. N and Civic Center Blvd., tel. 205/323–6665. Admission: $5 adults, $4 students. Open Mon.–Sat. 9–5, Sun. 1–5. Closed major holidays.*

2 The **Birmingham Museum of Art,** two blocks south, has one of the world's largest collections of Wedgwood, the largest collection of contemporary Chinese paintings outside the People's Republic of China, some extraordinary examples of Western American art, plus Italian Renaissance and pre-Columbian art. *2000 Eighth Ave. N, tel. 205/254–2565. Admission free. Open Tues.–Sat. 10–5 (until 9 on Thurs.), Sun. 1–5; closed Christmas, New Year's Day.*

At the corner of 16th Street North and Sixth Avenue North is
3 the **16th Street Baptist Church** (tel. 205/251–9402), site of one of the saddest and most memorable occurrences of the civil rights movement. Here, on the morning of September 15, 1963, a bomb exploded and killed four little black girls who were attending Sunday school in the basement. A plaque erected to their memory bears this legend: *May Men Learn to Replace Bitterness and Violence with Love and Understanding.*

4 Across the street is the new **Birmingham Civil Rights Institute** (Sixth Ave. and 16th St. N, tel. 205/328–9696). Having opened in fall 1992, the institute traces the civil rights movement from the 1920s through the present day via exhibits, multimedia presentations, music, and storytelling.

From here, head south. One block past First Avenue North,
5 running east and west between 20th and 24th streets, is **Morris Avenue,** a turn-of-the-century brick roadway lined with brick buildings of the period. Many of these buildings have been renovated and are now used as professional offices. Gaslights add to the old-fashioned atmosphere.

Driving east on First Avenue North, over the viaduct, you'll
6 see signs for **Sloss Furnaces,** a **National Historic Landmark.** The massive ironworks plant produced pig iron from ore dug from the hills surrounding Birmingham between 1882 and 1971. Retired blast-furnace workers who knew the heat of the flowing molten metal firsthand conduct guided tours through the plant, spicing the narrations with tales of their own experi-

Alabama Sports Hall of Fame Museum, **1**
Arlington, **7**
Birmingham Civil Rights Institute, **4**
Birmingham Museum of Art, **2**
Birmingham Zoo, **19**
Botanical and Japanese Gardens, **20**
Brother Bryan statue, **10**
Five Points South, **8**
Five Points Theatre, **14**
Highlands United Methodist Church, **11**
Morris Ave., **5**
Nabob Hill, **12**
Pickwick Hotel, **15**
Pickwick Place, **9**
Red Mountain Museum, **17**
Rube Burrows Food and Spirits, **16**
16th St. Baptist Church, **3**
Sloss Furnace, **6**
Southside Baptist Church, **13**
Vulcan statue, **18**

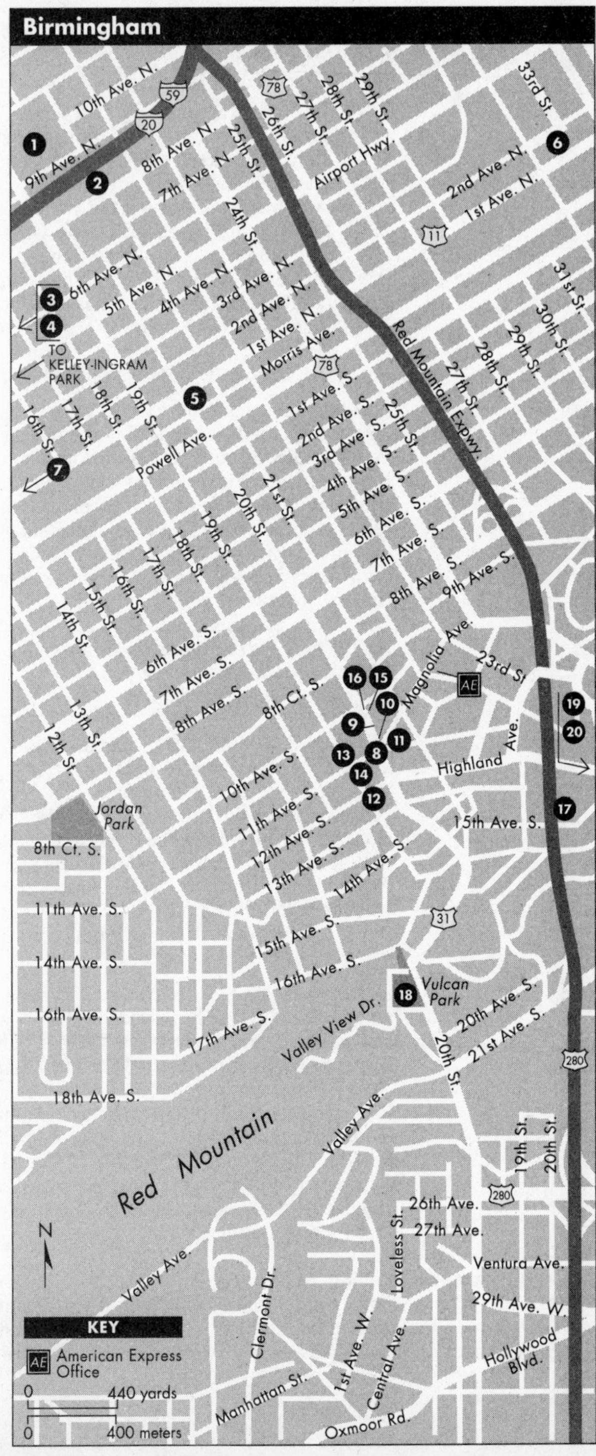

ences. *First Ave. N and 32nd St., tel. 205/324–1911. Admission free. Open Tues.–Sat. 10–4, Sun. noon–4. Closed Thanksgiving, Christmas, and New Year's Day.*

If you head west again on First Avenue North, you'll come to
7 **Arlington,** Birmingham's only remaining antebellum mansion.
It was used as headquarters by Union General James H. Wilson in March of 1865 as he and his raiders swept south through Alabama to Selma, destroying iron furnaces along the way. In the 1950s the city purchased the classic Greek Revival structure, and 50 prominent citizens donated funds for its renovation. Today it houses Civil War memorabilia, some prime examples of 19th-century furniture, and a museum dedicated to the women of Alabama. *331 Cotton Ave. SW, tel. 205/780–5656. Admission: $3 adults; $2 children 6–18, under 6 free. Open Tues.–Sat. 10–4, Sun. 1–4; closed major holidays.*

Heading east again on First Avenue North, turn right onto
8 20th Street and continue for about 12 blocks to reach **Five
Points South,** an outdoor museum of turn-of-the-century archi-
9 tecture. Start with the **Pickwick Place,** a miniature open-air
shopping mall between 20th Street South and Magnolia Avenue. On this site the Pickwick Ballroom once stood. Big bands played swing tunes while the belles and their beaux danced the nights away beneath the large mirrored ball that now hangs in the mall's entranceway.

Time Out At **Cosmos Pizza House** (2012 Magnolia Ave., tel. 205/930–9971), Jack makes gourmet pizza with sun-dried tomatoes, exotic cheeses, and crawfish.

Outside CAPS Restaurant and Lounge at Five Points is the
10 kneeling stone **statue of Brother Bryan,** Birmingham's good-
11 Samaritan minister. Across Magnolia, in front of the **Highlands
United Methodist Church,** is a concrete Art Deco fountain. The church, built in 1909 in the Spanish Renaissance Revival style, was designed by the same architect who was responsible for Atlanta's Fox Theatre. In the first block of 11th Avenue, in what is called the Spanish Stores for its stucco walls and tiled roofs, is **Highlands: A Bar and Grill** (*see* Dining, *below*), which has won national awards.

If you are lucky, you'll arrive on a "special weekend" (most are unannounced, with the exception of Halloween). As soon as the sun falls, the locals come out. Street bands play. Teenagers mimic denizens of London's Soho with their multihued hair and loose-fitting, wildly colored costumes. And men in drag dance in the streets. Is it any wonder local pundits have named Five Points "Bourbon Street without the sleaze"? With all the street people out, it is comforting to know that the Five Points South owners have their own security patrol, which immediately alerts the police department in case of a crime. You can walk these streets without fear.

Time Out Behind 20th Street Antiques, through a narrow walkway, is Cobb Lane, where **The Back Alley Restaurant** (tel. 205/933–6211) has dining indoors and on an oak-shaded patio. The fare is soups, salads, sandwiches, quiche, and one or two Continental entrées each day.

Walking north on 19th Street, you'll see a ridge on your left at
12 12th Avenue. Once called **Nabob Hill,** it was the site of five
mansions in which the families of high-ranking Confederate officers lived. Today there's only a playground. A block beyond
13 (at 1016 19th St. S) stands the large, columned **Southside Baptist Church.** Built in 1911, it is a prime example of Classical Revival architecture, resembling a Roman Ionic temple.

Turning right and back toward the center of Five Points, you
come to the Art Deco facade of multicolored Carrara glass that
14 was once the **Five Points Theatre** (1914 11th Ave. S), a popular
movie house in the 1920s and '30s. Today the building houses
Clyde Houston's bar and restaurant (tel. 205/251–0278).

15 Back on 20th Street is the **Pickwick Hotel** (1123 20th St. S; *see* Lodging, *below*), built in 1931 as the Medical Arts Building, with offices for physicians, surgeons, and pharmacists. Today it retains the original polished-marble lobby, but renovations have created roomy suites and a cozy little lounge with an etched-glass mirror showing Pickwick dancers in their finest formals.

Half a block down 20th Street, near where the walking tour of
16 Five Points began, is **Rube Burrows Food and Spirits** (1005 20th
St. S, tel. 205/933–5570), a watering hole and hamburger oasis
named for Alabama's infamous 19th-century train robber.

After leaving the area, you can head south on U.S. 31 a short
17 way until you come to the **Red Mountain Museum,** which showcases rocks, fossils, and minerals of the many types found in the
area. Also here is the only solar telescope in North America
open to the public; don't miss this chance to get a look at the
sun's surface. *1421 22nd St. S, tel. 205/933–4104. Donation:
adults $2, children $1.50; includes admission to Discovery
Place (*see *What to See and Do with Children*, below*). Open
Tues.–Fri. 9–3, Sat. 10–4, Sun. 1–4.*

A pleasant way to end a day is to wend your way up Red Moun-
18 tain to visit **Vulcan.** From the enclosed observation deck at the
base of the world's tallest cast-iron statue, there's a panoramic
view of the city. There's also a circular stairway inside for the
hardy. *Valley Ave. at U.S. 31S, tel. 205/328–6198. Admission:
$1 (under 6 free). Open daily 8 AM–10:30 PM.*

The next part of the tour, a day in itself, takes you to Mountain
Brook. This elegant suburb is a place for wandering along tree-
shaded country roads, driving past great old and new Southern
mansions. Here, too, nestled beneath a hammock of huge oaks,
19 is the **Birmingham Zoo.** A miniature train snakes through the
wooded acreage, or you may walk the paths at a leisurely pace.
The zoo is known for the breeding of Siberian tigers, a number
of which live here, along with the world's only self-sustaining
breeding colony of golden spider monkeys in captivity. *2630
Cahaba Rd., tel. 205/879–0408. Admission: $3 adults; $1.50
over 64 and children 2–17, under 2 free. Open daily 9:30–5.*

20 At the nearby **Botanical and Japanese Gardens,** under a great glass dome, waterfalls cascade into pools with plants of every shade of green and flowers of every color imaginable. Outside, there is a quiet Japanese garden with small bridges over bubbling brooks and an authentic teahouse set amid Japanese ferns, mosses, and trees. For the blind, there is a touch-and-see

nature trail. *2612 Lane Park Rd., tel. 205/879–1227. Admission free. Open daily sunrise to sunset.*

Birmingham for Free

Temple Sibyl. About five miles south of Vulcan on U.S. 31, atop Shades Mountain in the suburb of Vestavia Hills, is a replica of the Temple of Sibyl at Tivoli, near Rome. From this round, open-air temple, there's a grand view of the Georgian-style campus of Samford University and the whole valley below. It's a good spot for a picnic.

Vulcan Park (*see* Exploring, *above*).

What to See and Do with Children

Discovery Place of Birmingham, Inc. At this hands-on museum, a child can dress up in a policeman's hat and coat, climb on a fire truck, sit in an ambulance and sound the siren, or put together the bones of a skeleton. *1320 22nd Ave. S, tel. 205/939–1176. Admission (includes admission to Red Mountain Museum): $2 adults, $1.50 children under 16. Open Tues.–Fri. 9–3, Sat. 10–4, Sun. 1–4, summer; closed Sept., major holidays.*

Red Mountain Museum (*see* Exploring, *above*).

Ruffner Mountain Nature Center. Cutaway sections of the mountain ridge are labeled to explain the area's geologic history. There are also well-marked nature trails, a wildflower garden, and bird observation stations. *1214 81st St. S, tel. 205/833– 8112. Admission free. Open Tues.–Sat. 9–5, Sun. 1–5. Closed major holidays.*

Off the Beaten Track

Birmingham Horse Track. Thoroughbred racing is offered early May through July 4th weekend; simulcast racing, throughout the remainder of the year. In the future, greyhound racing may be added. A large video screen shows instant replays, displays odds, and announces upcoming races; there are smaller screens within view of spectators. Dining is offered at the Rib and Rail, Saratoga, and the glass-enclosed Ascot Room overlooking the track. *1000 John Rogers Dr., tel. 205/838–7500. Admission: $2; clubhouse: $4. Not open to anyone under 19.*

Legion Field. If you're a fan, you know that Birmingham is known as the Football Capital of the South—perhaps even the world. Legion Field (400 Graymont Ave. W, tel. 205/251–0537; tickets, tel. 205/254–2391) is the site of the annual Alabama–Auburn Iron Bowl Classic, in which Paul "Bear" Bryant won his record-breaking game to become the winningest coach in college football. Not far from the famous stadium is **Elmwood Cemetery** (600 Martin Luther King Jr. Dr. SW), where the Alabama legend is buried.

Southern Museum of Flight. Housed here is the Alabama Aviation Hall of Fame, the first Delta Airlines passenger plane, and World War II bombers built at a factory in Birmingham. *4343 73rd St. N, tel. 205/934–5181. Admission: $2 adults, $1 children 6–18, preschoolers free. Open Tues.–Sat. 9:30–5, Sun. 1–5.*

Tannehill Historical State Park. Built around reconstructed ironworks and blast furnaces that produced munitions for the Confederacy, the park offers a museum, crafts demonstrations, a gristmill, a pioneer farm, a country store, and a train ride. The log-walled **Furnace Master Inn** specializes in home cooking. *Bucksville exit off I–59 (about 30 mi west of Birmingham), tel. 205/477–5711. Admission: $1 adults, 50¢ children 6–12; under 6 and over 65 free. Open Tues.–Sun. 8 AM–sunset.*

Shopping

These days, shopping is done mostly in malls and centers in the suburban areas rather than downtown. Stores are usually open weekdays 10–6, Saturday 10–7, and closed Sunday. Sales tax is 6%. Banks are generally open weekdays 9–2.

Shopping Districts

Riverchase Galleria. About 10 miles from downtown, at the intersection of I–459 and U.S. 31S (Information Center: tel. 205/985–3039), is one of the largest shopping malls in the Southeast. Here you'll find more than 200 stores, including Macy's, Rich's, JC Penney, McRae's, Yieldings, and Parisian's department stores, plus specialty shops such as Banana Republic and other purveyors of fashion high and low. At the core is a 100-foot-high glass-domed atrium bordered by a dozen fast-food restaurants.

Mountain Brook Village. This small, villagelike shopping area, tucked away in the hollows of Birmingham's ritziest neighborhood (on Cahaba Rd.), has a number of small specialty shops, including Pappagallo. Also here is Browdy's, a New York–style deli-restaurant with imported beer (tel. 205/879–8585).

Discount Stores

Off Valley Avenue at Green Springs, **Palisades Shopping Center** (tel. 205/879–3040) is a complex of 15 or 20 discount shops, including Stein Mart (with name-brand clothing).

Antiques

For Depression glass, Oriental silver chests, and 19th-century memorabilia, try **20th Street Antiques** (20th St. at Cobb La., near Back Alley Restaurant, tel. 205/933–1472).

Day Trips from Birmingham

The sites listed below are within 150 miles of Birmingham. For information on them, *see* Elsewhere in the State, *below.*

U.S. Space and Rocket Center, Huntsville
Ave Maria Grotto, Cullman
De Soto Caverns, Childersburg
De Soto Falls, Fort Payne
Demopolis
Ivy Green, Tuscumbia
Little River Canyon, Fort Payne
Lookout Mountain Trail
Montgomery (*see* Montgomery section, below)
Mound State Monument, Moundville
Noccalula Falls and Park, Gadsden
Point Mallard Park, Decatur
Russell Cave National Monument, Bridgeport
Sequoyah Caverns, Valley Head
Sturdivant Hall, Selma
Tuscaloosa
Tuskegee

Participant Sports

Bicycling Although the terrain is very hilly, many bikers enjoy the quiet thoroughfares around Five Points South. For rentals, try **Alabama Cycle & Equipment Co.** (tel. 205/833–1122).

Canoeing North of Birmingham at Warrior, there are several outfitters on the Black Warrior River—including **Cahaba Canoe & Kayaks Too** (tel. 205/991–5461)—that offer whitewater canoeing. South of Birmingham, beginning and intermediate canoeing can be found on the Cahaba River, especially near Montevallo. The best guidebook is John Foshee's *Canoeing in Alabama.*

Fishing The best fresh-water crappie or bass fishing is northeast of Birmingham at **Logan Martin Lake** (tel. 205/831–6860) or south at the smaller lakes in **Oak Mountain State Park** (tel. 205/663–6783) off I–65. Rentals are available at **Rabbit Branch Marina** (tel. 205/525–5562) or **Aeromarine Inc.** (tel. 205/595–2141).

Golf Good public courses include **Boswell Highland** (tel. 205/326–3998) and **Hawkins Park and Recreational Center** (tel. 205/836–1661).

Hiking and Jogging **Oak Mountain State Park** (tel. 205/663–6783), 15 miles south of the city in Pelham, offers trails for hiking or jogging. Joggers also favor the quiet streets in and around Five Points South.

Tennis Birmingham's Park and Recreation Department (tel. 205/254–2391) maintains a number of public courts.

Spectator Sports

Baseball The **Birmingham Barons** of the Southern League are at home at Hoover Metropolitan Stadium (tel. 205/988–3200) in Hoover, south of Birmingham on AL 150.

Basketball The University of Alabama at Birmingham has had a fine basketball team since it imported former UCLA coach Gene Bartow. The **Blazers** (tel. 205/934–7252) play home games at the 19,000-seat Coliseum in the Birmingham–Jefferson Civic Center (tel. 205/251–4100).

Football The annual **Iron Bowl Classic,** held at Legion Field (tel. 205/254–2391) on the Friday after Thanksgiving, matches the Auburn Tigers against the Alabama Crimson Tide. Some of Alabama's home games are also played here.

Dining

Birmingham dining moved into the big time with the opening a few years ago of Highlands: A Bar and Grill, which won praise in national magazines, sparking competition among other top Birmingham restaurants. As throughout Alabama, north of Mobile, Old South dishes prevail here: fried chicken, barbecue, roast beef, and country fried steak.

The most highly recommended restaurants in each price category are indicated by a star ★.

Category	Cost*
Expensive	$25–$35
Moderate	$15–$25
Inexpensive	under $15

**per person without tax (7% in Birmingham), service, or drinks*

Downtown
Expensive
★ **Highlands: A Bar and Grill.** Exceptionally grand gourmet feasts are prepared here by owner-chef Frank Stitt, who worked at Chez Panisse in Berkeley and with Richard Olney in France and has received honors from *Playboy* and *Gourmet.* The room is a sophisticated peach and white, with paintings, an ornamental fireplace, brass candleholders, and fresh flowers—plus unhurried but efficient service. There's fillet of sole with a wine sauce so light it almost floats away; quail with raspberry sauce; and tomatoes stuffed with chunks of lobster, crab, shrimp, and corn—all superbly prepared. *2011 11th Ave. S, tel. 205/939–1400. Dress: casual. Reservations preferred. AE, DC, MC, V. Closed Sun.*

Moderate–Expensive
Bombay Cafe. The interior is attractive, with muted colors and an Italian marble fireplace, white tablecloths, and the food—such as simple, perfectly grilled amberjack, and snapper *en papillote* (snapper marinated in bèchamel sauce and baked in parchment with oysters and crabmeat)—is superb. *2839 Seventh Ave. S, tel. 205/322–1930. Dress: casual but neat. Reservations recommended. AE, D, MC, V. Closed Sun.*

G.G. in the Park. If there's a football game in town, there's a postgame party at G.G.'s. Prepare for lots of noise, and don't believe all the gossip you pick up between appetizer and main course. The sea scenes and oversize marlin that deck the walls will get you in the mood for seafood. Pick out your own Maine lobster from the tank and settle into a feast, or go for the angel-hair pasta Alfredo with lump crabmeat—it's all superior at G.G.'s. French onion soup, baked potato, garden salad, and hot rolls accompany each meal. *3625 Eighth Ave. S, tel. 205/254–3506. Dress: casual. Reservations suggested for groups of 5 or more. AE, DC, MC, V. Closed Sun.*

Moderate
Fish Market Restaurant. Fresh fish of all types is served here, from West Indies salad (with lump crabmeat) to seafood gumbo, grilled snapper to blackened redfish, fried scallops to raw oysters. Chef George Sarris is at his best with the Greek-style fish. The decor is restaurant nautical: fish nets, lobster traps, and carved fish. *611 21st St. S, tel. 205/322–3330. Dress: casual. No reservations. AE, D, MC, V. Closed Sun.*

★ **John's.** Though rather plain in atmosphere, this restaurant has been consistently rated best in local popularity polls. After a recent expansion, the family dining establishment seats 460 and serves some 1,200 meals daily. Owner Phil Hontzas serves the freshest seafood available and constantly gets raves on the trout amandine, whole red snapper, and jumbo shrimp fried in light batter. The cole slaw, with John's famous dressing, should be ordered with any meal. And the corn sticks, an Alabama specialty, are done up proudly here. *112 21st St. N, tel. 205/322–6014. Dress: casual. Reservations for more than 5. AE, DC, MC, V. Closed Sun.*

Michael's Sirloin Room. This is one of the most popular steak houses in Birmingham. It is also a sports bar, with photos of all

Dining
Bombay Cafe, **11**
Browdy's Fine Foods, **19**
Cabana Café, **21**
Cosmo's, **14**
Fish Market Restaurant, **10**
G.G. in the Park, **12**
Golden Rule Barbecue, **24**
Highlands: A Bar and Grill, **16**
Irondale Café, **9**
John's, **4**
Joy Young Restaurant, **22**
Michael's Sirloin Room, **5**
Ollie's B-B-Q, **6**
Rossi's South, **18**
Winston's Restaurant, **23**

Lodging
Comfort Inn–Perimeter, **20**
Courtyard Marriott, **25**
Days Inn, **7**
Holiday Inn–Redmont, **2**
Motel Birmingham, **3**
Mountain Brook Inn, **17**
Pickwick Hotel, **15**
The Radisson Hotel, **13**
Ramada Inn Airport, **8**
Tutwiler, **1**
Wynfrey Hotel, **23**

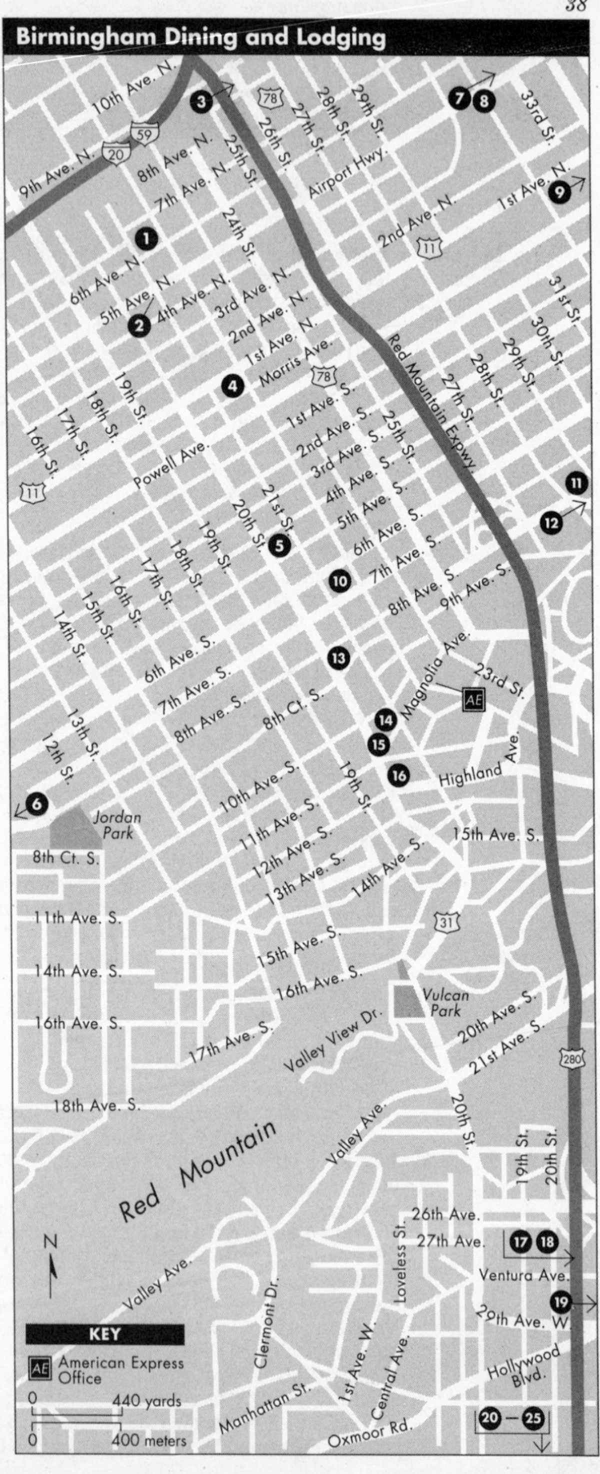

the local sports greats from Bear Bryant to Willie Mays on the wall of fame. The talk centers on what kind of team Alabama or Auburn will have this year, and the television is always tuned to the sport of the day. The specialty is a hearty cut of prime steer butt, usually at least two inches thick, charbroiled for a smoky taste, but other dishes are served, including veal, lamb, and pork cooked Greek style: heavy on the oregano and garlic. *431 20th St. S, tel. 205/322–0419. Dress: casual. Reservations for more than 5. AE, DC, MC, V. Closed Sun.*

Rossi's South. Recently moved from an in-town location, this locally popular Italian restaurant retains its casually tasteful atmosphere. Walls are decorated with paintings from Napoli, and there's piped-in music from the old country. Longtime fans can still feast on very good shrimp scampi, chicken cacciatore, veal piccante (medallions of veal in lemon butter with fettuccine), and superior veal Marsala. Go for the pasta and the Italian salad. *2737 U.S. Hwy. 280, tel. 205/879–2111. Dress: casual. Reservations accepted Fri. and Sat. AE, DC, MC, V. Closed Sun.*

Inexpensive

Cosmo's. This is an in place with UAB students in the Five Points South neighborhood. The walls are paneled in pastel Formica, and the neon lighting makes for a colorful, lively mix. A glass wall fronting on Magnolia Street encourages people-watching. The specialty is gourmet pizza: pesto with prosciutto, sweet peppers, goat cheese, sun-dried tomatoes, and Italian sausage. *2012 Magnolia Ave., tel. 205/930–9971. Dress: casual. No reservations. AE, MC, V.*

Ollie's B-B-Q. A tradition in Birmingham, Ollie McClung's barbecue restaurant is a place where people go to meet while they eat. A strongly religious man, Ollie sells Bibles as well as barbecue; on the walls are his favorite verses. The waitresses are very friendly, and the sauce is tangy. George Bush eats here when he's in town. *515 University Blvd. off I–65, tel. 205/324–9485. Dress: casual. No reservations. No credit cards. Open Mon.–Sat. 9:30–8, but never on Sunday. Inexpensive.*

Mountain Brook

Moderate

★ **Joy Young Restaurant.** Once a Birmingham tradition downtown, this Chinese restaurant, in its new location, is still one of the best in Birmingham. The windows give the place lots of light (though, unfortunately, the view is of a busy parking lot in a shopping mall), and there are modern Chinese paintings on the wall. The food is very good, especially the steamed red snapper. *547 Brookwood Blvd., tel. 205/879–7500. Dress: casual. Reservations suggested for 5 or more. AE, D, MC, V. Closed Mon. No dinner Sun.*

Inexpensive–Moderate

★ **Browdy's of Mountain Brook.** This Birmingham establishment, dating to 1913 and now in a new location, has shed its old grocery/bakery for a spiffy, contemporary look, executed in black and white walls with hot-pink and purple neon lights. The rotating daily specials, which always come with fresh vegetables, are very popular, as are the kosher sandwiches, baked beef short ribs, and beef brisket *au jus* with brown new potatoes and baby carrots. The restaurant also does a brisk carry-out business, including picnics and parties. *2713 Culver Rd., tel. 205/879–8585. Dress: casual. No reservations. AE, D, DC, MC, V.*

Cabana Café. Now in a new location, this casual eatery, with high ceilings and track lighting, offers a 120-item menu to choose from, including Mexican dishes. The Saturday champagne-brunch crowd crow over the eggs Benedict and seafood salad. Amberjack is coated with herb butter and grilled to a golden brown. The shrimp gumbo is good, and the Low Country Carolina chicken better. *217 Lakeshore Pkwy., tel. 205/870–1390. Dress: casual. No reservations. AE, MC, V. Closed Sun.*

Points Beyond
Inexpensive

Golden Rule Barbecue. This side-of-the-road joint doesn't invite leisurely dining, but it has the best barbecue in Birmingham—succulent, smoked long and evenly, and served with a mild red sauce that doesn't overpower. Booths, tables, and counters seat 70, or you can sit at picnic tables outside or take some away for a picnic of your own. *1571 Montgomery Hwy. (U.S. 31), tel. 205/823–7770. Dress: casual. No reservations. AE, MC, V. Closed Sun.*

Irondale Café. No lie, this restaurant *is* the inspiration for Fannie Flagg's Whistlestop Cafe in *Fried Green Tomatoes.* And yes, fried green tomatoes are always available, as well as a dozen other fresh vegetables, at least six entrées, and an array of desserts—all served cafeteria-style. Bill McMichael, who runs the restaurant with his family, plans to redecorate the place to include one room replicating the original café, which dates to Depression days; a '50s–'60s-style room; and a formal dining room. *1906 1st Ave. N, Irondale (east of Birmingham), tel. 205/956–5258. Dress: casual. Reservations advised for groups. No credit cards. Lunch only on Sun.; breakfast and lunch only on Mon.; closed Sat. and major holidays.*

Lodging

Many Birmingham hotels and motels offer weekend specials; inquire about special rates. In fall or winter, beware of football weekends: If the Alabama Crimson Tide or the Auburn Tigers are in town, you may find all hotels booked or at least very crowded.

The most highly recommended properties in each price category are indicated by a star ★. For a map pinpointing locations, *see* Dining, *above.*

Category	Cost*
Very Expensive	\$96–\$178
Expensive	\$80–\$95
Moderate	\$53–\$79
Inexpensive	under \$53

**double room; add 7% for taxes*

Downtown
Very Expensive
★

Pickwick Hotel. Part of the Five Points South area, the eight-story Pickwick was built in 1931 as an office building and converted in 1986 to a bed-and-breakfast hotel. Rooms have been decorated in an art deco style, with pink walls, green carpets, elegant period furnishings (including armoires), and Liberty of London bedspreads. Suites have kitchenettes, wet bars, and dining tables. High tea is served every afternoon. *1023 20th St. S, 35205, tel. 205/933–9555 or 800/255–7304. 35 rooms, 28 suites. Facilities: breakfast room, bar, sitting room with complimentary wine and cheese, meeting room. AE, DC, MC, V.*

The Tutwiler. A National Historic Landmark, the Tutwiler was built in 1913 as luxury apartments and converted into a hotel in

1987. The lobby is elegant, with marble floors, chandeliers, brass banisters, antiques, and lots of flowers. Rooms are furnished in antique reproductions, including armoires and high-back chairs, plus velour love seats and king-size or double beds. *Park Place at 21st St. N, 35203, tel. 205/322–2100 or 800/866–7666. 96 rooms, 53 suites. Facilities: restaurant, pub, reduced rate at nearby YMCA. AE, DC, MC, V.*

Expensive **Radisson Hotel.** This 14-story hotel near the University Medical Center and Five Points South was newly redecorated in 1988. The pink and green lobby, with a piano lounge, has a marble floor and Queen Anne–style furnishings. Rooms have a contemporary look, in mauve and peach tones. *808 20th St. S, 35205, tel. 205/933–9000 or 800/333–3333. 298 rooms, including 11 suites on the executive floor (3 with wet bars). Facilities: cable TV, outdoor pool, sauna, steam rooms, privileges at nearby fitness center, cocktail lounge, oyster bar. AE, DC, MC, V.*

Sheraton Civic Center Hotel. Completed in 1991, this 17-story downtown convention hotel is geared to the business traveler, with its large rooms and spacious public areas. It is located 4 miles from the airport. *2101 Civic Center Blvd., 35203, tel. 205/324–5000 or 800/325–3535. 770 rooms. Facilities: 3 restaurants, 2 lounges, indoor pool, health club, airport transportation. AE, D, DC, MC, V.*

Moderate–Expensive **Courtyard by Marriott.** Business travelers and families alike enjoy this attractive alternative to over-priced hotels. Located across from Brookwood Village Mall, it offers beautifully landscaped grounds and attractive public areas. *500 Shades Creek Pkwy., 35209, tel. 205/879–0400 or 800/321–2211. 142 rooms. Facilities: restaurant, pool, whirlpool, exercise room, laundry. AE, D, DC, MC, V.*

Moderate **Comfort Inn–Perimeter.** You can still enjoy the luxury of an indoor Jacuzzi, fitness center, and well-appointed rooms at this economy motel, which offers free in-room coffee and Continental breakfast. *4627 Hwy. 280, 35242, tel. 205/991–9977 or 800/221–2222. 100 rooms. Facilities: pool. AE, D, DC, MC, V.*

Holiday Inn–Redmont. The city's oldest hotel, dating to 1925, has undergone a $9-million renovation and now sports a fresh look, with traditional furnishings and decor. The two-room suites, which include parlors and large baths, are very popular. The property is downtown, one block from the financial district and four blocks from I–59. Guests are treated to a welcome reception and full breakfast and have use of the YMCA nearby. *2101 5th Ave. N, tel. 205/324–2101. 103 rooms, 9 suites. Facilities: restaurant, lounge, free airport transportation.*

Inexpensive **Motel Birmingham.** This old courtyard motel offers free airport transportation and Continental breakfast. *7905 Crestwood Blvd., 35210, tel. 205/956–4440 or 800/338–9275. 242 rooms. Facilities: outdoor pool, restaurant. AE, D, DC, MC, V.*

Farther Out
Very Expensive
★

Wynfrey Hotel. This deluxe hotel rises 15 stories above the Riverchase Galleria complex of 200 shops and restaurants (*see* Shopping, *above*). The lobby is elegant, with Italian marble floor, Chippendale furniture, Oriental rug, enormous arrangement of fresh flowers, and brass escalator. Rooms are furnished in English and French traditional styles. The top two floors constitute the Chancellor's Club and have two bi-level suites each. *U.S. 31 S, 1000 Riverchase Galleria, 35244, tel. 205/987–*

1600 or 800/476–7006. 310 rooms, 19 suites. Facilities: outdoor pool, complete health club with whirlpool, concierge, café, Winston's restaurant, piano lounge, "high-energy" lounge. AE, DC, MC, V.

Expensive **Mountain Brook Inn.** This eight-story glass hotel in the foothills of Red Mountain caters to the business traveler. The lobby is tastefully furnished, with marble floors, chandeliers, brass, and Oriental carpet. Eight suites are bi-level, with spiral staircases and Oriental decor; they have wet bars and refrigerators. Two suites have conference tables. *2800 U.S. 280, 35223, tel. 205/870–3100 or 800/523–7771. 153 rooms, 8 suites. Facilities: outdoor pool, privileges at nearby health club, 4 meeting rooms, ballroom (capacity: 300), restaurant, lounge. AE, D, DC, MC, V.*

Moderate **Ramada Inn Airport.** Three minutes from the airport, this 12-story hotel is a typical Ramada, except for the eye-catching winding staircase in the chandeliered lobby. *5216 Airport Hwy., 35212, tel. 205/591–7900 or 800/272–6232. 192 rooms. Facilities: outdoor pool, exercise room, 6 meeting rooms, restaurant, and lounge. AE, D, DC, MC, V.*

Inexpensive **Days Inn.** A typical unit of the chain, it has standard contemporary decor, and is located a mile from the airport. *5101 Messer-Airport Hwy., 35212, tel. 205/592–6110 or 800/325–2525. 143 rooms (some with coffeemakers). Facilities: outdoor pool, small meeting room, restaurant, privileges at nearby fitness center. AE, D, DC, MC, V.*

The Arts

For an up-to-date listing of happenings in the arts, get the current issue of *Birmingham* magazine on the newsstand. For ticket information, contact the **Greater Birmingham Convention & Visitors Bureau** (tel. 205/252–9825).

Theater The **Birmingham Jefferson Civic Center** (tel. 205/458–8401)—a four-block complex with an exhibition hall, a theater, a concert hall, and the Coliseum—hosts touring Broadway companies, major rock concerts, and exhibitions. The **Terrific New Theatre** (tel. 205/328–0868) hosts touring drama groups. **Town and Gown Theatre** (tel. 205/934–5088), a semiprofessional community theater based on the UAB campus (but not a college theater group), puts on five musical and dramatic works from October through May. **Birmingham Children's Theater** (tel. 205/324–0470), the nation's largest professional children's theatrical group, performs for children from October through May at the Civic Center.

Opera The **Southern Regional Opera** (tel. 205/322–6737) presents four productions each season (Nov.–May).

Concerts The **Alabama Symphony Orchestra** (tel. 205/326–0100) performs at the Civic Center throughout the year, and sometimes at Sloss Furnaces' covered amphitheater (tel. 205/324–1911). Rock concerts are held at the Civic Center, Sloss Furnaces, and the **Oak Mountain Amphitheater** in Pelham (tel. 205/985–9797). Organ shows on a "mighty Wurlitzer" accompany silent pictures at the **Alabama Theatre** (tel. 205/252–0412).

Dance The **State of Alabama Ballet** (tel. 205/252–2475) performs at the Civic Center from September through March. The modern dance group **Southern Danceworks** (tel. 205/322–6483) performs October through February at the Alabama Theatre and other halls in the city.

Festival For a month or more each spring, Birmingham celebrates the ballet, opera, painting, sculpture, literature, symphony, and other art forms of a single country at its **Festival of the Arts.** Performances and exhibits are staged at various locations throughout the city, though the Civic Center is usually the hub of activity. In June the city hosts another arts celebration, **City Stages,** in downtown Linn Park. For more information, contact the Greater Birmingham Convention & Visitors Bureau (tel. 205/252–9825).

Nightlife

Comedy **The Comedy Club** (430 Green Springs Hwy., tel. 205/942–0008) showcases nationally known and up-and-coming comedians nightly except holidays.

Country Music **Spencer's Lounge** (corner Second Ave. S and 18th St. S, tel. 205/326–6860) is the place to hear great southern tunes.

Discos **Overtures** (Riverchase Galleria, tel. 205/987–1600), at the Wynfrey Hotel, is where Yuppies meet.

Jazz **Grundy's Music Room and Lounge** (1924 4th Ave. N, tel. 205/323–3109) is a lively local favorite watering spot that attracts top area musicians.

Montgomery

Known as the Cradle of the Confederacy, Montgomery is a town steeped in antebellum history. While its population has grown to almost 200,500, the capital city is still reminiscent of a sleepy little town on the banks of the Alabama River. In the final year of the Civil War, Union troops, led by General John Wilson, passed through the city and burned artillery factories in Selma, but they did not destroy Montgomery. Today many of the old houses have been restored to their original splendor.

The city bears witness to another of this country's great struggles as well. Here, in 1954, after black seamstress Rosa Parks was arrested for refusing to give up her seat on a city bus to a white man, a young black minister, Dr. Martin Luther King, Jr., led the 1½-year bus boycott that spearheaded the civil rights movement. Completed in 1989, the dramatic Civil Rights Memorial in front of the Southern Poverty Law Center (400 Washington Ave., tel. 205/264–0286) is the first phase of a long-range project. Created by Maya Lin, designer of the Vietnam Veterans' Memorial in Washington, D.C., the monument consists of an upper plaza and a pool from which water flows over a 40-foot-wide black granite wall. On it are inscribed words from Dr. King's "I have a dream . . . " speech and the names of many who gave their lives to the civil rights movement.

While Montgomery's history has been dramatic, its present makes it the capital of stage drama in the South. With the move of the Alabama Shakespeare Festival into world-class facilities (costing $21.5 million), some of the best actors in America have been lured to the area to perform at the 750-seat festival stage and the 225-seat Octagon theater. Also in the 250-acre Wynton

M. Blount Cultural Park—named for the former postmaster general of the United States, who donated the land and the festival building to the city—is the $6.1 million Montgomery Museum of Fine Arts. The gardens are beautifully landscaped.

Arriving and Departing

By Plane Dannelly Field is seven miles from downtown. It is served by **American Eagle, Atlantic Southeast, Delta, Northwest Airlink,** and **USAir.**

Between the Airport and Center City **Taxis** are readily available and relatively inexpensive to most downtown hotels. Many hotels provide transportation from the airport by prior arrangement. **By car,** take U.S. 80, which connects with U.S. 31, to the first major intersection. Turn right onto the South By-Pass, where some hotels are located. To travel to downtown, turn north onto I–65, follow signs to I–85, and take the first exit, Court Street.

By Train **Amtrak's** (tel. 800/872–7245) ***Gulf Breeze*** links Montgomery and Birmingham, with stops at Greenville, Evergreen, Atmore, and Mobile. It connects with ***Crescent,*** which serves Birmingham on its New Orleans–New York run.

By Bus **Greyhound/Trailways** (210 Court St., downtown, tel. 205/264–4518).

By Car I–65 runs north to Birmingham and south to Mobile. I–85 begins in Montgomery and runs northeast to Atlanta. U.S. 80 runs west past the airport to Selma.

Getting Around

By Taxi Taxis charge $2.30 for the first mile, $1 for each additional mile. One company is **Yellow Cab** (tel. 205/262–5225).

By Bus City buses (tel. 205/262–7321) run from 6 AM to 4:30–6 PM, depending on the route. Exact change is required (80¢ fare, 10¢ transfer).

By Trolley A quiet, comfortable, inexpensive (25¢ each boarding) way to see downtown is by old-style trolley (tel. 205/262–7321). (Montgomery was the site of the first electric trolley.) It runs from the Cramton Bowl parking lot (two blocks behind the capitol) to the capitol, west on Dexter Avenue, through downtown, and to the parking lot in front of the old Union Station, next to the river. Get on and off at any of its stops, walk around, see the area, shop, and then get back on when it next makes its rounds (9–11:30, 1:20–3:40).

Important Addresses and Numbers

Tourist Information **Montgomery Area Chamber of Commerce & Visitor Division. Visitor Information Center** (401 Madison Ave., tel. 205/262–0013). **Alabama Bureau of Tourism and Travel** (532 S. Perry St., tel. 205/242–4169 or 800/ALABAMA to request travel information).

Emergencies Dial 911 for **police** or **ambulance** in an emergency.

Pharmacy **Harco Drugs** (Capitol Plaza Shopping Center, South By-Pass, tel. 205/281–1312, open until midnight).

Guided Tours

The only guided tours available in Montgomery are restricted to groups. A cassette driving tour of the downtown area is available for purchase ($9 for tape and book, $2 for book only) from **Old Alabama Town** (310 N. Hull St., tel. 205/263-4355). You may also buy a cassette for $5 to enjoy a walking tour of the historic district (*see* A Walking Tour in Exploring, *below*). The **Visitor Information Center** (*see* Important Addresses and Numbers, *above*) has a free 15-minute video on the city that will help you organize your own tour.

Exploring Montgomery

Numbers in the margin correspond to points of interest on the Downtown Montgomery map.

A Walking Tour

1 Begin with the handsome **State Capitol,** at present undergoing extensive restoration and scheduled to reopen in late 1992. It was built in 1851 and from 1860 served as the first capitol for the Confederate States of America. Just inside the huge double doors (with a bronze star marking the spot where Jefferson Davis stood to take the oath of office as president of the Confederacy) there is an amazing piece of interior design. The stairway curling up the sides of the circular hallway is freestanding, without visible support. The state's rich history has been caught by an artist's brush in great, colorful murals. In the large House chamber and smaller Senate chamber, the gigantic brick fireplaces are now fully operational following the renovation. *Bainbridge St. at Dexter Ave., tel. 205/242–4169.*

Walk west on Dexter Avenue for one block. On your left, at no.
2 454, is the **Dexter Avenue King Memorial Baptist Church** (tel. 205/263–3970), where Dr. Martin Luther King, Jr., began his career as a minister in 1955. The church's sanctuary and the basement Sunday-school rooms are open to visitors. A mural covering one basement wall depicts people and events associated with Dr. King and the Civil Rights Movement. *Admission free. Open weekdays 9–noon, Sat. 10–2.*

Walk back to the capitol and turn right onto Bainbridge. At the
3 corner of Bainbridge and Washington is the **Alabama Department of Archives and History,** a memorial to the soldiers who lost their lives in World War I. It is lined with Alabama marble and contains outstanding exhibits of artifacts documenting the state's history from its Indian days. *624 Washington Ave., tel. 205/242–2443. Open weekdays 8–5, with free guided tours, weekends 9–5. Closed major holidays.*

At the corner of Washington Avenue and Union Street stands
4 the **First White House of the Confederacy,** built in 1840. The house was occupied by Jefferson Davis and his family while the Confederacy was being organized at the State Capitol across the street. Today it contains many of their possessions, plus artifacts of the Civil War period. *644 Washington Ave., tel. 205/242–4624. Free tours weekdays 8–4:30, weekends 9–4:30.*

Continue walking north on Union, then turn right onto Monroe
5 Street. A half-block east is the **Governor Lurleen Burns Wallace Memorial Museum,** housed (with the Alabama Historical Commission's offices) in the 1850s Rice-Semple-Haardt House. With its wide porch and angular roof, it reflects French- and

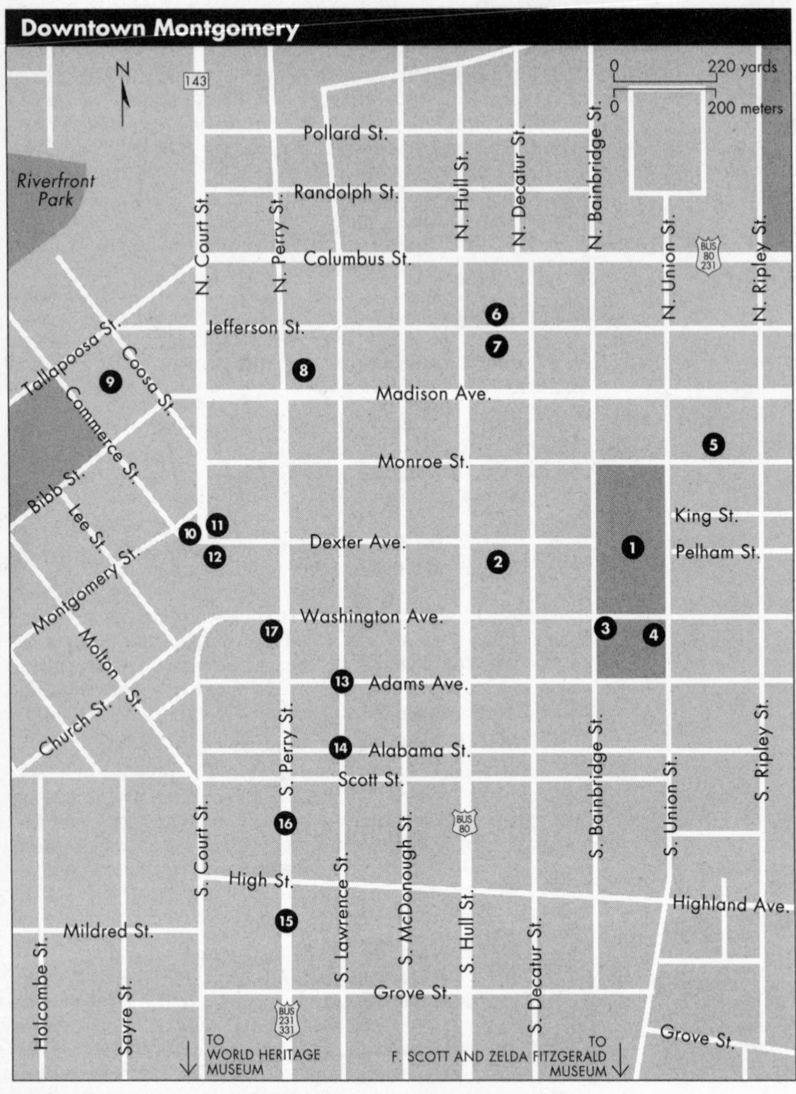

Alabama Dept. of Archives and History, **3**

Arts and Humanities State Council Building, **11**

Court Square Fountain, **10**

Dexter Ave. King Mem. Baptist Church, **2**

First White House of the Confederacy, **4**

Gov. Lurleen Burns Wallace Memorial Museum, **5**

Governor Shorter Mansion, **14**

House of Mayors, **15**

Lower Commerce St. Historic Dist., **9**

Lucas Tavern, **6**

Old Confederate Post Office, **17**

Ordeman-Shaw House, **7**

St. John's Episcopal Church, **8**

St. Peter's Roman Catholic Church, **13**

State Capitol, **1**

Teague House, **16**

Winter Building, **12**

Spanish-influenced designs; the latticed arches on the L-shaped porch were a feature of many early Montgomery homes. The museum displays many possessions of Alabama's first woman governor. *725 Monroe St., tel. 205/242–3183. Admission free. Open daily 8–5.*

The **Old North Hull Street Historic District** (also known as **Old Alabama Town**)—about six blocks northwest of the capitol, between Madison Avenue and Columbus Street—consists of 24 newly restored houses, barns, stores, and other structures from 1818 to the turn of the century. Most were moved here from their original sites.

6 The reception center for the district is in the old **Lucas Tavern**
(310 N. Hull St., tel. 205/263–4355), built in 1818 on the Old
Federal Road traveled by early settlers to the area; in 1825, the
French general Lafayette stayed at the tavern on his way to
Montgomery. A free slide show here tells the story of the district. A self-guided cassette walking tour covers 10 house mu-
7 seums. At the 11th—the **Ordeman-Shaw House** (230 N. Hull
St.), an Italianate town house with restored outbuildings and
gardens—volunteers lead tours of the house, when it's available. *Tel. 205/263–4355. Cassette tour: $5 adults; $2 children
6–18, under 6 free. Ordeman-Shaw House: $1 adults, children
free with adult. Open Mon.–Sat. 9–3:30, Sun. 1–3:30. Closed
major holidays.*

A Driving Tour

From North Hull Street, drive west on Madison Avenue for
three blocks. The imposing, high-spired church on the right is
8 **St. John's Episcopal Church** (113 Madison Ave., tel. 205/262–
1937). Built in 1856, it has colorful stained-glass windows and a
bronze plaque marking the pew where Jefferson Davis worshiped.

Continue west on Madison Avenue, veer left onto Bibb Street,
then turn right onto Commerce Street. On your right, between
9 Court Square and the Riverfront, is the **Lower Commerce
Street Historic District,** a group of renovated Victorian structures dating from the end of the last century and now used as office buildings. This area was the trade-and-transportation hub of the busy 19th-century town, which prospered from the business of the Alabama River; there cotton was loaded onto great riverboats and transported downstream and finally out to sea, headed for the textile mills of New England.

Drive south on Commerce Street to Dexter Avenue. At the
10 junction is **Court House Fountain,** built in 1885. Hebe, cupbear-
er to the gods, looks north down Commerce Street to the river.
11 To the left on Dexter is the extraordinary **Arts and Humanities
State Council Building** (1 Dexter Ave., tel. 205/242–4076), patterned after a Venetian palazzo. Works by Alabama artists are always on display in the magnificent lobby with its banistered balcony. Free tours can be arranged.

Across the avenue is another newly renovated structure, the
12 **Winter Building** (2 Dexter Ave.), built in the 1840s as the office
of the Southern Telegraph Company. It was from here that the Confederate leaders sent a telegram ordering their soldiers to fire on Fort Sumter, thereby starting the Civil War.

Drive east on Dexter Avenue, then south on Lawrence Street,
13 to **St. Peter's Roman Catholic Church** (219 Adams Ave., tel.
205/262–7304), built in 1852. Its unusual Spanish-style archi-

tecture may reflect the Cuban and Mexican origins of some of the building funds. To have a look inside, enter through the rectory.

Continue south on Lawrence Street past the new Montgomery County Courthouse. At the corner of Lawrence and Alabama
14 streets is the **Governor Shorter Mansion** (305 S. Lawrence St.) with its Greek Revival portico, home in the 19th-century to Governor John Gill Shorter. It has been renovated and now houses offices.

Turn right onto High Street and drive one block. To the left on
15 South Perry Street is the brick **House of Mayors.** Once the home of Jack Thorington and Mordecai Moses, both mayors of Montgomery during the 19th century, and Joseph Norwood, who became mayor of nearby Fort Deposit in the 1880s, this mansion now houses the Alabama Bureau of Tourism and Travel. Inside, free information about the state is available. *532 S. Perry St., tel. 205/242–4169. Open weekdays 8–5.*

16 One block north is the **Teague House** (468 S. Perry St.), a fine example of late Greek Revival architecture in the South and now owned by the Alabama Business Council. Continuing
17 north on Perry Street, you'll see the **Old Confederate Post Office** (39 S. Perry St., corner of Washington St.). One of the oldest buildings in town, it was once the law office of U.S. Congressman William Lowndes Yancey, who spoke eloquently in Congress in the mid-1800s about why the South should secede from the Union. The building served as the Confederate Post Office in 1861. Today it houses private offices.

Montgomery for Free

Concerts Each spring and fall, Blount International sponsors **concerts at Court Square** on Fridays at noon near the Court Square Fountain. During the Christmas season, the **First Baptist Church choir** (305 S. Perry St., tel. 205/834–6310) performs "The Living Christmas Tree," with the choir arranged in the shape of a tree.

Lectures **Auburn University** at Montgomery (off I–85N, 8 mi east of downtown, tel. 205/244–3000) offers entertaining and informative lectures throughout the year.

What to See and Do with Children

Montgomery Museum of Fine Arts. Alabama's oldest fine arts museum reopened in 1988 in an impressive new facility within the same park that houses the Alabama Shakespeare Festival Theatre. It features ARTWORKS, a hands-on gallery for children and adults; a permanent gallery exhibiting the Blount, Inc. Corporate Collection of American Art; and a gift shop, auditorium, and print gallery, as well as new galleries for changing exhibitions. Patrons enjoy dining in the Terrace Cafe. *One Museum Dr., tel. 205/244–5700. Admission free. Open Tues.–Wed., Fri.–Sat. 10–5, Thurs. 10–9, Sun. noon–5. Closed holidays.*

Montgomery Zoo. Expanded recently from 6 to 40 acres, the zoo is home to 800 animals from five continents. Dining, a gift shop, and a train ride are offered as well. *329 Vandiver Blvd., tel. 205/832–2637. Admission: $1.50 adults and children over*

12; 25¢ children 2–12, under 2 free; senior citizens free. Open daily 9:30–5:30 May–Sept., until 4:30 PM Oct.–Apr.; closed Christmas and New Year's Day.

W. A. Gayle Planetarium. Images of the sun, moon, planets, stars, and other heavenly bodies are projected on a 50-foot dome. Daily shows are continuously updated. *1010 Forest Ave., in Oak Park, tel. 205/832–2625. Admission free. Open Mon.–Sat. 9–5, Sun. 1–4. Shows weekends at 2 PM, closed last 2 weeks Aug., Dec. Show admission: $2 adults, $1 children 6–17. Not geared to pre-schoolers.*

Off the Beaten Track

Hank Williams Memorial. Montgomery was the home of country-music singer and songwriter Hank Williams, and after his untimely death at age 29 on New Year's Day, 1953, he was brought here for one of the city's grandest funerals. It was held at City Hall, with the top country stars of the time delivering eulogies and singing sad songs. He was buried in the Oakwood Cemetery Annex, (1305 Upper Wetumpka Rd., tel. 205/264–4938), beneath a stone that depicts his likeness and sheet music from his most popular songs, such as "Your Cheatin' Heart."

Jasmine Hill Gardens and Outdoor Museum. Here, atop a wooded hill, are 17 acres of beautiful gardens with replicas of Greek sculptures and of the ruins of the Temple of Hera. Musical performances are sometimes given at the outdoor theater. *1500 Jasmine Hill Rd., tel. 205/567–6463 or 205/567–9444. Admission: $3.50 adults; $2 children 6–12, under 6 free. Open Tues.–Sun. 9–5, closed Christmas and New Year's Day.*

Scott and Zelda Fitzgerald Museum. Zelda Fitzgerald grew up in these parts, and some of her artwork still hangs at Montgomery's Museum of Fine Arts (*see* What to See and Do with Children, *above*). Her husband, F. Scott, is famous for such works as *The Great Gatsby*, *Tender is the Night*, and numerous short stories. Once the home of this colorful couple, it's now a museum containing many of the Fitzgeralds' belongings; you can also view a 25-minute video on their life in Montgomery. *919 Felder Ave. (via South Union St.), tel. 205/264–4222. Admission free. Tours by appointment.*

World Heritage Museum. This museum on the outskirts of town showcases a number of historic artifacts, documents, and photographs of Civil War, Civil Rights, and general Alabama history. *110 W. Jeff Davis Ave. (via Court St. S), tel. 205/263–7229. Admission free. Tours by appointment.*

Shopping

Shopping Districts Almost all of Montgomery's shopping is done in the centers and malls surrounding the city. Here are the biggest and best:

Eastdale Mall. In addition to its anchor stores—Sears, Parisian's, McRae's, and Gayfer's—Eastdale has specialty stores, record and book stores, restaurants, three movie theaters, and a popular ice rink. *I–85N to Eastern By-Pass, take exit to Wetumpka, follow Eastern By-Pass north to Eastdale exit, tel. 205/277–7359.*

Montgomery Mall. This old shopping area has recently been enlarged and improved. A glass atrium at the center, flickering gaslights, and miniature trees, plus a replica of the famous old Klein's Jewelry clock that for many years stood outside One Dexter Avenue, give the mall a plush downtown-street look. The main stores are Gayfer's, McRae's, and JC Penney. *Intersection of South By-Pass and U.S. 231S, tel. 205/281–0242.*

Zelda Place. This Deco-style shopping area is Yuppie headquarters, with many small shops like Nancy Blount (women's high fashion), and the New York Kitchen Shoppe. Joe's delicatessen (tel. 205/244– 0440), a Montgomery tradition—serving super breakfasts and whopping corned beef and pastrami sandwiches, is also here. *I–85N to Ann St. exit, south on Ann St.*

Specialty Stores
Antiques

Herron House (422 Herron St., tel. 205/265–2063) has the city's largest stock of porcelain, glass, and silver, plus 18th- and 19th-century furniture. **Bodiford's Antique Mall** (919 Hampton St., tel. 205/265–4220) is several small stores gathered under one big roof. Depression pieces abound. **Blue Ridge Antique Junction** (Eastern By-Pass to U.S. 231N exit to Wetumpka; 7 mi from exit, on left atop Jasmine Hill, tel. 205/567–6106) packs antiques in two large buildings. There is also an old drugstore put together by the owners for your viewing pleasure.

Day Trips from Montgomery

The sites listed below are within 100 miles of Montgomery. For information on them, *see* Elsewhere in the State, *below.*

Birmingham (*see* Birmingham section, *above*)
De Soto Caverns, Childersburg
Demopolis
Mound State Monument, Moundville
Pike Pioneer Museum, Troy
Shorter Mansion, Eufaula
Sturdivant Hall, Selma
Tuscaloosa
Tuskegee

Participant Sports

Bicycling **Breakaway Bicycles** (tel. 205/271–2453) rents bicycles for rides in Oak Park or in the country.

Golf **Lagoon Park** (tel. 205/271–7004).

Miniature Golf **Mountasia Fantasy Golf** (tel. 205/277–4653) takes golfers on a safari through and around a man-made mountain, large model elephants and other animals, and a cave.

Tennis **Lagoon Park** (tel. 205/271–7004).

Spectator Sports

Dog Racing Greyhound races are held at **Victoryland,** about 20 miles east of Montgomery, just off I–85N in Shorter (tel. 205/727–0540 or 800/688–2946). There's racing and pari-mutuel betting every night but Sunday, and several matinees during the week.

Dining

The most highly recommended restaurants in each price category are indicated by a star ★.

Category	Cost*
Expensive	over $25
Moderate	$15–$25
Inexpensive	under $15

**per person without tax (8% in Montgomery), service, or drinks*

Downtown
Inexpensive

Chris' Hot Dog Stand. A Montgomery tradition for over 50 years, this stand is about 15 feet wide and 50 feet deep, with a counter always busy at lunchtime. Mr. Chris's famous sauce combines chili peppers, onions, and a variety of herbs that give his hot dogs a one-of-a-kind flavor. For a special treat, try the hot dog with "kitchen chili," a heavy, hot chili of beans and onions that you have to eat with a knife and fork. *138 Dexter Ave., tel. 205/265–6850. Dress: casual. No reservations. No credit cards. Closed Sun.*

Farmer's Market Cafeteria. Located in a downtown industrial-style metal building, the cafeteria is about as plain as a restaurant can be, except for the photos on the walls reminding diners of past sports heroes. Fried chicken, catfish, country smothered steak, and fresh vegetables are served. The hearty breakfast with smoked bacon and homemade biscuits is a local tradition. *315 N. McDonough St., tel. 205/262–9163. Dress: casual. No reservations. No credit cards. Closed Sun. Breakfast, lunch only.*

Martha's Place. You can't beat Martha Hawkins's good home-cooking, which she calls "a gift from God," so it's best to make reservations or come early to this vintage two-story house downtown. She's known far and wide for her fresh turnips, squash, peas, and corn, and entrées such as baked turkey, ham, fried chicken, barbecued ribs, meatloaf, and fried fish. If you want "soul" food (fresh collards and boiled or fried chitlins, served every Friday) call ahead. Lunch is served daily; dinner on Friday and Saturday. She serves buffet-style brunch on Sundays. *458 Sayre St., tel. 205/263–9135. Dress: casual. Reservations advised. No credit cards. Closed major holidays.*

Cloverdale
Expensive

★ **Sahara Restaurant.** Hands down, Joe and Mike Deep's Sahara—in the suburb of Cloverdale—is Montgomery's finest restaurant. The snapper, delivered twice weekly from the Gulf, is fried in a very light batter; the white meat flakes exactly as it should. Choice steaks are grilled over coals. And the seafood gumbo is wonderful: The okra is whole and not cooked to bits, and there's plenty of shrimp and oyster. *511 E. Edgemont Ave., tel. 205/262–1215. Jacket and tie required. Reservations recommended. AE, DC, MC, V. Closed Sun.*

★ **Vintage Year.** Chef Judy Martin has gone to a completely new menu, featuring snapper, tuna, shrimp, salmon, and other fish prepared in a Northern Italian style, as well as the ever-popular pasta varieties with or without shrimp. The decor is elegant, and the neighborhood bar is a popular meeting place. *405 Cloverdale Rd., tel. 205/264–8463. Jacket and tie required. Reservations required. AE, MC, V. Closed Sun.–Mon. Dinner only.*

Moderate

Jubilee Seafood Company. In a very pleasant, small café, Bud Skinner cooks some of the finest and freshest seafood dishes in town, including Dungeness crab, snapper prepared in a variety of ways (including Greek-style—sautéed in olive oil and spices

Dining

Bates House of Turkey, **17**
Chris' Hot Dog Stand, **6**
Farmer's Market Cafeteria, **5**
Green Lantern, **16**
Jubilee Seafood Company, **13**
Martha's Place, **8**
Martin's Restaurant, **14**
Sahara Restaurant, **10**
Sassafras Tearoom, **3**
Vintage Year, **9**

Lodging

Best Western-Montgomery Lodge, **11**
Courtyard by Marriott, **19**
Hampton Inn, **21**
Howard Johnson Hotel & Governor's House Conference Center, **15**
Inn South, **12**
La Quinta Motor Inn, **18**
The Madison Hotel, **4**
Ramada Inn East, **20**
Red Bluff Cottage, **2**
Riverfront Inn, **1**
State House Inn, **7**

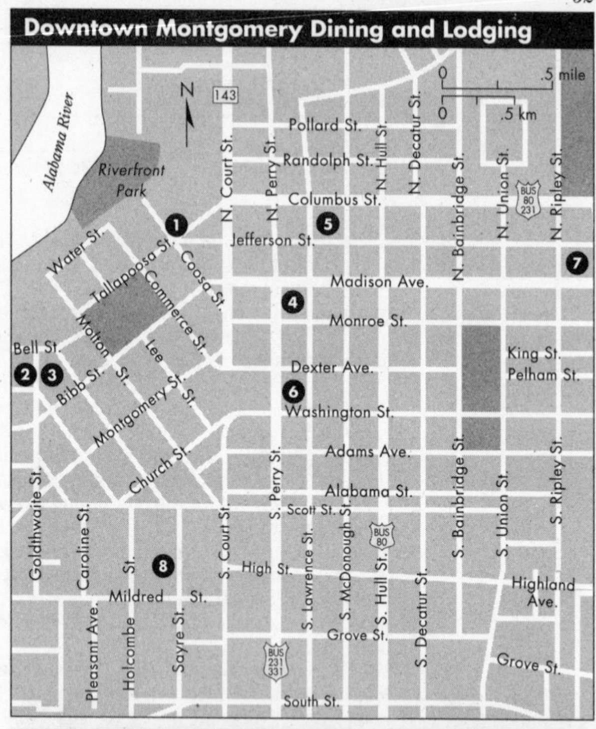

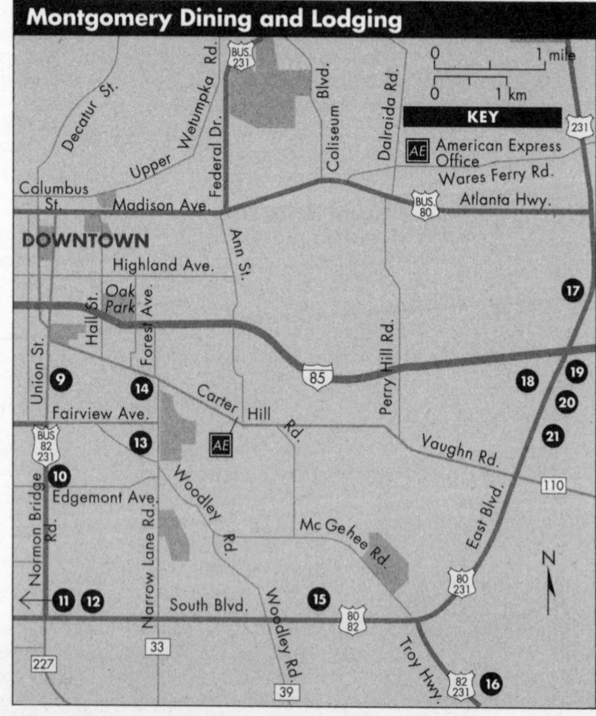

and topped with roasted almonds), soft-shell crabs, crab claws, and other delicacies. He is best known, however, for his Cajun-style dish—served only on special occasions— "oysters in rue": oysters lightly poached and dropped into a spicy, tomato-based sauce with mucho garlic, onions, peppers, and more. *1057 Woodley Rd., Cloverdale Plaza, tel. 205/262–6224. Dress: casual. No reservations. AE, DC, MC, V. Closed Sun.–Mon. Dinner only.*

Inexpensive **Martin's Restaurant.** In this plain but comfortable eatery in a small shopping center, you'll find generous helpings of home-cooked fresh vegetables, Southern fried chicken, and delicious panfried catfish fresh from Alabama ponds. The cornbread sticks literally melt in your mouth; you don't even need to put butter on them. *1796 Carter Hill Rd., tel. 205/265–1767. Dress: casual. No reservations. No credit cards. Closed Sat.*

Points Beyond

Moderate **Green Lantern.** In a rustic country setting, with jukebox music, fireplaces, and long tables, the Green Lantern is famous for its cheese biscuits, which many locals take home by the sackfuls. The waitresses bark out the menu, which is not printed. It consists of several types of steaks, all charbroiled, boiled shrimp, and fried chicken. The best is the steak, with huge baked potatoes and all the cheese biscuits you can eat. *5701 Troy Hwy., 5 mi southeast on U.S. 231, tel. 205/288–9947. Dress: casual. Reservations preferred, especially with large parties. AE, MC, V. Closed Sun. Dinner only.*

Sassafras Tearoom. You can buy the table you eat off of and enjoy a bit of Victoriana at this unusual century-old shop-cum-eatery in the Cottage Hill district. Operated by retired Colonel Jim Wallace and his wife Mary, the restaurant, which serves lunch only, caters to professionals and antiques hunters alike. Sassafras tea, either hot or cold, accompanies the crunchy chicken salad, buttermilk pie, and other home-cooked delectables, which are served promptly and graciously. *532 Clay St., tel. 205/265–7277. Dress: casual. Reservations suggested. MC, V. Lunch only. Closed evenings and weekends except for groups, as well as major holidays.*

Inexpensive **Bates House of Turkey.** There are only two like this in the world, so far as we know—here and 34 miles south at Greenville. In a small but well-polished down-home dining room, with photographs of the biggest turkey farm in central Alabama, Bates House of Turkey serves nothing but turkey for lunch and dinner: turkey sandwiches, turkey chili, turkey sausage, even quick-frozen smoked turkey breasts. *1060 Eastern By-Pass, 1 blk north of I–85, tel. 205/279–9775. Dress: casual. No reservations. MC, V. Closed Sun. evening.*

Lodging

The most highly recommended properties in each price category are indicated by a star ★. Several area lodgings offer special rates to theatergoers. For a map pinpointing locations, *see* Dining, *above*.

Category	Cost*
Very Expensive	over $70
Expensive	$50–$69

Moderate	$35–$49
Inexpensive	under $35

**double room; add 10% for taxes*

Downtown
Very Expensive

Madison Hotel. Elvis Presley slept here, but you're more likely to run into legislators and businessmen than rock stars. The six-story atrium lobby is furnished in Asian style and filled with lush greenery, and caged parrots and other birds that sing and talk throughout the day. The guest rooms carry on the Far East theme. The Civic Center is two blocks away. *120 Madison Ave., 36104, tel. 205/264–2231 or 800/228–5586. 184 rooms, 5 suites. Facilities: cable TV, outdoor pool, 2 restaurants, 2 lounges, large ballroom, 11 meeting rooms. AE, DC, MC, V.*

Expensive

★ **Red Bluff Cottage.** Located in the heart of downtown and overlooking the Alabama River, this raised cottage is bright and cheerful. The rooms are filled with antiques, some of them dating to the 18th century, collected by the Reverend Mark Waldo, who served an Episcopal parish in this city for many years, and his wife, Anne. Guests especially enjoy the music room/library containing a harpsichord, a piano, and lots of books. Full breakfast is served. *551 Clay St., Box 1026, 36101, tel. 205/263–1727. 3 rooms with bath. No credit cards.*

★ **Riverfront Inn.** A converted historic railway depot, the hotel retains many original elements, resulting in an 1890s feel in the lobby and lounge. Every guest room has a brass bed; other furnishings vary from room to room. Second-floor rooms have cathedral ceilings and original brick and beams. The Civic Center is just a block away. *200 Coosa St., 36104, tel. 205/834–4300. 130 rooms, including 6 suites. Facilities: cable TV, outdoor pool, restaurant, coffee shop, 2 lounges, 5 meeting rooms. AE, DC, MC, V.*

State House Inn. The hotel has been attractively redecorated with a pleasing color scheme of mauve and gray throughout the terra-cotta-tiled lobby and the large guest rooms. The location is central; the State Capitol is a block away. *924 Madison Ave., 36104, tel. 205/265–0741 or 800/552–7099. 164 rooms, 2 suites. Facilities: cable TV, outdoor pool, restaurant, lounge, 9 meeting rooms. AE, DC, MC, V.*

Outskirts
Expensive–Very Expensive

Courtyard by Marriott. This handsome, contemporary low-rise motor inn with a sunny gardenlike courtyard offers amenities popular with business travelers—spacious rooms, king-size beds, oversize work desks, excellent lighting, and hot water dispensers for in-room coffee. *5555 Carmichael Rd., near I–85 exit 6, tel. 205/272–5533 or 800/321–2211. 146 rooms, including 12 suites, a few with refrigerators. Facilities: coin laundry, pool, whirlpool, exercise room, restaurant, lounge. AE, DC, MC, V.*

★ **Howard Johnson Hotel & Governor's House Conference Center.** This brick, two-story hotel is located 15 minutes from the airport and within walking distance of shopping and entertainment. The lobby is decorated in Queen Anne style, guest rooms in contemporary white modular and light wood. The split-level bar features brass accents and marroon carpeting; guest rooms have multicolored carpet with matching drapes and bedspreads. Each room has a drip coffeemaker. *2705 E. South Blvd., 36116, tel. 205/288–2800 or 800/334–8459. 202 rooms, 3 suites, some with Jacuzzi, whirlpool, wet bar, refrigerator. Fa-*

cilities: cable TV, outdoor pool (in the shape of Alabama), restaurant, lounge, putting green, privileges at nearby health club possible, 10 meeting rooms (largest seats 1,000). AE, D, DC, MC, V.

Expensive **Ramada Inn East.** This two-story inn is off I–85, about 8 miles from downtown and 1½ miles from Lagoon Park (a sports facility with softball fields, tennis courts, and a golf course). The hotel, a blend of the Old South and the Tropics, features brightly lighted rooms with contemporary furnishings. There are coffeemakers in each room; suites have refrigerators, wet bars, and boardroom tables. *1355 Eastern By-Pass, 36117, tel. 205/277–2200 or 800/272–6232. 154 rooms, 2 suites. Facilities: free local calls, cable TV, outdoor pool, restaurant, lounge, reduced rate at adjacent health club. AE, D, DC, MC, V.*

Moderate **Best Western–Montgomery Lodge.** This is a two-story hotel three miles from the airport. The lobby bookcase is stocked for guests' use. Rooms have been redecorated in royal blue or cranberry; most have recliners, and three have king-size water beds. Complimentary Continental breakfast is served. *977 W. South Blvd., 36105, tel. 205/288–5740 or 800/528–1234. 100 rooms, 1 suite. Facilities: cable TV, outdoor pool, Jacuzzi, coin laundry, restaurant, lounge, 2 meeting rooms. Small pets allowed. AE, D, DC, MC, V.*

Hampton Inn. Off I–85, next door to the Ramada, this two-story inn—one of the chain's best—caters to businessmen. The lobby is homey, with lots of plants. Guest rooms are furnished in contemporary style. *1401 Eastern By-Pass, 36117, tel. 205/277–2400 or 800/426–7866. 103 rooms, 2 suites. Facilities: cable TV, outdoor pool, reduced rate at nearby health club, free local calls. AE, DC, MC, V.*

Inn South. This new no-frills property convenient to the airport, shopping malls, and downtown features double and king rooms decorated in blues and grays. A complimentary Continental breakfast is served in the contemporary-style lobby. *4243 Inn South Ave., 36105, tel. 205/288–7999. 127 rooms. Facilities: cable TV, free local calls. AE, D, DC, MC, V.*

La Quinta Motor Inn. The lobby has been remodeled in muted tones, with terra-cotta-tiled floor and silk flowers. Rooms are contemporary, in light earth tones. The location is near the Hampton Inn. *1280 Eastern By-Pass, 36117–2231, tel. 205/271–1620 or 800/531–5900. 130 rooms, 2 meeting suites. Facilities: cable TV, outdoor pool. AE, DC, MC, V.*

The Arts

For a listing of weekly events, get a current issue of *Montgomery!* magazine, which is given away in the lobbies of most hotels and motels.

Theater **Alabama Shakespeare Festival.** Shakespearean plays, modern drama, and musicals are performed on two stages at the multimillion dollar festival (tel. 205/277–2273) on the outskirts of Montgomery. (From downtown, drive east on I–85 to the Eastern By-Pass exit, then follow signs.) Stratford-upon-Avon drama authorities have called it the finest facility of its kind in the world. The season runs from November through August; tickets cost $15–$20.

A superb amateur-theater group performs at the **Montgomery Little Theatre** (tel. 205/263–4856) in fall and winter. Traveling theater groups play at the large auditorium at the **Civic Center** (tel. 205/241–2105). At the campus theater of **Auburn University at Montgomery** (tel. 205/244–3622), student actors perform drama and comedy.

Concerts The **Montgomery Community Symphony Orchestra** performs at the newly renovated Davis Theatre for the Performing Arts (tel. 205/262–5182). Other arts-related events are held at the 1,200-plus-seat auditorium as well.

Dance The **Montgomery School of Ballet** (tel. 205/265–3110) performs at different locations in the city.

Nightlife

Country and Western **Nashville Showcase** (3560 Atlanta Hwy., tel. 205/279–8001) features the Can Do Band and guest performers at weekly concerts. It's closed Sunday and Monday evenings.

Jazz **1048 East Fairview** (1048 E. Fairview, tel. 205/834–1048) offers live music nightly, with an emphasis on the blues Thursday, Friday, and Saturday evenings. Another option for jazz is **Dem Bonz** (4334 S. Court St., tel. 205/281–RIBS), featuring live music Thursday, Friday, and Saturday nights, as well as baby-back ribs and a variety of seafood.

Pop **Crockmire's Teepee Restaurant** (5620 Calmare Dr., tel. 205/277–1840) offers live music Wednesday through Sunday and prime rib steaks.

Kat and Harri's Nice Place (1061 Woodley Rd., tel. 205/834–2500), in the heart of the old Cloverdale neighborhood, offers live entertainment on weekends and snacks. Guests enjoy the open-air deck.

Mobile and the Gulf Coast

Mobile, one of the oldest cities in Alabama, is perhaps the most graceful. Its main thoroughfare, Government Street, is bordered with live oaks, and many antebellum buildings survive as a bridge to its treasured past. The city has profuse plantings of azaleas—a feature that is highlighted each spring with the Azalea Trail Festival. Nearby is Bellingrath Gardens, one of the most spectacular public gardens in the country, especially during spring.

In Mobile, Mardi Gras was created before New Orleans ever celebrated Fat Tuesday, and today the predominantly Catholic city celebrates the pre-Lenten season, usually in February, with parades and merrymaking day and night.

The area of the Gulf Coast around Gulf Shores, to the south of Mobile, encompasses about 50 miles of pure white-sand beach, including a former peninsula called Pleasure Island and Dauphin Island to the west. Though hotels and condominiums take up a good deal of the beachfront, some of it remains public. Here you'll find small-town Southern beach life, with excellent deep-sea fishing, as well as freshwater fishing in the bays and bayous, plus water sports of all types.

Those with more time might explore the eastern shore of Mobile Bay—Spanish Fort, Daphne, and Fairhope—which has a laid-back atmosphere of yesteryear: live oaks laced with Spanish moss; sprawling clapboard houses with wide porches overlooking the lazy, dark water of the bay; and interesting watering holes where local artists and writers meet informally. At Point Clear, south of Fairhope, is the Victorian-style Marriott's Grand Hotel, host for the past 145 years to the vacationing wealthy.

Getting Around

By Plane The Mobile Municipal Airport at Bates Field (tel. 205/633–0313), about 5 miles west of the city, is served by **American, Continental, Continental Express, Delta, Northwest Express,** and **Presidential/United Express. Air New Orleans, Continental, Delta, USAir,** and **Royale** have flights into the Pensacola Regional Airport (tel. 904/433–7800), some 40 miles east of Gulf Shores in Florida.

By Car I–10 travels east from Mobile into Florida through Pensacola, west into Mississippi. I–65 slices Alabama in half vertically, passing through Birmingham and Montgomery and ending at Mobile. Gulf Shores is connected with Mobile via I–10 and Route 59; Routes 180 and 182 are the main beach routes.

By Train **Amtrak**'s (tel. 800–872–8275) ***Gulf Breeze,*** links Birmingham, Montgomery, Greenville, Evergreen, Atmore, and Mobile. It connects with the ***Crescent,*** which serves Birmingham on its New Orleans–New York run.

By Bus **Greyhound/Trailways** has stations in Mobile (201 Government St., tel. 205/432–1861) and Pensacola (505 W. Burgess Rd., tel. 904/476–4800).

Guided Tours

Gray Line Tours (tel. 205/432–2229 or 800/338–5597), in Mobile, offers one- to 3½-hour trolley or motorcoach tours, departing from Fort Conde daily, to Mobile's historic points of interest, as well as to Bellingrath Gardens and the USS *Alabama.*

Important Addresses and Numbers

Tourist Information **Mobile Chamber of Commerce** is housed in **Fort Condé,** the official visitor center for Mobile (150 S. Royal St., tel. 205/434–7304 or 800/252–3862). **Alabama Gulf Coast Area Convention and Visitors Bureau** (Hwy. 59, 3150 Gulf Shores Pkwy., Drawer 457, Gulf Shores 36542, tel. 205/968–7511). **Orange Beach Chamber of Commerce** (Hwy. 182, P.O. Drawer 399, Orange Beach 36561, tel. 205/981–8000).

Emergencies Dial 911 for **police** or **ambulance** in an emergency.

Exploring Mobile and the Gulf Coast

Numbers in the margin correspond to points of interest on the Mobile and the Gulf Coast map.

Mobile The busy port city of **Mobile,** on the western bank of the Mobile
1 River and at the top of Mobile Bay, overlaps past and present. Despite a raking-over by Hurricane Frederick in 1979, gracious old mansions with iron-grillwork balconies and lovely gardens abound—belying the madness of the city's annual Mardi Gras (for 10 days preceding Shrove Tuesday, in Febru-

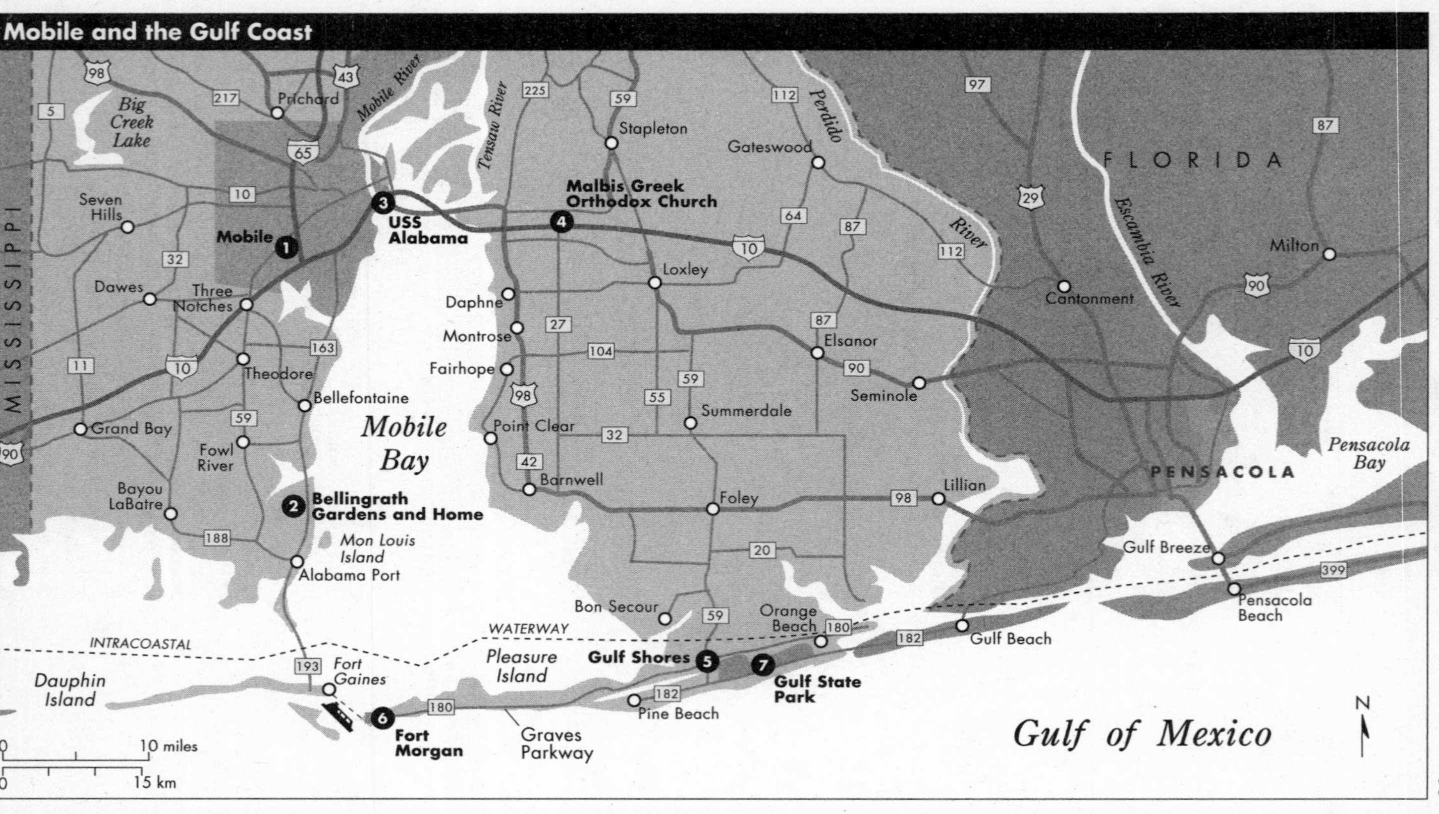

Mobile and the Gulf Coast
MISSISSIPPI
FLORIDA
Big Creek Lake
Prichard
Mobile River
Tensaw River
Stapleton
Gateswood
Perdido River
Seven Hills
Mobile
USS Alabama
Malbis Greek Orthodox Church
Loxley
Cantonment
Escambia River
Milton
Dawes
Three Notches
Daphne
Montrose
Fairhope
Elsanor
Seminole
Theodore
Bellefontaine
Grand Bay
Fowl River
Mobile Bay
Point Clear
Summerdale
Barnwell
Bayou LaBatre
Bellingrath Gardens and Home
Mon Louis Island
Alabama Port
Foley
Lillian
PENSACOLA
Pensacola Bay
Gulf Breeze
Pensacola Beach
Bon Secour
Orange Beach
Gulf Beach
INTRACOASTAL
WATERWAY
Dauphin Island
Fort Gaines
Pleasure Island
Gulf Shores
Gulf State Park
Pine Beach
Fort Morgan
Graves Parkway
Gulf of Mexico
N
10 miles
15 km

ary). Many businesses in town are conducted from buildings that predate the Civil War.

Fort Condé was the name the French gave the site in 1711; around it blossomed the first white settlement in what is now Alabama. For eight years it was the capital of the French colonial empire, and it remained under French control until 1763, long after the capital had moved to New Orleans. This French connection survives in the area's strong Creole-flavor cuisine that rivals New Orleans in fieriness.

Fort Condé, too, survives, thanks to a $2.2-million restoration, which preserved it when its remains were discovered—150 years after the fort was destroyed—during construction of the I–10 interchange (an I–10 tunnel now runs under the fort). A reconstructed portion houses the visitor center for the city, as well as a museum and several re-created rooms. Costumed guides interpret and enlighten. *150 S. Royal St., tel. 205/434–7304. Admission free. Open daily 8–5. Closed Christmas and Mardi Gras.*

Mobile today is noted for its tree-lined boulevards fanning out from **Bienville Square,** at the center of the city. Once upon a time, the square was a showplace, where the town's finest dressers would stroll beneath the live oaks and listen to bands playing on the ornate wrought-iron, gazebo-style bandstand. On special occasions—unfortunately few and far between these days—bands play again. One such occasion is the September Celebration, when weekend musical celebrations fill the air.

The city's main thoroughfare is Government Street, located in the Oakleigh Garden Historic District, a block north of Fort Conde. From here, signs lead to **Oakleigh,** a gorgeous white antebellum mansion with a stairway circling under ancient live oaks to a small portico. The high-ceilinged half-timbered house was built between 1833 and 1838 and is typical of the most expensive dwellings of its day. Fine period furniture, portraits, silver, jewelry, kitchen implements, toys, and more are displayed throughout. Tickets can be purchased next door at the **Cox-Deasy House,** another antebellum home that is not quite as old as Oakleigh (1850) and by no means as grand: A cottage, built for middle-class folk, it is furnished in simple 19th-century pieces. *350 Oakleigh Pl., tel. 205/432–1281. Admission: $4 adults, $3 over 65, $2 college students with ID, $1 children 6–18, under 6 free. Open Mon.–Sat. 10–4, Sun. 2–4. Guided tours conducted every half-hour. Closed major holidays and Christmas week.*

Several of Mobile's churches figure prominently in the area's rich African-American history: The **State Street A.M.E. Zion Church** (502 State St., tel. 205/432–3965) is one of the oldest and most striking African-American Methodist churches in town, the **St. Louis Street Missionary Baptist Church** (108 North Dearborn St., tel. 205/438–3823) hosted a conference that established Selma University. You can also visit the **Slave Market Site** (Corner St. Louis and Royal streets), where a memorial now stands commemorating Cudjoe Lewis, the last survivor of the *Clotilde,* America's last slave ship, which arrived in 1859.

Less than 20 miles south of Mobile off I–10 (turn south onto
2 Bellingrath Rd. at the town of Theodore) is **Bellingrath Gardens and Home,** site of one of the world's most magnificent aza-

lea gardens. Here, set amid a 905-acre semitropical landscape, are some 65 spectacular acres of gardens. Showtime for its azaleas is spring, when some 250,000 plantings of 200 different species are ablaze with color. But Bellingrath is a year-round wonder. In summer, 2,500 rosebushes are in bloom; in autumn, 60,000 chrysanthemum plants; in winter, fields of poinsettias. And countless other species and varieties of flowering plants spring up along a river or stream or around a lake populated by ducks and swans.

Guides are on hand throughout the gardens to assist or explain, but a free map lets you plan your own strolls along flagstone paths and charming bridges. One special area is the Oriental-American Garden, a lovely, tranquil setting with teahouses and bridges. The gardens are a sanctuary to over 200 species of birds; especially good times to visit for those ornithologically inclined are April and October, when large numbers of migratory birds drop by.

Coca-Cola bottling pioneer Walter D. Bellingrath began the nucleus of the gardens in 1917, when he and his wife bought a large tract as a fishing camp. Their travels, however, prompted them to create, instead, a garden rivaling some they had seen in Europe, and before long they opened it to the public. Today their brick home on the property is also open to visitors and offers one of the finest collections of antiques in the Southeast. Along with furniture, Meissen porcelain figurines, Dresden china, and other objets d'art amassed by Mrs. Bellingrath is the world's largest collection of Boehm porcelain birds. *Tel. 205/973–2217. Admission: gardens, $5 adults, $2.50 children 6–11, under 6 free; combination admission with house $11.25 adults, $8.75 children 6–11, $6.25 under 6. $6.25 home only. Gardens open daily 7 AM–sunset; house open daily 8 AM–1 hr. before sunset. AE, D, DC, MC, V. Closed Christmas.*

Mobile is at its loveliest during the **Azalea Trail Festival** in March or April, on the Saturday following the 10K Azalea Trail Run. The trail twines for 37 well-marked miles in and around the city, showing off azaleas at their best. Throughout the preceding week, scores of special events celebrate the yearly blossoming, from concerts to art exhibits, and in summer there's the crowning of America's Young Woman of the Year.

March is also the time of the **Historic Mobile Homes Tour,** when 19th-century Federal-style town houses, Creole cottages, and antebellum plantation homes—36 in all, public and private—are opened to visitors for daytime and candlelight tours. *For information, write to Historic Mobile Homes Tours, Box 2187, Mobile 36652, or call 205/438–7281.*

To the Shore From Mobile, there are two ways to reach Pleasure Island, a 30-mile region along the Gulf of Mexico. One is to take a scenic drive south along routes 163 and 193, perhaps stopping off at Bellingrath Gardens, and cross over the bridge to Dauphin Island, site of historic Fort Gaines, captured by Union forces during the Civil War Battle of Mobile Bay. Then you catch the **Mobile Bay Ferry** (tel. 904/434–7345 in FL, 205/421–6420; outside AL, 800/634–4027), for the 30-minute trip over to Fort Morgan, at the tip of Pleasure Island. This coastal route is shorter in mileage, though probably not in time. The other approach—the one our tour follows—is via U.S. 90E through the Bankhead Tunnel, then south on AL 59.

3 On the way, stop to pay a call aboard the **USS *Alabama*,** anchored in Mobile Bay just east of Mobile off I–10. Public subscription saved the mighty gray battleship from being scrapped ignominiously after her heroic World War II service, which ranged from Scapa Flow to the South Pacific. A tour of the ship gives a fascinating look into the life of a 2,500-member crew. Anchored next to the battleship is the submarine USS *Drum*, another active battle weapon during World War II, also open to visitors. Other exhibits in the 100-acre Battleship Park include a B-52 bomber called *Calamity Jane* and a P–51 Mustang fighter plane. *Battleship Pkwy., tel. 205/433–2703. Admission: $5 age 12 and up; $2.50 ages 6–11, under 6 free. Parking fee: $1. Open 8 AM–sunset. Closed Christmas.*

Twelve miles east of Mobile, on U.S. 90, the Mablis exit off I–
4 10, is the **Malbis Greek Orthodox Church,** a replica of a beautiful Byzantine church in Athens, Greece. It was built in 1965, at a cost of more than $1 million, as a memorial to the faith of a Greek immigrant and former monk, Jason Malbis, who founded the community but died before his dream for a cathedral could be realized. The marble for the interior was imported from the same quarries that provided stone for the Parthenon, and a master painter was brought over from Greece to paint murals on the walls and the 75-foot dome of the rotunda. The stained-glass windows are stunning. *County Route 27, tel. 205/626–3050. Admission free. Tours daily 9 AM–noon, 2–5 PM.*

When you're ready for some sun and surf, take AL 59 south to the end. At AL 182, head west. A block later, turn right for a
5 circular drive next to the **Gulf Shores** public beach area, crowded with Alabama high school and college students at spring break and everyone in summer. There's ample free parking—though the traffic is bumper-to-bumper at peak times—and the beach is as white as snow.

At the western tip of Pleasure Island, 20 miles from Gulf
6 Shores at the end of AL 180, is **Fort Morgan,** built in the early 1800s to guard the entrance to Mobile Bay. The fort saw fiery action during the Battle of Mobile Bay in 1864: Confederate torpedoes sank the ironclad *Tecumseh*, on which Admiral David Farragut gave his famous command "Damn the torpedoes! Full speed ahead!" The original outer walls still stand; inside, a museum chronicles the fort's history and displays artifacts from Indian days through World War II, with an emphasis on the Civil War. *Mobile Point, tel. 205/540–7125. Admission: $2 adults; $1 over 61 and children 6–18, under 6 free. Open daily 9–5 PM. Closed major holidays.*

7 Five miles east of Gulf Shores on AL 182 is **Gulf State Park Resort,** which covers more than 6,000 acres of Pleasure Island. Along with 2½ miles of pure white beaches and glimmering dunes, the park also has two freshwater lakes with canoeing and fishing, plus biking, hiking, and jogging trails through pine forests. There is a large beach pavilion with a snack bar, rest rooms, and showers, and nearby is a concrete fishing pier that juts 825 feet into the Gulf. There is also a resort inn and convention center, 468 campsites, and 21 cottages, plus tennis courts and an 18-hole golf course. *For information, write Gulf State Park, HC 79, Box 9, Gulf Shores 36542. Tel. 205/948–4853 or 800/544–4853. For cabins and bike, canoe, and motorless flat-bottom fishing boat rentals, tel. 205/968–7544; camping, tel. 205/968–6353; resort inn, tel. 205/968–7531. Open year-round.*

What to See and Do with Children

Exploreum Museum of Discovery offers hands-on exhibits that are educational and fun. *2.5 mi east of Spring Hill Ave. Exit off I–65, tel. 205/476–MUSE. Admission: $3 adults, $2 children ages 2–17, under 2 free. Open Tues.–Fri. 9–5, weekends 1–5. Closed Mon. and major holidays.*

Fort Condé (*see* Mobile in Exploring, *above*).

Fort Morgan (*see* To the Shore in Exploring, *above*).

Gulf State Park (*see* To the Shore in Exploring, *above*).

USS *Alabama* (*see* To the Shore in Exploring, *above*).

Waterville USA. This water park set on 17 acres has a 750,000-gallon wave pool (creates three-foot waves), seven exciting water slides, and a lazy river ride around the park. For younger children there are gentler rides in a supervised play area. There is also a 36-hole miniature golf course and a video-game arcade. *AL 59, Gulf Shores, tel. 205/948–2106. Admission: $9.95, children under 3 free. Open Memorial Day–Labor Day.*

Wildland Expeditions, led by Captain Gene Burrell on the *Gator Bait*, explores the Mobile–Tensaw Delta, with close-up views of plants and animals. *7536 Tung Ave. N, Theodore, 30582, tel. 205/460–8206. Admission: adults $17.50, students $10.50.*

Off the Beaten Track

Naval Aviation Museum. At the Naval Air Station in Pensacola, many planes used in both world wars and later—including a Gemini space capsule, F-18s, Corsairs, and Spitfires—are displayed on a rotating basis. And they're everywhere—outdoors, in hangars, or inside, on the floor or suspended from the ceiling. From Gulf Shores, follow the Beach Road east to Blue Angel Parkway, then to Sherman Field, where the precision-flying team the Blue Angels are based. (They practice here during the week when they are not doing shows elsewhere.) When the USS *Lexington* aircraft carrier is in port, you can go aboard between 9 and 3 on weekends. *Tel. 904/452–3604. Admission free. Open daily 9–5. Closed major holidays.*

Shopping

Mobile Most shopping in Mobile is done in malls and centers in the suburban areas. Stores are generally open Monday–Saturday 10–9, Sunday 1–6. Sales tax is 7%. Banks are generally open weekdays 9–2.

Shopping Districts. The **Bel Air Mall** (one block east of I–65 Beltline off Airport Blvd., tel. 205/478–1893) has some 175 stores under one roof, including JC Penney and Sears, plus a food court. **Springdale Mall-Plaza** (Airport Blvd. and I–65, tel. 205/479–9871), anchored by Gayfer's, McRae's, and Montgomery Ward, has more than 100 stores.

Antiques Antiques buffs love Mobile because it offers over 25 individual shops and three malls that specialize in antiques. There are at least 20 shops in the **Red Barn Antique Mall** (418 Dauphin Island Pkwy., tel. 205/473–9227). **Al Atchison Antiques** (601 Government St., tel. 205/438–9421 or 205/432–8423), one of the largest antiques dealers in the South, is packed with antique brass beds and other American and European antique furniture.

Souvenirs The **Tanner Mercantile Company** (5460 Old Shell Rd., tel. 205/476–5282), operated by Joel and Catherine Turner, specializes in Mobile souvenirs and gourmet coffees, including their trademark blend, Café Pecan Mobile. Another place to look for souvenirs, as well as books and local art, is the **Museum Gift Shoppe** (355 Government St., tel. 205/694–0069).

Gulf Shores
Beach Gear For swimsuits, air-brushed T-shirts, souvenirs, gifts, and camera supplies, try **Beach Bazaar** (Gulf Shores Pkwy., tel. 205/948–7233).

Gifts **Riviera Centre** (AL 59 S, Foley, AL, tel. 205/943–8888 or 800/5–CENTRE), a handsome complex of factory-direct stores 45 miles from Mobile, offers savings of up to 75% off regular retail prices. Stores include West Point Pepperell, L'Eggs Hanes Bali, Judy Bond, J. G. Hook, Dansk, Danskin, Calvin Klein, Liz Claiborne, American Tourister, Polo/Ralph Lauren, Manhattan, Bass Shoes, Pfaltzgraff, and other top names. *Open Mon.–Sat. 9 AM–9 PM, Sun. 10–6.*

Participant Sports

Biking **Gulf State Park Resort** (tel. 205/948–7275) in Gulf Shores has biking trails through pine forests and rents bicycles. **Island Recreation Services** (tel. 205/948–7334) in Gulf Shores rents bikes, mopeds, and water-sports equipment (*see* Water Sports, *below*).

Canoeing **Sunshine Canoe Rentals** (tel. 205/344–8664) runs canoe trips at Escatawpa River, 15 miles west of Mobile. The river has no rapids but makes for pleasant, leisurely travel past lots of white sandbars.

Fishing The freshwater and saltwater fishing in the Gulf area is excellent. **Gulf State Park Resort** has fishing from an 825-foot pier and rents flat-bottom boats for lake fishing. Deep-sea fishing from charter boats is very popular; in Gulf Shores, you can sign on board the *Marina Queen* (tel. 205/981–8499) for a full- or half-day fishing expedition, and Orange Beach has 40 boats to choose from. For a brochure on Orange Beach's offerings, call 205/981–8000; two choices are the 98-foot *Moreno Queen* (tel. 205/981–8499) and the 48-foot *Island Lady* (tel. 205/981–4510). Catches from these deep-sea expeditions include king mackerel, amberjack, tuna, white marlin, blue marlin, grouper, bonito, sailfish, and red snapper. Nonresidents 16 or over may not fish anywhere in Alabama without a valid fishing license; for information, call 205/242–3260.

Golf A good public 18-hole course in Mobile is the **Spring Hill College Golf Course** (tel. 205/343–2356); the 18-hole **Azalea City Golf Club** (tel. 205/342–4221) is rather flat and not a great challenge. **Gulf Shores Golf Club** (tel. 205/968–7366) has an 18-hole, 72-par championship course. The 18-hole course at the **Gulf State Park Resort** (tel. 205/948–4653) is one of the most beautiful, with moss-hung live oaks and giant magnolia trees. The newest links in the area, **Lakeview Golf Club** (off AL 59 on Rte. 20 south of Foley, tel. 205/943–4653), has 27 holes and six lakes and is well sand-trapped. Only 25 minutes from Gulf Shores, on the Beach Road East in Florida, is **Perdido Bay Resort** (tel. 904/492–1223), the home of October's Pensacola Open.

Horseback Riding **Horseback Beach Rides** (tel. 205/943–6674) offers guided group rides along country trails or along the beach at Gulf Shores.

Jogging **Gulf State Park Resort** has trails through a forest.

Sailing Sailboats that can be rented with captain include the *Cyrus King* (at **Island Sailing Center,** tel. 205/968–6775) and the *Daedalus* (tel. 205/986–7018) in Gulf Shores. **Island Recreation Services** (tel. 205/948–7334), in Gulf Shores; and **Land 'N' Sea** (tel. 205/943–3600), in Foley, rent sailboats without captain.

Tennis **Gulf State Park Resort** has courts.

Water Sports **Fun Marina** (tel. 205/981–8587) in Orange Beach rents Jet Skis, pontoon boats, and 16-foot bay-fishing boats. In Gulf Shores, **Island Recreation Services** (tel. 205/948–7334) rents boogie boards, body boards, surf boats, and sailboats.

Spectator Sports

Dog Racing At the **Mobile Greyhound Park** (off I–10W, about 10 mi from Mobile, tel. 205/653–5000) and at the **Pensacola Greyhound Track** (U.S. 98, about 40 mi east of Gulf Shores in Florida, tel. 904/455–8595 or 800/345–3997), there's pari-mutuel betting and a restaurant overlooking the finish line.

Dining

In Mobile and throughout the Gulf area, the specialty is fresh seafood, often prepared in Creole style, with peppery spices, crabmeat dressing, and sometimes a tomato-based sauce. Mobile, in fact, prides itself on being the only city in Alabama with a cuisine of its own, whose precedence (in time, at least) over New Orleans's it has been claiming for years. The basis of the claim is history: The founders of Mobile, French explorers Bienville and Iberville, came here first, then moved west to New Orleans.

The most highly recommended restaurants in each price category are indicated by a star ★.

Category	Cost*
Expensive	over $25
Moderate	$15–$25
Inexpensive	under $15

**per person without tax (9% in Mobile), service, or drinks*

Mobile
Expensive
★ **John Word's.** Word of mouth is fast spreading the fame of this restaurant in an ancient town house in downtown Mobile. You have to search for the place—the sign is so small, it looks like a lawyer's shingle. Inside, it's quietly elegant. The menu showcases an imaginative mélange of Creole and Italian specialties—pastas, steaks, and seafood dishes. *358 Dauphin St., tel. 205/433–7955. Jacket and tie suggested. Reservations suggested. AE, DC, MC, V. Closed Sun.*

La Louisiana. This antiques-filled old house on the outskirts is a delightful dinner setting. Fresh seafood is prepared with a touch of French Creole. Shrimp dishes are heavy with cream sauces unless you order them lightly fried. The seafood gumbo is made the Mobile way: heavy on shrimp, oysters, and okra. *2400 Airport Blvd., tel. 205/476–8130. Jacket and tie re-*

quested. Reservations preferred. AE, MC, V. Closed Sun. Dinner only.

★ **Pillars.** Sitting amid fine antiques from the 18th and 19th centuries in a huge old mansion with wide porches overlooking the live oaks in the yard, it is easy to imagine oneself in another time, listening to the latest news from the battlefront at Vicksburg or Shiloh. The beautifully cooked snapper with a white-wine-and-cream sauce and the snapper with crabmeat and a pecan Creole sauce are delicious. The lamb chops are cut thick and cooked just the way you like them over a charcoal grill. *1757 Government St., tel. 205/478–6341. Dress: jacket and tie suggested. Reservations preferred. AE, DC, MC, V. Closed Sun. Dinner only.*

Moderate

Malaga Restaurant. This is a small, intimate restaurant in the former carriage house of The Malaga Inn (*see* Lodging, *below*). At the end of one of its two rooms, a set of French doors lets in lots of light and a view out to the pool, landscaped with banana trees and other tropical plants. The walls are a mixture of old brick and a cream-and-green floral-print wallpaper. The menu is a mix of Creole-style seafood and Continental dishes. One of the most popular choices is snapper Brennan—fresh Gulf snapper served with a sauce of crabmeat, mushrooms, wine, and other delights. Continental choices include chateaubriand and steak Diane. *359 Church St., tel. 205/433–5858. Dress: casual. Reservations preferred for dinner. AE, DC, MC, V.*

Rousso's Restaurant. A local favorite, with a nautical look created by lots of fishnets and scenes of ships at sea, Rousso's is known for its crab claws, fried in a light batter and served with a catsup-horseradish sauce. *166 S. Royal St., tel. 205/433–3322. Dress: casual. Reservations accepted. AE, DC, MC, V.*

Inexpensive

Wintzell's Oyster House. Opened in 1938, this is a place to see and be seen. All the local celebrities (not to mention a movie or TV star or two) eat here—especially at the raw bar. Every piece of space on the walls and ceilings is covered with Wintzell's favorite sayings and photographs of celebrities and political figures. The seafood is fresh from the Gulf, fried or broiled—perfectly complemented by good draft beer. *605 Dauphin St., tel. 205/433–1004. Dress: casual. No reservations. AE, DC, MC, V. Closed Sun.*

Gulf Coast

Moderate–Expensive

Original Oyster House. A rustic but very clean, plant-filled restaurant overlooking the bayou, this has become a Gulf Shores tradition. Oysters on the half-shell, fresh out of nearby Perdido Bay, are the specialty of the house. The Cajun-style gumbo— a concoction of crab claws, shrimp, amberjack, grouper, redfish, okra and other vegetables, and Cajun spices—has won 20 major awards. *Bayou Village Shopping Ctr., AL 59, tel. 205/948–2445. Dress: casual. No reservations. AE, DC, MC, V.*

★ **Voyagers.** Roses in crystal vases and Art Deco touches set the tone for this airy, elegant dining room. Two-level seating allows beach or poolside views from every table. The specialties include trout with roasted pecans in Creole meunière sauce and soft-shell crab topped with Creole sauce Choron. Follow up with fried-apple beignet topped with French vanilla sauce or crepe soufflé praline. Service is deft, sophisticated, and there's an extensive wine selection. *Perdido Beach Hilton, Hwy. 182, Orange Beach, tel. 205/981–9811. Dress: jacket and tie suggested. Reservations advised. AE, DC, MC, V.*

Inexpensive

Dempsey's Restaurant. The setting is tropical, enhanced by a 20-foot waterfall, at this lakeside dining room. Cajun seafood specialties are arranged temptingly at the all-you-can-eat dinner buffet that includes such seafood dishes as stuffed jumbo shrimp. Live entertainment is offered nightly during the summer months and on weekends the rest of the year. *AL 182, Orange Beach, tel. 205/981–6800. Dress: casual. No reservations. AE, D, MC, V.*

Hazel's Family Restaurant. Former Alabama Governor Fob James, a resident of Gulf Shores, says Hazel's has "the best biscuits in the state." The plain but tasteful family-style restaurant serves a good, hearty breakfast, soup-and-salad lunches, and adequate buffet dinners featuring such seafood dishes as flounder Florentine or crab-stuffed broiled snapper. *Gulf View Square Shopping Ctr., Orange Beach, tel. 205/981–4628. Dress: casual. No reservations. AE, MC, V.*

Pompano's. All seats at this hotel restaurant have a view of the Gulf; one of the four high-ceilinged rooms has two glass walls. Furnishings are blond wood with green upholstery. The specialty is local seafood, served in a "coastal tradition." The Captain's Platter features Gulf jumbo shrimp, oysters, flounder, and bay scallops, all fried in a light batter. *Quality Inn Beachside, W. Beach Blvd., tel. 205/948–6874. Dress: casual. No reservations. AE, D, DC, MC, V.*

★ **Zeke's Landing Restaurant and Oyster Bar.** Overlooking the restaurant's marina on Cotton Bayou, the large rooms are highlighted by bleached woods, black lacquer, and brass. Service is deft, unhurried, and unfailingly friendly. There's an excellent, modestly priced selection of fried or grilled seafood, steaks, garden salads, and sandwiches, such as the seafood melt—crab and shrimp with Cheddar-cheese sauce over an open-faced English muffin. All entrées come with freshly baked bread, soup or salad, and a choice of potato. *Beach Hwy. 180, Orange Beach, 4 mi west of Perdido Beach Hilton, tel. 205/981–4001. Open daily for lunch and dinner; weekend brunch. Dress: casual. No reservations. AE, DC, MC, V.*

Lodging

The most highly recommended properties in each price category are indicated by a star ★.

Category	Cost*
Very Expensive	over $95
Expensive	$70–$95
Moderate	$50–$70
Inexpensive	under $50

**double room; add 10% for taxes in Mobile, 8% on the coast*

Mobile
Very Expensive
★

Stouffer's Riverview Plaza. A stylish new contemporary structure, the 28-story Riverview offers panoramic views of the Mobile River and downtown Mobile. The lobby and guest rooms are decorated in a contemporary style. *64 S. Water St., 36602, tel. 205/438–4000 or 800/468–3571. 365 rooms, 10 suites. Facilities: outdoor pool, sauna, whirlpool, deli, lounge, Julia's Restaurant, with sparkling chandeliers, mirrored columns, sweeping views of the riverfront. AE, DC, MC, V.*

Expensive
★

Radisson Admiral Semmes Hotel. An old hotel that was renovated several years ago, this is a favorite with local politicians. It is also popular with partygoers, particularly during Mardi Gras, because of its excellent location directly on the parade route. Rooms are furnished in Queen Anne and Chippendale styles. *251 Government St., Box 1209, 36633, tel. 205/432–8000 or 800/333–3333. 147 rooms, 22 suites. Facilities: cable TV/free movies, outdoor pool, Jacuzzi, Oliver's Restaurant, specializing in Cajun, Creole cuisines, Admiral's Corner Lounge, privileges at Y. AE, DC, MC, V.*

Ramada Resort and Conference Center. This glass-and-brick hotel, with a four-story main section and a two-story wing, houses Adam's Lounge, which plays top-40 dance tunes. Suites are large, and all rooms are decorated in a contemporary style. *600 S. Beltline Hwy. 36608, tel. 205/344–8030 or 800/272–6232. 230 rooms, 6 suites. Facilities: cable TV/free movies, heated indoor pool with Jacuzzi, outdoor pool, exercise room, putting green, lighted tennis court, restaurant, lounge, bar, 8 meeting rooms. AE, DC, MC, V.*

Inexpensive–Moderate
★

The Malaga Inn. A delightful, romantic getaway place, The Malaga comprises two town houses built by a wealthy landowner in 1862. The lobby is furnished with 19th-century antiques and opens onto a tropically landscaped central courtyard with a fountain. The rooms are large, airy, and furnished with massive antiques. Ask for the front suite, with 14-foot ceilings and crimson velveteen wallpaper. *359 Church St., 36602, tel. 205/438–4701. 40 rooms. Facilities: cable TV, outdoor pool, restaurant (*see *Dining*, above*), lounge. AE, DC, MC, V.*

Gulf Coast
Very Expensive
★

Marriott's Grand Hotel. Nestled amid 550 acres of beautifully landscaped grounds, the "Grand" has been a cherished tradition since 1847. Extensively refurbished by Marriott, it is one of the South's premier resorts. Its two-story cypress–paneled and beamed lobby evokes an aura of traditional elegance. Spacious rooms and cottages are also traditionally furnished. *On Mobile Bay, US Scenic 98, Point Clear 36564, tel. 205/928–9201 or 800/228–9290. 308 units, including some suites, 2 rooms with refrigerators. Facilities: cable TV, movies, pool, beach, sauna and whirlpool, marina with rental boats, sailing, charter fishing, social program, complimentary Grand Fun Camp for youngsters Mon.–Sat., rental bicycles, playground, 10 tennis courts, 36 holes golf, horseback riding, 3 dining rooms, including award-winning Magnolia Room, coffee shop, lounge with entertainment. AE, DC, MC, V.*

★ **Perdido Beach Hilton.** The eight- and nine-story towers are Mediterranean stucco and red tile. The lobby is tiled in terracotta and decorated with mosaics by Venetian artists and a brass sculpture of gulls in flight. Rooms are furnished in luxurious Mediterranean style, and all have a beach view and balcony. *AL 182E, Box 400, Orange Beach 36561, tel. 205/981–9811 or 800/634–8001. 345 units, including 16 suites. Facilities: heated indoor/outdoor pool, whirlpool, sauna, exercise room overlooking beach, 4 lighted tennis courts, pool bar, café, restaurant. AE, DC, MC, V.*

Expensive–Very Expensive

Gulf Shores Holiday Inn. This four-story beachfront hotel has Gulf-front, poolside, and king-size leisure rooms in a contemporary style. *Hwy. 182E, Gulf Shores Blvd., Box 417, Gulf Shores 36547, tel. 205/948–6191 or 800/465–4329. 118 rooms. Facilities: cable TV/free movies, outdoor pool, poolside, tennis* *courts nearby, restaurant, lounge, 3 meeting rooms. AE, DC, MC, V.*

Quality Inn Beachside. This spacious motel is made up of two buildings, one five years old (three stories) and a new one (six stories). All the guest rooms are modern, decorated in pastels, with private balconies; most face the Gulf; half have kitchens. In the Art Deco–style atrium lobby, with glass-brick walls, is a 70-foot swimming pool and a waterfall. Glass-walled elevators rise six stories. *921 W. Gulf Beach Blvd. (Hwy. 182), Box 1013, Gulf Shores 36542, tel. 205/948–6874 or 800/228–5151. 158 rooms. Facilities: cable TV, exercise room, large hot tub, outdoor and indoor pools, pool bar, piano bar, Pompano's restaurant (*see *Dining*, above*), deli. AE, D, DC, MC, V.*

Moderate–Expensive

Gulf Shores Plantation. This 320-acre family resort, 8 miles east of Fort Morgan on the Gulf, has condominiums with fully equipped kitchens in high rises overlooking the beach. Abundant recreational activities are available. *Rte. 180W, Box 1058, 36542, tel. 205/540–2291 or 800/554–0344. 518 units. Facilities: 2 restaurants, lounge, indoor and outdoor pools, tennis courts, access to golf course, other sports facilities, gift shop. AE, MC, V.*

Lighthouse. This complex of five two- to four-story buildings, surrounded by brightly colored exotic flowers, is set on a 580-foot private beach. The waterfront rooms have private balconies, and some units have kitchens. All have contemporary furnishings. *455 E. Beach Blvd., Box 233, Gulf Shores 36547, tel. 205/948–6188. 124 rooms. Facilities: cable TV/movies, 2 outdoor pools (1 heated, with large Jacuzzi). AE, D, DC, MC, V.*

Original Romar House. This unassuming beach cottage is filled with surprises—from the Caribbean-style upstairs sitting area to the Purple Parrot Bar to the luxurious Art Deco–style guest rooms. *23500 Perdido Beach Blvd. (Rte. 182), 36561, tel. 205/981–6156. 6 rooms. Facilities: Continental breakfast, hot tub, tandem bicycle. MC, V.*

The Arts

Theater The **Joe Jefferson Players** (tel. 205/471–1534), a well-established group of amateur actors and actresses, perform plays and musicals at various locations around Mobile throughout the year. They often perform at the Saenger Theater (tel. 205/433–2787) or the Mobile Municipal Auditorium (tel. 205/434–7381), as do The Playhouse in the Park's **Pixie Players** (tel. 205/344–1537), a children's theatrical group.

Nightlife

Hotel Lounges **Adam's** (Airport Blvd.–Beltline Hwy., tel. 205/344–8030), at Mobile's Ramada Inn Airport, is popular among younger partygoers who enjoy loud, fast music. There's live entertainment in **Admiral's Corner** at the Radisson Admiral Semmes Hotel (251 Government St., tel. 205/432–8000) and live entertainment and dancing in the **Jubilation** lounge of the Holiday Inn (I–10 and U.S. 90, tel. 205/666–5600).

Honky-tonk On the Alabama–Florida line is the **Flora-Bama Lounge** (Beach Rd., tel. 205/981–8555), with country-and-western music performed by a local band and vocalist. It's the place where Mobile native Jimmy Buffet got his start to stardom.

Swing At **Shirley & Wayne's** (AL 182, Romar Beach, tel. 205/981-4818), Wayne Perdew and his band play swing and country Monday–Saturday nights while you dine and/or dance.

Elsewhere in the State

Numbers in the margin correspond to points of interest on the Elsewhere in the State map.

8 **Ave Maria Grotto, Cullman.** Take a leisurely stroll through this hillside garden grotto to view over 125 miniature churches, buildings, and shrines, painstakingly created from originals in the United States and Europe by a Benedictine monk over the course of 50 years. Standing only a few feet in height, these tiny buildings were constructed from rare materials, such as marble and semiprecious stones, gathered from around the world. *50 mi from Birmingham via I–65N to U.S. 278E, St. Bernard's Abbey, Cullman, tel. 205/734–4110. Admission: $3.50 adults; $3 senior citizens; $2 children 6–12, under 6 free. Open daily 8 AM–sunset.*

5 **Demopolis.** This town takes great pride in its rich Southern heritage. A 5-mile self-guided-tour map provides detailed histories of the numerous antebellum homes in the area, and a cassette driving tour will take you past the 18th-century buildings in the historic downtown area. The 10,000-acre **Demopolis Lake** offers fishing, boating, swimming, picnicking, and campgrounds. *100 mi from Montgomery via U.S. 80W. 115 mi from Birmingham via I–59S to U.S. 43W. Maps, cassettes, and tape players are available, free of charge, from the Demopolis Area Chamber of Commerce, 213 N. Walnut St., Box 667, tel. 205/289–0270, open weekdays 8–5, or from the Information Center at the Best Western Hotel on Hwy. 80, tel. 205/289–5772, open evenings and weekends.*

Two fine antebellum homes in Demopolis are open to the public. **Gaineswood,** built in 1860, has been called one of the finest Greek Revival mansions in the South. The house has been extensively restored, down to reproductions of the original French wallpapers. It is unique in that it contains the original furnishings, including carved four-posters and a flutina—a one-of-a-kind musical instrument invented by the original owner (who also designed Gaineswood itself). Interior architectural elements include elaborate columns and pilasters; friezes and medallions of wood, plaster, cast iron, and leather; veined marble mantels; and ceiling-dome skylights. **Bluff Hall** was built in 1832 as a Federal-style house and remodeled in the Greek Revival style several years later. It stands on a chalky cliff above the Tombigbee River and features a columned front portico, a huge double parlor with Corinthian columns, and Empire and Victorian furnishings donated by friends and descendants of the original owner. Also on display is a collection of period clothing. Like Gaineswood, Bluff Hall is listed on the National Historic Register. *Gaineswood: 805 Whitfield St. E, tel. 205/289–4846. Admission: $3 adults, $2 students, 50¢ children under 13. Open Mon.–Sat. 9–5, Sun. 1–5. Closed holidays. Bluff Hall: 405 N. Commissioners Ave., tel. 205/289–1666. Admission: $2 adults, 50¢ children 5–12, children under 5 free. Open Mar.–Dec. Tues.–Sat. 10–5, Sun. 2–5; Jan.–Feb. Tues.–Sat. 10–4, Sun. 2–4. Closed Thanksgiving, Christmas, and New Year's Day.*

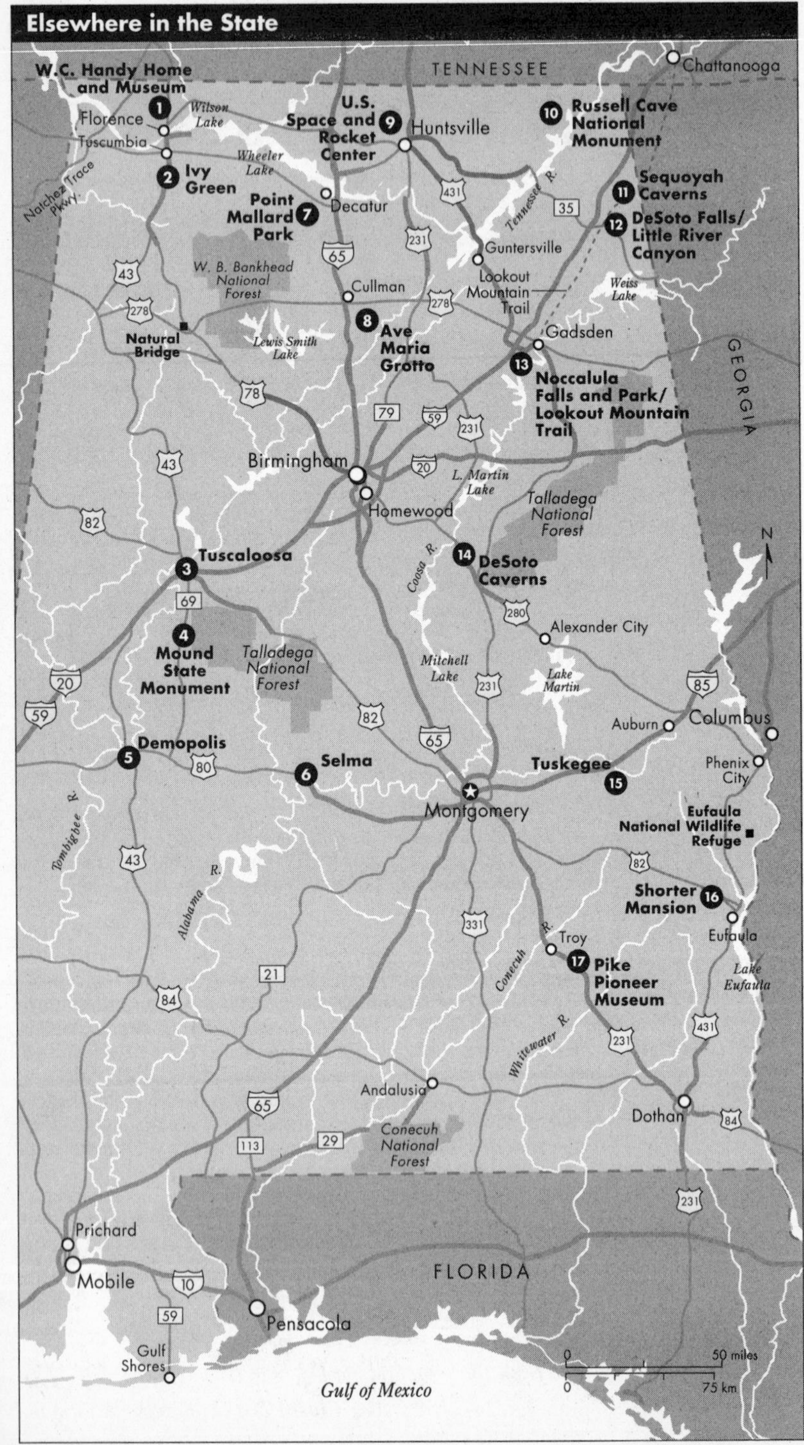
Elsewhere in the State
TENNESSEE
Chattanooga
W.C. Handy Home and Museum
1
Wilson Lake
Florence
Tuscumbia
U.S. Space and Rocket Center
9
Huntsville
10 Russell Cave National Monument
Wheeler Lake
2 Ivy Green
Natchez Trace Pkwy.
Point Mallard Park 7
Decatur
11 Sequoyah Caverns
Tennessee R.
12 DeSoto Falls/ Little River Canyon
Guntersville
W. B. Bankhead National Forest
Cullman
Lookout Mountain Trail
Weiss Lake
Natural Bridge
8 Ave Maria Grotto
Lewis Smith Lake
Gadsden
13 Noccalula Falls and Park/ Lookout Mountain Trail
GEORGIA
Birmingham
L. Martin Lake
Homewood
Talladega National Forest
3 Tuscaloosa
14 DeSoto Caverns
Coosa R.
Alexander City
4 Mound State Monument
Talladega National Forest
Mitchell Lake
Lake Martin
Auburn
Columbus
5 Demopolis
6 Selma
Tuskegee 15
Phenix City
Montgomery
Eufaula National Wildlife Refuge
Tombigbee R.
Alabama R.
Shorter Mansion 16
Eufaula
Troy
17 Pike Pioneer Museum
Conecuh R.
Lake Eufaula
Whitewater R.
Andalusia
Dothan
Conecuh National Forest
Prichard
Mobile
FLORIDA
Pensacola
Gulf Shores
50 miles
75 km
Gulf of Mexico

14 **DeSoto Caverns Park, Childersburg.** The site of a 2,000-year-old Indian burial ground, these vast onyx caves were rediscovered in 1540 by Hernando DeSoto and later served as a Confederate gunpowder mining center and a Prohibition speakeasy. Curious rock formations created by stalagmites and stalactites allow the imagination free rein. During the tour, the largest cave (over 12 stories high) hosts a sound, laser, light, and water show. *85 mi from Montgomery via U.S. 231N to Rte. 76. 60 mi from Birmingham via U.S. 280S to Rte. 76. Tel. 205/378–7252 or 800/933–CAVE. Admission: $8.50 adults; $5 children 4–11, under 4 free. (Tour, maze, and gemstone mining tickets $11.96 for adults and $8.46 for children.) Open Mon.–Sat. 9–5:30, Sun. 12:30–5:30 Apr.–Sept.; Mon.–Sat. 9–5, Sun. 12:30–5 rest of year. Closed Thanksgiving and Christmas.*

12 **DeSoto Falls, Fort Payne.** This 100-foot waterfall is one of the loveliest attractions in the 5,000-acre DeSoto State Resort Park. Unsupervised swimming is allowed in the lake, and there is a supervised pool, picnic area, and campgrounds nearby. *90 mi from Birmingham via I–59N to Exit 218 (AL 35) to Co. Rd. 89. Tel. 205/845–0051 or 800/ALA–PARK. Admission free, picnicking 50¢. Open daily 7 AM–dusk.*

2 **Ivy Green, Tuscumbia.** Visitors can tour the grounds and childhood home of Helen Keller. It was here, at the carriage house, where Annie Sullivan taught her the meaning of language. *The Miracle Worker* is performed on the grounds Friday and Saturday nights in June and July. *110 mi from Birmingham via I–65N to State Rd. 157N to U.S. 72W to Rte. 55N. 300 W. North Commons, tel. 205/383–4066. Admission: $3 adults, $1 children 6–11, under 6 free. Miracle Worker general admission: $5, $4 children 6–11, under 6 free. Open Mon.–Sat. 8:30–4, Sun. 1–4. Closed Labor Day, Christmas, and New Year's Day.*

12 **Little River Canyon, Fort Payne.** The deepest canyon east of the Rocky Mountains is found in DeSoto State Park. Almost 600 feet at its deepest point and 16 miles wide, the canyon is surrounded by a breathtaking 22-mile scenic drive. *95 mi northeast of Birmingham via I–59 to Hwy. 176 near Fort Payne, tel. 800/ALA–PARK. Admission free, 50¢ for use of picnic area.*

13 **Lookout Mountain Trail.** Stretching northeast from Gadsden, Alabama, to Chattanooga, Tennessee, this trail along a mountain ridge offers 100 miles of the prettiest scenery in the state for the adventurous hiker's delight; hiking trails abound. In Alabama the trail begins at Route 89 at the Georgia state line, travels into Mentone, Alabama, and continues via Route 89 to Dogtown and Routes 89 and 175 into Noccalula Falls at Gadsden. *Trail maps are available at the Welcome Center on I–59 at Valley Head, tel. 205/635–6522, or the Alabama Bureau of Tourism and Travel, tel. 800/ALABAMA.*

4 **Mound State Monument, Moundville.** The museum contains a number of prehistoric Indian artifacts discovered in the area. On the grounds are 20 earthen temple mounds, the largest of which supports a reconstructed Indian temple. Also on the grounds are a reconstructed Indian village, a nature trail leading to the Black Warrior River, picnic areas, and a campground. *100 mi from Montgomery via U.S. 82N to Hwy. 69S. 65 mi from Birmingham via I–59S to Hwy. 69S. Tel. 205/371–2572. Admission: $2 adults, $1 children 6–18 and senior citi-*

zens, under 6 free. Open daily 9–5. Closed Thanksgiving, Christmas, and New Year's.

13 **Noccalula Falls and Park, Gadsden.** Highlights of this 100-acre woodland park are a 90-foot waterfall, miniature golf, train rides, a small zoo, a botanic garden, a covered bridge, and a 1776 pioneer homestead—four log cabins were moved here from the backwoods of Tennessee. There are also campgrounds and picnic areas. *50 mi from Birmingham via I–59N to Exit 188. 1400 Noccalula Rd., Gadsden, tel. 205/546–5843. Admission to pioneer homestead and botanic garden: $1.50 adults, $1 over 60 and children under 12; train ride 75¢, 50¢ over 65 and under 12. Open daily 9–dark.*

17 **Pike Pioneer Museum, Troy.** This museum has captured the essence of 18th- and 19th-century Pike County in its 10,000 museum pieces, ranging from pioneer farm tools to turn-of-the-century household goods. These artifacts are displayed in 10 buildings that are themselves museum pieces, including a log house, a jail, a general store, and even an outhouse—all moved here from other parts of the state. *48 mi from Montgomery via U.S. 231S. Address: 248 U.S. 231N, Troy, tel. 205/566–3597. Admission: $2 adults, 50¢ students, children under 6 free. Open Mon.–Sat. 10–5, Sun. 1–5.*

7 **Point Mallard Park, Decatur.** Facilities at this 749-acre park include a swimming pool, a wave pool, and a water slide (summer only); plus an ice rink (mid-Nov.–mid-Mar.), campgrounds, an 18-hole championship golf course, miniature golf, a duck pond, and a four-mile hiking and biking trail. *130 mi from Birmingham via I–65N to Exit 334 to Rte. 67N. 1800 Point Mallard Dr., tel. 205/350–3000. Admission: $7 adults, $5 children 3–11. Fees for activities range from $1 to $13. Aquatic Center open Mon.–Sun. 10–6, Tues.–Thurs. 6–9 PM mid-May–Labor Day. Ice rink open mid-Nov.–mid-Mar. Closed Labor Day.*

10 **Russell Cave National Monument, Bridgeport.** This archaeological site was occupied by the American Indian's prehistoric ancestors for 8,000 years before the arrival of European settlers. Visitors today can tour the cave shelter—the entrance to over seven miles of cavernous passages—and view museum exhibits of prehistoric artifacts and an Indian burial ground. There are also tool and cooking demonstrations, a slide program, a nature trail, an Indian garden, a hiking trail, and picnic grounds. *130 mi from Birmingham via I–59N to Hwy. 117N to U.S. 72N to Co. Rd. 75. Tel. 205/495–2672. Admission free. Open daily 8–5. Closed Christmas.*

6 **Selma.** On March 21, 1965, following the aftermath of "Bloody Sunday" two weeks earlier, Dr. Martin Luther King, Jr., led a group of civil-rights demonstrators on a 50-mile march from downtown Selma's **Edmund Pettus Bridge** to Montgomery. The journey resulted ultimately in the passing of the nation's Voting Rights Act.

Selma may always be remembered for its controversial role in the civil-rights movement, but history buffs of all periods will find plenty to see in this small city's rich array of museums and antebellum mansions. Each year in late March a **Historic Selma Pilgrimage** (tel. 800/ALABAMA) takes visitors through several renowned homes. In late April one of the largest annual **Civil War re-enactments** (tel. 205/875–7241) in the nation draws thousands to the site of the Battle of Selma, on the Alabama

River. Year-round you can stop by the **Visitors Information Center** for advice on what to see. *50 mi from Montgomery via U.S. 80W. 80 mi from Birmingham via I–65S to Rte. 31S to U.S. 80W. 2207 Broad St., tel. 205/875–7485. Open daily 8–8.*

One of the state's finest examples of Greek Revival architecture is **Sturdivant Hall and Museum.** Built in 1853 by architect Thomas Helm Lee, Robert E. Lee's cousin, this antebellum-house museum has been restored to its original grandeur, featuring beautiful grillwork, lovely gardens, and period antiques and furnishings. *713 Mabry St., tel. 205/872–5626. Admission: $4.50 adults, $2.50 children 6–18, under 6 free. Open Tues.–Sat. 9–4, Sun. 2–4. Closed major holidays.*

11 **Sequoyah Caverns, Valley Head.** A half-mile guided tour through the caverns in Sand Mountain brings visitors past rock formations mirrored in lakes. In the 1930s, dances were held in the largest room, now called the Ballroom. Outside, there's a picnic area, a campground, a small zoo, a swimming pool, a playground, and hiking trails. *110 mi from Birmingham via I–59N to U.S. 11N. Sequoyah Rd., tel. 205/635–6423. Admission: $6 adults; $4.50 senior citizens; $4 children 6–12, under 3 free. Open daily 8:30–4 Memorial Day–Labor Day, weekends 8:30–5 rest of year.*

16 **Shorter Mansion, Eufaula.** This house museum, built in 1884, is a fine example of Neoclassical Revival architecture. It is dedicated to both Eufaula's and Barbour County's history, particularly as shown in the Governor's Parlor, a room containing portraits and memorabilia from the terms in office of the six Alabama governors who hailed from Barbour County. *90 mi from Montgomery via U.S. 82S. 340 N. Eufaula Ave., tel. 205/687–3793. Admission: $3 adults, 50¢ children under 12. Open Mon.–Sat. 10–4, Sun. 1–4. Closed major holidays.*

3 **Tuscaloosa.** Probably the most rewarding of the many day-trips based out of Birmingham is the jaunt to Tuscaloosa. Although this small river-city's leading export may well be football, its wealth of cultural offerings cannot be overlooked. History and architecture aficionados can take a tour with the **Tuscaloosa County Preservation Society** (tel. 205/758–2238 or 205/758–6138), music lovers can stop in to hear the estimable **Tuscaloosa Symphony Orchestra** (for schedule and box-office information, tel. 205/752–5515), crafts collectors can enjoy October's outstanding **Kentuck Festival of the Arts** (in nearby Northport, tel. 205/333–1252), and further information on the area can be obtained from the **Tuscaloosa Convention and Visitors Bureau.** *60 mi from Birmingham via I–20/I–59. 100 mi from Montgomery via U.S. 82. 600 Lurleen Wallace Blvd., Suite 140, tel. 205/391–9200. Open daily 8–5.*

If you are in town for a game, make it a point to see the **Paul W. "Bear" Bryant Museum,** which follows the University of Alabama's 100-year tradition of football preeminence. *323 Paul W. Bryant Dr., tel. 205/348–4668. Admission: $2 adults, $1 children under 18. Open Mon.–Sat. 9–4.*

The **Warner Collection,** which comprises several hundred paintings as well as dozens of artifacts and sculptures, is quite possibly the nation's largest private collection of American painting. It is displayed in two locations. The Asian-style, beautifully landscaped **Gulf State Paper Corporation Headquarters,** houses a range of art, including numerous works by the Wyeths, Albert Bierstadt, Frederic Remington, Thomas Cole, and George Catlin. A short drive away you'll find an even more impressive collection in the exquisitely furnished, 170-year-old **Mildred Warner House.** The comprehensive assortment of William Aiken Walker's revealing Southern folk paintings, which depict 19th-century African-American art, is worth the visit alone. The walls are virtually covered with works of American Impressionists, including Mary Cassatt, Maurice Prendergast, Winslow Homer, John Singer Sargent, Childe Hassam, Georgia O'Keefe, and James A. M. Whistler. *Admission to both collections free. Gulf State Paper Corporation: 1400 River Rd. NE, tel. 205/553–6200. Tours offered on the hour Mon.–Fri. 5 PM–7 PM, Sat. 10–7, Sun. 1–7. Mildred Warner House: 1925 8th St., tel. 205/345–4062. Tours offered on the hour Sat. 10–6, Sun. 1–6.*

15 **Tuskegee.** The **Tuskegee National Forest** (tel. 205/727–2652), spread over 11,000 acres, includes an 8½-mile hiking trail, a firing range, and a botanic garden, as well as a replica of the childhood home of Booker T. Washington. His actual home, **The Oaks,** is part of the **George Washington Carver Museum** on the Tuskegee University campus. This museum includes Carver's original laboratory, his artwork, and a historical study of the **Tuskegee Institute.** A walking tour of the Historic Campus district originates at the Carver Museum. *120 mi from Birmingham via I–65S to I–85E to U.S. 29S. 30 mi from Montgomery via I–85E to U.S. 29S. Tuskegee Institute National Historic Site, tel. 205/727–3200. Admission free. Open daily 9–5. Closed major holidays.*

9 **U.S. Space and Rocket Center, Huntsville.** Home to the U.S. Space Camp, where youngsters learn about space exploration, the center offers a bus tour of the NASA labs and shuttle test sites, a 45-minute Omnimax film (in which the screen extends above and around you) on space exploration, hands-on exhibits in the museum, and an outdoor park filled with spacecraft, including a full-size model of the Space Shuttle. *100 mi from Birmingham via I–65N to U.S. 72E. 1 Tranquillity Base, Huntsville, tel. 205/837–3400 or 800/63–SPACE. Admission: $11.95 adults, $7.95 over 60 and children 3–12, under 3 free; includes museum, film, NASA tour. Open daily 8–7 Memorial Day–Labor Day, 9–6 rest of year. Closed Christmas.*

1 **W. C. Handy Home and Museum, Florence.** The birthplace of the internationally acclaimed Father of the Blues has been furnished with items typical of the period when he grew up. In the museum behind the cabin, a treasure trove of his memorabilia has been preserved. Here you'll see his piano and famous golden trumpet, original manuscripts, and testimonials to his genius by such contemporaries as George Gershwin and Louis Armstrong. The annual W. C. Handy Music Festival (tel. 205/766–7642) held during the first full week in August, draws thousands. *College and Marengo sts., tel. 205/760–6434. Admission: $2 adults, 50¢ children under 18. Open Tues.–Sat. 9–noon, 1–4; closed major holidays.*

3 Georgia

By John English and William Schemmel

Updated by Mitzi Gammon

Diverse landscapes stretch from Georgia's pristine white-sand beaches and saltwater marshes to the rolling valleys tucked beneath the smoky blue peaks of the Appalachian Mountains—the tone varying from region to region. Atlanta bustles with metropolitan energy, Savannah glows with quaint historic charm, and the seaside resort communities blend southern elegance with a casual sensibility.

Progressive Atlanta is *the* boomtown of the southeast—Fortune-500 headquarters continue to spring up downtown, and office towers now punctuate the still vast canopy of green treetops. A rapid rail system whisks visitors around the maze of art, nature, and history museums; amusement parks; gardens; sports stadiums; and Buckhead's tony boutiques and restaurants. Yet Atlanta's heart and soul remain embedded in the 17 commercial and residential historic districts, in which turn-of-the-century Art Deco skyscrapers mingle with Italianate mansions. This unending variety, coupled with the region's unconditional hospitality, earned Atlanta the 1996 summer Olympic games.

A five-hour car ride allows ocean-seekers to escape the din of cosmopolitanism, along the 100-mile-long coastline that runs north from the mouth of the Savannah River southward to the mouth of the St. Mary's. Colonial Savannah is the Georgia coast's crown jewel, drawing many visitors to its cobblestone town squares and Spanish moss–draped parks, waterfront gift shops and jazz bars, and one of the nation's largest St. Patrick's Day parades.

St. Simons Island, about 70 miles south, attracts a more laid-back crowd, ranging from fishing, golf, and tennis enthusiasts to avid beach goers. On nearby Jekyll Island you'll glimpse the lavish lifestyle of America's early 19th-century rich and famous—stately Victorian and shingle "cottages" grace the island's Millionaire's Village. If you seek solitude and natural beauty visit Cumberland Island's protected forests and 16 miles of sandy coastline, or explore the black, 700-square-mile, gator-infested waters of Okefenokee Swamp.

Atlanta

"Her patron saint is Scarlett O'Hara," writer James Street once said of Atlanta, "and the town is just like her—shrewd, proud and full of gumption—her Confederate slip showing under a Yankee mink coat."

It's true that the Yankee influence has long given Atlanta its vitality, while its Southern traditions have made it one of America's most livable cities.

But make no mistake: Atlanta is located in the heart of the South. The state of Georgia continues to celebrate Confederate Memorial Day as a holiday every April. *The Atlanta Constitution's* Sunday section of regional news is still called "Dixie Living." And one of the top tourist attractions in this metropolis is the Cyclorama, a diorama depicting the famous Battle of Atlanta, which leveled the city during what locals call the "War Between the States."

Despite the mystique of *Gone With the Wind,* which Margaret Mitchell cranked out in a still-remaining apartment house at

10th and Peachtree streets, Atlanta has never really been part of the moonlight and magnolias myth common in many antebellum cities of the Old South.

Atlanta's chief asset has always been the accessibility of its location. From its earliest days, it was an important freight center, and it is still a major distribution center for trains, trucks, and planes. The city has long been called the "Crossroads of the South" because three interstates (I–85, I–75, and I–20) converge near downtown and because Atlanta's Hartsfield Airport has become the hub of the entire Southeast. There is an old local saying that goes, "It makes little difference whether you wind up in heaven or hell; in either case, you still have to pass through Atlanta."

In short order, Atlanta boasted other important assets. It became a banking center, and Peachtree Street is often tagged the "Wall Street of the South." In recent years, the city moved into the global arena with the opening of foreign banks and consulates and trade offices. Direct flights to Europe, South America, and Asia have stimulated new international business.

No mention of Atlanta would be complete without talking about its reputation as a "city too busy to hate." For the past three decades, Atlanta has been linked to the civil rights movement. It was Ralph McGill, the crusading editor of the *Constitution,* who guided the city through the civil rights struggle with unfaltering pragmatism. He insisted that folks simply do what needed to be done because it was right. In the 1960s, Atlanta quietly integrated its school system. The fact that peaceful desegregation and a soaring economy seemed to go hand in glove was not lost on anyone. Yet McGill was still a controversial figure during this critical period. It was often said that 50% of the local citizenry could not eat breakfast before reading Ralph McGill's daily column and that the other half couldn't eat after reading his column!

Among the accomplishments of Atlanta's black community was the Nobel Peace Prize that Martin Luther King, Jr., won in 1964. In 1972, Andrew Young was reelected the first black congressman from the South since Reconstruction. After serving as Ambassador to the United Nations during President Jimmy Carter's administration, Young was elected mayor of Atlanta.

In recent years, Atlanta has been ranked among the best places in the country to live. Some would attribute these high ratings to the area's pleasant year-round climate; but others insist that Atlanta just has the right mix of people who have worked together to build a pleasant community.

Arriving and Departing

By Plane Hartsfield International Airport, off I–85 and I–285, 13 miles south of downtown, is one of the world's busiest jet complexes. Airlines servicing it include **Aeromexico, Air Jamaica, American, Bahamasair, British Airways, Cayman Islands Airways, Continental, Delta, Japan Airlines, KLM, Lufthansa, Northwest, Sabena, Swissair, TWA, United,** and **USAir.**

Between the Airport and Center City **Atlanta Airport shuttle vans** (tel. 404/766–5312) operate every half hour between 7 AM and 11 PM. The downtown trip ($8 one-

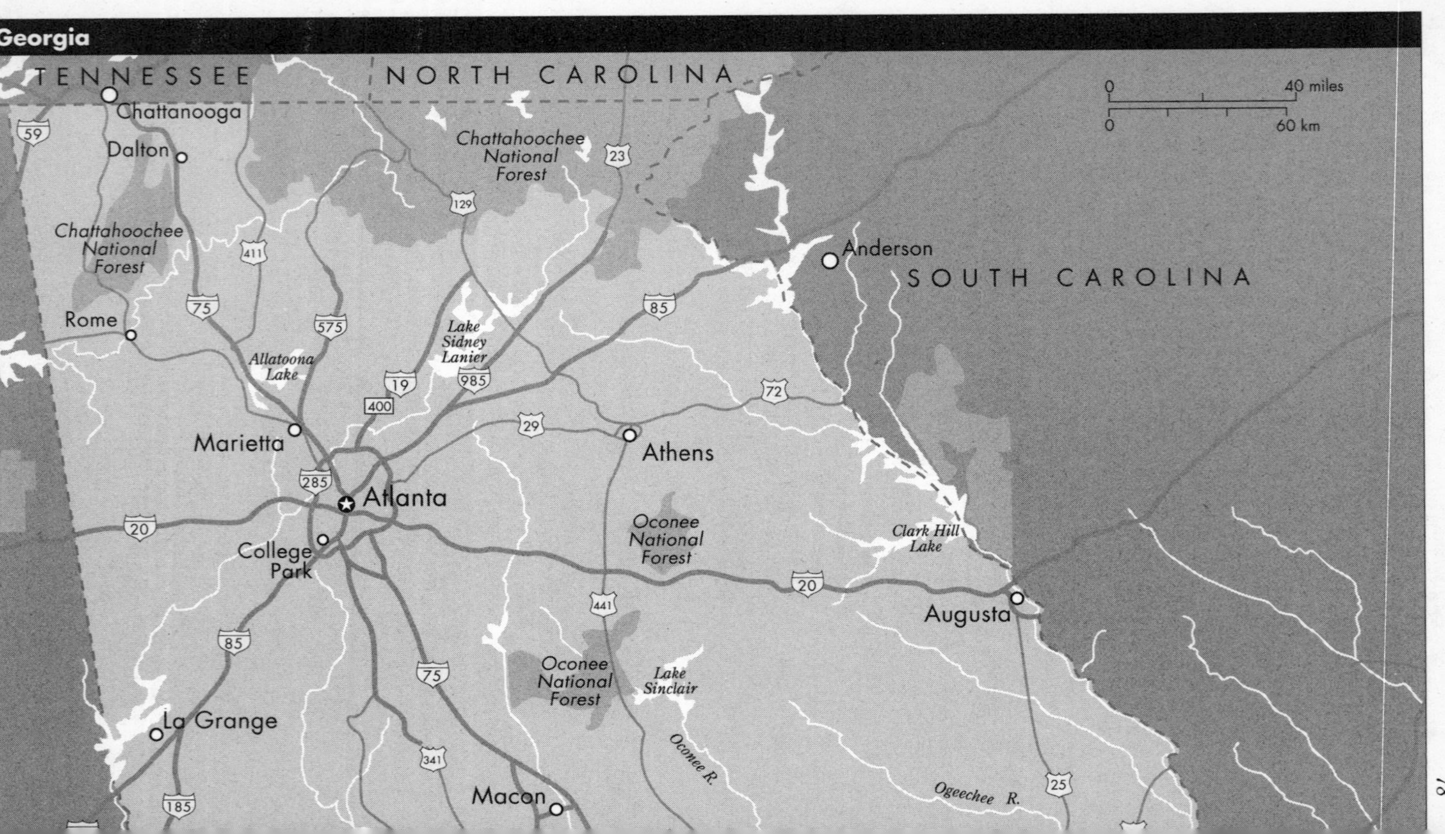
Georgia
TENNESSEE
NORTH CAROLINA
SOUTH CAROLINA
0 40 miles
0 60 km
Chattanooga
Dalton
Chattahoochee National Forest
Chattahoochee National Forest
Rome
Allatoona Lake
Lake Sidney Lanier
Anderson
Marietta
Athens
Atlanta
College Park
Oconee National Forest
Oconee National Forest
Clark Hill Lake
Augusta
Lake Sinclair
Oconee R.
Ogeechee R.
La Grange
Macon
59
75
411
575
129
23
19
400
985
85
72
29
285
20
441
20
85
75
341
185
25

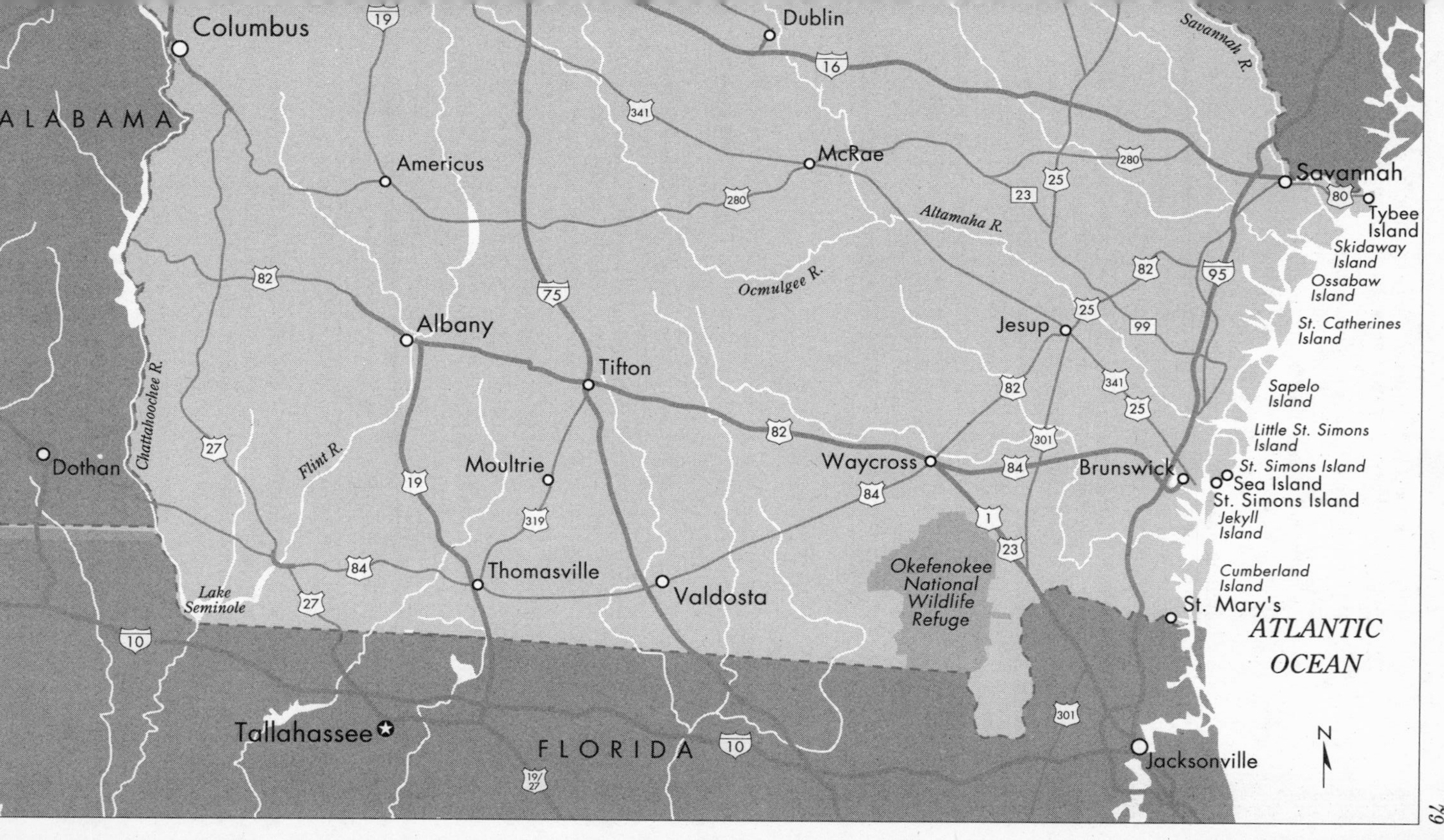
Columbus
Dublin
Savannah R.
ALABAMA
Americus
McRae
Savannah
Tybee Island
Skidaway Island
Ossabaw Island
Altamaha R.
Ocmulgee R.
Albany
Jesup
St. Catherines Island
Tifton
Sapelo Island
Little St. Simons Island
Dothan
Chattahoochee R.
Flint R.
Moultrie
Waycross
Brunswick
St. Simons Island
Sea Island
St. Simons Island
Jekyll Island
Thomasville
Valdosta
Okefenokee National Wildlife Refuge
Cumberland Island
Lake Seminole
St. Mary's
ATLANTIC OCEAN
Tallahassee
FLORIDA
Jacksonville
N
19
16
341
280
25
23
80
82
95
75
99
27
301
84
1
319
10
19/27

way) takes about 20 minutes and stops at major hotels. Vans also go to Emory University and Lenox Square ($12 one-way).

If your luggage is light, you can also take **MARTA**'s (Metropolitan Atlanta Rapid Transit Authority, tel. 404/848–4711) high-speed trains between the airport and downtown and other locations. Trains operate 5 AM–1 AM. The trip downtown takes about 15 minutes, and the fare is $1.

Taxi fare between the airport and downtown hotels is fixed at $15 for one person; $8 each for two people; $6 each for three people. Taxis aren't one of Atlanta's strong suits, so be certain your driver is familiar with your destination.

By Train **Amtrak's** *Crescent* (tel. 800/USA–RAIL) operates daily to New Orleans, Washington DC, and New York from Atlanta's Brookwood Station (1688 Peachtree St.).

By Bus Hop a bus to Atlanta via **Greyhound/Trailways Bus Lines** (81 International Blvd., tel. 404/522–6300).

By Car Atlanta is the hub of four interstate highways: I–85, running northeast to southwest from the South Carolina to the Alabama border; I–75, north–south from Tennessee to Florida; I–20, east–west from South Carolina to Alabama; and I–285, the Perimeter Highway, circling the metropolitan area for 65 miles.

Getting Around

By Bus The **Metropolitan Atlanta Rapid Transit Authority (MARTA,** tel. 404/848–4711) operates a modern, efficient bus system. The fare is $1, and exact change is required.

By Subway MARTA's clean, luxurious rapid-rail subway trains link downtown with most major landmarks. The rail system's two lines connect at the **Five Points Station** downtown, where information on public transportation is available at the **Ride Store** (weekdays 7 AM–7 PM and Sat. 8:30 AM–5 PM). Trains run 5 AM–1 AM, and parking ($1 all day) can be found around most suburban stations. The fare is $1 one-way, and exact change is required. Transfers, valid on buses or trains, are free.

By Taxi Taxis start at $1 and go up 20¢ for each ⅕ of a mile or 40 seconds of waiting time. Each additional person costs 50¢. When traveling in the Downtown, Convention Zone a flat rate of $3 for one person or $2 per person will be charged for any destination within the zone.

Guided Tours

Orientation **I Love Atlanta Tours** (tel. 404/872–5238) is a small local company offering customized tours in vans and motor coaches of such historic landmarks as Underground Atlanta and The King Center. Guides are friendly and knowledgeable.

Burton's Tours (tel. 404/523–8144), owned by the city's most famous soul-food chef, covers black historical landmarks such as the Martin Luther King, Jr., National Historic District and the Atlanta University Center area. Tours are in 46-passenger motor coaches, with guides who are full of anecdotes about the city's past and present.

Special-interest **Atlanta Carriage Co.** (tel. 404/584–9960) gives 30-minute horse-drawn carriage tours through downtown Atlanta ($25 a couple). The congested streets may lack the romantic charm of Savannah and Charleston, but with a little moonlight, a little champagne, who knows?

Walking Tours **The Atlanta Preservation Center** (401 Flatiron Bldg., tel. 404/876–2040) offers seven walking tours of historic areas and other places of interest from April through November ($5 adults, $3 senior citizens and students, children under 19 free). The tour of the Fox Theatre, with backstage looks at the city's elaborate 1920s picture palace, is especially recommended.

Important Addresses and Numbers

Tourist Information To plan your trip write to the Department of Tourism (233 Peachtree St. NE, Suite 2000, Atlanta 30303). When you are in Atlanta, the Convention and Visitors Bureau has three visitor information centers stocked with maps and brochures: **Peachtree Center Mall** (233 Peachtree St. NE, tel. 404/521–6684), **Underground Atlanta** (65 Upper Alabama St., tel. 404/577–2148), and **Lenox Square Mall** (3393 Peachtree Rd. NE, tel. 404/266–1398).

Emergencies Dial 911 for assistance. For hospital emergencies both **Grady Memorial Hospital** (80 Butler St., tel. 404/589–4070) and **Georgia Baptist Medical Center** (300 Boulevard NE, tel. 404/653–4000) have 24-hour emergency room service.

Pharmacy **Treasury Drug** (1061 Ponce de Leon Ave. NE, tel. 404/876–0381).

Exploring Atlanta

Orientation Atlanta's beltway is most often called "the Perimeter," but it's also known as "The Big O around the Big A," or simply I–285. The interstate's completion in 1969 reaffirmed the city's relentless development to the north. In fact, so many office parks, shopping centers, and multifamily housing developments have cropped up along the northern arc of I–285 that the name of one typical project, "Perimeter Center," may no longer just be an oxymoron. In the southern arc is the massive Atlanta Hartsfield International Airport.

Most of metro Atlanta is located within Fulton and DeKalb counties, but the southern part of the city is in Clayton County. Cobb and Gwinnett counties are in the burgeoning northern sector.

Some visitors are confused by Atlanta's lack of a strict grid system of streets or by its confluence of streets into five-point intersections. One generous explanation is that Atlanta's streets were originally cow paths and Indian trails, which were paved, renamed, and given lights; others blame topography and the meandering Chattahoochee River.

Atlanta is a city shaped like a cursive capital *I*. At the bottom is the downtown area, and at the top is the Lenox Square-Phipps Plaza area. Along the shank of the *I* runs the city's main thoroughfare, the famed Peachtree Street. Actually, Peachtree Street runs only about three miles north from downtown, then changes its name, without notice, to Peachtree Road. Past the Lenox Square area, the grand avenue becomes Peachtree Industrial Boulevard, a name that befits its environment. (Newcomers be forewarned: there are some three dozen arteries with "Peachtree" in their names.)

Seven distinct sections of the city are plotted along Atlanta's "big I": downtown, midtown, Ansley Park, Brookwood Hills, Peachtree Hills, Garden Hills, Buckhead, and Peachtree Park, which includes the Lenox area.

Numbers in the margin correspond to points of interest on the Downtown Atlanta and Atlanta Vicinity maps.

Downtown

The ideal way to get acquainted with Atlanta is to begin with its past. Atlanta is not a historic city like Savannah or Boston, yet its history can be traced to the mid-19th century. A good
1 way to start is with a saunter through **Oakland Cemetery.** Buried here are many of Georgia's notable politicians and businessmen. There is also a Jewish section and a section for Confederate soldiers. Margaret Mitchell, author of *Gone With the Wind* and a favorite daughter of the city, and golfer Bobby Jones are interred here. *248 Oakland Ave., tel. 404/577–8163. Tours available: tel. 404/876–2040.*

Continue to the Martin Luther King, Jr., National Historic District on Auburn Avenue, a couple of blocks north on Boulevard. Dr. King's white marble tomb with its eternal flame is
2 next to the **Ebenezer Baptist Church** (407 Auburn Ave.). For three generations the King family preached here. During the civil rights struggle, and after Dr. King was awarded the Nobel Peace Prize in 1964, Ebenezer Baptist was recognized as the spiritual center of the movement. After King's assassination in 1968, his widow, Coretta Scott King, established the ad-
3 joining **King Center.** It contains a museum with King memorabilia, a library, and a souvenir gift shop, and it frequently sponsors educational programs. *449 Auburn Ave., tel. 404/524–1956. Admission free. Open Oct.–Apr., daily 9–5:30; May–Sept., 9–8.*

4 A few doors up the street is **Dr. King's birthplace** (501 Auburn Ave.). The home, a Victorian structure in the Queen Anne style, is managed by the National Park Service and is open to the public daily.

Auburn Avenue is the heart of the black community's business
5 district. The landmark **Atlanta Life Insurance Company,** founded by Alonzo Herndon, was located in modest quarters at 148 Auburn Avenue until the new modern complex was opened in 1980 at No. 100.

6 At 145 Auburn Avenue is the **Atlanta Daily World** building, home of one the nation's oldest black newspapers. The church with the "Jesus Saves" sign on its steeple is the Big Bethel African Methodist Episcopal Church. Nearby is the **Royal Peacock Night Club,** a hot spot for black entertainers.

For a history of Auburn Avenue, stop in at the **African American Panoramic Experience** to see the permanent exhibit, as well as their other collections and displays. *135 Auburn Ave., tel. 404/521–2654. Admission: $2 adults, $1 children. Open Tues., Thurs.–Sat. 10–5. June–Aug. on Sun. 1–5.*

If you're interested in a free, guided walking tour of the so-called Sweet Auburn neighborhood, you can arrange one at the
7 **National Park Service Rangers Station** (440 Auburn Ave., tel.

404/331–3919) located across from the King Center or through the Atlanta Preservation Center (tel. 404/876–2040).

8 Closer to town, on Edgewood Avenue, is the **Municipal Market,**
a thriving produce market where you can buy every part of the
pig but the oink. At 125 Edgewood Avenue is the site of the first
bottling plant for the Coca-Cola Company; today the site is oc-
9 cupied by the **Baptist Student Center** for the adjoining campus
of **Georgia State University.** Mosey through the urban GSU
10 campus toward the gold dome of the **Georgia State Capitol**
building (206 Washington St.). If you read the state historical
markers on the grounds, you'll realize that Atlanta has been
virtually rebuilt since General Sherman's urban renewal program more than a century ago. The dome of the capitol is covered with gold leaf, originally mined from Dahlonega, in north
Georgia. In addition to housing politicos, it also contains a
Georgia history museum, which is open to the public. *Georgia*
State Capitol, tel. 404/656–2844. Free guided tours of the capi-
tol are given weekdays at 10 and 11 AM and at 1 and 2 PM.

11 Behind the capitol is the **Fulton County Stadium,** where the Atlanta Braves and Falcons play. Across the street from the capi-
12 tol is Atlanta's **City Hall** (68 Mitchell St.). When this 14-story
neo-Gothic structure with its lavish marble interior was first
built in 1926, wags dubbed it "The Painted Lady of Mitchell
Street."

Up Central Avenue to Upper Alabama Street is an entrance to
13 the city's newest attraction, **Underground Atlanta** (tel. 404/
523–2311). This reincarnated six-block entertainment-shop-
ping district, opened in June 1989, now accommodates some
100 specialty retail shops, 20 food-court vendors, and 22 restaurants and nightclubs on three levels. The entertainment area,
Kenny's Alley, is a sophisticated version of New Orleans's
Bourbon Street, with bars and night spots offering comedy
acts, a variety of music (Dixieland, country, pop, folk, jazz),
and dancing. Don't miss the ship decor at Dante's Down the
Hatch on Lower Pryor Street.

The main entrance of the $142-million joint venture between the city and The Rouse Co. is the Peachtree Fountains Plaza, with its distinctive 138-foot light tower. Across the street is an information center and on-site security pavilion. Two parking garages are on Martin Luther King Jr. Drive. The new Underground is almost three times larger than the first renovation, which opened in 1969 and closed in 1980.

Two other special attractions are near the Underground. **The World of Coca-Cola Pavilion** (55 Martin Luther King Jr. Dr., tel. 404/676–5151), which displays historical memorabilia from corporate archives and has interactive exhibits at a four-story, $10-million facility, is across the Depot Plaza on Central Avenue. **Atlanta Heritage Row** (55 Upper Alabama St., tel. 404/584–7879), within Underground Atlanta, features a multimedia presentation in a 100-seat theater while six historical vignettes tell the story of the spirit of the city's past and present.

At the Central Avenue entrance to the Underground Atlanta
14 complex is the **New Georgia Railroad** (90 Central Ave., tel. 404/
656–0769). The vintage locomotive and antique passenger
coaches make an 18-mile loop around the city three Saturdays a
month. One Saturday each month they travel to **Stone Moun-**
tain Park and Village, a suburb that's grown up around the

Downtown Atlanta

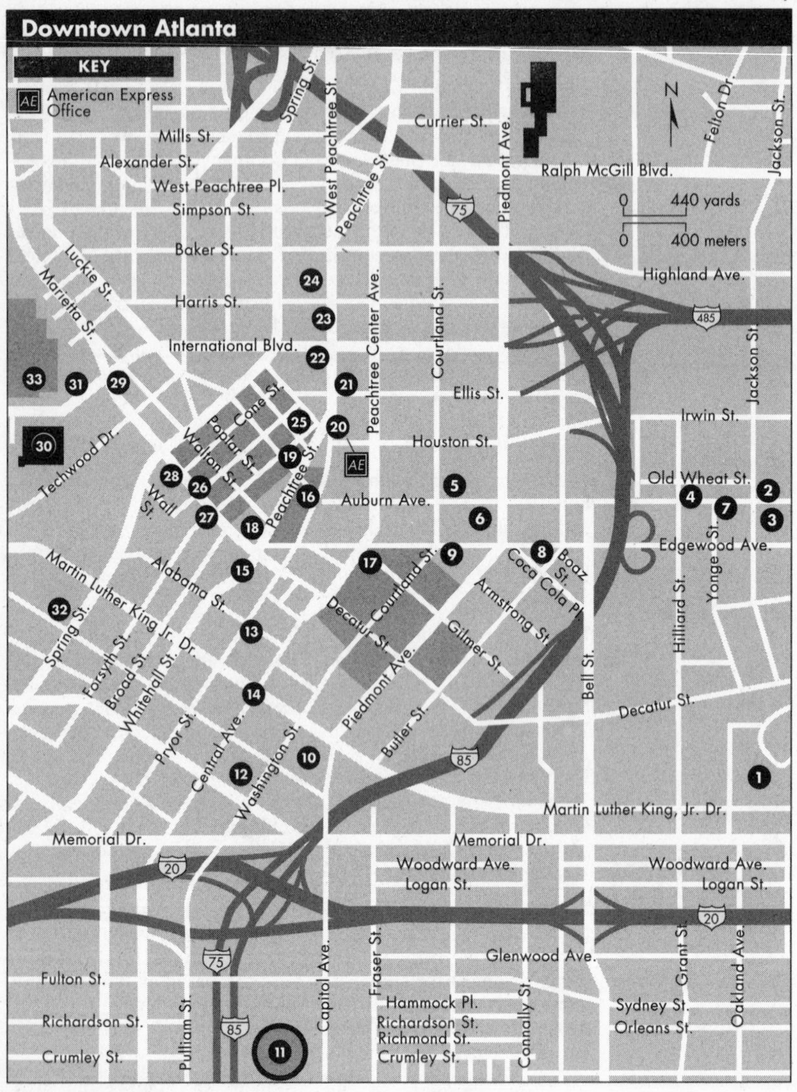

Atlanta Daily World, **6**
Atlanta-Fulton County Public Library, **25**
Atlanta History Center, **46**
Atlanta Life Insurance Company, **5**
Atlanta Newspapers Inc., **28**
Bank South Building, **26**
Baptist Student Center, **9**
Buckhead, **43**
Capital City Club, **24**
The "Castle", **37**
City Hall, **12**
CNN Center, **29**
Dr. King's birthplace, **4**
Ebenezer Baptist Church, **2**
Fay Gold, **44**
Federal Reserve Bank, **29**
Five Points MARTA, **15**
Flatiron Building, **19**
Fox Theater, **36**
Fulton County Stadium, **11**
Georgia Dome, **33**
Georgia Governor's Mansion, **45**

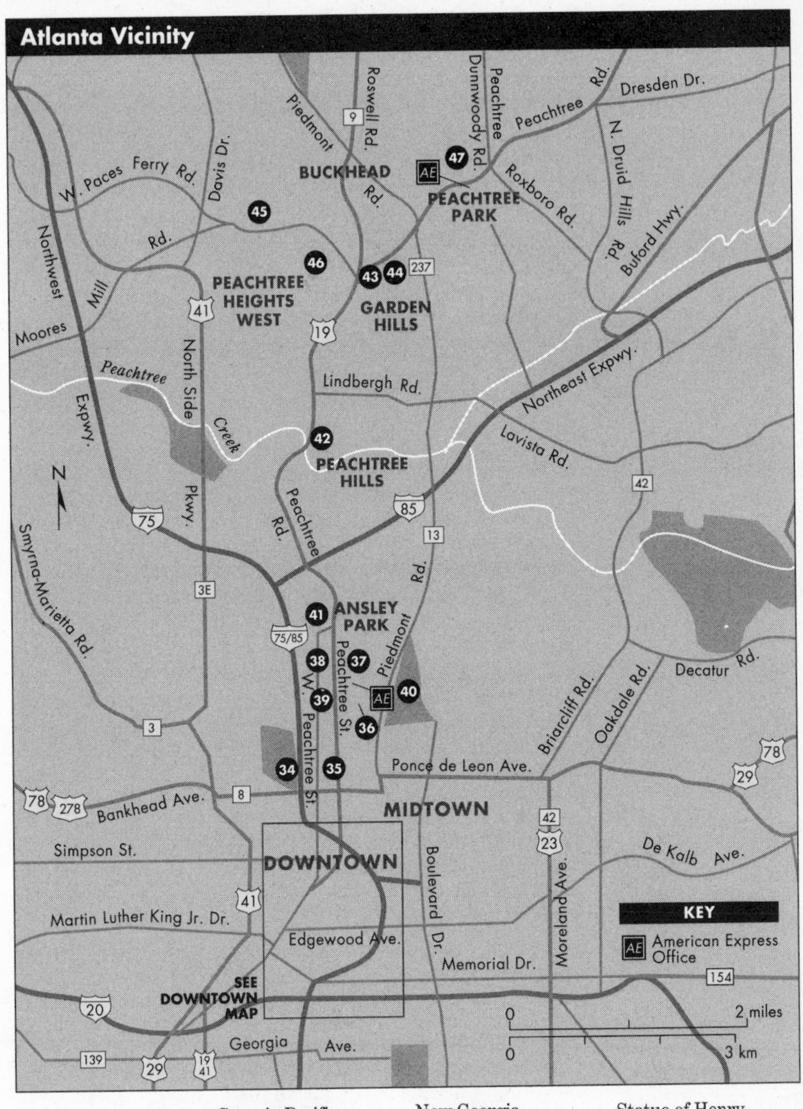

Georgia-Pacific Building, **20**

Georgia State Capitol, **10**

High Museum of Art, **39**

Hurt building, **17**

King Center for Nonviolent Social Change, **3**

IBM Tower, **35**

Municipal Market, **8**

National Park Service Rangers Station, **7**

Nation'sBank, **34**

New Georgia Railroad, **14**

Oakland Cemetery, **1**

Omni, **30**

Peachtree Battle Shopping Center, **42**

Peachtree Center, **23**

Phipps Plaza, **47**

Piedmont Park, **40**

Rhodes Hall, **41**

Richard B. Russell Federal building, **32**

Ritz-Carlton, **21**

Statue of Henry Grady, **27**

Underground Atlanta, **13**

Westin-Peachtree Plaza Hotel, **22**

William Oliver building, **18**

Woodruff Arts Center, **38**

Woodruff Park, **16**

World Congress Center, **31**

largest granite outcropping in the world, with a monumental Civil War sculpture carved on its side (*see* What to See and Do with Children, *below*). *Trips at 10 and 2. Loop fare is $10; Stone Mtn. $12.50. Both trips $5 children 3–12. Loop trips are nonstop and take about an hour.*

15 The **Five Points MARTA** station (Corner of Peachtree and Wall sts., downtown) is the city's major crossroads, the one tied to the economic lifeblood of the city, with its surrounding bank towers and offices of high-powered law firms. This is pinstripes and power-lunch territory.

On the corner of Peachtree and Alabama streets, outside the station, notice the old-fashioned gas street light, with its historical marker proclaiming it as the **Eternal Flame of the Confederacy.**

16 At **Woodruff Park** (corner of Peachtree St. and Park Pl.), named after the city's great philanthropist, Robert W. Woodruff, the late Coca-Cola magnate, you can see a cross section of Atlanta life. During lunchtime on weekdays, the park is filled with executives and secretaries, street preachers, politicians, Georgia State University students, and an array of other characters. If you want to join in, pick up lunch at one of the franchises or Chinese eateries around the park and find an empty bench. For people-watching, the scene rarely gets better than this.

Not much of old Atlanta still exists downtown, although a few
turn-of-the-century buildings remain. These elaborately decorated structures stand in sharp contrast to the severe modern-
17 ism of the skyscrapers of recent decades. **The Hurt Building** (45
Edgewood Ave.) features intricate architectural details, grill-
18 work, and an elaborate marble staircase. **The William Oliver
Building** (32 Peachtree St.) is an Art Deco gem. Walk through
its lobby and admire the ceiling mural, brass grills, and eleva-
19 tor doors. **The Flatiron Building** (at the Peachtree and Broad
sts. triangle) dates from 1897 and is the city's oldest high rise.
The elegant lobby of the Candler Building (127 Peachtree St.)
reeks of Old Atlanta money, power, and influence and is notable
for its decorative details.

20 The towering **Georgia–Pacific Building** (133 Peachtree St.) occupies hallowed ground, the precise site of the old Loew's Grand Theatre, where *Gone With the Wind* premiered back in 1939. One of the architectural oddities about this red marble high rise is that from certain angles the building appears to be two-dimensional or flat against the sky. There's a small branch of the **High Museum of Art** inside the building. *Tel. 404/577-6940. Admission free. Open weekdays 11–5.*

21 On the adjacent corner is the downtown **Ritz-Carlton Hotel** (181 Peachtree St.), a stylish place for a cocktail or high tea.

Next to **Macy's** department store (180 Peachtree St.), is the
22 **Westin–Peachtree Plaza Hotel** (210 Peachtree St.), at 73 stories the world's tallest hotel. Designed by Atlanta architect John Portman, the round tower with its trademark exterior elevator features a postmodern interior and a revolving bar/restaurant offering the best panoramic view of the city and the surrounding countryside.

23 In the next block, on both sides of the street, is **Peachtree Center,** a city within the city, also designed by John Portman. This complex of buildings, with its connecting skywalks, includes

the massive **Merchandise Mart;** the twin office towers of Peachtree Center, with an underground arcade and plaza; **the Apparel Mart;** and the **Hyatt Regency Hotel.** The Hyatt, with its bunkerlike exterior, low entrance, and soaring atrium, earned its place in history by being the first of its type back in 1967.

Within Peachtree Center, the **Atlanta International Museum of Art and Design** shows crafts from around the globe. *285 Peachtree Center Ave., tel. 404/688-2467. Admission free. Open Tues.–Sat. 11–5, Sun. noon–5.*

24 The **Capital City Club** (7 Harris St.) is another haunt of the city's power brokers. Its modest size makes it a holdout in the neighborhood, which attests to its clout.

Back down at the Georgia-Pacific intersection, pause at **Margaret Mitchell Park,** with its cascading waterfall and columned sculpture. Across the street, heading south, is the
25 **Atlanta-Fulton County Public Library** (126 Carnegie Way), which houses a large collection of *Gone With the Wind* memorabilia.

Head down Forsyth Street five blocks, to Marietta Street. Notice the renovated **Healy Building** (57 Forsyth St.), an early skyscraper in Commercial style with Tudor decoration.
26 Through the lobby is a pretty rotunda. The **Bank South Building** (55 Marietta St.) was briefly Atlanta's tallest building, from 1955 until 1964, until it was superseded by the National Bank of Georgia Building.

27 At the corner of Marietta and Forsyth streets is a bronze **statue of Henry Grady,** the post–Civil War editor of *The Atlanta Constitution* and early champion of the so-called "New South." Farther down Marietta Street are the offices of the **Atlanta**
28 **Newspapers Inc.** Next door is the **Federal Reserve Bank** (104 Marietta St.). Tours of its monetary museum can be arranged (tel. 404/521-8764). *Admission: free. Open Mon.–Fri. 9–4.*

Two blocks away, at the corner of Marietta Street and Tech-
29 wood Drive, is the **CNN Center** (1 CNN Center, 100 International Blvd.), the home of media mogul Ted Turner's Cable News Network. If you want to gawk at the high-tech world of "tee-vee" land and get a behind-the-scenes look at newscasters in action, take a 45-minute tour. The tour begins with a ride up the world's longest escalator to an eighth floor exhibit on Turner's global broadcasting empire. *Tours: tel. 404/827-2300. $5 adults, $2.50 senior citizens and children under 19. Open daily 9–5:30. Closed major holidays.*

30 Behind the CNN Center is the **Omni** (100 Techwood Dr.), where the Atlanta Hawks play and other special events such as
31 rock concerts are staged. The **World Congress Center** (285 International Blvd.), where Jimmy Carter held his rally the night he was elected president, and where the Democratic National Convention was held during the summer of 1988, is also nearby.
32 A short distance away is the **Richard B. Russell Federal Building** (Spring St. between Mitchell and Martin Luther King, Jr. Dr.), where former President Carter has an office. Its lobby has a tile mosaic that is worth seeing.

With a white, plum, and turquoise facade, the newly built
33 70,500-seat **Georgia Dome** is the site of Atlanta Falcons home games, major rock concerts, and conventions and trade shows. A design team of local architects crowned the 1-million-square-

foot facility with the world's largest cable-supported oval, giving the roof a circus-tent peak.

Midtown

The newly erected **Nation'sBank** tower (603 W. Peachtree St.),
34 easily visible from the expressway, stands as the South's tallest building. Down 14th Street is the city's acclaimed skyscrap-
35 er, the **IBM Tower** (1201 W. Peachtree St.), also known as One Atlantic Center. This postmodern high rise, which is visible from many parts of the city, was designed with a Gothic motif by Philip Johnson.

A couple of miles north, up Peachtree Street, is midtown. The
36 **Fox Theatre** (660 Peachtree St., tel. 404/881–2100) is a classic movie palace, built in the 1920s in Moorish-Egyptian style.

Time Out

If you want authentic Southern home-style cooking, don't miss **Mary Mac's Tea Room** (tel. 404/875–4337), just a few blocks from the Fox. Owner Margaret Lupo serves tasty plate lunches with cornbread. *224 Ponce de Leon Ave., tel. 404/875–4337. No credit cards accepted. Inexpensive.*

Peachtree Street at 10th Street used to be the heart of the hippie scene in Atlanta during the early 1970s. New construction has leveled vast areas of this district, but its residential blocks still include large 1920s bungalows and mansions converted into multiunit apartments. Gentrification has brought the Yuppie crowd into the area, so trendy and ethnic eateries and bars have followed.

Up Peachtree Street, across from the Woodruff Arts Center, is
37 an imposing old stone home known as **The Castle** (87 15th St.), which preservationists have saved.

38 The **Woodruff Arts Center** (1280 Peachtree St.) is home to the renowned **Atlanta Symphony** and the **Alliance Theatre,** which has more subscribers than does any other regional theater in the country. The Alliance has two venues: a main stage, where mainstream works are produced for general audiences, and a studio downstairs, which does offbeat productions for a more broad-minded public.

39 Next door is the white-enamel **High Museum of Art,** a high-tech showplace whose permanent collection is strong on the decorative arts and African folk arts. *1280 Peachtree St., tel. 404/892–3600. Admission: $4 adults, $2 students and senior citizens, $1 children 6–17; free on Thurs. after 1 PM. Special exhibits often have an additional charge. Open Tues.–Thurs. 10–5, Fri. 10–9, Sat. 10–5, Sun. noon–5.*

40 A few blocks off Peachtree Street is **Piedmont Park,** the city's outdoor recreation center. Here you'll find tennis courts, a swimming pool, and paths for biking, hiking, and jogging.

The Botanical Garden, located on 60 acres inside the park, has five acres of formal gardens, a 15-acre hardwood forest with walking trails, a serene Japanese garden, and the Fuqua Conservatory, which features unusual, flamboyant, and threatened flora from both tropical and desert climates. Don't overlook the whimsical dragon topiary at the entrance. *Tel. 404/876–5858. Admission: $4.50 adults, $2.25 children and senior citizens. Open Tues.–Sun. 9–6.*

41 North on Peachtree Street is **Rhodes Hall,** headquarters of the **Georgia Trust for Historic Preservation.** A permanent exhibit

focuses on Atlanta architecture of earlier eras. *1516 Peachtree St., tel. 404/881–9980. Admission $2. Open weekdays 11–4.*

In the Brookwood Hills area, across I–85, Peachtree Street becomes **Peachtree Road,** and turns into a strip of popular dining places. You'll also note that flowering peach trees once again thrive along various stretches of the road.

42 The **Peachtree Battle Shopping Center,** on your right, contains **Oxford Books** (2345 Peachtree Rd., tel. 404/262–3333).

Buckhead Past Peachtree Hills and Garden Hills is **Buckhead,** the heart of
43 affluent and trendy Atlanta. Many of Atlanta's finest restaurants and most popular watering spots are in this area. The
44 city's major art galleries are here, too. Start at **Fay Gold Gallery** (247 Buckhead Ave., tel. 404/233–3843) and pick up a guidebook for the location of other galleries.

A short drive out West Paces Ferry Road will bring you to the
45 **Georgia Governor's Mansion.** Built some 20 years ago, in Greek Revival style, the house features Federal-period antiques in its public rooms. *391 W. Paces Ferry Rd., tel. 404/261–1776. Open for free guided tours Tues.–Thurs. 10–11:30* AM.

46 In the same area is the **Atlanta History Center.** The center is currently expanding its facilities with the construction of a large exhibition hall due to open during the fall of 1993. Of interest on the 32-acre site are the **Swan House,** an Italianate villa filled with European furnishings and art; the **Tullie Smith Plantation,** an 1840s farmhouse; and **McElreath Hall,** an exhibition space for artifacts from Atlanta's history. *3101 Andrews Dr., tel. 404/261–1837. Admission: $6 adults, $4.50 senior citizens and students, $3 children 6–17, and under 6 free. Open Mon.–Sat. 9–5:30, Sun. noon–5:30.*

If you want to gaze at the lovely lawns, gardens, and mansions of Atlanta's well-to-do, drive around in this area, especially along Tuxedo, Blackland, and Habersham roads. Follow the green-and-white "Scenic Drive" signs past an impressive array of Greek Revival, Spanish, Italianate, English Tudor, and French château showplaces.

At the intersection of Peachtree Street and Lenox Road is
47 **Phipps Plaza,** which includes such fashionable shops as Lord & Taylor, Saks Fifth Avenue, Abercrombie & Fitch, Gucci, and Tiffany & Co. On the other corner is the **Ritz-Carlton Buckhead,** which features Atlanta's only five-star restaurant, **The Dining Room** (*see* Dining, *below*). If you intend to splurge, this is the place.

Atlanta for Free

Alonzo F. Herndon Home. Founder of the Atlanta Life Insurance Co., the nation's second-largest black-owned insurance company, Alonzo Herndon built this 15-room mansion in 1910. A museum contains furnishings, artwork, and memorabilia. *587 University Pl., tel. 404/581–9813. Open Tues.–Sat. 10–4.*

Concerts. On Sunday evenings during the summer, the **Atlanta Symphony Orchestra** performs free concerts for thousands of patrons who spread blankets and picnic suppers on the former golf course at Piedmont Park (Piedmont Ave. between 10th and 14th sts.).

Emory University Museum of Art and Archeology. The pristine interior of this Beaux Arts building on the Emory campus was designed by architect Michael Graves. Exhibits range from an Egyptian mummy to contemporary art. *Emory University, Kilgo Cir., tel. 404/727–4282. Admission: $2 suggested donation. Open Tues.–Sat. 10–4:30, Sun. noon–5.*

Telephone Museum. The advances of the telephone over the last century are chronicled in 10 exhibit areas. *Southern Bell Center, Plaza Level, 675 W. Peachtree St. NE, tel. 404/529–7334. Open weekdays 11–1.*

Georgia Governor's Mansion (*see* Exploring, *above*).

What to See and Do with Children

The "Weekend" tabloid section of Saturday's *Atlanta Journal–Constitution* has a listing called "Kids," which highlights special happenings around the city for young people.

Fernbank Science Center. The large planetarium here is the only one in the nation owned by a public school system. The museum focuses on a variety of areas, including geology, space exploration, and ecology. The forest behind the center is a treasure in itself. *156 Heaton Park Dr. NE, tel. 404/378–4311. Open Tues.–Fri. 8:30–10, Mon. 8:30–5, Sat. 10–5, and Sun. 1–5.*

Center for Puppetry Arts Museum. The large display of puppets from all over the world is designed to teach visitors about the craft. *1404 Spring St., tel. 404/873–3391. Admission: $3 adults, $2 children 13 and under. Open Mon.–Sat. 9–4.*

SciTrek. A new science and technology museum has some 100 hands-on exhibits in four halls—Simple Machines; Light, Color, and Perception; Electricity and Magnetism; and Kidspace, for 2–7-year-olds. *395 Piedmont Ave. NE, tel. 404/522–5500. Admission: $6 adults, $4 children 3–17, under 3 free. Open Tues.–Sat. 10–5, Sun. noon–5.*

Six Flags Over Georgia is Atlanta's major theme park, with over 100 rides, musical revues, performing tropical birds and dolphins; and concerts by top-name artists. *I–20W at Six Flags Dr., tel. 404/948–9290. Admission: (all-inclusive one-day pass) $22 adults, $11 for those 55 and older, $15.70 children 3–9, under 3 free; $5 parking fee. Opens 10 AM daily in summer and Nov. 25–Jan. 1, with weekend-only operations Mar.–May and Sept.–Oct. Closed Nov.–Feb.; closing times vary. Take MARTA's West Line to Hightower Station and connect with the Six Flags bus (No. 201).*

Stone Mountain Park is the largest granite outcropping on earth. The Confederate Memorial on the north face of the 825-foot-high, five-mile-around monolith is the world's largest sculpture. A 3,200-acre park includes a skylift to the mountaintop, a steam locomotive train ride around the base, an antebellum plantation, an ice-skating rink, golf course, swimming beach, campground, paddlewheel steamboat, and Civil War museum. *U.S. 78, Stone Mountain Freeway, tel. 404/498–5600. Admission: $5 per car, additional fees for attractions. Open daily 6 AM–midnight.*

Zoo Atlanta has nearly 1,000 animals inhabiting its redeveloped property. An ongoing $35-million renovation program has already resulted in the new Birds of Prey Amphitheater, the Ford African Rain Forest, Flamingo Lagoon, and the Sumtran Tiger Exhibit. *Grant Park, 800 Cherokee Ave., tel. 404/624–5600. Admission: $7 adults and children 12 and older, $4.50 children 3–11, under 3 free. Open daily 10–5. Closed major holidays.*

Off the Beaten Track

Deacon Burton's Grill. The holy grail of Atlanta soul food, this is the place to savor the authentic flavors of glorious Southern fried chicken, chitlins, fried fish, barbecue, turnip greens, cornbread, and cobblers. The chef and maitre d' is "Deacon" Lyndell Burton, an ageless wizard of the iron frying pan. *1029 Edgewood Ave. (across from Inman Park MARTA Station), tel. 404/525–3415. As the sign over the register says, The Credit Manager Is Out, Please Pay Cash. Inexpensive. Open weekdays 6 AM–4 PM.*

Carter Presidential Center. The museum and archives focus on Jimmy Carter's political career. But it sponsors other activities as well—projects on world food issues, children, foreign affairs conferences. Its Japanese garden is also a serene spot in which to unwind. *One Copenhill Ave. NE, tel. 404/331–3942. Admission: $2.50 adults, $1.50 senior citizens, children under 15 free. Open Mon.–Sat. 9–4:45, Sun. noon–4:45. Closed New Year's, Thanksgiving, and Christmas. Cafeteria open Mon.–Sat. 11–4, Sun. noon–4:30.*

Shopping

Atlanta's department stores, specialty shops, and flea markets are magnets for shoppers from across the Southeast. Most stores are open Monday–Saturday 10–9:30, and Sunday noon–6. Many downtown stores close Sunday. Sales tax is 6% in the city of Atlanta and Fulton County and varies in suburbs.

Shopping Districts

The downtown shopping area is anchored on the north by **Macy's** (180 Peachtree St., tel. 404/221–7221). The store carries top-name apparel and merchandise. Smaller stores include **Brooks Brothers** (235 Peachtree St., tel. 404/577–4040), on the ground floor of Peachtree Center's Gaslight Tower, **The Limited** (209 Peachtree St., tel. 404/523–1728), and a collection of retail shops inside Underground Atlanta.

At the intersection of Peachtree and Lenox roads, 8 miles north of downtown, is Atlanta's high-fashion shopping district. **Lenox Square Mall** has branches of **Neiman Marcus, Macy's, Rich's,** and 200 other specialty stores and restaurants. **Phipps Plaza** houses branches of **Saks Fifth Avenue, Lord & Taylor, Gucci,** and **Tiffany & Co.**

Specialty Shops

Antiques

Bennett Street in Buckhead is the address of a number of designer- or craftsmen-owned-and-operated shops selling antique pine furnishings, fine rugs, rare collectibles, and unique crafts. European furnishings, heirloom sterling, and fine art are the specialties in the more than 20 shops lining the cobblestone courtyard of Buckhead's **2300 Peachtree Road** complex. The **Miami Circle** district, also in Buckhead off Piedmont Road, is another enclave for antiques and decorative arts lovers.

If "junking" is your pleasure, you'll reach nirvana in the area around the intersection of Moreland and Euclid avenues, which is loaded with vintage clothing stores, used record and book shops, and some stores that defy description.

Books Atlanta's largest selection of books and newspapers is at **Oxford Books at Buckhead** (360 Pharr Rd., tel. 404/262–3333) and **The Renaissance Bookshop** (RIO Shopping Center, 595 Piedmont Ave., tel. 404/873–4161). Books are not the only inducement to visit the Oxford Bookstore; along the store's narrow balcony is a coffee shop, **The Cup and Chaucer.**

Food **DeKalb Farmers Market** (3000 E. Ponce de Leon Ave., Decatur, tel. 404/377–6400) has 106,000 square feet of exotic fruits, cheeses, seafood, sausages, breads, and delicacies from around the world. **Harry's Farmers Markets** (1180 Upper Hembree Rd., Alpharetta, tel. 404/664–6300; and 2025 Satellite Point, tel. 404/416–6900), north and northeast of the city, are more upscale versions offering prepared foods as well as exotic produce, vegetables, meats, and seafoods. *Both open daily.*

Participant Sports

Bicycling **Piedmont Park** (Piedmont Ave. between 10th and 14th Sts.) is closed to traffic and popular for biking. **Skate Escape** (across from the park at 1086 Piedmont Ave., tel. 404/892–1292) has rental bikes and skates. The **Southern Bicycle League** (tel. 404/594–8350) has regularly scheduled tours.

Golf The best public courses are **Stone Mountain Park** (U.S. 78, 16 mi east of downtown, tel. 404/498–5600), **Chastain Park** (216 W. Wieuca Rd., tel. 404/255–0723), and **Sugar Creek** (2706 Bouldercrest Rd., tel. 404/241–7671). Carts and rental clubs are available at all three.

Health Clubs Health clubs that are open to the public include **Boot Camp Fitness and Training** (597 Cooledge Ave., tel. 404/876–8686) and branches of the **YMCA** (tel. 404/588–9622). Hotels with health clubs open to guests include the **Westin Peachtree Plaza, Hotel Nikko,** the **Swissotel,** and the **Atlanta Marriott Marquis** (*see* Lodging, *below*).

Jogging Joggers quickly learn that this is a very hilly city, shaded by many trees. **Piedmont Park** is a traffic-free place perfect for running. Contact the **Atlanta Track Club** (3097 Shadowlawn Ave., tel. 404/231–9065) for other running zones.

Swimming Climate-controlled facilities are housed in the **Martin Luther King Jr. Natatorium** (70 Boulevard, tel. 404/688–3791). **White Water Park** (250 North Cobb Pkwy. U.S. 41, Marietta, tel. 404/424–9283) has a huge wave pool, several water slides, picnic areas, lockers, and showers.

Tennis **Bitsy Grant Tennis Center** (2125 Northside Dr., tel. 404/351–2774) is the area's best public facility. **Piedmont Park** (tel. 404/872–1507) has hard courts only (no locker facilities).

Spectator Sports

Atlanta's status as a spectator-sports capital grew during 1991 when the **Atlanta Braves** baseball team went from worst to first, becoming the National League champions. The Braves play home games at Atlanta–Fulton County Stadium (521 Capitol Ave., tel. 404/577–9100). The National Basketball Association's **Atlanta Hawks** play home games at the Omni Coliseum (100 Techwood Dr., tel. 404/827–DUNK). The National Football League's **Atlanta Falcons** play home games at the newly constructed Georgia Dome (285 International Blvd., tel. 404/261–5400).

Dining

By Christine Lauterbach

Atlanta offers a full range of eating options worthy of its new image as a dynamic international city. From a million-dollar diner to a humble meat-and-three, one can find almost anything in the capital of the New South: prestigious kitchens run by world-class chefs, a multitude of ethnic restaurants, and more fried chicken outlets than anywhere else in the country. But despite the best efforts of the convention and hospitality industry, the Old South is conspicuously absent.

The dining public is value oriented and prices are still low in Atlanta. A full plate means a lot to the average consumer and it is the rare restaurant that does not meet this expectation. The local taste for things sweet and fried cannot be discounted. Try to catch the flavor of the South at breakfast and lunch in modest establishments and to reserve your evenings for more ambitious culinary exploration.

The most highly recommended restaurants in each price category are indicated by a star ★.

Category	Cost*
Very Expensive	over $45
Expensive	$35–$45
Moderate	$25–$35
Inexpensive	under $15

**per person without tax (6%), service, or drinks*

Downtown
Very Expensive
★

City Grill. This posh but breezy restaurant has made the most of its grand location in the recently renovated historic Hurt building. The bustle of success greets you at the door while bucolic murals and stunning high ceilings help create a feeling of glamour. The menu is modern French: duck, fish, and beef entrées. There are a few weaknesses, but you can't go wrong with the free-range chicken, the lamb, or any of the delicious vegetable specialties. Club-style service is by a well-trained staff. *55 Hurt Plaza, tel. 404/524–2489. Valet parking. Jacket required. Reservations recommended, weeks ahead for weekend dining. AE, D, DC, MC, V. No lunch weekends.*

Expensive

Morton's. Signature porterhouse and prime dry-age steaks are served in a clubby, sophisticated setting of gleaming hardwood floors and comfortable banquettes. The lunch and dinner menus also offer fish and chicken entrées for those with lighter appetites. *245 Peachtree Center Ave., tel. 404/577–4366. Jacket and tie requested. Reservations accepted. AE, DC, MC, V.*

Savannah Fish Company. Have a drink in the revolving lounge at the top of the hotel, but come down to the ground floor for a smashingly good and simple meal of fresh fish, grilled or sautéed without ado. Entrées are served with a bamboo steamer of

Dining
Bice, **4**
Chef's Grill, **2**
City Grill, **19**
Dailey's, **14**
Delectables, **16**
Harold's Barbecue, **20**
Indigo, **7**
Mick's, **6**
Morton's, **10**
Partners, **8**
Savannah Fish Company, **13**
Thelma's, **11**
The Varsity, **5**

Lodging
Ansley Inn, **3**
Atlanta Marriott Marquis, **9**
Barclay, **12**
Colony Square, **1**
Hyatt Regency, **17**
Omni, **15**
Ritz-Carlton, **18**
Westin Peachtree Plaza, **13**

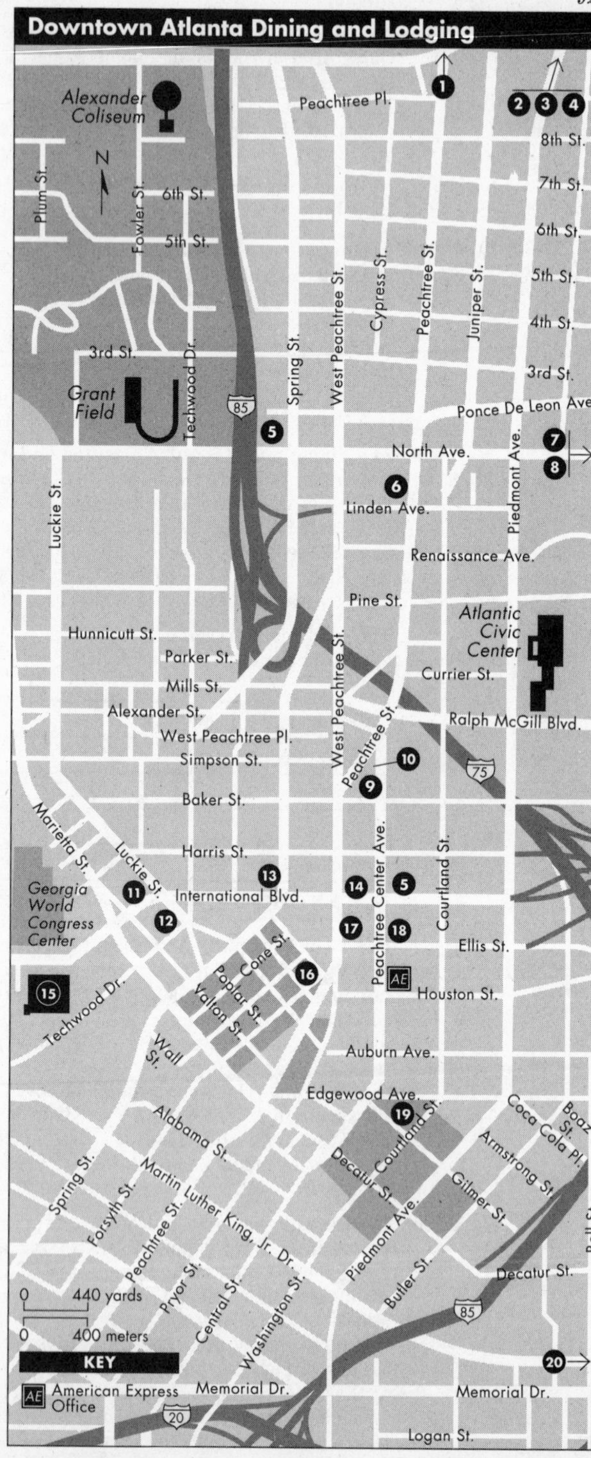

fresh vegetables. Ignore overpriced appetizers and enjoy the house's saffron and fennel-flavored fish stew. Pass up generic cakes for the simple Savannah fried puffs sprinkled with sugar and served with three sauces. There's a hint of Asian simplicity in the pared-down decor. *Westin Peachtree Plaza, Peachtree St. at International Blvd., tel. 404/589–7456. Jacket optional. Reservations accepted for lunch only. AE, D, DC, MC, V.*

Moderate **Dailey's.** There's always something going on at the bar and in the two dining rooms of this enormous converted warehouse. Downstairs is casual fun. Upstairs there's spectacular decor (merry-go-round horses, enormous shop lamps, both in perfect scale with the imposing space) and more serious dining: veal with Pommery mustard, amberjack au poivre, crisp duck, generous salad, and fried rolls. The menu is recited, the service flashy. Revved-up versions of pastry classics are paraded before the adoring eyes of the crowd on an astounding dessert bar. *17 International Blvd., tel. 404/681–3303. Dress: casual. No reservations; expect a wait. AE, D, DC, MC, V. No lunch weekends.*

Inexpensive ★ **Delectables.** One of downtown's best-kept secrets, don't let the location (inside the Central Public Library) or the format (cafeteria) deter you. This is a very sophisticated little operation serving ravishing salads, wholesome soups, yummy cookies, and freshly baked cakes. Sandwiches are fair. You can enjoy your meal immersed in jazz music and sunshine, on the patio. *Public Library, corner of Margaret Mitchell Sq. and Carnegie Way (enter through Carnegie Way), tel. 404/681–2909. Dress: casual. No reservations. No credit cards. Lunch and coffee break only. Weekdays only.*

Harold's Barbecue. It's a short distance from downtown, but worth the ride. Legislators, political groupies, and small fry from the capitol sit side by side, wolfing down delicious chopped pork sandwiches, huge platters of freshly sliced meat, and overflowing bowls of Brunswick stew. Don't miss the crackling bread. The knotty pine, tacky art, and management haven't changed in 25 years. *171 McDonough Blvd. near the Federal Penitentiary, tel. 404/627–9268. Dress: casual. No reservations. No credit cards. Closed Sun.*

Thelma's. Honest-to-goodness soul food is served in a squat cinder block building with a cafeteria counter and cramped dining room. Go early at lunchtime to beat the crowds lining up for baked chicken, okra cakes, twice-cooked potatoes, and some of the best flavored greens around town at this cheerful family-run eatery. *190 Luckie St., tel. 404/688–5855. Dress: casual. No reservations. No credit cards. Breakfast and lunch only. Closed weekends.*

Varsity. Part of Atlanta's collective past, people from all walks of life are likely to run into this enormous, sprawling diner to get one of the famous chili dogs, a glorified hamburger, or a gigantic order of fresh and delicious—but greasy—onion rings. Line up behind the locals and pay close attention to the lingo: "One naked dog, walking and a bag o' rags," will get you a plain hot dog and some french fries. Connoisseurs drink orange frosties. Folks in a hurry get curb service. *61 North Ave., tel. 404/881–1706. Dress: casual. No reservations. No credit cards. Open late.*

Midtown
Very Expensive
★ **Bice.** This new restaurant opened in July 1991 boasting an opulently decorated "look," created by design maestro Adam Tihany, that includes a 35-foot-high domed ceiling, modern artwork, and logo china. The nouvelle Italian cuisine is as delicious as it is artfully presented. Grilled Georgia foie gras with sweet-potato chips, fresh tuna ravioli, grilled sea bass, and veal chops receive top ratings, and the pasta entrées are stellar. *1100 Peachtree St., tel. 404/874–4580. Jacket and tie recommended. Reservations recommended. AE, DC, MC, V. Closed Sun. lunch.*

Moderate–Expensive
Chef's Grill. This casual San Francisco–style bistro located inside the Woodruff Arts Center is a popular pre- and post-theater dining spot. The menu changes with the seasons, but grilled fish, gourmet pizzas, and creative appetizers are always found. Grilled eggplant, warm Georgia goat cheese, and crab cakes are among the specialties. *1280 Peachtree St., tel. 404/881–0652. Dress: casual. Reservations recommended. AE, MC, V. Closed Sun. and Mon. for dinner, weekends for lunch.*

★ **Indigo.** Sizzling and trendy, the creative coastal cuisine proves it can be taken seriously. Owner Alix Kenagy is a former fashion editor with a great eye for catchy details. Lime and cilantro flavor many of the dishes. Conch fritters, lamb turnovers, grilled oysters with chipotle peppers and tequila, and fish and fresh herbs in a twist of parchment are particularly recommended. Don't miss the refreshing Key lime pie or the sautéed bananas with rum and lime. There's brown paper on the tables and porch furniture on the sidewalk. It's always crowded, but waiting for a table can become part of the fun. *1897 N. Highland Ave., tel. 404/876–0676. Dress: casual. No reservations. AE, MC, V. Dinner only.*

★ **Partners.** Next door to Indigo, it is also owned by Alix Kenagy. Upbeat and noisy, the creative decor is an appropriate backdrop for an excellent light menu that includes freshly made ravioli with a different stuffing and sauce every day, Cajun mixed grill, Vietnamese chicken cakes, and nostalgic, old-fashioned desserts. An appealing small wine list is full of good values. *1399 N. Highland Ave., tel. 404/875–0202. Dress: casual. No reservations; expect a wait. AE, MC, V. Dinner only.*

Inexpensive
Mick's. Casual and hip, with a well-researched and implemented menu, this restaurant serves the kind of food America never stopped loving: yummy burgers, great chicken sandwiches, big cream pies. The menu also includes fresh pasta, grilled vegetable plates, and soda fountain specials. Great people-watching opportunities abound in a pertly renovated old drugstore. *557 Peachtree St., tel. 404/875–6425 and Peachtree Center Ave. and International Blvd., tel. 404/688–MICK (three other locations: 3393 Peachtree Rd., tel. 404/262–6425; 4505 Ashford-Dunwoody Rd., tel. 404/394–6425 and 2110 Peachtree Rd., tel. 404/351–6425). Dress: casual. No reservations. AE, DC, MC, V. Open late.*

Buckhead
Very Expensive
Bone's. In this brash, New York–style steakhouse, the rich and powerful rub egos and compare lifestyles over steaks, chops, lobster, and potatoes baked in a crust of salt. Most patrons wear jackets, but if your idea of fun is spending big bucks in a sport shirt, they won't turn you down. *3130 Piedmont Rd., tel. 404/237–2663. Jacket and tie suggested. Reservations recommended. AE, DC, MC, V. No lunch weekends.*

★ **Chops.** This clubby steakhouse is a favorite of the city's power brokers. The interior's sleek Mission-style setting features a redwood bar and a carved glass screen. You're served generous portions of grain-fed Midwestern beef cooked on an indoor grill and a wide variety of seafood. *70 W. Paces Ferry Rd., tel. 404/262–2675. Jacket and tie suggested. Reservations recommended. AE, D, DC, MC, V. No lunch weekends.*

Coach & Six. This has been one of Atlanta's most famous and most idiosyncratic restaurants for nearly three decades. No place can make you feel more like an outsider, yet no place provides a better opportunity to see the Atlanta that was, and still is, a mercantile boomtown. Marvelous New York–style rolls, raw vegetables, olives, cheese toast, and spinach pie are presented before the meal even begins. The menu focuses on steaks, roasts, chops, and fresh fish. There's also an impressive pastry cart. The service aims for formality but is sometimes uncaring. *1776 Peachtree Rd., tel. 404/872–6666. Jacket and tie required. Reservations required well in advance for weekends. AE, D, DC, MC, V. No weekend lunch.*

★ **Dining Room, in the Ritz-Carlton Buckhead.** This is the best restaurant in town and among the country's ten greatest. Under Chef Guenter Seeger, haute cuisine is not flashy or ostentatious. Strictly limiting himself to the freshest regional products, Seeger doesn't like calling attention to the culinary process. The menu, handwritten every day, is likely to involve local sun-dried sweet potatoes (in ravioli), Vidalia onions (with lobster and lobster coral sauce), or persimmons (in a mousse with muscadine sorbet and Georgia golden raspberries). Quivering creamy textures (especially fresh duck liver or any kind of seafood) are the result of the chef's own cooking magic. Don't ask for your food to be well-done. Surrender to this imperious genius and the exquisite, discreet service. *3434 Peachtree Rd., tel. 404/237–2700. Jacket and tie requested. Reservations required, several days ahead for weekend dining. AE, D, DC, MC, V. Dinner only. Closed Sun.*

★ **La Grotta.** Despite its odd location in the basement of an apartment building, this is one of the best-managed dining rooms in town. Magnetic, dynamic Sergio Favalli is a superb host and the waiters are on their toes. The kitchen experiments cautiously with new concepts and trendy ingredients, but old Northern Italian favorites remain at the core of the menu. Don't miss the cold grilled wild mushrooms, the baby quails over polenta, or the special tiramisu dessert. Veal and fresh pasta are outstanding. There's an excellent wine list. *2637 Peachtree Rd., tel. 404/231–1368. Jacket and tie required. Reservations required well in advance. AE, D, DC, MC, V. Dinner only. Closed Sun.*

★ **103 West.** An ornate facade and porte cochere add to the proud image of Atlanta's poshest, most palatial restaurant. Antique tapestries, watered silks, and glorious details fill the dining rooms. The kitchen matches this lavish classicism. Here's the place to gorge on crab cakes with beurre blanc, sweet basil and red pepper rouille; or fresh veal sweetbreads with madeira sauce and fresh grapes on a bed of wilted spinach. Glamour dishes include smoked mountain trout with lump crabmeat, venison with wild mushrooms and mustard fruit, and an amazing "Grand Dessert" sampler. *103 W. Paces Ferry Rd., tel. 404/233–5993. Jacket and tie required. Reservations required. AE, D, DC, MC, V. Dinner only. Closed Sun.*

Expensive
★ **Abruzzi Ristorante.** "Understated elegance" is the buzz phrase for this modern yet traditional restaurant frequented by the city's old guard. If you're not taken with one of the myriad menu-offerings, have managing partner Nico Petrucci suggest a specialty. Excellent dishes include salmon carpaccio, green-and-white gnocchi in pesto, sautéed sweetbreads, veal chop, baked fish with rosemary, and ricotta cheesecake. *2355 Peachtree Rd., tel. 404/261–8186. Jacket and tie requested for dinner. Reservations recommended. AE, DC, MC, V. No weekend lunch. Closed Sun.*

Pano's and Paul's. An Atlanta classic, it's now in its 12th year of stylish pampering. Pano Karatassos and Paul Albrecht hit gold, thanks to their single-minded devotion to their customers' whims and needs, including dietary restriction. Lovely lights and rich fabrics fill the dining rooms designed by Penny Goldwasser. Many new ideas percolate through the kitchen; state-of-the-art dishes are introduced as specials and eventually included in the menu. Look for roasted Georgia quails with foie gras and trumpet mushrooms, smoked salmon crêpes with truffle horseradish sauce, and a combination of Maine lobster and capon breast with a mousseline of potato and celery. *1232 W. Paces Ferry Rd., tel. 404/261–3662. Jacket required. Reservations required (days, sometimes weeks ahead for a prime slot). AE, D, DC, MC, V. Dinner only. Closed Sun.*

Moderate–Expensive
★ **Buckhead Diner.** This million-dollar fantasy by the owners of Pano's and Paul's is still one of the hottest restaurants in town, a shimmering faux-diner wrapped in luscious hues of neon. Inlaid wood, Italian leather, hand-cut marble and mellow lights establish a languorous ambience reminiscent of the Orient Express. The cuisine is anything but diner: neo-Asian shrimp wonton, buffalo-milk mozzarella melted in fresh tomato coulis, veal meatloaf, and homemade banana-walnut ice cream are some of the treats prepared by gifted young Gerry Klaskala. Interesting wines are available by the glass. *3073 Piedmont Rd., tel. 404/262–3336. Dress: informal. No reservations; expect a long wait. AE, D, DC, MC, V.*

Pricci. The stamp of acclaimed designer Patrick Kuleto is apparent in the chic mirrored and windowed decor of this recently opened hot spot. Deceptively simplistic Italian fare is accompanied by Pricci's own breads. *3018 Maple Dr., tel. 404/237–2941. Jacket and tie requested. Reservations advised. AE, D, DC, MC, V. No lunch Sun.*

Inexpensive
★ **Azalea.** East meets West on the menu at this black-on-white contemporary restaurant, where Atlanta master chef Tom Catherall mans the kitchen, drawing crowds to the place-to-be-seen atmosphere. *3167 Peachtree Rd., tel. 404/237–9939. Reservations not accepted. AE, MC, V. Dinner nightly.*

OK Café. You'll go "back to the future" in this witty take-off on small-town cafés. There's a great cast of cheeky waitresses, whimsical art, and very comfortable booths. Particularly good breakfasts (fried French toast, stout omelets) are served, but blue plate specials are not always reliable. The desserts are excellent. *1248 W. Paces Ferry Rd., tel. 404/233–2888. Dress: casual. No reservations. AE, MC, V. Open 24 hours.*

Rocky's Brick Oven Pizzeria. This bastion of European-style pizza simply bustles with energy. The clientele includes well-heeled parents with tots in tow, art school students, and rocker Mick Jagger, who frequented it while filming a movie. The kitchen turns out thick, square Sicilian pizzas as well as thin-crusted Neapolitan pies with the city's most appealing combination of toppings. *1770 Peachtree St., tel. 404/876-1111. Dress: casual. No reservations. AE, MC, V. Open late.*

Lodging

One of America's three most popular convention destinations, Atlanta offers a broad range of lodgings. More than 12,000 rooms are in the compact downtown area, close to the Georgia World Congress Center, Atlanta Civic Center, Atlanta Merchandise Mart and Apparel Mart, and Omni Coliseum. Other clusters are in the affluent Buckhead corporate and retail area, and around Hartsfield International Airport.

Category	Cost*
Very Expensive	over $100
Expensive	$75–$100
Moderate	$50–$75
Inexpensive	under $50

**double room; add 11% for taxes*

Downtown and Midtown
Very Expensive

Atlanta Marriott Marquis. Immense and coolly contemporary, the Marquis seems to go on forever as you stand under the lobby's huge fabric sculpture that appears to be floating down from the sky-lit roof 50 stories above. Each guest room opens onto this atrium. *265 Peachtree Center Ave., 30303, tel. 404/521-0000 or 800/228-9290. 1,671 rooms, 71 suites. Facilities: 5 restaurants, 4 bars and lounges, health club, indoor/outdoor pool. AE, D, DC, MC, V.*

Colony Square Hotel. Theatricality and opulence are epitomized by the dimly lit lobby with overhanging balconies, piano music, and fresh flowers. The hotel is one block from MARTA's Art Center station, across from the Woodruff Arts Center and the High Museum of Art, and it anchors the Colony Square office/residential/retail complex. *Peachtree and 14th Sts. (1 block from MARTA's Art Center rail station), 30361, tel. 404/892-6000 or 800/422-7895. 428 rooms, 33 suites. Facilities: lobby lounge, restaurant, access (for a fee) to the Colony Club health club, racquetball courts, outdoor pool. AE, D, DC, MC, V.*

Hyatt Regency Atlanta. The Hyatt's 23-story atrium/lobby (built in 1965) launched the chain's "atrium look." The rooms were renovated in honor of the hotel's 20th anniversary. Most guests are conventioneers. *264 Peachtree St. (connected to MARTA's Peachtree Center Station), 30303, tel. 404/577-1234. 1,278 rooms, 58 suites. Facilities: 4 restaurants, outdoor pool, health club, sauna, 2 ballrooms. AE, D, DC, MC, V.*

Omni Hotel at CNN Center. The hotel is adjacent to the CNN Center, home of Ted Turner's Cable News Network. The lobby combines Old World and modern accents, with marble floors, Oriental rugs, exotic floral and plant arrangements, and contemporary furnishings. *100 CNN Center, near MARTA's Omni station stop, 30335, tel. 404/659-0000 or 800/843-6664. 465 rooms. Facilities: 2 restaurants, lounge, access to the Downtown Athletic Club. AE, D, DC, MC, V.*

Ritz-Carlton Atlanta. The mood here is set by traditional afternoon tea served in the intimate, sunken lobby beneath an 18th-century chandelier. Guest rooms are luxuriously decorated with marble writing tables, sofas, four-poster beds, and marble bathrooms. *181 Peachtree St., 30303, tel. 404/659–0400 or 800/241–3333. 447 rooms. Facilities: 2 restaurants, bar with live jazz, access (for a nominal fee) to the adjacent Phoenix Athletic Club. AE, D, DC, MC, V.*

Westin Peachtree Plaza. Every photograph of Atlanta's skyline taken in the last 10 years features this cylindrical glass tower, the tallest hotel in North America. The five-story atrium lobby is classic John Portman—the Atlanta-based architect who set a modern hotel style for the world. The hotel was recently renovated top to bottom to the tune of $35 million. For the best views, ask for the 45th floor or higher. *210 Peachtree St. at International Blvd., 30303, tel. 404/659–1400 or 800/228–3000. 1,074 rooms. Facilities: 3 restaurants, 3 bars, a rooftop indoor/outdoor pool, health club, sauna, shopping gallery, kosher kitchen. AE, D, DC, MC, V.*

Moderate–Expensive

Ansley Inn. Above a sloping lawn a block from Piedmont Park, Atlanta's premier greenspace, stands a handsome three-story brick Tudor manson. The 1987 restoration produced oversize guest rooms with private baths, and common areas furnished with all the comforts of home and more—Chinese porcelains, antiques, and original art. *253 15th St., 30309, tel., 404/872–9000. 11 rooms, 1 suite. Facilities: free use of athletic club. AE, D, DC, MC, V.*

Inexpensive

Barclay Hotel. This is a quiet, older downtown hotel patronized by budget travelers. The hotel's Wild Wild West Nightclub and Soda Club is geared toward teenagers under the drinking age. *Directly behind the Peachtree Center at 89 Luckie St. NW, 30303, tel. 404/524–7991. 73 rooms. Facilities: rooftop swimming pool and sun deck, restaurant. AE, DC, MC, V.*

Buckhead

Very Expensive

Hotel Nikko. A dual-height lobby looking out to an outside Japanese garden and a cascading 35-foot waterfall is the opening statement of this towering hotel. Opened in 1990, the building's design evokes the style of a Southern Colonial mansion. Authentic Japanese and Mediterranean cuisine is served in the restaurant. *3300 Peachtree Rd., 30305, tel. 404/365–8100 or 800/645–5687. 418 rooms, 22 suites. Facilities: restaurants, health club, pool, Library Bar, lounge, ballroom, and 14 meeting rooms. AE, D, DC, MC, V.*

JW Marriott. This elegant 25-story hotel opened in Lenox Square in December 1988. It is sumptuous, but in a subdued style emphasizing intimacy and comfort. Irregularly shaped rooms have spacious baths with separate shower stall and tub. Homey traditional decor and tasteful reproduction antique furniture add to its informal tone. *3300 Lenox Rd., 30326, tel. 404/262–3344 or 800/228–9290. 371 rooms, 30 suites. Facilities: indoor pool, health club, 2 lounges, Swan Room restaurant, ballroom, and meeting rooms. AE, D, DC, MC, V.*

Ritz-Carlton, Buckhead. Not to be confused with the Ritz-Carlton in Atlanta, its classy downtown cousin, this suburban hotel caters more to social events and shopping lovers. *3434 Peachtree Rd., 30326, tel. 404/237–2700 or 800/241–3333. 524 rooms, 29 suites. Facilities: The Café, with live music and dance floor; The Dining Room, The Bar, with evening entertainment, indoor swimming pool and deck, health center. AE, D, DC, MC, V.*

Swissotel. New on the Buckhead scene, this stunning luxury hotel boasts a chic contemporary glass-and-white-enamel exterior, reminiscent of the High Museum, and classically sophisticated Biedermeier-style interiors. It's adjacent to Lenox Square, a prime location for access to shopping and dining. *3391 Peachtree Rd., 30326, tel. 404/365-0065 or 800/253-1397. 362 rooms, 15 suites. Facilities: indoor pool, health club, 2 lounges, 2 restaurants, ballroom, meeting rooms. AE, D, DC, MC, V.*

Moderate **Embassy Suites.** This contemporary high-rise is located in Buckhead directly on a major thoroughfare, Peachtree Road, just blocks from the city's two top shopping centers—Phipps Plaza and Lenox Square. A variety of suites ranging from deluxe presidential (with wet bars) to more basic sleeping- and sitting-room combinations are available, as are a limited number of double-bed rooms. *3285 Peachtree Rd., 30326, tel. 404/261-7733 or 800/362-2779. 313 suites, 15 rooms. Facilities: restaurant, lounge, indoor and outdoor pools, fitness room. AE, D, DC, MC, V.*

The Arts

Culture here now means more than church suppers, stock-car racing, and country music. The Atlanta Symphony Orchestra plays the great halls of Europe and New York, the Atlanta Ballet is rated one of the top companies in the country, and the Alliance Theatre sells more season tickets than any other regional theater in the country.

For the most complete schedule of cultural events, check the "Weekend" tabloid section of Saturday's *Atlanta Journal-Constitution.* Also check *Creative Loafing,* a lively community weekly distributed at restaurants, bars, and stores throughout the metro area.

TicketMaster (tel. 404/249-6400) and **Tic-X-Press, Inc.** (tel. 404/231-5888) handle tickets for the Fox Theatre, Atlanta Civic Center, and other large houses. However, most companies sell tickets through their own box offices.

Theater Consistently one of the region's best, the **Alliance Theatre** performs everything from Shakespeare to the latest Broadway and off-Broadway shows in the Woodruff Arts Center (*see* Exploring, *above*).

Horizon Theatre Co. This experimental company produces new works by contemporary playwrights, as well as mime shows. *1038 Austin Ave. in Little Five Points, tel. 404/584-7450.*

Theatrical Outfit. Original and nationally known contemporary works are produced by this company. *1021 Peachtree at 10th St., tel. 404/872-0665.*

Touring Broadway musicals, pop music, and dance concerts are presented in **The Atlanta Civic Center** (395 Piedmont Ave., tel. 404/523-6275), **Center Stage** (1374 W. Peachtree St., tel. 404/873-2500), and at the **Fox Theatre** (660 Peachtree St., tel. 404/881-2100; see Exploring, *above*).

Concerts Modeled after the Vienna Boys' Choir, the **Atlanta Boys' Choir** (tel. 404/378-0064) performs frequently at Atlanta locations and makes national and international tours.

The long-established **Atlanta Chamber Players** (tel. 404/892-8681) perform classical works at various Atlanta locations.

The city's **Atlanta Symphony Orchestra** (tel. 404/892–2414) performs its fall–spring subscription series in the 1,800-seat Symphony Hall at Woodruff Arts Center. During the summer, the orchestra accompanies big-name artists in Chastain Park and plays free Sunday evening concerts in Piedmont Park.

Opera **The Atlanta Opera Association** (tel. 404/355–3311), made up of local singers and musicians, is augmented by internationally known artists.

Dance **The Atlanta Ballet Company** (tel. 404/873–5811), founded in 1929, has received international recognition for its high-quality productions of classical and contemporary works. Performances are at the Fox Theatre and Atlanta Civic Center.

Ballet Rotaru (tel. 404/266–8500), founded in 1988, is Atlanta's newest classical dance company and features 32 dancers trained in the Kirov tradition. Performances are at the Woodruff Arts Center and the Fox Theatre.

Nightlife

"We entertain at home," Atlantans proudly sniffed some 20 years ago. Today, the pursuit of entertainment—from midtown to Buckhead—is known as the "Peachtree Shuffle." Throughout the city you will find a vibrant nightlife, with everything from piano bars to high-energy dance clubs. Locals seem to take pride in the fact that Atlanta has always had more saloons than churches . . . and, in the South, that's saying something.

Most bars and clubs are open seven nights, until 2–4 AM. Those featuring live entertainment usually have a cover charge. For a listing of entertainment, consult both the "Weekend" section of Saturday's *Atlanta Journal-Constitution* and *Creative Loafing*.

Blues New Orleans–style blues send jam-packed crowds into a frenzy at **Blind Willie's** (828 N. Highland Ave., tel. 404/873–2583), a storefront club in trendy Virginia/Highland. Chicago-style blues and zydeco are on the musical menu at the popular **Blue's Harbor** (Underground Atlanta, tel. 404/524–3001).

Jazz **The Bar** at the Ritz-Carlton Buckhead *(see* Lodging, *above)* has dark wood paneling, a small museum's worth of original art, a real fire crackling in the hearth throughout the winter, and fashionably dressed patrons sipping drinks while a jazz combo plays. Atlanta doesn't get any more uptown than this. Tea is served in the afternoons 3–5.

Cafe 290 (290 Hilderbrand Ave., tel. 404/256–3942) showcases good local jazz bands in a relaxed and casual neighborhood restaurant/bar setting.

Dante's Down the Hatch (3380 Peachtree Rd., tel. 404/266–1600) and **Underground Atlanta** (Lower Pryor St., tel. 404/577–1800) are two of the city's best-known showplaces. In Buckhead, The Paul Mitchell Trio conjures silky-smooth sounds in the "hold" of a make-believe sailing ship. Downtown, jazz entertainers perform nightly. Fondues and a large wine selection add to the experience.

Just Jazz (2101 Tula St., tel. 404/355–5423) is a new, small Buckhead club off Bennett Street that features live performances by headline musicians.

Rock **The Cotton Club** (1021 Peachtree St., tel. 404/874–2523) is a loud, usually packed, midtown club that features both local and national performers in a variety of musical styles.

Limelight (1150 Peachtree St., tel. 404/873–6700) is a lavish nightclub and café complex with formal gardens, cobblestone walkways, and gilded archways. An "atmospheric" ceiling with stars hangs over the large dance floor.

The Point (420 Moreland Ave., tel. 404/577–6468) in Little Five Points showcases up-and-coming rock and progressive music groups in a small club setting.

Rupert's (3330 Piedmont Rd., tel. 404/366–9834) boasts a live 10-piece orchestra that plays big band and contemporary dance music. The interior of the strip-center club has a multitiered balcony overlooking the dance floor.

Bars and Lounges **Atkins Park Bar & Grill** (794 N. Highland Ave., tel. 404/876–7249), one of Atlanta's oldest neighborhood bars, is packed nightly with a mostly young crowd. It's a fun place to meet-and-mingle in a nonmeat-market atmosphere.

The antithesis of hip-and-trendy, 31-year-old **Manuel's Tavern** (602 N. Highland Ave., tel. 404/525–3447)—ancient by Atlanta standards—is a neighborhood saloon in the truest sense. A blend of families, politicians, writers, students, professionals, and blue-collar workers enjoy good drinks, bar food (chili dogs, french fries, strip steaks), and conversations. A lively summertime Shakespeare festival is staged in an adjoining room.

Three Dollar Cafe (3002 Peachtree Rd., tel. 404/266–8667) has an open-air deck equipped with TVs, a volley-ball court, and other warm-weather diversions that makes it the Buckhead spectators spot.

Nonalcoholic **Joyful Noise** (2669 Church St., tel. 404/768–5100), a Christian supper club on Atlanta's south side, has a buffet supper and live entertainment performed by gospel and other religious musical groups.

Savannah

By Honey Naylor

Updated by Mitzi Gammon

Savannah. The very sound of the word conjures up misty images of mint juleps, live oaks dripping with Spanish moss, handsome mansions, and a somewhat decadent city moving at a lazy Southern pace. Why, you can hardly say "Savannah" without drawling.

Well, brace yourself. The mint juleps are there all right, along with the moss and the mansions and the easygoing pace, but this Southern belle rings with surprises.

Take, for example, St. Patrick's Day: Why on earth does Savannah, of all places, have a St. Patrick's Day celebration second only to New York's? The greening of Savannah began more than 164 years ago and nobody seems to know why, although everybody in town talks a blue (green) streak about St. Patrick's Day. Everything turns green on March 17, including the faces of startled visitors when green scrambled eggs and green grits are put before them. One year, some well-oiled revelers even tried to dye the Savannah River green.

Savannah's beginning was February 12, 1733, when English General James Edward Oglethorpe and 120 colonists arrived at Yamacraw Bluff on the Savannah River to found the 13th and last colony in the New World. As the port city grew, Englishmen, Scottish Highlanders, French Huguenots, Germans, Austrian Salzburgers, Sephardic Jews from Spain and Portugal, Moravians, Italians, Swiss, Welsh, and the Irish all arrived to create what could be called a rich gumbo.

In 1793, Eli Whitney of Connecticut, who was tutoring on a plantation near Savannah, invented a mechanized means of "ginning" seeds from cotton bolls. Cotton soon became king, and Savannah, already a busy seaport, flourished under its reign. Waterfront warehouses were filled with "white gold," and factors, or brokers, trading in the Savannah Cotton Exchange set world prices. The white gold brought in solid gold, and fine mansions were built in the prospering city.

It was a Yankee who ushered in Savannah's Golden Age, and it was Yankees who shattered it. In 1864, Savannahians, having seen what Sherman did to the rest of Georgia, surrendered their city to the Union general rather than see it torched. In December of that year, Sherman sent a now-famous telegram to Lincoln. It read, "I beg to present to you as a Christmas gift, the City of Savannah with 150 heavy guns and plenty of ammunition and also about 25,000 bales of cotton."

Following Reconstruction and the collapse of the cotton market, Savannah itself virtually collapsed. The city languished for more than 50 years. Elegant mansions were either razed or allowed to decay, and cobwebs replaced cotton in the dilapidated riverfront warehouses.

But in 1955, Savannah's spirits rose again. News that the exquisite Isaiah Davenport home (324 E. State St.) was to be destroyed prompted seven outraged ladies to raise enough money to buy the house. They saved it the very day before the wrecking ball was to swing.

Thus was born the Historic Savannah Foundation, the organization responsible for the restoration of downtown Savannah. More than 1,000 structures have been restored in the 2.5-square-mile Historic District, the nation's largest urban Historic Landmark district, and many of them are open to the public during the annual tour of homes.

When visiting the city, you'll hear a lot about the "Savannah colors." As old buildings were scraped down in preparation for restoration, Savannah showed its true colors—rich mauves, blues, grays, and golds appearing beneath old layers of paint. Those colors are in full view now, making Savannah one of the nation's most colorful cities.

Arriving and Departing

By Plane Savannah International Airport, (tel. 912/964–0514), 10 miles west of downtown, is served by **American, Continental, Delta, United,** and **USAir.** There is no international passenger service.

Between the Airport and Center City **Vans** operated by **McCalls Coastal Express** (tel. 912/966–5364 or 800/673–9365) leave the airport 6 AM–10 PM daily destined for downtown locations. The trip takes 20–30 minutes, and the one-way fare is $12.

Taxi fare from the airport to downtown hotels is $15 for one person, $3 for each additional person.

By car, drive south on Dean Forest Drive to I–16, then east on I–16 into downtown Savannah.

By Train **Amtrak** (800/USA–RAIL) has regular service along the Eastern Seaboard, with daily stops in Savannah. The Amtrak station (2611 Seaboard Coastline Dr., tel. 912/234–2611) is 4 miles southwest of downtown. Cab fare into the city is $5–$10.

By Bus The **Greyhound/Trailways** station (tel. 912/233–7723) is downtown at 610 W. Oglethorpe Avenue.

By Car I–95 slices north–south along the Eastern Seaboard, intersecting 10 miles west of town with east–west I–16, which dead-ends in downtown Savannah. U.S. 17, the Coastal Highway, also runs north–south through town. U.S. 80, which connects the Atlantic to the Pacific, is another east–west route through Savannah.

Getting Around

Despite its size, the downtown Historic District should be explored on foot. Its grid shape makes getting around a breeze, and you'll find any number of places to stop and rest.

By Bus Buses require 75¢ in exact change, and 5¢ extra for a transfer. **Chatham Area Transit (CAT)** (tel. 912/233–5767) operates buses in Savannah and Chatham County Monday–Saturday from 5:30 AM to midnight, Sunday 7 AM to 7 PM.

By Taxi Taxis start at 60¢ and cost $1.20 for each mile. **Adam Cab Co.** (tel. 912/927–7466) is a reliable, 24-hour taxi service.

Important Addresses and Numbers

Tourist Information For trip planning information, write to the **Savannah Area Convention and Visitors Bureau** (222 W. Oglethorpe Ave., Savannah 31499, tel. 912/944–0456 or 800/444–2427). The **Savannah Visitors Center** (301 Martin Luther King Jr. Blvd., tel. 912/944–0455) has free maps and brochures, lots of friendly advice, and an audiovisual overview of the city. The center is also the starting point for a number of guided tours. *Open Mon.–Fri. 8:30–5, weekends and holidays 9–5.*

Emergencies Dial 911 for **police** and **ambulance** in an emergency.

Hospitals Area hospitals with 24-hour emergency rooms are **Candler General Hospital** (5353 Reynolds St., tel. 912/354–9211) and **Memorial Medical Center** (4700 Waters Ave., tel. 912/356–8000).

Pharmacies **Revco Discount Drug Center** (Medical Arts Shopping Center, 4800 Waters Ave., tel. 912/355–7111) and **Pharmor** (7400 Abercorn St., tel. 912/352–8127).

Guided Tours

Orientation **Gray Line Tours** (tel. 912/234–8687) is the official tour organization for the Historic Savannah Foundation, which is the nonprofit organization that began, and continues, restoration of the city's fine old buildings. Guides are both knowledgeable and enthusiastic, and you'll ride in sleek, 20-passenger, climate-controlled vans. Tours of the Historic District and of the Victorian District each take about two hours. **Colonial Historic Tours** (tel. 912/233–0083) will take you on a two-hour tool around town on minibuses or on an "Old Time Trolley."

Special-interest The **Garden Club of Savannah** (tel. 912/238–0248) takes you into private gardens tucked behind old-brick walls and wrought-iron gates. The **Negro Heritage Trail** (tel. 912/234–8000), tracing the city's 250-year black history, is a van tour with a knowledgeable guide who will tell you about the Gullah culture of the Georgia and Carolina sea islands. Tours commence at the Black Heritage Museum in the King-Tisdell Cottage (514 E. Huntingdon St.).

Savannah River Cruise Line (tel. 912/234–4011) operates *The Magnolia,* an 82-foot paddlewheel boat, up and down the Savannah River. Guides offer a wealth of information and trivia about Savannah's historic ties to the river. There are daily two-hour narrated harbor tours and formal moonlight dinner cruises Thurs.–Sat. that include a four-course dinner for $32 per person. Departures are from 504 E. River St.

Carriage Tours of Savannah (tel. 912/236–6756 or 800/442–5933) show you the Historic District by day or by night at a 19th-century clip-clop pace, with coachmen spinning tales and telling ghost stories along the way. A romantic evening champagne tour in a private carriage will set you back $50–$60, plus $16 per bottle of bubbly. Regular tours are a more modest $10 adults, $5 children 11 and under. Daily departures are from City Market, Savannah Visitor's Center, and Madison Square; evening departures are behind the Hyatt Regency Hotel.

Lowcountry The **Associated Guides of the Low Country** (tel. 912/234–4088 or 800/627–5030), and **Gray Line** (tel. 912/234–8687) make four-hour excursions to the fishing village of Thunderbolt; the Isle of Hope, with stately mansions lining Bluff Drive; the much-photographed Bonaventure Cemetery on the banks of the Wilmington River, with 200-year-old oaks draping Spanish moss over the graves of many notable Savannahians; and Wormsloe Plantation, with its mile-long avenue of arching oaks.

Walking Tours The **Square Roots** (tel. 912/232–6866 or 800/868–6867) offers strolls through the Historic District and along Tybee Beach. The in-town tour focuses on the city's architecture and gardens. Tours usually last two hours and range in price from $9.50 to $17.

Exploring Savannah

Numbers in the margin correspond to points of interest on the Savannah Historic District map.

General Oglethorpe himself designed the original town of Savannah and laid it out in a perfect grid. The Historic District is neatly hemmed in by the Savannah River, Gaston Street, and East and West Broad streets. Streets are arrow-straight, public squares of varying sizes are tucked into the grid at precise intervals, and each block is sliced in half by an alley. Bull Street, anchored on the north by City Hall and the south by Forsyth Park, charges down the center of the grid and lunges around the five public squares that stand in its way. (Maneuvering a car around Savannah's squares is a minor art form.)

The Historic District

There are two excellent reasons for making your first stop the **Savannah Visitors Center** *(see* Tourist Information in Important Addresses and Numbers, *above*), the most obvious being the maps and brochures you'll need for exploring. The other reason is the structure that houses the Center. The big redbrick building with its high ceilings and sweeping arches was the old Central of Georgia railway station, completed in 1860.

1 (marker beside the preceding paragraph)

The Visitors Center lies just north of the **site of the Siege of Savannah.** During the American Revolution, the Redcoats seized Savannah in 1778, and the Colonial forces made several attempts to retake it. In 1779, the Colonials, led by Polish Count Casimir Pulaski, laid siege to the city. They were beaten back, and Pulaski was killed while leading a cavalry charge against the British.

On the battle site, adjacent to the Visitors Center in a restored
2 shed of the railway station, the **Great Savannah Exposition** offers an excellent introduction to the city. Two theaters present special-effects depictions of Oglethorpe's landing and of the siege. There are various exhibits, ranging from old locomotives to a tribute to Savannah's own world-famous songwriter Johnny Mercer, as well as two restored dining cars that aren't going anywhere, but you can climb aboard for a bite to eat. *303 W. Broad St., tel. 912/238–1779. Admission: $2.75 adults; $2.50 senior citizens; $1 children 6–12, under 6 free. Open weekdays 8:30–5, weekends 9–5.*

Turn left on Broad Street and walk two blocks to the
3 **Scarbrough House.** The exuberant Regency mansion was built during the 1819 cotton boom for Savannah merchant prince William Scarbrough and designed by English architect William Jay. A Doric portico is capped by one of Jay's characteristic half-moon windows. Four massive Greek Doric columns form a peristyle in the atrium entrance hall. Three stories overhead is an arched, sky-blue ceiling with sunshine filtering through a skylight. *41 Martin Luther King Dr., tel. 912/233–7787. Admission: free. Open Mon.–Sat. 10–4.*

Continue east across Franklin Square and stroll through City Market, with its sidewalk cafés, jazz joints, and shops. Now
4 head east on St. Julian Street to **Johnson Square.** Laid out in 1733 and named for South Carolina Governor Robert Johnson, this was the earliest of Oglethorpe's original 24 squares. The square was once a popular gathering place, where Savannahians came to welcome President Monroe in 1819, to greet the Marquis de Lafayette in 1825, and to cheer for Georgia's secession in 1861. It was here that Lafayette laid the cornerstone for the monument that marks the grave of his friend and Revolutionary War hero, Major-General Nathaniel Greene. (It was on Greene's plantation after the war that Eli Whitney invented the cotton gin.)

Time Out

Food carts are parked in Johnson Square; you can pick up an ice cream cone, a hot dog, or a cold drink and relax on one of the park benches.

Andrew Low House, **18**
Cathedral of St. John the Baptist, **16**
Chippewa Square, **14**
Colonial Park Cemetery, **15**
Emmet Park, **8**
Factors Walk, **5**
Forsyth Park, **24**
Great Savannah Exposition, **2**
Green-Meldrim House, **20**
Isaiah Davenport House, **9**
Johnson Square, **4**
Juliette Gordon Low House, **13**
Lafayette Square, **17**
Madison Square, **19**
Massie Heritage Interpretation Center, **23**
Owens-Thomas House, **10**
River Street, **6**
Savannah Visitor's Center, **1**
Scarbrough House, **3**
Ships of the Sea Museum, **7**
Telfair Mansion and Art Museum, **12**
Temple Mickve Israel, **21**
Wesley Monumental Church, **22**
Wright Square, **11**

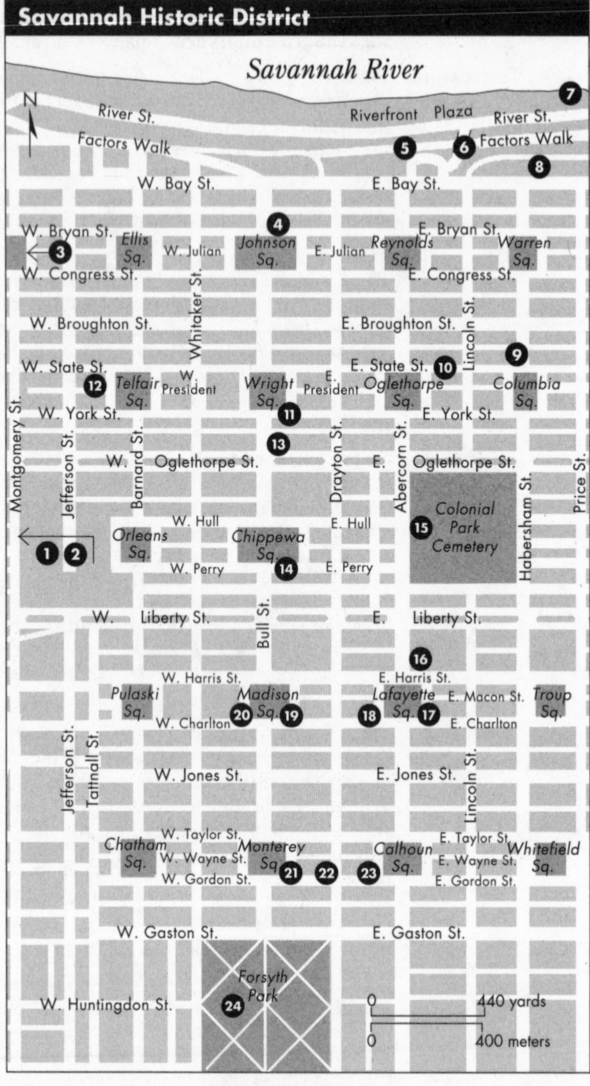

That building to the north with the glittering gilt dome at the foot of Bull Street is **City Hall,** dating from 1905. (The dome was regilded in 1987.) The lower stories of City Hall face the spot from which the SS *Savannah* set sail in 1819, the first steamship to cross any ocean. Just to the west of City Hall, on Yamacraw Bluff, is a marble bench, appropriately called **Oglethorpe's Bench,** that marks the site of the general's field tent.

5 6 Cobblestone ramps lead from Bay Street down to **Factors Walk** and, below it, to **River Street.** Cars can enter Factors Walk via the ramps, and so can pedestrians. (These are serious cobblestones, and you will suffer if you wear anything but the most comfortable shoes you own.) There is also a network of iron

walkways connecting Bay Street with the multistoried buildings that rise up from the river level, and iron stairways plunge (word used advisedly) from Bay Street down to Factors Walk.

Foreign vessels still call at the Port of Savannah, the largest port between Baltimore and New Orleans. Paper and other products have replaced the cotton exports, and in 1977 a multimillion-dollar riverfront revitalization transformed the decayed warehouses into a nine-block marketplace with everything from sleek boutiques to musty taverns.

Learning about the port and the river is a breeze aboard *The Magnolia*, so you may want to break up your walking tour at this point to board the paddlewheeler (*see* Guided Tours, *above*).

There are benches all along **Riverfront Plaza** where you can watch the parade of freighters and pug-nosed tugs, and the tugboat-shape sandboxes where youngsters can play. Each weekday, Dixieland music can be heard from the cabin of the ***River Street Rambler,*** a brightly painted freight train that rumbles down River Street to the port. River Street is the main venue for many of the city's celebrations, including the First Saturday festivals when flea marketeers, artists, and crafts-men display their wares and musicians entertain the crowds.

Even landlubbers can appreciate the fine craftsmanship of the
7 ship models in the **Ships of the Sea Museum.** The four floors of the museum contain models of steamships, nuclear subs, China clippers with their sails unfurled, Columbus's ships, a showcase filled with ships-in-bottles, and a collection of fine Royal Doulton porcelain seafarers. *503 E. River St. and 504 E. Bay St., tel. 912/232–1511. Admission: $3 adults, $1.50 children 7–12, under 7 free. Open daily 10–5. Closed St. Patrick's Day and major holidays.*

If you entered the museum at the River Street entrance and worked your way up all four floors, you'll be topside again on
8 Bay Street. The tree-shaded park along Bay Street is **Emmet Park,** named for Robert Emmet, a late 18th-century Irish patriot and orator. Walk west along Bay Street and turn left onto Abercorn Street. In **Reynolds Square** you'll see the statue of John Wesley, who preached in Savannah and wrote the first English hymnal here in 1736. The monument to the founder of the Methodist Church is shaded by greenery and surrounded by park benches. On the square is the **Olde Pink House** (23 Abercorn St.). Built in 1771, it is one of the oldest buildings in town. The porticoed pink stucco Georgian mansion has been a private home, a bank, and headquarters for a Yankee general during the war. It is now a restaurant (*see* Dining, *below*).

From Reynolds Square walk south on Abercorn Street, turn left onto Broughton Street, and two blocks down turn right
9 onto Habersham Street. This will bring you to the **Isaiah Davenport House.** Semicircular stairs with wrought-iron trim lead to the recessed doorway of the redbrick Georgian mansion that master builder Isaiah Davenport built for himself in 1815. Three dormer windows poke through the sloping roof of the stately house, and inside there are polished hardwood floors, fine woodwork and plasterwork, and a soaring elliptical staircase. The furnishings are Hepplewhite, Chippendale, and Sheraton, and in the attic there is a collection of antique dolls and a dollhouse with tiny 19th-century furnishings. *324 E.*

State St., tel. 912/236–8097. Admission: $4 adults, $3 children 6–18, under 6 free. Open Tues.–Sat. 10–4, Sun.–Mon. 2–4:30.

10 Walk west on State Street two blocks to the **Owens-Thomas House.** This was William Jay's first Regency mansion in Savannah, built in 1817, and it is the city's finest example of that architectural style. The thoroughly English house was built largely with local materials, including tabby—a mixture of oyster shells, sand, and water that resembles concrete. The entry portico is of Doric design with curving stairs leading to a recessed door topped by a fanlight. Of particular note are the curving walls of the house, Greek-inspired ornamental molding, Jay's half-moon arches, stained-glass panels, and Duncan Phyfe furniture. You'll see hoopskirt chairs (whose short arms accommodated the circular skirts of many Southern belles), canopied beds, a pianoforte, and displays of ornate silver. From a wrought-iron balcony, in 1825, the Marquis de Lafayette bade a two-hour au revoir to the crowd below. *124 Abercorn St., tel. 912/233–9743. Admission: $5 adults; $3 students; $2 children 6–12, under 6 free. Open Sun.–Mon. 2–4:30; Tues.–Sat. 10–4:30.*

Stroll through **Oglethorpe Square,** across State Street, and con-
11 tinue two blocks west to **Wright Square.** The square was named for James Wright, Georgia's last Colonial governor. Centerpiece of the square is an elaborate monument erected in honor of William Washington Gordon, founder of the Central of Georgia Railroad. A slab of granite from Stone Mountain marks the grave of Tomo-Chi-Chi, the Yamacraw chief who befriended General Oglethorpe and the colonists.

Continue west on State Street, strolling, if you like, through
12 **Telfair Square** to reach the **Telfair Mansion and Art Museum.** The South's oldest public art museum is housed in yet another of Jay's Regency creations, this one designed in 1819. Within its marbled halls there are American, French, and German Impressionist paintings; a large collection of works by Kahlil Gibran; plaster casts of the Elgin Marbles, the Venus de Milo, and the Laocoön, among other classical sculptures; and a room that contains some of the Telfair family furnishings, including a Duncan Phyfe sideboard and Savannah-made silver. The mansion is also notable for Jay's distinctive moldings, cornices, and mantelpieces. *121 Barnard St., tel. 912/232–1177. Admission: $2.50 adults, $1 students, 50¢ children 6–12; free on Sun. Open Tues.–Sat. 10–5, Sun. 2–5.*

At the next corner, turn left onto Oglethorpe Avenue and cross
13 Bull Street to reach the **Juliette Gordon Low House.** This majestic Regency mansion is attributed to William Jay (and why not?) and in 1965 was designated Savannah's first National Historic Landmark. "Daisy" Low, founder of the Girl Scouts, was born here, and the house is now owned and operated by the Girl Scouts of America. Mrs. Low was also an artist, and her paintings and other artworks are on display in the house, along with original family furnishings of the 19th century. *142 Bull St., tel. 912/233–4501. Admission: $4 adults, $3.75 senior citizens, $3 children under 18; discounts for Girl Scouts. Open Mon.–Sat. 10–4, Sun. 12:30–4:30. Closed every Wed., and Sun. in Dec. and Jan.*

14 **Chippewa Square** is a straight shot south on Bull Street. There you can see the imposing bronze statue of the general himself, James Edward Oglethorpe.

From Chippewa Square, go east on McDonough Street to reach
15 the **Colonial Park Cemetery.** Savannahians were buried here from 1750 to 1853. Shaded pathways lace through the park, and you may want to stroll through and read some of the old inscriptions. There are several historical plaques in the cemetery, one of which marks the grave of Button Gwinnett, a signer of the Declaration of Independence.

16 The **Cathedral of St. John the Baptist** soars like a hymn over the corner of Abercorn and Harris streets, two blocks south of the cemetery. The French Gothic cathedral, with the pointed arches and free-flowing traceries characteristic of the style, is the seat of the Diocese of Savannah. It is the oldest Roman Catholic church in Georgia, having been founded in the early 1700s. Fire destroyed the early structures, and the present cathedral dates from the late 19th century. Most of the cathedral's impressive stained-glass windows were made by Austrian glassmakers and imported around the turn of the century. The high altar is of Italian marble, and the Stations of the Cross were imported from Munich.

17 Across from the cathedral is **Lafayette Square,** named for the Marquis de Lafayette. The graceful three-tier fountain in the square was donated by the Georgia chapter of the Colonial Dames of America.

18 Across the square is the **Andrew Low House.** The house was built for Andrew Low in 1849, and later belonged to his son William, who married Juliette Gordon. After her husband's death, "Daisy" Low founded the Girl Scouts in this house on March 12, 1912. Robert E. Lee and William Thackeray were both entertained in this mansion. In addition to its historical significance, the house boasts some of the finest ornamental ironwork in Savannah. Members and friends of the Colonial Dames have donated fine 19th-century antiques and stunning silver to the house. *329 Abercorn St. Admission: $2 adults, $1 students, 75¢ children and Girl Scouts. Open daily 10:30–4:30. Closed Christmas, Thanksgiving, and New Year's Day.*

19 Two blocks to the west is **Madison Square,** laid out in 1839 and named for James Madison. The statue depicts Sergeant William Jasper hoisting a flag and is a tribute to his bravery during the Siege of Savannah. Though mortally wounded, he rescued the colors of his regiment in the assault on the British lines.

20 On the west side of the square is the **Green-Meldrim House,** designed by New York architect John Norris and built about 1850 for cotton merchant Charles Green. The house was bought in 1892 by Judge Peter Meldrim, hence the hyphenated name. Meldrim's heirs sold the house to St. John's Episcopal Church, for which it is now the parish house. It was here that General Sherman established residence after taking the city in 1864. Here the general lived in a splendid Gothic Revival mansion, complete with crenellated roof and oriel windows. The gallery that sweeps around three sides of the house is awash with filigreed ironwork. The mantels are Carrara marble, the woodwork is carved black walnut, and the doorknobs and hinges are silver-plated. There is a magnificent skylight above a gracefully curved staircase. The house is furnished with 16th- and 17th-

century antiques. *1 West Macon St. on Madison Sq., tel. 912/232–1251. Admission: $3. Open Oct.–Feb. Tues., Thurs., Fri., and Sat. 10–4; Mar.–Sept., Mon. and Wed. 1–4. Closed during special church functions.*

Time Out Students from the Savannah College of Art and Design buy art supplies and books at **Design Works Bookstore.** There is also a soda fountain and tables in this old Victorian drugstore, where you can get short orders, burgers, and deli sandwiches. *Corner of Bull and Charlton Sts., tel. 912/238–2481. Open Mon.–Thurs. 8–7:30, Fri. 9–4, Sat. 10–2.*

The fifth and last of Bull Street's squares is **Monterey Square,** which commemorates the victory of General Zachary Taylor's forces in Monterrey, Mexico, in 1846. The square's monument honors General Casimir Pulaski, the Polish nobleman and Revolutionary War hero who lost his life during the Siege of Savannah.

21 On the east side of the square stands **Temple Mickve Israel,** which was consecrated in 1878. Five months after the founding of Savannah, a group of Spanish and German Jews arrived, bringing with them the prized "Sephar Torah" that is in the present temple. The splendid Gothic Revival synagogue contains a collection of documents and letters pertaining to early Jewish life in Savannah and Georgia. *20 E. Gordon St. Admission free. Open weekdays 10–noon.*

A block east of the temple is a Gothic Revival church memori-
22 alizing the founders of Methodism. The **Wesley Monumental Church,** patterned after Queen's Kirk in Amsterdam, celebrated a century of service in 1968. The church is noted for its magnificent stained-glass windows. In the Wesley Window there are busts of John and Charles Wesley.

23 At the **Massie Heritage Interpretation Center,** in addition to a scale model of the city, maps and plans, and architectural displays, is a "Heritage Classroom" that offers schoolchildren hands-on instruction about early Colonial life. *207 E. Gordon St., tel. 912/651–7380. Admission free, but a donation of $1.50 is appreciated. Open weekdays 9–4:30.*

24 The southern anchor of Bull Street is **Forsyth Park,** with 20 luxuriant acres. The glorious white fountain, dating from 1858, was restored in 1988. In addition to its Confederate and Spanish-American War memorials, the park contains the Fragrant Garden for the Blind, a project of Savannah garden clubs. There are tennis courts and a tree-shaded jogging path. The park is often the scene of outdoor plays and concerts.

The Victorian District The **King-Tisdell Cottage,** perched behind a picket fence, is a museum dedicated to the preservation of black history and culture. The Negro Heritage Trail (*see* Special-interest Tours in Guided Tours, *above*) begins here, in this little Victorian house. Broad steps lead to a porch that's loaded with gewgaws, and dormer windows pop up through a steep roof. The interior is furnished to resemble a late 19th-century black coastal home. *514 E. Huntingdon St., tel. 912/234–8000. Admission: $1.50 adults, $1 children. Open weekdays 10:30–4:30, weekends 1–4.*

Other houses of interest in the Victorian district are at **118 E. Waldburg Street** and **111 W. Gwinnett Street.** A stroll along **Bolton Street** will be especially rewarding for fans of fanciful architecture. Of particular note is the entire 200 block, 114 W. Bolton Street, 109 W. Bolton Street, and 321 E. Bolton Street.

Day-tripping to Tybee Island

Tybee Island, which lies 18 miles east of Savannah right on the Atlantic Ocean, offers all manner of water and beach activities. The drive to Tybee takes about a half hour, and there are two historic forts to visit on the way.

To reach Tybee Island, drive east on Victory Drive (U.S. 80) all the way to the Atlantic. (The highway sometimes goes under the alias of Tybee Road.)

Fort Pulaski is 15 miles east of downtown Savannah. You'll see the entrance on your left just before Tybee Road reaches Tybee Island. A must for Civil War buffs, the fort was built on Cockspur Island between 1829 and 1847, and named for General Casimir Pulaski. Robert E. Lee's first assignment after graduating from West Point was as an engineer here. During the Civil War the fort fell on April 12, 1862, after a mere 30 hours of bombardment by newfangled rifled cannons. It was the first time such cannons had been used in warfare—and the last time a masonry fort was thought to be impregnable. The restored fortification, operated by the National Park Service, is complete with moats, drawbridges, massive ramparts, and towering walls. There is an interpretive center that offers historical demonstrations, self-guided trails, and ample picnic areas. *U.S. 80, tel. 912/786–5787. Admission: $1 adults, children 16 and under free. Open daily 8:30–5:15 in winter; 8:30–6:45 in summer. Closed Christmas.*

Three miles farther along U.S. 80 is **Tybee Island.** "Tybee" is an Indian word meaning salt. The Yamacraw Indians came to the island to hunt and fish, and legend has it that pirates buried their treasure here.

The island is about five miles long and two miles wide, with a plethora of seafood restaurants, chain motels, condos, and shops. The entire expanse of white sand is divided into a number of public beaches, where visitors go shelling and crabbing, play on waterslides, charter fishing boats, swim, or just build sand castles.

The **Tybee Museum and Lighthouse** are at the very tip of the island. In the museum you'll see Indian artifacts, pirate pistols, powder flasks, old prints tracing the history of Savannah, even some sheet music of Johnny Mercer songs. The Civil War Room has old maps and newspaper articles pertaining to Sherman's occupation of the city. On the second floor there are model antique cars and ship models, and a collection of antique dolls. The lighthouse across the road is Georgia's oldest and tallest, dating from 1773, with an observation deck 145 feet above the sea. Bright red steps—178 of them—lead to the deck and the awesome Tybee Light. The view of the ocean will take away whatever breath you have left after the climb. *Meddin Dr. and the jumping off place, tel. 912/786–4077. Admission to both lighthouse and museum: $1.50 adults, $1 senior citizens, 50¢ children 6–12. Both open daily in summer 10–6; weekdays noon–4, in winter weekends 10–4. Closed Tues.*

Time Out **Spanky's Pizza Galley & Saloon,** overlooking the beach, has seafood platters, burgers, chicken dishes, and salads. *404 Butler Dr., tel. 912/236–3009. AE, MC, V. Open daily 11 AM–midnight.*

Heading west back to Savannah, take the Islands Expressway, which becomes the President Street Extension. About 3½ miles outside the city you'll see a sign for **Fort Jackson,** located on Salter's Island. The Colonial fort was purchased in 1808 by the federal government, and is the oldest standing fort in Georgia. It was garrisoned in 1812, and was the Confederate headquarters of the river batteries. The brick fort is surrounded by a tidal moat, and there are 13 exhibit areas. Battle reenactments, blacksmithing demonstrations, and programs of 19th-century music are among the fort's schedule of activities. The Trooping of the Colors and military tattoo take place at regular intervals during summer. *1 Ft. Jackson Rd., tel. 912/232–3945. Admission: $2 adults, $1.50 students, senior citizens, and military personnel. Open daily 9–5.*

Savannah for Free

Beach at Tybee Island (*see* Exploring, *above*).

There are many **celebrations** in Savannah, and most of them take place on River Street. Arts-and-crafts displays, music, and entertainment are always part of such special events as the February Georgia Day Festival, Oktoberfest, the Great American 4th of July, the Seafood-Fest, and First Saturday festivals every month. About 40,000 greenish folk flock to Riverfront Plaza after the St. Patrick's Day parade. Contact the Savannah Visitors Center (*see* Important Addresses and Numbers, *above*) or the **Artsline** (tel. 912/233–2787).

Free Concerts are given during summer months in Johnson Square.

Oatland Island Education Center. Located only 15 minutes from downtown Savannah, this 175-acre maritime forest is not only a natural habitat for coastal wildlife (including timber wolves and panthers), it also offers environmental education for visitors. The center also houses the coastal offices of the Georgia Conservancy. *711 Sandtown Rd., tel 912/897–3773. Open weekdays 8:30–5; Second Saturday events Oct.–May 11–5.*

Skidaway Island Marine Science Complex. On the grounds of the former Modena Plantation, the complex features a 12-panel, 12,000-gallon aquarium with marine and plant life of the Continental Shelf. Other exhibits highlight archaeological discoveries and undersea life of the Georgia coast. *McWhorter Dr., Skidaway Island, tel. 912/598–2325. Open weekdays 9–4, weekends noon–5.*

Telfair Mansion and Art Museum charges no admission on Sundays (*see* Exploring, *above*).

Watch the parade of ships on the Savannah River.

What to See and Do with Children

Explore Savannah, Inc. (418 E. State St., tel. 912/354–4560 or 912/233–5238) designs individualized activity packages and tours for children ages 4–16. Professional guides conduct full- or half-day tours, and ticket prices, which start at $10, include transportation, meals, and snacks.

Fort Pulaski and Jackson (*see* Exploring, *above*).
Juliette Gordon Low Girl Scout National Center (*see* Exploring, *above*).
Oatland Island Education Center (*see* Savannah for Free, *above*).
Exhibits at the **Savannah Science Museum** include live and mounted reptiles and amphibians, a "walk-in" human heart and mouth, a solar energy unit, Indian artifacts, plans, and planetarium shows. *4405 Paulsen St., tel. 912/355–6705. Admission: $2.50 adults; $1.50 senior citizens, students, and children 12 and under. Open Tues.–Sat. 10–5, Sun. 2–5; planetarium shows Sun. at 3 PM.*
Tybee Island Museum and Lighthouse (*see* Exploring, *above*).

Off the Beaten Track

If your tastebuds are fixin' for real down-home barbecue, head for **Wall's.** There's a counter where you place your order and a couple of orange plastic booths. Entertainment is provided by a small black-and-white TV set. You reach in the refrigerator case to get your canned beverage, and your food comes served in Styrofoam cartons. A sign taped up over the counter reads, "When I work, I works hard. When I sit, I sits loose—when I think, I falls asleep." Plain? Not really. There is richness in them thar barbecued spare ribs, barbecued sandwiches, and deviled crabs (the three items make up the entire menu). A large carton of ribs costs $7.50. *515 E. York La., between Oglethorpe Ave. and York St., tel. 912/232–9754. Dress: bibs. No credit cards. Open Thurs. 11–10, Fri. and Sat. 11–11.*

Shopping

Regional wares to look for are handcrafted items from the Low Country—handmade quilts and baskets; wreaths made from Chinese tallow trees and Spanish moss; preserves, jams, and jellies. The favorite Savannah snack, and a popular gift item, is the benne wafer. It's about the size of a quarter and comes in a variety of flavors.

Shopping Districts

Riverfront Plaza/River Street is nine blocks of shops housed in the renovated waterfront warehouses, where you can find everything from popcorn to pottery. **City Market,** located on West St. Julian Street between Ellis and Franklin squares, has sidewalk cafés, jazz haunts, shops, and art galleries. If you're in need of anything from aspirin to anklets, head for **Broughton Street** and wander through its many variety and specialty stores.

Oglethorpe Mall (7804 Abercorn St. Ext.) is an enclosed center with four department stores (Sears, JCPenney's, Belk, and Maas Bros./Jordan Marsh) and over 140 specialty shops, fast-food and full-service restaurants. The newly opened **Savannah Mall** (14045 Abercorn St.) just off I–95 also has four major anchor stores (JB White's, Belks, Parisians, and Montgomery Ward), along with 100 specialty shops, fast-food and full-service restaurants.

Specialty Shops

Antiques

Arthur Smith (1 W. Jones St., tel. 912/236–9701) houses four floors of 18th- and 19th-century furniture. At **Claire West** (413 Whitaker St., tel. 912/236–8163) you will find two floors filled with fine linens, antique prints, and old and new decorative tabletop objects, as well as a strong collection of European and American antiques.

Artwork **Exhibit A** (342 Bull St., tel. 912/238–2480), the gallery of the Savannah College of Art and Design, has hand-painted cards, handmade jewelry, and paintings by regional artists. **Gallery 209** (209 E. River St., tel. 912/236–4583) is a co-op gallery with paintings, watercolors, and sculptures by local artists. Original artwork, limited- and unlimited-edition prints, and books by prolific painter Ray Ellis are sold in the **Compass Prints Ray Ellis Gallery** (205 W. Congress St., tel. 912/234–3537). Famous for his collaborations with Walter Cronkite, this shop is the part-time Savannah resident's only retail operation.

Benne Wafers You can buy boxed bennes in most gift shops, but **The Cooky Shanty** (2233 Norwood Ave., tel. 912/355–1716) is where they originated. You can buy them and watch them being made here.

Books The nine rooms of **E. Shaver's** (326 Bull St., tel. 912/234–7257) bookstore are stocked with books on architecture and regional history, as well as used and rare books. **The Book Lady** (17 W. York St., tel. 912/233–3628) specializes in used, rare, and out-of-print books; it also provides a search service.

Country Crafts **Callaway Gardens Country Store** (301 E. River St., tel. 912/236–4055) carries lots of gift-packaged preserves and jellies, sauces, bacon and hams, cookbooks, and gifts. At **Charlotte's Corner** (1 W. Liberty St., tel. 912/233–8061) there are handmade quilts and baskets made from quilts, regional cookbooks, aprons, and Savannah-made potpourris. **Georgia Crafts** (217 W. St. Julian St., tel. 912/236–1220) is another crafty shop for handmade baskets, antique dolls, jams, jellies, preserves, and wreaths.

Participant Sports

Bicycling Pedaling is a breeze on these flatlands. Rental bikes are available at the **DeSoto Hilton Hotel** (Bull and Liberty Sts.) and the **Hyatt Regency Hotel** (2 W. Bay St.).

Boating **Coastal Excursions** conducts water-taxi service to secluded area beaches and nearby barrier islands such as Tybee, Little Tybee, and Wilmington islands (534 Jackson Blvd., Savannah 31405, tel. 912/356–1174). **Saltwater Charters** (111 Wichersham Dr., tel. 912/598–1814) operates everything from 2-hour sightseeing tours to 13-hour deep-sea fishing expeditions. Pedal boats can be rented for pedaling around **Lake Mayer** (Lake Mayer Park, Sallie Mood Dr. and Montgomery Crossroads Dr., tel. 912/352–0032). There are public boat ramps at **Bell's Landing** on the Forest River (Apache Rd. off Abercorn St.); **Islands Expressway** on the Wilmington River (Islands Expressway adjacent to Frank W. Spencer Park); and **Savannah Marina** on the Wilmington River in the town of Thunderbolt.

Golf There's a 27-hole course at **Bacon Park** (Shorty Cooper Dr., tel. 912/354–2625), and a 9-hole course at **Mary Calder Park** (W. Lathrop Ave., tel. 912/238–7100).

Health Clubs The following private clubs are open to guests for a fee:

Savannah Downtown Athletic Club (7 E. Congress St., tel. 912/236–4874). Nautilus and free-weight equipment, whirlpool, sauna, aerobics, and karate classes.

Racquet Plus (4 Oglethorpe Professional Bldg., tel. 912/355–3070). Racquetball courts, Nautilus equipment, whirlpool, and sauna.

YMCA Family Center (6400 Habersham St., tel. 912/354–6223). Gymnasium, exercise classes, pool, and tennis—for men and women.

Jewish Educational Alliance (5111 Abercorn St., tel. 912/355–8111). Racquetball courts, gymnasium, weight room, sauna, steam, whirlpool, and aerobic dance classes.

Jogging Flat-as-a-pancake **Forsyth Park** is a favorite jogging path, with plenty of shade trees and benches. The beach at **Tybee Island** is another great favorite of joggers. Suburbanites favor the jogging trails in **Lake Mayer Park** (Montgomery Crossroads Rd. at Sallie Mood Dr.) and **Daffin Park** (1500 E. Victory Dr.).

Tennis There are 14 lighted courts in **Bacon Park** (Skidaway Rd., tel. 912/351–3850); four lighted courts in **Forsyth Park** (Drayton and Gaston Sts., tel. 912/351–3852); and eight lighted courts in **Lake Mayer Park** (Montgomery Crossroads Rd. and Sallie Mood Dr., tel. 912/925–8706).

Dining

Situated on a river, 18 miles inland from the Atlantic Ocean, Savannah naturally has excellent seafood restaurants. Barbecue is also a local favorite, and there are a number of Continental restaurants as well. The Historic District is loaded with eateries, especially along River Street. Savannahians also like to drive out to eat in Thunderbolt and on Skidaway, Tybee, and Wilmington islands.

The most highly recommended restaurants in each price category are indicated by a star ★.

Category	Cost*
Very Expensive	over $30
Expensive	$25–$30
Moderate	$15–$25
Inexpensive	under $15

**per person without tax, service, or drinks*

American
Very Expensive

Olde Pink House. The brick Georgian mansion, built for James Habersham in 1771, is one of Savannah's oldest structures. The cozily elegant tavern has original Georgia pine floors and crystal chandeliers, and antique furniture that was shipped from England. Lunch and cocktails are served below in the romantic Planters Tavern, where black leather chairs are pulled up around an open fire in the wintertime. Veal Thomas Jefferson is a sautéed cutlet topped with fresh crabmeat and béarnaise sauce, and garnished with asparagus and shrimp. "Mr. and Mrs. Habersham's Dinner," purportedly the favorite of the original occupants, begins with a shrimp appetizer and moves on to black-turtle bean soup, salad, "an intermission of sorbet," chateaubriand carved tableside, and a dessert. *23 Abercorn St., tel. 912/232–4286. Jacket required for dinner. Reservations suggested for dinner. AE, DC, MC, V.*

Dining
Crystal Beer Parlor, **17**
Elizabeth on 37th, **23**
45 South, **9**
Johnny Harris, **7**
LaToque, **12**
Mrs. Wilkes Boarding House, **18**
Olde Pink House, **11**
Pirates' House, **10**
River House, **2**
Seashell House, **24**
Shrimp Factory, **4**

Lodging
Ballastone Inn, **13**
Days Inn, **1**
DeSoto Hilton, **15**
Eliza Thompson House, **19**
Foley House, **14**
Forsyth Park Inn, **20**
The Gastonian, **21**
Hyatt, **3**
Jesse Mount House, **16**
Mulberry, **8**
Olde Harbour Inn, **5**
Radisson Plaza, **22**
River Street Inn, **6**

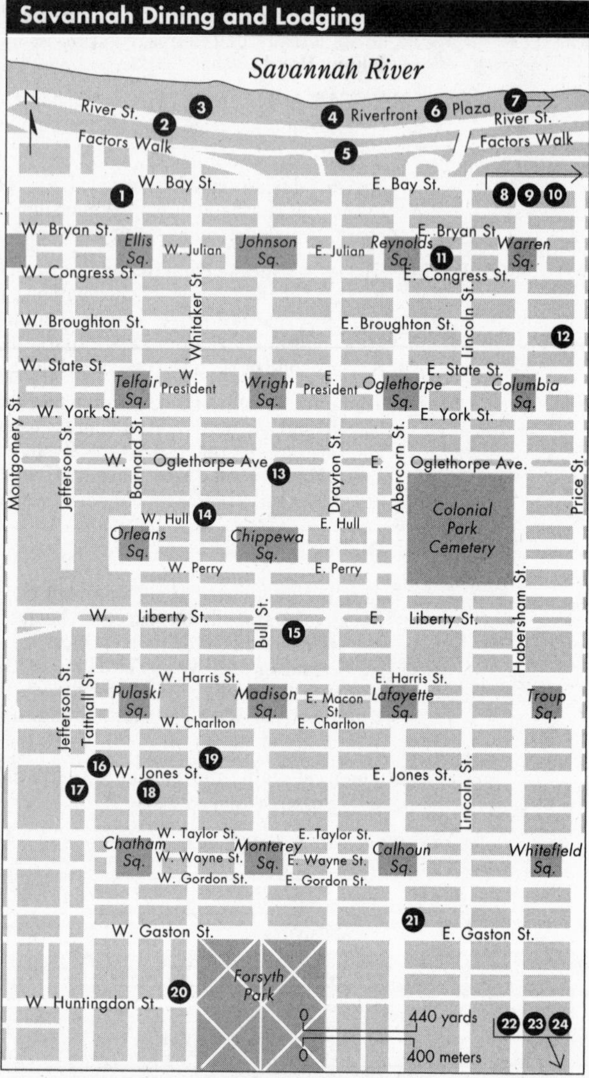

Expensive ★ **45 South.** This was a popular southside eatery that moved in 1988 to the sprawling Pirates' House complex. 45 South is a small, stylish restaurant with contemporary decor in lush mauve and green Savannah colors. There is a changing menu that might include contemporary American dinner entrées such as peppered breast of duck with acorn squash and fresh spinach, and trout with a ragout of zucchini and basil. *20 E. Broad St., tel. 912/233–1881. Jacket and tie required. Reservations accepted. AE, MC, V.*

Inexpensive ★ **Crystal Beer Parlor.** A comfortable family tavern famed for hamburgers, thick-cut french fries, onion rings, and frosted mugs of draft beer. The menu also offers fried oyster sandwiches, gumbo, and shrimp salad. *301 W. Jones St. at Jefferson*

St., tel. 912/232–1153. Dress: informal. No reservations. No credit cards.

Johnny Harris. What started as a small roadside stand in 1924 has grown into one of the city's mainstays, with a menu that includes steaks, fried chicken, seafood, and a variety of barbecued meats spiced with the restaurant's famous sauce. *1651 E. Victory, tel. 912/354–7810. Dress: casual. No reservations. AE, DC, MC, V. Closed Sun.*

★ **Mrs. Wilkes Boarding House.** There's no sign out front, but you won't have any trouble finding this famed establishment. At breakfast time and noon (no dinner is served) there are long lines of folks waiting to get in for a culinary orgy. Charles Kuralt and David Brinkley are among the celebrities who have feasted on the fine Southern food, served at big family-style tables. For breakfast there are eggs, sausage, piping hot biscuits, and grits. At lunch, bowl after bowl is passed around the table. Fried or roast chicken, collard greens, okra, mashed potatoes, cornbread, biscuits—the dishes just keep coming. *107 W. Jones St., tel. 912/232–5997. Dress: informal. No reservations. No credit cards.*

Continental
Moderate–Expensive

★ **LaToque.** Swiss-born owner/chef Christian Bigler prepares fish, shellfish, lamb, veal, and beef in traditional European style, with light sauces or grilled. The dining room has an understated elegance, with starched white tablecloths and dark red decor. *420 E. Broughton St., tel. 912/238–0138. Jacket and tie required. Reservations accepted. AE, MC, V. Closed Sun.*

Seafood
Expensive

★ **Elizabeth on 37th.** Elizabeth and Michael Terry's restaurant is in an elegant turn-of-the-century mansion, with hardwood floors and spacious rooms. Elizabeth is the chef, called by *Town & Country* magazine, "One of America's great new women chefs." Among her specialties is flounder Elizabeth, a filet broiled in a crab, cream, and sherry sauce. While the emphasis is on sea creatures served in delicate sauces, there are other excellent offerings, including steak au poivre, quail, lamb, and chicken dishes. *105 E. 37th St., tel. 912/236–5547. Dress: informal, no shorts. Reservations required. AE, MC, V. Closed Sun.*

Pirates' House. You'll probably start hearing about the Pirates' House about 10 minutes after you hit town. There are all sorts of legends about it involving shanghaied sailors and ghosts. It's a sprawling complex with nautical and piratical trappings, and 23 rooms with names like The Jolly Roger and The Black Hole; children love the place. The menu is almost as big as the building, with heavy emphasis on sea critters. For starters there are oysters, escargots, and soft-shell crabs. The large portions of gumbo and seafood bisque come in iron kettles. Flounder Belle Franklin is crabmeat, shrimp, and filet of flounder baked in butter with herbs and wines and a glaze of cheeses and toasted almonds. You can pick out your live Maine lobster from a big saltwater tank. There are 40 listings on the dessert menu; try the warm chocolate-chip pie topped with whipped cream. The large bar upstairs has a ceiling all a-twinkle with ersatz stars. *20 E. Broad St., tel. 912/233–5757. Dress: informal. Reservations accepted. AE, DC, MC, V. Sun. jazz brunch.*

Moderate–Expensive

River House. This stylish restaurant sits over the spot where the SS *Savannah* set sail for her maiden voyage across the ocean in 1819. For starters try the snails wrapped in puff pastry, baked and served with beurre blanc sauce; or oysters on the half shell. There are a number of mesquite-grilled entrées, including swordfish topped with raspberry-butter sauce and grouper Florentine, served with creamed spinach and a fresh dill and lemon-butter sauce. Entrées are served with freshly baked loaves of sourdough bread, and fish dishes come with freshly made angel-hair pasta. *125 W. River St., tel. 912/234–1900. Dress: informal for lunch; jacket and tie required for dinner. Reservations accepted. AE, DC, MC, V.*

Inexpensive–Moderate ★ **Seashell House.** It may not look like much from the outside, but the steamed seafood inside is regarded by many to be the best in the city. It specializes in crab, shrimp, and oysters, as well as a Low Country Boil that includes shrimp, sausage, corn, and whatever else comes to mind that day. It also features a seafood platter second to none. Be prepared to roll up your sleeves and dig in. *3111 Skidaway Rd., tel. 912/352–8116. Dress: casual. No reservations. AE, MC, V.*

Shrimp Factory. Like all of Savannah's riverfront restaurants, this was once an old warehouse. Now it's a light and airy place with exposed brick, wood paneling, beamed ceilings, and huge windows that let you watch the parade of ships on the water. A house specialty is pine bark stew—five native seafoods simmered with potatoes, onions, and herbs, and served with blueberry muffins. The extensive lunch and dinner menus have few offerings that don't come from the sea. Blackened dolphin filet is smothered with herbs and julienned sweet red peppers in butter sauce. Baked deviled crabs are served with chicken baked rice. Fish entrées are accompanied by angel-hair pasta, and there is a delicious whipped-cheese spread for the warm French bread. *313 E. River St., tel. 912/236–4229. Dress: informal. Reservations accepted. AE, DC, MC, V.*

Lodging

While Savannah has plenty of chain hotels and motels, ranging from the simple to the sublime, the city's most distinctive lodgings are the historic inns. There are more than two dozen historic inns, guest houses, and bed-and-breakfasts in the Historic District.

If "historic inn" brings to your mind images of roughing it in picturesque but shabby genteel mansions with slightly antiquated plumbing, you're in for a surprise. Most of the inns are in mansions, most of them with high ceilings, spacious rooms, and ornate carved millwork. Most have canopied, four-poster, or Victorian brass beds and 19th-century antiques. Most of them *also* have enormous marble baths with whirlpools, hot tubs, or Jacuzzis (if not all of the above), and many of them have a film library for the in-room VCRs. Virtually all have turndown service with a chocolate or praline and, in some, a discreet brandy is placed on your nightstand. In most cases, Continental breakfast and afternoon aperitifs are included in the rate.

The most highly recommended properties in each price category are indicated by a star ★.

Category	Cost*
Very Expensive	over $100
Expensive	$75–$100
Moderate	$50–$75
Inexpensive	under $50

**double room; add taxes or service*

Inns and Guest Houses
Very Expensive

★ **Ballastone Inn.** This sumptuous inn is located within a mansion, dating from 1835, that was once, so it is said, a bordello. The Ballastone is notable for the wildly dramatic designs of its Scalamandre wallpaper and fabrics, which show off the Savannah colors to full advantage. Each of the 19 rooms has a different theme, with distinctive colors, ambience, and 18th- or 19th-century antiques. In Scarborough Fair, a vivid red and yellow room, the fabric pattern was adapted from a Victorian china serving platter in the Davenport House. That exquisite third-floor room has two queen-size Victorian brass beds, a Queen Anne lowboy and writing desk, and a Victorian slipper chair. On the garden level (there are three stories in addition to the garden level), rooms are small and cozy, with exposed brick walls, beamed ceilings, and in some cases windows at eye level with the lush courtyard. One such room is the Sorghum Cane, trimmed in the bronze color of sugarcane molasses; it has two queen-size brass beds, wicker furniture, and wall fabric patterned after the etched glass window of a restored local house. Afternoon tea or wine served daily; bedtime turn-downs with chocolate and brandy. *14 E. Oglethorpe St., 31401, tel. 912/236–1484. 17 rooms with bath. Facilities: concierge, courtyard Jacuzzis, in-room VCRs, film library. AE, MC, V.*

Foley House. In the parlor of this four-story 1896 house, carved gargoyles flank the original fireplace and there is a graceful brass-and-crystal chandelier. On the newel post in the hall there is an elaborate lamp that worked as an extra in *Gone With the Wind.* There are four rooms in the carriage house and 16 spacious rooms (four with Jacuzzis) in the main house, all with canopied or four-poster beds, polished hardwood floors covered with Oriental rugs, and 19th-century antiques. There is a splendid tapestry in the Essex Room (an especially romantic room with a balcony on Chippewa Square), a king-size bed and day bed, and an extra large bath with whirlpool. When you call to reserve, ask about the special package deals. *14 W. Hull St., 31401, tel. 912/232–6622 or 800/647–3708. 20 rooms with bath. Facilities: concierge, courtyard with hot tub, VCRs, film library. AE, MC, V.*

★ **Gastonian.** Hugh and Roberta Lineberger's inn will probably, to put it modestly, knock your socks off. The mansion was built in 1868, and each of its 13 sumptuous suites is distinguished with vivid Scalamandre colors. The Caracalla Suite is named for the marble bath with an eight-foot whirlpool tub. The huge bedroom has a king-size canopy bed, working fireplace, and a lounge with a mirrored wet bar. The French Room, resembling a 19th-century French boudoir, is done in blues and whites, with Oriental rugs and flocked wallpaper. All rooms have working fireplaces and antiques from the Georgian and Regency periods. In the morning, a full breakfast is served in the formal dining room—pancakes, eggs, waffles, country ham, grits, fresh fruit, biscuits, and juice—or you can opt for a Continental breakfast in your room. Each guest receives a fruit basket and split of wine upon arrival. *220 E. Gaston St., 31401, tel. 912/232–2869, fax 912/234–0006. 10 rooms, 3 suites with bath. Facilities: concierge, VCRs, film library, whirlpools, courtyard, and sun deck with hot tub. AE, MC, V.*

Expensive–Very Expensive

Olde Harbour Inn. The building dates from 1892, when it was built on the riverfront as a warehouse and processing plant, but the old inn is actually a thoroughly modern facility that housed condos until 1987. Each suite has a fully equipped kitchen, including dishwasher and detergent. All suites overlook the river and have wall-to-wall carpeting, exposed brick walls painted white, and a canopied or four-poster bed. There are studio suites; regular suites with living room, bedroom, kitchen, and bath; and loft suites. (The latter are lofty indeed, with 25-foot ceilings, balconies overlooking the water, huge skylights, and ample room to sleep six.) Each evening a dish of sherbet is brought to your room and placed in the freezer, and each morning croissants, blueberry muffins, juice, and coffee are served in a cozy breakfast room. *508 E. Factors Walk, 31401, tel. 912/234–4100 or 800/553–6533. 24 suites with bath. Facilities: concierge, room service, fully equipped kitchen, cable TV with remote control, VCRs, film library, honor bar, valet laundry, and parking. AE, DC, MC, V.*

Expensive

★ **Eliza Thompson House.** This 25-room guest house, located on one of the Historic District's prettiest tree-lined streets, was originally built in 1847 for "Miss Eliza." There are king- and queen-size four-poster and canopied beds; some rooms with wall-to-wall carpeting, others with Oriental rugs covering the Georgia pine floors. The choice rooms overlook the large brick courtyard, which is a popular place for wedding receptions. In nice weather the complimentary breakfast is served at tables placed around a tiered fountain. *5 W. Jones St., 31401, tel. 912/236–3620 or 800/348–9378. 25 rooms with bath. Facilities: concierge. AE, MC, V.*

★ **Forsyth Park Inn.** As the name suggests, this Victorian mansion sits across the street from Forsyth Park. In the foyer is a grand piano, and afternoon wines and cheeses are taken to the accompaniment of Mercer and Gershwin music. Rooms are outfitted with 19th-century furnishings, including king- and queen-size four-poster beds, and have working fireplaces, large marble baths (some with whirlpools). The carriage house, just off the courtyard, has a suite with bath, complete kitchen, and a screened porch. *102 W. Hall St., 31401, tel. 912/233–6800. 9 rooms with private bath; 1 private guest cottage. Facilities: Jacuzzi. AE, MC, V.*

Bed-and-breakfasts

Expensive

★ **Jesse Mount House.** The Georgian home of Lois and Howard Crawford (the house is named for the original owner in 1854) has a three-bedroom suite on the upper level with a sunny sitting room. The suite has white-iron furniture, a shower-bath, refrigerator, coffeemaker, wineglasses, and dishes; two of the bedrooms have fireplaces with gas logs. Breakfast (freshly squeezed orange juice, croissants, blueberry muffins, coffee) can be taken either in your quarters or with the Crawfords in the formal dining room. *209 W. Jones St., 31401, tel. 912/236–1774. 3-bedroom suite. Facilities: cable TV, private phones. No credit cards.*

R.S.V.P. Savannah (417 E. Charlton St., 31401, tel. 912/232–7787 or 800/729–7787, fax 912/236–2880) is a bed-and-breakfast service that can reserve accommodations for you in Savannah, Tybee, and the surrounding area.

Hotels and Motels
Expensive–Very Expensive

DeSoto Hilton. Three massive chandeliers glisten over the jardinieres, fresh flowers, and discreetly placed conversation areas of the spacious lobby. The chandeliers are from the historic DeSoto Hotel that stood on this site long ago. Guest rooms are on the cushy side, in Savannah peach and green, with wall-to-wall carpeting, traditional furniture, and king, queen, or two double beds. (The best view is from the corner king rooms, which have the added attraction of coffeemakers, refrigerators, and such.) Suites have kitchens and custom-made contemporary furnishings in the bedroom, sitting room, and dining area. *15 E. Liberty St., 31401, tel. 912/232–9000 or 800/445–8667. 254 rooms; 9 suites with bath. Facilities: concierge, free parking, restaurant and lounge, outdoor pool with sundeck, golf and tennis privileges at area clubs. AE, DC, MC.*

Hyatt. When this riverfront hotel was built in 1981, preservationists opposed a seven-story structure in the historic district. Its modern design has a towering atrium and a pleasant central lounge, as well as glass elevators. Its rooms have mauve furnishings and balconies overlooking the atrium, the Savannah River, or Bay St. MD's Lounge is the ideal spot to have a drink and watch the river traffic drift by. *2 W. Bay St., tel. 912/238–1234 or 800/228–9000. 346 rooms. Facilities: 2 restaurants, 2 lounges, indoor pool, gift shop, AE, DC, MC, V.*

★ **Mulberry.** There are so many objets d'art in the public rooms that the management has obligingly provided a walking tour brochure. There are, to mention but a few, 18th-century oil paintings, an English grandfather clock dating from 1803, Chinese vases from the Ching Dynasty, an ornate Empire game table—and to think this was once a Coca-Cola bottling plant. The restaurant is a sophisticated affair with crystal chandeliers and mauve velvet Regency furniture. There is a spacious courtyard covered with a mosquito net, which keeps it about 10 degrees cooler in the summer. The guest rooms are in a traditional motif; suites have queen-size beds, wet bars, amenity packages, and river views. *601 E. Bay St., 31401, tel. 912/238–1200 or 800/554–5544 (in GA 800/282–9198). 119 rooms, 25 suites with bath. Facilities: concierge, bar, restaurant, outdoor pool, rooftop deck with Jacuzzi, accommodations for nonsmokers and the handicapped. AE, DC, MC, V.*

Radisson Plaza. This is Savannah's newest hotel. Located in the Historic District, the 8-story lodging is on the city's riverfront adjacent to River Street and Factor's Walk. *100 Gen. McIntosh Blvd., 31401, tel. 912/233–7722 or 800/333–3333. 385 rooms, 46 suites. Facilities: 2 restaurants, lobby lounge, indoor and outdoor pools, fitness club. AE, D, DC, MC, V.*

River Street Inn. This elegant Legacy Hotel offers panoramic views of the Savannah River. Rooms are furnished with antiques and reproductions from the era of King Cotton. Amenities include turn-down service. The interior is so lavish, it's difficult to believe it was only recently a vacant warehouse dating back to 1830. One floor includes charming shops, another a New Orleans–style restaurant and blues club. *115 E. River St., tel. 912/234–6400 or 800/253–4229. 44 rooms. Facilities: restaurant, lounge, shops. AE, MC, V.*

Moderate

Days Inn. This downtown hotel is located in the Historic District near the City Market, only a block off River Street. Its compact rooms have modular furnishings and most amenities, including HBO/ESPN on the tube and valet service. Interior corridors and an adjacent parking garage minimize its motel qualities. *201 W. Bay St., tel. 912/236-4440 or 800/325-2525. 235 rooms. Facilities: restaurant, pool, gift shop. AE, DC, MC, V.*

Nightlife

Savannah's nightlife is a reflection of the city's laid-back, easy-going personality. Some clubs feature live reggae, hard rock, and other contemporary music, but most stay with traditional blues, jazz, and piano bar vocalists. After-dark merrymakers usually head for watering holes on Riverfront Plaza or the southside.

Jazz Clubs

The Crossroads (219 W. St. Julian St., tel. 912/234-5438) is Savannah's newest blues night club featuring live entertainment Tuesday through Saturday.

Hard-Hearted Hannah's (312 W. St. Julian St., tel. 912/232-3470, also in the City Market) showcases local talents such as keyboardist Joe Jones.

Bars and Nightclubs

Congress Street Station (121 W. Congress St., tel. 912/233-0486) is a small dark club that formerly was called Nightflight. It's still the city's liveliest music hall, featuring a variety of name performers in rock, blues, jazz, reggae, folk, country, and comedy. The age of the crowd on the tiny dance floor depends on who's on the bandstand.

Kevin Barry's Irish Pub (117 W. River St., tel. 912/233-9626), a cozy pub with a friendly bar and traditional Irish music, is *the* place to be on St. Patrick's Day. The rest of the year there's a mixed bag of tourists and locals, young and old. **Hollywood's** (9 W. Bay St., tel. 912/233-8347), across from the Hyatt Regency, is a very active singles bar, where young locals and out-of-towners mix it up to taped Top-40 music.

The Golden Isles and Okefenokee Swamp

The Golden Isles are a string of lush, subtropical barrier islands meandering lazily down Georgia's Atlantic coast from Savannah to the Florida border. Three of the islands—Jekyll Island, Sea Island, and St. Simons Island—are connected to the mainland by bridges in the vicinity of Brunswick; these are the only ones accessible by automobile. The Cumberland Island National Seashore is accessible by ferry from St. Mary's. Little St. Simons Island, a privately owned retreat with a guest lodge, is reached by a private launch from St. Simons.

The islands have a long history of human habitation; Indian relics have been found on them that date to about 2500 BC. According to legend, the various Indian nations agreed that no wars would be fought there and that tribal members would visit only in a spirit of friendship.

Each Golden Isle has a distinctive personality, shaped by its history and ecology. About 50 miles inland is the Okefenokee Swamp National Wildlife Refuge, which has a character all its own.

Cumberland Island National Seashore

Numbers in the margin correspond to points of interest on the Golden Isles map.

1 The largest, most southerly, and most accessible of Georgia's primitive coastal islands is **Cumberland**, a 16-by-3-mile sanctuary of marshes, dunes, beaches, forests, lakes and ponds, estuaries and inlets. Waterways are home to gators, sea turtles, otters, snowy egrets, great blue herons, ibis, wood storks, and more than 300 other species of birds. In the forests are armadillos, wild horses, deer, raccoons, and an assortment of reptiles.

After the ancient Guale Indians came 16th-century Spanish missionaries, 18th-century English soldiers, and 19th-century planters. During the 1880s, Thomas Carnegie of Pittsburgh built several lavish homes here, but the island remained largely as nature created it. In the early 1970s, the federal government established the Cumberland Island National Seashore and opened this natural treasure to the public.

Getting Around The only public access to the island is by *The Cumberland Queen*, a reservations-only, 150-passenger ferry based near the National Park Service Information Center at the docks at St. Mary's on the mainland. From mid-May through Labor Day, the *Queen* departs from St. Mary's daily at 9 and 11:45 AM and departs from Cumberland at 10:15 AM and 4:45 PM. The trip takes 45 minutes. For the remainder of the year there is no ferry on Tuesday and Wednesday.

Important Addresses and Numbers To make ferry reservations or obtain further information, contact the **National Park Service** (Cumberland Island National Seashore, Box 806, St. Mary's 31558, tel. 912/882–4335). Ferry bookings are very heavy during summer, but cancellations and no-shows often make last-minute space available.

Exploring From the Park Service docks at the island's southern end, you can follow wooded nature trails, swim and sun on 18 miles of undeveloped beaches, go fishing and bird-watching, and view the ruins of Carnegie's great estate, **Dungeness.** You can also join history and nature walks led by Park Service rangers. There is no transportation on the island, so the length of your explorations will be determined by your own interests and energy. Bear in mind that summers are hot and humid, and that you must bring your own food, soft drinks, sunscreen, and a reliable insect repellent. All trash items must be transported back to the mainland by campers and picnickers. *Nothing can be purchased on the island.*

Lodging

Camping Novice campers usually prefer **Sea Camp,** a five-minute walk from the *Cumberland Queen* dock, with rest rooms and showers adjacent to campsites. The beach is just beyond the dunes. Experienced campers will want to hike 3–10 miles to several areas where cold-water spigots are the only amenities. Contact the National Park Service (*see* Important Addresses and Numbers, *above*).

Hotels **Greyfield Inn.** The island's only hotel lodgings are in a turn-of-the-century Carnegie family home. Greyfield's public areas are filled with family mementoes, furnishings, and portraits (you may feel as though you've stepped into one of Agatha Christie's mysterious Cornwall manors). Prices include all meals, sales tax, mandatory gratuity, and pickup and drop off by the inn's

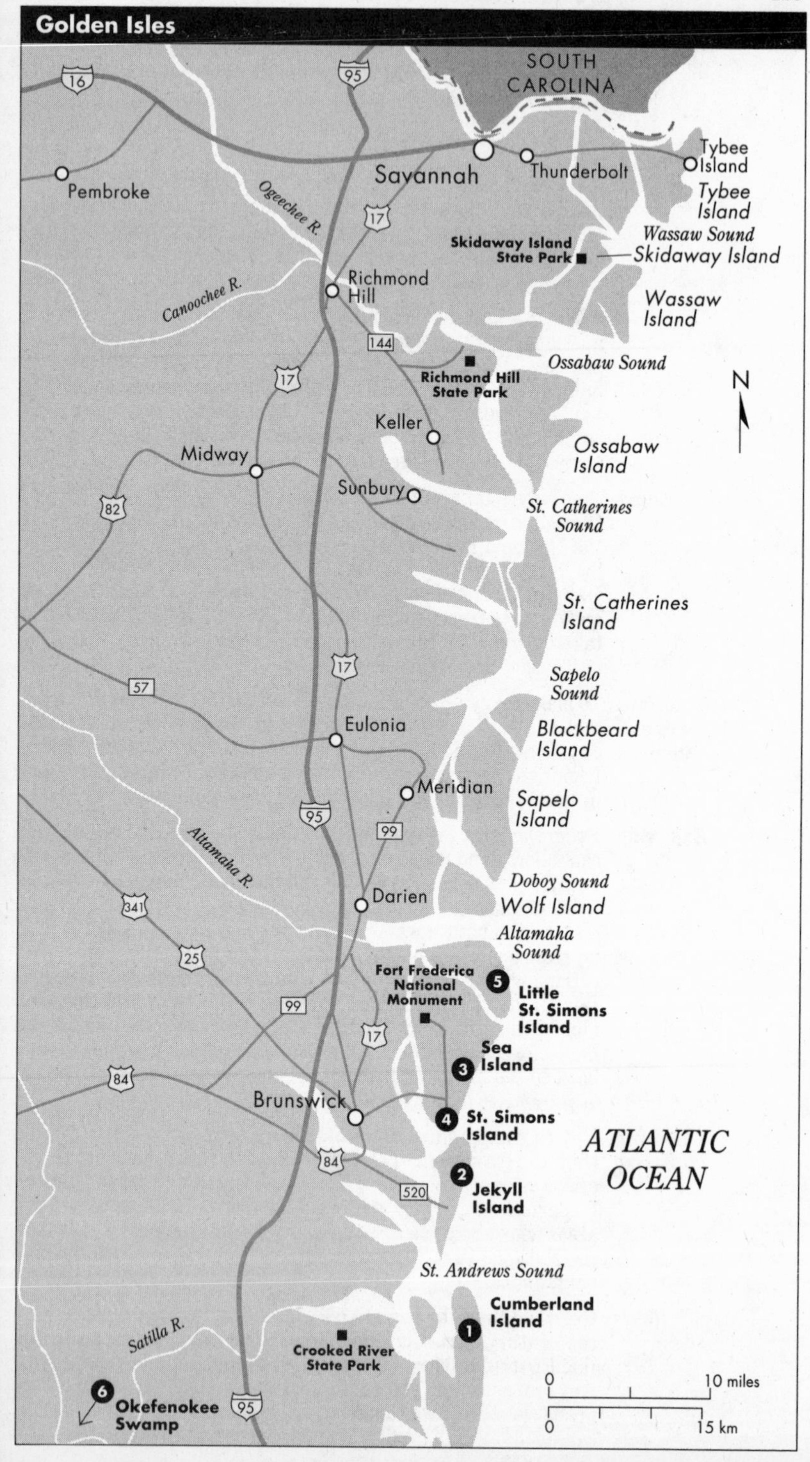
Golden Isles
SOUTH CAROLINA
16
95
Savannah
Thunderbolt
Tybee Island
Tybee Island
Pembroke
Ogeechee R.
17
Wassaw Sound
Skidaway Island State Park
Skidaway Island
Richmond Hill
Canoochee R.
Wassaw Island
144
Ossabaw Sound
Richmond Hill State Park
17
N
Keller
Ossabaw Island
Midway
Sunbury
82
St. Catherines Sound
St. Catherines Island
17
Sapelo Sound
57
Blackbeard Island
Eulonia
Meridian
Sapelo Island
95
99
Altamaha R.
Doboy Sound
Darien
Wolf Island
341
Altamaha Sound
25
Fort Frederica National Monument
5
Little St. Simons Island
99
17
Sea Island
3
84
Brunswick
4
St. Simons Island
ATLANTIC OCEAN
84
2
520
Jekyll Island
St. Andrews Sound
Cumberland Island
1
Satilla R.
Crooked River State Park
0
10 miles
0
15 km
6
Okefenokee Swamp
95

ferry at Fernandina Beach, Florida. *Drawer B, Fernandina Beach, FL 32034, tel. 904/261-6408. 5 rooms, 1 suite. MC, V. Very Expensive (over $150).*

The Charter House. The accommodations of the 120-room motel are spartan but air-conditioned. It is located 2 miles from the Cumberland ferry dock. The on-site restaurant serves reasonably priced breakfasts, lunches, and dinners and presents live evening entertainment in the lounge. *2710 Osborne St., St. Mary's 31588, tel. 800/768-6250. 119 rooms, 1 suite. Facilities: restaurant, lounge, swimming pool. AE, D, DC, MC, V. Moderate ($38-$48).*

Jekyll Island

For 56 winters, between 1886 and 1942, America's rich and fa-
2 mous faithfully came south to **Jekyll Island.** Through the Gilded Age, the Great War, the Roaring '20s, and the Great Depression, Vanderbilts and Rockefellers, Morgans and Astors, Macys, Pulitzers, and Goodyears shuttered their Fifth Avenue castles and retreated to the serenity of their wild Georgia island. There they built elegant "cottages," played golf and tennis, and socialized. Early in World War II, the millionaires departed for the last time. In 1947, the state of Georgia purchased the entire island for the bargain price of $650,000.

Getting Around

By Plane Jekyll has its own airstrip for private planes, with refueling facilities (Davis Aviation, tel. 404/635-2500). **Glynco Jetport,** 6 miles north of Brunswick, is served by **Atlantic Southeast Airlines** (tel. 800/282-3424) flights from Atlanta and by Charlotte, NC-based **USAir** (tel. 800/428-4322).

By Car From Brunswick by car, take the Jekyll Island Causeway ($1 per car).

Important Addresses and Numbers **The Jekyll Island Convention and Visitors Bureau** (901 Jekyll Island Causeway, Jekyll Island 31520, tel. 912/635-3636), at the end of the causeway, is open daily 9-5.

Guided Tours Tours of the **Jekyll Island Club Historic District** originate at the Museum Orientation Center on Stable Road. Ninety-minute tours are given in open-air trolleys. Sites include several restored homes and buildings in the 240-acre historic district: Indian Mound; William Rockefeller's shingled cottage; and Faith Chapel, illuminated by stained-glass windows signed by Louis Comfort Tiffany. Audiovisual orientations are presented a half-hour before each tour departs. *Exit 35, tel. 912/635-2236. Admission: $7 adults, $5 children 6-18, under 6 free. Tours operate daily 10-3. Closed New Year's, Thanksgiving, and Christmas.*

Exploring Jekyll Island is still a vast playground, but no longer restricted to the rich and famous. For recreation, there is golf (63 holes), tennis, fishing, biking, and jogging. There is also a new water park, picnic grounds, and tours of the historic homes.

One side of the island is flanked by nearly 10 miles of hard-packed Atlantic beaches; the other, by the Intracoastal Waterway and picturesque salt marshes. Deer and wild turkeys inhabit interior forests of pine, magnolia, and moss-veiled live oaks. Egrets, pelicans, herons, and sandpipers skim the gentle surf.

Jekyll's clean, mostly uncommercialized beaches are free and open to the public year-round. Bathhouses with rest rooms, changing areas, and showers are open at regular intervals along the beach. Beachwear, suntan lotion, rafts, snacks, and drinks are available at the **Jekyll Shopping Center,** facing the beach at Beachview Drive.

Participant Sports

Golf

Jekyll's 63 holes of golf include three 18-hole courses (tel. 912/635–2368) with a main clubhouse on Capt. Wylly Rd. and a 9-hole course (tel. 912/635–2170) on Beachview Dr.

Tennis

Nine courts include J.P. Morgan's indoor court (tel. 912/635–2600).

Water Park

Summer Waves, an 11-acre water park, opened in June 1988 and has an 18,000-square-foot wave pool; eight water slides; a children's activity pool with 2 slides; and a 1,000-foot river for tubing and rafting. *210 Riverview Dr., tel. 912/635–2074. Admission: $9.95 adults, $7.95 children 4–8. Open Sun.–Fri. 10–6, Sat. 10–8 May 23–Aug. 30 and Labor Day weekend.*

Dining

The Grand Dining Room. In the Jekyll Island Club Hotel the dining room sparkles with silver and crystal. What sets the meals apart from the ordinary are the sauces that flavor the dishes of fresh seafood, beef, veal, and chicken. *371 Riverview Dr., tel. 912/635–2600, ext. 1002, or 800/333–3333. Jacket requested at dinner. Reservations recommended. AE, DC, MC, V. Expensive ($30–$40).*

The Wharf. Opened in 1989 as the Golden Isles' only over-the-water dining experience, this restaurant provides a saltwater marsh view from its dock location. Fresh seafood is featured nightly in the dining room and screened-porch raw bar. Cocktails are served in the lounge. *One Pier Rd., tel. 912/635–3800. Dress: casual. AE, MC, V. Inexpensive–Moderate ($10–$15).*

Lodging

Jekyll Island Club Hotel. Built in 1887, the four-story clubhouse, with wraparound verandas, towers, and turrets, once served as dining area, social center, and guest accommodations for some of the wealthiest families in the United States. In 1985, a group of Georgia businessmen spent $17 million restoring it to a splendor that would astonish even the Astors and Vanderbilts. The guest rooms and suites are custom-decorated with mahogany beds, armoires, and plush sofas and chairs. Some have flowery views of the Intracoastal Waterway, and several suites have Jacuzzis. The adjacent Sans Souci Apartments, former "bachelor quarters" built in 1886 by J.P. Morgan and William Rockefeller, have been converted into guest rooms. The hotel is operated as a Radisson Hotels resort. *371 Riverview Dr., Jekyll Island 31520, tel. 912/635–2600 or 800/333–3333. 134 rooms. Facilities: restaurant, outdoor pool, gift shops, croquet lawn, free shuttle to nearby beaches, tennis courts. AE, DC, MC, V. Expensive–Very Expensive ($69–over $100).*

Jekyll Inn. This is the largest facility on the island. Located on a landscaped 15-acre site, these oceanfront units, including some villas with kitchenettes, also underwent a $2.5 million renovation. Rooms were redecorated with new lighting and carpeting, and saunas and Jacuzzis in some bathrooms. Island decor was added to the second-floor Ocean View lounge. *975 Beachview Dr., Jekyll Island 31520, tel. 912/635–2531 or 800/528–1234. 264 rooms. Facilities: restaurant, large pool, playground. AE, DC, MC, V. Moderate–Very Expensive ($60–over $100).*

Holiday Inn Beach Resort. Nestled amid natural dunes and oaks in a secluded oceanfront setting, this hotel has a private beach, but its rooms with balconies still don't have an ocean view. Its recreational activities include outdoor pool and playground, tennis courts and 63 holes of golf. *200 S. Beachview Dr., Jekyll Island 31520, tel. 912/635–3311 or 800-HOLIDAY. 205 rooms. Facilities: restaurant, lounge with live entertainment, satellite cinema, some in-room saunas and whirlpools, bike rentals. AE, D, DC, MC, V. Expensive ($64–$100).*

Sea Island

3 **Sea Island** has been the domain of the **Cloister Hotel** since 1928. Attached to St. Simons Island by a bridge over a narrow waterway, and a good many steps up the social ladder, the resort lives up to its celebrity status. Guests lodge in spacious, comfortably appointed rooms and suites in the Spanish Medi-terranean main hotel and in beachside cottages and villas.

For recreation, there's a choice of golf, tennis, swimming in pools or at the beach, skeet shooting, horseback riding, sailing, biking, lawn games, and surf and deep-sea fishing. After dinner, a big-band orchestra plays for dancing in the lounge.

Like a person of some years, the Cloister has its eccentricities. Guest rooms were only recently equipped with TVs. Credit cards are not honored, but personal checks are accepted. Gentlemen must cover their arms in the dining rooms, even at breakfast. And for the most part, nouvelle cuisine, new American cuisine, and other culinary trends of the '80s have yet to breach the hotel's traditional menus. A complete spa facility opened in 1989 and features a fully equipped workout room, daily aerobics classes, facials and massages, and other beauty treatments.

There is no admission gate, and nonguests are free to admire the beautifully planted grounds and to drive past the mansions lining Sea Island Drive. Space permitting, they may also play at the Sea Island Golf Course and on the tennis courts and dine in the main dining room. *The Cloister, Sea Island 31561, tel. 912/638–3611, reservations 800/SEA–ISLAND. 264 rooms, 450 cottages, 44 condos. Facilities: restaurants, pools, golf, tennis, fitness center and spa; shuttle service to and from Jacksonville, Savannah, and Brunswick airports. Full American Plan. No credit cards, but personal checks are accepted. Very Expensive (over $100).*

St. Simons Island

As large as Manhattan, with over 14,000 year-round residents,
4 **St. Simons** is the Golden Isles' most complete and commercial resort destination. Fortunately, the accelerated development of condos, shopping districts, and other amenities in recent years has failed to spoil the natural beauty of the island's regal live oaks, beaches, and wavering salt marshes. Visits are highlighted by swimming and sunning on hard-packed beaches, biking, hiking, fishing, horseback riding, touring historic sites, and feasting on fresh local seafood at a growing number of restaurants. All of Georgia's beaches are in the public domain.

Getting Around
By Plane
Glynco Jetport, 6 miles north of Brunswick, is served by **Atlantic Southeast Airlines** (tel. 800/282–3424) flights from Atlanta and by **USAir's** (tel. 800/428–4322) Charlotte, NC, flights.

By Car
Reach St. Simons by crossing the Torras Causeway from Brunswick. The island's accommodations and sights are widespread, so you'll need a car.

Important Addresses and Numbers
St. Simons Island Chamber of Commerce (Neptune Park, St. Simons Island 31522, tel. 912/638–9014) can provide helpful information about the area.

Exploring
Many sights and activities are in **the village** area along Mallery Street at the south end of the island. Shops sell groceries, beachwear, and gifts. There are also several restaurants, pubs, and a popular public pier.

Also at the island's south end is **Neptune Park,** which includes picnic tables, a children's play park, miniature golf, and beach access. In the summer, a freshwater swimming pool, with showers and rest rooms, is open in the **Neptune Park Casino** (tel. 912/638–2393), in addition to a roller-skating rink, bowling lanes, and snack bars. Also in the park is **St. Simons Lighthouse,** a beacon since 1872. The **Museum of Coastal History** in the lightkeeper's cottage has permanent and changing exhibits of coastal history. *Tel. 912/638–4666. Admission (including the lighthouse): $1.50 adults, $1 children 6–12. Open Tues.–Sat. 10–5, Sun. 1:30–5.*

Ft. Frederica National Monument, at the north end of the island, includes the tabby ruins of a fort built by English troops in the mid-1730s as a bulwark against a Spanish invasion from Florida. Around the fort are the foundations of homes and shops built by soldiers and civilians. Start your tour at the **National Park Service Visitors Center,** which has a film and displays. *Tel. 912/638–3639. Admission: $3 per car. Open daily 9–5.*

On your way to Frederica, pause at **Christ Episcopal Church** on Frederica Road. Consecrated in 1886 following an earlier structure's desecration by Union troops, the white frame Gothic structure is surrounded by live oaks, dogwoods, and azaleas. The interior is highlighted by beautiful stained-glass windows. Donations welcome.

Dining
Alfonza's Olde Plantation Supper Club. Seafood, superb steaks, and plantation fried chicken are served in a gracious and relaxed environment. The club also has a cocktail lounge. *Harrington La., tel. 912/638–9883. Dress: informal. Reservations recommended. MC, V. Moderate ($11–$20).*

Blanche's Courtyard. Located in the village, this lively restaurant/nightclub is gussied up in "Bayou Victorian" dress, with lots of antiques and nostalgic memorabilia. True to its bayou decor, the menu features Cajun-style seafood as well as your basic steak and chicken. A ragtime band plays for dancers on the weekends. *440 Kings Way, tel. 912/638–3030. Dress: informal. Reservations accepted. AE, DC, MC, V. Moderate ($20–$30).*

Emmeline & Hessie. A large dining room and bar offer patrons a spectacular view of the marina and marshes. Specialties are seafood, steak, and lobster. There's also a bakery, a deli, and a seafood market on the premises. There's usually a line here, but it's well worth the wait to watch the sun set over the marshes as you dine. During the summer months, live bands play on the outdoor terrace. *Golden Isles Marina, tel. 912/638–9084. Dress: informal. Reservations accepted for dinner only. AE, MC, V. Inexpensive–Moderate ($15–$30).*

CJ's. This tiny village-area restaurant serves the island's best Italian food. Deep-dish and thin-crust pizzas, pastas, and all of the menu's sandwiches draw a faithful local clientele. The limited seating capacity creates lengthy waits, but the cuisine is worth your patience and take-out is available. *405 Mallory St., tel. 912/634–1022. Dress: informal. No reservations. No credit cards; personal checks accepted. Inexpensive (under $20).*

Crab Trap. One of the island's most popular spots, the Crab Trap offers a variety of fried and broiled fresh seafood, oysters on the half shell, clam chowder, heaps of batter fries, and hush puppies. The atmosphere is rustic-casual—there's a hole in the middle of every table to deposit corn cobs and shrimp shells. *1209 Ocean Blvd., tel. 912/638–3552. Dress: informal. No reservations. Inexpensive (under $20).*

Lodging

King and Prince Hotel and Villas. This hotel facing the beach stepped into the deluxe resort category with a recently completed, multimillion-dollar modernization and expansion. Guest rooms are spacious, and villas offer from two to three bedrooms. *Box 798, 201 Arnold Rd., St. Simons Island 31522, tel. 912/638–3631 or 800/342–0212. 130 rooms, 50 villas. Facilities: restaurant, lounge, indoor/outdoor pool, tennis, golf, bike rentals. AE, DC, MC, V. Expensive ($95–$275).*

Sea Palms Golf and Tennis Resort. A contemporary resort complex with fully furnished, ultramodern villas nestles on an 800-acre site. *5445 Frederica Rd., St. Simons Island 31522, tel. 912/638–3351 or 800/282–1226. 263 rooms. Facilities: 2 pools, health club, 27-hole golf course, tennis, children's recreation programs. AE, DC, MC, V. Expensive ($89–$269).*

Country Hearth Inn. Located on wooded land just off one of the island's main streets, this newer antebellum-style motel offers convenience and privacy plus the advantage of efficiency accommodations. Continental breakfast is included. *301 Main St., tel. 912/638–7805 or 800/673–6323. 73 rooms. Facilities: color cable TV, pool, hot tub, meeting facilities. AE, D, DC, MC, V. Moderate (under $70).*

Days Inn of America. This new facility opened in 1989 on an inland stretch of the island's main thoroughfare. Each room has built-in microwaves and refrigerators. Continental breakfast is included in the cost. *1700 Frederica Rd., St. Simons Island 31522, tel. 912/634–0660. 101 rooms. Facilities: pool, color cable TV. AE, MC, V. Moderate (under $75).*

Queen's Court. This family-oriented complex in the village has clean, modest rooms, some with kitchenettes. The grounds are beautiful. *437 Kings Way, St. Simons Island 31522, tel. 912/638–8459. 23 rooms. Facilities: color cable TV, shower baths, pool. MC, V. Moderate (under $70).*

Little St. Simons Island

Six miles long, two to three miles wide, skirted by Atlantic beaches and salt marshes teeming with birds and wildlife,
5 **Little St. Simons** is custom-made for Robinson Crusoe–style getaways. The island has been owned by one family since the early 1900s, and the only development is a rustic but comfortable guest compound. The island's forests and marshes are in-

habited by deer, armadillos, horses, raccoons, gators, otters, and over 200 species of birds.

Guests are free to walk the 6 miles of undisturbed beaches, swim in the mild surf, fish from the dock, and seine for shrimp and crabs in the marshes. There are also horses to ride, nature walks with experts, and other island explorations that can be made by boat or in the back of a pickup truck.

Dining and Lodging

River Lodge and Cedar House. Up to 24 guests can be accommodated in the lodge and house. Each has four bedrooms with twin or king-size beds, private baths, sitting rooms, and screened porches. Older hunting lodges have some private and some shared baths. None of the rooms are air-conditioned, but ceiling fans make sleeping comfortable. The rates include all meals and dinner wines (cocktails available at additional cost). Meals, often featuring fresh fish, pecan pie, and home-baked breads, are served family-style in the lodge dining room. *Box 1078, Little St. Simons Island 31522, tel. 912/638–7472. Facilities: stables, pool, beach, transportation from St. Simons Island, transportation on the island, fishing boats, interpretive guides. Minimum two-night reservations. MC, V. Very Expensive (over $100).*

Okefenokee Swamp National Wildlife Refuge

Covering more than 700 square miles of southeast Georgia, spilling over into northeast Florida, the mysterious rivers and
6 lakes of the **Okefenokee Swamp** bristle with seen and unseen life. Scientists agree that Okefenokee is not duplicated anywhere else on Earth. The swamp is actually a vast peat bog, remarkable in geologic origin and history. Once part of the ocean floor, it now rises more than 100 feet above sea level.

As you travel by canoe or speedboat among the water-lily islands and the great stands of live oaks and cypress, be on the lookout for otters, egrets, muskrats, herons, cranes, and gators cruising the dark channels like iron-clad subs. The Okefenokee Swamp Park, 8 miles south of Waycross, is a major visitor gateway to the refuge. The Swamp Park is a nonprofit development operating under a long-term lease. There are two other gateways to the swamp: an eastern entrance in the Suwanee Canal Recreation Area, near Folkston; and a western entrance at Stephen C. Foster State Park, outside the town of Fargo.

Seminole Indians, in their migrations south toward Florida's Everglades, once took refuge in the Great Okefenokee. Noting the many floating islands, they provided its name—"Land of the Trembling Earth."

Exploring

Okefenokee Swamp Park. South of Waycross, via U.S. 1, the park offers orientation programs, exhibits, observation areas, wilderness walkways, an outdoor museum of pioneer life, and boat tours into the swamp that reveal its ecological uniqueness. A boardwalk and 90-foot tower are excellent places to glimpse cruising gators and a variety of birds. Gate admission includes a guided boat tour and all exhibits and shows. You may also arrange for lengthier explorations with a guide and a boat. *Waycross 31501, tel. 912/283–0583. Admission: $8 adults, $6 children 5–11. Open daily summer, 9–6:30; spring, fall, and winter, 9–5:30.*

Suwanee Canal Recreation Area. This area, 8 miles south of Folkston, via GA 121/23, is administered by the U.S. Fish and Wildlife Service. Stop first at the Visitor Information Center, which has an orientation film and exhibits on the Okefenokee's flora and fauna. A boardwalk takes you over the water to a 40-foot observation tower. At the concession building you may purchase snacks and sign up for guided boat tours into an 11-mile waterway, which resulted from efforts to drain the swamp a century ago. Hikers, bicyclists, and private motor vehicles are welcome on the Swamp Island Drive; several interpretive walking trails may be taken along the way. Picnicking is allowed. *Park Supt., Box 336, Folkston 31537, tel. 912/496-7156. Admission to the park is free (there's a $3 charge per car). 1-hr tours: $6.75 adults, $3.50 children 5–11, $2.25 children 1–4; 2-hr tours: $13.50 adults, $7 children 5–11, $4.50 children 1–4. Refuge open 7 AM–7:30 PM Mar. 1–Sept. 10; 8–6 Sept. 11–Feb. Closed Christmas.*

Stephen C. Foster State Park. Eighteen miles from Fargo, via GA 11, is an 80-acre island park entirely within the Okefenokee Swamp National Wildlife Refuge. The park encompasses a large cypress and black gum forest, a majestic backdrop for one of the thickest growths of vegetation in the southeastern United States. The lush terrain and the mirrorlike black waters of the swamp provide at least a part-time home for more than 225 species of birds, 41 species of mammals, 54 species of reptiles, 32 species of amphibians, and 37 species of fish. Park naturalists leading boat tours will spill out a wealth of swamp lore as riders observe gators, many bird species, and native trees and plants. You may also take a self-guided excursion in rental canoes and fishing boats. Camping is also available here (*see* Lodging, *below*). *Fargo 31631, tel. 912/637-5274. Admission free. Open 6:30 AM–8:30 PM Mar. 1–Sept. 1; 7 AM–7 PM Sept. 2–Feb. 29. Admission: $3 to National Wildlife Refuge.*

Lodging
Camping

Stephen C. Foster State Park. The park has furnished two-bedroom cottages ($50 a night Sun.–Thurs.; $60 weekends) and campsites with water, electricity, rest rooms, and showers ($10 a night). Because of roaming wildlife and poachers, the park's gates close between sunset and sunrise. If you're staying overnight, stop for groceries in Fargo beforehand. *Park Supt., Fargo 31631, tel. 912/637-5274. Inexpensive–Moderate.*

Laura S. Walker State Park. Near Okefenokee Swamp Park, but not in the swamp, are campsites ($10) with electrical and water hookups. Be sure to pick up food and supplies on the way to the park. *Park Supt., Waycross 31501, tel. 912/287-4900. Facilities: playground, fishing docks, pool, picnic areas. Inexpensive.*

4 Louisiana

By Honey Naylor

The various regions within most states are vaguely referred to by locals as "upstate," "to the south," and so on. Such is not the case in Louisiana. In "Sportsman's Paradise" (or the "Bayou State" or the "Pelican State," as it is also called), the land is clearly divided. Louisianians almost to a person say *North* Louisiana and *South* Louisiana, and even in conversation you can detect a capitalized distinction. The truth is, North Louisiana and South Louisiana have about as much in common as North Dakota and South Carolina. *North* Louisiana is southern, and *South* Louisiana is not. (A South Louisiana exception is the area north of Baton Rouge, in the Feliciana Parishes [counties], where both terrain and customs are akin to those in North Louisiana.) Peace reigns 'twixt the twain, of course. But it is no accident that construction of I–49, the north–south interstate, dragged on for years. Now, at least the North and the South are physically—though not philosophically—connected.

Louisiana's Mason-Dixon line is Alexandria, in the state's midsection, known to all as Alex and pronounced *Elleck* by most. North of Alexandria are rolling hills and piney woods, acres of hiking and happy hunting grounds, and lakes where you can fish and camp.

The terrain flattens out and becomes marshy south of Alexandria. In Cajun Country (also known as Acadiana and French Louisiana), Cajun fiddles tune up for *fais-do-do* (dances); tables are laden with crawfish, jambalaya, and gumbo; and pirogues (small, flat-bottom boats) are poled through bayous. Gracious antebellum homes decorate the Great River Road between Baton Rouge and New Orleans, frilly riverboats play upon the Mississippi, and tour boats sneak beneath lacy gray Spanish moss into mysterious cypress swamps and sloughs.

Not a month goes by without a festival of some sort. South Louisiana is particularly festive. It's home, after all, to the state's most famous city—New Orleans—and the splashiest celebration in all of North America—Mardi Gras.

New Orleans

When Rhett Butler took Scarlett O'Hara to New Orleans on their honeymoon, the city was scarred by war, carpetbaggers were looting the town, and decent folk feared for their lives. But gone with the wind the city wasn't. Captain Butler and his bride were entertained at a continuous round of lavish parties, suppers, and plays.

Since the 1980s, New Orleans, like most cities, has had its problems with crime and a depressed economy. But its reputation as a good-time town has remained intact. Despite its problems, New Orleans is forever finding something to celebrate. As well as world-famous Mardi Gras, new festivals crop up at the drop of a Panama hat. New Orleans party animals even celebrated a new addition to the Audubon Zoo.

The city's most famous party place is the French Quarter. Also called the Vieux Carré (Old Square), the Quarter is the original colony, founded in 1718 by French Creoles. As you explore its famous restaurants, antiques shops, and jazz haunts, try to imagine a handful of determined early 18th-century settlers living in crude palmetto huts, battling swamps, floods, hurri-

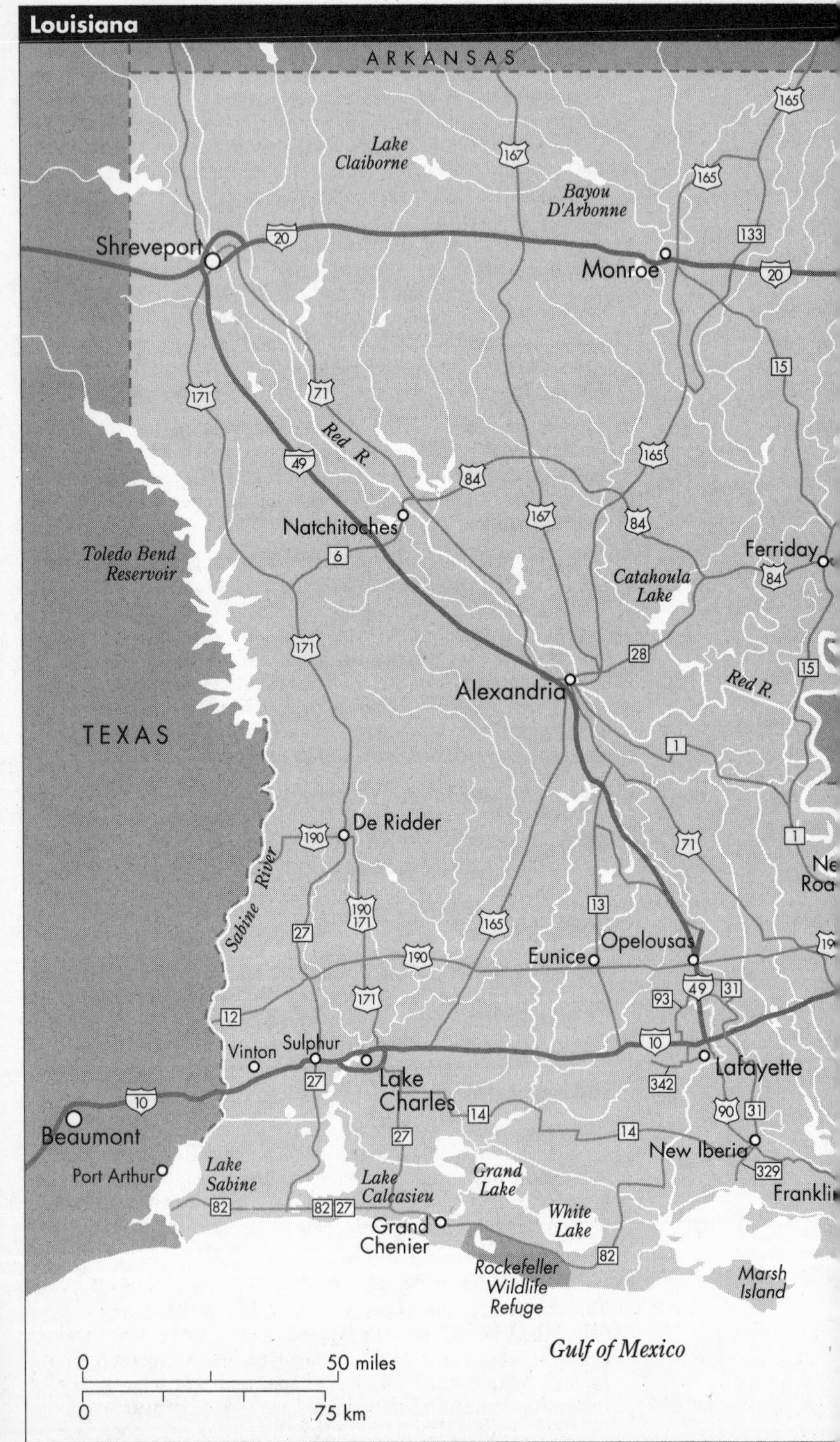
Louisiana
ARKANSAS
TEXAS
Lake Claiborne
Bayou D'Arbonne
Shreveport
Monroe
Red R.
Natchitoches
Toledo Bend Reservoir
Ferriday
Catahoula Lake
Alexandria
Red R.
De Ridder
Sabine River
Eunice
Opelousas
Vinton
Sulphur
Lake Charles
Lafayette
Beaumont
Port Arthur
Lake Sabine
Lake Calcasieu
Grand Lake
New Iberia
Franklin
White Lake
Grand Chenier
Rockefeller Wildlife Refuge
Marsh Island
Gulf of Mexico
0
50 miles
0
75 km

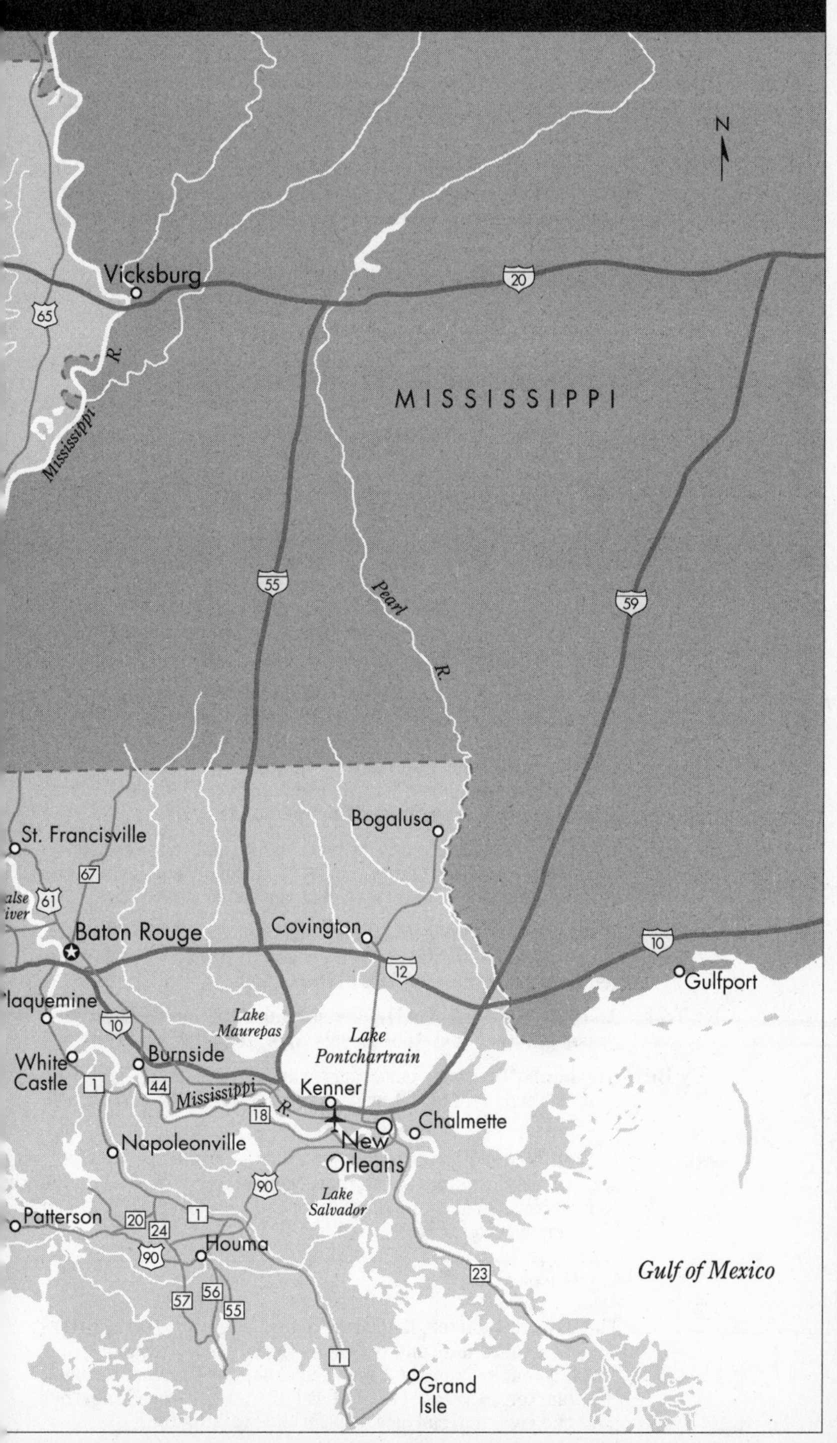
N
Vicksburg
20
65
Mississippi R.
MISSISSIPPI
55
Pearl R.
59
Bogalusa
St. Francisville
67
61
alse
iver
Covington
Baton Rouge
10
12
Gulfport
laquemine
10
Lake
Maurepas
Lake
Pontchartrain
White
Castle
Burnside
1
44
Mississippi R.
Kenner
18
Chalmette
New
Orleans
Napoleonville
90
Lake
Salvador
Patterson
20
24
1
90
Houma
23
Gulf of Mexico
57
56
55
1
Grand
Isle

canes, and yellow fever. Two cataclysmic fires in the late 18th century virtually leveled the town. The Old Ursuline Convent on Chartres Street is the only remaining original French Colonial structure. Survival was a struggle for the Creoles, and the sobriquet "The City That Care Forgot" stems from a determination not only to live life but to celebrate it, come what may.

Necessity may be the mother of invention, but it was the Father of Waters that forced Crescent City denizens to devise a new vocabulary for dealing with directions. The Mississippi River moves in mysterious waves, looping around the city and wreaking havoc with ordinary directions. New Orleanians, ever resourceful, refer instead to lakeside (toward Lake Pontchartrain), riverside (toward the Mississippi), upriver (also called uptown), and downriver (downtown).

Arriving and Departing

By Plane **New Orleans International Airport** (Moisant Field), located 15 miles west of New Orleans in Kenner, is served by American, Continental, Delta, Midway, Northwest, Royale, Southwest, TWA, United, and USAir. Foreign carriers serving the city include Aviateca, Lacsa, Sahsa, and Taca.

Between the Airport and Center City **Buses** operated by Louisiana Transit (tel. 504/737–9611) run every 22 minutes between the airport and Elk Place in the Central Business District (CBD). Hours of operation are 6 AM to 6:20 PM; the last bus leaves the airport at 5:40 PM. The $1.10 trip downtown takes about an hour.

Limousines of Rhodes Transportation (tel. 504/469–4555) leave the airport every 5–10 minutes, 24 hours a day, for the 20- to 30-minute trip into town. The limos, which are really small vans, drop passengers off at their hotels, so arrival time at your destination will depend upon the number of stops the van makes en route. The fare is $7 per person.

Taxi fare is $18 for up to three passengers, and $6 for each additional person. If you share a cab with three or four people, the driver may agree to charge each of you the $7 limo rate.

Driving from Kenner into New Orleans is via Airline Highway (U.S. 61) or I–10. Hertz, Avis, Budget, and other major car-rental agencies have outlets at the airport.

By Train **Amtrak** (800/USA–RAIL) trains pull into the CBD's Union Passenger Terminal (1001 Loyola Ave., tel. 504/528–1610).

By Bus **Greyhound/Trailways** buses arrive and depart from Union Passenger Terminal (1001 Loyola Ave., tel. 504/525–9371 or 800/237–8211).

By Car I–10 runs from Florida through New Orleans and on to California. I–55 is the north–south route, connecting with I–10 to the west of New Orleans; I–59 heads for the northeast. U.S. 61 and 90 also run through New Orleans.

Getting Around

The French Quarter, laid out in a perfect grid pattern, covers about a square mile and is best explored on foot. Should your feet fail you, look for the Vieux Carré shuttle that loops around the Quarter. Several of the CBD sights are clustered together near the river and can also be seen on a walking tour.

By Bus Buses require 60¢ exact change (except for the CBD shuttle, which is 30¢). Transfers are 5¢ extra. The CBD shuttle bus operates weekdays from 6:30 AM to 6 PM, and the Vieux Carré shuttle operates weekdays from 5 AM to 7:23 PM. The Regional Transit Authority (RTA) puts out a color-coded *RideGuide*, available free at the tourist welcome centers (*see* Tourist Information in Important Addresses and Numbers, *below*), and has a 24-hour information service (tel. 504/569–2700; for the hearing impaired, 504/569–2838). **Easy Rider,** a shuttle bus between the Riverwalk and the New Orleans Convention Center complex, charges 50¢ and connects with other bus routes.

By Streetcar The St. Charles Streetcar, New Orleans's moving Historic Landmark, clangs up St. Charles Avenue through the Garden District, past the Audubon Zoo and other Uptown sights. The streetcar can be boarded in the CBD at Canal and Carondelet Streets ($1). A round-trip sightseeing jaunt covers just over 13 miles and takes 90 minutes. The streetcar operates daily, every five minutes 7:30 AM to 6 PM, every 15–20 minutes 6 PM to midnight, and hourly midnight to 7 AM.

The Riverfront Streetcar rolls along the river between Esplanade Avenue and the Robin Street Wharf. It makes ten stops, five above and five below Canal St. The fare is $1, and it operates weekdays from 6 AM–midnight; weekends 8 AM–midnight.

By Taxi Taxi fares start at $1.25, adding 25¢ for each fifth of a mile or 40 seconds of waiting time.

By Ferry A free ferry crosses the Mississippi from the Canal Street Wharf to Algiers, leaving the pier every 25 minutes.

Important Addresses and Numbers

Tourist Information To plan your trip, write to **The Greater New Orleans Tourist and Convention Commission** (1520 Sugar Bowl Dr., New Orleans, LA 70112). The Tourist Commission staffs a desk near the customs desk at New Orleans International Airport, but its main outlet is the **New Orleans Welcome Center.** *529 St. Ann St. in French Quarter, tel. 504/566–5068. Open daily 9–5. Closed major holidays.*

Emergencies Dial 911 for **police** or **ambulance** in an emergency.

Doctor The following hospital emergency rooms are open all night: **Tulane Medical Center** (220 Lasalle St., tel. 504/588–5711), in the CBD near the French Quarter; **Touro Infirmary** (1401 Foucher St., tel. 504/897–8250), near the Garden District.

24-hour Pharmacy **Eckerd's** (3400 Canal St., tel. 504/488–6661).

Guided Tours

Orientation If you prefer a "known" in an unknown city, go in an air-conditioned, 45-passenger **Gray Line** bus (tel. 504/587–0861) for a two-hour tour of New Orleans's major sights. **Tours by Isabelle** (tel. 504/391–3544) uses air-conditioned, 14-passenger vans for a more personalized and multilingual three-hour tool around town. Both companies provide hotel pickup, and reservations can be made through your hotel.

Special-interest **Statistics for the Superdome** (tel. 504/587–3810) are staggering and you can learn all about the huge facility during daily tours. On the flatboats of **Wagner's Honey Island Swamp Tours** (tel.

504/641–1769), steered by a professional wetland ecologist, you can tour one of the country's best-preserved river swamps. **Tours by Isabelle** (tel. 504/391–3544) takes you to the bayous for a visit with a Cajun alligator hunter. **Acadian-Creole Tours** (tel. 504/524–1700 or 504/524–1800) travels to a famous old sugar plantation. **Classic Tours** (tel. 504/899–1862) is operated by two native Orleaneans who are in love with the city. Their chatty tours cover art, antiques, architecture, and history. **Le 'Ob's Tours** (tel. 504/288–3478) runs a daily black-heritage/city tour highlighting sites and history important to the African-American experience.

Exploring New Orleans

Numbers in the margin correspond to points of interest on the French Quarter and Central Business District map.

Tucked in between Canal Street, Esplanade Avenue, Rampart Street, and the Mississippi River, the Vieux Carré is a carefully preserved historic district. But the Quarter is also home to some 7,000 residents, some of the most famous of the French Creole restaurants, and many a jazz club. An eclectic crowd, which includes some of the world's best jazz musicians, ambles in and out of small two- and three-story frame, old-brick, and pastel-painted stucco buildings. Baskets of splashy subtropical plants dangle from the eaves of buildings with filigreed galleries, dollops of gingerbread, and dormer windows. Built flush with the *banquettes* (sidewalks), the houses, most of which date from the early to mid-19th century, front secluded courtyards awash with greenery and brilliant blossoms.

In the early 19th century, the American Sector was just upriver of the French Quarter. For that reason, street names change as you cross Canal Street from the French Quarter: Bourbon Street to Carondelet Street, Royal Street to St. Charles Avenue, and so on.

Nerve center of the nation's second-largest port and main parade route during Mardi Gras, the CBD cuts a wide swath between Uptown and Downtown, with Canal Street the official dividing line. Bordered by Canal Street, the river, Howard Avenue, and Loyola Avenue, the CBD has the city's newest high-tech convention hotels, along with ritzy new shopping malls, age-old department stores, foreign agencies, fast-food chains, monuments, and the monumental Superdome.

Nestled in between St. Charles Avenue, Louisiana Avenue, Jackson Avenue, and Magazine Street, the Garden District is aptly named. The Americans who built their estates upriver surrounded their homes with lavish lawns, forgoing the Creoles' preference for secluded courtyards. Many of the elegant Garden District homes were built during New Orleans's Golden Age, from 1830 until the Civil War. Magazine Street is heaven on earth for shoppers. Joggers, golfers, tennis buffs, and horseback riders head for Audubon Park, and animal lovers can get close to many different species at the Audubon Zoo.

The French Quarter Make your first stop the **New Orleans Welcome Center** (529 St. Ann St.), for free maps, brochures, and friendly advice.

1 2 The **Welcome Center** is in the heart of **Jackson Square,** near a large equestrian statue of General Andrew Jackson, for whom the square is named. Jackson Square was known as Place

d'Armes to the Creoles; it was renamed in the mid-19th century for the man who defeated the British in the Battle of New Orleans. Place d'Armes was the center of all Colonial life, home to parading militia, religious ceremonies, social gatherings, food vendors, entertainers, and pirates. The square remains a social hub today. Pirate attire is not uncommon in the colorful crowd that flocks to the square. The only thing missing is the militia.

3 **St. Louis Cathedral,** soaring above the earthly activity taking place right in its front yard, is a quiet reminder of the spiritual life of New Orleans citizens. The present church dates from 1794, and it was restored in 1849. Tours are conducted daily except during services.

Alongside the church are **Pirate's Alley** and **Père Antoine's Alley.** Those cracked-flagstone passageways seem redolent of infamous plots and pirate intrigue—but, alas, the streets were laid long after Jean Lafitte and his Baratarian band had vanished. William Faulkner wrote his first novel, *A Soldier's Pay*, while living at **624 Pirate's Alley.**

4 The church is flanked by two buildings of the **Louisiana State Museum.** As you face the church, the **Cabildo** is on the left, the **Presbytere** on the right. Transfer papers for the Louisiana Purchase of 1803 were signed on the second floor of the Cabildo. It now holds historic documents, works of art, and artifacts pertinent to the region, including a death mask of Napoleon, who was a hero for many a New Orleanian. A four-alarm fire in 1988 damaged the roof and top floor of the Cabildo. The structure is expected to be renovated entirely by Labor Day 1993.

The Presbytere was built as a home for priests of the church, but was never used for this purpose. Like the Cabildo, it is also a museum, with changing exhibits. The odd-shaped structure in the arcade of the Presbytere is a Confederate submarine. Hours and admission charges for the Cabildo and Presbytere are the same. *Jackson Sq., tel. 504/568–6968. Admission: $3 adults; $1.50 students and senior citizens (children under 12 free). Open Tues.–Sun. 10–5. Closed legal holidays.*

You can see what life was like for upscale 19th-century Creole apartment dwellers on a guided tour in the **1850s House.** Located in the lower Pontalba Buildings (lower because it's on the downriver side of the square), the building contains period furnishings, antique dolls, and evidence of cushy Creole living. It, too, is part of the Louisiana State Museum complex. *523 St. Ann St., Jackson Sq., tel. 504/524–9118. Admission: $3 adults, $1.50 students and senior citizens (children under 12 free). Open Tues.–Sun. 10–5. Closed legal holidays.*

The **Pontalba Buildings** that line Jackson Square on St. Ann and St. Peter streets are among the oldest apartment houses in the country. Built between 1849 and 1851, they were constructed under the supervision of the baroness Micaela Pontalba, who occasionally lent the laborers a helping hand.

The promenade of **Washington Artillery Park,** across Decatur Street, affords a splendid perspective of the square on one side and Old Man River rolling along on the other. On the **Moon Walk** promenade, across the tracks from the park, you can sit on a bench or stroll down the steps to the water's edge.

The French Quarter and Central Business District

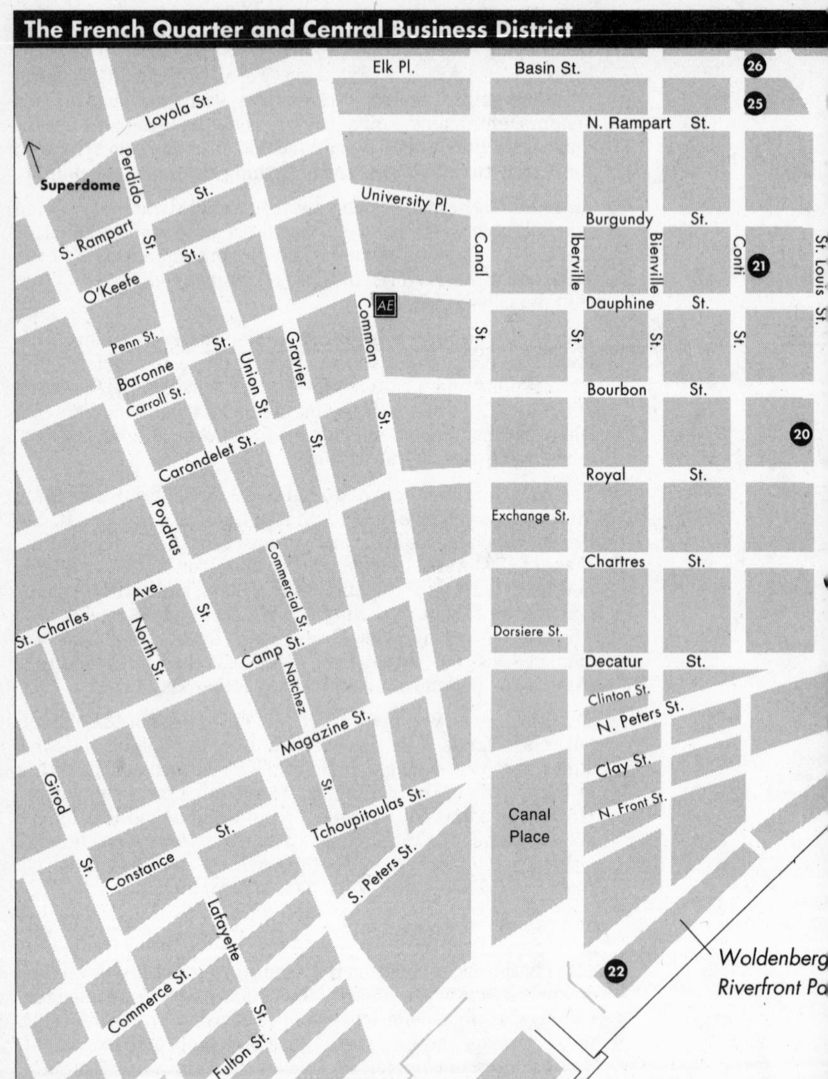

Aquarium of the Americas, **22**
Beauregard-Keyes House, **8**
Café du Monde, **5**
Cornstalk Fence, **11**
First Skyscraper, **15**
Gallier House, **9**
Hermann-Grima House, **20**
Historic New Orleans Collection, **17**
Jackson Square, **2**
LaBranche House, **14**
Lafitte's Blacksmith Shop, **10**
Louis Armstrong Park, **23**
Louisiana State Museum, **4**
Madame John's Legacy, **13**
Musée Conti, **21**
Napoleon House, **19**
New Orleans Pharmacy Museum, **18**
Old Ursuline Convent, **7**
Old U.S. Mint, **6**
Our Lady of Guadalupe, **25**
Preservation Hall, **16**
St. Louis Cathedral, **3**
St. Louis Cemetery No. 1, **26**
Theatre for the Performing Arts, **24**
Voodoo Museum, **12**
Welcome Center, **1**

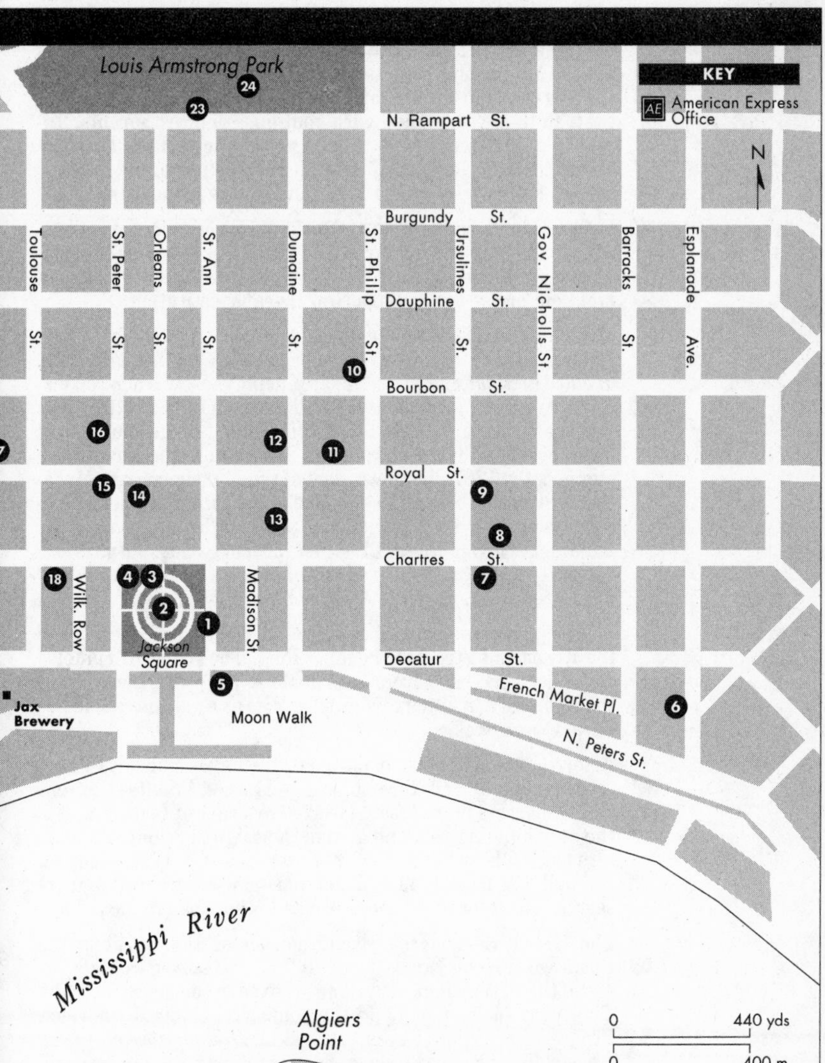

Louis Armstrong Park
KEY
American Express Office
N
N. Rampart St.
Burgundy St.
Dauphine St.
Bourbon St.
Royal St.
Chartres St.
Decatur St.
French Market Pl.
N. Peters St.
Toulouse St.
St. Peter St.
Orleans St.
St. Ann St.
Dumaine St.
St. Philip St.
Ursulines St.
Gov. Nicholls St.
Barracks St.
Esplanade Ave.
Wilk. Row
Madison St.
Jackson Square
Jax Brewery
Moon Walk
Mississippi River
Algiers Point
0
440 yds
0
400 m

Washington Artillery Park is anchored on the upriver side by the **Jackson Brewery and Millhouse,** and downriver by the **French Market.** Jax Beer used to be brewed in the brewery, and the market is on the site of a late-17th-century Indian trading post. Both are now filled with boutiques and restaurants. Toward Canal Street on Decatur Street is the Jackson Brewery Corporation's latest addition, **The Marketplace,** on Decatur Street, home of yet more restaurants and retail outlets.

5 **Café du Monde** in the French Market, a 24-hour haven for café au lait and *beignets* (square, puffy, holeless doughnuts sprinkled with powdered sugar), is a traditional last stop after a night out on the town, and a New Orleans institution.

Make a right and continue down Decatur Street to Esplanade Avenue. *This area on the fringe of the Quarter should be avoided at night,* but you'll be safe during the day when you vis-
6 it the Jazz and Mardi Gras Exhibits in the **Old U.S. Mint.** This was the first branch of the U.S. Mint, and it turned out money hand over fist from 1838 until Something (the Civil War) stopped it in 1861. It's now a part of the Louisiana State Museum. **A Streetcar Named Desire,** one of the cars from the old Desire line, is in mint condition and on display behind the building. *400 Esplanade Ave., tel. 504/568–6968. Admission: $3 adults; $1.50 students and senior citizens, children under 12 free. Open Tues.–Fri. 10–5. Closed major holidays.*

Speaking of streetcars, the upriver trip is now a breeze since the Riverfront Streetcar began rolling. The streetcar rumbles right along the river from Esplanade Avenue all the way up to the Robin Street Wharf, where the *Mississippi Queen* and the *Delta Queen* dock.

After viewing the mint, make a left; turning left again at Char-
7 tres Street and walk three blocks to **The Old Ursuline Convent** (1114 Chartres St.). Erected in 1749 by order of Louis XV, it is the only building remaining from the original colony. The Sisters of Ursula, who arrived in New Orleans in 1727, occupied the building from 1749 to 1824. It is now an archival and research center for the archdiocese and is not open to the public.

The Greek Revival raised cottage across the street is the
8 **Beauregard-Keyes House.** General P.G.T. Beauregard, who ordered the first shot at Fort Sumter, lived in the house after the Civil War. In the mid-1940s the house was bought by novelist Frances Parkinson Keyes (author of *Dinner at Antoine's*), whose office was in the slave quarters. Costumed docents will tell you all about the dwelling and its dwellers. *1113 Chartres St., tel. 504/523–7257. Admission: $4 adults, $3 senior citizens and students, $1.50 children under 12. Open Mon.–Sat. 10–3. Closed major holidays.*

At the corner turn right onto Ursulines Street and walk one
9 block to Royal Street, where you'll find the **Gallier House.** Built about 1857 by famed architect James Gallier, Jr., this is one of the best-researched house museums in the city. The Galliers were Irish, but this is a fine example of how well-heeled Creoles lived. *1118 Royal St., tel. 504/523–6722. Admission: $4 adults; $3 senior citizens, AAA members, and students; $2.50 children 6–12. Tours Mon.–Sat. 10–4:30, Sun. 12:30–4:30. Closed major holidays.*

Back on Ursulines Street, turn right and walk one block to Bourbon Street, turn left, and go one more block. The tattered
10 cottage is **Lafitte's Blacksmith Shop** (941 Bourbon St.). The house dates to 1772, and it is typical of houses built by the earliest settlers. According to a cherished legend, the cottage was once a front for freebooter Jean Lafitte's smuggling and slave trade. Today it's a neighborhood bar, and for a long time it has been a favorite haunt of artists and writers, the well-known and the never-known (*see* Nightlife, *below*).

Go down St. Philip Street one block and turn right for a look at
11 the **Cornstalk Fence** (915 Royal St.). Morning glories and ears of corn are intricately intertwined in the cast-iron fence.

At the corner of Royal Street turn right onto Dumaine Street.
12 The **Voodoo Museum** is an "only in New Orleans" phenomenon and either spooky or campy (or both), depending upon what spirits move you. Remembrances of voodoo queen Marie Laveau are prominently displayed, along with altars, artifacts, and everything you need for a voodoo to-do. *724 Dumaine St., tel. 504/523–7685. Admission: $5 adults, $4 students and senior citizens; $3 children. Open daily 10–7.*

As you leave the museum, turn right and walk one block on
13 Dumaine Street. **Madame John's Legacy** (632 Dumaine St.) is so named for a character in the short story " 'Tite Poulette,' " by 19th-century New Orleans writer George Washington Cable. The West Indies–style house was built in 1788 on the site of the birthplace of Renato Beluche, a Lafitte lieutenant who helped Andrew Jackson in the Battle of New Orleans. Part of the Louisiana State Museum (tel. 504/568–6968), the house is open sporadically, depending upon the state's financial situation.

Go back to Royal Street, turn left and walk two blocks past the quiet, green **Cathedral Garden,** which is at the rear of St. Louis Cathedral. One block more will bring you to St. Peter Street and the most-photographed building in the city. The
14 **LaBranche House** (700 Royal St.), dating from about 1840, wraps around the corner of Royal Street and runs halfway down St. Peter Street. Its filigreed double galleries are cast iron with an oak-leaf-and-acorn motif.

15 Directly across the street is the **First Skyscraper** (640 St. Peter St.). Built between 1795 and 1811, it was a three-story high rise; rumor has it that the fourth floor was added later so that it might retain its towering title. Behind weathered walls is
16 **Preservation Hall** (726 St. Peter St.), home of the world's best traditional and Dixieland jazz (*see* Nightlife, *below*).

17 Continue on Royal Street one block to the **Historic New Orleans Collection.** The **Merieult House** was one of the few buildings to survive the fire of 1794 and now contains an extensive collection of documents and research materials pertaining to the city. Exhibits in the **Williams Gallery** on the ground floor can be seen for free, and for a nominal fee you can take a guided tour and hear the legends of the historic house. *533 Royal St., tel. 504/523–4662. Admission: $2. Open Tues.–Sat. 10–5. Closed major holidays.*

Turn left and then right onto Toulouse Street, walk toward the
18 river, and turn right onto Chartres Street. The **New Orleans Pharmacy Museum** is a musty old place where Louis Dufilho had his pharmacy in 1823. It's full of ancient and mysterious

medicinal items, and there is an Italian marble fountain used by 19th-century soda jerks. *514 Chartres St., tel. 504/524–9077. Admission: $1. Open Tues.–Sun. 10–5. Closed Mon.*

19 At the corner of Chartres and St. Louis streets is the **Napoleon House** (500 Chartres St.), a long-time favorite haunt of artists and writers. The bar fairly oozes atmosphere from every splinter, with peeling sepia walls, Napoleonic memorabilia, and taped classical music to back up your libation. It is entirely possible—and this is a proven fact—to laze away an entire afternoon sitting by an open door and watch rain splatter down on the pavement.

If you can wrench yourself away, turn right at the corner and
walk along St. Louis Street past Antoine's Restaurant and go
20 one more block to the **Hermann-Grima House.** Guides will steer
you through the American-style town house, built in 1831, and on winter Thursdays you can get a taste of Creole during cooking demonstrations. *820 St. Louis St., tel. 504/525–5661. Admission: $4 adults, $3 senior citizens and students, children under 8 free. Open Mon.–Sat. 10–4. Last tour at 3:30. Closed major holidays.*

Turn left as you leave the house, left again on Dauphine Street,
21 and then right on Conti Street to reach the **Musée Conti Wax
Museum.** The museum waxes lifelike on Louisiana legends, among them Andrew Jackson, Jean Lafitte, Marie Laveau, and former governor Edwin Edwards. *917 Conti St., tel. 504/525–2605. Admission: $5.70 adults, $3.42 children 6–12. Open daily 10–5. Closed Christmas and Mardi Gras.*

Foot of Canal At the end of Canal Street is the **Aquarium of the Americas,**
22 whose spectacular design lets viewers feel part of the watery
world by offering close-up encounters with the 7,000 aquatic creatures in 60 separate displays in four major environments. The beautifully landscaped 16-acre **Woldenberg Riverfront Park** around the aquarium is a tranquil spot with an excellent view of the river. *Foot of Canal St., tel. 504/861–2538. Admission: $8 adults, $6.25 senior citizens, $4.25 children 3–12. Open daily except Christmas, 9:30–5.*

Time Out Nearby **Arnaud's Grill** has mosaic-tile floors, ceiling fans, and a player piano as the backdrop for its mixed drinks. *813 Bienville St., tel. 504/523–5433. Jacket required. Reservations required. AE, DC, MC, V.*

We'll now take a look at some of the attractions on unattractive, run-down Rampart Street, but we'll do so with a warning: The section of the street between St. Peter and Canal streets is relatively safe during daylight hours, but *should be avoided at night. Avoid the section between St. Peter Street and Esplanade Avenue day* and *night.*

At St. Ann Street, a large arch hovers over the entrance to
23 **Louis Armstrong Park,** which is named for native son Louis
"Satchmo" Armstrong. Inside the park are the **Municipal Audi-
24 torium** and the **Theatre for the Performing Arts.** The auditorium
is on the site of Congo Square, scene of 18th- and 19th-century slave gatherings. Congo Square is believed to have been the birthplace of jazz, with the voodoo Afro-Caribbean rhythms of the slaves' songs and chants influencing the new music. Large crowds attend the opera and ballet at the theater, and many a

Carnival ball is still held at the auditorium. *Do not venture into the park alone, even in the daytime.*

25 **Our Lady of Guadalupe Catholic Church** (411 N. Rampart St.) was dedicated in 1827, when it was known as the Mortuary Chapel. It was originally used only for funerals, usually for victims of yellow fever and cholera. This church is home to one of the city's legends, St. Expedite. The story is that a statue was delivered to the church in a crate marked simply "Expedite." It was expeditiously mounted, and it can be seen to the right as you enter the church.

26 Just behind the church on Basin Street is **St. Louis Cemetery No. 1,** between St. Louis and Conti streets. This is New Orleans's oldest City of the Dead, so called because the stark white aboveground tombs resemble tiny houses. The cemetery dates from 1789, and well-worn paths lead through a maze of tombs and mausoleums, many with the same ornate grilles and ironwork as the houses where live folks live. Many a well-known early New Orleanian is buried here, and voodoo doings mark the tomb believed to be that of Marie Laveau. (Some say she is buried in St. Louis Cemetery No. 2.) *Warning: The cemetery is adjacent to a crime-ridden housing project, and you should not visit it alone. Go on a group tour, which can be arranged through an agency (see* Guided Tours, *above).*

Audubon Park and Zoo

Rolled out across St. Charles Avenue from Tulane and Loyola universities is **Audubon Park and Zoo.** You can board the **St. Charles Streetcar** at Poydras Street and St. Charles Avenue to tool off Uptown. The Friends of the Zoo operate a free shuttle that boards in front of Tulane every 15 to 20 minutes for a ride to the zoo, which lies on the 58 acres of the park nearest the river. It is entirely possible to while away an entire day exploring Audubon Zoo. A wooden walkway strings through the zoo, and a miniature train rings around a part of it. More than 1,500 animals roam free in natural habitats, such as the **Australian exhibit,** where kangaroos hop-nob with wallabies, and the **Louisiana Swamp exhibit,** where alligators bask on the bayou. A special treat is the feeding of the sea lions, which is marked by a great deal of flapping about and barking. The **Wisner Children's Village** has a petting zoo and elephant and camel rides. *Tel. 504/861–2537. Admission: $7 adults, $3.25 senior citizens and children 2–12. Open weekdays 9:30–5; weekends (winter) 9:30–5, during daylight savings time 9:30–6. Closed major holidays.*

The 400-acre Audubon Park, with live oaks and lush tropical plants, was once part of the plantation of Etienne de Bore and his son-in-law Pierre Foucher. In 1795, de Bore figured out how to granulate sugar for commercial purposes, thereby revolutionizing the sugar industry.

In addition to the 18-hole golf course, there is a two-mile jogging track with 18 exercise stations along the way, a **stable** that offers guided trail rides, and 10 tennis courts. The park is also eminently suitable for lolling about under a tree and doing nothing. Note, however, that you should stay *out* of the park after dark.

Around Town

City Park Avenue, Bayou St. John, Robert E. Lee Boulevard, and Orleans Avenue embrace the 1,500 luxuriant acres of **City Park,** which can be reached via the Esplanade or the City Park bus. You can spend a great deal of time simply admiring the lagoons and majestic live oaks, whose gnarled branches bow and scrape to Mother Earth, but there is plenty to keep you busy if you are not an idler. There are four 18-hole golf courses, a double-deck driving range, 39 lighted courts in the Wisner Tennis Center, Botanical Gardens, baseball diamonds, and stables. At the casino on Dreyfous Avenue you can rent **bikes, boats,** and **canoes**—or just have a bite to eat—and at the amusement park, you can ride the turn-of-the-century carousel and miniature train. **Storyland** offers puppet shows, talking storybooks, storybook exhibits, and storytelling—hence its name. Unfortunately, it is no fairy tale that City Park is *not safe at night.*

The **New Orleans Museum of Art** (NOMA), in the park, displays from its collections Italian paintings from the 13th to 18th centuries, 20th-century European and American paintings and sculptures, Chinese jades, and the Imperial Treasures by Peter Carl Fabergé. *Lelong Ave., City Park, tel. 504/488-2631. Open Tues.–Sun. 10–5:30. Admission: $4 adults, $2 senior citizens and children 3–17; admission free on Thurs. to Louisiana residents. Closed major holidays.*

To reach the **Pitot House** from NOMA, walk along Lelong Avenue, cross over the Bayou St. John Bridge, and make a right turn on Moss Street. Continue following Moss Street as it winds alongside the bayou, and look for the house on your left. The West Indies–style house was built in the late 18th century and bought in 1810 by New Orleans mayor James Pitot. It is furnished with Louisiana and other American 19th-century antiques. *1440 Moss St., tel. 504/482-0312. Admission: $3 adults, $1 children under 12. Open Wed.–Sat. 10–3, last tour 2:15. Sometimes closed Sat.; call ahead. Closed major holidays.*

Longue Vue House & Gardens sits right on the border between Orleans and Jefferson parishes, about a $5 cab ride from the Quarter. To describe this mansion, the word "opulent" immediately comes to mind. The house is furnished with elegant antiques and sits on eight acres of landscaped gardens. Yes, opulent is the word. *7 Bamboo Rd., tel. 504/ 488-5488. Admission: $6 adults, $3 students and children. Open Mon.–Sat. 10–4:30, Sun. 1–5. Closed major holidays. Last tour begins 3:45.*

New Orleans for Free

A free **ferry** runs from the foot of Canal Street across the Mississippi to Algiers Point. A round-trip excursion takes about 25 minutes.

New Orleans **street musicians** perform regularly in Jackson Square and on Bourbon, Royal, and Chartres streets. There are free **concerts** on weekends in Dutch Alley in the French Market. You can also lean against a lamppost on Bourbon Street and listen to the music that pours out of jazz clubs.

Free **tours** of the French Quarter and the Garden District (although you must hand over $1 for the streetcar fare for the last) are given by park rangers. Reservations are necessary for the cemetery and Garden District tours. *Walks begin at the Folklife & Visitor Center, 916–18 N. Peters St., in the French Market, tel. 504/589-2636.*

What to See and Do with Children

Aquarium of the Americas (*see* Foot of Canal in Exploring, *above*).
Audubon Zoo (*see* Audubon Park and Zoo in Exploring, *above*).
City Park (*see* Around Town in Exploring, *above*).
Jackson Square (*see* The French Quarter in Exploring, *above*).
Le Petit Théâtre du Vieux Carré (616 St. Peter St., tel. 504/522-2081). The Children's Corner often puts on plays for the little ones.
Louisiana Nature and Science Center (1100 Lake Forest Blvd., tel. 504/246-9381).
Musée Conti Wax Museum (*see* the French Quarter section in Exploring, *above*).
Ripley's Believe It or Not Museum. Exhibits of oddities from Robert Ripley's collections. *501 Bourbon St., tel. 504/529-5131. Admission: $5 plus tax adults, $3 plus tax children 7–12, 6 and under free. Open daily 10 AM–midnight.*
Riverboat Rides. Steamboat and ferry rides on the Mississippi hold a particular fascination for children. Aside from the view of the city and the water lapping at the sides of the boats, kids love to watch the big sternwheel turning. The mighty *Natchez* (tel. 504/586-8777), with its off-key steam calliope blasting out tunes, and the *Cotton Blossom* (tel. 504/586-8777), with its hour-long trip upriver to the Audubon Zoo, are great fun.
St. Charles Streetcar (*see* Getting Around, *above*).
Roman Candy Man. Look for the old-fashioned horse-drawn cart of the candy man just outside the zoo.
Parades and Festivals (*see* Festivals and Seasonal Events in Before You Go, Chapter 1).

Off the Beaten Track

Ever get nostalgic for the old-fashioned drugstore, which is not to be confused with today's discount chains? Well, there's a tiny one in New Orleans. At **Schweickhardt Drugs,** you can shop for sundries on one side and have a sundae at the soda fountain on the other. A big sign in the window proclaims the fame of its Nectar Soda, which is indeed quite well-known to locals. (It's $1.65 at the counter, $1.91 to go.) Sandwiches and plate lunches are also served at the lunch counter. The drugstore is easily reached, because it's right on the streetcar line. *1438 S. Carrollton Ave., tel. 504/866-1833. Open daily 8–6:30.*

Shopping

Pralines, chicory coffee, Mardi Gras masks, nostalgia clothing, and jazz records are usually hot tickets for tourists (as well as for locals). The packaging of New Orleans food to go is a growing trend.

Shopping Districts New Orleans shops string along the Mississippi all the way from the French Quarter to Riverbend (at the Uptown bend in the river) and beyond. **The French Quarter** is the place to search for antiques shops, art galleries, designer boutiques, bookstores, and all sorts of shops in all sorts of edifices. Among **Canal Place**'s (333 Canal St.) lofty tenants you'll find Saks Fifth Avenue, Laura Ashley, Gucci, Charles Jourdan, and Benetton. **Riverwalk** (1 Poydras St.) is a long, tunnellike marketplace brightened by over 200 splashy shops, restaurants, food courts, and huge windows overlooking the Mississippi. The tony **New Orleans Centre,** between The Hyatt Regency Hotel and the Superdome on Poydras St., boasts more than 100 occupants, including Macy's and Lord & Taylor. Along six miles of **Magazine Street** are Victorian houses and small cottages filled with antiques and collectibles. Stop at the **New Orleans Welcome Center** for a copy of the shopper's guide published by the Magazine Street Merchants Association. Turn-of-the-century Creole cottages cradle everything from toy shops to designer boutiques and delis in the **Riverbend** (Maple St. and Carrollton Ave.). At **Uptown Square** (200 Broadway), boutiques and restaurants surround—guess what?—a square. Macy's and Mervyn's are among the 155 shops in Metairie's glittering three-level **Esplanade Mall** (1401 W. Esplanade Ave.).

Department Stores **Woolworth's** (737 Canal St., tel. 504/522–6426) has budget shopping to a New Orleans beat.

Specialty Stores

Antiques **As You Like It** (3025 Magazine St., tel. 504/897–6915) carries obsolete patterns in silver and silverplate.

Shoulder to shoulder along **Royal Street** are some of the finest—and oldest—antiques stores in New Orleans. Among them are: **French Antique Shop** (225 Royal St., tel. 504/524–9861); **Manheim Galleries** (403–409 Royal St., tel. 504/568–1901); **Moss Antiques** (411 Royal St., tel. 504/522–3981); **M.S. Rau, Inc.** (630 Royal St., tel. 504/523–5660); **Royal Antiques** (307–309 Royal St., tel. 504/524–7033); and **Waldhorn Company** (343 Royal St., tel. 504/581–6379).

Art The French Quarter is known for its many art galleries, most of which are located on Royal Street: **Bergen Galleries** (730 Royal St., tel. 504/523–7882) offers posters and collectibles by local artists; **The Black Art Collection** (738 Royal St., tel. 504/529–3080) displays and sells works by local and national black artists; **Dyansen Gallery** (433 Royal St., tel. 504/523–2902) features the work of modern and contemporary artists; **Kurt E. Schon, Ltd.,** (523 Royal St., tel. 504/523–5902) has classic paintings from the 17th through the 20th centuries; **Merrill B. Domas American Indian Art** (824 Chartres St., tel. 504/586–0479) offers antique and contemporary art and crafts by Native American artists; **Southern Expressions** (521 St. Anne St. at Jackson Sq., tel. 504/525–4530) shows the work of regional artists.

Flea Market Jazz is within earshot and "junque" at your fingertips, at the **French Market Flea Market** on weekends from 7 to 7.

Food to Go **Bayou To Go** (New Orleans International Airport, Concourse C, tel 504/468–8040) has a full line of Louisiana food products, including fresh, frozen, and cooked seafood packed to check or carry on the plane.

Jazz Records You'll find the hard-to-find vintage stuff at **Record Ron's** (1129 Decatur St. and 407 Decatur St., tel. 504/524–9444).

Masks For exotic handmade masks to decorate your face or your wall, try **Rumors** (513 Royal St., tel. 504/525–0292).

Pralines For the best pralines in town, try **Old Town Praline Shop** (627 Royal St., tel. 504/525–1413).

Participant Sports

Biking In the French Quarter, Bourbon and Royal streets are closed to all but pedalers and pedestrians. Rentals are available at **Bicycle Michael's** (618 Frenchmen St., tel. 504/945–9505; $3.50 hour, $12.50 day).

Golf There are four 18-hole golf courses in City Park, plus a double-decker driving range. You can rent clubs, handcarts, and electric carts at the **City Park** (1040 Filmore Dr., tel. 504/483–9396). To rent clubs and tee off on Audubon Park's luscious links, check into **Audubon Park's Clubhouse** (473 Walnut St., tel. 504/861–9511). The **Joe Bartholomew Municipal Golf Course** (6514 Congress Dr., tel. 504/288–0928) has an 18-hole course in Pontchartrain Park.

Tennis There are 39 courts in the **City Park Wisner Tennis Center** (1 Dreyfous Ave. in City Park, tel. 504/483–9383). **Audubon Park** (tel. 504/895–1042) has 10 courts near Tchoupitoulas Street.

Spectator Sports

Baseball The **Tulane Green Wave** plays home games at the school's St. Charles Avenue campus (tel. 504/861–3661). The **University of New Orleans Privateers** take on foes at the Lakefront (tel. 504/286–7240).

Basketball The **Sugar Bowl Basketball Classic** is played in the Superdome the week preceding the annual football classic.

Football The **New Orleans Saints** play NFL games in the Superdome (tel. 504/522–2600). Home games of **Tulane University** are also played in the Dome (tel. 504/861–3661). The annual **Sugar Bowl Football Classic** (tel. 504/525–8573) is played in the Dome on New Year's Day, and in late November the **Bayou Classic** (tel. 504/587–3663) pits Southern University against Grambling University.

Dining

By Lisa LeBlanc-Berry

The "Urbane Gourmet" food critic for Gambit *newspaper, Lisa LeBlanc-Berry is currently the editor of* Where Magazine *in New Orleans.*

New Orleans usually means excellent dining. The Big Easy is recognized almost as much for hot and spicy culinary delights as it is for hot and steamy jazz. Louisiana styles of cooking are becoming increasingly popular worldwide—but what is a fad elsewhere is a tradition here.

As a general rule, expect to tip from 15% to 20%. Most establishments do not automatically add a service charge.

Apart from K-Paul's and Galatoire's, where people stand in line to be served on a first-come basis, you are strongly advised to make reservations and to book well in advance for weekends, particularly during holiday periods or conventions.

Most of the more pricey restaurants adhere to a moderate dress code—jackets for men, and in some places, a tie. New Orleans is a conservative city; dining out is an honored ritual, and people are expected to dress the part. A man in faded jeans and sports coat may not be turned away, but he may not feel terribly comfortable either. Credit cards are accepted in most, but not all, dining establishments; it's wise to check in advance.

Lunch hours are 11:30 AM to 2:30 PM. Dinner is almost always served from 6 to 10 PM, although some restaurants will close an hour earlier or later depending on volume of business and season.

The following terms will appear frequently throughout this section:

andouille (an-*dooey*)—Cajun sausage made with pork blade meat, onion, smoked flavorings, and garlic.
boudin (boo-*dan*)—hot, spicy pork with onions, rice, and herbs stuffed in sausage casing.
bananas Foster—a dessert of bananas sautéed with butter, brown sugar, and cinnamon, flambéed in white rum and banana liqueur, and served on ice cream.
barbecue shrimp—large shrimp baked in the shell, covered with butter, rosemary, herbs, and spices. They are not barbecued at all.
court bouillon (coo–bee–*yon*)—a thick, hearty soup made with a roux, vegetables, and fish, and served over rice.
crawfish—also known as "mud-bugs," because they live in the mud of freshwater streams. They resemble miniature lobsters and are served in a great variety of ways.
étouffée (ay-too-*fay*)—crawfish étouffée is made with a butter and flour roux of celery and onion, then cooked for a short period of time and served over rice. Shrimp étouffée is heartier, made with an oil and flour roux or tomato paste, celery, onion, bell pepper, tomatoes, and chicken stock, cooked for approximately an hour and served over rice.
filé (fee-*lay*)—ground sassafras, used to season gumbo and many other Creole specialties.
grillades (gree-*yads*)—bite-size pieces of veal rounds or beef chuck, braised in red wine, beef stock, garlic, herbs, and seasoning, served for brunch with grits and with rice for dinner.
gumbo—a hearty soup prepared in a variety of combinations (okra gumbo, shrimp gumbo, chicken gumbo, to name a few).
jambalaya (jum-bo-*lie*-yah)—a spicy rice dish cooked with stock and chopped seasoning, and made with any number of ingredients including sausage, shrimp, ham, and chicken.
muffuletta—a large, round loaf of bread filled with cheese, ham, and salami smothered in a heavy, garlicky olive salad.
rémoulade—a cold dressing that accompanies shrimp (sometimes crabmeat) over shredded lettuce, made of mayonnaise and Creole mustard, oil and vinegar, horseradish, paprika, celery, and green onion.
praline (praw-*leen*)—candy patty most commonly made from sugar, water or butter, and pecans. There are many different flavors and kinds.

New Orleans is renowned for *Creole* cuisine. A Creole, by definition, is a person of French or Spanish ancestry born in the New World. However, Creole is also a word of elastic implications, and in culinary terms, Creole refers to a distinctive cuisine indigenous to New Orleans that has its roots in European dishes, enhanced by the liberal usage of local seasonings such as *filé*. The French influence is also strong, but the essence of Creole is in sauces, herbs, and the prominent use of seafood.

In recent years the term *Nouvelle Creole* has been popularized by local restaurateurs. Instead of gumbo or jambalaya, a nouvelle menu might include hickory-grilled items, seafood served with pasta, or smoked meats and fish. There has also been a strong Italian influence in Creole cuisine in the last decade, creating yet another marriage of styles.

The initial restaurant listings here are divided into five Creole categories: *Classic Creole*, restaurants devoted to traditional Louisiana cuisine with minimal French overtones; *French Creole*, indicating a more expansive Continental accent; *Italian Creole*, Creole with an Italian flair; *Soul Creole*, black cuisine of Creole origin; and *Creole-Inspired*, meaning the newer breed of cooking styles that incorporate Nouvelle Creole dishes, new American cooking, and classic Creole. Please note that the above categories often overlap; it is not unusual to find a blend of varying Creole cuisines on any given menu.

Cajun cuisine was brought from Nova Scotia to the bayou country by the Acadians over 250 years ago. Cajun cooks generally use less expensive ingredients than their Creole counterparts, and they are heavy-handed on the herbs and spices.

Cajun cuisine is rarely served in its purest form in New Orleans; rather it is often blended with Creole to create what's known as "New Orleans–style" cooking. There is a difference, though, between the two: Creole is distinguished by its rich and heavy sauces; Cajun, by its tendency to be spicy and hot.

The most highly recommended restaurants in each price category are indicated by a star ★.

Category	Cost*
Very Expensive	over $35
Expensive	$25–$35
Moderate	$15–$25
Inexpensive	under $15

**per person without tax (9% in New Orleans), service, or drinks*

Louisiana Cuisine
Cajun-inspired

K-Paul's Louisiana Kitchen. National celebrity chef Paul Prudhomme made blackened redfish so famous that a fishing ban was levied and restaurateurs can no longer acquire the fish. K-Paul's now serves blackened yellowfin tuna. Strangers often must share tables, and the "no reservations" policy makes for long lines outside. But K-Paul's is a shrine to the popular concept of New Orleans Cajun cooking. *416 Chartres St., French Quarter, tel. 504/942–7500. Dress: informal. No reservations. AE. Closed Sat. and Sun. Expensive.*

Dooky Chase's. The roots of many of the home-style dishes at Dooky Chase's go back more than a century. The food, prepared with a technique handed down by generations of local cooks, is served in a warm and elegantly proportioned dining room hung with artworks by local black artists. Crab soup and Creole gumbo are dependable starters. Good meat entrées include the buttery pannéed veal and pork chops sautéed with onions. The sausage jambalaya, stewed okra, and sweet potatoes are as delicious as they are definitive. Homey desserts include bread pudding and a decent apple pie. Late lunch or early dinner at Dooky's on Sunday afternoons has become a tradition for neighborhood families, and the weekday luncheon buffets are a bargain. *2301 Orleans Ave., Treme, tel. 504/821–2294. Reservations advised. Dress: casual. AE, MC, V. Moderate.*

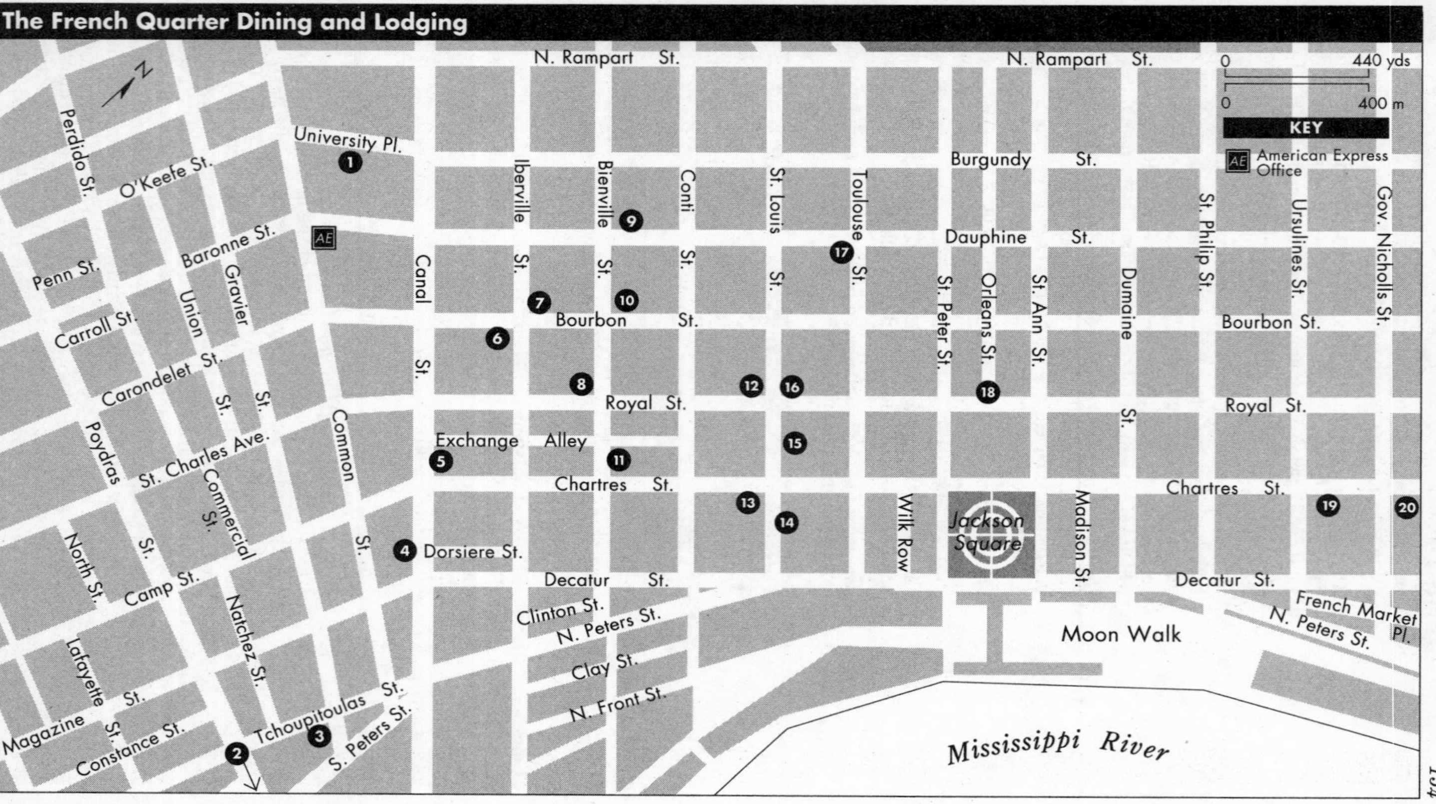
The French Quarter Dining and Lodging
KEY
AE American Express Office
0 440 yds
0 400 m
N
N. Rampart St.
Burgundy St.
Dauphine St.
Bourbon St.
Royal St.
Exchange Alley
Chartres St.
Decatur St.
Dorsiere St.
Clinton St.
N. Peters St.
Clay St.
N. Front St.
Gov. Nicholls St.
Ursulines St.
St. Philip St.
Dumaine St.
St. Ann St.
Orleans St.
St. Peter St.
Toulouse St.
St. Louis St.
Conti St.
Bienville St.
Iberville St.
Canal St.
Madison St.
Wilk Row
Jackson Square
Moon Walk
French Market Pl.
Mississippi River
University Pl.
Common St.
Perdido St.
O'Keefe St.
Baronne St.
Gravier St.
Union St.
Penn St.
Carroll St.
Carondelet St.
St. Charles Ave.
Poydras St.
Commercial St.
Natchez St.
Camp St.
North St.
Tchoupitoulas St.
S. Peters St.
Lafayette St.
Magazine St.
Constance St.
1
2
3
4
5
6
7
8
9
10
11
12
13
14
15
16
17
18
19
20

New Orleans Dining and Lodging

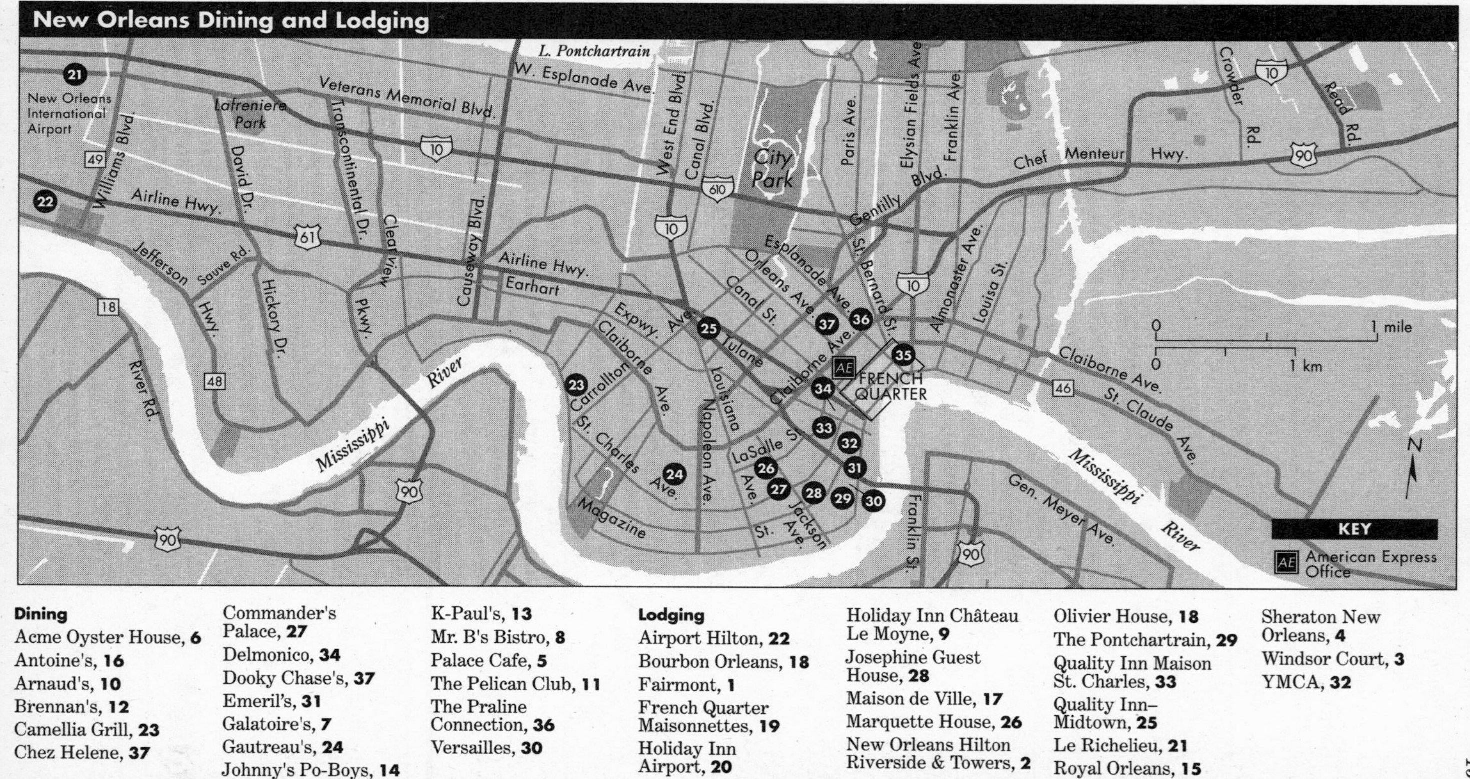

Dining
Acme Oyster House, **6**
Antoine's, **16**
Arnaud's, **10**
Brennan's, **12**
Camellia Grill, **23**
Chez Helene, **37**
Commander's Palace, **27**
Delmonico, **34**
Dooky Chase's, **37**
Emeril's, **31**
Galatoire's, **7**
Gautreau's, **24**
Johnny's Po-Boys, **14**
K-Paul's, **13**
Mr. B's Bistro, **8**
Palace Cafe, **5**
The Pelican Club, **11**
The Praline Connection, **36**
Versailles, **30**

Lodging
Airport Hilton, **22**
Bourbon Orleans, **18**
Fairmont, **1**
French Quarter Maisonnettes, **19**
Holiday Inn Airport, **20**
Holiday Inn Château Le Moyne, **9**
Josephine Guest House, **28**
Maison de Ville, **17**
Marquette House, **26**
New Orleans Hilton Riverside & Towers, **2**
Olivier House, **18**
The Pontchartrain, **29**
Quality Inn Maison St. Charles, **33**
Quality Inn–Midtown, **25**
Le Richelieu, **21**
Royal Orleans, **15**
Sheraton New Orleans, **4**
Windsor Court, **3**
YMCA, **32**

Classic Creole

★ **Arnaud's.** Beveled glass, ceiling fans, and tile floors cast an aura of traditional Southern dining. The lively Sunday jazz brunch is a classic New Orleans experience. Pompano *en croûte*, veal Wohl, and filet Charlemond topped with two sauces are savory entrée selections, and there is little on the menu there that isn't excellent. *813 Bienville St., French Quarter, tel. 504/523-5433. Jackets required. Reservations required. AE, MC, V. Expensive.*

Delmonico. This is the closest many visitors get to dinner in a handsomely decorated home in the Garden District. Elegance and warmth characterize the atmosphere in Delmonico, which is decorated with traditional wallpapers in relaxing colors, botanical prints, period furniture, and other domestic touches. It's the perfect place for vegetable soup or delicately seasoned okra gumbo. The rest of the menu has its weaknesses, but look for the competently done beef fillet in burgundy sauce, a toothsome broiled red snapper, spicy broiled and stuffed shrimp, and home-style chocolate and coconut cream pies. Don't expect frills in the table service. *1300 St. Charles Ave., Lower Garden District, tel. 504/525-4937. Reservations advised for weekends. Dress: casual. AE, DC, MC, V. Moderate.*

★ **Galatoire's.** Operated by the fourth generation, Galatoire's is a tradition in New Orleans. Creole specialties, moderately priced by New Orleans standards, are served in a big, brightly lit room with mirrors on all sides. Lunch is served all afternoon, and you can avoid the lines by arriving after 1:30. An extensive menu offers every imaginable Creole dish. Seafood is the most diverse category, but there is also a fine lineup of steaks, sweetbreads, and chicken dishes. *209 Bourbon St., French Quarter, tel. 504/525-2021. Jacket and tie required after 5 and on Sun. No reservations. No credit cards. Closed Mon. Moderate.*

French Creole

★ **Antoine's.** Established in 1840, Antoine's is the oldest restaurant in the United States under continuous family ownership. You can best appreciate this fine old restaurant if you are accompanied by a regular. Oysters Rockefeller originated here, as did pompano *en papillote* and puffed-up soufflé potatoes. *Tournedos marchand de vin* is a legend in its own wine. Be sure and tour the restaurant after dinner. *713 St. Louis St., French Quarter, tel. 504/581-4422. Jacket required for dinner. Reservations required. AE, DC, MC, V. Very Expensive.*

Brennan's. Opened in 1946, Brennan's is one of the city's premier dining establishments. Breakfast at Brennan's is a tradition unto itself. The extensive menu includes rich, creamy eggs Benedict, Sardou, and Houssarde. The traditional breakfast dessert is bananas Foster, flamed with liqueur in a tableside ritual. The oysters tournedos Chanteclair, three prime cuts, each with a different sauce, is one of the restaurant's strong suits: excellent French sauces with a Creole stamp. Brennan's also serves brunch on weekends. *417 Royal St., French Quarter, tel. 504/525-9711. Jacket required at dinner. Reservations advised. AE, DC, MC, V. Very Expensive.*

★ **Commander's Palace.** Housed in a renovated Victorian mansion, this elegant restaurant offers the best sampling of old Creole cooking prepared with a combination of American and French styles. Entrée selections include veal chop Tchoupitoulas, trout with roasted pecans, and tournedos. Commander's serves a one-of-a-kind bread pudding soufflé.

Jazz brunch Saturday and Sunday, a festive affair with balloons and lots of Creole egg dishes, is best enjoyed in the Garden Room overlooking the patio. *1403 Washington Ave., Garden District, tel. 504/899–8221. Jackets required. Reservations required. AE, DC, MC, V. Very Expensive.*

★ **Gautreau's.** This is one of the most popular restaurants in the Uptown area: a small café converted from an old pharmacy. The food is straightforward but imaginative, while being comfortably Creole. Lunches are light and include many good soups and salads with the entrées. The dinner menu consists entirely of specials; perhaps the best of those regularly appearing are the various manifestations of filet mignon, but the fish and veal are also consistent winners. *1728 Soniat St., Uptown, tel. 504/899–7397. Jacket suggested. Reservations strongly advised. MC, V. Closed for lunch; closed for dinner Sun. Moderate.*

Avant-garde

★ **Emeril's.** For many seasoned restaurant goers in New Orleans, Emeril's is the pace-setter for Creole cuisine. Proprietor-chef Emeril Lagasse, formerly at Commander's Palace, opened this large, noisy and decidedly contemporary restaurant in early 1990 with an ambitious menu that gives equal emphasis to Creole and modern American cooking. On the plate, this translates as a fresh corn crepe topped with Louisiana caviar, grilled andouille sausage in the chef's own sauce, a sauté of crawfish over jambalaya cakes, fresh fruit cobblers, and a cornucopia of other creative dishes. You can grab a stool at a food bar and get close-up views of the chef at work. The looks of the place are appropriately avant-garde—brick and glass walls, gleaming wood floors, burnished-aluminum lamps, and a huge abstract-expressionist oil painting. *800 Tchoupitoulas St., Warehouse District, tel. 504/528–9393. Advance reservations strongly advised. Jackets suggested. AE, DC, MC, V. Closed Sun., no lunch Sat. Expensive.*

The Palace Cafe, a split-level two-story restaurant in the historic Werlein Building, has the feeling of a large Parisian café, with a spiral staircase, a black-and-white tile floor, wood paneling, and splashy murals. Starters include grilled andouille with sweet potato cakes, and oyster shooters (served in a shot glass with shallots, lemon, and cracked-pepper sauce). Specialties are rotisserie chicken basted in garlic oil, superb catfish in a pecan crust, seafood, and game. Wait till you see the separate chocolate-dessert listing. *605 Canal St., Central Business District, tel. 504/523–1661. Dress: casual but neat. Reservations suggested. AE, DC, MC, V. Moderate.*

Creole-inspired

★ **Mr. B's Bistro.** You can tell you're near this classy bistro by the aroma of fish and steaks roasting on hickory and pecan logs. The shrimp Chippewa and hickory-grilled fish are highly recommended, and the gumbo ya-ya is first-rate. The wine list is solid, with some very good wines by the glass available at the bar. The lively jazz brunch offers New Orleans classic egg dishes, and then some. *201 Royal St., French Quarter, tel. 504/523–2078. Dress: informal. Reservations required. AE, MC, V. Sun. brunch. Moderate.*

Soul Creole

Chez Helene. Stuffed bell peppers, fried chicken, Creole gumbo, and smothered okra are just some of the fine recipes of Helene Howard, whose nephew, Austin Leslie, opened the second Chez Helene (316 Chartres St. in the de la Poste Hotel, French Quarter, tel. 504/525–6130). The soul and Cajun specialties are marked by spiciness and fresh herbs. The Creole jambalaya and crawfish étouffée are among the city's simplest and best; the fresh corn bread is a joy. *1540 N. Robertson St., Mid-City, tel. 504/945–0444. Dress: informal. Reservations advised. AE, MC, V. Moderate.*

★ **Praline Connection.** Down-home cooking in the Southern-Creole style is the forte of this laid-back and likable restaurant where the food is the no-nonsense kind that has fueled generations of Southern families. The fried or stewed chicken, smothered pork chops, barbecued ribs, and collard greens are definitively done. And the soulful filé gumbo, crowder peas, bread pudding, and sweet-potato pie are among the best in town. Add to all this some of the lowest prices anywhere, a congenial service staff, and a neat-as-a-pin dining room and the sum is a fine place to spend an hour or two. *542 Frenchmen St., Faubourg Marigny, tel. 504/943–3934. No reservations. Dress: casual. AE, MC, V. Inexpensive.*

Continental

★ **Versailles.** Continental sumptuosity and Creole heartiness never kept better company than they do in this plush restaurant, done in Old World–style elegance. The moods in the several elaborate dining rooms vary from cheery to rather somber. The softly lit main room affords leafy views of St. Charles Avenue, while the brighter rooms behind are sheathed in pale wallpapers and pastel-hued flowers. Crab dishes shine, especially the cold, marinated crabmeat *à la grecque,* prepared in a scallop shell with spinach mousse and a mustard-dill sauce. Soups range from the subtle clarity of the artichoke Monte Cristo to the richness of shrimp and mirliton in cream. The supreme duckling andalouse and medallions of beef Madagascar are two of the many excellent meat dishes. The appropriately elaborate desserts include a marvelous bittersweet chocolate mousse in a raspberry sauce and a Bavarian cream in a custard sauce tinged with orange liqueur. *2100 St. Charles Ave., Uptown, tel. 504/524–2535. Reservations strongly advised. Jacket required. AE, DC, MC, V. Dinner only. Closed Sun. Very Expensive.*

★ **Pelican Club.** Sassy New York flourishes are found throughout the menu of this smarlty decorated but eminently comfortable place in the heart of the French Quarter. Still, evidence of chef Richard Hughes's South Louisiana origins also keeps popping up. Hughes spent seven years in Manhattan as the top chef of the acclaimed Memphis. In three handsome dining rooms inside a balconied old town house, he turns out a stew of shellfish that's a clever improvisation of both San Francisco's cioppino and Louisiana's bouillabaisse. A touch of saffron in his jambalaya of chicken, sausage, and shellfish makes it a cousin of Spain's paella. Closer to home are red snapper stuffed with crabmeat; a bisque of bourbon, crab, and corn; and a crème brûlée in the grandest French-Creole tradition. Each of the dining rooms, hung with consignment art from local galleries, has its own ambience. *615 Bienville St., French Quarter, tel. 504/523–1504. Jacket suggested. Reservations advised. AE, MC, V. No lunch weekends. Expensive–Very Expensive.*

Back to Basics
Seafood

Acme Oyster and Seafood Restaurant. The granddaddy of local oyster bars, the Acme has a big old marble counter where you stand and eat dozen after dozen of oysters, opened before your eyes by old pros. Next to that is another bar where you get your beer, the preferred drink with cold oysters. You order your sandwiches from the cooking station, where you can see them frying the oysters. The wait is aggravating if it's a crowded day, but it's worth it. A recent addition is a limited salad bar.

You can eat oysters on the half shell at a table, but this isn't the style of the natives. *724 Iberville St., French Quarter, tel. 504/522-5973. Dress: informal. No reservations. AE, DC, MC, V. Closes 10 PM Fri., Sat., earlier on other nights. Inexpensive.*

Grills and Coffee Shops

★ **Camellia Grill.** This is the class act among lunch counters, with linen napkins and a maître d'. The omelets are the best in town. Especially good is the ham, cheese, and onion—huge and fluffy. Good red beans and rice on Monday. Great hamburgers, pecan pie, cheesecake, and banana-cream pie. The chocolate freezes are also popular. Dining here is entertaining, mainly due to the somewhat theatrical waiters. Expect long lines on weekends for breakfast. *626 S. Carrollton Ave., Uptown, tel. 504/866-9573. Dress: informal. No reservations. No credit cards. Inexpensive–Moderate.*

Johnny's Po-Boys. Strangely enough, good po-boys are hard to find in the French Quarter. Johnny's compensates for the scarcity with a cornucopia of them, put together in the time-honored New Orleans manner. Inside the soft-crusted French bread come the classic fillings—lean boiled ham, well-done roast beef in a garlicky gravy, crisply fried oysters or shrimp, and a wide variety of others. The chili may not cut it in San Antonio, but the red beans and rice are respectable. The surroundings are rudimentary. *511 St. Louis St., French Quarter, tel. 504/523-9071. No credit cards. Breakfast, lunch, dinner Mon.–Sat. Closed for dinner Sun. Inexpensive.*

Lodging

Visitors to New Orleans have a wide variety of accommodations to choose from: posh high-rise hotels, antiques-filled antebellum homes, Creole cottages, or old slave quarters.

When planning a stay in New Orleans, try to reserve well in advance, especially during Mardi Gras or other seasonal events. Frequently, hotels offer special packages at reduced rates, but never during Mardi Gras, when almost every accommodation raises its rates higher than listed here. Many chain or associated hotels and motels offer the additional convenience of advance reservations at affiliated hostelries of your choosing along your route.

The most highly recommended properties in each price category are indicaded by a star ★.

Category	Cost*
Very Expensive	over $120
Expensive	$90–$120
Moderate	$50–$90
Inexpensive	under $50

**for a double room; not including 11% tax*

Hotels
Central Business District

Staying in the Central Business District will appeal to visitors who prefer accommodations in luxurious high-rise hotels. All the hotels listed here are within walking distance of the French Quarter, but shuttles, taxis, buses, and the streetcar are available. *Walking in this area after dark is not recommended.*

★ **Fairmont Hotel.** The Fairmont is one of the oldest grand hotels in America. The red and gold Victorian splendor of the massive lobby evokes a more elegant and gracious era. The hotel is composed of three separate buildings. The Baronne and University sections have spacious rooms. Rooms in the Shell section are smaller and were completely redone in 1989; there is no elevator service in this building. Special touches in every room include four down pillows, electric shoe-buffers, and bathroom scales. Impressive murals depicting life in the South enliven the walls of the famed Sazerac Bar; the herbs used in the restaurants are grown on the roof and delivered to the kitchens within 20 minutes of being cut. The Sazerac Restaurant has had a face-lift that removed the old world ambience and replaced it with a contemporary look. *University Pl., 70140, tel. 504/529–7111 or 800/527–4727. 685 rooms, 50 suites. Facilities: 4 restaurants with bars, heated outdoor pool, 2 tennis courts, beauty salon, gift shop, lobby pastry shop, jewelry store, public stenographer, valet parking. AE, DC, MC, V. Very Expensive.*

★ **Windsor Court Hotel.** Exquisite, gracious, elegant, eminently civilized—these words are frequently used to describe Windsor Court, but all fail to capture its wonderful quality. Le Salon's scrumptious high tea is served each afternoon in the lobby. Plush carpeting, canopy and four-poster beds, stocked wet bars, marble vanities, oversize mirrors, dressing areas—all contribute to the elegance and luxury of the Windsor Court. The hotel is located across from the Rivergate and four blocks from the French Quarter. In 1990 the hotel and its fine Grill Room restaurant received the AAA 5 Diamond award. *300 Gravier St., 70140, tel. 504/523–6000 or 800/262–2662. 58 rooms, 266 suites. Facilities: 2 restaurants, lounge, entertainment, Olympic-size outdoor pool, health club, Jacuzzi, steambath, sauna, gift shop, shoe shine, valet laundry, parking. AE, DC, MC, V. Very Expensive.*

New Orleans Hilton Riverside & Towers. It's located on the banks of the Mississippi, with Riverwalk sprawled out around it and the New Orleans Convention Center just down the street. Pete Fountain's Club is here. The River Center Tennis & Racquetball Club is a handy spot for working off all the calories you'll consume at Winston's. VIPs check into the Tower suites, where a concierge looks after things, but the best views of the river are in the appropriately named Riverside section. *Poydras St. at the Mississippi River, 70140, tel. 504/561–0500 or 800–HILTONS. 1602 rooms, 86 suites. Facilities: 3 restaurants, 6 lounges, 2 outdoor pools, tennis and racquetball club, golf clinic, business center. AE, DC, MC, V. Moderate–Very Expensive.*

★ **Sheraton New Orleans.** On Canal Street, across from the French Quarter, the Sheraton has a lobby that is large and user-friendly. A tropical atmosphere permeates its Gazebo Lounge, which features jazz nightly. Café Promenade encircles the second level. Executive rooms on the top floors come with many special amenities. The year 1991 saw the completion of a multimillion-dollar renovation that added a health club, two restaurants, and a conference center, and redecorated all the guest rooms. Expect top-quality service. *500 Canal St., 70130, tel. 504/525–2500 or 800/325–3535. 1,100 rooms, 72 suites. Facilities: 3 restaurants, 2 lounges, entertainment, outdoor swimming pool with restaurant, gift shop, video checkout,* *nonsmoking rooms, valet service, and parking. AE, DC, MC, V. Moderate–Very Expensive.*

Quality Inn–Midtown. Too far to walk but only a short drive from the French Quarter. *3900 Tulane Ave., 70119, tel. 504/486–5541 or 800/228–5151. 102 rooms. Facilities: restaurant, lounge, entertainment, outdoor pool, whirlpool, nonsmoking rooms, airport shuttle. AE, DC, MC, V. Moderate.*

French Quarter Since most people who visit New Orleans stay in the Quarter, the 96-square-block area abounds with every type of guest accommodation. The selections that follow are all quality establishments chosen to provide variety in location, atmosphere, and price. Reservations are usually a must.

★ **Bourbon Orleans.** The splendid lobby of this historic hotel is of white marble with crystal chandeliers and a grand piano. A magnificent spiral staircase leads to the 1815 Orleans Ballroom, which was the site of innumerable masquerade and quadroon balls. The large guest rooms have Queen Anne furnishings; bathrooms are fitted with telephones and mini-TVs. Even-numbered rooms face a beautiful courtyard, but you can still hear the Bourbon Street noise. The suites are bilevel and have two entrances. *717 Orleans St., 70116, tel. 504/523–2222 or 800/521–5338. 164 rooms, 47 suites. Facilities: restaurant, lounge, entertainment, outdoor pool, secretarial service, valet service. AE, DC, MC, V. Very Expensive.*

★ **Hotel Maison de Ville.** This small, romantic hotel lies in seclusion amid the hustle and bustle of the French Quarter. Tapestry-covered chairs, a fire burning in the sitting room, and antiques-furnished rooms all contribute to a 19th-century atmosphere. Some rooms are in former slave quarters in the courtyard; others are on the upper floors of the main house. The Continental breakfast is served with a rose on a silver tray. Other meals can be enjoyed at Le Bistro. Visitors who seek a special hideaway will love the Audubon housekeeping cottages—in a private, enclosed area, with statuary and individual patios—two blocks from the hotel. *727 Toulouse St., 70130, tel. 504/561–5858 or 800/634–1600. 14 rooms, 2 suites, 7 cottages. Facilities: restaurant, pool at cottage location, valet service, parking. AE, MC, V. Expensive–Very Expensive.*

★ **Royal Orleans Hotel (Omni).** This elegant, white-marble hotel, built in 1960 re-creates an aura that reigned in New Orleans more than a century ago. Rooms, though not large, are well appointed with marble baths (telephone in each) and more marble on dressers and tabletops. Balcony rooms cost the most. The well-known Rib Room Restaurant makes its home on the lobby level. *621 St. Louis St., 70140, tel. 504/529–5333 or 800/THE-OMNI. 350 rooms, 16 suites. Facilities: 2 restaurants, 3 lounges, rooftop heated pool, exercise room, florist, gift shop, jewelry store, beauty salon and barbershop, valet service, parking. AE, DC, MC, V. Expensive–Very Expensive.*

Le Richelieu. Here the friendly, personal atmosphere of a small hotel is combined with amenities usually associated with a luxury high rise—many at a moderate rate. Some rooms have mirrored walls and walk-in closets, many have refrigerators, and all have brass ceiling fans. Luxury suites (like the one Paul McCartney stayed in) are also available. An intimate bar and café off the courtyard has tables on the terrace by the pool. *1234 Chartres St., 70116, tel. 504/529–2492 or 800/535–9653, fax 504/524–8179. 69 rooms, 17 suites. Facilities: restaurant,* *lounge, outdoor pool, valet service, free parking. AE, DC, MC, V. Moderate–Very Expensive.*

Olivier House. The entrance of this small hotel, in two 1836 town houses, contains an enormous carved mirror and chandeliers that are original to the house. Room design and decor vary; some rooms have lofts, many have complete kitchens; gas-burning fireplaces are found throughout. Most rooms are a comfortable mix of antiques and traditional decor; some have a tropical feeling, with wicker furnishings and sunny colors. Pets are welcome. Noisy birds inhabit the three pretty courtyards filled with tropical plants. Don't expect a spic-and-span luxury hotel; in this family-owned and operated charmer, the homey, casual atmosphere is the thing. *828 Toulouse St., 70112, tel. 504/525–8456. 40 rooms. Facilities: pool, shaded courtyards, elevator. AE, DC, MC, V. Moderate–Very Expensive.*

★ **Holiday Inn Château Le Moyne.** Old World atmosphere and decor; 8 suites located in slave quarters off a tropical courtyard. *301 Dauphine St., 70112, tel. 504/581–1303 or 800/HOLIDAY. 160 rooms, 11 suites. Facilities: restaurant, lounge, outdoor heated pool. AE, DC, MC, V. Moderate–Expensive.*

★ **French Quarter Maisonnettes.** All the maisonnettes (some with two and three rooms) open directly onto a private flagstone courtyard. Functional furnishings, private baths, and TVs are included; private phones are not available. Children over 12 and well-trained pets are welcomed. *1130 Chartres St., 70116, tel. 504/524–9918. 1 room, 7 suites. No credit cards. Closed July. Inexpensive.*

Garden District/Uptown

★ **Pontchartrain Hotel.** Maintaining the grand tradition is the hallmark of this quiet, elegant European-style hotel that has reigned on St. Charles Avenue for more than 60 years. From the canopied entrance to the white-gloved elevator operator, the hotel's commitment to quality, service, and taste shows clearly. Accommodations range from lavish, sun-filled suites to small, darkish rooms with shower baths. The internationally known Caribbean Room restaurant provides memorable dining. *2031 St. Charles Ave., 70140, tel. 504/524–0581 or 800/952–8092, telex 266068PONT. 63 rooms, 37 suites. Facilities: 2 restaurants, piano bar, 24-hr concierge, limousine, valet service, parking. AE, DC, MC, V. Moderate–Very Expensive.*

★ **Josephine Guest House.** In this restored Italianate mansion, built in 1870, French antiques fill the rooms, and Oriental rugs cover gleaming hardwood floors. Four rooms and a parlor are in the main house; there are two smaller but spacious rooms in the garçonnière (quarters where the original owners' sons stayed). The bathrooms are impressive in both size and decor. A complimentary Creole breakfast of orange juice, café au lait, and homemade biscuits can be brought to your room (Wedgwood china on a silver tray) or served on the secluded patio. Phones can be installed in rooms upon request. *1450 Josephine St., 70130, 1 block from St. Charles Ave., tel. 504/524–6361. 6 rooms. AE, DC, MC, V. Moderate.*

★ **Quality Inn Maison St. Charles.** Lovely property in five historic buildings along St. Charles Avenue. Home of Patout's fine restaurant. *1319 St. Charles Ave., 70130, tel. 504/522–0187 or 800/228–5151. 121 rooms, 11 suites. Facilities: lounge, outdoor pool, heated whirlpool, nonsmoking rooms, valet parking. AE, DC, MC, V. Moderate.*

Kenner/Airport

New Orleans Airport Hilton & Conference Center. This $32 million facility is directly opposite the New Orleans International

Airport. *901 Airline Hwy., Kenner 70062, tel. 504/469–5000 or 800/HILTON. 312 rooms, 2 suites. Facilities: restaurant, lounge, heated outdoor pool, tennis court, fitness center, business center, valet service, airport shuttle. AE, DC, MC, V. Moderate–Expensive.*

Holiday Inn–Airport Holidome. Many of the rooms here face the dome-covered pool area. *2929 Williams Blvd., Kenner 70062, tel. 504/467–5611 or 800/HOLIDAY. 302 rooms, 1 suite, Facilities: restaurant, lounge, indoor pool, exercise room, sauna, Jacuzzi, airport shuttle, free parking. AE, DC, MC, V. Moderate.*

Bed-and-breakfasts Bed-and-breakfast means overnight lodging and breakfast in a private residence. Begin by writing or calling a reservation service and discussing price range, type of residence, location, and length of stay. The service in turn will provide you with descriptions of several choices of B&Bs that meet your criteria. From these choices you'll make a decision and send a 20% deposit. You'll receive the address and other pertinent details before you arrive.

New Orleans Bed & Breakfast. Among 300 properties citywide are private homes, apartments, and condos. Prices range from $35 to $150. *Contact Sarah-Margaret Brown, Box 8163, New Orleans 70182, tel. 504/838–0073. AE, MC, V. Inexpensive–Very Expensive.*

Bed & Breakfast, Inc.—Reservations Service. This service offers a variety of accommodations in all areas of New Orleans. Some homes are 19th-century, others are contemporary. Guest cottages, rooms, and suites are also available. Prices range from $40 to $110. *Write or call Hazel Boyce, 1021 Moss St., Box 52257, New Orleans 70152, tel. 504/525–4640 or 800/749–4640. No credit cards. Inexpensive–Expensive.*

Hostels **International Center YMCA.** Accommodations are for both men and women. *936 St. Charles Ave., 70130, tel. 504/568–9622. 150 rooms, no private baths. Facilities: restaurant, gym, weight room, track, indoor pool, parking. MC, V. Inexpensive.*

Marquette House, New Orleans International Hostel. This is the fourth-largest youth hostel in the country, run by Steve and Alma Cross. *2253 Carondelet St., 70130, tel. 504/523–3014, fax 504/529–5933. 160 dorm beds, 5 private rooms with shared bath, 12 apartments. Facilities: 2 lounge areas with TV (1 nonsmoking), 2 equipped community kitchens, dining room, coin-operated laundry, lockers, garden patio with picnic tables. AE, MC, V. Inexpensive.*

The Arts

Comprehensive listings of events can be found in the weekly newspaper *Gambit*, which is distributed free at newsstands, supermarkets, and bookstores. The Friday edition of the daily *Times-Picayune* carries a "Lagniappe" tabloid that lists weekend events. The monthly *New Orleans Magazine* also has a Calendar section. Credit-card purchases of tickets for events at the Saenger Performing Arts Center, the Orpheum Theater, and UNO Lakefront Arena can be made through TicketMaster (tel. 504/888–8181).

Theater The avant-garde, the off-beat, and the satirical are among the theatrical offerings at **Contemporary Arts Center** (900 Camp St., tel. 504/523–1216). At **Le Petit Théâtre du Vieux Carré** (616

St. Peter St., tel. 504/522–9958), classics, contemporary drama, children's theater, and musicals are presented. Touring Broadway shows, dance companies, and top-name talent appear at the **Saenger Performing Arts Center** (143 N. Rampart St., tel. 504/524–2490).

Concerts Free jazz concerts are held on weekends in **Dutch Alley.** Pick up a schedule at the information kiosk (French Market at St. Philip St., tel. 504/522–2621). The New Orleans Symphony performs at the **Orpheum Theatre** (129 University Pl., tel. 504/525–0500), which also presents jazz and pop concerts.

Nightlife

Jazz was born in New Orleans, and the music refuses to be confined to nighttime. Weekend jazz brunches are enormously popular and are featured all over town. But a stroll down Bourbon Street will give you a taste of the city's eclectic rhythms. You'll hear Cajun, gutbucket, R&B, rock, ragtime, New Wave, and you name it, and you'll hear it almost around the clock. During the annual Jazz and Heritage Festival, held from the last weekend in April through the first weekend in May, musicians pour in from all over the world to mix it up with local talent, and the music never misses a beat.

New Orleans is a 24-hour town, meaning that there are no legal closing times and it ain't over till it's over. Closing times, especially on Bourbon Street, depend on how business is. Your best bet is to call and ask before tooling out to bar-hop at 2 AM. It is also a superb idea to call and ask about current credit-card policy, cover, and minimum.

Gambit, the free weekly newspaper, has a complete listing of who's doing what where. Things can change between press and performance times, so if there's an artist you're especially eager to hear, it's wise to call and confirm before turning up.

Jazz Aboard the ***Creole Queen*** (Poydras St. Wharf, tel. 504/529–4567) you'll cruise on the river with Andrew Hall's Society Jazz Band and there's a buffet to boot. If you've an ounce of romance racing through your veins, do it.

There's live music five nights a week at the **Palm Court Jazz Cafe.** Traditional jazz is the rule, with blues thrown in on Wednesday. The fine Creole and international kitchen stays open until the music stops. *1204 Decatur St., tel. 504/525–0200. Open noon–11 PM. Live music starts Wed., Thurs. and Sun. 8 PM; Fri. and Sat. 7 PM; Sun. brunch noon–3 PM. Closed Mon. and Tues.*

Pete Fountain's (2 Poydras St., tel. 504/523–4374) is a New Orleans legend with his clarinet and his band that plays in a plush 500-seat room on the third floor of the Hilton Hotel. This is Pete's home base, and the man's on the stand Tuesday, Wednesday, Friday, and Saturday when he's in town. But he makes frequent appearances around the country, so it's wise to call first.

Speaking of legends, the old-time jazz greats lay out the best traditional jazz in the world in a musty, funky hall that's short on comfort, long on talent. **Preservation Hall** (726 St. Peter St., day tel. 504/522–2238, night tel. 504/523–8939) is *the* place for traditional jazz, and it costs you a mere $3 at the door. You may have to stand in line to get in, but it will help if you get there around 7:30.

Dixieland is the name of the tune at the **Seaport Cajun Cafe & Bar** (424 Bourbon St., tel. 504/568–0981). You can dine on seafood and Cajun dishes while sitting on a balcony and watching the movable feast down on "the Street."

Rambling, rustic, and raucous **Snug Harbor** (626 Frenchmen St., tel. 504/949–0696) is where graybeards and undergrads get a big bang out of the likes of the Dirty Dozen, Charmaine Neville, the David Torkanowsky Trio, and Maria Muldaur.

R&B, Cajun, Rock, New Wave

Industrial-strength rock rolls out of the sound system at the **Hard Rock Cafe** (440 N. Peters, tel. 504/529–8617). Hard Rock Hurricanes are dispensed at a guitar-shaped bar, and the place is filled with rock 'n' roll memorabilia. Hamburgers, salads, and steaks are served.

The college crowd raises the rafters at **Jimmy's Music Club** (8200 Willow St., tel. 504/861–8200). The music, by national as well as local groups, is rock, New Wave, reggae, R&B . . . whatever.

Benny's Bar (938 Valence, tel. 504/895–9405) is a laid-back lair for blues and reggae. There's never a cover here.

An institution, **Tipitina's** (501 Napoleon Ave., tel. 504/897–3943) is sort of a microcosm of the Jazz Fest, featuring progressive jazz, reggae, R&B, rock, New Wave, and blues. Its name comes from a song by Professor Longhair, who was posthumously awarded a Grammy for Best Traditional Blues Recording, and the place is dedicated to his memory. Funky, mellow, loaded with laid-back locals. $3–$10 cover.

Bars

One of the world's best-known bars and home of the Hurricane (a sweetly potent concoction of rum and fruit juices) is **Pat O'Brien's** (718 St. Peter St., tel. 504/525–4823). There are three bars, including a lively piano bar and a large courtyard bar, and mobs of collegians and tourists line up to get in. Very lively, very loud, very late.

Dancing

Forty-one Forty-one (4141 St. Charles Ave., tel. 504/897–0781) is a stylish bastion for disco dancing and mingling singles.

Two-stepping to a Cajun band is billed as the "spécialité de la maison," but the **Maple Leaf Bar** (8316 Oak St., tel. 504/866–9359) moves with rock, R&B, reggae, and gospel as well. (Cajun nights *are* special.) There's a $2–$5 cover, depending on what's up.

If you're into heavy-duty dancing to Top-40s discs, check out **Club Galleria West** (The Galleria, 1 Galleria Blvd., Metairie, tel. 504/836–5055). The glitzy disco draws a loyal crowd of young locals.

South Louisiana

Just as the state has two distinct regions, so, too, does South Louisiana. We'll make two separate tours of South Louisiana, beginning with Acadiana. Also called French Louisiana, the region is the cradle of the Cajun craze that's swept the nation. Our second tour will cover Baton Rouge, the state capital, and continue to plantation country—the only Southern section of South Louisiana.

Cajuns are descendants of 17th-century French settlers who established a colony they called l'Acadie in the present-day Canadian provinces of Nova Scotia and New Brunswick. The Acadians—"Cajun" is a corruption of "Acadian"—were expelled by the British in the mid-18th century. Their exile was described by Henry Wadsworth Longfellow in his epic poem *Evangeline*. They eventually found a home in South Louisiana, and there they have been since 1762, imbuing the region, the state, and the nation with their unique cuisine and culture. The flavor of the region is summed up in the Cajun phrase *"Laissez les bons temps rouler!"* (Let the good times roll!)

Cajun Country is made for meandering. We're going to take some scenic routes and state highways, and we encourage you to take to the country roads along the way to further explore the backroads and byways of bayou country.

Getting Around

By Air **Lafayette Regional Airport** (tel. 318/266–4400) and **Lake Charles Regional Airport** (tel. 318/477–6051) are served by American Eagle, Atlantic Southeast, and Continental. Flying time to Lake Charles is an hour and 20 minutes; to Lafayette 40 minutes; and to Baton Rouge a half hour.

By Car The fastest route from New Orleans through Cajun Country to Lafayette and Lake Charles is via I–10, which cuts coast-to-coast across the southern United States. However, if you've time, do take the leisurely scenic drives for exploring.

Great Drives: LA 56 to LA 57 is a circular drive out of Houma, along which you can see shrimp and oyster boats docked along the bayous from May to December. Another circular drive is the Creole Nature Trail (LA 27) out of Lake Charles. LA 82 (Hug-the-Coast Highway) runs through the coastal marshes along the Gulf of Mexico.

By Train **Amtrak** (tel. 800/USA–RAIL) serves Franklin, Schriever (12 miles from Houma), Lafayette, New Iberia, and Thibodaux (the station is 5 miles from town).

By Bus **Greyhound Southeast Lines** has frequent daily departures to Franklin, Houma, Lafayette, Lake Charles, Morgan City, New Iberia, Opelousas, and Thibodaux.

Guided Tours

Acadiana to Go (tel. 318/981–3918) gives guided tours of Acadiana, as well as the rest of Louisiana. **Allons à Lafayette** (tel. 318/269–9607) offers customized tours, with bilingual guides and itinerary planning for Lafayette and Cajun Country. **Annie Miller's Terrebonne Swamp & Marsh Tours** (tel. 504/879–3934) is especially popular with the kids. The lady who gets along great with gators does daily tours March 1–November 1 out of Houma into the swamps. **Atchafalaya Basin Backwater Adventure** (tel. 504/575–2371) gives two-hour tours of the swamps surrounding Gibson and four-hour forays into the Great Chacahoula Swamp. **Hammond's Flying Service** (tel. 504/876–0584) has air tours, which soar out of Houma over the swamps, marshlands, and the Gulf of Mexico. **McGee's Landing** (tel. 318/

228–2384) conducts pontoon-boat tours from the levee in Henderson into the 800,000-acre Atchafalaya Basin.

Important Addresses and Numbers

Tourist Information

The **Iberia Parish Tourist Commission,** 2690 Centre St., New Iberia, tel. 318/365–1540. Open daily 9–5. The **Lafayette Convention and Visitors Commission,** 16th Street and Evangeline Thruway, tel. 318/232–3808 or 800/346–1958 (U.S., outside LA); 800/543–5340 (CAN). Open weekdays 8:30–5, weekends 9–5. The **Southwest Louisiana Convention & Visitors Bureau,** 1211 N. Lakeshore Drive, Lake Charles, tel. 318/436–9588. Open weekdays 8–5; weekends 9–3.

Emergencies

Dial 911 for assistance, or try the emergency room at **Hamilton Medical Center** (2810 Ambassador Caffery Pkwy, Lafayette, tel. 318/981–2949); in Lake Charles, **St. Patrick's Hospital** (524 S. Ryan St., tel. 318/436–2511).

24-hour Pharmacy

Eckerd's, (3601 Johnston St., Lafayette, tel. 318/984–5220). In Lake Charles, when pharmacies are closed at night contact **St. Patrick's Hospital** (*see* Emergencies, *above*).

Exploring South Louisiana

Numbers in the margin correspond to points of interest on the South Louisiana map.

U.S. 90 drops down into Houma in the marshlands south of New Orleans, an area that abounds with campgrounds and charter boats for fresh- and saltwater fishing. Our route will take us through Morgan City, where the first Tarzan film was made; Franklin, an official Main Street USA town; and the state's only Indian reservation. We'll follow the rambling Bayou Teche (pronounced "tesh") into St. Martinville in Evangeline Country, and next we'll head for Lafayette, which proudly calls itself, with some justification, the capital of French Louisiana. The scenic route to Lake Charles is LA 14, which is fishing, camping, and bird-watching territory. Looping back toward Baton Rouge, we'll go through the area famed for the *Courir du Mardi Gras*, or Mardi Gras Run, during which masked and costumed horseback riders make a mad dash throughout the countryside. The trip ends near Baton Rouge on the Mississippi River, where we'll begin our second tour.

1 **Houma,** in Terrebonne Parish, dates from 1795 and is located in the heart of the old Hache Spanish Land Grant. The town is named for the Houmas Indians (the stressed first syllable of Houma sounds like "home"). Terrebonne Parish is a major center for shrimp and oyster fisheries, and the blessing of the shrimp fleets in Chauvin and Dulac is a colorful April event.

The 21-room **Southdown Plantation** was built in 1859 as a one-story Greek Revival house, but the addition in 1893 of the second floor transformed it into a castlelike Queen Anne mansion. The house contains a display of 135 Boehm and Doughty porcelain birds. U.S. Senator Allen Ellender called Houma home, and the house contains a re-creation of his Washington office. *LA 311 at St. Charles St., Houma, tel. 504/851–0154. Admission: $4 adults, $2.50 senior citizens, $2 students, $1 children 6–12. Open daily 10–4 (last tour at 3). Closed major holidays.*

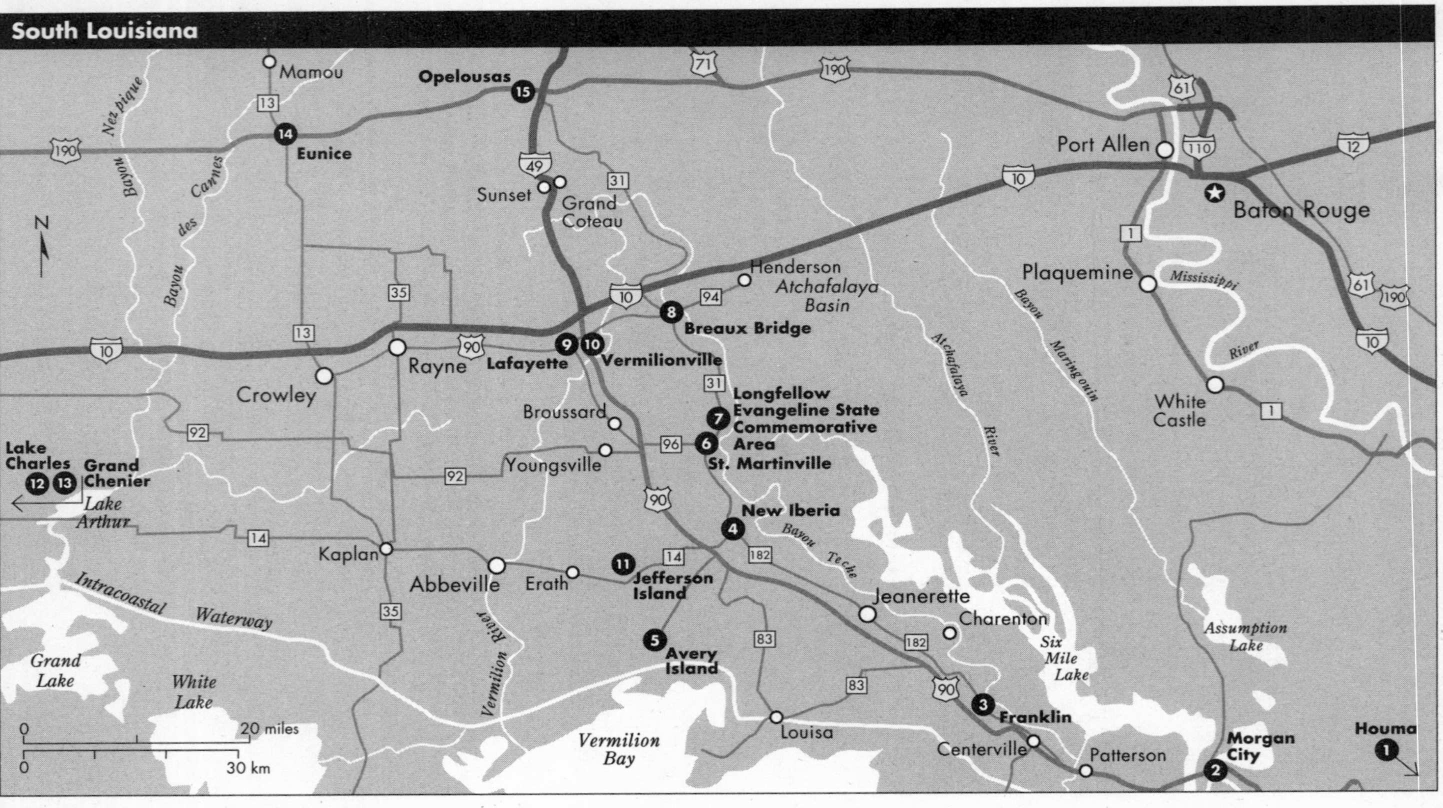

South Louisiana
Mamou
Opelousas
Eunice
Nez pique
Bayou des Cannes
Bayou
Sunset
Grand Coteau
Port Allen
Baton Rouge
Plaquemine
Mississippi River
White Castle
Henderson
Atchafalaya Basin
Breaux Bridge
Rayne
Lafayette
Vermilionville
Crowley
Broussard
Longfellow Evangeline State Commemorative Area
St. Martinville
Youngsville
Lake Charles
Grand Chenier
Lake Arthur
New Iberia
Bayou Teche
Atchafalaya River
Bayou Maringouin
Kaplan
Abbeville
Erath
Jefferson Island
Jeanerette
Charenton
Intracoastal Waterway
Vermilion River
Avery Island
Six Mile Lake
Assumption Lake
Grand Lake
White Lake
Vermilion Bay
Louisa
Franklin
Centerville
Patterson
Morgan City
Houma
20 miles
30 km
N

2 Traveling northwesterly now on U.S. 90, we'll come to **Morgan City,** smack on the Atchafalaya River. This city struck it rich when the first producing offshore oil well was completed on November 14, 1947, and the Kerr-McGee Rig No. 16 ushered in the "black gold rush." Front Street runs alongside the 22-mile-long floodwall. Atop the **Great Wall,** Moonwalk is a lookout with a great view of the Atchafalaya, as well as displays depicting the history of the region. At the **Morgan City Information Center** (725 Myrtle St., tel. 504/384–3343, open daily 8–4) you can see a video of the first Tarzan movie, which was filmed in Morgan City in 1917.

Across from the information center, the 3½-acre **Swamp Gardens** is a heritage park that depicts the settlement of Atchafalaya Basin; displays include pirogues and other aspects of bayou life. *725 Myrtle St., tel. 504/384–3343. Admission: $2 adults, $1 children, under 5 free. Open daily 8–4.*

3 The little town of **Franklin** lies 20 miles northwest of Morgan City on U.S. 90. However, we recommend that you get there via LA 182, which you pick up just outside of Patterson. This is Bayou Teche country, and the state highways follow the writhing bayou along some stretches. (*Teche* is an Indian word meaning snake. According to an ancient Indian legend, the death throes of a giant snake carved the bayou.)

If you're of a nostalgic bent, Franklin's Main Street may bring tears of joy to your eyes. The official Main Street USA status was bestowed on it by the National Trust for Historic Preservation. The street rolls out beneath an arcade of live oaks, and old-fashioned street lamps with No Hitching signs line the boulevard. Franklin is nestled along a bend in the bayou, and there is a splendid view of it from **Parc sur le Teche.** (To reach the park as you drive north through town, turn right on Willow Street by the courthouse square.)

The **Chitimacha Indian Reservation,** three miles northeast of Franklin, is the state's only Indian reservation. For centuries the Chitimacha flourished along the shores of Bayou Atchafalaya. The tribe's main settlement was in Charenton, site of the present reservation. The tribe was famed for its weaving, and Chitimacha baskets, as well as other small craft items, can be found in the reservation's craft shop. *LA 326, Charenton, tel. 318/923–4830. Admission free. Open daily 8–4:30. Closed major holidays.*

4 **New Iberia**—the "Queen City of the Teche"—is the next stop along LA 182. New Iberia was founded in 1779 by Spanish settlers, who named the town after the Iberian Peninsula. The town is a blend of Spanish, French, and Acadian cultures.

Set in two lush acres on the bank of the bayou, in the shadows of moss-draped oaks, **Shadows-on-the-Teche** is one of the South's best-known plantation homes. Built in 1834 for sugar planter David Weeks, this fine old home is the epitome of what went with the wind. *317 E. Main St., New Iberia, tel. 318/369–6446. Admission: $5 adults; $4 senior citizens, $3 children 6–11, children under 6 free. Open daily 9–4:30. Closed Christmas, Thanksgiving, and New Year's Day.*

City Park is a 45-acre area across the Teche from Main Street, with tennis courts, playgrounds, baseball and softball fields, a fishing pond, boat ramps, and picnic shelters with barbecue facilities. *Admission free. Open weekdays 8 AM–9 PM, Sat. 1–9, Sun. 1–5. Closed major holidays.*

Make a short detour, nine miles south of New Iberia, to see
5 **Avery Island.** The factory on the "island" (it's actually a salt dome) is the birthplace of Tabasco sauce, and descendants of Edmund McIlhenny continue making the hot sauce he invented in the mid-1800s. Other attractions are the 200-acre Jungle Garden, lush with tropical plants, and Bird City, a sanctuary with flurries of snow-white egrets. *LA 329, tel. 318/369–6243. Admission to the gardens and sanctuary: $5 adults; $3.50 children 6–12, under 6 free. Admission to the Tabasco factory is free. Open daily 8–5:30.*

LA 31 hugs, as best it can, the Teche from New Iberia north to
6 **St. Martinville** in the heart of Evangeline Country. This little town is awash with legends. Longfellow's poem was based on the true story of Emmeline Labiche and Louis Arceneaux, two young lovers who were separated for years during the Acadian exile. St. Martinville was a major point of debarkation for Acadian refugees in the mid-18th century. Louis arrived in the town first and waited many long years hoping to find Emmeline. He eventually despaired of ever seeing her again and became engaged to another woman. Emmeline finally did reach St. Martinville, and, the story is told, Louis saw her by chance as she stepped ashore. Pale with shock, he told her that he was betrothed to another, turned on his heel, and disappeared. Their last, unhappy meeting place was beneath the **Evangeline Oak** (Evangeline Blvd. at Bayou Teche). The *Romance of Evangeline* was filmed in St. Martinville in 1929. Dolores Del Rio starred as Evangeline, and posed for the bronze statue that the cast and crew donated to the town.

You can see the statue in the cemetery behind the church of **St. Martin de Tours** (123 S. Main St.), near the grave of Emmeline Labiche. St. Martin de Tours, Mother Church of the Acadians, is one of the oldest Catholic churches in the country. Inside there is a replica of the Lourdes Grotto and a baptismal font said to have been a gift from Louis XVI. In the late 18th century, St. Martinville was known as Petit Paris because it was a major refuge for royalists who escaped during the French Revolution. "Little Paris" was the scene of many regal balls, soirees, and operas.

Just north of the city limits, on LA 31 and the banks of the
7 Teche, the **Longfellow-Evangeline State Commemorative Area** is a 157-acre park shaded by majestic, moss-draped live oaks. The park contains picnic tables and pavilions, a boat launch, and early Acadian structures. *Tel. 318/394–3754. Admission to the grounds: $2 per vehicle. Open daily 9–7 Apr. 1–Sept. 30, 9–5 rest of year.*

Continue northward on LA 31 for a look at the little town of
8 **Breaux Bridge.** Breaux Bridge is home to world-famous **Mulate's** (*see* Dining, *below*) and calls itself the Crawfish Capital of the World. The **Crawfish Festival,** held in May, draws upwards of 100,000 people.

9 About 15 minutes from Breaux Bridge on LA 94 is **Lafayette,** a major center of Cajun lore and life. Stop in at the **Lafayette Convention and Visitors Bureau** (16th St. and Evangeline Thruway) and load up your tote bag with maps and brochures.

The **Acadian Village,** nestled in 10 wooded acres, is a re-creation of an early 19th-century bayou settlement. There is a general store, a blacksmith shop, a chapel, and houses representing different styles of Acadian architecture. *200 Greenleaf Rd. (LA 342), tel. 318/981–2364. Admission: $5 adults, $4 senior citizens, $2.50 children 6–14. Open daily 10–5. Closed major holidays.*

Time Out **Dwyer's Café** serves Cajun plate lunches, burgers, and sandwiches. *323 Jefferson St., tel. 318/235–9364. Open weekdays 4 AM–4 PM, Sat. 4 AM–2 PM. No credit cards. Inexpensive.*

The Louisiana Live Oak Society was founded in Lafayette more than 50 years ago. A charter member of that silent but leafy set dominates the 900 block of St. John Street. The **St. John Oak** is 400 years old and has a matronly waistline of about 19 feet. It is on the grounds of the **Cathedral of St. John the Evangelist** (914 St. John St.), a Romanesque church with Byzantine touches.

The **Lafayette Natural History Museum** is a busy place, with workshops, movies, concerts, light shows, and a planetarium. It's also the venue for the annual September Louisiana Native Crafts Festival. *637 Girard Park Dr., Lafayette, tel. 318/268–5544. Admission free. Open Mon., Wed., Thurs., and Fri. 9–5, Tues. 9–9, weekends 1–5.*

The museum's sister facility is **The Acadiana Park Nature Station,** a three-story cypress pole structure with an interpretive center and discovery boxes to help children get acquainted with the wildflowers, birds, and other things they'll see along a 3½-mile trail. *E. Alexandre St., Lafayette, tel. 318/235–6181. Admission free. Open weekdays 9–5, weekends 11–3.*

The Lafayette Art Gallery gives visitors a close look at local arts and crafts. *700 Lee Ave., tel. 318/269–0363. Open weekdays 10–4:30.*

10 **Vermilionville** is Acadiana's answer to Colonial Williamsburg in Virginia. On the banks of Bayou Vermilion, the 22-acre living history museum presents early Cajun, Creole, and Chitimacha Indian life in the region through architecture, food, and daily programs featuring music and dance, as well as lectures on religion, language, and social history. **La Cuisine Maman** serves up Cajun and Creole fare, and even the fast-food facilities dish out the likes of boudin. Costumed, French-speaking craftspeople demonstrate Acadian craft-making in restored and replica buildings, and engage in conversation with visitors (this is a great place to brush up on your French). A chapel patterned after the Acadian settlers' first church, and an adjacent cemetery interpret local religious customs—including voodoo and Cajun *traiteurs* (healers). A hand-pulled ferry crosses Petite Bayou to an outdoor theater-in-the-round, where reenactments of the everyday life of 19th-century pioneers are presented. *1600 Surrey St. (just off U.S. Hwy. 90, near the airport), tel. 318/233–4077 or 800/99–BAYOU. Admission: $8 adults, $6.50 senior citizens, $5 students 6–18. Open daily 9–5. Closed Christmas and New Year's Day.*

We'll hitch up with U.S. 90 now and go 15 miles south to the junction with LA 675, where a right turn will take us to **Live Oak Gardens.** American actor Joseph Jefferson, who toured the country in the 19th century portraying Rip Van Winkle,

bought several thousand acres of land in South Louisiana and
11 built his winter home on what came to be called **Jefferson Island.** In 1980, the salt dome on which the "island" rested collapsed, causing severe damage. The area, now called Live Oak Gardens, has been completely restored to its former grandeur, with formal and informal gardens and groves of live oaks. Jefferson's house is a three-story, comfortably opulent, Southern Gothic home with Moorish touches. A café in the reception area overlooks Lake Peigneur. A 45-minute boat ride on the lake is included in the admission. *5505 Rip Van Winkle Rd., off LA 14, tel. 318/365–3332. Admission: $8 adults, $7 senior citizens, $4.50 children 5–16. Open daily 9–5 during daylight savings time, 9–4 during winter. Closed major holidays.*

12 At this point, we'll strike out on LA 14 and head for **Lake Charles,** the state's third seaport. The city dates from the 1760s, when the first French settlers arrived. The first home was built by Charles Sallier on the shell beach by the lake, and the town was originally called Charlie's Lake. The city is blessed with more than 50 miles of rivers, lakes, canals, and bayous, making it a paradise for sailing, fishing, canoeing, shrimping, and crabbing.

North Beach (admission $1 per vehicle) is a white-sand beach on the north shore of the lake, where you can loll in the sun, swim, or rent a sailboat. Twelve miles north of the city on LA 378, **Sam Houston Jones State Park** is a 1,068-acre area that beckons sports and nature enthusiasts.

The **Imperial Calcasieu Museum,** on the site of Charles Sallier's home, has an extensive collection pertaining to Lake Charles and Calcasieu Parish. The museum includes an old-fashioned pharmacy, an Audubon collection, a Gay Nineties barbershop, and a modern fine-arts gallery. *204 W. Sallier St., Lake Charles, tel. 318/439–3797. Admission $1, children under 6 free. Open Tues.–Fri. 10–5, weekends 1–5. Closed Mon., and major holidays.*

The **Creole Nature Trail** is a 105-mile loop beginning on LA 27 in **Sulphur,** dipping down along the Gulf of Mexico on LA 82, and winding up back in Lake Charles. Beautiful in the spring, this drive takes you to the **Sabine Wildlife Refuge** (admission free) where a paved 1½ mile trail takes you right into the wilds. There is an audiovisual center and a tower at the end of the trail, which gives you an excellent view of the wilderness. (Take along some insect repellent!)

You can make a detour off the Creole Nature Trail and continue east on LA 82 (Hug-the-Coast Highway), which whips along
13 the windswept coastal marshes through **Grand Chenier** to the **Rockefeller Wildlife Refuge,** an 84,000-acre tract where thousands of ducks, geese, 'gators, wading birds, otters, and others while away the winter months.

We'll leave Lake Charles on I–10E, and exit on U.S. 165 headed north. An 18-mile drive will put us at the intersection of U.S. 190, where we'll head east again.

14 This route will take us through the tiny town of **Eunice,** home of the **Cajun Radio Show** (*see* Nightlife, *below*) and of the **Eunice Museum.** The museum is in a former railroad depot and contains displays on Cajun culture, including Cajun music and Cajun Mardi Gras. *220 S. C.C. Duson Dr., Eunice, tel. 318/*

457–6540. Admission free. Open Tues.–Sat. 8–noon and 1–5. Closed major holidays.

The area surrounding Eunice is the major stomping grounds for the annual Courir du Mardi Gras, which takes place the Sunday before Fat Tuesday (Mardi Gras Day). *Le Capitain* leads a band of masked and costumed horseback riders on a mad dash through the countryside, stopping at farmhouses along the way to shout, *"Voulez-vous recevoir cette bande de Mardi Gras?"* (Do you wish to receive the Mardi Gras?) The answer is always Yes, and the group enlarges and continues, gathering food for the street festivals that wind things up.

15 Farther east on U.S. 190 is **Opelousas,** the third-oldest town in the state. Poste de Opelousas was founded in 1720 by the French as a trading post. The town is named for the Appalousa Indians, who lived in the area centuries before the French and Spanish arrived. For a brief period during the Civil War, Opelousas served as the state capital.

On the east side of town on U.S. 190, look for the **Acadiana Tourist Center** (tel. 318/948–6263), where you can get plenty of information and also arrange for tours of some of the town's historic homes.

Adjacent to the tourist center is the **Jim Bowie Museum.** This was Bowie's boyhood home, and the museum has memorabilia pertaining to his life and times, including the famous Bowie knife. *U.S. 190E, tel. 318/948–6263. Admission free. Open daily 8–4.*

A 15-minute drive south of Opelousas on I–49, exiting on LA 93, will put you on Main Street in **Grand Coteau.** Grand Coteau is a religious and educational center, and the entire peaceful little village is on the National Register of Historic Places. Of particular note here is the **Church of St. Charles Borromeo,** a simple wooden structure with an ornate high-baroque interior. There are 36 works of art in the church, most of which were done by Erasmus Humbrecht, whose works can also be seen in St. Louis Cathedral in New Orleans. The church's unusual bell tower is one of the area's most-photographed sights. The church can be toured (for a $1 donation per person), but you must call (tel. 318/662–5279 weekdays; 318/662–3875 weekends) to make arrangements in advance.

Time Out **The Kitchen Shop,** in a quaint cypress cottage, sells unique gifts, Louisiana specialties, and garden art. There's also a tiny sun-filled room, an herb garden, and a patio where you can relax over desserts, tea, and gourmet coffee. *Corner of King and Cherry sts., Grand Coteau, tel. 318/662–3500. MC, V. Open Mon.–Sat. 9–5. Inexpensive.*

Chretien Point Plantation, not far away, is noted not only for its grandeur but also for the role it played in *Gone With the Wind.* In the 1930s, a photographer infatuated with the house took pictures of it and sent them to Hollywood. As a result, its staircase was the model for the one in Scarlett O'Hara's Tara. The house now takes bed-and-breakfast guests. *About 4 mi from Sunset on the Bristol/Bosco Rd., tel. 318/662–5876 or 318/233–7050. Admission: $5.50 adults, $5 senior citizens, $2.75 children 5–12, under 4 free. Open daily 10–5. Closed major holidays.*

You can continue on to Baton Rouge via either U.S. 190 or I–10, as Grand Coteau is cradled in between the two thoroughfares. We'll begin our next tour in Baton Rouge and continue into plantation country.

What to See and Do with Children

Acadian Village, Lafayette (*see* Exploring, *above*).
Annie Miller's Terrebonne Swamp & Marsh Tours (*see* Guided Tours, *above*).
Atchafalaya Basin Backwater Adventure (*see* Guided Tours, *above*).
Avery Island (*see* Exploring, *above*).
Chitimacha Indian Reservation, Charenton (*see* Exploring, *above*).
City Park, New Iberia (*see* Exploring, *above*).
Creole Nature Trail, Lake Charles (*see* Exploring, *above*).
Hammond's Flying Service, Air Tours, Houma (*see* Guided Tours, *above*).
Jim Bowie Museum, Opelousas (*see* Exploring, *above*).
Lafayette Natural History Museum & Nature Station (*see* Exploring, *above*).
Live Oak Gardens (*see* Exploring, *above*).
McGee's Landing, Atchafalaya Basin Tours (*see* Guided Tours, *above*).
North Beach, Lake Charles (*see* Exploring, *above*).
Vermilionville (*see* Exploring, *above*).

Off the Beaten Track

People all over the world have a hankering for Cajun chank-a-chanking (dancing). To Cajun music, musicians need those special triangles, accordions, and fiddles. A number of places in Cajun Country make not only music but musical instruments as well. Among them is the **Savoy Music Center Accordion Factory** in Eunice. The front half of the building is a music store, and behind it, Cajun accordions are made from scratch. Proprietor Marc Savoy says his factory turns out about five accordions a month and fills orders all the way from Alaska to New Zealand. On Saturday mornings, accordions and other instruments tune up and take off during the weekly jam sessions held in the shop. There's beer to drink, two-stepping to do, and musicians from all over the area dropping over to sit in on the informal sessions. *U.S. 190, 3 mi east of Eunice, tel. 318/457–9563. Admission free. Open Tues.–Fri. 9–5, Sat. 9–noon.*

Participant Sports

Louisiana is not called Sportsman's Paradise for nothing. Hunting and fishing are a way of life in this state. There are approximately 1.7 million acres of publicly owned or managed lands open to hunting. For information on permits, limits, and seasons, contact the **Louisiana Department of Wildlife & Fisheries,** Box 15570, Baton Rouge 70895, tel. 504/342–5868.

Biking These flatlands and lush parks make for easy riding. There are 60 miles of marked bike trails in Lafayette. Guides, rental bikes, and maps are available at **Pack & Paddle** (601 E. Pinhook Rd., Lafayette, tel. 318/232–5854).

Canoeing Paddling is almost a breeze on the easy-going Whisky Chitto Creek. Canoes can be rented at **Arrowhead Canoe Rentals** (9 mi. west of Oberlin on Rte. 26, tel. 318/639–2086 or 800/637–2086).

Fishing Trips to fish, sightsee, bird-watch, or hunt can be arranged at **Gator Guide Service** (Box 9224, New Iberia 70562, tel. 318/365–6400). **Sportsman's Paradise** (tel. 504/594–2414) is a charter fishing facility 20 miles south of Houma, with eight boats available year-round. **Salt, Inc. Charter Fishing Service** (tel. 504/594–6626 or 504/594–7581), LA 56 south of Houma at Coco Marina, offers fishing trips in the bays and barrier islands of lower Terrebonne Parish, as well as into the Gulf of Mexico.

Golf You can tee off at **Pine Shadows Golf Center** (750 Goodman Rd., Lake Charles, tel. 318/433–8681), **City Park Golf Course** (Mudd Ave. and Eighth St., Lafayette, tel. 318/268–5557), and **Vieux Chene Golf Course** (Youngsville Hwy., Broussard, tel. 318/837–1159).

Hiking/Nature Trails The Old Stagecoach Road in **Sam Houston Jones State Park** is a favorite for hikers who want to explore the park and the various tributaries of the Calcasieu River. The **Louisiana State Arboretum** (Ville Platte, tel. 318/363–2503) is a 600-acre facility with four miles of nature trails.

Horseback Riding There are trail rides, pony rides, and even hayrides at **Broken Arrow Stables** (Segura Rd. off LA 3013, New Iberia, tel. 318/369–PONY).

Dining and Lodging

Dining Graced as the state is with waterways, Louisiana tables are laden with seafood in every imaginable and innovative variety. In South Louisiana, sea creatures are prepared with a Cajun flair, which usually means hot and spicy.

Category	Cost*
Very Expensive	over $35
Expensive	$25–$35
Moderate	$15–$20
Inexpensive	under $15

**per person without tax (7½%), service, or drinks*

Lodging Sleeping accommodations run from homey bed-and-breakfasts to chain motels to luxury hotels to elegant antebellum mansions open for overnighters.

Category	Cost*
Very Expensive	over $120
Expensive	$90–$120
Moderate	$50–$90
Inexpensive	under $50

**double room; add 6% for taxes*

Breaux Bridge
Dining
★

Mulate's. A roadhouse with flashing yellow lights outside and plastic checkered cloths inside, Mulate's is an eatery, a dance hall, an age-old family gathering spot, and a celebrity, having been featured on the "Today" show and "Good Morning, America," among other airings. A dressed-down crowd digs into the likes of stuffed crabs and the Super Seafood Platters. Live music at lunch and dinner. *325 Mills Ave., tel. in LA 800/634-9880 or in USA 800/42-CAJUN. Dress: informal. Reservations not required. AE, MC, V. Open Sun.-Thurs. 7 AM-10:30 PM, Fri. and Sat. 7 AM-11 PM. Closed Christmas Day. Moderate.*

Carencro
Dining

Prudhomme's Cajun Cafe. In a suburb of Lafayette, celebrity chef Paul Prudhomme's sister Enola—a major contributor to *The Prudhomme Family Cookbook*—has her country kitchen in a cypress cottage. Her specialties are blackened fish dishes, eggplant pirogue, and panfried rabbit in cream sauce—plus homemade jalapeño-and-cheese bread. *4676 N.E. Evangeline Thruway, tel. 318/896-7964. Dress: informal. Reservations not required. AE, MC, V. Closed Mon. Moderate.*

Donaldsonville
Dining

Lafitte's Landing. Pirate Jean Lafitte is said to have frequented this raised Acadian cottage, which dates from 1797. Chef John Folse, who is renowned the world over in culinary circles, prepares such delicacies as Shrimp Anne (pecan-smoked shrimp served on fried zucchini) and pecan-smoked tournedos finished with a pecan tasso glace. *Sunshine Bridge Access Rd., tel. 504/473-1232. Dress: casual but neat. Reservations advised. D, MC, V. Expensive.*

Lafayette
Dining

Cafe Vermilionville. A 19th-century inn with crisp white napery, old-brick fireplaces, and a casual elegance. Among the specialties are Redfish Anna, with lump crabmeat, artichoke hearts, and béarnaise sauce, and fried soft-shell crab with crawfish fettuccine. *1304 W. Pinhook Rd., tel. 318/237-0100. Dress: informal. Reservations advised. AE, MC, V. Closed Christmas and New Year's Day. Moderate.*

Prejean's. Housed in a cypress cottage, this local favorite has a cozy oyster bar, red-checkered cloths, and live music nightly. Specialties include Prejean's Platter (seafood gumbo, fried shrimp, oysters, catfish, and seafood-stuffed bell peppers) and Crawfish Dinner, with étoufféed, bisqued, and fried mudbugs. *3480 U.S. 167N, next to Evangeline Downs, tel. 318/896-3247. Dress: informal. Reservations not required. AE, DC, MC, V. Closed Christmas and Thanksgiving. Moderate.*

Lodging

Holiday Inn Central-Holidome. Seventeen acres containing virtually everything you'd ever need for a long and yuppie life. *Box 91807, 70509, tel. 318/233-6815 or 800/HOLIDAY. 250 rooms. Facilities: airport shuttle, cable TV, cocktail lounge, restaurant, heated indoor pool with whirlpool, sauna, 2 lighted tennis courts, 24-hr jogging track, game rooms, playgrounds, picnic areas. AE, DC, MC, V. Moderate-Very Expensive.*

Hotel Acadiana. A cushy lobby is lit by a huge brass chandelier, and there's concierge floor and standard rooms with thick carpeting, marble-top dressers, minirefrigerators, and wet bars. Even-numbered rooms face the pool. *1801 W. Pinhook Rd., 70508, tel. 318/233-8120, in LA 800/874-4664 or in USA 800/826-8386. 304 rooms. Facilities: free airport shuttle, cable TV with ESPN, cocktail lounge, restaurant, free parking, facilities for handicapped, outdoor pool, 2 outdoor Jacuzzis. AE, DC, MC, V. Inexpensive-Moderate.*

Lake Charles
Dining

Cafe Margaux. Candlelight, soft pinks, white linens, French waiters, and a 9,000-bottle mahogany wine cellar. Specialties include rack of lamb *en croute* and fillet of flounder with lump crabmeat and brown meunière sauce. *765 Bayou Pines East, tel. 318/433–2902. Jacket and tie suggested. Reservations recommended. AE, MC, V. Closed Sun., Christmas. Moderate–Expensive.*

Lodging

Holiday Inn, Lake Charles. Built in 1982 between the lake and the interstate, the Holiday Inn has traditional furnishings in rooms done in soothing earth tones. The four-story structure offers 10 rooms for nonsmokers and five for the handicapped. Rooms on the lakeside are infinitely preferable to those on the interstate side. *505 N. Lakeshore Dr., 70601, tel. 318/433–7121 or 800/367–1814 or 800/433–8809 (LA). 269 rooms. Facilities: free airport shuttle, cable TV, coffee shop, restaurant, free parking, gift shop, laundry, room service, safety deposit box, outdoor swimming pool. AE, DC, MC, V. Moderate.*

Chateau Charles Hotel and Conference Center. A New Orleans–style structure with wrought-iron trim and beamed ceilings, the hotel is located on 25 wooded acres, three minutes from downtown. There are four two-bedroom suites with wet bars, microwaves, minirefrigerators; six nonsmokers' rooms, and easy access for the handicapped in the all-ground-level hotel. The facility was built in 1955 and completely renovated in 1983. *Box 1381, 70602, tel. 318/882–6130. 260 rooms. Facilities: free airport shuttle, free shuttle to local health clubs, cable TV, restaurant, cocktail lounge, laundry, and room service. AE, DC, MC, V. Inexpensive–Moderate.*

Downtowner Motor Inn. Smack on the lake, adjacent to the Hilton but about 10 years its senior, the Downtowner boasts a boat dock, splashy garden, large sun deck, and contemporary rooms in green and rust. Ask for a room overlooking the lake. *507 N. Lakeshore Dr., 70601, tel. 318/433–0541. 134 rooms. Facilities: free airport shuttle, cable TV, cocktail lounge, 24-hr restaurant, room service. AE, DC, MC, V. Inexpensive.*

Opelousas
Dining

Palace Café. A down-home coffee shop on the town square, operated by the same family for 65 years. Locals flock here for the café's famous homemade baklava. Among the eclectic specialties are baked eggplant stuffed with Alaskan king crabmeat dressing, and Greek salad with feta cheese, black and green olives, and anchovies. There are also steaks, fried chicken, sandwiches, burgers, and seafood. *167 W. Landry St., tel. 318/ 942–2142. Dress: informal. Reservations not required. MC, V. Closed Easter, July 4th, Thanksgiving, Christmas Eve, Christmas Day, and New Year's Day. Inexpensive.*

St. Martinville
Dining

La Place d'Evangeline. In the historic redbrick Old Castillo Hotel, on the banks of the Bayou Teche beneath the branches of the Evangeline Oak, dine in high-ceiling rooms where 18th-century royalists once held lavish balls and operas. An extensive menu includes steak Evangeline, stuffed with lump crabmeat; red snapper Gabriel, with seafood sauce; and alligator meat. Do not pass up the homemade bread. Proprietors Peggy and Gerald Hulin have renovated the upstairs part of the old hotel, and five rooms are now open for guests. *220 Evangeline Blvd., tel. 318/394–4010. Dress: informal. Reservations not necessary. AE, MC, V. Closed Christmas. Moderate.*

The Arts

Concerts Major concert attractions are booked into the **Cajundome** in Lafayette (444 Cajundome Blvd., tel. 318/265–2100) and the **Lake Charles Civic Center** (900 Lakeshore Dr., tel. 318/491–1256).

Theater **The Lake Charles Little Theater** (813 Enterprise Blvd., Lake Charles, tel. 318/433–7988) puts on a variety of plays and musicals. **The Theatre 'Cadien** (tel. 318/893–5655) performs plays in French in various venues. **Lafayette Community Theatre** (529 Jefferson St., tel. 318/235–1532) offers contemporary plays with a Cajun flair.

Nightlife

Louisiana is alive with all kinds of music, but while we're in Cajun Country our focus will be on the music of the Cajuns. And we'll introduce you to chank-a-chanking at a fais do-do. Translation? The little iron triangles in most Cajun bands make a rhythmic "chank-a-chank" sound, and most folks call dancing to the rhythm chank-a-chanking. As for fais do-do (pronounced "fay doh-doh"), that's the dance, or party, where you go to chank-a-chank. Fais do-dos crop up all over Cajun Country, sometimes in the town square, sometimes at somebody's house. There are also restaurants, dance halls, and lounges that regularly feature live Cajun music. The *Times of Acadiana* is a free newspaper that comes out every Wednesday and is available in hotels, restaurants, and shops. Check the "On the Town" section to see what's doing in the area.

The following restaurants and lounges regularly feature music for two-stepping, waltzing, and chank-a-chanking. ("Regularly" does not necessarily mean every night.) Sunday afternoon (*all* afternoon) is often devoted to dancing. Be sure and call to find out what the schedule is.

Mulate's (*see* Beaux Bridge Dining, *above*).
Prejean's (*see* Lafayette Dining, *above*).
Randol's (2320 Kaliste Saloom Rd., Lafayette, tel. 318/981–7080). Hot dancing in a greenhouse setting.
La Poussière (1301 Grand Pointe Rd., Breaux Bridge, tel. 318/332–1721). One of the oldest dance halls around.
Belizaire's (2307 N. Parkerson Ave., Crowley, tel. 318/788–2501). Take a look at the Cajun Music Hall of Fame before you take to the floor.
Slim's Y-Ki-Ki (LA 167, Washington Rd., Opelousas., tel. 318/942–9980). *Louisiana Life* magazine rated this black Cajun club the best Cajun dancing place in the state.
Fred's Lounge (420 Sixth St., Mamou, tel. 318/468–5411). Saturday morning radio broadcasts (complete with music, of course), have been aired from Fred Tate's place for more than 40 years. It starts at 8 AM and goes on till 1 PM.
Cajun Music Show. A live radio show, mostly in French, that's been described as a combination of the "Grand Ole Opry," the "Louisiana Hayride," and the "Prairie Home Companion." *Eunice, tel. 318/457–6575. Admission: free. Saturday nights from 6 to 8 in the Liberty Theatre, Park Ave. at Second St.*

Baton Rouge and Plantation Country

Our meandering amble through South Louisiana brings us now to Baton Rouge, the state capital. Legend has it that in 1699 French explorers observed that a red stick planted in the ground on a high bluff overlooking the Mississippi served as a boundary between two Indian tribes. Sieur d'Iberville, leader of the expedition, noted *le baton rouge*—the red stick—in his journal, and *voila!* Baton Rouge.

This is the city from which Huey P. Long ruled the state and also the site of his assassination. Even today, more than half a century after Long's death, legends abound of the colorful, cunning, and controversial governor and U.S. senator.

The parishes to the north of Baton Rouge are quiet and bucolic, with gently rolling hills, high bluffs, and historic districts. John James Audubon lived in West Feliciana Parish in 1821, tutoring local children and painting 80 of his famous bird studies. In both terrain and traits, this region is more akin to North Louisiana than to South Louisiana—which is to say, the area is very Southern.

As you are by now aware, Louisiana is graced with many stately mansions. But the area designated Plantation Country begins with a reservoir of fine old homes north of Baton Rouge that cascades all the way down the Great River Road to New Orleans.

Getting Around

By Plane Baton Rouge Metropolitan Airport (tel. 504/355–0333), 12 miles north of downtown, is served by **American, Continental, Delta,** and **Northwest.**

By Car I–10 and U.S. 190 run east–west through Baton Rouge. I–12 heads east, connecting with north–south I–55 and I–59. U.S. 61 leads from New Orleans to Baton Rouge and north. Ferries across the Mississippi cost $1 per car; most bridges are free.

Great Drives: LA 1 travels along False River, which is a blue "oxbow lake" created ages ago when the mischievous, muddy Mississippi changed its course. Water lazily nudges the shore along the route, which wanders past gracious homes and small lake houses.

By Bus **Greyhound Southeast Lines** (tel. 504/343–4891) has frequent daily service to Baton Rouge and surrounding towns.

Guided Tours

Lagniappe Tours (tel. 504/382–8687) has daily van tours of Baton Rouge, Cajun Country, and plantations.
Louisiana Backroads Unlimited (tel. 504/638–6254) specializes in off-the-beaten-track tours of the state's backroads and byways.
Southern Hospitality Tours (504/635–3582 or 800/288–8196) covers the state in style in luxury 15-passenger vans outfitted with TV, bar, and such. The company specializes in customized tours.

Important Addresses and Numbers

Tourist Information The **Louisiana Visitor Information Center** will supply you with maps and brochures to just about anywhere. *Louisiana State Capitol, State Capitol Dr., Baton Rouge, tel. 504/342–7317. Tourist information can be obtained by calling 800/33-GUMBO (outside LA) or 504/342–8119 (in LA). Open daily 9–4:30. Closed Thanksgiving, Christmas, New Year's Day, Mardi Gras.*

West Feliciana Historical Society Information Center is another useful stop for advice and information. *364 Ferdinand St., St. Francisville, tel. 504/635–6330. Open Mon.–Sat. 9–4, Sun. 1–4.*

Emergencies Dial 911 for assistance. Hospital emergency rooms are open 24 hours a day. **Baton Rouge General Medical Center** (3600 Florida Blvd., tel. 504/387–7000); **Our Lady of the Lake Medical Center** (5000 Hennessy Blvd., tel. 504/765–6565).

Pharmacy **Eckerd's** (3651 Perkins Rd., tel. 504/344–9459; 14455 Greenwell Springs Rd., tel. 504/261–6541).

Exploring Baton Rouge and Plantation Country

Numbers in the margin correspond to points of interest on the Baton Rouge and Plantation Country map.

After touring the state capital, we'll take LA 67 to see the historic districts and plantations in the parishes north of Baton Rouge. An overnight stay in one of the plantation bed-and-breakfasts is recommended. From St. Francisville, we'll take the free ferry at the tip of town and start south on LA 1 to see the antebellum gems that decorate the Great River Road between Baton Rouge and New Orleans.

1 Start your tour of **Baton Rouge** at the Visitors Information Center in the lobby of the **State Capitol Building.** Armed with maps and brochures, you can take a tour of the first floor, which includes the spot where Huey Long was shot. This building is America's tallest state capitol, standing 34 stories tall. There is an observation deck on the 27th floor that affords a spectacular view of the Mississippi River and the city. *State Capitol Dr., tel. 504/342–7317. Admission free. Open daily 8–4:30; last tour at 4 PM. Closed major holidays.*

A museum in the **Pentagon Barracks** has exhibits that acquaint visitors with the Capitol complex. The barracks were originally built in 1823–24 to quarter U.S. Army personnel, and when Louisiana State University moved from Pineville to Baton Rouge in 1869, it was located in these buildings. *Riverside North on the State Capitol grounds, tel. 504/342–1866. Admission free. Open Tues.–Sat. 10–4, Sun. 1–4. Closed major holidays.*

Only one battle of the American Revolution was fought outside the 13 original colonies, and it was fought on these capitol grounds. One of the historic buildings, the **Old Arsenal Museum** (tel. 504/387–2464), a heavy-duty structure dating from about 1835, was restored and rededicated in April 1992.

The castlelike, Gothic Revival **Old State Capitol** (150 North Blvd., tel. 504/342–8211) was being renovated at press time. When it was completed in 1849, it was considered by some to be

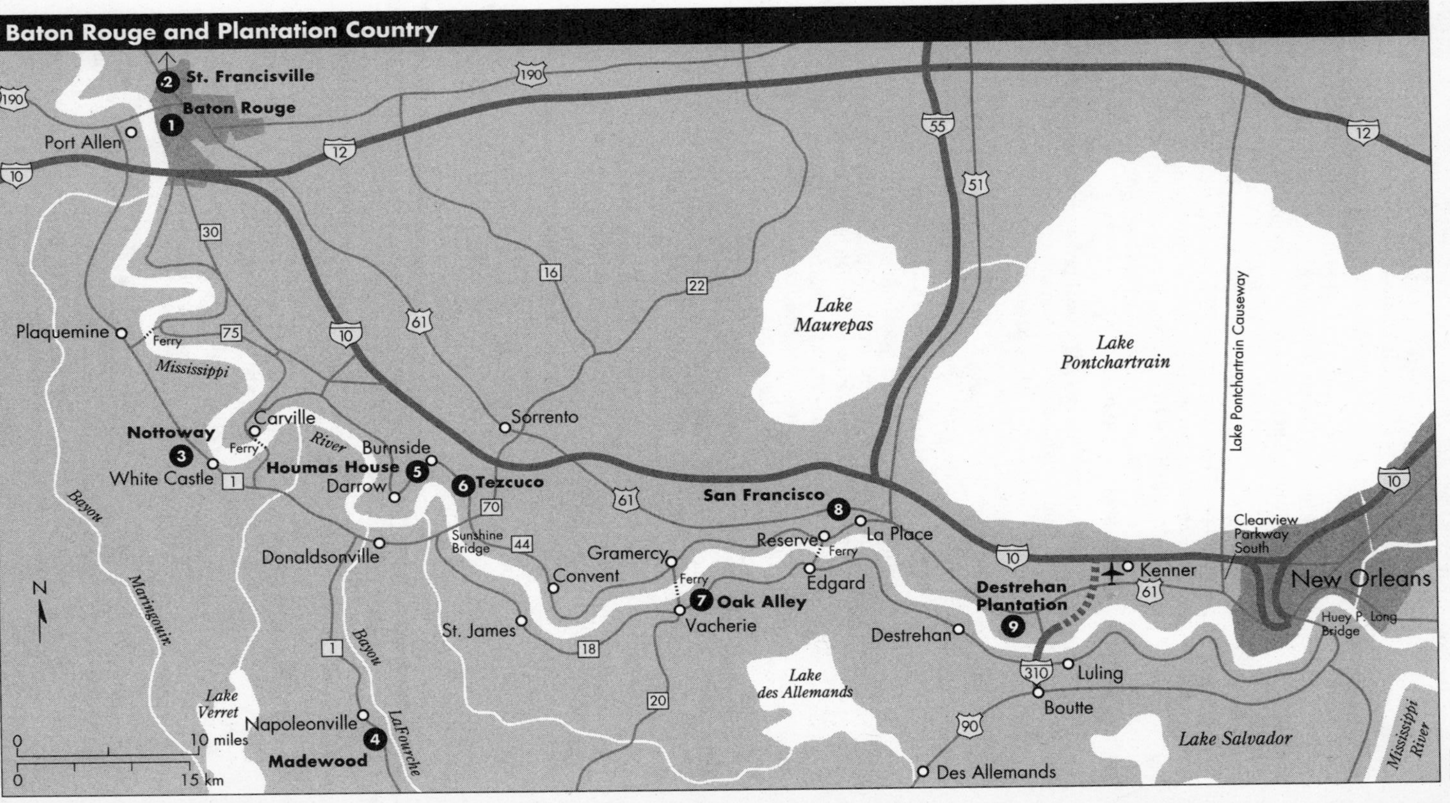
Baton Rouge and Plantation Country
St. Francisville
Baton Rouge
Nottoway
Madewood
Houmas House
Tezcuco
Oak Alley
San Francisco
Destrehan Plantation
Lake Pontchartrain
Lake Maurepas
Lake Pontchartrain Causeway
Clearview Parkway South
New Orleans
Huey P. Long Bridge
Mississippi River
Lake Salvador
Lake des Allemands
Lake Verret
Bayou Maringouin
Bayou LaFourche
Kenner
Luling
Boutte
Des Allemands
Destrehan
La Place
Reserve
Edgard
Vacherie
Gramercy
Convent
St. James
Sunshine Bridge
Sorrento
Burnside
Darrow
Donaldsonville
Carville
White Castle
Napoleonville
Plaquemine
Port Allen
Ferry
10 miles
15 km

a masterpiece, by others a monstrosity. When it reopens, probably in 1994, it will house a museum dedicated to Louisiana politics.

Across the street from the Old State Capitol is the **Louisiana Arts & Science Center Riverside Museum,** housed in an old railroad station. There is a fine arts museum with changing exhibits, an Egyptian tomb exhibit, restored trains from the 1890s to the 1950s, and a Discovery Depot with a children's art gallery and workshop. *100 S. River Rd., tel. 504/344–9463. Admission: $1.50 adults; 75¢ students, senior citizens, and children 6–12; children under 6 free. Museum does not charge admission on Sat. 10–noon. Open Tues.–Fri. 10–3, Sat. 10–4, Sun. 1–4. Closed major holidays.*

The ***Samuel Clemens Riverboat*** gives one-hour narrated tours of Baton Rouge harbor and evening supper cruises. *Departures from Florida Blvd. at the River, tel. 504/381–9606. Admission: $6 adults, $4 children under 12. 1-hr. tours 10 AM, noon, and 2 PM; Apr.–Aug. daily Sept.–Nov. and March, Wed.–Sun.; call for schedule Dec.–Feb. Closed Thanksgiving and Christmas.*

The **Louisiana Arts & Science Center** is in the restored Old Governor's Mansion, which was built in 1930 during Huey Long's administration. Rooms in the antiques-filled house are dedicated to the memories of Louisiana governors. *502 North Blvd., tel. 504/344–9463. Admission: $1.50 adults; 75¢ students, senior citizens, and children 6–12. Open Sat. 10–4, Sun. 1–4. Closed major holidays.*

Time Out At the **Blackforest** you can get German food, deli sandwiches, plate lunches, and imported beer. *321 North Blvd., tel. 504/334–0059. MC, V. Inexpensive.*

About 1½ miles from the center of town, **Magnolia Mound Plantation** is an early 19th-century raised cottage furnished with American Federal antiques and Louisiana artifacts. On Tuesday and Thursday from October through May cooking demonstrations are conducted in the outbuildings. *2161 Nicholson Dr., tel. 504/343–4955. Admission: $3.50 adults, $2.50 senior citizens, $1.50 students, 75¢ children. Open Tues.–Sat. 10–4, Sun. 1–4. Closed major holidays.*

Continuing south on Nicholson Drive you'll come to **Louisiana State University.** LSU was founded in Pineville in 1860 as the Louisiana State Seminary of Learning and Military Academy. Its president was William Tecumseh Sherman, who resigned when war broke out and four years later made his famous march through Georgia. The 200-acre campus has several museums of interest, as well as Indian Mounds that are of particular interest to archaeologists and archaeology buffs.

Baton Rouge's other major institution of higher learning is **Southern University,** about five miles north of town on U.S. 61. Founded in 1880, Southern U. is the nation's largest predominantly black university.

Fourteen miles north of Baton Rouge on U.S. 61, you'll come to the **Port Hudson State Commemorative Area.** The 650-acre park is the site of a fiercely fought Civil War battle, and the longest siege in American military history. There are high viewing towers, gun trenches, and, on a more peaceful note, seven miles of hiking trails. *756 W. Plains-Port Hudson Rd. (U.S. 61), tel. 504/654–3775. Admission $2. Open Wed.–Sun. 9–5. Closed major holidays.*

2 About 10 miles farther brings you to **St. Francisville,** which has been described as a town two miles long and two yards wide. Much of the long, skinny town is listed on the National Register of Historic Places. Allow plenty of time for your visit to **Rosedown Plantation and Gardens.** This house and its surroundings bring on a bad attack of hyperbole. Suffice it to say that the opulent house dates from 1835, is beautifully restored, and nestles in 28 acres of exquisite formal gardens. *LA 10, just off U.S. 61, tel. 504/635–3332. Admission: $9 to the house and gardens, $5 for the gardens only. Open daily 9–5 Mar.–Oct., 10–4 Nov.–Feb. Closed Christmas Eve and Christmas Day.*

A few miles south of St. Francisville, off U.S. 61, you'll find the 100-acre **Audubon State Commemorative Area,** where Audubon did a major portion of his "Birds of America" studies. The three-story Oakley Plantation House on the grounds is where Audubon tutored the young Eliza Pirrie. *LA 956, tel. 504/635–3739. Admission to the park and plantation: $2. Grounds open daily 9–7 Apr. 1–Sept. 30, 9–5 daily Oct. 1–Mar. 31. Oakley open daily 9–5. Closed major holidays.*

The Myrtles bills itself as America's Most Haunted House and hosts Mystery Weekends, Halloween Tours, and such. The Myrtles is best noted for its 110-foot gallery with Wedgwood blue cast-iron grillwork. The house was built around 1796, and has elegant formal parlors with rich molding and faux marble paneling. *5 mi north of St. Francisville on U.S. 61, tel. 504/635–6277. Admission: $6 adults, $3 under 13. Open daily 9–5. Closed Christmas.*

Drive aboard the ferry ($1 per car) just outside St. Francisville for a breezy ride across the Mississippi. Pick up LA 1 in New Roads and head south. You'll be driving right alongside **False River,** which was an abandoned riverbed that became a lake. In contrast to the muddy Mississippi, the waters of False River are dark blue. This is an excellent fishing area, and you'll see long piers and fishing boats tied up all along the route.

3 Sixteen miles south of Baton Rouge is **Nottoway,** the South's largest plantation home, built in 1859 by famed architect Henry Howard. The Greek Revival/Italianate mansion has 64 rooms filled with antiques and is especially noted for its white ballroom, which has original crystal chandeliers and hand-carved Corinthian columns. Several of the rooms are open for overnighters. Before you leave the lush grounds of Nottoway, walk across the road and go up on the levee for a splendid view of Old Man River. *LA 1, 2 mi north of White Castle, tel. 504/545–2730. Admission: $8 adults, $3 children under 12. Open daily 9–5. Closed Christmas Day.*

4 Henry Howard was also the architect for **Madewood,** a magnificent 21-room Greek Revival mansion with double galleries and white columns. *A Woman Called Moses*, starring Cicely Tyson, was filmed in the house. This, too, is an elegant antebellum bed-and-breakfast. *4250 LA 308, 2 mi south of Napoleonville, tel. 504/369–7151. Admission: $5 adults, $4 students, $3 children under 12; 10% discount for senior citizens. Open daily 10–5. Closed major holidays.*

On the East Bank of the River, docents in antebellum garb
5 guide you through **Houmas House,** a Greek Revival masterpiece famed for its three-story spiral staircase. *Hush Hush, Sweet Charlotte,* with Bette Davis and Olivia de Haviland, was filmed here, as was the pilot for the TV series "Longstreet." *LA 942, ½ mi off LA 44 in Burnside, tel. 504/522–2262. Admission: $6.50 adults, $4.50 ages 13–17, $3.25 children 6–12. Open daily Feb.–Oct. 10–5, Nov.–Jan. 10–4. Closed major holidays.*

6 Built in 1835, **Tezcuco** is a graceful raised cottage with delicate wrought-iron galleries, ornate friezes, an antiques shop, and overnight cottages. *LA 44, about 7 mi above Sunshine Bridge, tel. 504/562–3929. Admission: $5 adults, $2.50 children 4–12, $3.50 students and senior citizens. Open Mar.–Oct. 10–5, Nov.–Feb. 10–4. Closed major holidays.*

7 **Oak Alley** is also a movie star, having served as the setting for the Don Johnson-Cybil Shepherd TV remake of *The Long Hot Summer.* The house dates from 1839, and the 28 gnarled and arching live oaks trees that give the house its name were planted in the early 1700s. There is a splendid view of those trees from the upper gallery. *LA 18, 6 mi upriver of the Gramercy-Vacherie ferry, tel. 504/523–4351. Admission: $6.50 adults, $3.50 children 13–18, $2 children 6–12, 5 and under free. Open daily 9–5. Closed major holidays.*

8 **San Francisco,** completed in 1856, is an elaborate "Steamboat Gothic" house noted for its ornate millwork and ceiling frescoes. *LA 44 near Reserve, tel. 504/535–2341. Admission: $6.50 adults, $3.75 students, $2.50 children 6–11. Open daily 10–4. Closed major holidays.*

9 **Destrehan Plantation** is the oldest plantation left intact in the lower Mississippi Valley. The simple West Indies–style house, dating from 1787, is typical of the homes built by the earliest planters in the region. *9999 River Rd., tel. 504/764–9315. Admission: $5 adults, $3 children 13–18, $2 children 6–12. Open daily 9:30–4. Closed major holidays.*

Destrehan is about an hour's drive from New Orleans, and U.S. 61 will take you right into the city.

What to See and Do with Children

Blue Bayou Water Park (*see* Participant Sports, *below*).
Samuel Clemens Riverboat (*see* Exploring, *above*).
Louisiana Arts & Science Center Riverside Museum (*see* Exploring, *above*).

Off the Beaten Track

LA 942 is a peaceful back road that drifts off U.S. 61 just north of Baton Rouge and winds through woodlands and past green pastures with grazing horses and lazing cattle. At the intersection of LA 3004, there is a tiny community called **Plains.** A marker notes that during the Civil War the Battle of Plains took place here.

Plains's small-town features include the **Volunteer Fire Department** building; the **Plains Super Market,** and next to it the **Plains Presbyterian Church.**

Participant Sports

Golf Baton Rouge boasts two 18-hole championship golf courses that are open to the public: **Howell Park** (5511 Winbourne Ave., Baton Rouge, tel. 504/357-9292); and **Webb Park** (1351 Country Club Dr., Baton Rouge, tel. 504/383-4919). St. Francisville has a new 18-hole Arnold Palmer course that visitors are welcome to play (The Bluffs, LA 965, six miles east of U.S. 61, tel. 504/634-5222).

Hiking There are seven miles of hiking trails in the **Port Hudson State Commemorative Area** (756 W. Plains-Port Hudson Rd. Hwy 61, tel. 504/654-3775).

Swimming **Blue Bayou Water Park** (18142 Perkins Rd. off I-10, Baton Rouge, tel. 504/753-3333) splashed on the scene in 1990 with a wave pool and all sorts of flumes, sleds, and slides—including a corkscrew critter, a wave pool, and a seven-story slide. For the little ones there's a 7,000-square-foot Pollywog pool. There's also a restaurant and a fast-food facility. *Admission: $12.50 for anyone over 4 feet, $10.95 for anyone under 4 feet. Open mid-May–Labor Day; 10–6 daily.*

Tennis You can lob and volley at **City Park** (1440 City Park Ave., Baton Rouge, tel. 504/344-4501 or 923-2792); **Highland Road Park** (Highland and Amiss Rd., Baton Rouge, tel. 504/766-0247); and **Independence Park** (549 Lobdell Ave., Baton Rouge, tel. 504/923-1792).

Dining and Lodging

Dining Cajun is *the* way to go here. Dine and dance at the new Mulate's in Baton Rouge, or try the po'boys at The Cabin in Burnside.

Category	Cost*
Very Expensive	over $35
Expensive	$25–$35
Moderate	$15–$20
Inexpensive	under $15

**per person without tax (7% in Baton Rouge), service, or drinks*

Lodging Staying on the plantation is your best bet for lodging in South Louisiana, but if you are stuck in the city or are budget conscious, you'll have no problem finding suitable accommodations.

Category	Cost*
Very Expensive	over $120
Expensive	$90–$120
Moderate	$50–$90
Inexpensive	under $50

**double room; add 9% for taxes*

The most highly recommended establishments in each price category are indicated by a star ★.

Baton Rouge
Dining

Chalet Brandt. Swiss-born Charles Brandt has created an Alpine house that lacks only the Alps. The elegant dining rooms gleam with brass and china collectibles from around the globe, and many of the edibles are also imported. Brandt's motto is "Continental cuisine with Louisianians in mind." There is a changing menu that might include fresh poached Norwegian salmon with mousseline sauce; veal tournedos topped with foie gras, truffles, and madeira sauce; or speckled trout with crawfish Cardinale sauce. *7655 Old Hammond Hwy. tel. 504/927-6040. Jacket and tie required. Reservations suggested. AE, DC, MC, V. Expensive.*

Mike Anderson's. Former LSU football player Mike Anderson believes in serving up enormous portions and almost single-handedly supports the folks who manufacture doggie bags. His rustic, barnlike restaurant features the freshest of Louisiana seafood, with specialties like trout Norman (fried trout filet with crabmeat au gratin). Don't pass up the fried onion rings. Lowly cole slaw is elevated here to heavenly realms. *1031 W. Lee Dr., tel. 504/766–7823. Dress: informal. Reservations not required. AE, MC, V. Closed Thanksgiving, Christmas, New Year's Day, Easter. Inexpensive.*

★ **Mulate's.** A rustic place with cypress beams, red-checkered cloths, and artwork by Cajun artist George Rodrigue, Mulate's offers shrimp and oyster en brochette, a Super Seafood Platter, and live Cajun music every night. *8322 Bluebonnet Road, tel. 504/767–4794 or 800/634–9880. Dress: informal. Reservations not required. AE, MC, V. Inexpensive.*

Lodging

Crown Sterling Suites. Built in 1985 as an Embassy Suites Hotel, this centrally located property has a southwestern motif. Each two-room suite, with complexions of peaches and greens, has a galley kitchen with microwave, and custom-made mahogany furniture. The complimentary full breakfast is cooked to order. *4914 Constitution Ave., 70808, tel. 504/924–6566 or 800/433–4600. 224 suites. Facilities: free airport shuttle, cable TV, cocktail lounge, coffee shop, restaurant, free parking, gift shop, handicapped facilities, laundry, room service, indoor pool, sauna, and steam room. AE, DC, MC, V. Expensive.*

Baton Rouge Hilton. This Hilton bills itself as a city resort hotel and boasts that it's the only capital city hotel with 24-hour room service. Centrally located at I–10 and College Drive, the tall, skinny white high rise offers a nonsmoking floor and half a floor with facilities for the handicapped. Traditional furnishings throughout, in hues of plum and blue. *5500 Hilton Ave., 70808, tel. 504/924–5000, 800/621–5116, or in LA 800/221–2584. 305 rooms. Facilities: free airport shuttle, cable TV, cocktail lounge, coffee shop, restaurant, concierge, free parking, gift shop, laundry, room service, lighted tennis courts, sauna, health club, jogging track. AE, DC, MC, V. Moderate–Expensive.*

★ **Marriott's Residence Inn.** One- and two-bedroom suites with dens, dining rooms, wood-burning fireplaces, and kitchens equipped with everything right down to popcorn poppers. The two-bedroom suites come with Jacuzzis. Traditional furnishings in the centrally located hotel, which opened in 1984. *5522 Corporate Blvd., 70808, tel. 504/927–5630 or 800/331–3131. 80 suites. Facilities: cable TV, concierge, free parking, handicap* *facilities, laundry service, spa/health club, outdoor pool. AE, DC, MC, V. Moderate.*

Burnside
Dining
★

Cabin. Rustic 150-year-old slave cabin-cum-restaurant with yellowed newspapers covering the walls and ancient tools dangling here and there. Crawfish stew and crawfish étouffée are featured, but there are po'boys, steaks, and burgers, too. *Junction of LA 44 and 22, tel. 504/473–3007. Dress: informal. Reservations not required. AE, MC, V. Closed Christmas, Thanksgiving, New Year's. Moderate.*

Lodging
Cheneyville

Loyd's Hall Plantation. In 1992 *Travel & Leisure* named this bed-and-breakfast among the 10 top spots for a wedding anniversary. In a country setting adjacent to a historic plantation mansion, you'll enjoy total privacy in this rustic replica of a 19th-century farmhouse. The little cottage is furnished with a blend of antiques and modern comforts: a wood-burning fireplace, porch with rocking chairs, four-posters, a modern kitchen, air-conditioning, and TV. *292 Loyd Bridge Rd., 71325, tel. 318/776–5641 or 800/749–1928, fax 318/279–2335. Housekeeping cottage (2 bedrooms share bath). Facilities: pool, stocked kitchen, AE, MC, V. Moderate.*

Natchitoches

Cloutier Townhouse. On Front Street, overlooking Cane River Lake, this elegant three-story townhouse offers B & B accommodations. The exterior is adorned with filigreed cast-iron galleries, and the interior has high ceilings, hardwood floors, and Louisiana Empire antiques. The larger and quieter of the two bedrooms is the master bedroom, which has a full-tester bed, gas fireplace, wing chairs, and a settee. The master bath has a Jacuzzi and lighted shower stall. Breakfast includes homemade multigrain bread and fresh fruit. *8 Ducournau Sq., 71457, tel. 318/352–5242. 2 double rooms with bath. MC. V. Moderate.*

Holiday Inn. Comfortable and predictable rooms are available in this link of the familiar chain. On the outskirts of town, it offers a restaurant, outdoor pool, and cable TV. *Hwy. 1 Bypass S, tel. 318/357–8281 or 800/HOLIDAY. 143 rooms, 2 suites, AE, DC, MC, V. Moderate.*

Fleur-de-Lis. The granddaddy of local B & B is an unpretentious turn-of-the-century house with a front porch and swing. The downstairs family room looks and feels lived-in. Full breakfast is served family-style in an adjacent dining room. Guest rooms have a four-poster or a brass bed and wicker furnishings; baths are small but modern. *336 2nd St., 71457, tel. 318/352–6621. 5 double rooms with bath. AE, MC, V. Inexpensive.*

Jefferson House. B & B within walking distance of the historic district, Jefferson House is a split-level frame structure in a serene setting. Guests occupy the entire first floor, which is decorated in a tasteful blend of traditional furnishings and East Asian *objets d'art.* A large stately parlor has a high beamed ceiling, brick fireplace, and doors opening to a veranda with rocking chairs and a view of Cane River Lake. Bedrooms have quilted spreads and matching drapes; baths are large and modern. *229 Jefferson St., 71457, tel. 318/352–3957 or 318/352–5756. 2 rooms with bath. MC, V. Inexpensive.*

Napoleonville
Lodging

Madewood. Expect gracious Southern hospitality in this antiques-filled Greek Revival mansion, which is both elegant and cozy. The $159 price for a room in the main house includes not only breakfast but wine and cheeses in the parlor, followed by a candlelit Southern dinner in the stately dining room. There are also suites in restored outbuildings on the plantation grounds

($90 per couple including Continental breakfast, $159 for full breakfast and dinner). *4250 LA 308, Napoleonville 70390, tel. 504/369–7151; 800/749–7151; in LA, 800/375–7151. All rooms with private bath. AE, MC, V. Closed major holidays. Expensive.*

White Castle
Lodging

Nottoway. A massive Italianate mansion with 64 rooms filled with antique treasures, this is reputed to be one of the most stunning B&Bs in the nation. Thirteen of its elegant rooms are let to overnight guests, who are welcomed with complimentary sherry upon arrival. Your first breakfast of croissants, juice, and coffee is served in your room; second breakfast is a full feast in the Magnolia Room. *2 mi north of White Castle on LA 1, White Castle 70788, tel. 504/545–2730. All rooms have private baths. AE, DC, MC, V. Closed Christmas Day. Expensive–Very Expensive.*

The Arts

Theater

Top name stars such as Alabama and Neil Diamond are booked into the **Centroplex Theatre for the Performing Arts.** (tel. 504/389–3030).

The **Baton Rouge Little Theatre** (7155 Florida Blvd., tel. 504/924–6496) has been presenting musicals, comedies, and dramas for more than 40 years.

Concerts

Guest soloists perform frequently with the **Baton Rouge Symphony Orchestra** (Centroplex Theatre for the Performing Arts, tel. 504/387–6166). LSU's annual **Festival of Contemporary Music** (tel. 504/388–5118), which takes place in February, is more than 40 years old.

Nightlife

Baton Rouge
Cajun Clubs

Mulate's (8322 Bluebonnet Rd., tel. 504/767–4794) in Baton Rouge is a chip off the famed old Breaux Bridge block.

Country/Western

The **Texas Club** (456 N. Donmoor Ave., tel. 504/928–4655) is the hot spot for top-name country artists.

Bars and Nightclubs

An LSU crowd congregates at the **Bayou** (124 W. Chimes St., tel. 504/346–1765), where there is occasional live music Saturday night. The **Bengal** (2286 Highland Rd., tel. 504/387–5571) draws a young disco crowd to its dance floor, game room, and patio. Live bands and DJs alternate at **Sports Illustrated Bar** (1176 Bob Pettit Blvd., tel. 504/766–6794). The young and not so young dance in a tropical setting at **TD's** (Baton Rouge Hilton Hotel, tel. 504/924–5000). An older, upscale crowd collects at the **Quarternote Lounge** (3827 S. Sherwood Forest Blvd., tel. 504/291–0312). The **Ascot Club** (711 Jefferson Hwy. (Goodwood Shopping Village, suite 4A, tel. 504/924–4540) and **ZeeZee Gardens** (2904 Perkins Rd., tel. 504/346–1291) are both restaurants with lively bars. And there's Dixieland at **Rick's Cafe Americain** (2363 College Dr., tel. 504/924–9042).

Excursion to Natchitoches and North Central Louisiana

Getting There

By Car Route 1 and I–49, which cut north–south through the state's midsection, bisect Natchitoches.

By Bus Natchitoches is served by **Greyhound/Trailways** (tel. 318/352–8341).

Exploring The **Natchitoches Parish Tourist Office** (781 Front St., tel. 318/352–8072) provides information about the region, including self-guided walking/driving-tour brochures.

The earliest permanent European settlement in the Louisiana Purchase territory was not New Orleans but the little town of **Natchitoches** (pronounced **Nak**-uh-tish), which predates the Crescent City by four years. Nestled in rolling green hills and thick pine forests, Natchitoches has two other claims to fame. The town hosts a sparkling Christmas Festival of Lights, which was featured in the film *Steel Magnolias*, and it's the hometown of that film's screenwriter, Robert Harling. The friendly residents are happy to point out where Dolly Parton, Sally Field, Julia Roberts, and the other magnolias hung out during filming.

Front Street, which is lined with small, wrought iron–face buildings, lies alongside pretty Cane River Lake. The lake's sloping grass-green banks are shaded by giant weeping willow trees. The downtown area is part of a 33-block historic district, which contains a number of homes open to the public. Trolley, boat, and minibus tours, all of which focus on *Steel Magnolia* sites, are available (Cane River Cruises, tel. 318/352–7093).

Fort St. Jean Baptiste is a reconstruction of the outpost that stood near this site in 1716. The several replica buildings were constructed using 18th-century hardware, including handmade door latches and hinges. Structures include a church, powder magazine, warehouse, and kitchen. *Corner Mill and Jefferson Sts., tel. 318/357–3101. Admission: $2, children under 12 free. Open daily 9–5.*

Natchitoches is on the fringe of the 100,000-acre **Kisatchie National Forest** (tel. 318/352–2568). In addition to its hardwood and pine forests, it offers equestrian, hiking, and nature trails; picnic and camping sites; and splendid vistas.

The Cane River Lake drifts southward from Natchitoches, lined by tall trees, stately plantations, and humble cottages. Several plantation homes are open for tours in "Cane River Country." Melrose Plantation, the home of artist Clementine Hunter, is 14 miles south of Natchitoches. Hunter, a black freed slave, began construction of the seven buildings with her family in 1796. Several patrons of the arts, whose guests included Erskine Caldwell, Lyle Saxon, and Alexander Woollcott, have owned Melrose during this century. The African House, an unusual Congo-style structure the second floor of which is decorated with Hunter's murals, is of particular interest. *Rte. 119, Melrose, tel. 318/379–0055. Admission: $4* *adults, $2 children 13–18, $1 children 6–12. Open daily noon–4. Closed major holidays.*

Handmade brick, heart cypress, and wood pegs were used to build the **Bayou Folk Museum, the Kate Chopin House,** which was completed in 1813. In the 1880s this raised cottage was the home of Kate Chopin, author of *The Awakening*. The house is cluttered with an eclectic collection of treasures and trifles donated by locals. The museum contains photographs and memorabilia and a first edition of *Bayou Folk*, a collection of Chopin's short stories about Cane River Country. *Cloutierville, tel. 318/379–2233. Admission: $2 adults, $1 children. Open Mon–Sat. 9–5, Sun. 1–5. Closed major holidays.*

The still-working **Magnolia Plantation** is a National Bicentennial Farm, one of only two west of the Mississippi. The mansion's 27 rooms are furnished with an extensive collection of Louisiana and Southern Empire antiques. Outbuildings include brick cabins and a barn containing the only cotton press in the United States still in its original location. *Hwy. 119 near Derry, 22 miles south of Natchitoches, tel. 318/379–2221. Admission: $4 adults, $2 students, $1 children. Open daily 1–4. Closed major holidays.*

Dining

Lecompte

Mariner's Seafood and Steakhouse. A popular local spot on the banks of pretty Sibley Lake, just outside of town, this spacious, glassed-in restaurant offers hearty seafood and steak dishes. The salad bar is a crowd-pleaser, as is the Sunday brunch. *700 Rte. 3110 Bypass, tel. 318/357–1220. Reservations accepted. AE, DC, MC, V. No lunch. Moderate.*

Lea's Lunch Room. Louisianians who frequently make the trek from north to south Louisiana often plan to arrive in Lecompte (pronounced le-**count**) at lunchtime. There's nothing fancy here: just a huge sun- and noise-filled room, where country food has been served since 1928. The cornbread and homemade pies are legendary. Expect brusque service and plate lunches of prodigious proportions. *U.S. 71 S, Lecompte, tel. 318/776–5178. Dress: casual. Reservations not accepted. No credit cards. Closed Mon. Inexpensive.*

Natchitoches

Lasyone's Meat Pie Kitchen. Natchitoches is famed for its succulent meat pies, and the best place to sample them is this ultracasual country-kitchen café. Other offerings include meat, chicken, and seafood; for dessert, select from a display of Cane River cream pies. *622 2nd St., tel. 318/352–3353. Reservations not necessary. No credit cards. Closed Sun. Inexpensive.*

5 Mississippi

By Janet Clark

Updated by Sylvia Higginbotham

Mississippians are fascinated with each other and spend a lot of time telling what they know. Once I corrected a friend who was recounting an event with no regard for the facts. "Hush!" she said. "This is a *story*." Stories are important here, so hush and listen.

If you mind your manners, Mississippi folks will get interested in you, too. As soon as you hit Iuka or Olive Branch you're sure to be asked, "Where y'all from?" even if there's just one of "y'all" at the moment. This is how Mississippi's famous hospitality begins. We see you, like some fabulous creature, with your story spread bright behind you like a tail. And spend some time considering whether you've got Mississippi relatives. The next questions are "What's your name? Any kin to those Henleys over in Tutwiler?"

You'll want to try out some Mississippi storytellers before you come. You'll feel exalted reading William Faulkner's Nobel Prize address, you'll laugh at the characters in Eudora Welty's short stories, and find pathos aplenty in Tennessee Williams's plays. B.B. King, Mose Allison, Son Thomas, John Lee Hooker, and Muddy Waters will give you the authentic Mississippi blues. Jimmie Rodgers is called "the father of country music," and then, of course, there's Tupelo-born Elvis Presley, "The King" of rock 'n roll.

Prepare for weather. Mississippi is fickle where that's concerned. You can swelter from May to October and then suddenly freeze, just for a few days at Fair time in October. On any day record highs and lows can vary by 60 degrees. February is generally interrupted by "blackberry winter" and everyone rushes to plant marigolds, which die in the short March cold snap. In spring and fall you're generally talking *wonderful*, with temperatures in the 60s and 70s and azaleas bursting out everywhere.

Check on festivals, those down-home celebrations when Mississippians are most themselves. The Mississippi Department of Economic and Community Development, Division of Tourism (Box 849, Jackson, MS 39205, tel. 601/359–3297 or 800–647–2290) can give you a monthly blow by blow, which includes such events as annual "pilgrimages" to antebellum mansions. Pilgrimages coincide with the blossoming of spring flowers in twelve historic towns. Kosciusko's big Natchez Trace Festival is one of many such celebrations in April. The month of May brings the popular Blessing of the Fleet in Biloxi, the Gumtree Festival in Tupelo, and Jubilee!JAM in Jackson. Expect hot July weather, and outstanding surprises at the Choctaw Indian Fair near Philadelphia, followed by the Neshoba County Fair—the world's largest houseparty—in August. Fall is full of fairs and festivals and antiques shows. Try Macon's Dancing Rabbit Festival in October, or the Great Mississippi River Balloon Race in Natchez. Most towns celebrate Christmas with seasonal specials beginning in early December.

Forget the interstate routes, and hit the back roads to discover the "real" Mississippi along the beautiful Natchez Trace, the Great River Road, and an abundance of quiet and scenic country trails.

Mississippi

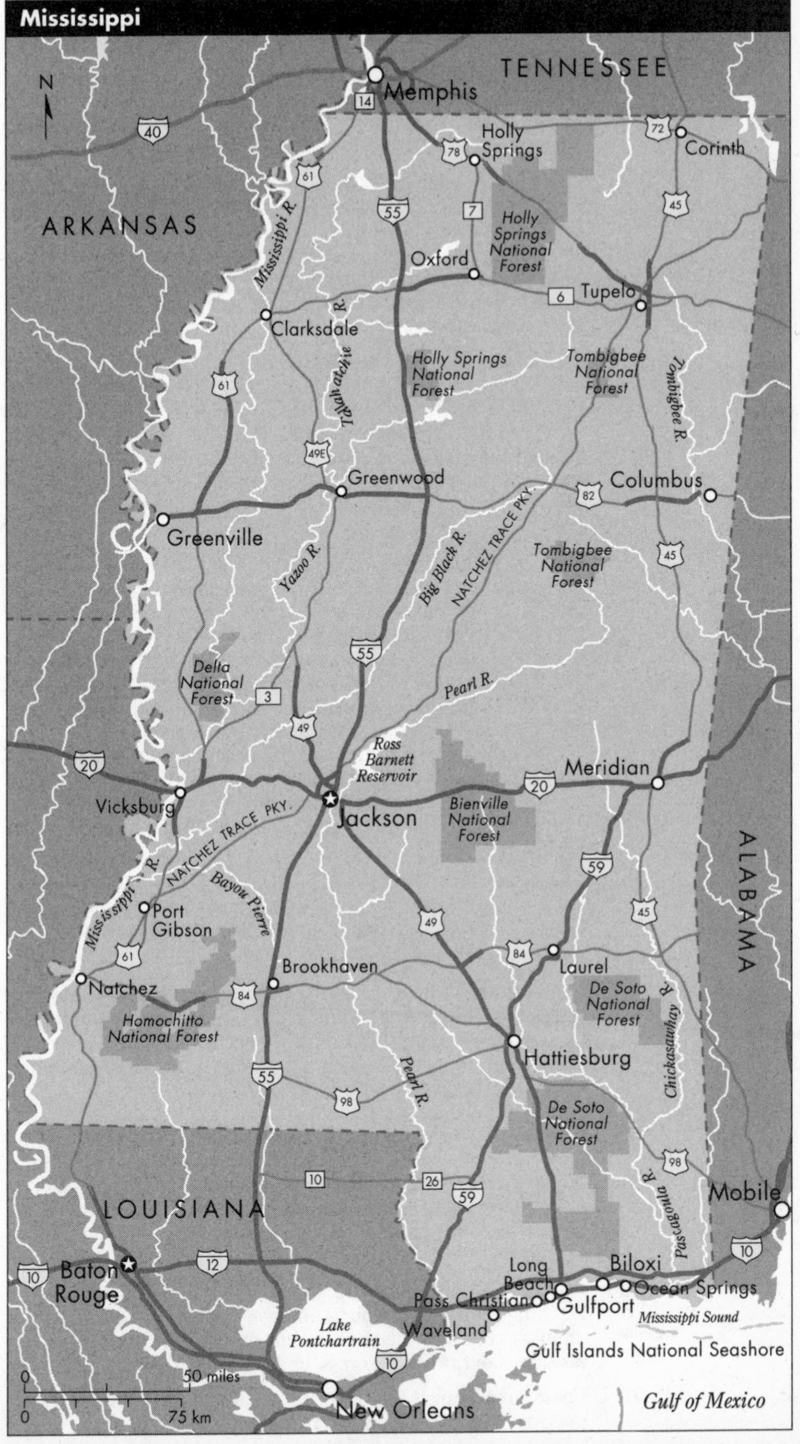

The Gulf Coast

The Mississippi Gulf Coast runs along U.S. 90 from Alabama to Louisiana. The traveler seeking a boisterous good time will find it in the restaurants, bars, hotels, motels, and souvenir shops that jostle for space along U.S. 90's busy four lanes.

Don't let the clamor of this neon strip hide the coast's quieter treasures: the ancient land, sculpted by wind and water, continually changing; serene beachfront houses set on green and shady lawns; the teeming wildlife of the Mississippi Sound and its adjacent bayous and marshes; the unspoiled natural beauty of the seven barrier islands that separate the Gulf of Mexico from the Mississippi Sound.

On a clear day, if you have good eyesight or a good imagination, you can see these islands. Their names (from east to west) are Petit Bois (anglicized as "Petty Boy"), Horn, East and West Ship, and Cat. Two others, Round and Deer, lie within the Mississippi Sound. The islands' shapes are constantly shifting as the tides and prevailing winds work on their fragile sands. In 1969 Hurricane Camille's furious onslaught cut Ship Island in two.

During the 1700s France, England, and Spain ruled the area, according to their fortunes in international wars. Street names, family names, and traditions still reflect this colorful heritage. In the late 19th and early 20th centuries, the coast became a fashionable vacation spot for wealthy New Orleanians and Delta planters eager to escape yellow fever epidemics. Elegant hotels, imposing beachfront mansions, and smaller summer homes sprang up. Edgewater Plaza shopping mall now stands on the site of the queen of the early hotels, the Edgewater Gulf, which in its heyday had its own stop on the L & N Railroad. Today the homes that have endured the vagaries of time and hurricanes stand along the beach—brave and beautiful survivors.

The coast's people today are known as easygoing and tolerant, artistic and hardy. Though individualistic, they are linked by a reliance on the sea and its bounty, and by a love of the water and its Gulf shores.

Take your cue from the natives and ignore any urge to swim in the sound. It's too murky (at best). Instead, admire the stately live oaks and accept the salutes of crabs. Go floundering and spear your supper. Above all, slow down. On the Mississippi Coast only the traffic on U.S. 90 moves quickly.

Getting Around

By Car You can drive across the entire coast in 1½ hours on I–10 and U.S. 90, reaching New Orleans in just over an hour from Gulfport. Jackson is three hours straight up U.S. 49, north from Gulfport.

By Plane Fly into Gulfport-Biloxi Regional Airport (Airport Road, off Washington Ave., Gulfport) and you can be on the beach in 15 minutes. Fly into the regional airport on **ASA/The Delta Connection, Continental Express,** or **Northwest Airlink.**

By Bus **Coast Area Transit** (DeBuys Rd., Gulfport, tel. 601/896–8080) provides a coastwide public transportation system.

Greyhound-Trailways connects the coast with Jackson, New Orleans, and Mobile (Biloxi: 502 W. Railroad Ave., tel. 601/436–4335; Gulfport: 11205 25th Ave., tel. 601/863–1022; Bay St. Louis: 512 Ulman Ave., tel. 601/467–4272).

Important Addresses and Numbers

Tourist Information Get a free *Attractions and Accommodations* guide to the Gulf Coast area at the **Mississippi Gulf Coast Convention and Visitors Bureau.** *Box 6128, Gulfport, 39506, tel. 601/896–6699 or 800/237–9493. Open weekdays 8–5.*

Emergencies For assistance dial 911, call the **Mississippi Highway Patrol** (601/864–1314), or go to the emergency room at **Biloxi Regional Medical Center** (150 Reynoir St., Biloxi, tel. 601/436–1191).

Guided Tours

Celebrity Limousine and Tours Service (111 South Shore Dr., Biloxi, tel. 601/388–1384) charters bus tours of the coastal area and New Orleans.

Coasting, Inc. (Box 7408, 1524 2nd St., Gulfport, tel. 601/864–2044) custom-plans tours and entertainment for groups.

Exploring the Gulf Coast

Ocean Springs To begin at the beginning, at least as far as Mississippi is concerned, start in **Ocean Springs.** Here, in 1699, the French commander Pierre LeMoyne Sieur D'Iberville established Fort Maurepas to shore up France's claim to the central part of North America. This first colony was temporary, but it's fondly remembered by Ocean Springs in its spring festival celebrating D'Iberville's landing. Magnificent oaks shade the sleepy town center, a pleasant area of small shops to explore on foot.

Ocean Springs is famous as the home of Walter Anderson (1903–1965), an artist of genius and grand eccentricity who enjoyed an ecstatic communion with nature, which he revealed in thousands of drawings and watercolors, most of them kept secret until his death. You can discover his work at the **Walter Anderson Museum of Art,** to which murals from the **Anderson Cottage** were moved, and the adjoining **Old Community Center.** Anderson painted the intricate murals in the Community Center for a fee of $1; they are appraised at $1 million. *510 Washington Ave., tel. 601/872–3164. Admission: $3 adults, $1 children 12 and under. Open Tues.–Sat. 10–5, Sun. 1–5.*

The nearby **Shearwater Pottery and Showroom** offers a wide selection of original and reproduction Anderson family hand-thrown and cast pottery. Visitors can watch the pottery being made in the workshop. *102 Shearwater Dr., tel. 601/875–7320. Showroom open Mon.–Sat. 9–5:30, Sun. 1–5:30. Workshop open weekdays 9–12, 1–4.*

A brochure from the **Ocean Springs Chamber of Commerce** (tel. 601/875–4424) will guide you on a driving tour of the D'Iberville Trail, shaded by moss-draped trees and bordered by summer houses.

Gulf Islands National Seashore—which includes Ship, Horn, and Petit Bois Islands—has its headquarters on Ocean Springs's Davis Bayou. In the summer you can explore the marshes by boat with a U.S. Park Ranger as your guide. When heat and humidity allow, picnic here and explore the nature trails. *3500 Park Rd., Ocean Springs, tel. 601/875–9057. Ranger boat tours begin at 6:30 PM Thurs.–Sun.; rangers start taking reservations at 6 PM (limit of 20 people).*

Biloxi From Ocean Springs, cross the Biloxi–Ocean Springs bridge to **Biloxi,** practicing the correct pronunciation, "Bi-LUX-i," as you go. Biloxi is the oldest continuous settlement on the Gulf Coast and the second-largest city in Mississippi. When Pierre LeMoyne Sieur D'Iberville met the Indians who called themselves Biloxi, or "first people," he gave their name to the area and to the bay. The French constructed Fort Louis here; it served as the capital of the Louisiana Territory from 1720 to 1722, when the capital was moved to New Orleans.

At the foot of the Biloxi–Ocean Springs Bridge, on the south, is **Gulf Marine State Park,** jutting over the water on wooden decks. Through its telescopes you can glimpse **Deer Island** 12 miles away or watch gulls and pelicans, sailboats and sailboards. This is a great spot for fishing, 24 hours a day. Bait and tackle are sold here and fishing poles may be rented daily 9–5. *Just south of U.S. 90 at the west end of the Biloxi–Ocean Springs Bridge. Open daily.*

Adjacent to Gulf Marine State Park is the **J. L. Scott Marine Education Center and Aquarium,** featuring live exhibits of Gulf Coast animals and a spectacular 40,000-gallon aquarium. *115 E. Beach Blvd., Biloxi, tel. 601/374–5550. Admission: $2 adults, $1 children and senior citizens. Open Mon.–Sat. 9–4.*

Across U.S. 90 is **Point Cadet Plaza,** a waterfront complex now under development, which has a marina and the **Seafood Industry Museum.** In the 1880s Point Cadet was home to European emmigrants who flocked to Biloxi to work in the seafood canneries. *Point Cadet Plaza, tel. 601/435–6320. Admission: $2.50 adults, $1.50 children and senior citizens. Open daily 9–5. Closed Sun.*

At the intersection of the I-10 loop and U.S. 90 you can hop aboard the good ship ***L.A. Cruise*** for an afternoon or evening of gaming, dining, and dancing. *Tel. 800/752–1778. Tickets: $19.95 per person.*

Biloxi's **Small Craft Harbor,** off U.S. 90 on the sound, captures the atmosphere of a lazy fishing village. Catch the **Sailfish Shrimp Tour** boat here to experience 80 minutes as a shrimper. Cast your nets upon the waters and let the crew identify your catch, however bizarre, for you. *Biloxi Small Craft Harbor. Tel. 601/374–5718. Call for admission prices and schedule.*

Biloxi's landmark 65-foot-tall **Lighthouse** on U.S. 90 was erected in 1848. During the Civil War, Federal forces, operating from Ship Island, blockaded the Mississippi Sound and cut Biloxi off from much-needed supplies. When the Yankees demanded that Biloxi submit or starve, the reply was that the Union would have to "blockade the mullet" first. Ever since, mullet has been known as "Biloxi bacon" and honored with its own festival each October. The city defended itself with what appeared to be a formidable cannon array near the lighthouse but what was actually only two cannons and many logs painted black! *U.S. 90, tel. 601/435–6293. Admission: free, donations accepted. Open Tues.–Sat. 10–5, Sun. 1–5, May–Labor Day.*

The Lighthouse is the starting point for the **Biloxi Tour Train,** which bumps you past historic mansions and shrimp trawlers. *U.S. 90 at Porter Ave. Six tours daily, Mar. 1–Labor Day. Admission: $1.50 adults, $1 children.*

Mardi Gras is as grand a celebration in Biloxi as in nearby New Orleans, and the Krewe costumes are equally festive. See costumes and crowns at the **Mardi Gras Museum,** housed in the old Magnolia Hotel, an 1847 structure listed on the National Register of Historic Places. *119 Rue Magnolia, tel. 601/432–8806. Admission: free, donations accepted. Open weekdays 10–4.*

Time Out Mary Mahoney's **Old French House Restaurant** is in a renovated 1737 mansion with several elegant dining rooms and enclosed patios. Locals swear by it, perhaps more for the comfort of its old brick and age-darkened wood and for the memory of Mary herself (who always went from table to table, chatting with customers) than for the food. Come for drinks in the Old Slave Quarter (11 AM–11 PM) and for Le Café's beignets, coffee, gumbo, and po'boys served 24 hours a day (there's take-out, too). *138 Rue Magnolia, tel. 601/374–0163. Reservations recommended for lunch and dinner in the elegant main dining rooms. AE, DC, MC, V. Very Expensive.*

Four miles from Gulfport is **Beauvoir,** the antebellum beachfront mansion that was the last home of Jefferson Davis. Here the president of the Confederacy wrote his memoirs and his book *The Rise and Fall of the Confederate Government.* The serene, raised cottage-style house, with its sweeping front stairs, is flanked by pavilions and set on a broad lawn shaded by ancient live oaks. A Confederate cemetery on the grounds includes the Tomb of the Unknown Soldier of the Confederacy. *On U.S. 90 between Biloxi and Gulfport, tel. 601/388–1313. Admission: $4 adults, $2 children, $3.50 senior citizens. Open daily 9–5. Closed Christmas Day.*

Gulfport **Gulfport** merges seamlessly with Biloxi along U.S. 90. If you have time for only one activity on the coast, make it a getaway to **Ship Island** on the passenger ferry from the Gulfport Harbor. At **Ship Island** a U.S. Park Ranger will guide you through Fort Massachusetts, built in 1859 and used by Federal troops to blockade the sound during the Civil War. The rangers will treat you to tales of the island's colorful past, including the story of the *filles aux casquettes*—young women sent by the French government as brides for the lonely early colonists. Each girl *(fille)* carried a small hope chest *(casquette).* Spend the day sunning, swimming in the clear green water, and beachcombing for treasures washed up by the surf. You'll feel a world away (just remember to return on the last boat). *Ticket office at Gulfport Harbor in the Joseph T. Jones Memorial Park, just east of the intersection of U.S. 49 and U.S. 90, tel. 601/864–1014. Cost (round-trip): $12 adults, $6 children 3–10. 1–3 trips daily, Mar.–Oct.*

West of Gulfport the landscape grows increasingly broad, wild, and lovely. The highway runs between stately homes on the north and shimmering water on the south from Long Beach through Pass Christian and from Bay St. Louis to Waveland.

Pass Christian (Chris-chi-ANN) suffered the full fury of Hurricane Camille on August 17, 1969, but not even Camille could erase its history. Here sailboat racing began in the South, and here the second yacht club in the country was formed (it still exists today). Louisiana landowner Zachary Taylor was at the yacht club when he was persuaded to run for the presidency. In 1913, President Woodrow Wilson and his family spent a Christmas vacation here, but his Dixie White House, the Herndon Home, was destroyed by Camille.

Waveland boasts the best beach in Mississippi, located on E. Beach Boulevard, two miles south of U.S. 90. Take a beach walk or drive through Buccaneer State Park's mossy live oaks to enjoy the splendid, unimpeded view of sparkling waters.

What to See and Do with Children

Boating (*see* Participant Sports, *below*).
The Doll House accommodates a collection of contemporary and antique dolls and stuffed animals. *3201 Bienville Blvd., on U.S. 90, Ocean Springs, tel. 601/872–3971. Cost: donation for YMCA Pet Shelter. Open 1–5. Closed Mon.*
Fishing (*see* Participant Sports, *below*).
Funtime USA will entertain children for hours, with its water slides, playground, bumper boats and cars, and over 100 arcade games. *1300 Beach Blvd., Gulfport, tel. 601/896–7315. Open daily, 9AM–midnight.*
Gulf Islands National Seashore (*see* Exploring, *above*).
J. L. Scott Marine Education Center and Aquarium (*see* Exploring, *above*).
Marine Life offers continuous shows with performing dolphins, sea lions, and macaws. *Joseph T. Jones Memorial Park, just east of the intersection of U.S. 49 and U.S. 90., tel. 601/863–0651. Admission: $8.95 adults, $5.75 children 3–11, children under 2 free. Open daily 9–4. Closed Thanksgiving and Christmas.*

Shopping

Gifts At **Ballard's Pewter** (1110 Government St., Ocean Springs, tel. 601/875–7550) you can find necklaces and earrings made from sand dollars and crabs, or have the pewtersmith fashion a "bespoke" (custom-made) piece.

Outfit yourself at **Realizations** (1000 Washington St., Ocean Springs, tel. 601/875–0503) in T-shirts, skirts, blouses, and dresses silk-screened with Walter Anderson's swirling block print designs. Books, reproductions, and posters of the artist's work are also available. Next door is **Gayle Clarke Artisans** (tel. 601/875–3900), where you can purchase crafts, blown glass, pottery, and handmade jewelry—including dragonfly necklaces.

Beaches

Twenty-six miles of man-made beach extend from Biloxi to Pass Christian. Toward the west the beaches become less commercialized and crowded; **Waveland**'s is the best of all. Tan, sail, jet-ski, or beachcomb, but *don't* swim; it's shallow and not clean.

Participant Sports

Boating Sailboats, sailboards, jet skis, and catamarans may be rented from the many vendors who station themselves along the beach. You can also rent 14-foot motorboats at **End of the Wharf** (315 E. Beach Blvd., Biloxi), just behind Fisherman's Wharf Restaurant.

Camping Take U.S. 90 to Waveland, turn south on Nicholson, and follow the signs to **Buccaneer State Park** (tel. 601/467–3822), which conceals 129 campsites in a grove of live oaks streaming with moss. An Olympic-size wave pool may lure you from the nature trail and picnic sites. There are no cabins, but toilet and shower facilities are available. **Gulf Islands National Seashore** (*see* Exploring, *above*) offers campsites for trailers and RV's.

Fishing and Crabbing For **floundering** you'll need nighttime, a light, and a gig. Head for the sound, roll up your jeans, and spear your supper! A chicken neck and a string will put you in the **crabbing** business at any public pier. If you want to be lazy, substitute a crab trap for the string.

Charter boats for half-day and full-day **deep-sea fishing** can be found at marinas and harbors all along the Gulf Coast. Prices range upward from $30 per person, averaging $55; group rates are usually available. The Mississippi Gulf Coast Convention and Visitors Bureau (tel. 601/896–6699 or 800/237–9493) can assist you.

Golf The coast's climate allows for year-round golfing, and many golf packages are offered by hotels and motels. The Mississippi Coast Coliseum sponsors **indoor golf clinics,** day and night, February–April. Contact the Mississippi Gulf Coast Convention and Visitors Bureau (tel. 601/896–6699 or 800/237–9493) for details. Diamondhead's **Pine** and **Cardinal courses** (7600 Country Club Circle, Bay St. Louis, tel. 601/255–2525) offer 36 holes that can challenge all but the pros. Wooded, gently rolling, and well-kept, they are ringed by the large, elegant houses and condominiums of Diamondhead resort community.

Hickory Hill Country Club and Golf Course (900 Hickory Hill Dr., Gautier, tel. 601/497–5575, ext. 204) offers visitors fairways lined with whispering pines, tall oaks, magnolias, and dogwoods. Flowers surround the teeing areas.

Pine Island Golf Course (Gulf Park Estates, 2¼ mi east of Ocean Springs, 3 mi south of U.S. 90, tel. 601/875–1674) was designed by Pete Dye, who created the tournament players course in Jacksonville. This course spans three islands, and its abundant wildlife, beautiful setting, and club house can console you for any bogeys. Call ahead for tee time.

Windance Country Club (94 Champion Circle, Gulfport, tel. 601/832–4871) has a public golf course ranked among the top 100 in the United States by *Golf Digest.* Call ahead for tee time.

Dining and Lodging

Dining Fresh Gulf seafood, particularly redfish, flounder, and speckled trout dishes, stars in coast restaurants. Soft-shell crab is a coast specialty, and crab claws are a traditional appetizer. Coast natives are fond of quaffing Barq's root beer with their seafood.

Category	Cost*
Very Expensive	over $20
Expensive	$15–$20
Moderate	$10–$15
Inexpensive	$5–$10

**per person without tax (8%), service, or drinks*

Lodging Recent tough economic conditions have battered the Gulf Coast like a hurricane, but good lodgings can still be found.

Category	Cost*
Very Expensive	over $70
Expensive	$50–$70
Moderate	$30–$50
Inexpensive	$20–$30

**double room; add 9% for taxes*

Bay St. Louis *Lodging*

Diamondhead Inn. This standard-issue motel attracts golfers who play the nearby Diamondhead Pine and Cardinal courses (*see* Participant Sports, *above*). The wooden walks and balconies are nicked by cleats; some walls are scarred, presumably by golfers' rages or rowdies. Each room has a balcony and kitchenette (actually just a fridge for beer). *4300 Aloha Circle, Bay St. Louis 39520, tel. 601/255–1421 or outside MS 800/647–9550. 67 rooms. Facilities: yacht club, marina, tennis courts, 36-hole golf course, stable. AE, MC, V. Expensive.*

Biloxi *Dining*

Fisherman's Wharf. A neighboring shrimp factory perfumes the parking lot here, but race inside to fresher air and views of oyster shuckers at work on the pier. Crabmeat salad for lunch; broiled catch-of-the-day for dinner; and always, the only dessert, the mysterious Fisherman's Wharf pie. *315 E. Beach Blvd., tel. 601/436–4513. Dress: informal. Reservations recommended. AE, MC, V. Expensive.*

Baricev's. The restaurant's large, plain dining room is enhanced by display cases of fish heaped on ice, and by sweeping views of the ocean where the creatures so recently cavorted. Fried soft-shell crab, a specialty, is succulent inside a thick, flaky crust. If you scorn "fry," other specialties are snapper Baricev, rolled in seasoned cracker crumbs and broiled in olive oil; and oysters Baricev, a casserole of plump oysters, green onions, garlic, cheese, and olive oil. Baricev's is Yugoslavian, but the hearty gumbo bespeaks a proper French *roux. 899 Central Beach Blvd., tel. 601/435–3626. Dress: informal. No reservations. AE, DC, MC, V. Moderate.*

McElroy's Harbor House Seafood Restaurant. Biloxi natives and real shrimpers eat hearty breakfasts, lunches, and dinners here in functional surroundings. Notable are the po'boys, oysters on the half shell, broiled stuffed flounder, and stuffed crabs. You can also try "Biloxi bacon." *Biloxi Small Craft Harbor, tel. 601/435–5001. Dress: informal. AE, DC, MC, V. Inexpensive.*

Ole Biloxi Schooner. Coast residents flock to this family-run restaurant on Biloxi's serene back bay. It's tiny—little more than a shack—but the food is good, especially the gumbo and the po'boys, which come "dressed" and wrapped in paper. *159 E. Howard, tel. 601/374–8071. Dress: informal. No credit cards. Inexpensive.*

Lodging **Mississippi Beach Resort Hotel.** Formerly the Biloxi Hilton, this high-rise hotel with its flanking motellike wings, gains distinction from tropical plantings. Rooms can be tired and musty. *2060 W. Beach Blvd., Biloxi 39531, tel. 601/388–7000. 450 rooms. Facilities: lounge with entertainment, 6 lighted tennis courts, championship golf course nearby, swimming pool, 2 playgrounds, game room. AE, MC, V. Expensive–Very Expensive.*

Royal d'Iberville Hotel. This hotel has gone upscale since a recent decoration that left the spacious rooms bright with chintz. Furniture is hotel-functional; the large public areas are comfortably contemporary. *1980 W. Beach Blvd., Biloxi 39530, tel. 601/388–6610; 800/647–3955; in MS, 800/222–3906. 264 rooms. Facilities: beachfront lounge, entertainment, 2 swimming pools, restaurants, tennis, golf, meeting facilities, babysitting. AE, DC, MC, V. Expensive–Very Expensive.*

Beachwater Inn. Set among live oaks that contrast with its contemporary lines, this family-owned motel attracts repeat customers. Its owners are experts on coast attractions and events. The rooms are fresh and neat, though not elegant. *1678 W. Beach Blvd., Biloxi 39530, tel. 601/432–1984. 31 rooms, some with cooking nooks and porches; beach views. Facilities: babysitting, swimming pool, golf packages, deep-sea fishing, and activity director. No restaurant. AE, MC, V. Moderate.*

Gulfport
Dining

Vrazel's. In 1969, Hurricane Camille blew away the restaurant that had long stood here; the brick building that replaced it gets its charm from soft lighting and dining nooks with large windows facing the beach. Added attractions include the red snapper, Gulf trout, flounder, and shrimp prepared every which way: étouffée, au gratin à la Cajun, amandine, à la Vrazel, blackened, Pontchartrain, meuniere. Snapper Lenwood is a specialty, teaming broiled snapper with crabmeat and crawfish in a Cajun-style sauce. For the best of land and sea, try veal Aaron (crabmeat, mushrooms, and lemon sauce combined with tender veal medallions). *3206 W. Beach Blvd. (U.S. 90), tel. 601/863–2229. Jacket and tie required. Dinner reservations recommended. AE, MC, V. Moderate.*

Lil Ray's, Etc. Coast tacky decor includes running lights and other nautical trappings. But for giant po'boys (9" or 14" long) on thick French bread, the only place as good as this Lil Ray's in Gulfport is the original Lil Ray's in Waveland *(see* Waveland Dining, *below*). Try fried soft-shell crabs or fried oysters your first time round. Regulars wolf down enormous seafood platters (stuffed crab and fried catfish, shrimp, and oysters) and mountains of boiled shrimp, crabs, and crawfish in season. The gumbo is excellent. *U.S. 49 across from Norwood Village Shopping Center, tel. 601/831–1160 or 601/831–1161. Dress: informal. No reservations. MC, V. Closed Sun. Inexpensive.*

Long Beach
Dining

Chappy's. Special-occasion dining for Coast residents often means a visit to this pleasant restaurant with its twinkling white lights outside, its black-clad waiters inside. Specialties include rich gumbo, redfish pan-fried Cajun style, and barbecued shrimp. The fish, fresh from the Gulf, is cooked by Chappy himself. *624 E. Beach, tel. 601/865–9755. Dress: dressy for the*

Coast, informal by world standards. Reservations recommended. AE, MC, V. Expensive.

Ocean Springs
Dining

Germaine's. Formerly Trilby's, this little house surrounded by live oaks has served many a great meal to its faithful clientele. The atmosphere is reminiscent of New Orleans, with unadorned wooden floors, walls decked in local art-for-sale, fireplaces, and attentive service. Specialties include mushrooms *le marin*, crabmeat au gratin, trout *desoto*, veal Angela, and chicken Chardonnay. *U.S. 90E, tel. 601/875–4426. Jacket and tie required. Reservations recommended. AE, DC, MC, V. Expensive.*

Jocelyn's Restaurant. Jocelyn scandalized Mississippians when she left Trilby's kitchen (now Germaine's, *see above*), but they love her cooking just as much in this old frame house. This is as good as coast seafood gets. The specialty is the day's catch of flounder, trout, and redfish subtly seasoned and served with garnishes as bright and original as modern art. Chicken pot pie is another specialty. *U.S. 90E, opposite Eastover Bank, tel. 601/875–1925. Reservations recommended. Dress: neat but casual. No credit cards. Expensive.*

La Casa de Elva. Pink stucco and round arches say Mexico, but the wooded views say Gulf Coast at this large restaurant that's open for lunch and dinner. Specialties include marinated shrimp stuffed with cheese and jalapeño, wrapped in bacon and broiled under a cheese topping; shrimp baked in a delicate butter-citrus sauce with cilantro; and traditional Mexican dishes like boneless breast of chicken baked in an *achiote* sauce and beef strips in *ranchero picante* salsa. There's a piano bar until midnight, with dancing. *U.S. 90, 1 mi east of Biloxi–Ocean Springs Bridge, tel. 601/875–0144. Reservations not required. Dress: casual. MC, V. Inexpensive.*

Waveland
Dining

Lil Ray's. The appointments in the *original* Lil Ray's are limited to trestle tables and benches. This is a place to dream about when you're hungry for seafood platters and po'boys. The menu is the same as Lil Ray's in Gulfport *(see* Gulfport Dining, *above*). A waitress, asked by a customer for a diet drink, said it best: "Mister, this ain't no diet place." *1015 U.S. 90, tel. 601/467–4566. Dress: informal. Reservations not required. MC, V. Inexpensive.*

Nightlife

Live Entertainment

David M's (857 Beach Blvd., Biloxi, tel. 601/374–8832) includes five bars and restaurants that offer varied entertainment: music of the '60s and '70s, dancing on a black-marble dance floor, relaxing in a large hot tub. There's also a barefoot bar at the end of a pier (in case you wish to arrive by boat).

Bars

Steep yourself in antebellum splendor at **Mary Mahoney's Irish Pub** adjacent to the Old French House *(see* Time Out in Exploring, *above*), or tip a frosty beer with the locals in the fishhouse-plain bar at **Baricev's** *(see* Biloxi Dining, *above*). Swim up to barstools in the pool for summer drinks at the **Mississippi Beach Resort Hotel** *(see* Lodging, *above*).

The Natchez Trace

The **Natchez Trace Parkway** is what God meant highways to be. Flower-sprigged and forested, it is a long thin park running from Nashville to Natchez, crossing the early paths worn by Choctaw and Chickasaw Indians, flatboatmen, outlaws, itinerant preachers, postriders, soldiers, and settlers. Landscaped by the National Park Service, the Trace is meticulously manicured to show off the straightest pines and spookiest cypresses, to alternate peaceful vistas of reeds and still waters with dense woodlands where the dogwood stars shine. The Trace grows increasingly wild and mysterious as it nears Natchez; the cutthroats and murderers who frequented the early trails come unwanted to mind.

When completed, the Trace will be 449 miles long, with 313 miles in Mississippi. There are no billboards along its route, and commercial vehicles are forbidden to use it. Park rangers are serious about the 50 mph speed limit; you'll probably get acquainted with one if you drive any faster.

You can make the drive in seven hours from Tupelo to Natchez by driving diagonally across the state. However, to fully appreciate the beauty and history of the Trace requires a more leisurely approach, perhaps a week-long odyssey.

Getting Around

By Car This is the only way to tour the Trace properly, though you can reach the major cities along the highway by plane and by bus. Corinth is located at the intersection of U.S. 72 and U.S. 45, and Tupelo is five miles south of the Natchez Trace Parkway at the intersection of U.S. 45 and U.S. 78.

The Trace is incomplete at Jackson, connected by I–55 and I–20, which run through the city. Jackson is also on U.S. 49 and U.S. 51. Natchez, the beginning of the Natchez Trace Parkway (but the end of this tour), is also served by U.S. 61.

By Plane
Columbus Golden Triangle Regional Airport (U.S. 82, 10 miles west of Columbus) is served by **Northwest Airlink, American Eagle,** and **Atlantic Southeast Airlines,** with connections nationwide through Memphis and Atlanta.

Jackson **American, Continental Express, Delta,** and **Northwest Airlines** offer nonstop daily flights to Dallas, Atlanta, and New Orleans, with direct service available to almost every major city in the United States. The airport, Allen C. Thompson Field, is east of Jackson off I–20, 10 minutes from downtown.

Tupelo Tupelo Municipal Airport, 15 minutes from Elvis Presley's birthplace, is served by **Northwest Airlink** and **American Eagle.**

By Bus **Greyhound-Trailways** offers daily service to Tupelo, Corinth, Columbus, Philadelphia, Jackson, Port Gibson, and Natchez. Stations are located at 201 Commerce St., Tupelo, tel. 601/842–4557; 904 Main St., Columbus, tel. 601/328–4732; 204 U.S. 72E, Corinth, tel. 601/287–1466; 201 S. Jefferson St., Jackson, tel. 601/353–6342; and 103 Lower Woodville Rd., Natchez, tel. 601/445–5291.

Guided Tours

Special-interest In Jackson, **Southern Tours, Incorporated** (Box 16623, Jackson 39236, tel. 601/977–9233 or 800/426–9111), offers a "Mansions Along the Mississippi" tour designed for groups of up to 30. Group tours are conducted in motor coaches. Spend two nights each in mansions and historic inns in Vicksburg and Natchez. (The tour may also include New Orleans's French Quarter.) Customized group tours are available, including visits to Civil War sites and Southern gardens, and a close look at Black Heritage.

Vicksburg Historic Tours (#9 Crestwood Dr., Vicksburg 39180, tel. 601/638–8888 or 800/527–4702) gives morning bus tours daily, which cover the Vicksburg National Military Park, the USS *Cairo*, and antebellum homes throughout the city. Afternoon tours, offered Monday through Saturday, drive through the city visiting antebellum homes. Reservations are recommended.

In Natchez, **Natchez Pilgrimage Tours, Inc.** (Box 347, Natchez 39121, tel. 601/446–6631 or 800/647–6742) takes groups of 20 or more to tour 13 antebellum homes year-round (during Pilgrimage, between 24 and 30 homes are open). Tours are conducted mornings and afternoons, and bus tickets can be bought at six of the area's hotels. Tour tickets can be bought only at the Pilgrimage Tour office on the corner of Canal and State streets.

Important Addresses and Numbers

Tourist Information **Corinth/Alcorn Area Chamber of Commerce.** *810 Tate St., Corinth 38834, tel. 601/287–5269. Open weekdays 8–5. Closed for lunch.* **Metro Jackson Convention and Visitors Bureau.** *Box 1450, Jackson 39205, tel. 601/960–1891 or 800/354–7695. Open weekdays 8:30–5.* **Jackson Visitor Information Center.** *Located at the entrance to the Mississippi Agriculture and Forestry Museum, 1150 Lakeland Dr. east of I–55, tel. 601/960–1800. Open weekdays 8:30–4:30.* **Natchez Trace Parkway Visitor Center.** *Rte. 1, NT-143, Tupelo 38801; on the Natchez Trace Pkwy., milepost 266, tel. 601/845–1572. Open daily 8–5. Closed Christmas Day.* **Natchez Convention & Visitors Bureau.** *311 Liberty Rd., Natchez 39120, tel. 601/446–6345 or 800/647–6724. Open weekdays 8–5.* **Natchez Pilgrimage Tours.** This is the only place to purchase tickets for Pilgrimage tours and activities. *Canal St. at State St., Box 347, Natchez 39120, tel. 601/446–6631 or 800/647–6742 (out-of-state). AE, MC, V. Open daily 8:30–5:30.* **Tupelo Convention and Visitors Bureau.** *399 E. Main St., Box 1485, Tupelo 38801, tel. 601/841–6521 or 800/533–0611. Open weekdays 8–5.*

Emergencies In Tupelo, Jackson, and Natchez, dial 911 for **police** or **ambulance** in an emergency. For help on the Natchez Trace, dial 0 and ask for the nearest Park Ranger.

Seek medical help at **North Mississippi Regional Medical Center** (830 S. Gloster St., Tupelo, tel. 601/841–3000), **Mississippi Baptist Medical Center** (1225 N. State St., Jackson, tel. 601/968–1776), and **Jefferson Davis Hospital** (Sgt. Prentiss Dr., Natchez, tel. 601/442–2871).

24-hour Pharmacy **Jim Bain's Pharmacy** (519 N. Gloster St., Tupelo, tel. 601/844–4530) has a 24-hour answering service. In Jackson, **Eckerd's**

(DeVille Plaza, I–55N, E. Frontage Rd., tel. 601/956–5143). In Natchez, **Lessley's Pharmacy** (115 Jefferson Davis Blvd., tel. 601/446–6331 or after 6 PM 601/442–4272).

Exploring the Natchez Trace

Numbers in the margin correspond to points of interest on the Natchez Trace map.

The Mississippi segment of the Natchez Trace begins near Tupelo, in the northeast corner of the state. It wanders through a hilly landscape of dense forests and sparkling streams.

Named for J.P. Coleman, Mississippi's governor from 1955 to
1 1959, **J.P. Coleman State Park** vies with Tishomingo State Park for the title of most spectacular Mississippi state park. There are wooded campsites for tents and RVs, and 10 secluded cabins, some of them old and rustic (no air-conditioning); others from the 1970s have fireplaces and central air and heat. Rooms at the balconied lodge overlook the shale beaches of serene Pickwick Lake. Visitors explore nature trails, rent canoes and boats, fish, swim, and waterski. *Rte. 5, Box 504, Iuka 38852 (13 mi north of Iuka off U.S. 25), tel. 601/423–6515.*

2 **Tishomingo State Park** lies in the Appalachian foothills, making its terrain unique in Mississippi. If you're feeling peppy, a 13-mile nature trail winds through a canyon along steep hills by waterfalls, granite outcrops, and a swinging bridge; otherwise, take the winding roads through forests so leafy they can hide the brightest day in shadow. Eight-mile canoe trips and float trips are offered from mid-March to October. Around Haynes Lake are primitive campsites, hookups, and five rustic cabins to rent. Bring your own provisions. *Box 880, Tishomingo, MS 38873 (mi marker 394 off Natchez Trace), tel. 601/438–6914.*

3 **Corinth** is a town of special interest for Civil War enthusiasts. The Battles of Shiloh and Corinth are commemorated with markers and displays throughout the area. Corinth was settled just seven years before the war and assumed military importance because of its two railroad lines.

In April 1862, after the bloody battle of Shiloh, near Shiloh Church in Tennessee, 21 miles to the north, the Confederates turned Corinth into a vast medical center. In May 1862, the Confederates, under General P.G.T. Beauregard, were forced to withdraw further; their retreat involved the most ingenious hoax of the war: To fool the Federal forces, campfires were lighted, dummy cannoneers were placed at fake cannons, empty trains were cheered as if they brought reinforcements, and buglers moved along the deserted works, playing taps. Union forces occupied the town and, in October 1862, a Confederate attempt to recapture the town failed.

To visit all of Corinth's Civil War sites, follow the street markers, using the self-guided tour brochure available free at the **Northeast Mississippi Museum.** *Fourth St., at Washington St., tel. 601/287–2231. Admission: $1.50 adults, 50¢ children. Open daily 1–4. Closed Thurs. and the month of Jan.*

4 Between Corinth and Tupelo is **Jacinto,** a ghost town with a restored Federal-style courthouse (1854) surrounded by pre-1870 buildings that are slowly being restored.

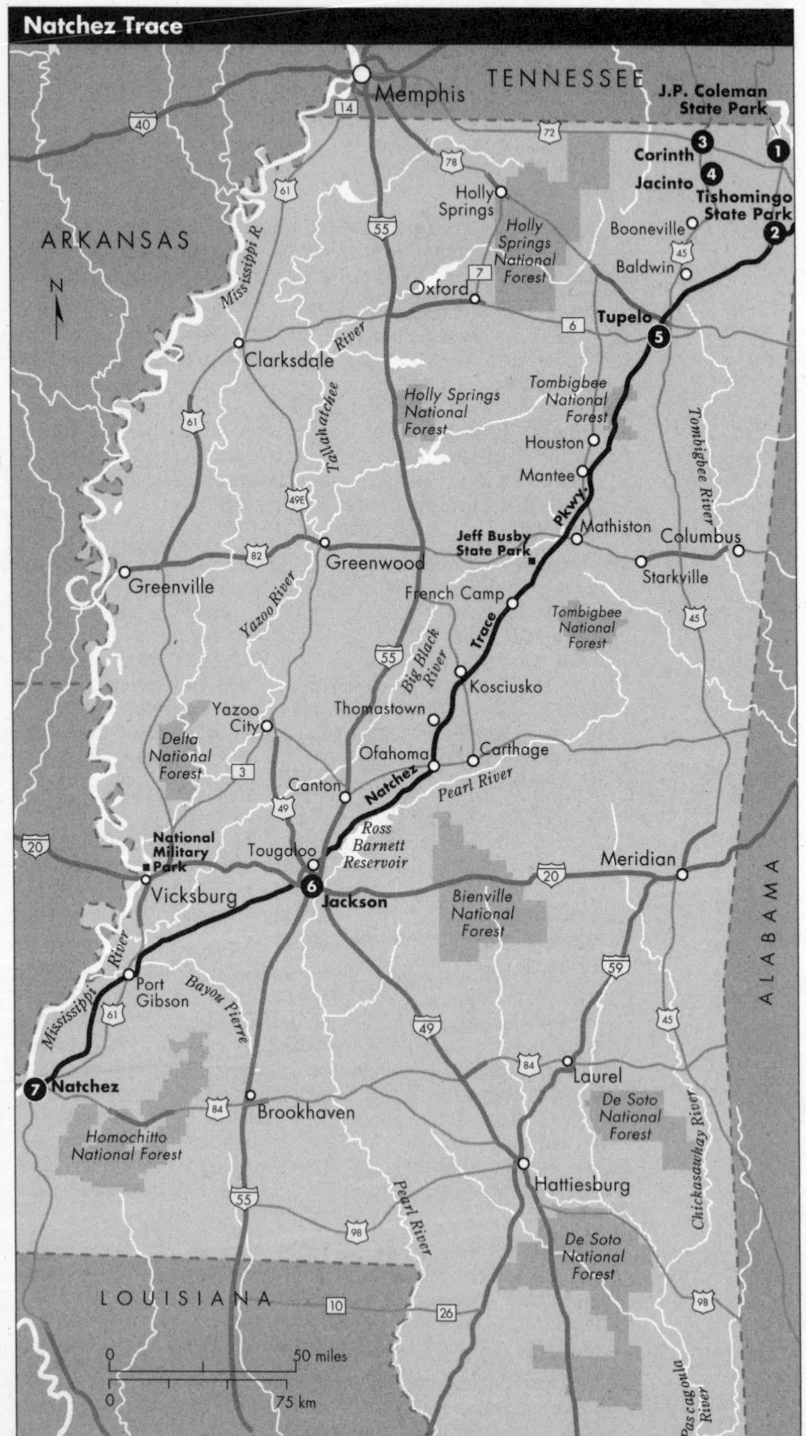
Natchez Trace
TENNESSEE
Memphis
J.P. Coleman State Park
Corinth
Jacinto
Tishomingo State Park
Holly Springs
Booneville
Baldwin
ARKANSAS
Mississippi R.
Holly Springs National Forest
Oxford
Tupelo
Clarksdale
Tallahatchee River
Holly Springs National Forest
Tombigbee National Forest
Houston
Mantee
Tombigbee River
Pkwy.
Mathiston
Columbus
Jeff Busby State Park
Greenwood
Greenville
Starkville
Yazoo River
French Camp
Tombigbee National Forest
Trace
Big Black River
Kosciusko
Thomastown
Yazoo City
Delta National Forest
Ofahoma
Carthage
Canton
Natchez
Pearl River
Ross Barnett Reservoir
National Military Park
Tougaloo
Meridian
Vicksburg
Jackson
Bienville National Forest
ALABAMA
Mississippi River
Port Gibson
Bayou Pierre
Natchez
Laurel
Brookhaven
De Soto National Forest
Homochitto National Forest
Hattiesburg
Chickasawhay River
Pearl River
De Soto National Forest
LOUISIANA
0 50 miles
0 75 km
Pascagoula River

Jacinto also has nature trails that lead to mineral springs, and a swinging bridge. A new recreational park provides hookups for eight campers, a playground, and a picnic area with grills. *On MS 356, 9 mi east of U.S. 45 between Corinth and Tupelo, tel. 601/286–8662. Admission free. Open Tues.–Sun. 1–5, Sat. 10–5, other times by appointment. Closed Jan.–Mar.*

The **Natchez Trace Parkway Visitor Center** (*see* Tourist Information, *above*) is located five miles north of Tupelo on the Trace. The Visitor Center offers exhibits, a 12-minute film, a hands-on area for children, and the *Official Map and Guide,* which opens to a four-foot length to give detailed, mile-by-mile information from Nashville to Natchez.

Tupelo 5 The largest city in north Mississippi, **Tupelo** (named after the tupelo gum tree), was founded in 1859 and is a city of accomplishment. Progressive leaders have successfully lured business and industry to an area that only 30 years ago was predominantly agricultural. The arts flourish here, and the medical center is the largest in the state. The scenic hill country provides beautiful places to camp, swim, fish, jog, and bike.

Why do so many tourists flock here? Because this is a city of destiny: the birthplace of Elvis Presley, the one-and-only king of rock and roll. The **Tupelo Convention and Visitor's Center** is a good place to start your tour *(see* Tourist Information, *above).* From here, head to **Elvis Presley's birthplace,** a tiny, two-room "shotgun" house built by his father, Vernon Presley, for $180. Elvis Aaron Presley was born here on January 8, 1935. The home has been restored and furnished much as it was when the Presleys lived in it. The house is now surrounded by **Elvis Presley Park,** land purchased with proceeds from Elvis's 1956 concert at the Mississippi-Alabama Fair. The park includes a swimming pool, tennis courts, playground, and a gift shop (for Elvis souvenirs) in the Youth Center, and the new **Elvis Presley Museum,** opened in August 1992, with more than 3,000 pieces of previously unseen Elvis memorabilia. The **Elvis Presley Memorial Chapel,** suggested by the singer in 1971 as a place for his fans to meditate, was dedicated in 1979, two years after Presley's death. *Off Old Hwy. 78, at 306 Elvis Presley Dr., tel. 601/841–1245. Admission: $1 adults, 50¢ children. Museum admission: $4 adults, $2 children. Open Mon.–Sat. 9–5:30, Sun. 1–5.*

Five miles north of the Presley birthplace is **Elvis Presley Lake and Campground** where you can swim, ski, sun, and fish—and think about Elvis. *Off Canal St. extended, tel. 601/841–1304. Primitive and full-service campsites. Separate fees for swimming, camping, fishing, and boat launching.*

The **Tupelo Museum** displays further Presley memorabilia along with other exhibits, including a turn-of-the-century Western Union office, a working sorghum mill, a train depot and caboose, and an old-time country store. *Located in James J. Ballard Park, off MS 6W, tel. 601/841–6438. Admission: $1 adults, 50¢ children 3–11, under 3 free. Group tours by appointment. Open Tues.–Fri. 10–4, weekends 1–5.*

Once you've satisfied your Elvis mania, turn your thoughts to the Civil War Battle of Tupelo. In 1864, Union General A. J. Smith marched 14,000 troops against Nathan Bedford Forrest's forces near Tupelo. Smith's goal was to end the constant Southern harrassment of supply lines to Sherman's army besieging Atlanta. The battle, on July 14, 1864, was the last major battle in Mississippi and one of the bloodiest. A **National Battlefield** site on West Main Street (MS 6), inside the city limits, commemorates the battle with monuments and displays.

From Tupelo, the trip to Jackson takes three hours if you don't stop. It can easily take an entire day, however, if you stop to read the brown wooden markers, explore nature trails, and admire the neat fields, trees, and wildflower meadows.

Bynum Mounds (milepost 232.4) are ceremonial hills that were constructed between 100 BC and AD 200 by prehistoric people. Exhibits describe their daily existence.

Jeff Busby State Park (milepost 193.9) was named for the Mississippi congressman who introduced legislation creating the Natchez Trace Parkway. The park includes an overlook at one of the state's highest points (603 feet) and a 20-minute nature trail that identifies native plants and describes their use by pioneers. Campers may wish to spend the night. For more information contact the State Parks (Box 451, Jackson 39205, tel. 601/364–2120).

The **Little Mountain Service Station** is located at the campground entrance. This privately owned station is the only place to fuel up right on the parkway.

At **French Camp** (milepost 180.7), where Frenchman Louis LeFleur established a stand (or inn) in 1812, you can watch sorghum molasses being made on Saturdays in late September and October.

At **Beaver Creek** (milepost 145.1) a short (5- to 10-minute), self-guided nature trail explains beavers' habits.

Cypress Swamp (milepost 122.0), a pleasure today, was once a treacherous, mosquito-infested morass for early travelers. A 20-minute self-guided nature walk takes you through the gloom of a tupelo/bald cypress swamp.

The **Ridgeland Crafts Center** displays and sells high quality crafts in a dogtrot log cabin. Members of the Craftsman's Guild of Mississippi have created Choctaw Indian baskets of seamless doubleweave, splint baskets of Mississippi white oak, wooden plates and utensils, handwoven and handscreened clothing, pottery, pewter jewelry, and sturdy, whimsical wooden toys. The Center sponsors free demonstrations (usually on weekends) of basketweaving, Indian dances and games, bread baking in an outdoor stone oven, and glassblowing. *Natchez Trace at Ridgeland (milepost 102.4), tel. 601/856–7456. Restrooms, picnic tables, water fountain. Admission free. Open daily 9–5.*

The parkway is incomplete from milepost 101.5 to 87.0. I–55, I–20, and I–220 are connecting routes. To reach Jackson, follow I–55 south from the Trace.

Jackson 6

At its spangled edges, **Jackson** has little to distinguish it, but the state capital becomes increasingly original toward its shady heart. The downtown area has many small museums and most of the city's notable architecture.

The city is named for Andrew Jackson, who was popular with Mississippians long before he became president. As Major General Jackson, he helped negotiate the Treaty of Doak's Stand by which the Choctaw Indians ceded large chunks of Mississippi to the United States, on October 18, 1820. The City of Jackson is the county seat of Hinds County, named for another negotiator, Major General Thomas Hinds, an enterprising and daring hero of the Battle of New Orleans in the War of 1812.

The **Jackson Visitor Information Center** is a small log cabin with anachronistic plate glass windows and a good stock of brochures. *At the Mississippi Agriculture and Forestry Museum, 1150 Lakeland Dr., east of I–55, tel. 601/960–1800. Open weekdays 8:30–4:30.*

The Agriculture and Forestry Museum looks like an old farm marooned in the midst of expanding suburbs, but the city was actually here first. The 10 farm buildings were brought here to stand exactly as they once did in Jefferson Davis County, Mississippi. They are still surrounded by a working farm with fields of corn and cotton, and pastures for sheep, goats, and horses. A crossroads town, similar to small Mississippi towns in the 1920s, has also been assembled. Work goes on in a blacksmith's shop and a cotton gin, meetings are held in the old Masonic Lodge, and the 1897 Epiphany Episcopal church building can be rented for weddings. The General Store sells soft drinks, snacks, and souvenirs. A complete tour of the museum will take about 90 minutes. *1150 Lakeland Dr., Tour Coordinator, Box 1609, Jackson 39215, tel. 601/354–6113. Admission: $3 adults; $1 children 6–18, under 6 free. Group tours available. Open Mon.–Sat. 9–5, Sun. 1–5. Summer hours: Tues.–Sat. 10–7, Sun. 1–5.*

The **Old Capitol Building** sits serenely on Capitol Green, with the **War Memorial Building** (1940) to the north and the **Mississippi Archives Building** (1971) to the south. Begun in 1833 and completed in 1840, the Old Capitol, with its simple columns and elegant proportions, is an excellent example of Greek Revival architecture. The building was restored in 1959–61 for use as the **State Historical Museum.** Capitol Green is a leafy reminder of the checkerboard pattern of alternating squares of buildings and parks recommended by President Thomas Jefferson and proposed for Jackson by Peter A. Vandorn. Vandorn submitted a map and plan for the new city in April 1822. The Vandorn map and other exhibits depicting Mississippi's history are on display in the museum. *100 North State St., tel. 601/354–6222. Admission free. Guided tours available. Open weekdays 8–5, Sat. 9:30–4:30, Sun. 12:30–4:30.*

The **Spengler's Corner Building** (101 N. State St.) is one of Jackson's oldest commercial structures. In 1840 Joseph Spengler opened a tavern here that was popular with legislators, but when the New Capitol was built, the inn closed. Many other businesses occupied the building, which was restored as a law office in 1976. Adjoining it to the north are attractive late-19th- and early 20th-century buildings, with the stucco and bay windows making them primarily Victorian-Italianate in style.

The old **Central Fire Station** (201 S. President St.) is a three-story brick structure completed in 1905; it served as Central Station No. 1 until 1975. The Jackson Chamber of Commerce restored it in 1978.

City Hall (203 S. President St.) is a white Greek Revival building that has served continuously as Jackson's center of government since its opening in 1847. A Masonic Hall originally occupied the third floor. During the Civil War, City Hall was used as a hospital. Look into the tiny City Council chamber with its black and white floors and heavy red velvet curtains. On the west side of the building is the formal Josh Halbert Garden, with a statue of Andrew Jackson designed in 1968.

In the **Mississippi Arts Center** you will find the **Mississippi Museum of Art** and the **Impressions Gallery.** The museum has changing exhibits and a permanent collection of regional paintings. In the high-tech, hands-on Impressions Gallery, you can create music by walking through beams of light, wave your arms to send colors rippling from your shadow, and more—all in the name of education and art. *201 E. Pascagoula St., tel. 601/960–1515. Admission: $2 adults, $1 children. The Impressions Gallery is free. Museum open Tues.–Fri 10–5, weekends noon–4. Closed Mon.*

Davis Planetarium is the largest planetarium in the Southeast and one of the world's best-equipped, but its shows vary wildly in quality. *201 E. Pascagoula St., tel. 601/960–1550. Admission: $4 adults, $2.50 children 12 and under and senior citizens. Closed Mon.*

The **U.S. Federal Courthouse** (245 E. Capitol St.) is a good example in concrete and sandstone of the streamlined Art Deco style that was popular between the world wars, a time when many Jackson buildings were constructed. This building was completed in 1934 and served as Jackson's post office and as a federal court building until 1988, when a new post office was built. The motifs of eagles, stars, and geometric designs on the exterior are repeated throughout the interior and on the free-standing aluminum light fixtures around the building.

St. Andrew's Episcopal Cathedral (305 E. Capitol St.) offers free musical programs at noon each Wednesday (except in the summer), followed by sandwiches at a nominal fee. The original building is an important example of Gothic Revival architecture enhanced by fine stained-glass windows.

The Lamar Life Building, adjacent to St. Andrew's, was designed to complement the cathedral. Although it has lost the alligators that once flanked its doors, it still exhibits other Gothic designs and a crenellated clock tower. The president of Lamar Life during the building's construction (1924–25) was C.W. Welty, father of Eudora Welty, Pulitzer Prize–winning author and lifelong Jackson resident.

The **Mississippi Governor's Mansion** has been continuously in use as the official home of the state's first family since its completion in 1841. At that time, Jackson was a tiny city and this grand Greek Revival dwelling was an optimistic statement. General Sherman presumably lived here during his occupation of Jackson in 1863. An addition in the rear serves the governor's family. The original building was carefully restored in the 1970s and furnished with museum-quality antiques that the state could never have afforded in the 1800s. Invest 30 minutes in the lively tours, strong on legend as well as fact. *300 E. Capitol St., tel. 601/359–3175. Admission free. Tours Tues.–Fri. 9:30–11:30.*

Smith Park is the only public square that remains from the 1822 checkerboard plan of the city. It is the center of the Smith Park Historic District. The park was a grazing area for animals until 1884, when James Smith of Glasgow, Scotland, a former Jacksonian, donated $100 to fence and beautify it, and the park was named for him. It is the setting for a famous short story, "The Winds," by Eudora Welty. The park hosts frequent concerts, festivals, picnics, and art exhibits. A popular "Fridays in Smith Park" program offers noontime entertainment in April and October.

The **Cathedral of St. Peter the Apostle** (203 N. West St.), built 1897–1900, is the third building of the congregation, which organized in 1846. Their first building was burned by Federal troops in 1863, as were many others in the city. Their second church, now in the very center of the downtown area, at the site of the present rectory (123 N. West St.), was criticized for its remoteness from town.

Across Yazoo Street from Smith Park is a Greek Revival building with graceful columns. Constructed of slave-made brick in 1843–44, this simple, elegant structure housed the First Baptist Church until 1893, then a Methodist church, followed by the Central Church of Christ. After several years as an apartment house, it became an office building in 1959, and it now belongs once more to the Methodists.

The **Galloway House** (304 N. Congress St.) is a two-story house built in the Victorian "Second Empire" style. Completed in 1889, this house was built for Methodist Bishop Charles Galloway, a distinguished churchman of international renown. In 1983 it was renovated for use as a law office.

The **New Capitol** sits in Beaux Arts splendor at the junction of Mississippi and North Congress streets, its dome surmounted by a gold-plated copper eagle with a 15-foot wingspan. Completed in 1903 at a cost of $1 million, the Capitol enjoyed a $19-million renovation from 1979 to 1983. It was designed by the German architect Theodore C. Link, who was strongly influenced by the national capitol in Washington, DC. Elaborate architectural details inside the building include a Tiffany window. Ride up in the ornate brass-and-wood elevator if the grand staircase outside daunts you. *400 High St., tel. 601/359–3114. Admission free. Open weekdays 8–5, Sat. 10–4, Sun. 1–4. Guided tours: weekdays 9, 10, 11, 1:30, 2:30, 3:30.*

Eudora Welty Library (300 N. State St.), the largest public library in Mississippi, is named in honor of the city's famed short-story writer and novelist *(The Ponder Heart, Losing Battles, The Optimist's Daughter)*. The library opened in 1986; it has a 42-foot-long circulation desk, handcrafted of African rosewood and curly maple by local craftsman Fletcher Cox. It houses the Mississippi Writer's Room exhibit on Miss Welty, William Faulkner, Tennessee Williams, Margaret Walker Alexander, Ellen Douglas, and many others. *300 N. State St., tel. 601/968–5811. Open Mon.–Thurs. 10–9, Fri. and Sat. 10–6, and (Sept.–May) Sun. 1–5.*

A few Victorian homes stand on North State Street between College Street and Fortification Street, the survivors of the many large houses that lined this street in its heyday as Jackson's best address. The **Morris House** (505 N. State St.) is a Classic Revival house built about 1900. The **Virden-Patton House** (512 N. State St.), built about 1849, was undamaged in the Civil War, suggesting that Union officers may have used it as headquarters. The **Millsaps-Buie House** (628 N. State St.), built in 1888, has been restored as a bed-and-breakfast inn *(see*

Lodging, *below*). It was built by Major Reuben Webster Millsaps, the founder of Millsaps College in Jackson. Two doors north is the **Garner Green House** (1910), with an imposing portico of Corinthian columns. This house was moved across the street from its original location and restored in 1988 to become an office building. **Greenbrook Flowers** (c. 1895–97; 705 N. State St.) occupies the former St. Andrew's Episcopal rectory; it has been greatly altered.

Time Out **Kitchen Delights** offers takeout food as appealing as its tomato-red building. The fresh herbs in the front garden show up in plate lunches such as tarragon chicken breast over rice and salads such as fresh tomato and mozzarella with basil. Other specialties are crawfish and crabmeat quiche (in season), fresh-baked breads, and raisin-walnut cookies. *709 Poplar Blvd., tel. 601/353–FOOD. Open weekdays 9–5:30. AE, MC, V. Inexpensive (unless you stock up on fresh cheeses and pâtés).*

The **Manship House** was built about 1857 by Charles H. Manship, the Jackson mayor who surrendered the city to General William Tecumseh Sherman on July 16, 1863. The museum is a careful restoration of a small Gothic Revival–style home with examples of wood graining painted by Manship himself. *420 E. Fortification St. (enter parking area from Congress St.), tel. 601/961–4724. Admission free. Tours: Tues.–Fri. 9–4, weekends 1–4. Closed Mon.*

C.W. Welty and his wife Chestina built the house at **741 North Congress Street** in 1907. Their daughter Eudora was born here in 1909 in the master bedroom on the second floor. Welty used images of this house and neighborhood in many of her literary works, including *The Golden Apples*. It has been restored for use as a law office.

The **Smith Robertson Museum,** the state's only Afro-American museum, has displays that focus on black life in Mississippi throughout its history. The building, which was the first public school for black children in Jackson, has been creatively adapted for use as a museum and meeting place. *528 Bloom Street, tel. 601/960–1457. Admission: $1.50 adults, 50¢ children. Open Mon.–Fri. 9–5, Sat. 9–12, Sun. 2–5.*

Jackson's oldest house, **The Oaks,** was built by James Hervey Boyd, mayor of Jackson between 1853 and 1858. *823 N. Jefferson St., tel. 601/353–9339. Admission: $2, children $1. Open Tues.–Sat. 10–4, Sun. 1:30–4. Closed Mon.*

Jackson is a city of neat, tree-shaded neighborhoods, excellent for walking, jogging, or "Sunday driving," especially the **Belhaven area** bounded by Riverside Drive, I–55, Fortification Street, and North State Street. **Carlisle, Poplar, Peachtree,** and **Fairview streets** are distinguished by fine homes.

Rocky Springs (milepost 54.8) was a stop for post riders during the early 1800s, and General Grant's army camped here on its march to Jackson and Vicksburg during the Civil War. You can camp here, too. It's a first-come, first-served race, especially on weekends, but at least you needn't worry about Confederate sharpshooters. Overhung by ancient trees, the stream ripples and sings like mountain waters. Trails meander through the woods and up a steep hill to a tiny old cemetery and **Rocky**

Springs Methodist Church (1837), where services are still held on Sundays.

At milepost 41.5 is a portion of the **Old Trace,** a short section of the original Indian Trace of loess soil (easily eroded and compacted earth). You can park and walk along it for a short way.

Port Gibson is the earliest town to grow up along the Trace that is still in existence. On Church Street is the much-photographed **First Presbyterian Church** (1859), its spire topped by a 12-foot hand pointing heavenward. The church chandeliers came from the old steamboat *Robert E. Lee*. Among the churches and houses along Church Street that have been recently restored are **Gage House** (602 Church St.), 1830, with double galleries and a handsome brick dependency; **Temple Gemiluth Chassed** (706 Church St.), 1892, a synagogue with Moorish Byzantine architecture unique in Mississippi; **St. James Episcopal Church** (808 Church St.), c. 1897, a high Victorian Gothic structure designed by a Boston architect, thus reflecting Massachusetts architecture; **Port Gibson Methodist Church** (901 Church St.), 1860, Romanesque Revival in style; the **Hughes Home** (907 Church St.), 1825, once owned by Henry Hughes, author of the first sociology textbook, and once the residence of black poet Irvin Russell; and **St. Joseph's Catholic Church** (909 Church St.), 1850, Gothic in style, with pointed arches and buttresses. The **Disharoon House** (1002 Church St.), 1830s, one of the finest in Claiborne County, is a 2½-story house with double galleries that have Tuscan colonnettes. **Oak Square** (1207 Church St.), 1850–1906, is now a bed-and-breakfast inn (*see* Lodging, *above*). The **African-American Quilters' Workshop** (507 Market St., tel. 601/437–8905, open weekdays 8–5) has a renowned collection of quilts on display and for sale. The **Chamber of Commerce** is housed in a small 1805 home built by Port Gibson's founder and moved to this site in 1980. *South end of Church St., tel. 601/437–4351. Open Mon.–Fri. 8–4, Sat. 9–4.*

The **Port Gibson Chamber of Commerce** provides maps to historic sites in the vicinity, among them the impressive Rosswood Plantation (circa 1857).

Grand Gulf Military Monument commemorates the once-thriving town of Grand Gulf that was left in ruins by Federal gunboats during the Civil War. On a steep hill, the old town site has become a museum with an 1863 cannon, a collection of carriages, an 1820s dogtrot cabin, an old Catholic church, and a Spanish house from the 1790s. *North of Port Gibson off U.S. 61. Rte. 2, Box 389, Port Gibson 39150. Admission: $1.50 adults, 75¢ children. Open Mon.–Sat. 8–noon, 1–5; Sun. 9–noon, 1–6.*

Time Out Handmade bonnets swing in the breeze on the porch of **The Old Country Store,** which has been in business at Lorman since 1890. Its longleaf-pine flooring is jammed with display cases, most installed when the store was built, and you can buy souvenirs, soft drinks, and snacks, including mellow hoop cheese sliced with an antique cutter. *U.S. 61, in Lorman, tel. 601/437–3661. MC, V.*

Ask directions at the Old Country Store to the restored **Rodney Presbyterian Church** (about 12 miles southwest of Lorman). The town of **Rodney,** once home to wealthy plantation owners and river merchants, became a ghost town when the Mississippi River shifted its course. Your visit to Rodney will be enhanced by reading Eudora Welty's powerful essay "Some Notes on River Country" and her short story "At the Landing."

Northwest of Lorman, on MS 552, are 23 vine-clad columns that are the romantic ruins of **Windsor,** a huge Greek Revival mansion that was built in 1861 and burned down in 1890.

Just off the Trace near milepost 20 is **Springfield,** a plantation home built in Jefferson County in 1791. Tradition says Andrew Jackson married Rachel Donelson Robards here soon after the house was completed. *Rte. 1, Box 201, Fayette 39069, west of Natchez Trace on MS 553, tel. 601/786–3802. Admission: $5 adults, $2.50 children under 12. Open year-round 9:30–dusk.*

Emerald Mound (milepost 10.3) is the second-largest Indian mound in the country, covering almost eight acres. It was built around 1300 for religious ceremonies practiced by ancestors of the Natchez Indians. It's a good place to picnic, view a sunset, fly a kite, and let your children run loose.

The Parkway abruptly ends, putting you on U.S. 61 as you near Natchez. Here is the little town of **Washington,** with the buildings of **Historic Jefferson College** meticulously restored. Washington was the capital of the Mississippi Territory from 1802 to 1817, and Jefferson College was chartered in 1802 as the territory's first educational institution. Here Aaron Burr, who served as Thomas Jefferson's vice president, was arraigned for treason, under an oak tree, which still stands. Burr was lionized by Natchez society while he awaited trial. *U.S. 61 at Natchez, tel. 601/442–2901. Admission free. Buildings open Mon.–Sat. 9–5, Sun. 1–5.*

Natchez
7

Natchez is named for the mound-building, sun-worshiping Natchez Indians who lived here, undisturbed, in small villages before the French built Fort Rosalie in 1716. Later the city came under British rule (1763–1779), and the district known today as **Natchez-under-the-Hill** grew up at the Mississippi River landing beneath the bluff. The Spanish took control in 1795; they left their mark on the city by establishing straight streets—which intersect at right angles, atop the bluff—and green parkland that overlooks the river. The United States claimed Natchez by treaty in 1795. The city gave its name to the Natchez Trace and prospered as travelers heading for Nashville passed through with money in their pockets and a willingness to spend it on a rowdy good time.

The real glory days came between 1819 and 1860, when cotton plantations and the bustling river port poured riches into Natchez. Wealthy planters built stylish town houses and ringed the city with opulent plantation homes. Because the city had little military significance, it survived the Civil War almost untouched, but its economy was wrecked. The city entered a decline that actually saved its architectural treasures. No one could afford to tear houses down or even to remodel them. In 1932, the women of Natchez originated the idea of a pilgrimage, which would raise money for preservation. The Natchez Pilgrimage is now held twice a year, three weeks in October and four weeks in March and April. Many houses are open only during Pilgrimage weeks, when crowds flock to see them, but others are open year-round.

Begin your sightseeing at one of the tourist information centers (*see* Important Addresses and Numbers, *above*). The Chamber of Commerce offers a free self-guided walking tour. At the **Pilgrimage Tour Headquarters** (Canal and State Sts., tel. 601/446–6631 or 800/647–6742) you can purchase ***Natchez: Walking Guide to the Old Town*** and a plethora of additional books and maps of this fascinating city.

Stanton Hall (1857) is one of the most palatial and most photographed houses in America. Four giant fluted columns surmount double porticos enclosed by delicate, lacy wrought-iron railings. This magnificent preservation project of the Pilgrimage Garden Club is furnished with important Natchez antiques and objets d'art. *401 High St., tel. 601/446–6631 or 800/647–6742. Admission: $4 adults, $2 children. Open daily 9–5.*

Rosalie (1823) established the ideal form of the "Southern mansion" with its white columns, hipped roof, and red bricks. Furnishings purchased for the house in 1858 include a famous Belter parlor set. *100 Orleans St., tel. 601/445–4555. Admission: $4 adults, $2 children over 10. Open daily 9–5.*

Magnolia Hall (c. 1858) was shelled by the Union gunboat *Essex* during the Civil War. The shell reportedly exploded in a soup tureen, scalding several diners. The Greek Revival mansion has stucco walls and fluted columns topped with curving Ionic capitals. Note the plaster magnolia blossoms on the parlor ceiling. *215 S. Pearl St., tel. 601/442–7259. Admission: $4 adults, $2 children. Overnight lodgings. Daily tours 9–5.*

Natchez National Historical Park was established in 1988 to help preserve and interpret this city so historically significant to the development of the American South. Currently, two properties are featured: **Melrose** (1845), a mansion that symbolizes the era when cotton ruled, and the **William Johnson House** (1841). Johnson was a prominent "free man of color," and his restored house (due to open in late 1993) will serve as a Black-history museum. *Melrose: 1 Melrose-Monteballo Parkway. William Johnson House: 210 State St., tel. 601/442–7047. Admission to Melrose: $4. Open daily 9–5.*

Longwood (1860–61) is the largest octagonal house in the United States. When the Civil War broke out, Northern workers fled to their homes, preventing the immensely wealthy Dr. Haller Nutt from completing the mansion. Hoping to finish the house at the war's end, Nutt moved his family into the basement, but he died in 1864. Still unfinished, Longwood is now a museum for the Pilgrimage Garden Club. *140 Lower Woodville Rd., tel. 601/442–5193. Admission: $4 adults, $2 children. Open daily 9–5.*

What to See and Do with Children

Jackson

Space Port. Large video arcade. *N. Park Mall, 1200 E. County Line Rd., tel. 601/956–7315. Open Mon.–Sat. 10–9:30, Sun. 1–6.*

Chuck E. Cheese's Pizza Time Theatre. Arcade and entertainment for the under-12 set. *5465 I–55N, tel. 601/956–5252. Open Mon.–Thurs. 11–9:30, Fri. and Sat. 11–11, Sun. noon–9:30.*

Impressions Gallery (*see* Exploring, *above*).

Mississippi Agriculture and Forestry Museum (*see* Exploring, *above*).

The New Capitol is awe-inspiring enough in its decorations (4,500 bare light bulbs, and plenty of gilt) to interest even young children (*see* Exploring, *above*).

Zoological Park. Family recreational spot features animals in natural settings, including many endangered species. *2918 W. Capitol St., tel. 601/352–2580. Admission: $3 adults, $1.50 children 3–12. Open summer 9–6, winter 9–5.*

Natchez **Carriage rides** are a fun way to see downtown Natchez. Tours begin at Natchez Pilgrimage Tour Headquarters (Canal St. at State St.) or the Eola Hotel (110 N. Pearl St.). A tour lasts about 30 minutes and costs $8 adults, $4 children 12 and under.

Grand Village of the Natchez Indians. The archaeological park and museum depicts the culture of the Natchez Indians, which reached its zenith in the 1500s. *400 Jefferson Davis Blvd., tel. 601/446–6502. Admission free. Open Mon.–Sat. 9–5, Sun. 1:30–5.*

Longwood. An air of mystery surrounds this uncompleted octagonal house, making it the only Natchez mansion guaranteed to interest children (*see* Exploring, *above*).

Port Gibson **Grand Gulf Military Monument.** Children love the steep trail, the observation tower, the old waterwheel, and the blood-stained uniforms (*see* Exploring, *above*).

Tupelo **Elvis Presley Birthplace.** One tourist said to her grandchild, "I'm not paying 50¢ for you to see furniture that wasn't even his." You, however, may want to (*see* Exploring, *above*).

Elvis Presley Park (*see* Exploring, *above*).

Elvis Presley Lake and Campground (*see* Exploring, *above*).

Off the Beaten Track

Columbus, 45 miles east of the Natchez Trace on U.S. 82, is one of Mississippi's most undisturbed antebellum towns, and one which claimed the moniker "Possumtown" until the city was chartered in 1821 and a more dignified name was chosen. This river city (on the Tombigbee) boasts 100 pre–Civil War mansions and many historic sites. Columbus is called the town "where flowers healed a nation" because of a group of gracious women who, in 1866, placed flowers on the graves of both Confederate and Union soldiers. The gesture inspired the poem "The Blue and the Gray," and Columbus's Decoration Day at Friendship Cemetery is now observed as the nation's Memorial Day. The Convention and Visitors Bureau (402 2nd Ave. N, Box 789, Columbus 39703, tel. 601/329–1191 or 800/327–2686) has additional information.

Magnificent **Waverley Mansion** (1852) is often featured in national and international publications. It is privately owned, immaculately and lovingly restored, and a genuine Mississippi showplace where twin spiral staircases gracefully proceed up three stories. *Approx. 10 mi from Columbus, off MS 50, Rte. 2, West Point 39773, tel. 601/494–1399. Admission: $4.50. Open year-round, 8–sunset.*

Shopping in Jackson

Antiques **Bobbie King's** (Woodland Hills Shopping Center, Old Canton Rd. at Duling Ave., tel. 601/362–9803) specializes in heirloom textiles and exhibits them in lavish displays with one-of-a-kind accessories to wear or with which to decorate your home. **Cot-**

tage Antiques (4074 N. State St., tel. 601/362–6510; closed Sat.) carries fine American antiques, accessories, and textiles. **C.W. Fewel III & Co., Antiquarians** (840 N. State St., tel. 601/355–5375) specializes in fine 18th- and 19th-century furnishings and accessories.

Books Books by Mississippi authors and about Mississippi are available from knowledgeable booksellers at **Lemuria** (202 Banner Hall, tel. 601/366–7619). **Choctaw Books** (406 Manship St., tel. 601/352–7281) stocks first editions of Southern writers' works.

Gifts The members of the Craftsman's Guild of Mississippi have raised crafts from their "arts and crafts" status to "craft *as* art." Their work is sold in the Jackson area (*see* Exploring, *above*) at **Ridgeland Crafts Center**, the **Old Capitol Museum** shop, and the **Mississippi Arts Center** shop.

The Everyday Gourmet stocks state products, including pecan pie, bread, and biscuit mixes; muscadine jelly; jams and chutneys; cookbooks; fine ceramic tableware, and a complete stock of kitchenware and gourmet foods (2905 Old Canton Rd., tel. 601/362–0723).

Mississippi-made products, from jams and jellies to Delta farm-raised catfish pâté, are stock items at **Taylor Maid** (1667 Lakeland Dr., tel. 601/366–9395). Imported coffees, chocolates, and other outstanding culinary gifts are plentiful.

Participant Sports

Golf In Jackson: **Lefleur's Bluff State Park,** 18 holes (Highland Dr., tel. 601/987–3998).

Jogging In Jackson: Jog on paths that curve under tall pines and stretch down to a sunny meadow in **Parham Bridges Park** (5055 Old Canton Rd.).

In Natchez: An asphalt road runs about one-and-a-half miles through **Duncan Park** (Duncan St. at Auburn Ave.).

Tennis In Jackson: **Tennis Center South** (2827 Oak Forest Dr., off McDowell Rd., tel. 601/960–1712) and **Parham Bridges Park** (5055 Old Canton Rd., tel. 601/956–1105).

In Natchez: There are courts in **Duncan Park** (Duncan St. at Auburn Ave.).

Dining and Lodging

Dining In Tupelo, Jackson, and Natchez you can find everything from caviar to chitlins. Fine food often comes in casual surroundings. Jackson boasts several elegant restaurants, and Natchez offers plantation breakfasts in antebellum opulence. Tupelo offers a wide variety, but specializes in down-home cooking. If you're eating on the run, Jackson's County Line Road east of I–55 and the East Frontage Roads along I–55N are jammed with fast-food joints. Blue plate dinners of fresh Mississippi vegetables are a widely available alternative.

Category	Cost*
Very Expensive	over $20
Expensive	$15–$20

Moderate	\$10–\$15
Inexpensive	under \$10

**per person without tax (8%), service, or drinks*

Lodging National hotel and motel chains are found in Jackson and Tupelo. The choice is greater in Jackson. In Natchez, travelers will find plantation homes that open their doors in bed-and-breakfast courtesy.

Category	Cost*
Very Expensive	over \$70
Expensive	\$50–\$70
Moderate	\$30–\$50
Inexpensive	under \$30

**double room; add 7% for taxes*

Jackson
Dining

400 East Capitol. This elegant restaurant occupies a historic building that has been carefully restored on the outside and beautifully adapted for business use within. Signature dishes are regional: Mississippi farm-raised rabbit, quail salad, angelhair pasta with shrimp. All are subtly seasoned and sauced, and artistically presented. Desserts are rich confections such as Linzer torte or Chocolate Paradise laced with crème Anglais and chocolate sauce. This is food for a special occasion; give yourself plenty of time to enjoy. *400 East Capitol St., tel. 601/355–9671. Jacket and tie recommended. Reservations recommended for lunch and dinner. AE, MC, V. Very Expensive.*

Ralph & Kacoo's. Ralph & Kacoo's originated in South Louisiana, so Cajun fare is naturally de rigueur. Crawfish étouffée is prepared to perfection, *cher! 100 Dyess Rd. (and County Line Rd.), tel. 601/957–0702. Reservations not accepted. Dress: casual. AE, MC, V. Expensive.*

Hal and Mal's Restaurant and Oyster Bar. This vast warehouse has been converted with the help of neon, 1930s antiques and memorabilia, and terrific entertainment. A mixed crowd of artistic, business, and collegiate types comes to this trendy spot for such specialties as grilled fresh fish, grilled chicken, and oyster po'boys. *200 S. Commerce St., tel. 601/948–0888. Dress: informal. Reservations recommended for dinner. MC, V. Closed Sun. Moderate.*

Mayflower. A perfect 1930s period piece with black and white tile floors, straight-back booths, and formica-topped coffee counter, this café specializes in Greek salads, fresh fish sautéed in lemon butter, and people-watching till all hours. *123 W. Capitol St., tel. 601/355–4122. Dress: informal, elegant, or odd. No reservations. MC, V. Moderate.*

Palette. This restaurant, in a gallery in the Mississippi Arts Center, is one of the state's finest lunch spots. Everybody likes the large, light-filled spaces, the art on the white walls, the friendly bustle of the arts community and businesspeople, the piano music, and most of all the carefully prepared and beautifully presented creations of chef Jim Hudson. You may find Mississippi catfish sautéed in pecan butter; fresh vegetable lasagne; or chicken with penne in garlic brie sauce; but the delicacies change frequently. *201 E. Pascagoula St., tel. 601/960–*

2003. No reservations required. Dress: casual. MC, V. Closed Mon. Inexpensive–Moderate.

Gridley's. Mexican tile tables and floors enhance small, sunny dining areas. Eat pancakes as big as a plate ($1 each) for breakfast, and spicy barbecued pork and ribs anytime else. *1428 Old Square Rd., tel. 601/362–8600. Dress: informal. No reservations. AE, MC, V. Inexpensive.*

People's Cafe. Crammed with artsy memorabilia, this tiny café packs in Jackson's downtown crowd with its amazing lunch buffet at which specialties ranging from Deep South–country to multi-national are served. Try fresh local vegetables and homemade breads, soups, and desserts. A Jackson tradition, The People's Cafe is now run by a fine chef who not only upgrades Mississippi blue-plate fare to gourmet standards, but also takes time to make friends of his customers. *232 W. Capitol St., tel. 601/353–7100. No reservations. Dress: casual. MC, V. No dinner. Inexpensive.*

Lodging

Millsaps-Buie House. This Queen Anne–style home, with its corner turret and tall-columned porch, was built in 1888 for Jackson financier and philanthropist Major Reuben Webster Millsaps, founder of Millsaps College in Jackson; it is listed on the National Register of Historic Places. Restored as a B&B in 1987, its guest rooms are individually decorated with antiques. An attentive staff serves morning coffee and pastries in your room or in the Victorian dining room. *628 N. State St., 39202, tel. 601/352–0221. 11 rooms, each with telephone and private bath. AE, DC, MC, V. Expensive–Very Expensive.*

Holiday Inn Downtown. Convention hotel with cheerful guest rooms (those on the east side overlook the Cathedral of St. Peter the Apostle and Smith Park) and a convenient downtown location. *200 E. Amite St., 39201, tel. 601/969–5100 or 800/HOLIDAY. 358 rooms. Facilities: restaurant, pool, lounge. AE, DC, MC, V. Expensive.*

Ramada Renaissance Hotel. This new high-rise convention motel is sleekly contemporary. *1001 County Line Rd., 39211, tel. 601/957–2800 or 800/272–6232. 300 rooms. Facilities: airport courtesy van, restaurant with live entertainment, jazz in the lobby bar, gift shop, barber shop. AE, DC, MC, V. Expensive.*

Edison Walthall Hotel. The cornerstone and huge brass mailbox near the elevators are almost all that remain of the original Walthall Hotel. The dismal motel that occupied the site next was transformed into the new hotel. The marble floors, gleaming brass, a paneled library/writing room, and cozy bar almost fool you into thinking this is a restoration. *225 E. Capitol St., 39201, tel. 601/948–6161 or 800/932–6161. 208 rooms. Facilities: heated pool, Jacuzzi, transportation to airport, copy machines, notary public. AE, DC, MC, V. Moderate–Expensive.*

Natchez

Dining

Pompous Palate. This is a pleasant surprise. Nestled quietly in a grand old bank building with still-intact marble columns, Natchez's newest restaurant is already a favorite. The specialty: Continental cuisine with a Southern touch, and truly delectable desserts. *409 Franklin St., tel. 601/445–4946. Reservations recommended during spring and fall. Dress: casual. AE, MC, V. Expensive.*

Cock of the Walk. The famous original of a regional franchise, this marvelous old train depot overlooking the Mississippi River specializes in fried catfish fillets, fried dill pickles, hush puppies, mustard greens, and coleslaw. Waiters in red long john shirts serve cornbread to the constant strum of banjos. *200*

North Broadway, on the Bluff, tel. 601/446–8920. Dress: informal. Reservations not required. AE, MC, V. Moderate.

Natchez Landing. The porch tables provide a view of the Mississippi River, which is at its very best when both the *Delta Queen* and *Mississippi Queen* steamboats dock. Specialties are barbecue (pork ribs, chicken, beef) and fried and grilled catfish. *11 Silver St., Natchez-under-the-Hill, tel. 601/442–6639. Dress: informal. Reservations not required. AE, MC, V. Closed Sun. Moderate.*

Scrooge's. The old storefront-cum-restaurant has a pub atmosphere downstairs and a more subdued intimate ambience upstairs. The menu includes red beans and rice, and mesquite-grilled chicken or shrimp with angel-hair pasta. *315 Main St., tel. 601/446–9922. Dress: informal. Reservations not required. AE, MC, V. Moderate.*

Brothers. It's reminiscent of a New Orleans café: light and airy, very busy most evenings, and complete with a courtyard. Food is influenced by New Orleans, too; Cajun and Creole dishes are the most popular on the menu. The seafood, steaks, and pastas are terrific. *209 Franklin St., tel. 601/442–1777. AE, MC, V. Inexpensive–Moderate.*

Fare. The red, white, and blue color scheme of this Victorian café creates a carnival air. The menu includes homemade soups, sandwiches, beignets (French doughnuts), and café au lait. *109 N. Pearl St., tel. 601/442–5299. Dress: informal. No reservations. MC, V. Inexpensive.*

Parlor. This parlor is a comfortable mishmash of unmatching tables and chairs, racks of magazines, jazz posters, and an enclosed patio with picnic tables and umbrellas. Mexican food is a specialty (the fajitas are fresh); so is grilled catfish with vegetables and seafood pasta. *116 S. Canal St., tel. 601/446–8511. Dress: informal. Reservations recommended. AE, MC, V. Closed Sun. Inexpensive.*

Lodging This list includes the area's most popular bed-and-breakfast inns. **Natchez Pilgrimage Tours** (Canal St. at State St., Box 347, Natchez 39120, tel. 800/647–6742) can answer questions and handle reservations. Contact **Creative Travel** (Canal St. Depot, Natchez 39120, tel. 601/442–3762) about stays in private homes, which are less expensive than the mansions.

Burn. This elegant 1832 mansion offers a seated plantation breakfast, private tour of the home, and swimming pool. *712 N. Union St., 39120, tel. 601/442–1344 or 800/647–6742. 6 bedrooms, all with private baths. AE, MC, V. Very Expensive.*

Monmouth. This plantation mansion (c. 1818) was owned by Mississippi governor John A. Quitman from 1826 to his death in 1858. Guest rooms are decorated with tester beds and antiques. The grounds are tastefully landscaped, with a New Orleans–style courtyard, a pond, and a gazebo. Plantation breakfast; tour of home. *36 Melrose, 39120, tel. 800/828–4531. 4 bedrooms, 1 suite in main house; 5 bedrooms in servants' quarters; 4 in garden cottages. No children under 14. AE, MC, V. Expensive–Very Expensive.*

Dunleith. Stately, colonnaded Dunleith is a popular Natchez bed-and-breakfast inn. Guests are served breakfast in the former poultry house, featuring old brick walls and a fireplace. Beautiful gardens enhance this Greek Revival mansion. *84 Homochitto St., 39120, tel. 601/446–6631. 12 guest rooms with private bath. AE, MC, V. Moderate–Very Expensive.*

Natchez Eola Hotel. This beautifully restored 1920s hotel has an elegant, formal lobby and small guest rooms with antique reproduction furniture. The Natchez Eola, one of the South's grand old hotels, is one of only sixty in the United States to be selected by the National Trust for Historic Preservation as one in which architecture and historic integrity have been maintained. *110 N. Pearl St., 39120, tel. 601/445–6000 or 800/888–9140. 122 rooms. AE, DC, MC, V. Moderate.*

Ramada Hilltop. The typical motel decor is forgotten if your room overlooks the Mississippi River. *130 John R. Junkin Dr., 39120, tel. 601/446–6311 or 800/272–6232. AE, DC, MC, V. Moderate.*

Port Gibson
Lodging

Oak Square. Constructed about 1850, this home, with its numerous outbuildings and lovely gardens, occupies an entire block on historic Church Street. Now a bed-and-breakfast inn, it offers a full southern breakfast. *1207 Church Street, Port Gibson 39130, tel. 601/437–4350 or 800/729–0240. 8 rooms. AE, MC, V. Expensive–Very Expensive.*

Tupelo
Dining

Chez Bernard. In a new brick building with white columns, classic French cuisine is prepared by a Swiss chef who was formerly with the Drake Hotel in New York. The dining room, with natural moldings, a brick wine rack, green marbleized wallpaper, and European paintings, is lighted by 8-foot French windows and a crystal chandelier. To begin, you might try the Parma ham with melon or the pâté in pastry; then there's sliced duck breast in a Pinot noir sauce or a delicate fillet of sole *bonne femme. 150 S. Industrial Rd., tel. 601/841–0777. Reservations required at dinner. Jacket required. AE, MC, V. Closed Sat. lunch and Sun. Very Expensive.*

Jefferson Place. This austere 19th-century house is lively inside, with red-checked tablecloths and bric-a-brac. The place is popular with the college crowd; short orders and steaks are the specialties. *823 Jefferson St., tel. 601/844–8696. Dress: informal. Reservations not required. AE, MC, V. Closed Sun. Expensive.*

Papa Vanelli's Pizzaria. Family pictures and scenes of Greece decorate the walls of this comfortably nondescript restaurant where tables wear traditional red-and-white checkered tablecloths. Specialties (all homemade) include pizza with 10 toppings, lasagna, moussaka, manicotti, and Greek salad. Vanelli's own bakery produces breads, strudels, and pastries. *1302 N. Gloster, tel. 601/844–4410. Dress: informal. Reservations not required. AE, D, MC, V. Inexpensive.*

Lodging

Executive Inn. Guest rooms in this large, contemporary hotel are plain and functional, yet new and clean. *1011 N. Gloster, 38801, tel. 601/841–2222. 119 rooms. Facilities: indoor pool, whirlpool, sauna, cable TV, restaurant, lounge. AE, DC, MC, V. Moderate–Expensive.*

Ramada Inn. This modern three-story hotel caters to business travelers and conventions as well as families. Dancing nightly (except Sunday) in Bogart's Lounge. Breakfast and lunch buffets are served. *854 N. Gloster, 38801, tel. 601/844–4111 or 800/272–6232. 230 rooms, 10 executive suites. Facilities: large outdoor pool, coin laundry, valet service, in-room movies, barber and beauty shops. AE, DC, MC, V. Moderate.*

Best Western Trace Inn. This old, rustic inn on 15 acres near the Natchez Trace offers neat rooms and friendly service. *3400 W. Main St., 38801, tel. 601/842–5555. 134 rooms. Facilities: in-room movies, playground, pool, restaurant, entertainment* *and dancing nightly (except Sun.), courtesy car. AE, MC, V. Inexpensive–Moderate.*

Nightlife

Jackson **Hal and Mal's** is the city's most popular night spot (*see* Dining, *above*). There's live entertainment at **The Dock** (Main Harbor Marina at Ross Barnett Reservoir, tel. 601/856–7765) Thursday–Sunday, when some 2,000 people pass through. The restaurant, which sits on a pier, generally attracts a young crowd, but draws an older one on Sundays. The mood is set by the people who step off their boats to dine, drink, and listen to the rock and roll and rhythm and blues.

Poet's (1855 Lakeland Dr., tel. 601/982–9711) presents food, drink, and a jazz trio in an old-fashioned atmosphere, created by antiques, old signs, pressed tin ceiling, and wooden floors.

Shucker's (1216½ N. State St., tel. 601/353–7536) is a tiny room with neon lights, pool table, and outdoor deck. Blues and classic rock are performed by local bands on Friday and Saturday; drinks, po'boys, and oysters are served.

Natchez **Brothers's** (209 Franklin St., tel. 601/442–1777) courtyard and bar is indeed a gathering place. It's casual, often crowded, and always fun.

King's Tavern (619 Jefferson St., tel. 601/446–8845) is located in the oldest house in the Natchez Territory (1789). The lounge is rustic yet inviting, especially if you're an "Old Natchez" aficionado.

Under-the-Hill Saloon (33 Silver St., tel. 601/446–8023) features live entertainment on weekends in one of the few original buildings left in Natchez-Under-the-Hill.

Holly Springs and Oxford

Holly Springs and Oxford, just east of I–55 in north Mississippi, are sophisticated versions of the Mississippi small town; both are courthouse towns incorporated in 1837. They offer visitors historic architecture, arts and crafts, literary associations, a warm welcome, and those unhurried pleasures of Southern life that remain constant from generation to generation—entertaining conversation, good food, and nostalgic walks at twilight.

Getting Around

By Car A 30-minute drive from Memphis, Holly Springs is located in north Mississippi near the Tennessee state line on U.S. 78 and MS 4, MS 7, and MS 311. Oxford is 29 miles south of Holly Springs on MS 7. Oxford is also accessible from I–55; it is 23 miles east of Batesville on MS 6.

By Bus **Greyhound** has stations at Holly Springs (490 Craft St., tel. 601/252–1353) and Oxford (925 Van Buren, tel. 601/234–1424).

Guided Tours

Guided tours of the University of Mississippi campus are available upon request from the admissions office (tel. 601/232–7226).

Important Addresses and Numbers

Tourist Information **Holly Springs Chamber of Commerce** is located at 154 S. Memphis Street, tel. 601/252–2943. Open Monday–Wednesday and Friday 9–4. Closed Thursday afternoon and weekends.

Oxford has an information center in a cute cottage on the square next to City Hall, and also a Tourism Council (tel. 601/234–4651).

Oxford-Lafayette County Chamber of Commerce is at 440 N. Jackson Avenue in Oxford, tel. 601/234–4651. Open weekdays 9–4.

Contact the **Public Relations Department of the University of Mississippi** (tel. 601/232–7236) for information about university plays, lectures, sporting events, and special events.

Emergencies In Holly Springs, dial 0 for assistance. In Oxford, dial 911. Medical help is available at **Oxford-Lafayette Medical Center** (U.S. 75, 1 mi south of the Oxford Square on S. Lamar Ave., tel. 601/234–6721).

24-hour Pharmacy **Chaney's Eastgate Pharmacy** (Eastgate Shopping Center, University Ave. E, tel. 601/234–7221, after hours 601/234–0058).

Exploring Holly Springs and Oxford

Holly Springs **Holly Springs** arose from a crossroads of old Indian trails originally called Spring Hollow. Here Chickasaw Indians and travelers stopped to rest and bathe in the medicinal waters of springs in glades of holly trees. After the Chickasaw Cession in 1832, settlers came from the Carolinas, Virginia, and Georgia. Holly Springs became an educational, business, and cultural center as the newly arrived planters gained great wealth. Cotton barons built palatial mansions and handsome commercial buildings. Today Holly Springs has more than 300 structures listed on the National Register of Historic Places.

Holly Springs survived at least 50 raids during the Civil War. In December 1862, the Confederate army under General Earl Van Dorn destroyed $1 million worth of Union supplies intended for General Grant's use in his march against Vicksburg. Bent on reprisals against the city, Grant ordered General Benjamin Harrison Grierson to burn it in 1864. A clever Holly Springs matron, Maria Mason, invited the general into her home to chat. They discovered that they shared a love of music and that they had studied piano under the same teacher; so instead of destroying Holly Springs, Grierson enjoyed its hospitality at a series of afternoon gatherings and piano concerts. Many of Holly Springs's historic homes are open only during Pilgrimage (the last weekend in April), but the following landmarks are open daily.

Montrose (1858) was built by Albert Brooks as a wedding present for his daughter. Now leased by the Holly Springs Garden Club, this mansion has an elegant spiral staircase as well as elaborate cornices and plaster ceiling medallions. *307 E. Salem Ave., tel. 601/252–2943. Admission: $3 adults, children under 12 free. Open by appointment only.*

Rust College (N. Memphis St.), founded in 1868, contains **Oak View** (c. 1860), one of the oldest buildings in the state associated with black education. Metropolitan Opera star Leontyne Price, a native of Laurel, Mississippi, graduated from Rust.

The Yellow Fever House (104 E. Gholson Ave.), built in 1836, was Holly Springs's first brick building. It was used as a hospital during the 1878 yellow fever epidemic.

Hillcrest Cemetery (380 S. Maury St.) contains graves of 13 Confederate generals. Many of the iron fences surrounding the graves were made locally before the Civil War.

The Kate Freeman Clark Art Gallery is dedicated solely to the work of Holly Springs resident Kate Freeman Clark, who was trained in New York City during the 1890s. Clark completed more than 1,000 works on canvas and paper, including landscapes and portraits. She returned to Holly Springs in the 1920s and never painted again. Many of her friends did not know of her talent until her paintings were discovered after her death. In her will she left funds to establish a museum. *292 E. College Ave., tel. 601/252–2511. Admission free. Open by appointment (contact Holly Springs Chamber of Commerce;* see *Important Addresses and Numbers*, above*).*

Even the briefest visit to Holly Springs should include a look at the exteriors of several homes that are not usually open to the public. **Oakleigh,** on Salem Avenue across the street from Montrose, is a mansion with fine details: acanthus leaves on the graceful, grooved columns, a cornice emphasized by recessed dentil moldings and projecting pendants, and the pediment with a semicircular window. The interior is equally grand. Also on Salem Avenue are **Cedarhurst** and **Airliewood,** brick houses constructed in the Gothic style popularized in the 1850s by Andrew Jackson Downing. General Grant used Airliewood as his headquarters and General Ord used Cedarhurst as his during their occupation of Holly Springs.

Oxford Oxford and Lafayette County were immortalized as "Jefferson" and "Yoknapatawpha County" in the novels of Oxford native William Faulkner, but even if you're not a Faulkner fan, this is a great place to experience small town living. You won't be bored; the characters who fascinated Faulkner still live here, and the University of Mississippi keeps things lively.

Faulkner received the Nobel Prize for Literature in 1949, and his readers will enjoy exploring the town that inspired *The Hamlet*, *The Town*, and *The Mansion*. "I discovered that my own little postage stamp of native soil was worth writing about, and that I would never live long enough to exhaust it," said Faulkner. "I created a cosmos of my own."

Many people who knew the eccentric Mr. Bill still live in Oxford and are willing to share stories about him. You may encounter them around **Courthouse Square.** The Square is a National Historic Landmark, and at its center is the white sandstone **Lafayette** (pronounced "Luh-FAY-it") **County Courthouse,** named for the French Revolutionary War hero the Marquis de Lafayette. The courthouse was rebuilt in 1873 after Union troops burned it; on its south side is the monument to Confederate soldiers. The courtroom on the second floor is original.

Time Out At **Square Books** the knowledgeable staff can tell you about Oxford's "writers in residence." While enjoying cappuccino, espresso, or delicious desserts, keep an eye out for well-known writers who may stroll over from the university, among them Willie Morris (*North Toward Home*), Barry Hannah (*Geronimo Rex*), or John Grisham (*The Firm*). *South side of Courthouse*

Square, tel. 601/236–2262. Open Mon.–Thurs. 9–9, Fri. and Sat. 9–10, Sun. 12–6. MC, V.

University Avenue from South Lamar Boulevard just south of the Courthouse Square to the University of Mississippi is one of the state's most beautiful sights when the trees flame orange and gold in the fall, or when the dogwoods blossom in the spring.

The **University Museum** displays the brightly colored primitive paintings of local artist Theora Hamblett. Hamblett gained international fame for her works depicting dreams and visions, children's games, Mississippi landscapes, and scenes from her childhood. *University Ave. at 5th St., tel. 601/232–7073. Admission free. Open Tues.–Sat. 10–4.*

Just beyond the museum is **The University of Mississippi,** the state's beloved "Ole Miss," which opened in 1848 with 80 students. **The Grove,** the tree-shaded heart of the campus, is almost as important a meeting place as Courthouse Square. (It was supposedly here that Faulkner, just fired from his job as postmaster for writing novels on the job, said, "Never again will I be at the beck and call of every son-of-a-bitch who's got two cents to buy a stamp.")

Facing the Grove, antebellum **Barnard Observatory** houses **The Center for the Study of Southern Culture,** with exhibits on Southern music, folklore, and literature, and the world's largest blues archive (40,000 records). The center's annual Faulkner seminar attracts Faulkner scholars from around the world (*see* The Arts, *below*). The center's remarkable new *Encyclopedia of Southern Culture* is for sale here. *Barnard Observatory, University of Mississippi, tel. 601/232–5993. Admission free. Open weekdays 8:15–4:45.*

The **Mississippi Room** in the John Davis Williams Library contains both a permanent exhibit on Faulkner, including his Nobel Prize medal, and first editions of other Mississippi authors. *On the University of Mississippi campus. Admission free. Open weekdays 8:30–5, Sat. 10–4.*

Rowan Oak was the home of William Faulkner from 1930 until his death in 1962. Although this is one of Mississippi's most famous attractions, there are no signs to direct you to the home and only an unobtrusive historical marker at the site. The house and its surrounding 31 acres are as serene and private as they were when Faulkner lived and wrote there.

Built around 1844 by Colonel Robert Sheegog, the two-story, white-frame house with square columns represents the so-called planter style of architecture common to many Mississippi antebellum homes. After the Civil War it fell into disrepair and, in 1930, was purchased by Faulkner and his bride of one year, Estelle Oldham Franklin. The house was both a sanctuary and a financial burden to the author; it is now a National Historic Landmark owned by the University of Mississippi.

Faulkner made improvements and additions to the house, including a porch on the east side that he surrounded with a brick wall to shield him from curious strangers. After winning the Nobel Prize, he added the study where his bed, typewriter, desk, and other personal items, such as his sunglasses, a Colgate shave stick refill, an ink bottle, and a can of dog repellent, still evoke his presence.

Faulkner wrote an outline for his novel *The Fable* on the walls of the study, which is reputed to be the most photographed room in the state. The days of the week are neatly printed over the head and length of the bed, and to the right of the door leading into the room is the notation, "Tomorrow." *Old Taylor Rd., tel. 601/234–3284. Admission free. Open Tues.–Sat. 10–noon and 2–4, Sun. 2–4.*

Faulkner's funeral was held at Rowan Oak, and he was buried in the family plot in **St. Peter's Cemetery** at Jefferson and North 16th streets, beside his relatives. Also buried here is Caroline Barr, "Mammy Callie," Faulkner's childhood nurse. The tomb of the author's brother, Dean Faulkner, who was killed in an airplane crash, bears the same epitaph as the one Faulkner had given to John Sartoris in the novel *Pylon.*

Off the Beaten Track

William Faulkner was married in little **College Hill Presbyterian Church** (8 mi northwest of Oxford on College Hill Rd.) on June 20, 1929. The slave gallery doors and original pews are intact, although it's believed that Sherman stabled horses here during his occupation of College Hill in 1862. Behind the church is one of north Mississippi's oldest cemeteries.

From Oxford take MS 7S, to MS 328 to reach Taylor. Downtown **Taylor** is just three stores, but they house artists' studios and the old Taylor Grocery, which has a restaurant in the back (tel. 601/236–1716; no credit cards; closed Mon.). Here you can eat crisp fried catfish and mounds of hush puppies. In sculptor **William Beckwith's studio** you can see his statue of Temple Drake, the character who waited for the train in Taylor in Faulkner's novel *Sanctuary.* Small as it is, Taylor is achieving cult status; it's proper to brag about coming here!

What to See and Do with Children

Holly Springs **Chewalla Lake and Recreation Area** *(see* Participant Sports, *below).*

Oxford **Avent Park** *(see* Participant Sports, *below).*

Square Books has a large collection of children's books *(see* Exploring, *above).*

The Union, the University of Mississippi's student center, has pool rooms, a video arcade, and a book store. *Open weekdays 8 AM–10 PM, Sat. 4 PM–midnight, Sun. 4 PM–9 PM. Bookstore open weekdays 7:45–5.*

Participant Sports

Holly Springs's Chewalla Lake and Recreation Area are part of Holly Springs National Forest and have nature trails, picnic areas, swimming, boating, camping, and fishing (license required). *From Holly Springs take MS 4 to Higdon Rd. Turn east; go 7 mi to entrance. Information: National Forests, Mississippi, 100 W. Capitol St., Suite 1141, Jackson 39269, tel. 601/960–4391.*

Oxford's Avent Park (Park Dr., the continuation of Bramlett

Rd., which runs north of E. Jackson Ave.) offers tennis courts, a playground, picnic areas, and a jogging trail.

Dining and Lodging

Dining You don't have to travel far in these small towns to find one-of-a-kind dining experiences. Food, not decor, is usually the focus.

Category	Cost*
Very Expensive	over $20
Expensive	$15–$20
Moderate	$10–$15
Inexpensive	under $10

**per person without tax (8%), service, or drinks*

Lodging When staying overnight in Oxford try the Oliver-Britt House, especially if you'd like to hear town gossip from your innkeeper. For more conventional lodgings, try the Alumni House on the University of Mississippi campus or, more conventional yet, the Holiday Inn.

Category	Cost*
Very Expensive	over $70
Expensive	$50–$70
Moderate	$30–$50
Inexpensive	$20–$30

**double room; add 8% for taxes*

Holly Springs *Dining* **Phillips Grocery.** The building was constructed in 1882 as a saloon for railroad workers. Today it's decorated with antiques and crafts, and serves big, old-fashioned hamburgers. *541-A Van Dorn across from the old depot, tel. 601/252–4671. Dress: informal. No reservations. Open weekdays 9–5, Sat. 9–6. Inexpensive.*

Oxford *Dining* **Downtown Grill.** With its comfortable plaid chairs and dark walls, the Grill's bar could be a club in Oxford, England. But then there's the light and airy balcony overlooking the square—pure Oxford, Mississippi. Downstairs in the restaurant, specialties include Jesse's Famous Seafood Gumbo; *panéed* (breaded) veal with fresh zucchini, yellow squash, onion, and shrimp; Mississippi catfish either grilled or Lafitte (topped with shrimp, julienned ham, and a savory cream sauce); and an array of rich desserts. *1115 Jackson Ave., tel. 601/234–2659. Dress: informal. Reservations recommended. AE, MC, V. Moderate.*

Smitty's. Homestyle cooking features red-eye gravy and grits, biscuits with blackberry preserves, fried catfish, chicken and dumplings, cornbread, and black-eyed peas. The menu says, If'n You Need Anything That Ain't on Here, Holler at the Cook. *S. Lamar Blvd., just south of the Square, tel. 601/234–9111. Dress: informal. No credit cards. Inexpensive.*

Starnes Catfish Place. This rustic retreat is a local favorite known for its fried catfish with the traditional trimmings—crisp hush puppies and creamy coleslaw. BYOB. *Hurricane Landing Rd. off MS 7N, tel. 601/234–7251. Dress: informal. No reservations. Closed Mon., Tues. MC, V. Inexpensive.*

Lodging **Holiday Inn.** These functional rooms have no surprises. The restaurant, however, can do a surprisingly good breakfast, though you'll probably choose Smitty's for the biscuits *(see* Dining, *above). 400 N. Lamar, 38655, tel. 601/234–3031. 100 rooms. Facilities: pool, lounge, travel agency, HBO. AE, DC, MC, V. Moderate.*

Oliver-Britt House. There are five pleasant rooms, each with bath and color TV, in a restored home built about 1900 and run in a helter-skelter fashion as a B&B. The location, midway between the university and Courthouse Square, is convenient. Lunch (Tuesday–Friday) and Sunday brunch are served. *512 Van Buren Ave., 38655, tel. 601/234–8043. AE, MC, V. Moderate.*

Alumni House. Rooms are plain and clean; the only real plus is their location on the Ole Miss campus. *The University of Mississippi, 38677, tel. 601/234–2331. MC, V. Inexpensive–Moderate.*

The Arts

Faulkner and Yoknapatawpha Conference. This week-long event includes lectures by Faulkner scholars and field trips in "Yoknapatawpha County." For information, write to the Center for the Study of Southern Culture, University, Oxford 38677.

Nightlife

Oxford Current entertainers at **The Gin** (E. Harrison St. and S. 14th St., tel. 601/234–0024) follow in the footsteps of Mose Allison and Taj Mahal, who once played here.

The Hoka, (304 S. 14th St., tel. 601/234–3057), a warehouse turned movie theater-restaurant, has been called the "only Bohemian café in Mississippi" by author Barry Hannah. Hard wooden booths, jukebox, unbelievable clutter. BYOB to enjoy arty movies and short-order food, especially the cheesecake.

In an old livery stable once owned by Murry Faulkner (William's father), **Syd's** (1118 Van Buren Ave., tel. 601/236–3194) restaurant/bar has plenty of exposed brick, wooden floors, and a spare Mississippi charm. Music is rock and roll and the blues.

The Delta

"The Delta begins in the lobby of the Peabody Hotel in Memphis and ends on Catfish Row in Vicksburg," said journalist David Cohn of Greenville. In between is a vast agricultural plain created by the Mississippi River and an intimate set of personal relationships.

If life should give you only one day in the Delta, use it to cruise down U.S. 61 and the Great River Road (MS 1) from Memphis to Vicksburg. Time it right for lunch in Clarksdale, Merigold, or Boyle, and dinner at Doe's in Greenville. Then on a Saturday night you'll be able to pick up public radio's "Highway 61" with host Bill Ferris, creator and director of the Center for Southern Folk Culture. He'll be playing the blues about the time you glimpse the first kudzu near Vicksburg.

Getting Around

By Car U.S. 61 runs from Memphis through the Delta to Vicksburg, Natchez, and Baton Rouge, LA. The Great River Road (MS 1) parallels U.S. 61 and the river through part of this route.

By Plane Greenville is served by **Northwest Airlink** (tel. 601/335–5362).

By Bus **Greyhound/Trailways** stops in Belzoni (West Side Grocery, 711 Francis St., tel. 601/247–2150), Clarksdale (1604 State St., tel. 601/627–7893), Cleveland (U.S. 61N, tel. 601/843–5113), Greenville (1849 U.S. 82E, tel. 601/335–2633), and Vicksburg (1511 Walnut St., tel. 601/638–8389).

Guided Tours

Vicksburg **Vicksburg Historic Tours, Inc.** Tours of Vicksburg National Military Park and historic homes. *9 Crestwood Dr., tel. 601/638–8888. Admission: $25 adults, $12 children. Open Feb.–mid-Nov.*

Important Addresses and Numbers

Tourist Information **Clarksdale-Coahoma County Chamber of Commerce.** Sunflower Ave., Box 160, Clarksdale 38614, tel. 601/627–7337. Open weekdays 8:30–5.

Cleveland-Bolivar County Chamber of Commerce. Third St., Box 490, Cleveland 38732, tel. 601/843–2712. Open weekdays 8:30–5 (closed noon–1).

Greenville Chamber of Commerce. Box 933, Greenville 38701, tel. 601/378–3141. Open weekdays 9–5.

Greenwood Convention & Visitors Bureau. Box 739, Greenwood 38930, tel. 601/453–9197 or 800/844–7141.

Mississippi Welcome Center. 4210 Warrenton Rd., Vicksburg 39180, tel. 601/638–4269. Open Monday–Saturday 8–5, Sunday 1–5.

Vicksburg Convention & Visitors Bureau. Clay St. and Old U.S. 27, Box 110, Vicksburg 39180, tel. 601/636–9421 or 800/221–3536. Open daily 8–5.

Washington County Welcome Center. U.S. 82 at Reed Rd., Box 6022, Greenville 38701, tel. 601/332–2378. Open weekdays 8–5, Sun. 1–5.

Emergencies In Greenville and Vicksburg, dial 911. Seek emergency medical help at **Delta Regional Medical Center** (1400 E. Union Ave., Greenville, tel. 601/334–2000) and at **Mercy Regional Medical Center** (100 McAuley Dr., Vicksburg, tel. 601/631–2131).

Exploring the Delta

Numbers in the margin correspond to points of interest on the Mississippi Delta map.

Head down U.S. 61 from Memphis through the Mississippi Delta. Fifty miles south you'll enter **Coahoma County** (from the Choctaw word "Co-i-humma," meaning "red panther"). At **Rich,** swing west on U.S. 49 for a spectacular view of the Mis-
1 sissippi River from the **Mississippi-Arkansas Bridge.** Continue south on MS 1 to skirt serene **Moon Lake** and **Friars Point.** The

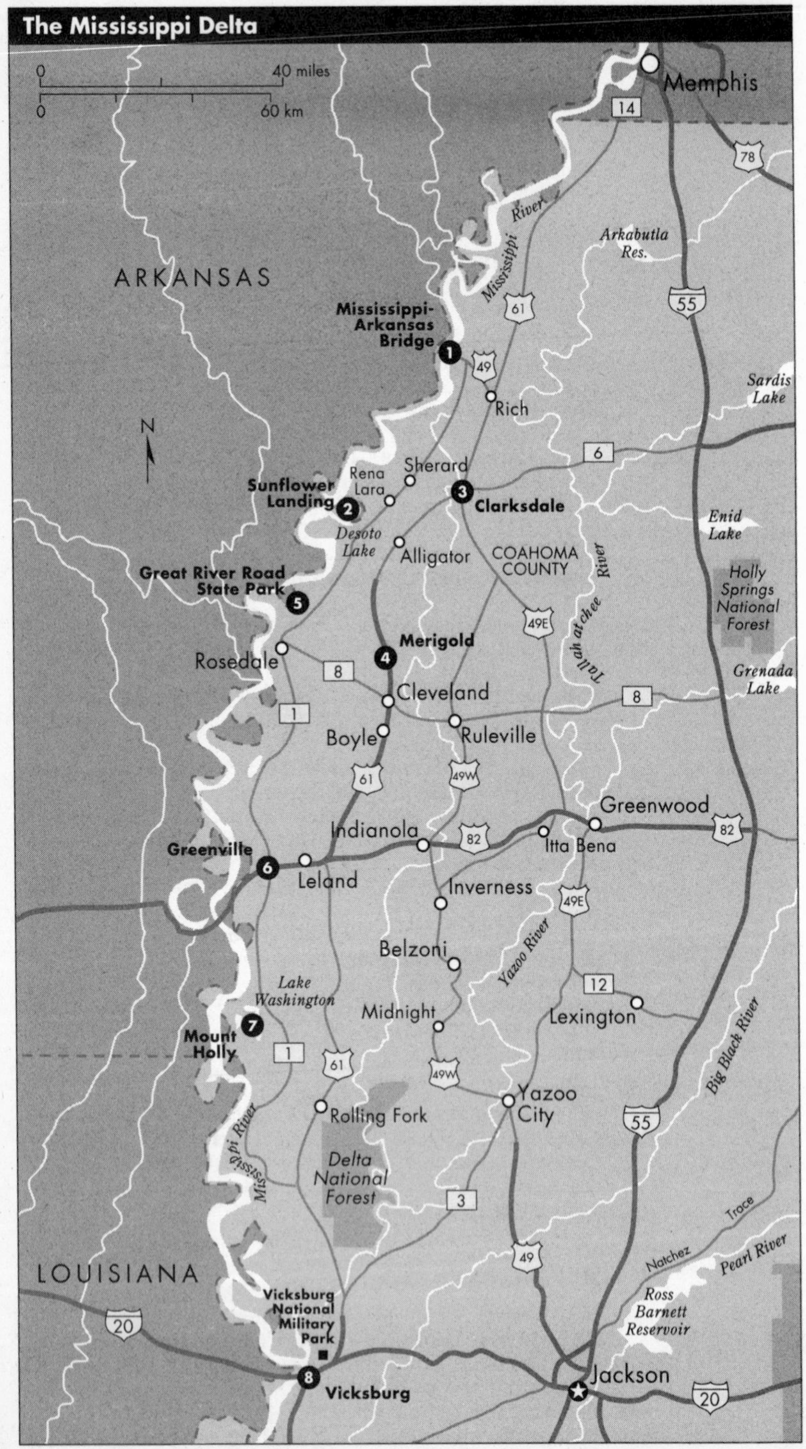
The Mississippi Delta
0
40 miles
0
60 km
N
ARKANSAS
LOUISIANA
Memphis
Mississippi River
Arkabutla Res.
Mississippi-Arkansas Bridge
1
Rich
Sardis Lake
Sherard
Rena Lara
Sunflower Landing
2
3
Clarksdale
Desoto Lake
Alligator
COAHOMA COUNTY
Enid Lake
Tallahatchee River
Holly Springs National Forest
Great River Road State Park
5
Merigold
4
Rosedale
Cleveland
Grenada Lake
Boyle
Ruleville
Greenwood
Indianola
Itta Bena
Greenville
6
Leland
Inverness
Yazoo River
Belzoni
Lake Washington
Midnight
Lexington
Big Black River
7
Mount Holly
Yazoo City
Rolling Fork
Delta National Forest
Mississippi River
Natchez Trace
Pearl River
Ross Barnett Reservoir
Vicksburg National Military Park
8
Vicksburg
Jackson
14
78
55
61
49
6
49E
8
1
49W
82
12
3
20

levee parallels MS 1 for most of the southbound trip; park and climb up for a look at the "Father of Waters."

2 At **Rena Lara,** turn west to **Sunflower Landing** on Desoto Lake.
Near here, in May 1541, Hernando DeSoto "discovered" the
Mississippi River. Return to Rena Lara, backtrack to **Sherard,**
3 and head east on MS 322 to **Clarksdale.**

As a child, author Tennessee Williams spent time here, visiting his grandfather, the rector of St. George's Episcopal Church. (In Williams's *Cat on a Hot Tin Roof,* Brick was running high hurdles at nearby Friars Point when he broke his leg.)

The Delta Blues Museum is a testament to the important role played by Clarksdale and Coahoma County in the history of the blues. The museum features exhibits and programs highlighting the history of the blues, tracing its influence on rock, jazz, and pop music through videotapes, slides, records, and books. *Housed in the Carnegie Public Library, Clarksdale, tel. 601/624–4461. Admission free. Open weekdays 9–5.*

4 Continue to **Merigold** on U.S. 61. The **McCartys of Merigold** are famous throughout the state for their pale stoneware. Their shop features their pottery and handcrafted jewelry; in the spring and summer you may get a peek at their gardens. *Corner of Goff and St. Mary Sts., tel. 601/748–2293. Open Tues.–Sat. 9:30–5. Closed Sun., Mon., and month of Jan.*

From Merigold continue through Cleveland to Boyle if you're
planning to lunch at the Sweet Olive (*see* Dining and Lodging,
below), or turn west on MS 8 to pastoral **Rosedale** for sweeping
5 views of the Mississippi River. **The Great River Road State Park**
(the world's longest park) has a 75-foot-high overlook tower.
*Located off MS 1 in Rosedale, Box 292, Rosedale, 38769, tel.
601/759–6762. Open daily 8–5.*

6 From Rosedale, follow MS 1 into **Greenville,** the seat of Washington County. The city is named for Revolutionary War hero General Nathaniel Greene, a close friend of George Washington, for whom the county is named. The city's history has been dominated by the Mississippi River. The river created the rich soil in which cotton flourished, and Greenville was—and is—the port used by the massive Delta plantations to ship their bales to market. During the Civil War battle for Vicksburg, Union troops burned Greenville to the ground. The citizens rebuilt the town only to suffer a yellow fever epidemic in 1877. Then, in 1890, the city suffered disastrous flooding; levees finally solved the problem after the great flood of 1927. At the turn of the century Greenville developed into a major river port.

Greenville probably has produced more writers than any other city of its size in the country. These include William Alexander Percy *(Lanterns on the Levee)*, his nephew Walker Percy *(The Last Southern Gentleman, The Moviegoer)*, Ellen Douglas *(A Family's Affair, The Magic Carpet)*, Hodding Carter (Pulitzer Prize–winning, crusading journalist), Shelby Foote *(The Civil War, Love in a Dry Season)*, and Hodding Carter III (television news commentator and journalist). The best reason to visit Greenville, however, is to eat at **Doe's** *(see* Dining, *below*).

Continue south on MS 1, 17 miles to Lake Washington to tour
7 **Mount Holly** (1856), one of the best Mississippi examples of a

Victorian-Italianate house. *Box 140, Chatham 38731, tel. 601/827–2652. Admission: $4 adults, $2 children 12 and under. Tours Tues.–Sun. 1–5. Closed Mon. Bed-and-breakfast lodgings by reservation.*

At MS 436, go west two miles to photograph the vine-covered ruins of **St. John's Episcopal Church.** Only its walls and bell tower remain; its windows were removed during the Civil War so that the leading could be melted to make bullets.

At MS 14, go east to Rolling Fork, then south on U.S. 61
8 through fields and wildlife areas to **Vicksburg.**

Vicksburg Near the site of present-day Vicksburg, the Spanish established Fort Nogales in 1790. Vicksburg itself began as a mission founded by the Reverend Newitt Vick in 1814. He chose a spot high on the bluffs above a bend in the Mississippi River, a location that would have important consequences for the young city and for the nation not 50 years later.

During the War Between the States, the Confederacy and the Union vied for control of this strategic location. U.S. Grant's men doggedly slogged through canals and bayous in five futile attempts to capture the city, which was called the Gibraltar of the Confederacy because of its almost impregnable defenses. Then, in a series of raids and battles, Grant laid waste the area between Vicksburg and Jackson to the east and Port Gibson to the south. Grant's attacks on Vicksburg were repulsed once again; he then laid siege to the city for 47 days. On July 4, 1863, the city surrendered, giving the Union control of the river and sounding the death knell for the Confederacy.

The suffering at Vicksburg was profound. The land was devastated; today's green and serene countryside was a region of blasted trees and blackened hills. Vicksburg's **National Military Park** marks the spot where the town was under siege. Battle positions are marked, and monuments line the park's 16-mile drive. The Visitor Center offers orientation programs and exhibits. A guided tour is a good investment, should time and money ($15 for two hours) permit. The self-guided driving tour is well marked, however, and a cassette tape may be rented for $4.50. *Entrance and Visitor Center located on Clay St. (U.S. 80), 1 mi from I–20, Exit 4B, tel. 601/636–0583. 18-min film shown on the hour and half-hour. Admission: $3 per car load. Open daily 8–5; summer 8–6. Closed Christmas Day.*

The Union gunboat, the **USS *Cairo,*** was the first ironclad ever sunk by an electrically-detonated mine. It has been raised from the Yazoo River and restored. A small museum adjacent to it displays Civil War artifacts recovered from the *Cairo. 3201 Clay St., Vicksburg Military Park, tel. 601/636–2199. Admission free. Open daily 9–5, summer 9–6.*

The Vanishing Glory is a multimedia, 15-projector show portraying the sights and sounds of Vicksburg under siege. *Waterfront Theatre, 717 Clay St., tel. 601/634–1863. Admission: $3.50 adults, $2 students. Open daily 10–5.*

Vicksburg's historic homes may have cannonballs imbedded in their walls, but they have been beautifully restored. Worth a visit are **Cedar Grove** (2200 Oak St.), **Balfour House** (Crawford and Cherry Sts.), and the **Martha Vick House** (1300 Grove St.).

Mississippi River adventures await those who wish to travel aboard a 40-foot tour boat as it jets down the river. **Hydro-Jet Boat Tours** depart Vicksburg daily at 9 AM, 2 PM, and 5 PM March 1–November 15 on a narrated, 40-mile tour. *Tel. 601/638–5443 or 800/521–4363. Admission: $25 adults, $15 children.*

In 1894 Coca-Cola was first bottled at the **Biedenharn Candy Company,** which is now a Coke museum. *1107 Washington St., tel. 601/638–6514. Admission: $1.75 adults, $1.25 children under 12. Open Mon.–Sat. 9–5, Sun. 1:30–4:30.*

What to See and Do with Children

National Military Park (*see* Exploring, *above*).
Biedenharn Candy Company (see Exploring, *above*).
The new **Jim Henson/Muppets Museum** in Leland (S. Deer Creek Dr. E, tel. 601/686–2687) is open daily; admission free.
The USS *Cairo* and the ***Cairo*** Museum *(see* Exploring, *above*).
Hydro-Jet Boat Tours *(see* Exploring, *above*).
Toys and Soldiers Museum. Thousands of toy soldiers, a miniature circus, antique trains, and old toys are on display. *1100 Cherry St., Vicksburg, tel. 601/638–1986. Admission: $2 adults, $1.50 grades 1–12, free for preschoolers. Open Mon.–Sat. 9–4:30, Sun. 1:30–4:30.*

Off the Beaten Track

The **Ethel Wright Mohamed Stitchery Museum** in Belzoni contains pictures embroidered by Mrs. Mohamed, who took up needlework in her 60s to record her life in the Delta with her storekeeper husband and eight children. Some of Mrs. Mohamed's work is in the Smithsonian's permanent collection. The gallery is in the Mohamed family home, and the pictures cover every wall. *307 Central St., Belzoni 39038, tel. 601/247–1433. Admission free. Open by appointment.*

The **American Costume Company Museum** in Ruleville is the brain-child of former Hollywood costume designer Luster Bayless. See costumes worn by film stars John Wayne, Marilyn Monroe, and many more. *104 N. Ruby St., Ruleville, tel. 601/756–2171. Admission: $5 adults, $2.50 senior citizens, $2 children. Open 10–5. Closed Mon. and Wed.*

In Indianola, the **Crown Restaurant** in the **Antique Mall** serves lunch in a setting reminiscent of an English pub. You can buy your plate, chair, or table, or the antique English furnishings and accessories that fill the large restaurant/shop. If you come here on U.S. 82 from Greenville, you'll pass through prime antiqueing territory. *MS 448, Indianola. Antique Mall open Tues.–Sat. 9–5. The Crown Restaurant, tel. 601/887–2522.*

Near Greenwood, **Florewood River Plantation State Park** is an exact replica of an 1850s working plantation, complete with reenactments in the school, blacksmith shop, plantation store, and more. This living history park is well worth the trip. *Box 680, Greenwood, tel. 601/455–3821. Admission: $3.50 adults, $3 senior citizens, $2.50 children. Seasonal activities Mar. 1–Dec. 1. Open Tues.–Sat. 9–5, Sun. 1–5. Cotton Museum (on site) open year-round.*

Shopping

Antiques **The Antique Mall,** Indianola *(see* Off the Beaten Track, *above).*

Gifts Climb up into the **Attic Gallery** (1406 Washington St., Vicksburg, tel. 601/638–9221) to see regional art and fine crafts chosen with a discriminating eye—a Southern rival to New York galleries.

Participant Sports

Jogging The hilly roads in the **Vicksburg National Military Park** (I–20, Exit 4-B, Clay St.) are a challenging course for joggers.

Tennis **Carrie Stern Courts** (Eureka St., Greenville), **Ward Park** (MS 1S, Greenville), and **Clear Creek** (I–20, Bovina exit 7, Vicksburg).

Dining and Lodging

Dining Whether they need to celebrate the cotton crop or bemoan it, Delta folks love to get together and will drive for hours to party or eat out. Good food and drink are required; fancy surroundings aren't.

Category	Cost*
Very Expensive	over $20
Expensive	$15–$20
Moderate	$10–$15
Inexpensive	under $10

**per person without tax (7%), service, or drinks*

Lodging

Category	Cost*
Very Expensive	over $70
Expensive	$50–$70
Moderate	$30–$50
Inexpensive	under $30

**double room; add 7% for taxes*

Boyle
Dining
Sweet Olive. Lunch and dinner are served in the living and dining rooms of this restored Victorian home. Lunch varies with the chef's whim—chicken in a sour-cream sauce with fruit salad, perhaps, or for dessert, praline cheesecake or ice cream pie. *328 N. Bayou Ave., off U.S. 61 at Boyle, tel. 601/846–1100. Dress: informal. Reservations recommended. Open Tues.–Sat. 11:30 AM–2 PM. Closed Sun. and Mon. No credit cards. Inexpensive.*

Clarksdale
Dining
Rest Haven. The Delta's large Lebanese community influences the food, which is considered regional fare. Among the favorites: *kibbie* (seasoned lean ground steak with cracked wheat); spinach and meat pies; and cabbage rolls. Daily plate lunch specials include chicken and dumplings, and red beans and sausage over rice. *419 State St. (Hwy. 61), tel. 601/624–8601. Dress: informal. Reservations recommended for groups. Inexpensive.*

Greenville *Dining*

Doe's. This is a tumbledown building, visually as uninspiring as any restaurant you'll find—Formica-top tables, mismatched chairs, mismatched cutlery, mismatched plates—and you're practically eating in the kitchen. But when you see that huge steak hanging off your plate, you'll know why this place is famous. Hot tamales (a popular take-out item) and the house salad dressing (olive oil, lemon juice, garlic) are specialties. *502 Nelson St., tel. 601/334–3315. Dress: informal. Reservations recommended. MC, V. Moderate–Expensive.*

Vicksburg *Dining*

Tuminello's. Since 1899 Vicksburg residents and visitors have come here for fresh seafood and Italian fare. The old brick building, once Tuminello's Grocery, now with sparkling chandeliers and paneling made from willow trees along the Mississippi, is a pleasant atmosphere for dining. Specialties include veal sautéed with crabmeat and asparagus spears; baked stuffed redfish; and shrimp *francesca* (sautéed in Imperiale sauce and flamed with brandy). *500 Speed St., tel. 601/634–0507. Dress: informal, although jacket and tie are suitable. AE, MC, V. Expensive–Very Expensive.*

Delta Point. This large, elegant restaurant sits high on the bluff, and its picture windows provide excellent views of the Mississippi River. Service is impeccable, the menu varied and ambitious, and the food erratic. China, crystal, and flowers contribute to the gracious mood. Specialties are beef tenderloin stuffed with marinated Bing cherries; shrimp and fettuccine; and cherries jubilee and bananas Foster. *4144 Washington St., tel. 601/636–5317. Jacket and tie required. Reservations recommended. Sun. brunch. AE, DC, MC, V. Expensive.*

Maxwell's. This candlelit place looks neither tacky nor chic; however, its food is consistently well prepared. It serves a homestyle noon buffet (baked ham and raisin sauce; chicken livers with mushrooms) and goes fancy at night with such specialties as oysters Rockefeller, stuffed mushrooms, fresh redfish with shrimp sauce, and prime rib. *4207 Clay St., tel. 601/636–1344 or 601/636–9656. Dress: informal. Reservations recommended. Closed Sun. AE, MC, V. Expensive.*

Lodging

Anchuca. Guests stay in the slave quarters or a turn-of-the-century cottage of this antebellum mansion. Rooms are decorated in period antiques and fabrics. A plantation breakfast and house tour are included. *1010 1st East St., 39180, tel. 601/636–4931 or 800/262–4822. 9 rooms, each with private bath. Facilities: pool, hot tub. AE, MC, V. Very Expensive.*

Cedar Grove. Guest rooms are furnished with antiques in this 1840 Greek Revival mansion. Service is erratic, staff noisy, but the gaslit surroundings make up for lapses. Plantation breakfast and tour of home included. *2300 Washington, tel. 601/636–2800 or 800/448–2820 (800/862–1300 in MS). Facilities: pool, garden, courtyard, live music 5–8. AE, MC, V. Very Expensive.*

Duff Green Mansion. This 1856 mansion was used as a hospital during the Civil War. Each guest room is decorated with antiques, including half-tester beds. A large, Southern-style breakfast and a tour of the home are included. *1114 1st East St., 39180, tel. 601/638–6662. 5 rooms, 1 suite, all with private baths. Facilities: pool, courtyard. AE, MC, V. Very Expensive.*

Comfort Inn. Functional, clean rooms in a new motel. *I–20 Frontage Road S., 39180, tel. 601/634–8607 or 800/228–5150. 70* *rooms. Facilities: swimming pool, exercise room, whirlpool, sauna. AE, DC, MC, V. Inexpensive–Moderate.*

Nightlife

Maxwell's in Vicksburg *(see* Dining, *above)* offers live entertainment in its lounge each weekend. **Miller's Still,** in the Velchoff Corner Restaurant (1101 Washington St., Vicksburg, tel. 601/638-8661), opens at 11 AM Monday–Saturday and at 4 PM Sunday, with live entertainment Thursday–Saturday.

Beechwood Restaurant & Lounge (4449 Hwy. 80 E, Vicksburg, tel. 601/636-3761) is a hot spot for Monday Night Football fans. Open at 6 PM Monday, 7 "til" Tuesday–Saturday. Live entertainment nightly.

6 North Carolina

By Carol Timblin

The author won first place in the Lowell Thomas Travel Journalism Competition and the Discover America Award in 1988, and has a weekly travel feature in The Leader, *a Charlotte newspaper.*

Bluish purple mountains covered with mist. Clear streams and large expanses of freshwater lakes. Growing cities surrounded by industrial plants and patches of red clay. Pine barrens and golf courses scattered in the Sandhills that were once the beaches of the Atlantic. Great flat fields of soybeans, corn, and tobacco in the east. Fleets of boats and ships anchored at marinas on the Intracoastal Waterway. Tall dunes, sprinkled with sea oats, and long stretches of sandy beaches. A string of lighthouses along a chain of barrier islands, over a hundred miles long.

This is North Carolina. Though its profile is currently changing to high-tech, with a concentration of activities at the Research Triangle Park near Raleigh and the University Research Park at Charlotte, there are no huge megalopolises. North Carolina politics are often puzzling to outsiders, as the extremes of view range from ultraliberal to ultraconservative. Charlotte, the largest city, with a population of about 410,000, is one of the leading financial centers of the Southeast. With megabanks such as NationsBank and First Union National Bank, its influence is felt far beyond the geographical boundaries of North Carolina.

In Colonial days, North Carolina produced mostly tar, pitch, and turpentine. During the Civil War, Confederate Army General Robert E. Lee gave the state its nickname—the Tar Heel State. He borrowed the tar heel image from compatriot Jefferson Davis, who alleged he would coat the heels of his soldiers with tar to help them stand their ground.

Geography has dramatically carved out three distinct regions in North Carolina. The Appalachian Mountains give way to the rolling hills of the Piedmont Plateau, which in turn evolve into the Coastal Plain—a stretch of more than 500 miles from the Tennessee border to the Atlantic Ocean. Each region has its own unique place in the state's rich history, spanning four centuries. Charlotte and the capital city of Raleigh lead the state in growth and development, with Greensboro, Winston-Salem, and High Point (the Triad) following. Wilmington is a bustling port city, in marked contrast to the tranquil villages along the Outer Banks. Golf is the recreational focus of the Sandhills, while snow skiing has taken hold in The High Country (Alleghany, Ashe, Avery, Mitchell, and Watauga counties). Asheville has maintained its status as a resort city for over 100 years and continues to grow in popularity as a travel destination.

North Carolina has courted visitors since the first English settlers arrived here in 1584. During the Depression of the 1930s, state officials began to realize anew the importance of tourism and put up a hospitality sign. Since then, a good highway system and excellent airport facilities have been developed. Eight welcome centers now serve visitors throughout the state. Tourism is the third-largest industry behind tobacco and textiles. The welcome mat is out in North Carolina, so make the most of it while exploring and enjoying the treasures of the Tar Heel State.

For a time called "Variety Vacationland," North Carolina offers a wealth of leisure activities and attractions—historic sites, natural wonders, all kinds of sports, and luxury resorts and hotels. The state is famous for its down-home cuisine, and its

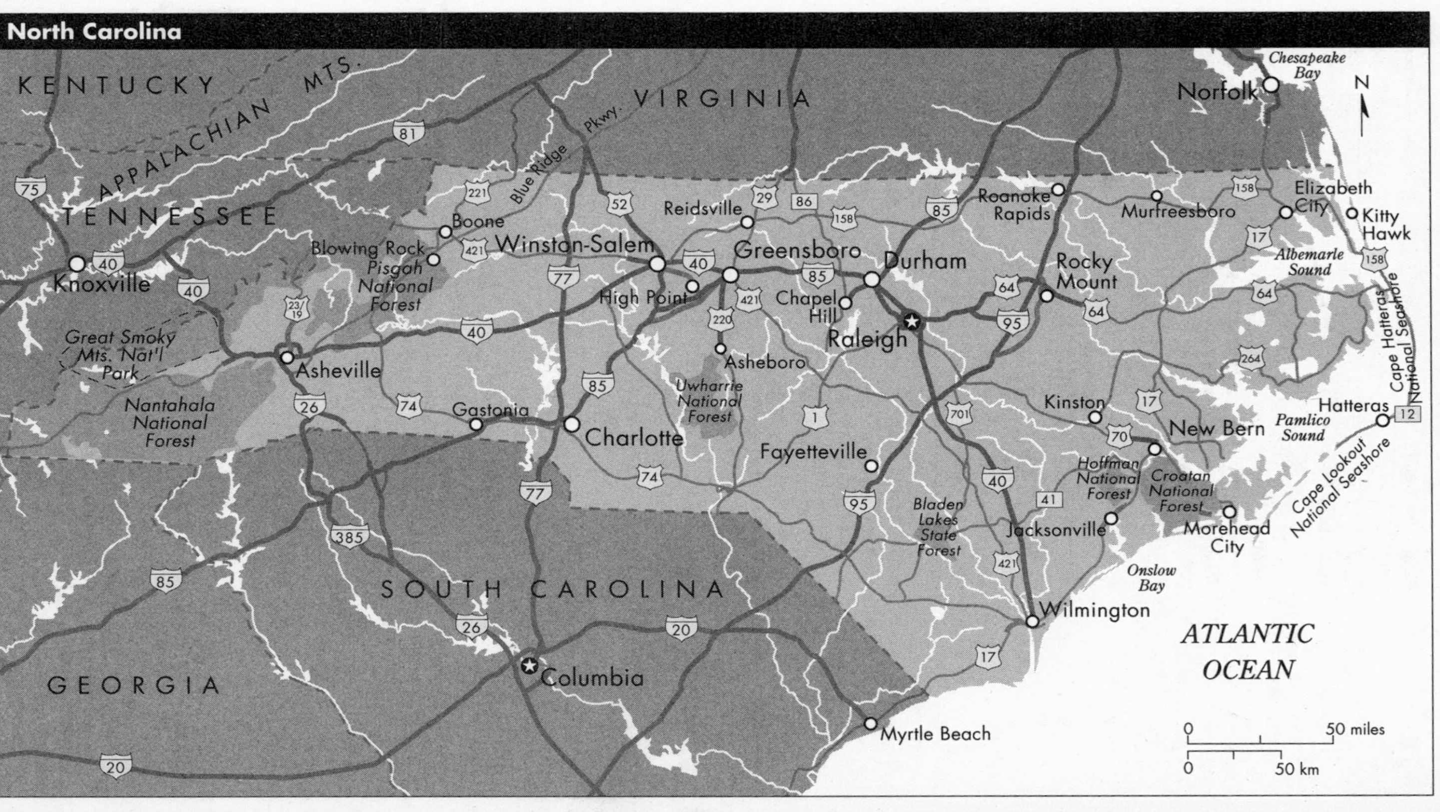
North Carolina
KENTUCKY
APPALACHIAN MTS.
VIRGINIA
TENNESSEE
SOUTH CAROLINA
GEORGIA
ATLANTIC OCEAN
Chesapeake Bay
Norfolk
N
Blue Ridge Pkwy.
Knoxville
Great Smoky Mts. Nat'l Park
Nantahala National Forest
Asheville
Boone
Blowing Rock
Pisgah National Forest
Winston-Salem
High Point
Reidsville
Greensboro
Asheboro
Uwharrie National Forest
Gastonia
Charlotte
Chapel Hill
Durham
Raleigh
Fayetteville
Roanoke Rapids
Rocky Mount
Murfreesboro
Elizabeth City
Kitty Hawk
Albemarle Sound
Cape Hatteras National Seashore
Hatteras
Pamlico Sound
Kinston
New Bern
Hoffman National Forest
Croatan National Forest
Morehead City
Cape Lookout National Seashore
Bladen Lakes State Forest
Jacksonville
Onslow Bay
Wilmington
Columbia
Myrtle Beach
0 50 miles
0 50 km

tangy barbecue, served with a vinegar-base sauce, is legendary.

Charlotte

Charlotte, once a sleepy Southern crossroads, is growing up to be one of the nation's most sophisticated cities—with luxury hotels, world-class restaurants, sporting events, and varied cultural activities. Even stock car racing at the Charlotte Motor Speedway has become trendy; some fans watch the races from the exclusive Speedway Club overlooking the track. Charlotte is the banking capital of the Southeast and home to national and international corporations that have played a vital role in shaping the city's history. Charlotte-Douglas International Airport is one of the fastest-growing in the country.

Though Charlotte dates to Revolutionary times (it is named for King George III's wife, Queen Charlotte), its Uptown is sparkling new with an ever-changing skyline. In recent years, urban revival has brought people back to the city to enjoy entertainment and cultural events. The new North Carolina Blumenthal Center for the Performing Arts (227 N. Tryon St.) opened in fall 1992. Since the arrival of the National Basketball Association team—the Charlotte Hornets—in 1989, Hornet mania has gripped the city, with fans wearing team colors and sporting various likenesses of Hugo the hornet on their cars.

In spite of all the new glitz and glamour, Charlotte has not outgrown its down-home flavor, and people still love the traditional pleasures of spreading a picnic in Freedom Park as they listen to the Charlotte Pops, politicking and munching barbecue at Mallard Creek Church, or watching the fireworks at Memorial Stadium on the Fourth of July.

Arriving and Departing

By Plane
Airports and Airlines

Charlotte-Douglas International Airport (tel. 704/359–4000), located on the west side of the city off I–85, serves the metropolitan area. Carriers include **American, Delta, Lufthansa German Airlines, TWA, United,** and **USAir. USAir Express** provides service to nearby cities and towns. Direct service is available to London, Frankfurt, Nassau, Puerto Rico, and Bermuda.

Between the Airport and Center City

By Bus. You can take a bus into the city during peak business hours (6–9 AM and 3–6 PM). The fare is 70¢ per person.

By Taxi. It costs around $11 per person ($2 each additional person) to take a taxi; limousines are approximately $4 per person. Most major hotels provide complimentary transportation to and from the airport.

By Car. Follow the road leading from the airport to the Billy Graham Parkway and then go north. Then, follow Wilkinson Boulevard (U.S. 74) east to I–277, which leads to the heart of Uptown.

By Train

Amtrak (1914 N. Tryon St., tel. 704/376–4416 or 800/872–7245) offers daily service to Washington, DC, to Atlanta, GA, and points beyond. Daily round-trip service is also available to Raleigh.

By Bus **Greyhound-Trailways Bus Lines** (601 W. Trade St., tel. 704/527–9393) serves the Charlotte area.

By Car Charlotte is a transportation hub of the Southeast. I–85 and I–77, north–south routes, run through the city, and I–40, an east–west route, is 40 miles to the north. U.S. 74, a major east–west route, also serves the city. I–277 and Charlotte 4 are inner-city loops. An outer beltway is planned, but at this time NC 51 is something of a perimeter route around part of the city, connecting Pineville, Matthews, and Mint Hill. Harris Boulevard is another semiperimeter from the northern to the eastern end of the county, connecting I–77 to University City, Hickory Grove, and Independence Boulevard (U.S. 74).

Getting Around

By Bus **Charlotte Transit** (tel. 704/336–3366) provides public transportation throughout the city. The Transit Mall has bus shelters on Trade and Tryon streets in Uptown. Fares are 80¢ for local rides and $1.15 for express service; senior citizens with ID cards pay 30¢ between 9 and 3, after 6, and on weekends. Free bus service is available between Mint and Kings Drive on Trade and between Stonewall and 11th on Tryon weekdays 9–3.

By Taxi Visitors may choose from a half dozen different taxi companies. **Yellow Cab** (tel. 704/332–6161) has a shiny fleet of cars, plus vans that serve the airport. **Crown Cab** (tel. 704/334–6666) gets high marks. Passengers pay a set flat rate.

Important Addresses and Numbers

Tourist Information The **Visitor Information Center** is operated by the Charlotte Convention & Visitors Bureau (122 E. Stonewall St., tel. 704/371–8700 or 800/231–4636. Open weekdays 8:30–5, Sat. 10–4, and Sun. 1–4. Parking is available). The **N.C. Welcome Center** (on I–77 north at the North Carolina-South Carolina line, tel. 704/588–2660, open daily 8–5 except Christmas, New Year's Day, and a half day on Thanksgiving) provides information on Charlotte and the entire state. The **Charlotte-Douglas International Airport** has unmanned information kiosks (open at all times).

Emergencies Dial 911 for **police** and **ambulance** in an emergency. Hospital emergency rooms are open 24 hours a day. **Care Connection,** operated by Presbyterian Hospital, will give physician referrals and make appointments (tel. 704/384–4111, open weekdays 8:30–4:30). **Healthfinder,** run by Mercy Hospital, is a similar operation (tel. 704/379–6100, open weekdays 8:30–5). Another option is the Mecklenburg County Medical Society, which also gives physician referrals (tel. 704/376–3688, open weekdays 9–noon).

Pharmacy **Eckerd Drugs** (Park Road Shopping Center, tel. 704/523–3031; and 3740 Independence Blvd., tel. 704/536–1010).

Guided Tours

Guided tours are given by **"Day Trippin" in the Carolinas** (tel. 704/362–2352), **Gray Line** (tel. 704/332–8687), **Adam's Stage Lines** (tel. 704/537–5342), and **Queens Carriages** (tel. 704/391–1232).

Several balloon companies give aerial tours, which end with champagne: **Air Fair Balloons** (tel. 704/522–0965), **Balloons Over Charlotte** (tel. 704/541–7058), **Adventures Aloft of Charlotte** (tel. 704/545–6418), and **Fantasy Flights** (tel. 704/552–0469).

Exploring Charlotte

Numbers in the margin correspond to points of interest on the Charlotte map.

Uptown Charlotte is ideal for walking, but some form of transportation is needed for visiting surrounding sites. Buses are adequate for getting around within the city limits; otherwise, you will need a car. Discovery Place provides free parking for its visitors; the Convention Center offers parking at a reasonable rate. The original city was laid out into four wards from The Square, at Trade and Tryon streets. The Visitor Information Center, on Stonewall Street, can provide information on a self-guided walking tour of Fourth Ward and a historic tour of Uptown, as well as maps and brochures covering other areas.

Uptown Charlotte Walking Tour

A walking tour of Charlotte may take a half hour or a full day, depending on whether you're interested in shopping, architecture, or history. Take time to stroll down **Tryon Street** and enjoy the ambience of this revitalized area. Take note of the outdoor sculptures and the creative architecture of some of the newer buildings, particularly the **First Union Tower,** and **NationsBank Corporate Center.** During the warm months there will probably be some lunchtime entertainment going on at various plazas. Be sure to wander through the **Overstreet Mall,** a labyrinthine maze of shops and restaurants between the major office buildings. The best entrance to the mall is through the Radisson Plaza Hotel.

1 Begin your tour at **Discovery Place,** across the street from the **Visitor Information Center** on Church Street. You'll want to make the hands-on Science Museum a priority, so plan to set aside at least two hours for this experience. The museum is for children of all ages. Enjoy the aquariums, the rain forest, the Omnimax Theatre, and Kelly Space Voyager Planetarium, and check the schedule for special exhibits. *301 N. Tryon St., tel. 704/372–6261; Omnimax, tel. 704/845–6664. Admission: $5–$8 adults, $4–$7 senior citizens and students, $2.50–$5 children 3–5. Open daily except Thanksgiving and Christmas, weekdays 9–5; Omnimax and planetarium open Mon.–Wed. 9–5, Thurs. 9–8, Fri.–Sat. 9–9, and Sun. 1–6.*

2 **Fourth Ward,** Charlotte's new "old" city, which lies just west of Discovery Place, offers a refreshing change from the newly developed parts of town. A self-guided tour, available from the Visitor Information Center, points to 18 historic sites in the area, including the **Old North Carolina Medical College Building** (229 N. Church St.), where the center itself is located. Be sure to stop by **Old Settlers Cemetery,** behind First Presbyterian Church, containing stones that date to the 1700s, including the grave of Thomas Polk, a founding father. **First Presbyterian Church,** which takes up a city block and faces W. Trade Street, reflects the prosperity of the early settlers and their descendants. By the turn of the last century, they had built this Gothic Revival complex with stained glass to replace a much simpler meeting house. **Fourth Ward Park** is an oasis in the middle of the

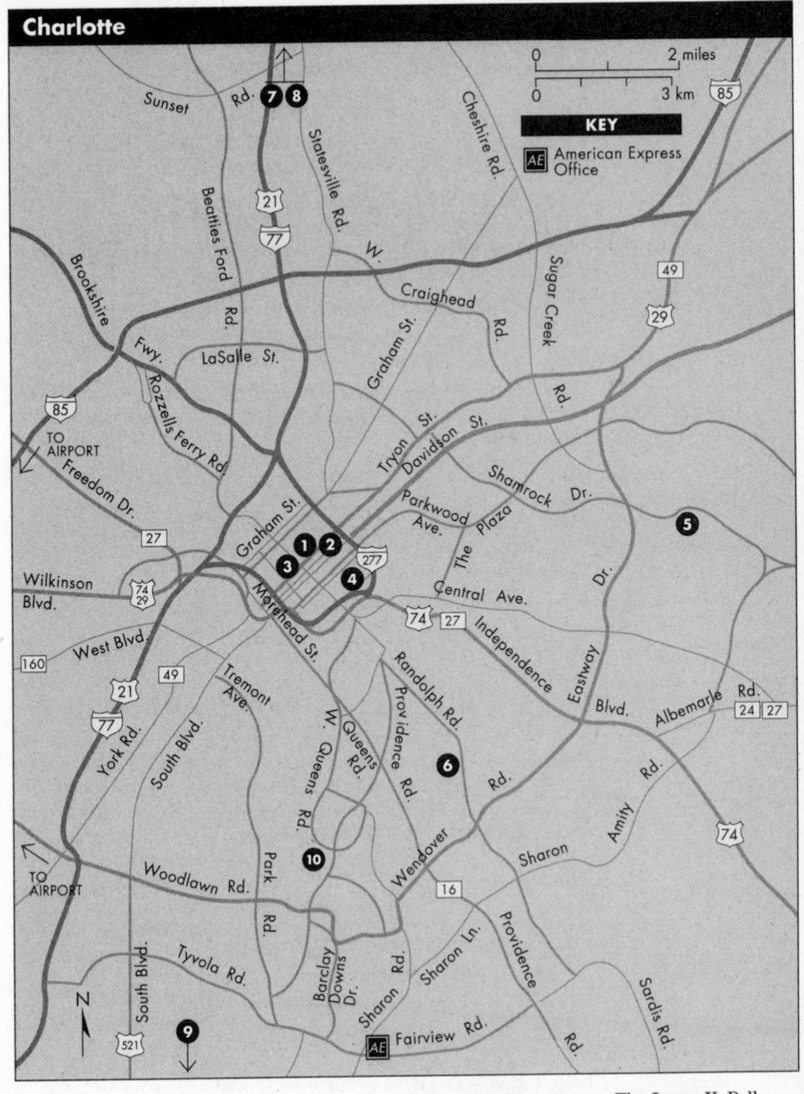

Afro-American Cultural Center, **4**

Discovery Place, **1**

The Energy Explorium, **8**

Fourth Ward, **2**

Hezekiah Alexander Homesite and History Museum, **5**

The James K. Polk Memorial, **9**

Latta Plantation Park, **7**

Mint Museum of Art, **6**

Overstreet Mall, **3**

Wing Haven Gardens and Bird Sanctuary, **10**

city. You can't miss the flamingo pink **Overcarsh House** (1879), perched above the park. It is one of two bed-and-breakfast houses in Fourth Ward. **Alexander Michael's** (401 W. Ninth St.) is a favorite eatery. **Poplar Street Books** is housed in the Victorian Young-Morrison House (226 W. Tenth St.). U.S. President Taft spent the night in the **Liddell-McNinch House** (51 N. Church St.) when he visited Charlotte in 1909.

Spirit Square (345 N. College St.) includes galleries, a performing arts center, and classrooms. The **Public Library,** which includes a mural of a Romare Bearden painting, is open weekdays 9–9, Saturday 9–6, and Sunday 2–6.

The North Carolina Blumenthal Center for the Performing Arts (227 N. Tryon St.) is a gleaming new home for the performing arts.

3 The **Overstreet Mall** is a good place to wind up a walking tour. You'll find some expensive specialty shops and several informal restaurants here.

Other Charlotte Area Attractions Driving Tour

Other attractions are spread out across the city, so you may want to concentrate on one or two. You can reach the Afro-American Cultural Center, Hezekiah Alexander Homesite, Mint Museum, and Charlotte Nature Museum by city bus; for visits elsewhere, a car is needed.

From Uptown Charlotte, follow Seventh Street east until you
4 get to N. Myers Street. The **Afro-American Cultural Center,** a black arts center, including galleries, a theater, and bookstore, is housed in the restored building that formerly served as the Little Rock AME Zion Church. *Tel. 704/374–1565. Open Tues.–Sat. 10–6, Sun. 1–5.*

From Seventh Street, take Central Avenue east to Eastway Drive. Turn left on Eastway and follow it for several blocks un-
5 til you turn right on Shamrock Drive, where the **Hezekiah Alexander Homesite and History Museum** is preserved as a memorial to one of Mecklenburg County's earliest settlers. The stone house, built in 1774, is the oldest dwelling in the county. Here, Alexander and his wife Mary reared 10 children and farmed the land. Costumed docents give guided tours of the homesite, including the reconstructed spring house and log kitchen. Special seasonal events, held during the spring, summer, and at Christmastime, commemorate the early days. *3500 Shamrock Dr., tel. 704/568–1774. Admission: $2 adults, $1 children 6–16. Open Tues.–Fri. 10–5, weekends 2–5.*

Follow Eastway Drive (Charlotte 4) south for several miles to
6 Randolph Road and turn right to reach the **Mint Museum of Art.** Built in 1837 as a U.S. Mint, it has served as a home for art since 1936 and in recent years has attracted such exhibits as "Ramesses the Great." *2730 Randolph Rd., tel. 704/337–2000. Admission: $4 adults, children under 12 free. Open Tues. 10–10, Wed.–Sat. 10–5, and Sun. 1–6. Closed Christmas and New Year's Day.*

7 **Latta Plantation Park,** located northwest of town (off I–77, near Huntersville), centers around a Catawba River plantation house, built by merchant James Latta in the early 1800s. Costumed guides give tours of the house, which is on the National Register of Historic Places. In addition to the house, visitors enjoy the farm animals, an equestrian center, Audubon center, and the Carolina Raptor Center, where injured and orphaned

birds of prey are cared for. *5225 Sample Rd., Huntersville, tel. 704/875-2312. Admission: $1 adults, 50¢ for children. Park open daily 7 AM to dark. House tours are offered Tues.–Sun. at 2, 3, and 4 PM.*

8 Continue on I–77N to **the Energy Explorium,** operated by Duke Power Company on Lake Norman. Hands-on exhibits allow you to experience the excitement of creating nuclear power and other kinds of energy. A wildflower garden and picnic area offer diversion of a different kind. *McGuire Nuclear Plant, off I-77 and NC 73, Cornelius, tel. 704/875-5600. Admission free. Open Mon.–Sat. 9–5, Sun. noon–5. Closed major holidays.*

What to See and Do with Children

Carowinds, an 83-acre theme amusement park, straddles the North Carolina–South Carolina line. Young children love the Kids Karnival and teenagers seek thrills on the Vortex, a super coaster, which takes its passengers on a stand-up ride. For grown-ups, there are serene rides and Broadway-style shows. The Paladium offers musical concerts with star entertainers. *Carowinds Blvd., tel. 704/588-2600. Open daily 10–8 except Fri. June–Aug.; closed weekdays Mar.–Apr., Sept.–early Oct. Call 800/822-4428 for ticket prices.*

The Nature Museum, a sister to Discovery Place, is a delight to young children. It features some live animals and exhibits, plus a small planetarium. *1658 Sterling Rd., tel. 704/372-6261. Admission: $1. Open Mon.–Fri. 9–5, Sat. 10–5, Sun. 1–5. Closed major Holidays.*

Freedom Park, across the footbridge from the Nature Museum, offers acres of space and a shimmering lake where you can feed the ducks. Children love climbing on the train engine, fire trucks, and airplanes, as well as using the playground equipment. *2435 Cumberland Ave., tel. 704/336-2663. Admission free.*

9 The **James K. Polk Memorial,** now a state historic site, marks the humble 1795 birthplace of the 11th president. Guided tours of the log cabins are available, and the buildings are decorated with fresh pine boughs and candles at Christmastime. Exhibits in the center depict early life in Mecklenburg County. *U.S. 521, Pineville, tel. 704/889-7145. Admission free. Open Mon.–Sat. 9–5, Sun. 1–5 Apr.–Oct.; Tues.–Sat. 10–4, Sun. 1–4 Nov.–Mar.*

Reed Gold Mine, east of Charlotte in Cabarrus County, is where America's first gold rush began following Conrad Reed's discovery of a 17-pound nugget in 1799. Visitors may explore the underground mine shaft and gold holes, pan for gold during the summer months, learn about the history of gold mining, or enjoy a picnic. *Off NC 27 between Midland and Stanfield, tel. 704/786-8337. Gold panning is $3 (group rate $1 per person), but admission is free. Open Mon.–Sat. 9–5, Sun. 1–5 Apr.–Oct.; Tues.–Sat. 10–4, Sun. 1–4 Nov.–Mar.*

The **Schiele Museum of Natural History and Planetarium** in Gastonia offers some outstanding exhibits, including one on the natural history of the state and another on land mammals of North America. Visitors also enjoy the living history demonstrations at the pioneer site, as well as the nature trail. *Garrison Blvd., Gastonia, tel. 704/866-6902. Admission to museum* *free; $2 charge for planetarium shows and movies. Open Tues.–Fri. 9–5, weekends 1–5. Closed on Thanksgiving Day and Christmas week.*

The **Spencer Shops–N.C. Transportation Museum,** north of Salisbury, was once Southern Railway's largest repair facility between Washington, DC, and Atlanta, GA. A restored train takes passengers on a short ride over the 57-acre complex, with a stop at the round house. The museum, a state historic site, traces the development of transportation in North Carolina from Indian times to the present. The gift shop features some unique train memorabilia. *Off I–85 at Spencer, tel. 704/636–2889. Admission free. Train rides $1.50–$3. Open Mon.–Sat. 9–5, Sun. 1–5 Apr. 1–Oct. 10; Tues.–Sat. 10–4, Sun. 1–4 Nov.–Mar.*

Off the Beaten Track

10 A visit to **Wing Haven Gardens and Bird Sanctuary** will take you into Myers Park, one of Charlotte's loveliest neighborhoods. The three-acre garden, developed by the Clarkson family, is home to more than 135 species of birds. *248 Ridgewood Rd., tel. 704/331–0664. Admission free. Open Sun. 2–5, Tues.–Wed. 3–5 or by appointment.*

Davidson is a delightful college town several miles north of Charlotte, via I–77. Throughout the year, Davidson College offers a number of cultural activities—including plays, concerts, art exhibits, lectures, and sporting events (tel. 704/892–2000).

Shopping

Charlotte is the largest retail center in the Carolinas, with the majority of stores in suburban malls. Villages and towns in outlying areas offer some regional specialties. Uptown shops are open 10–5:30 daily except Sunday. Malls are open Monday–Saturday 10–9 and Sunday 1–6. Sales tax is 6%.

Shopping Districts

Midtown Square offers savings at such outlets as the Dress Barn and Burlington Coat Factory. Outlets are also clustered in **Windsor Square** near Matthews and at **Outlet Marketplace** on I–77 near Carowinds.

Park Road Shopping Center features an old-fashioned Woolworth's store, JC Penney's, Bush Stationers, and other shops. **Cotswold Shopping Mall** is home to the outlet stores, Marshalls and Stein Mart. **SouthPark,** located in the most affluent section of the city, caters to upscale customers. Belk, Dillard's, Thalhimers, Montaldo's, and Sears are here. **Specialty Shops on the Park,** across from Southpark, is another cluster of expensive shops. **The Arboretum,** also on the south side, offers upscale mall shops and restaurants, as well as a Walmart. **Eastland Mall,** on the east side of town, features an ice skating rink, plus Dillard's, Belk, JC Penney's, Sears, and other retail stores. Outlets are clustered in **Windsor Square** near Matthews and at **Outlet Marketplace** on I–77 near Carowinds.

Department Stores

Belk, Dillard's, Montaldo's, Hecht's, and Upton's all offer quality merchandise.

Specialty Stores
Antiques

The towns of Waxhaw, Pineville, and Matthews are the best places to find antiques. Each has a number of shops, and Waxhaw sponsors an annual antiques fair each February. If you want to combine shopping with lunch, Matthews offers a choice of restaurants. Shops are usually open Monday through Saturday in Pineville and Matthews. In Waxhaw, some shops are open on Sunday but closed on Monday. You can also find a good selection of antiques at the Metrolina Expo on the first and third weekends of the month.

Books There are some excellent bookshops in Charlotte. Sure bets are the **Intimate** at Eastland, South Park, and University Place and **Poplar Street Books** in Fourth Ward. The International Newsstand at Providence Square Shopping Center carries publications from around the world.

Crafts The best buys are in the **Metrolina Expo,** open the first and third weekends of every month. Crafts are also offered at the **Carolina Craft Shows,** held in the fall and spring at the Convention Center, as well as the **Southern Christmas Show** and the **Southern Spring Show** at the Merchandise Mart.

Participant Sports

Bicycling There is a 10-mile designated route between Southpark and Uptown Charlotte. North Carolina has designated tours stretching from the coast to the mountains. Route maps are available from the NC Department of Transportation (Box 25201, Raleigh 27611).

Camping Near Charlotte, try McDowell Park and Nature Reserve, Carowinds and Duke Power State Park. In neighboring South Carolina, try Kings Mountain State Park.

Canoeing Inlets on Lake Norman and Lake Wylie are ideal for canoeing, as are some spots of the Catawba River. The Pee Dee River east of Charlotte and the New River in the mountains offer other options.

Fishing Enthusiasts enjoy fishing in Charlotte's neighboring lakes and streams, as well as farther away on the coast and in mountain streams. A state license is required and may be purchased at local bait and tackle shops. For details, contact the North Carolina Division of Boating and Inland Fishing (tel. 919/733–3633).

Golf Charlotte has several good public golf courses, among them Crystal Springs, Renaissance, and Pebble Creek. The Visitor Information Center (tel. 704/371–8700) can provide a complete list. The renowned Pinehurst–Southern Pines golf area is only a two-hour drive from Charlotte.

Hiking Crowder's Mountain and Kings Mountain near Gastonia and the Uwharrie Mountains east of Charlotte offer plenty of varied terrain and challenge for hikers.

Jogging Jogging trails and tracks can be found in most city and county parks and at many local schools. Contact the Mecklenburg County Park and Recreation Department (tel. 704/336–3854) or Charlotte Park and Recreation (tel. 704/336–2464).

Physical Fitness The Charlotte YWCAs and YMCAs will permit guests with Y memberships in another location to use their facilities for a $5 fee. Many hotels in town also offer fitness centers.

Tennis Courts are available in several city parks, including Freedom, Hornet's Nest, Park Road, and Veterans. A growing number of hotels and motels provide courts as well. For details, call the

Charlotte Park and Recreation Department (tel. 704/336–2464).

Spectator Sports

Baseball The Charlotte Knights play April–August at Knights Castle, I–77 and Gold Hill Road, in South Carolina (tel. 704/332–3746). The Gastonia Rangers play during the same period at Sims Legion Park in Gastonia (tel. 704/867–3721).

Basketball The Charlotte Hornets play from November to April at the Charlotte Coliseum on Tyvola Road, off the Billy Graham Parkway (tel. 704/357–0489 or 800/543–3041).

Racing NASCAR races, such as the **Coca-Cola 600** and **Winston Champion Spark Plug 300,** draw huge crowds at the Charlotte Motor Speedway near Concord. For tickets, call 704/455–3200. Visitors also enjoy **Winston Cup** tours and thrilling track rides (tel. 704/455–3204) and **Backing Up Classics,** an antique car museum (tel. 704/788–9500).

Dining

By Peg Robarchek

Updated by Carol Timblin

The choice of good places to eat in Charlotte is extremely varied, including many restaurants specializing in international cuisine. Local specialties include barbecued pork and chicken, fresh seafood, fried chicken, and country ham. Hush puppies, made from cornmeal batter and fried in deep fat, almost always accompany fish and barbecue. Grits is another Southern specialty widely served in North Carolina, usually with breakfast. There is also a wide selection of places that feature steaks and roast prime ribs of beef. The number of ethnic restaurants is increasing.

The most highly recommended restaurants in each price category are indicated by a star ★.

Category	Cost*
Very Expensive	over $20
Expensive	$15–$20
Moderate	$10–$15
Inexpensive	under $10

**per person without tax (6% in Charlotte), service, or drinks*

American
Very Expensive
★ **Jonathan's Uptown.** Next door to Spirit Square performing arts center, Jonathan's is an easy walk from most Uptown hotels. And it is as noted for the lively entertainment in its Jazz Cellar and bar as it is for its food. Dinner specialties include sautéed venison loin, grilled or blackened mahi mahi, a variety of steaks, and roast duck with regional sauces and stuffings. *330 N. Tryon St., tel. 704/332–3663. Jacket and tie suggested. Reservations recommended. AE, DC, MC, V.*

Moderate–Expensive
★ **Longhorn Steaks Restaurant and Saloon.** Longneck beers, buckets of roasted peanuts, and Margaritas that live up to the Texas tradition of being the biggest and the strongest will help you make it through the wait, which stretches to an hour on weekends at this popular watering hole. The atmosphere is loose but not raucous. The menu concentrates on steaks, in-

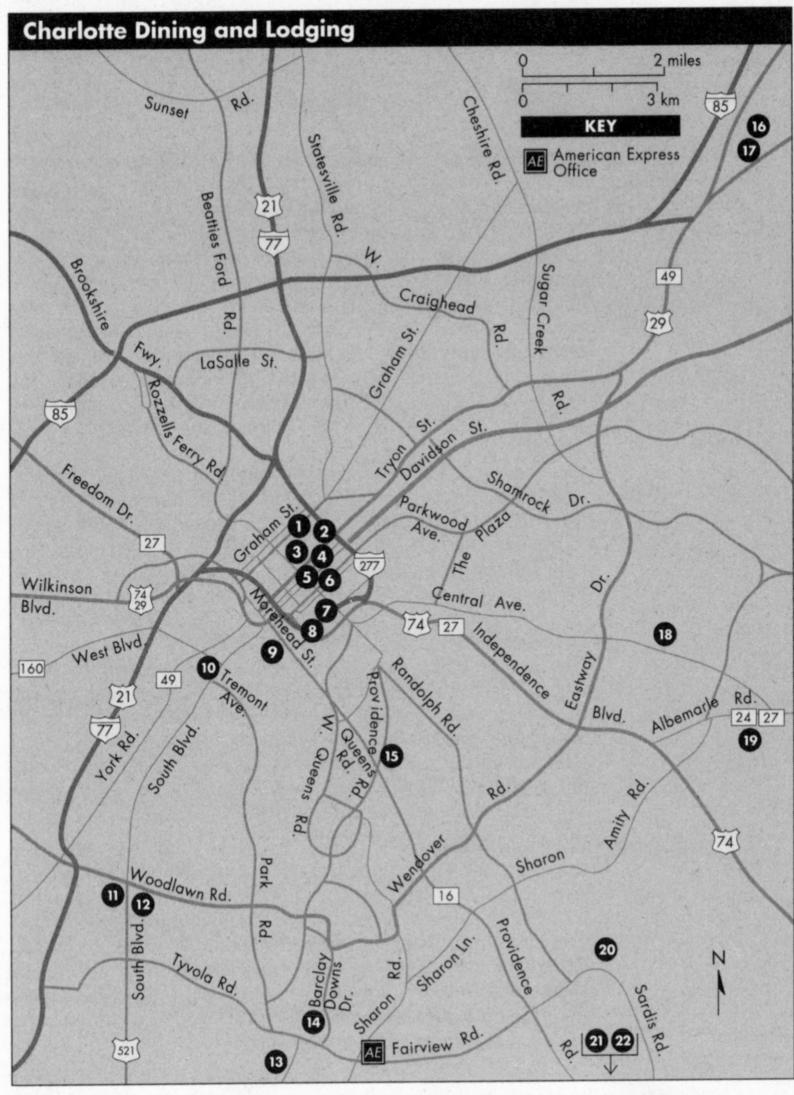

Dining

Catherine's on Providence, **15**

Grady's Goodtimes, **19**

Jonathan's Uptown, **2**

Kabuto's Japanese House of Steaks, **17**

The Lamplighter, **8**

The Landmark Restaurant, **18**

Longhorn Steaks Restaurant & Saloon, **9**

Newmarket Grill, **22**

Pewter Rose Bistro, **10**

PizZarrelli Trattoria, **13**

Prisms Restaurant and The Bistro, **5**

Villa Antonio, **11**

Lodging

Adam's Mark, **7**

The Dunhill, **1**

Embassy Suites, **12**

Hilton at University Place, **16**

The Homeplace, **20**

Hyatt Charlotte, **14**

Inn on Providence, **22**

Marriott City Center, **4**

Omni Charlotte Hotel, **6**

Radisson Plaza Hotel, **3**

cluding a filet mignon as thick and tender as any you'll ever order. Other Longhorns are located in Crown Pointe in Matthews and on Highway 51 near Pineville. *700 E. Morehead St., tel. 704/332–2300. Dress: informal. Reservations not accepted. AE, MC, V.*

Inexpensive–Moderate ★ **Catherine's on Providence.** Elegant food is seldom served under the same roof with low prices, but Catherine's has cornered the market on this unlikely pairing. Vegetables get an image boost at Catherine's, where the menu changes daily. Smothered cabbage, marinated cucumbers, and Greek tomato salad are good examples of the way ordinary produce is transformed into gourmet food. Tender rib roast and roast pork loin with mustard sauce are menu regulars. Breakfast also ventures away from the usual. Soft candlelight and warm woods create a cozy feeling, but the noise level is a bit high for intimacy. *829 Providence Rd., tel. 704/372–8199. Dress: informal. Reservations not accepted. Closed Mon. No dinner Sun., Tues., and Wed. AE, MC, V.*

Grady's Goodtimes. Packed every night of the week, this restaurant has earned praise from patrons for its friendly service and excellent food. Favorites are the greenhouse salad served with honey-mustard dressing, the mesquite-grilled chicken or fish, and the hot chocolate bar cake. There's usually a wait of 30 minutes to an hour, but the time passes quickly at the lively bar. *5546 Albemarle Rd., tel. 704/537–GOOD. Dress: informal. Reservations not accepted. AE, DC, MC, V.*

Newmarket Grille. You can enjoy a variety of moderately priced dishes, including soups, sandwiches, salads, pastas, steak, and fish, within the rich mahogany walls of this restaurant in the Arboretum Shopping Center on the south side. Outdoor dining is also an option, and there's a cozy, dark bar for getting together with friends. *8136 Providence Rd., tel. 704/543–4656. Dress: informal. Reservations not accepted. AE, DC, MC, V.*

Inexpensive **Landmark Restaurant–Diner.** This New York–style eatery in the Eastland Mall neighborhood is a cut above most inexpensive restaurants, and it's open until 3 AM on weeknights and 24 hours on weekends. Decorated in contemporary colors, this spacious restaurant is a good place for an informal breakfast, lunch, dinner, or after-hours dessert. (Ask for the New York–style cheesecake from the in-house bakery.) *4429 Central Ave., tel. 704/532–1153. Dress: casual. Reservations not accepted. AE, MC, V. Closed Christmas Day.*

Continental
Very Expensive ★ **The Lamplighter.** You don't have to go abroad to find gourmet cuisine served in an elegant setting. Just step into the softly lit, sophisticated atmosphere of The Lamplighter, located in an old Dilworth home. The trio combination entrées (beef, veal, and lamb, or different seafoods) are exceptional, and the wine list is extensive. Diners enjoy beginning and ending their evening with cocktails in the quiet, intimate lounge. *1065 E. Morehead St., tel. 704/372–5343. Reservations advised. Jackets suggested. AE, DC, MC, V.*

Moderate **Pewter Rose Bistro.** Housed in the second-floor loft of a renovated textile mill in historic Dilworth, just a five-minute drive from Uptown, the Pewter Rose Bistro is a favorite hangout for Charlotte's young professionals. Subtly offbeat in decor, the Pewter Rose specializes in fresh seasonal foods. The menu features a variety of chicken and seafood dishes. Especially popular is the fettuccine with cognac dill cream sauce and optional smoked salmon and caviar. The bar is pleasant and roomy, filled with comfy sofas and chairs to make the wait enjoyable. *1820 South Blvd., tel. 704/332–8149. Dress: informal. Reservations not accepted. AE, MC, V. Closed Sun., Mon.*

Prisms Restaurant and the Bistro. Distinguished by its massive glass windows, this new Charlotte restaurant gets rave reviews from the Uptown crowd for its varied lunch and dinner menus. The wild mushroom fettuccini is delectable. There's entertainment on Friday and Saturday evenings and brunch on Sunday. Diners park free in the parking garage. *2 First Union Center, tel. 704/335–9918. Reservations accepted. Dress: informal. AE, MC, V.*

Italian
Very Expensive

Villa Antonio. Violin music, waiters with accents from around the world, the intimate candlelight setting, and the personalized welcome by owners Antonio and Charlene Garcia make this upscale restaurant a favorite dinner spot, especially among the international community. The most requested dishes are osso bucco in a Grand Marnier sauce, *cioppino* (containing a variety of seafoods), and homemade *foccaccio* (a crackerlike bread). Live music is offered on Friday and Saturday evenings. *4707 South Blvd., tel. 704/523–1594. Reservations suggested. Dress: informal. AE, DC, MC, V.*

Inexpensive–Moderate

PizZarrelli Trattoria. The secret to the unique flavor of the made-from-scratch pizzas is in the two wood-burning brick ovens, built by Italian masons in the Old World style. The menu also features calzone, lasagna, spaghetti, and other Southern Italian dishes—all family recipes and especially good when served with the mellow house wine. The tables are covered with red-checked gingham, and the walls are adorned with posters and photographs that chronicle the professional singing career of owner Neal Zarrelli, a former opera star who often sings for his customers. *9101 Pineville-Matthews Rd., Pineville, tel. 704/543–0647. Dress: casual. Reservations not required. No credit cards.*

Japanese
Moderate–Expensive

Kabuto Japanese House of Steaks. The chef's preparation and cooking of food tableside is all the entertainment you need at this ethnic restaurant. Fish, chicken, and steak are prepared along with fresh vegetables. Sushi and sashimi are also available. *77 Tyvola Pl., tel. 704/529–0659; in Town Center Plaza, U.S. 49 near UNC–Charlotte, tel. 704/548–1219. Dress: informal. Reservations suggested. AE, D, DC, MC, V. Closed major holidays.*

Lodging

Approximately 16,000 hotels rooms are available in the Charlotte area. You can choose from economy motels, convention hotels, or bed-and-breakfast houses. Most of the major chains are represented, including Hilton, Hyatt, Marriott, Omni, Sheraton, and Wyndham, as are less expensive options—EconoLodge, Comfort Inn, Days Inn, La Quinta, Luxbury, Motel 6, Hampton, Sterling Inn, and Red Roof Inn. Mid-priced motel chains include Holiday Inn, Howard Johnson, Ramada Inn, and Quality Inn. Some hotels offer great weekend packages. A 6% accommodations tax and 6% sales tax are added to every room charge. Pick up the "Charlotte Visitors Guide" for a more comprehensive list.

Category	Cost*
Very Expensive	over $100
Expensive	$60–$100
Moderate	$30–$60
Inexpensive	under $30

**double room; add 12% for taxes*

Hotels
Expensive

Charlotte Marriott City Center. This high-rise hotel sits in the middle of The Square in Uptown Charlotte. An atrium links the hotel with shops and offices. The lobby is dazzling but not imposing. Guests enjoy the casual atmosphere of Sweetbay, which serves great hamburgers. Nightlife is centered in Chatfield's lounge. The **Charlotte Marriott Executive Park** on I–77 south (300 rooms) is a comparable option. Other Marriott properties in the city include **Fairfield Inn** on I–85, **Residence Inn** on U.S. 29, and **Courtyard** on Park Road. *100 W. Trade St., 28202, tel. 704/333–9000 or 800/228–9290. 431 rooms and suites. Facilities: indoor pool, whirlpool, sauna, health club, meeting rooms, airport shuttle. AE, DC, MC, V.*

Dunhill. Charlotte's oldest and most historic hotel (built in 1929) features artwork by Philip Moose and 18th- and 19th-century reproduction furniture in the lobby, restaurant, and guest rooms. Guests enjoy being transported to and from the airport and around town in a standard limousine or a 1985-Sterling taxicab from London, though the hotel is within walking distance of Uptown attractions. The restaurant, **Monticello's,** gets rave reviews for its beautifully presented California cuisine. A complimentary Continental breakfast is served here as well. *237 N. Tryon St., 28202, tel. 704/332–4141. 59 rooms and 1 penthouse with Jacuzzi. Facilities: restaurant, lounge. AE, D, DC, MC, V.*

Embassy Suites. An eight-story atrium distinguishes this all-suite hotel, located near the airport and the Coliseum. Guests have the option of regular suites (which feature two rooms, plus a coffee maker, refrigerator, microwave, and regular amenities) or 12 upgraded suites, four of which have Jacuzzis. Guests are served a cooked-to-order full breakfast and are treated to an afternoon reception. *4800 S. Tryon St., 28217, tel. 704/527–8400 or 800/EMBASSY. 274 suites. Facilities: indoor pool, whirlpool, sauna, health club, restaurant, lounge, meeting rooms, airport transportation. AE, DC, MC, V.*

Hilton at University Place. The hotel dominates the European-style shopping and entertainment village near the University of North Carolina at Charlotte. Movies, restaurants, shops, a bank, and even a hospital are just a few steps from the hotel door. The interior of this high-rise features a three-story atrium. Dining is offered in Justin's, overlooking the adjacent lake. There is a happy hour buffet at the Lakeside Lounge. The 11th and 12th floors offer a number of special amenities, including concierge services, complimentary breakfast, evening hors d'oeuvres, and cocktails. *8629 J.M. Keynes Blvd., 28262, tel. 704/547–7444 or 800/HILTONS. 243 rooms and suites. Facilities: fitness center, outdoor lap pool, meeting rooms, airport transportation. AE, DC, MC, V.*

Hyatt Charlotte Hotel. The focal point of the four-story atrium is a Mexican-imported water fountain surrounded by 25-foot olive trees. Meeting rooms and the lower lobby open onto the open-air courtyard. Scalini's restaurant features Northern Italian cuisine. The Club piano bar is a favorite with the after-hours crowd. Guest rooms are equipped with data ports for laptop computers and fax machines. *5501 Carnegie Blvd., 28209-3462, tel. 704/554-1234 or 800/233-1234. 267 rooms and suites. Facilities: indoor pool, Jacuzzi, health club, meeting rooms, airport transportation. AE, MC, V.*

Omni Charlotte Hotel. The pink marble used in the public rooms makes this one of Charlotte's classiest Uptown hotels. Guests can enjoy the ambience of C. Banknight's Bistro and Bar and then work out with Charlotte's movers and shakers in the adjoining 50,000-square-foot YMCA, which includes an indoor track and a lap pool. For special pampering, stay on the Club levels (21 and 22) or in the Presidential Suite. *222 E. 3rd St. 28202, tel. 704/377-6664 or 800/843-6664. 410 rooms. Facilities: indoor pool, health club, meeting rooms, airport transportation. AE, DC, MC, V.*

Radisson Plaza Hotel Charlotte. Having just completed an extensive renovation, this 15-story hotel is a first-class property offering convenience and contemporary elegance. If you join the Radisson Hospitality Club, you get a complimentary breakfast, happy hour drinks, unlimited local calls, and reduced car rental. All guests enjoy complimentary newspapers and free parking. *2 NCNB Plaza, 28280, tel. 704/377-0400 or 800/333-3333. 368 rooms and suites. Facilities: restaurant, bar, outdoor pool, health club, meeting rooms, airport transportation. AE, DC, MC, V.*

Moderate–Expensive

Adam's Mark Hotel. This is one of the best places in town to have a meeting. Rooms on the west side, overlooking Marshall Park, afford great views of the Charlotte skyline. There's a one-mile fitness trail in the park nearby. Guests enjoy dining in Bravo!, an Italian restaurant featuring professional singers who double as waiters and waitresses, which is one of the city's favorite gathering spots. The classic Continental cuisine includes a variety of entrées including veal scallopine and seafood pasta. The high-energy disco atmosphere of C. J.'s attracts a large following. *555 S. McDowell St., 28204, tel. 704/372-4100 or 800/444-ADAM. 600 rooms and suites. Facilities: indoor and outdoor pools, Nautilus-equipped health club, whirlpool, sauna, racquetball courts, meeting rooms, airport transportation. AE, DC, MC, V.*

Bed-and-breakfasts

Moderate–Expensive

The Inn on Providence. Darlene and Dan MacNeill offer five luxurious bedrooms, each with private bath, plus a home-cooked breakfast. Guests enjoy the spacious grounds and swimming pool in this quiet southeast Charlotte neighborhood. *6700 Providence Rd., 28226, tel. 704/366-6700. 5 rooms. MC, V.*

Moderate

The Homeplace. This spotless turn-of-the-century Victorian gem is now a bed-and-breakfast inn filled with antiques and memorabilia from yesteryear. The inn offers four guest rooms, each with a private bath, and breakfast prepared by owners Peggy and Frank Darien. The Homeplace is located in a country/suburban neighborhood. *5901 Sardis Rd., 28226, tel. 704/365-1936. 3 rooms. AE, MC, V.*

Nightlife

Bailey's Billiard and Bar (5873 Albemarle Rd., tel. 704/532–1005 and 8500 Pineville-Matthews Rd., tel. 704/541–0794) offers billiards in an upscale setting and deli-style food.

Murder/Comedy Theater (1000 S. Kings Dr., tel. 704/358–1100) combines dinner with musical-comedy murder mysteries. Guests are the actors.

Comedy Zone (5624 Westpark Dr., tel. 704/527–8000; and 5317 E. Independence Blvd., tel. 704/568–4242). Choose one of two locations for an evening of laughs.

Giorgio's Northern Italian Ristorante & Piano Bar (5301 E. Independence Blvd., tel. 704/535–7525) is a great place to get together with friends.

Lizzie's (4809 S. Tryon St., tel. 704/527–3064), a restaurant on the south side, is best known for its piano bar, featuring owner Liz King, and swing dance music.

Plum Crazy (I–77 and Tyvola Rd., tel. 704/525–4386) is a popular spot for the young set.

Raleigh

Including Durham and Chapel Hill

Raleigh had much to celebrate during its 200th anniversary in 1992, with new office towers and renovated buildings in the downtown area, and the addition of a new aquatic center in Pullen Park, a new amphitheater in Walnut Creek Park, a new facility for the North Carolina Museum of History, and several shopping malls.

The cosmopolitan flavor of today's Raleigh is evidenced by the international traffic of American Airlines, which operates a major hub at the Raleigh-Durham International Airport, offers service to Paris, Cancun, Bermuda, Puerto Rico, Nassau, and the U.S. Virgin Islands.

There's a vibrance in this overgrown college town and capital city that's unique in the state. The Duke, NC State, and UNC (Carolina) basketball teams have all become Atlantic Coast Conference (ACC) champions in recent seasons, and Duke won the NCAA title in 1991. Scientific breakthroughs are commonplace at Research Triangle Park in Durham, as is important medical research at local universities. People, however, still get as excited over barbecue as they do about politics. The City of Oaks, so called because of its profusion of oak trees, is small town and big town, Old South and New South, down-home and urbane, all in one.

Arriving and Departing

By Plane
Airports and Airlines

Raleigh is served by the Raleigh–Durham International Airport (RDU, tel. 919/840–2123), located between the two cities near the Research Triangle Park, off I–40. **American, Delta, TWA, United,** and **USAir** together offer approximately 250 daily flights. **American Eagle, Command, United Express, USAir Express,** and **WRA Airlines** provide regional commuter service.

Between the Airport and Downtown Since airport bus service is not available, the best way to get downtown is by taxi or limousine. Taxis cost $15–$18; limousine service is about half that price.

By Car. From the airport, take I–40 east to Exit 285. Then follow Wade Avenue east and turn right on Downtown Boulevard, which leads into the heart of the city. The drive takes about 20 minutes.

By Train **Amtrak** (320 W. Cabarrus St., tel. 919/833–7594 or 800/872–7245) connects Raleigh with Washington, DC, and New York to the north and with Florida to the south. There are two daily trains, one northbound and one southbound. Service to Charlotte is also offered daily.

By Bus **Carolina Trailways/Greyhound Bus Lines** (321 W. Jones St., tel. 919/828–2567 or 800/528–0447).

By Trolley The **Trolley Through Raleigh** makes six stops around the city, including the Amtrak office (by advance reservation), City Market, and the Capital Area Visitor Center. On third Saturday of each month, between noon and 4, a historic tour of Raleigh is given. *Tel. 919/834–4844. Trolley runs weekdays, 11–2. Fare: 10¢. Tour admission: $1.*

By Car I–40 and U.S. 401 form something of a perimeter route around the city. I–40 runs west of downtown, joining I–85 on the west side and I–95 on the east side. U.S. 1, which runs north and south, also links to I–85 going northeast. U.S. 64 and U.S. 70 run east and west through Raleigh.

Getting Around

By Bus **Capital Area Transit** (919/833–5701) is Raleigh's public transport system. Fares are 75¢ for adults, 30¢ for senior citizens, and 60¢ for adults between 9 AM and 3:30 PM. Children under 4 ride free.

By Taxi Approximately 16 taxi companies serve the Raleigh area. Fares are calculated by the mile.

Important Addresses and Numbers

Tourist Information **The Raleigh Convention and Visitors Bureau** offers information on the area. *225 Hillsborough St., Suite 400, tel. 919/834–5900 or 800/868–6666.*

The **Raleigh Visitor Information Center** is operated by the Greater Raleigh Chamber of Commerce, *800 S. Salisbury St., tel. 919/833–4636. Open weekdays 8:30–5. Free parking.*

Capital Area Visitor Center offers information about tours through state government buildings. *301 N. Blount St., tel. 919/733–3456. Open weekdays 8–5, Sat. 9–5, Sun. 1–5.*

The City of Raleigh Arts Commission gives information on arts events (tel. 919/831–6789).

The **Durham Convention & Visitors Bureau** provides information on that city and country. *101 E. Morgan St., Durham 27701, tel. 919/688–BULL or 800/772–BULL.*

Emergencies Dial 911 for **police** or **ambulance** in an emergency.

Doctor Hospital emergency rooms are open 24 hours a day. For minor emergencies, the city has 10 urgent-care centers. If you are in need of a local doctor, call the **Wake County Medical Society** (tel. 919/821–2227) for a referral.

Pharmacy **Eckerd Drugs** (3427 Hillsborough Rd., Durham, tel. 919/383–5591).

Guided Tours

Capital Area Visitor Center provides free tours of the executive mansion, state capitol, legislative building, and other government buildings. *Tel. 919/733–3456. Open weekdays 8–5, Sat. 9–5, Sun. 1–5.*

Executive Guest Tours & Services (tel. 919/839–5805), **Tailored Services, Inc.** (tel. 919/787–5180), and **Tours and Functions** (tel. 919/782–8145) offer customized tours for groups in Raleigh and the surrounding area.

Exploring Raleigh

Raleigh is spread out, so a car is almost a necessity unless you limit your sightseeing to downtown. The city offers plenty of parking, including public lots at the corner of Edenton and Wilmington streets and in the 400 block of N. Salisbury Street (50¢ cents per hour or $4 per day). There's also a big parking garage at the Raleigh Civic and Convention Center. Watch for one-way streets when driving. Getting around Raleigh without a map is often difficult, but the streets in the downtown area are laid out in an orderly grid fashion with the State Capitol as the hub (a good landmark).

Most of the attractions in the downtown Raleigh walking tour are state government and historical buildings and are free to the public. You'll need several hours just to hit the high spots, even more time if you tend to get hooked on museums.

State Capitol Walking Tour After stopping in at the **Capital Area Visitor Center** to pick up maps and brochures, begin your tour at the **State Capitol,** which occupies the block facing Fayetteville Street Mall in the center of downtown between Wilmington and Salisbury streets. Finished in 1840 and restored during the 1976 Bicentennial, it exudes a special warmth not found in the more contemporary 1960s State Legislative Building. The old building that once housed all the functions of state government could tell many tales if its walls could talk. *Capitol Sq., tel. 919/733–4994. Open weekdays 8–5, Sat. 9–5, Sun. 1–5. Closed certain holidays.*

The **State Legislative Building,** on the corner of Salisbury and Jones streets, sits one block north of the capitol. When the legislature is in session, the building hums with lawmakers and lobbyists. *Salisbury and Jones Sts., tel. 919/733–7928. Open weekdays 8–5, Sat. 9–5, Sun. 1–5.*

A half block away is the **North Carolina Museum of Natural Sciences,** a favorite hangout for children, who love its resident snakes and animal exhibits. The gift shop offers some unusual souvenirs. *102 N. Salisbury St., tel. 919/733–7450. Open Mon.–Sat. 9–5, Sun. 1–5.*

Now step back in time at the **North Carolina Museum of History.** Here you'll see exhibits on period costumes, guns, and on many other subjects that chronicle the state's 400-plus years of history. The gift shop is worth a look. *109 E. Jones St., tel. 919/733-3894. Open Tues.–Sat. 9–5, Sun. 1–6.*

The **Executive Mansion** (200 N. Blount St., tel. 919/733-3456), a brick turn-of-the-century Queen Anne cottage-style structure with gingerbread trim, is home to the governor. Tour hours vary; check with the Capital Area Visitor Center. A stroll through the nearby **Oakwood Historic District** will introduce you to more fine examples of Victorian architecture.

The revitalized **City Market** (Martin St. and Moore Sq.) is home to specialty shops, art galleries, and restaurants. Trolleys shuttle between downtown and the market at lunchtime; the fare is only 10¢. *Tel. 919/828-4555. Stores open Mon.–Sat. 10–5:30; restaurants, Mon.–Sat. 7 AM–1 AM and Sun. 11:30–10.*

Fayetteville Street Mall extends from the State Capitol to the Raleigh Civic and Convention Center. Open to pedestrians only, it offers a chance to get in touch with the city at an easy pace. In the middle of the mall is a bronze statue of Sir Walter Raleigh, who started the first colony in North Carolina and for whom the city is named.

The **North Carolina Museum of Art** can be reached by driving west on Hillsborough Street to Blue Ridge Boulevard. The museum exhibits art from ancient Egyptian times to the present. The **Museum Cafe** is open for lunch Tuesday–Sunday, for dessert and tea Friday–Sunday, and for dinner on Friday. *2110 Blue Ridge Blvd., tel. 919/833-1935 (restaurant tel. 919/833-3548). Free guided tours daily at 1:30 PM. Open Tues.–Thurs. and Sat. 9–5, Fri. 9–9, and Sun. 12–5.*

What to See and Do with Children

Pullen Park (520 Ashe Ave., near NCSU, tel. 919/831-6468 or 919/831-6640) attracts large crowds during the summer to its 1911 Dentzel carousel and train ride. You can swim here, too, and enjoy an arts and crafts center and the Theater in the Park. A new aquatic center will open in 1992.

At the **North Carolina Museum of Life and Science** (433 Murray Ave., off I-85 in Durham, tel. 919/220-5429) visitors encounter life-size models of dinosaurs on the nature trail and get to ride a train through the 40-acre wildlife sanctuary. The hands-on museum is an animal habitat that features native North Carolina animals. The aerospace exhibit is also outstanding, as is Bodytech, an interactive exhibit.

Off the Beaten Track

Bennett Place. On this spot in Durham in April 1865, Confederate General Joseph E. Johnston disobeyed President Jefferson Davis's order to retreat and instead surrendered to U.S. General William T. Sherman. The two then set forth the terms for a "permanent peace" between the South and the North. Historic reenactments are held annually. *4409 Bennett Memorial Rd., Durham 27705, tel. 919/383-4345. Admission free. Open Apr.–Oct., Mon.–Sat. 9–5, Sun. 1–5; Nov., Tues.–Sat. 10–4, Sun. 1–4.*

North Carolina Central University Art Museum. African-American art is showcased here. *1801 Fayetteville St., Durham*

27705, tel. 919/683-6211. Admission free. Open Tues.-Fri. 9-5, Sun. 2-5.

Shopping

Shopping Districts Because so many stores have moved to the suburbs, downtown shopping isn't what it used to be, and the stores that remain now close by 5 or 6 in the evening. The best of the suburban malls:

Cameron Village Shopping Center (1900 Cameron St.), Raleigh's oldest shopping center and one of the first in the Southeast, is anchored by JC Penney and Thalhimers and contains a Talbot's and Fresh Market.

Crabtree Valley Mall (Glenwood Ave.; U.S. 70) is the city's largest enclosed mall, with over a million square feet of retail space and more planned for the future. Stores include Belk, Sears, and Thalhimers.

North Hills Mall (Six Forks Rd. and Beltline) offers the latest in high fashion. Stores include Montaldo's, Tyler House, and Dillard's.

Brightleaf Square (905 W. Main St., Durham) is an upscale shopping-entertainment complex housed in old tobacco warehouses in the heart of downtown. Shoppers enjoy relaxing at Taverna Nikos, a Greek restaurant.

Specialty Stores
Art/Antiques **City Market** (311 Blake St., tel. 919/828-4555). Look for antiques and art in this revitalized shopping area.

Flea Markets **North Carolina State Flea Market.** You can find anything and everything here—from fine antiques to "early attic" furniture. *Hillsborough St. and Blue Ridge Rd., tel. 919/832-0361. Open weekends 9-5.*

Another option is the **Raleigh Flea Market Mall.** *1924 Capital Blvd., tel. 919/839-0038. Open weekends 9-6.*

Food **Farmer's Market.** This $4 million market, which opened in 1991, replaces an old Raleigh institution. The 60-acre site includes a garden center and restaurant. *Lake Wheeler Rd. and I-40, tel. 919/733-7417 (market) or 919/833-7973 (restaurant). Open 24 hrs, June-Sept.; 5 AM-6 PM, Mon.-Sat., Oct.-May.*

Participant Sports

Bicycling The city has designated 20 miles of greenways for biking, and maps are available at Raleigh Parks and Recreation (tel. 919/890-3285).

Camping Try the North Carolina State Fairgrounds, William B. Umstead State Park, Eno River State Park at Durham, Clemmons State Forest near Clayton, or Jordan Lake between Apex and Pittsboro. Other options are Lake Gaston and Kerr Lake near the Virginia line. *For details, call the Raleigh Convention and Visitors Bureau, tel. 919/834-5900, or the North Carolina Division of Travel and Tourism, tel. 919/733-4171 or 800/VISIT-NC.*

Canoeing Lake Wheeler and Shelley Lake are the best places for canoeing. The Eno River State Park near Durham is another option. The Haw River is popular as well, but can be treacherous after a heavy rain.

Fishing Fishing licenses may be purchased at local bait-and-tackle shops. Call the North Carolina Division of Boating and Inland Fishing (tel. 919/733-3633) for more information.

Golf The Raleigh area has about 10 golf courses open to the public, including **Wildwood Green Golf Club** and **Wake Forest Country Club.** A complete list of courses is available from the Raleigh Convention and Visitors Bureau (tel. 919/834-5900). Pinehurst-Southern Pines, the Golf Capital of the World, offering more than 35 courses, is only a short drive away.

Hiking Jordan Lake, Lake Wheeler, William B. Umstead State Park, and Duke Forest in Durham offer thousands of acres for hiking. For trail information, call the North Carolina Division of Travel and Tourism (tel. 919/733-4171 or 800/VISIT-NC).

Jogging Runners enjoy Shelley Lake, the track at NCSU, and the Capitol Area Greenway system, which is partially completed.

Physical Fitness The YMCA (1601 Hillsborough St., tel. 919/832-6601) will permit visitors to use their facilities for $3-$10, provided they have a YMCA membership elsewhere. The Y also accepts guests staying at certain local hotels. Hotels with fitness centers are noted in the accommodations listings.

River Rafting The Haw River is the closest place for shooting the rapids.

Skiing (*See* the North Carolina High Country and Asheville sections.)

Tennis More than 80 courts in city parks are available for use. Millbrook Exchange Park (1905 Spring Forest Rd.) holds city tournaments. (For more details on tennis courts in Raleigh, call 919/876-2616.)

Spectator Sports

Baseball The Durham Bulls play at the Durham Athletic Park (426 Morris St., Durham, tel. 919/688-8211).

Basketball The Triangle (Raleigh, Durham, and Chapel Hill) is basketball heaven with teams such as UNC-Chapel Hill, Duke, NC State, and NC Central University to cheer to victory. For information on Raleigh's favorite team—NCSU—contact the university ticket office (tel. 919/515-2106).

Tennis The Raleigh Edge professional tennis team plays in the Raleigh Civic & Convention Center (tel. 919/878-7788).

Dining

Dining in the Raleigh area is both sophisticated and down-home. There are many upscale restaurants, as well as informal places where barbecue, Brunswick stew, fried chicken, and lots of country vegetables are served in great quantities for very low prices.

Category	Cost*
Very Expensive	over $25
Expensive	$15-$25

Moderate	\$8–\$15
Inexpensive	under \$8

**per person without tax (6%), service, or drinks*

Expensive

Angus Barn, Ltd. This Raleigh tradition is housed in a huge rustic barn. Gingham- and denim-clad waiters and waitresses add authenticity to the farmlike scene. The astonishing wine and beer list covers 35 pages of the menu. The restaurant serves the best steaks, baby back ribs, and prime rib for miles around. Desserts are heavenly. Take-home products are sold in the Country Store. *U.S. 70W at Airport Rd., tel. 919/781–2444. Dress: informal. Reservations recommended. Sat.—first come, first served. AE, DC, MC, V.*

42nd St. Oyster Bar. This much talked-about restaurant is the place to see and be seen in Raleigh. Politicians, businessmen, and laborers sit side by side downing succulent oysters and other seafood dishes. *West and Jones Sts., tel. 919/831–2811. Dress: casual. Reservations not necessary. AE, DC, MC, V.*

Moderate

Bo's Cafe America–The Restaurant at Artspace. Located in the City Market, this upscale eatery is the "in" spot for lunch and dinner. Favorite menu selections include baked fish Bayou Teche, white fish stuffed with crabmeat, shrimp, spinach, and mushrooms, and the seafood pasta San Francisco, whose ingredients vary daily. Live jazz is performed on Friday and Saturday evenings. *329 S. Blount St., tel. 919/821–2662. Reservations recommended. Dress: informal. AE, DC, MC, V. Closed Sun. except Mother's Day.*

Bullock's Bar-B-Cue (Durham). If you want to experience local cuisine, try the Brunswick stew, barbecue, southern fried chicken, and hush puppies at this casual eatery that offers eat-in or carry-out service. *3330 Wortham St., tel. 919/383–3211. First-come, first-served (come early). No credit cards. Closed Sun.*

Est Est Est Trattoria. The best place in town for authentic northern Italian pasta. *19 W. Hargett St., tel. 919/832–8899. Dress: informal. Reservations not required. Closed Sun. MC, V.*

Inexpensive

Big Ed's City Market Restaurant. A must for breakfast, this Raleigh favorite in the City Market features three home-cooked meals. *220 Wolf St., tel. 919/836–9909. Reservations not required. Dress: casual. No credit cards. Closed Sun.*

Irregardless Cafe. This eatery is a delight to vegetarians and weight-conscious eaters. *901 W. Morgan St., tel. 919/833–8898. Dress: casual. Reservations not required. Sat. dinner only. Sun. brunch. MC, V.*

Lodging

Raleigh offers lodgings in all price ranges—from convention hotels to bed-and-breakfast houses to economy chains. Major hotel chains represented here are Holiday Inn, Hilton, Radisson, Marriott, Embassy Suites, and Sheraton. Inexpensive lodging is offered by Comfort Inn, EconoLodge, Crickett Inn, Days Inn, and Hampton Inn. Since Raleigh is a business town, many hotels and motels advertise special weekend rates.

You've Let Your Imagination Go, Now Get Up And Follow Your Dreams.

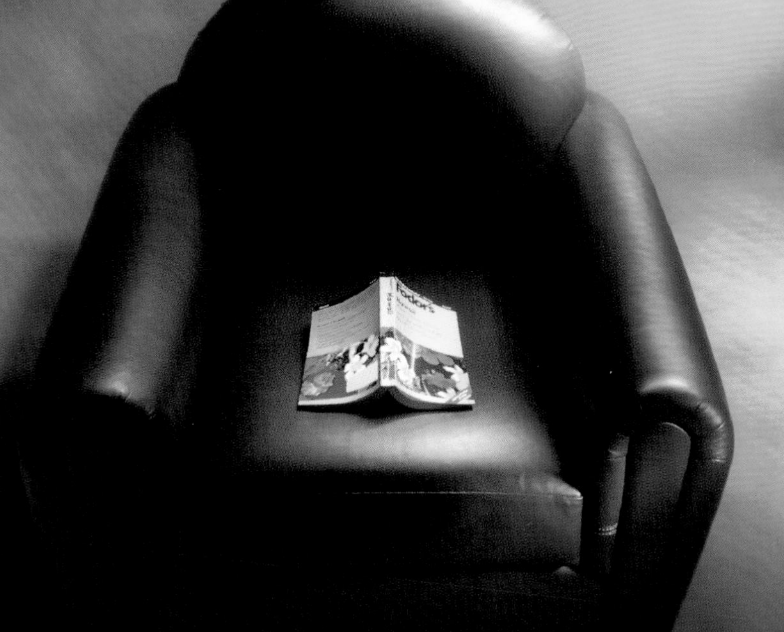

For The Vacation You're Dreaming Of, Call American Express® Travel Agency At 1-800-YES-AMEX.*

American Express will send more than your imagination soaring. We'll fly you, sail you, drive you to any Fodor's destination and beyond. Because American Express believes the best vacations happen from Europe to the Orient, Walt Disney® World to Hawaii and everywhere in between.

For dependable service, expert advice, and value wherever your dreams take you, call on American Express. After all, the best traveling companion is a trustworthy friend.

©1992 American Express Travel Related Services, Inc. All rights reserved.
*Calls from the continental United States only. All others please see your nearest American Express Travel Service Office.

It's easy to recognize a good place when you see one.

American Express Cardmembers have been doing it for years.

The secret? Instead of just relying on what they see in the window, they look at the door. If there's an American Express Blue Box on it, they know they've found an establishment that cares about high standards.

Whether it's a place to eat, to sleep, to shop, or simply meet, they know they will be warmly welcomed.

So much so, they're rarely taken in by anything else.

Always a good sign.

Category	Cost*
Very Expensive	over $100
Expensive	$60–$100
Moderate	$30–$60
Inexpensive	under $30

**double room; add 8% for taxes*

Very Expensive

Fearrington House (Chapel Hill). This French-style country inn is a member of Relais & Chateaux. It features a restaurant that serves regional food prepared in a classic manner. *8 mi south of Chapel Hill on US 15–501 (postal address: Fearrington Village Center, Pittsboro 27312), tel. 919/542–2121 or 800/334–5475. 14 rooms. MC, V.*

Expensive

North Raleigh Hilton and Convention Center. This is a favorite capital city spot for corporate meetings. The Tower Suites offer a complimentary Continental breakfast, free hors d'oeuvres, concierge, newspapers, and light secretarial service. Guests enjoy dining in Lofton's restaurant and listening to the piano afterward in the lobby bar. Bowties is one of the city's hottest nightspots. *3415 Wake Forest Rd., 27609, tel. 919/872–2323. 337 rooms and suites. Facilities: indoor pool, health club, complimentary airport shuttle, meeting rooms. AE, DC, MC, V.*

Oakwood Inn. Located in Historic Oakwood, one of the city's oldest downtown neighborhoods, this is an alternative to hotel/motel living. Built in 1871 and now on the National Register of Historic Places, the inn is furnished with Victorian period pieces. Guests are served a sumptuous breakfast and assisted with dinner reservations and evening entertainment plans. *411 N. Bloodworth St., 27604, tel. 919/832–9712. 6 rooms with bath. AE, MC, V.*

Radisson Plaza Hotel Raleigh. This is an architecturally exciting hotel in the heart of downtown, with brick walls and arches, cascading fountains, and an expansive atrium. The hotel is connected to the civic center via a plaza. The hotel offers the Provence Restaurant, Cafe Promenade, and the Goodies-To-Go deli. *420 Fayetteville St. Mall, 27601, tel. 919/834–9900 or 800/333–3333. 362 rooms and suites. Facilities: indoor pool, whirlpool, free parking, meeting rooms, airport shuttle. AE, DC, MC, V.*

Raleigh Marriott Crabtree Valley. This is one of the city's most luxurious hotels. Fresh floral arrangements adorn the elegantly decorated public rooms. Guests enjoy the intimacy of the Scotch Bonnets restaurant, the family atmosphere of Allie's, and Champions Sports Bar. The concierge floor offers complimentary Continental breakfast and hors d'oeuvres. *4500 Marriott Dr. (U.S. 70W near Crabtree Valley Mall) 27612, tel. 919/781–7000 or 800/228–9290. 375 rooms and suites. Facilities: indoor/outdoor pool, whirlpool, exercise room, game room, golf and racquetball nearby, complimentary airport shuttle. AE, DC, MC, V.*

Velvet Cloak Inn. This hotel is in a class of its own. Curtis, the doorman who dresses to the nines in a tux and top hat, has been greeting guests here for years. Local brides have wedding receptions around the enclosed pool, and politicians frequent the bar at Baron's Restaurant and Nightclub. The Charter Room, an elegant restaurant, often features live entertainment. Afternoon tea and cookies are served in the lobby. Rooms in the brick structure, decorated with delicate wrought iron, are frequently refurbished. *1505 Hillsborough St., 27605, tel. 919/828–0333; 800/334–4372; in NC, 800/662–8829. 172 rooms and suites. Facilities: 2 restaurants, enclosed pool and tropical garden, complimentary coffee and newspaper in the lobby, guest privileges at the YMCA next door, airport shuttle, meeting rooms. AE, DC, MC, V.*

Washington Duke Hotel & Golf Club (Durham). Located on the campus of Duke University, this luxurious inn overlooks the Robert Trent Jones golf course. On display in the public rooms are memorabilia belonging to the Duke family for whom the hotel and university are named. The bar is called the Bull Durham. *3001 Cameron Blvd., Durham 27706, tel. 919/490–0999. 171 rooms. Facilities: outdoor pool, jogging trails, restaurant, bar, golf course. AE, DC, MC, V.*

Moderate

Arrowhead Inn. This bed-and-breakfast inn, located a few miles outside Durham, offers alternative lodging in a homelike setting. Guests are served a hearty breakfast. *106 Mason Rd., Durham, 27712, tel. 919/477–8430. 6 rooms, some with private baths. Closed Christmas week. AE, MC, V.*

Quality Suites Hotel. Minutes from downtown, this hotel features luxurious two-room suites that are equipped with VCRs, cassette stereos, microwaves, wet bars, and refrigerators. The manager's evening reception and the cooked-to-order breakfast are included in the tariff. *4400 Capital Blvd., 27604, tel. 919/876–2211 or 800/228–5151. 114 suites. Facilities: restaurant, outdoor pool, health club, meeting rooms, complimentary airport shuttle. AE, DC, MC, V.*

Ramada Inn Crabtree. This hotel gets the award for being the friendliest motel in town. It's also where football and basketball teams like to stay when they're here for a game, as evidenced by the helmet collection and other sports memorabilia in the Brass Bell Lounge. The Colonnade Restaurant is known for its Sunday buffets. *3920 Arrow Dr. (U.S. 70 and Beltline), 27612, tel. 919/782–7525 or 800/2–RAMADA. 177 rooms and suites. Facilities: restaurant, lounge, outdoor pool, jogging trail, meeting rooms, airport shuttle. AE, DC, MC, V.*

Inexpensive

Hampton Inn. This budget motel offers inexpensive rates without sacrificing quality. A Continental breakfast, local calls, and in-room movies are available at no extra charge. *1001 Wake Towne Dr., 27609, tel. 919/828–1813 or 800/426–7866, 131 rooms. Facilities: outdoor pool and meeting rooms. AE, DC, MC, V.*

Nightlife

Much of the nightlife is centered in the larger hotels, such as the Hilton or the Marriott. **Charlie Goodnight's Comedy Club** (861 W. Morgan St., tel. 919/833–8356) combines dinner with a night of laughs. Another option is **Comedy Sportz** (329 Blake St., City Market, tel. 919/872–4764).

Winston-Salem

The manufacture of cigarettes, textiles, furniture, and other products has built a solid economic base in the Winston-Salem area. There's also a healthy respect for the arts here, and the North Carolina School of the Arts commands international attention. The Crosby golf tournament, formerly played at Pebble Beach, California, attracts the rich and famous. Old Salem, a restored 18th-century Moravian town within the city of Winston-Salem, has been drawing tourists since the early 1950s.

Arriving and Departing

By Plane Five major airlines serve the Piedmont Triad International Airport (tel. 919/665–5666): **American, Delta, Continental, United,** and **USAir.**

By Bus Contact **Greyhound/Trailways** (tel. 919/725–5692).

By Train **Amtrak** serves Greensboro (tel. 919/855–3382), about 25 miles away.

Getting Around

By Trolley Trolleys run between the Winston-Salem Visitor Center and Old Salem, weekdays 9:40–5:30. *Fare: 25¢.*

Important Addresses and Numbers

Tourist Information **Winston-Salem Convention & Visitors Bureau** (Box 1408, Winston-Salem 27102, tel. 919/725–2361 or 800/331–7018). A visitors reception center is located in the City Market (601 N. Cherry St., Suite 100, tel. 919/777–3796).

Emergencies Dial 911 for **police** and **ambulance** in an emergency.

Guided Tours

Contact **Carolina Treasures and Tours** (1001 S. Marshall St., Suite 117, Winston-Salem 27101, tel. 919/631–9144) or **Margaret Glenn Tours** (Box 1134, Winston-Salem 27116, tel. 919/724–6547).

Exploring Winston-Salem

Begin your tour of the city at the **Winston-Salem Visitor Center,** where you'll see a 12-minute film on the area. *601 N. Cherry St., Suite 100, tel. 919/777–3796. Open daily.*

Old Salem is just a few blocks from downtown Winston-Salem and only a stone's throw from I–40 (take the Old Salem/Salem College exit). The 1700s live again in this village of 60 original brick and wooden structures. The aromas of freshly baked bread, sugar cakes, and ginger snaps mix with those of beeswax candles and newly dyed flax. Tradesmen work in their shops making pewterware, cooking utensils, and other items, while the womenfolk embroider and weave cloth. New to the tour are African-American interpretations at each site. The Moravians, a Protestant sect, fled to Georgia to find religious freedom. From there they went to Bethlehem, Pennsylvania, but finally found the peace they sought in the Piedmont region of North Carolina. In 1753, they built Bethabara, located on Bethabara Road, off University Parkway, and then in 1766 they built Salem. Tour tickets will get you into several restored buildings at Old Salem, but you may wander through the streets free of charge. Old Salem will undergo expansion over the next few years. *600 S. Main St., tel. 919/721-7300. Admission: $10 adults, $5 children ages 6-14; families $25; check into a combination ticket to MESDA. Open Mon.-Sat. 9:30-4:30, Sun. 1:30-4:30.*

Time Out **Winkler Bakery** will satisfy your craving for hot, freshly baked Moravian sugar cake. The bakery is included on tours and is also open to the public. *525 S. Main St., tel. 919/721-7302. Open Mon.-Sat. 9-5, Sun. 1:30-5.*

Another way to step back into time is to enter the **Museum of Early Southern Decorative Arts (MESDA).** Six galleries and 19 rooms are decorated with period furnishings. *924 S. Main St., tel. 919/721-7360. Admission: full tour $5 adults, $3 children, ages 6-14; combination tickets to MESDA and Old Salem: $13 adults, $6 children. Open Mon.-Sat. 10:30-4:30, Sun. 1:30-4:30.*

Stroh Brewery, approximately 5 miles south of downtown via U.S. 52, rolls out 5.5 million barrels of beer a year as the second-largest brewery in the country. A single machine can fill and seal up to 1,500 12-ounce cans of beer per minute. You can see it made and enjoy a complimentary drink. *Schlitz Ave., U.S. 52S at S. Main St., tel. 919/788-6710. Admission free. Open spring-fall, weekdays 11-4:30; winter, noon-3.*

R. J. Reynolds Whitaker Park is one of the world's largest and most modern cigarette manufacturing centers. On the guided tour you see how 8,000 cigarettes are produced every minute. *Reynolds Blvd., tel. 919/741-5718. Admission free. Open weekdays 8-6, 8-8 late May-early Sept.*

Historic **Bethabara Park** is another vision from the 1700s. You can explore the foundations of the town, as well as the three remaining historic structures. Kids love the reconstructed Indian fort. A greenway, extending from Wake Forest University to Reynolda Road is now under construction. *2147 Bethabara Rd., tel. 919/924-8191. Admission free. Open weekdays 9:30-4:30, weekends 1:30-4:30. Guided tours Apr.-Dec. 15 or by appointment. Self-guided walking tour available year-round.*

Reynolda House Museum of American Art, formerly the home of tobacco magnate R. J. Reynolds, reopened in 1992 after an extensive renovation that opened more rooms to the public. *Reynolda Rd., tel. 919/725-5325. Admission: $5 adults, $3 students, $4 senior citizens. Open Tues.-Sat. 9:30-4:30, Sun. 1:30-4:30.*

SECCA (the Southeastern Center for Contemporary Art) is near Reynolda House. This unique museum is the place to see the latest in Southern painting, sculpture, and printmaking. The Tudor-style facility, the former home of the late James G. Hanes, a textile industrialist, is as interesting as the exhibits. *750 Marguerite Dr., tel. 919/725-1904. Admission: $3 adults, $2 students and senior citizens, children under 12 free. Open Tues.-Sat. 10-5, Sun. 2-5.*

Tanglewood Park (Hwy. 158, Clemmons, tel. 919/766–0591), a 10-minute drive west from the city via I–40, is the former home of the late William and Kate Reynolds and today serves as a public park. Visitors enjoy horseback riding, golf, tennis, boating, miniature golf, swimming, camping, and other activities, including PGA golf events and an annual steeplechase.

What to See and Do with Children

Nature Science Center of Winston-Salem. Look at the stars, handle live starfish in the tidal pool, pet the lambs and goats. The museum underwent a $6 million expansion in fall, 1992. *Museum Dr., Winston-Salem, tel. 919/767–6730. Admission: $3.50 adults, $2.50 students and senior citizens, children under 3 free. Open Mon.–Sat. 10–5, Sun. 1–5.*

Shopping

Crafts The *New York Times* called the **Piedmont Craftsmen's Shop and Gallery** a "showcase for Southern crafts." *1204 Reynolda Rd., tel. 919/725–1516. Open Tues.–Sat. 10–6, Sun. 1–5, daily from Thanksgiving through Christmas.*

Outlets This is a textile center, so there are many clothing outlets clustered along the interstates. **Marketplace Mall** (2101 Peters Creek Pkwy., tel. 919/722–7779) and **Hanes Mill/Sara Lee Outlet** (Ricks Dr., tel. 919/744–3306) are good options. The 100 stores in **Burlington Manufacturers Outlet Center** (tel. 919/227–2872) and **Waccamaw Pottery and the Burlington Outlet Mall** (tel. 919/229–0418) make the area off I–85 near Burlington truly the outlet capital of the South. *Most stores are open Mon.–Sat. 10–9, Sun. 1–6.*

Dining

Traditional dining in these parts is Southern—fried chicken, ham, vegetables, biscuits, fruit cobblers, and the like. Chopped or sliced pork barbecue is also a big item. However, there's a growing number of gourmet restaurants.

Category	Cost*
Very Expensive	over $25
Expensive	$15–$25
Moderate	$8–$15
Inexpensive	under $8

**per person without tax (6%), service, or drinks*

Expensive **La Chaudiere.** Elegantly prepared French country dishes of pheasant, rabbit, veal, and other delicacies are served here in a country French atmosphere. Soft white walls, original paintings, and fresh flowers set off this restaurant in Reynolda Village. *120 Reynolda Rd., tel. 919/748–0269. Dress: jacket and tie suggested. Reservations strongly recommended. Closed Mon. AE, DC, MC, V.*

Leon's Cafe. This casual eatery near Old Salem serves some of the best gourmet food in town—fresh seafood, chicken breasts with raspberry sauce, lamb, and other specialties. *825 S. Mar-*

shall, tel. 919/725–9593. Dress: casual. Reservations not accepted. No lunch. Closed Sun.–Mon. and the last two weeks in Aug. MC, V.

Moderate–Expensive

Old Salem Tavern Dining Room. Eat Moravian food in a Moravian setting served by waiters in Moravian costumes, all in the heart of Old Salem. Standard menu items are chicken pie, ragout of beef, and rack of lamb. From April through October you can dine outside under the arbor. *736 S. Main St., tel. 919/748–8585. Dress: casual. Reservations recommended. Sun. brunch. AE, MC, V.*

Moderate

Café Piaf. Inside the Stevens Center, this restored Art Deco performing-arts center offers pretheater dinners (5:30–7), featuring pasta primavera, chicken Piaf, and other French entrées. Dessert and coffee follow performances. *401 W. 4th St., tel. 919/750–0855. Dress: casual. Reservations advised. AE, MC, V.*

Newmarket Grille. Fresh vegetables and meats, plus homemade breads and desserts, make this establishment a winner. The varied menu includes fresh grilled fish, poultry, beef, and pork dishes, as well as some stir-fry items, plus burgers and sandwiches. The bar is a popular gathering spot for the city's movers and shakers. *300 S. Stratford Rd., 27103, tel. 919/724–5220. Dress: casual. Reservations not accepted. AE, DC, MC, V.*

Noble's Grille. New on the dining scene, this upscale French restaurant serves a variety of entrées grilled or roasted over an oak-and-hickory fire, including braised rabbit with black-pepper fettuccine and Carolina poussin with polenta. *380 Knollwood St., tel. 919/777–8477. Dress: jacket and tie suggested. Reservations recommended. AE, MC, V. Closed Sun.*

Lodging

Category	Cost*
Very Expensive	over $100
Expensive	$60–$100
Moderate	$30–$60
Inexpensive	under $30

**double room; add 8% for taxes*

Very Expensive

Marque of Winston-Salem. This downtown property near the convention center and Stevens Center features an atrium and garden terrace, as well as large guest rooms. *300 W. 5th St., 27101, tel. 919/725–1234 or 800/228–9000. 288 rooms. Facilities: indoor pool, Jacuzzi, exercise room; garage parking and airport transportation extra. AE, DC, MC, V.*

Stouffer Winston Plaza. Centrally located off I–40, this hotel has almost 10,000 square feet of meeting space that can be augmented by facilities at the Convention Center across the street. *460 N. Cherry St., 27101, tel. 919/725–1234 or 800/527–2341, fax 919/722–9182. 318 rooms. Facilities: 2 restaurants, bar, indoor/outdoor pool, steam room, sauna, game room, and gift shop. AE, DC, MC, V.*

Moderate–Expensive

Brookstown Inn. Sleep under a comfy handmade quilt in front of the fireplace or enjoy wine and cheese in the spacious lobby of this unusual bed-and-breakfast hotel, built in 1837 as one of the first textile mills in the South. Breakfast is included. *200 Brookstown Ave., 27102, tel. 919/725–1120. 72 rooms. Facilities: some rooms with whirlpools, airport transportation, meeting rooms. AE, MC, V.*

Moderate **Comfort Inn–Cloverdale Plaza.** Located off I–40 near downtown and Old Salem, this immaculately kept economy inn offers a free Continental breakfast. *110 Miller St., 27103, tel. 919/721–0220. 122 rooms. Facilities: outdoor pool, health club, meeting room. AE, MC, V.*

Outer Banks and Historic Albemarle

North Carolina's Outer Banks are made up of a series of barrier islands stretching from the Virginia state line southward to Cape Lookout. Throughout history they have posed a threat to ships, and hence the area became known as the Graveyard of the Atlantic. A network of lighthouses and lifesaving stations was built to make the Outer Banks safer for navigators. English settlers attempted to colonize the region more than 400 years ago, but the first colony disappeared mysteriously, without a trace. Their plight is retold in an annual outdoor drama, "The Lost Colony." The islands offered seclusion and privacy to pirates who hid out in the coves and inlets. The notorious pirate Blackbeard lived and died here. For many years the Outer Banks remained isolated, home only to a few families who made their living by fishing. Today the islands, linked by bridges and ferries, are popular among summer tourists. Much of the area is included in the Cape Hatteras National Seashore. The largest towns on the islands are Kill Devil Hills and Nags Head.

On the inland side of the Outer Banks is the Historic Albemarle Region, a remote area of small villages and towns surrounding Albemarle Sound. Edenton served as the Colonial capital for a while, and today many of its early structures are preserved for posterity.

Getting Around

By Plane The closest commercial airports are the Raleigh-Durham International Airport (tel. 919/840–2123) and Norfolk International (tel. 804/857–3200), both of which are served by major carriers, including **American, Continental, Delta,** and **USAir. Dawn Air** (tel. 919/473–3222 or 800/927–3296) provides commuter service from Norfolk to the Dare County Regional Airport at Manteo.

By Train **Amtrak** service (tel. 800/872–7245) is available to Norfolk, VA, about 75 miles to the north.

By Car U.S. 158 links Manteo with Norfolk and other places north. U.S. 64 and 264 are western routes. NC 12 goes south toward Ocracoke Island and north toward Corolla. Toll ferries connect Ocracoke to Cedar Island and Swan Quarter. There is a free ferry across Hatteras Inlet.

By Taxi **Beach Cabs** (tel. 919/441–2500), based in Nags Head, offers 24-hour service from Norfolk to Ocracoke and towns in between.

Another option is **Outer Banks Limousine Service** (tel. 919/261–3133).

By Boat Seagoing visitors travel the Intracoastal Waterway through the Outer Banks and Historic Albemarle region. Boats may dock at Elizabeth City, Manteo (the Salty Dawg Marina), and other ports.

Guided Tours

Historic Albemarle Tour, Inc. (Box 759, Edenton 27932, tel. 919/482–7325) offers guided tours of Edenton and publishes a brochure on a self-guided tour of the Albemarle Region.

Kitty Hawk AeroTours (tel. 919/441–4460) leave from the First Flight Airstrip or Manteo for Kitty Hawk, Corolla, Cape Hatteras, Ocracoke, Portsmouth Island, and other areas along the Outer Banks. *Mar.–Labor Day.*

Ocracoke Trolley Tours (of Ocracoke Island) depart from Trolley Stop One, NC 12, Ocracoke, tel. 919/928–6711. *Easter–Labor Day, Mon.–Sat.*

Important Addresses and Numbers

Tourist Information **Dare County Tourist Bureau,** (Box 399, Manteo, 27954, tel. 919/473–2138). **Historic Albemarle Tour, Inc.** (Box 759, Edenton 27932, tel. 919/482–7325). **Outer Banks Chamber of Commerce** (Box 1757, Kill Devil Hills 27948, tel. 919/441–8144). **North Carolina Coast Host** (Box 1198, Morehead City 28557, tel. 919/726–6831).

Emergencies Dial 911 for Oregon Inlet, Roanoke Island, and Hatteras Island; 919/928–4631 for Ocracoke. The Outer Banks Medical Center at Nags Head is open 24 hours a day, tel. 919/441–7111.

Coast Guard Tel. 919/995–5881.

Exploring the Outer Banks

Numbers in the margin correspond to points of interest on the Outer Banks map.

You can begin your tour of the Outer Banks from either the southern end of the barrier islands at Cedar Island or the northern end at Nags Head. Unless you're camping, overnight stays will probably be in Ocracoke or in the Nags Head-Manteo area, where motels and hotels are concentrated. (There's also a motel at Cedar Island on the mainland where you catch the ferry to Ocracoke.) You can drive the 70-mile stretch of barrier islands in a day, but be sure to allow plenty of time during the summer season in case you have to wait for the next ferry to the mainland. A complete schedule is included on the state map. For reservations, call 919/225–3551 for departures from Cedar Island, 919/928–3841 from Ocracoke, or 919/926–1111 from Swan Quarter. Be wary of getting stranded on the islands during major storms and hurricanes when the roads and bridges become clogged with traffic.

1 **Kill Devil Hills,** on U.S. 158 Bypass, midway between Kitty Hawk and Nags Head, is such an unimpressive location, it's hard to believe its historical significance as the site of man's first flight. The **Wright Brothers National Memorial,** a granite

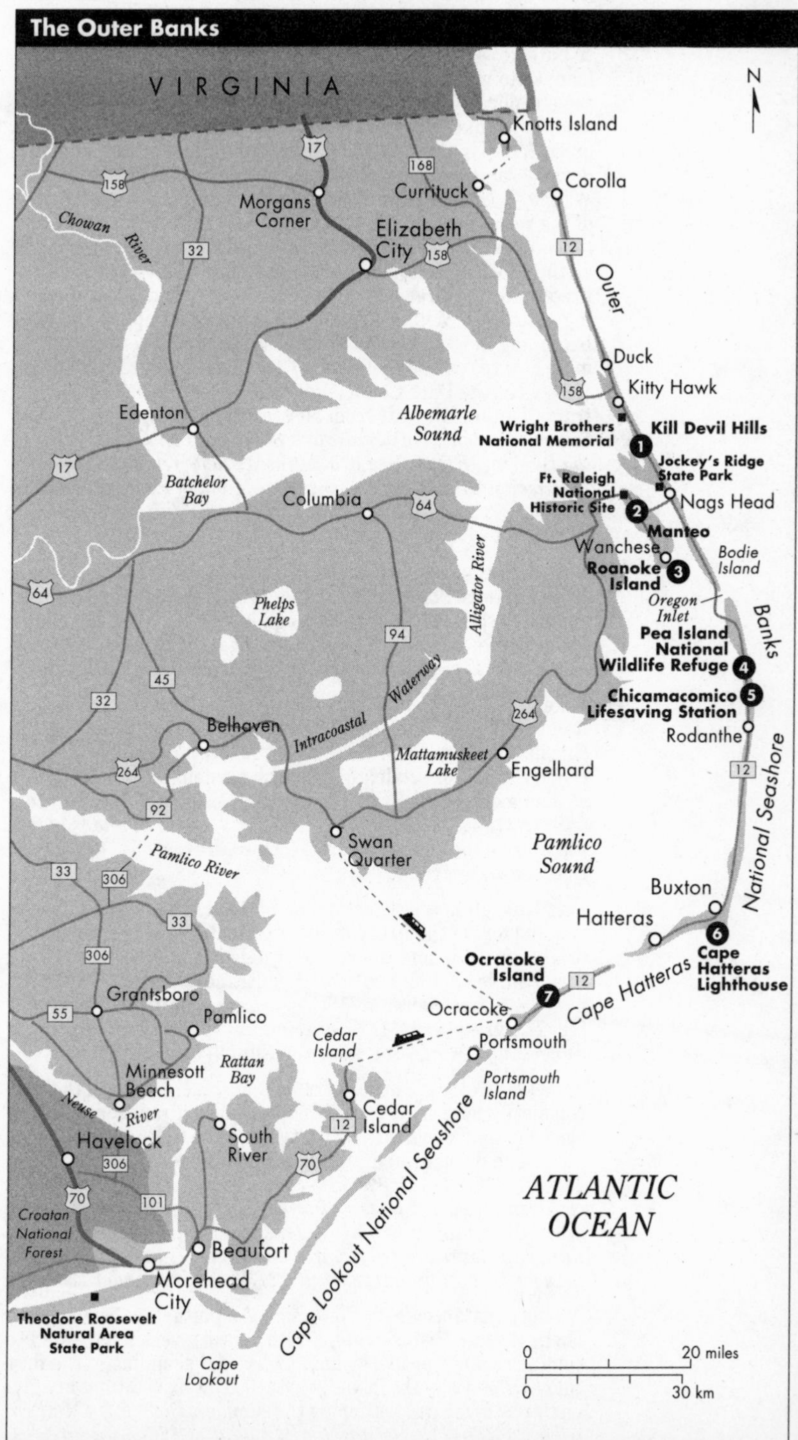
The Outer Banks
VIRGINIA
Knotts Island
Corolla
Currituck
Morgans Corner
Elizabeth City
Chowan River
Outer
Duck
Kitty Hawk
Edenton
Albemarle Sound
Wright Brothers National Memorial
Kill Devil Hills
Jockey's Ridge State Park
Ft. Raleigh National Historic Site
Nags Head
Batchelor Bay
Columbia
Manteo
Wanchese
Bodie Island
Roanoke Island
Alligator River
Oregon Inlet
Banks
Phelps Lake
Pea Island National Wildlife Refuge
Chicamacomico Lifesaving Station
Rodanthe
Intracoastal Waterway
Belhaven
Mattamuskeet Lake
Engelhard
National Seashore
Swan Quarter
Pamlico River
Pamlico Sound
Buxton
Hatteras
Cape Hatteras Lighthouse
Ocracoke Island
Cape Hatteras
Grantsboro
Pamlico
Ocracoke
Cedar Island
Portsmouth
Rattan Bay
Minnesott Beach
Portsmouth Island
Neuse River
Cedar Island
Havelock
South River
Cape Lookout National Seashore
ATLANTIC OCEAN
Croatan National Forest
Beaufort
Morehead City
Theodore Roosevelt Natural Area State Park
Cape Lookout
0
20 miles
0
30 km
N

monument that resembles the tail of an airplane, stands as a tribute to Wilbur and Orville Wright, two bicycle mechanics from Ohio who took to the air on December 17, 1903. You can see a replica of *The Flyer* and stand on the exact spot where it made four take-offs and landings, the longest being a distance of 852 feet. Exhibits and an informative talk by a National Park Service ranger make the thrilling event come to life again. The Wrights' accomplishment was no easy task in this remote area of the world in those days. Without roads or bridges, they had to bring in the airplane unassembled. They also had to bring in all their food and supplies and build a camp (the Wrights at first used tents and later built a wooden storage shed, as well as living quarters). Wilbur and Orville made four trips to the site, beginning in 1900, each time conducting experiments to determine how to achieve their goal. The annual Wilbur Wright Fly-In, held at the Dare County Regional Airport every spring, attracts vintage aircraft from all over the country. Contact the *Superintendent, National Park Service, U.S. Department of the Interior, Rte. 1, Box 675, Manteo 27954, tel. 919/441–7430. Admission $3 per car, $1 per person, Golden Passport holders and those under 16 and over 65 free. Open daily 9–5 with extended hours in the summertime. Closed major holidays.*

A few miles south of Kill Devil Hills, via U.S. 158 Bypass, is **Jockey's Ridge State Park,** the tallest sand dune in the East and a popular spot for hang gliding and kite flying. You can join in the activities and have a picnic here. *Rte. 158 Bypass, Milepost 12, tel. 919/441–7132. Admission free. Open daily 8 AM–sunset.*

2 Take U.S. 64-264 from U.S. 158 Bypass to reach **Manteo** and
3 **Roanoke Island,** the site of several attractions, including the Elizabethan Gardens, "The Lost Colony" Waterside Amphitheatre, and Fort Raleigh. The lush gardens were established as a memorial to the first English colonists. *U.S. 64, Manteo, tel. 919/473–3234. Admission: $2 adults, children under 12 free when accompanied by an adult. Open Mar.–Nov., daily 9–5; Dec.–Jan., weekdays 9–5.*

Fort Raleigh is a reconstruction of what is thought to be the original fort of the first Carolinian colonists. Be sure to see the orientation film and then take a guided tour of the fort. A nature trail leads to an outlook over Roanoke Sound. On special occasions, musicians play 16th-century music in the visitor center. *Tel. 919/473–2111. Admission free. Open Sept.–May 9–5; June–Aug., Mon.–Sat. 9–8; and Sun. 9–6.*

"The Lost Colony" outdoor drama reenacts the story of the first colonists who settled here in 1584 and then disappeared during the time that some of their party returned to England for supplies. The drama celebrated its own 50th anniversary in 1987. *Tel. 919/473–3414 or 800/488–5012. Admission: $10 adults, $4 children under 12. Reservations suggested. Performances are given from mid-June until late Aug., Mon.–Sat. at 8:30 PM. Backstage tours are offered afternoons, mid-June–Aug. (see the play first). Admission: $3 adults, $1.50 children under 12.*

A short distance from Waterside Amphitheatre is the **Elizabeth II State Historic Site,** a 16th-century vessel recreated to commemorate the 400th anniversary of the landing of the first colonists on Roanoke Island. Historical interpretations are given by costumed guides during the summer. *Downtown Manteo, tel. 919/473–1144. Admission: $3 adults, $2 senior citizens,*

$1.50 children.Open Nov.–Mar., Tues.–Sun. 10–4; Apr.–Oct., daily 10–6.

Resume your journey southward on the Outer Banks via NC 12, a road that will take you all the way to Ocracoke Island. On the way you will pass over **Bonner Bridge,** which arches for three miles over Oregon Inlet and carries traffic to Hatteras Island, the "Blue Marlin Capital of the World."

4 **Pea Island National Wildlife Refuge,** on NC 12 between Oregon Inlet and Rodanthe, is made up of more than 5,000 acres of marsh that serves as wildlife refuge. In this vicinity was the Pea Island Life Saving Station, whose courageous crew, led by Richard Etheridge, made daring rescues during the late 1800s and early 1900s. *Pea Island Refuge Headquarters, tel. 919/987–2911. Open Apr.–Nov. weekdays 8–4.*

5 A few miles south of Pea Island is the 1911 **Chicamacomico Lifesaving Station.** Now restored, the museum tells the story of the 24 stations that once lined the Outer Banks. Living-history reenactments are performed June–August. *Tel. 919/987–2203. Admission: free. Open 11–5.*

6 **Cape Hatteras Lighthouse,** about 30 miles south of Rodanthe, sits as a beacon to ships offshore. The 208-foot lighthouse is the tallest in the East. Offshore lie the remains of the *Monitor,* a Confederate ironclad ship that sank in 1862. The visitor center offers information on the national seashore. *Hatteras Island Visitor Center, tel. 919/995–4474. Open Sept.–May 9–5, June–Aug. 9–6.*

At Hatteras, board the free ferry to Ocracoke Island. Boats leave every 40 minutes, and the journey takes about half an hour.

7 **Ocracoke Island** was cut off from the world for so long that native residents still speak in quasi-Elizabethan accents; today, however, the island is a refuge for tourists. There is a village of shops, motels, and restaurants around the harbor where the infamous pirate Blackbeard met his death in 1718. The Ocracoke Lighthouse is a photographer's dream. *For information, contact the Ocracoke Visitor Center on Cedar Island, tel. 919/928–4531.*

Off the Beaten Track

Somerset Place. The Collins family kept meticulous records on the 300 slaves that worked this plantation (now a state historic site) in the 1800s. Their descendants still hold family reunions here. *Off U.S. 64 at Creswell, tel. 919/797–4560. Admission free. Open Apr.–Oct., Mon.–Sat. 9–5, Sun. 1–5; Nov.–Mar., Tues.–Sat. 10–4, Sun. 1–4.*

Beaches

More than 70 miles of unspoiled beaches stretch from Nags Head to Ocracoke Island. Preserved as Cape Hatteras National Seashore, this coastal area is ideal for swimming, surfing, windsurfing, diving, boating, and any number of water activities. If you want to swim, stay in areas where there are lifeguard stations—Coquina Beach, Salvo, Cape Hatteras, Frisco, and Ocracoke. Nags Head (so named because Bankers would tie lanterns around the heads of their horses to lure merchant ships), is the most commercial beach area, with lifeguards stationed near motels and hotels. You can explore the *Laura Barnes* shipwreck site at Coquina Beach, considered the best swimming hole on the Outer Banks. Facilities here include picnic shelters, rest rooms, showers, and bath houses. Ghost-fleet maps are available at the Wright Brothers National Memorial gift shop. Divers and surfers enjoy practicing their antics around Cape Hatteras.

Participant Sports

Camping Camping is permitted in designated areas all along the Cape Hatteras National Seashore. All campgrounds in the park have cold showers, drinking water, tables, grills, and restrooms (except Ocracoke, which has pit toilets). Sanitary stations for recreational vehicles are located at Oregon Inlet, Cape Point at Cape Hatteras, and Ocracoke. Oregon Inlet, Cape Point, and Ocracoke are open from mid-April through mid-October; Salvo and Frisco, mid-June to late August. Be sure to take along extra-long tent stakes for sand, and don't forget the insect repellent. All sites are available on a first-come, first-served basis (except Ocracoke where reservations are required). Contact Cape Hatteras National Seashore, Route 1, Box 675, Manteo 27954, tel. 919/473–2311. In addition to campsites in the National Seashore, there are many private campgrounds scattered along the Outer Banks. *For information contact the North Carolina Travel and Tourism Division, tel. 800/847–4862.*

Fishing This area is a paradise for fishermen who enjoy surf casting or deep-sea fishing. You can board a charter boat or head your own craft out of Oregon Inlet. (Call 919/441–6301 for information on chartered trips.) North Carolina fishing licenses are available from local bait-and-tackle shops and marinas or from the N.C. Division of Boating and Inland Fishing (tel. 919/733–3633).

Hang Gliding Only a few miles from where Wilbur and Orville Wright first took flight, you can try your hand at hang gliding. There's probably not a safer place to attempt this aerial feat than from the giant sand dune at Jockey's Ridge State Park, where national champions gather every May for the Hang Gliding Spectacular. Lessons are given by the **Kitty Hawk Kites,** purported to be the world's largest hang gliding school. Their shop is located on U.S. 158 at Milepost 13, Nags Head, tel. 919/441–4124 or 800/733–3633.

Scuba Diving With over 600 known shipwrecks off the coast of the Outer Banks, diving opportunities are virtually unlimited. The *Monitor* is off-limits, however. Dive shops include: **Hatteras Divers** (tel. 919/986–2557) and **Nags Head Pro Dive Shop** (tel. 919/441–7594).

Surfing and Windsurfing The Outer Banks offer ideal conditions for these sports. Contact **Kitty Hawk Sports** (U.S. 158 at Milepost 13, tel. 919/441–4124 or 800/334–4777).

Dining

Plan to get your fill of seafood during your visit to the Outer Banks; it's in abundant supply here, and a number of restaurants prepare it quite well.

Category	Cost*
Very Expensive	over $25
Expensive	$15–$25
Moderate	$8–$15
Inexpensive	under $8

**per person without tax (6%), service, or drinks*

Kill Devil Hills
Moderate–Expensive

Etheridge Seafood Restaurant. The fish comes straight from the boat to the kitchen at this family-owned, upscale seafood house, in operation for over half a century. It's decorated with Etheridge family memorabilia, depicting their successful fishing and warehousing operation. *U.S. 158 Bypass at Milepost 9.5, tel. 919/441–2645. Open Mar.–Oct. Reservations not accepted. MC, V.*

Manteo
Expensive

Elizabethan Inn. Enjoy "Pastime with Goode Companie," a show with an authentic 16th-century Elizabethan feast at this inn. *US 64, tel. 919/473–2101 or 800/346–2466. Reservations required. Closed late Aug.–early June, Sat.–Tues.; late Sept.–mid-Oct., weekdays. Cost: $25 adults, $14 children.*

Moderate

Weeping Radish Brewery and Restaurant. This Bavarian-style restaurant is named for the radishes sprinkled with salt and served with Hoplen beer, brewed right on the premises. Waiters dressed in Bavarian costumes serve German dishes while German music plays in the background. Tours of the brewery are given upon request. *US 64, tel. 919/473–1157. Reservations required for parties of six. MC, V. Closed major holidays.*

Nags Head
Expensive

Owens' Restaurant. Housed in an old Nags Head–style clapboard cottage, Owens' has been in the same family for over 40 years. The seafood is outstanding—especially the coconut shrimp and lobster bisque. Nightly entertainment is offered in the brass and glass Station Keeper's Lounge. *U.S. 158, Milepost 17, tel. 919/441–7309. Reservations accepted for large parties only. No lunch. Closed Dec.–Mar. AE, DC, MC, V.*

Moderate–Expensive

Lance's Seafood Bar & Market. You can contemplate the fishing and hunting memorabilia while you dine on steamed or raw seafood and then drop the shells through the hole in the table. *U.S. 158 bypass, milepost 14, tel. 919/441–7501. MC, V. Closed Christmas.*

Lodging

The majority of motels and hotels are clustered in the Nags Head–Manteo area, but a small number of rooms are available in the Cape Hatteras area. There are 60 cottages for rent on Ocracoke Island, plus a dozen or so motels and inns. Condos and beach cottages may be rented by the week or month through area realty companies. The Outer Banks Chamber of Commerce (tel. 919/441–8144) can steer you in the direction of rental agencies.

Category	Cost*
Very Expensive	over $100
Expensive	$60–$100

Moderate	$30–$60
Inexpensive	under $30

**double room; add 8% for taxes*

Duck
Very Expensive

Sanderling Inn and Restaurant. If you enjoy being pampered, come to this inn, located in a remote beach area north of Duck. Guests are treated to lounging robes, fruit and wine, and complimentary hors d'oeuvres. For recreation you can play tennis, go swimming, or take a nature walk through the Pine Island Sanctuary and then curl up with a good book from the inn's library—or enjoy a videotape. Though it was built in 1985 and has all the contemporary conveniences, the inn has the stately, mellow look of old Nags Head. The restaurant, one of the best in the region, serves three meals a day, and reservations are required for dinner. Entrées include crab cakes, roast Carolina duckling with black cherry sauce, and fricassee of shrimp. *1461 Duck Rd., 27949, tel. 919/261–4111. 60 rooms and 28 efficiencies. Facilities: pool, tennis, Jacuzzi, hot tub, health club, golf privileges, bicycles, meeting rooms. AE, MC, V.*

Kill Devil Hills
Moderate–Expensive

Ramada Inn. Rooms in this convention-style hotel have ocean views and come with refrigerators and microwave ovens. Peppercorns Restaurant, overlooking the ocean, serves breakfast and dinner, and lunch is available on the sun deck next to the pool. *US 158, Milepost 9½, Box 2716, 27948, tel. 919/441–2151 or 800/635–1824. 173 rooms. Facilities: pool, golf privileges, Jacuzzi, meeting rooms. AE, MC, V.*

Manteo
Expensive

Tranquil House Inn. This 19th-century-style waterfront inn is only a few steps from shops, restaurants, and the Elizabeth II State Historic Site, but bikes are provided for adventures beyond. Guests receive fresh flowers and complimentary wine upon arrival. A Continental breakfast is also on the house. Guests often gather around the fireplace in the library to talk about the day's activities. *Queen Elizabeth Ave., the Waterfront, Box 2045, Manteo 27954, tel. 919/473–1404 or 800/458–7069. 28 rooms. Facilities: outdoor grill, observation deck. AE, DC, MC, V.*

Ocracoke
Moderate

Island Inn and Dining Room. The inn has been in operation since 1940, though it was built as a private lodge back in 1901. The best rooms are located in the Crow's Nest on the third floor; these large rooms offer cathedral ceilings and look out over the island. The dining room is known for its oyster omelet, crab cakes, and hush puppies. Reservations are advised, particularly for dinner. *NC 12, Box 9, 27960, tel. 919/928–4351 (inn) or 919/928–7821 (dining room). Open year-round. 35 rooms. Facilities: outdoor pool. MC, V.*

Asheville

In recent years this mountain city has been rated, among cities of its size, as America's number-one favorite place to live. It has scenic beauty, low levels of pollution, a good airport and road system, a moderate four-season climate, a variety of hotels and restaurants, and plenty of cultural opportunities. It is a city where banjo pickers are as revered as violinists, where mountain folks mix with city slickers, and where everyone finds a common ground in a love for the city.

Getting Around

By Plane The Asheville Regional Airport (tel. 704/684–2226) is served by **American Eagle, Atlantic Southeast Airlines, Comm Air, Delta, United–United Express,** and **USAir.**

By Car I–40 runs east and west through the city. I–26 runs from Charleston to Asheville. I–240 forms a perimeter around the city. U.S. 23-19A is a major north and west route.

By Bus **Greyhound/Trailways** (tel. 704/253–5353).

Guided Tours

Three companies provide group tours: **Travel Professionals, Inc.** (tel. 704/298–3438), **Western Carolina Tours** (tel. 704/254–4603), and **Young Transportation** (tel. 704/258–0084 or 800/622–5444).

Important Addresses and Numbers

Tourist Information The **Visitor Information Center** (151 Haywood St., tel. 704/258–3858) and the **Asheville Convention and Visitors Bureau** (Box 1010, Asheville 28802, tel. 800/257–1300).

Emergencies Dial 911.

Exploring Asheville

Downtown Asheville is noted for its eclectic architecture. The **Battery Park Hotel,** built in 1924, is neo-Georgian; the **Flatiron Building** (1924) is neoclassical; the **Church of St. Lawrence** (1912) is Spanish Baroque; **Old Pack Library** (1925) is in Italian Renaissance–style; the **S & W Cafeteria** (1919) is Art Deco. A brochure entitled "Asheville Heritage Tour," details six different historic districts in the city. A guided walking tour is given every Sunday at 2 PM from June through mid-October. For details, contact the Preservation Society of Asheville and Buncombe County (Box 2806, Asheville 28802, tel. 704/254–2343).

The **Thomas Wolfe Memorial** (48 Spruce St.), built in 1880 in the Queen Anne style, is one of the oldest houses in downtown Asheville. Wolfe's mother ran a boarding house here for years, and he used it as the setting for his novel *Look Homeward, Angel.* Family pictures, clothing, and original furnishings fill the house, now a state historic site. Guided tours are available. *Tel. 704/253–8304. Admission: $1 adults, students 50¢. Open Apr.–Oct. Mon.–Sat. 9–5, Sun. 1–5; Nov.–Mar. Tues.–Sat. 9–4, Sun 1–4.*

From downtown, follow I–40 east to Exit 50 (U.S. 25). The entrance to the architecturally famous **Biltmore Estate** faces Biltmore Village, about three blocks from the interstate. Built as the private home of George Vanderbilt, the 255-room French Renaissance château is today a museum. Richard Morris Hunt designed the castle, and Frederick Law Olmsted landscaped the original 125,000-acre estate (now 8,000 acres). It took 1,000 men five years to complete the gargantuan project. On view are the priceless antiques and art treasures collected by the Vanderbilts, and 17 acres of gardens. Visitors also enjoy visiting the state-of-the-art winery and Christmas candlelight tours of the house. *Tel. 704/255–1700 or 800/543–2961. Admis-*

sion: $19.95 adults, $15 students ages 12–17, children 11 and under free when accompanied by an adult. Open daily 9–5; sunset views and live music Fri.–Sat., late May–Aug. 6:30–10:30.

Take U.S. 19-23 Bypass north, off I–240, from Asheville to Weaverville, a distance of about 18 miles. The **Zebulon B. Vance Birthplace** is located on Reems Creek Road (Route 1103). This state historic site, which includes a two-story log cabin and several outbuildings, is where Vance—North Carolina's governor during the Civil War—grew up. Crafts and chores typical of his period are often demonstrated. Picnic facilities are available. *Tel. 704/645–6706. Admission free. Open Apr.–Oct., Mon.–Sat. 9–5, Sun. 1–5; Nov.–Mar., Tues.–Sat. 9–4, Sun. 1–4.*

Time Out Enjoy fresh mountain trout or chicken with pineapple raisin sauce in the turn-of-the-century **Weaverville Milling Company,** near the Vance Homestead. Waitresses dress in gingham. The craft shop on the premises sells locally made quilts and quilted pillows. *Tel. 704/645–4700. Reservations suggested. Open weekdays 5–9 (except Wed.) and weekends 5–9:30 Apr.–Dec.; Thurs.–Fri. 5–9, weekends 5–9:30 Jan.–Mar. MC, V. Moderate.*

Flat Rock About 25 miles south of Asheville, Flat Rock can be reached via I–26. This vacation-retirement community, long popular with Charlestonians, is home to the Flat Rock Playhouse and to the estate of poet and Lincoln biographer Carl Sandburg. **Connemara** is the home where the Pulitzer Prize winner spent the last years of his life with his wife Lilian. The house is at the same time warm and austere. Guided tours are given by the National Park Service, which manages the property. "The World of Carl Sandburg" and "Rootabaga Stories" are presented here by the Vagabond Players during the summer. *Tel. 704/693–4178. Admission: $1 per person, ages 16–71. Open daily 9–5.*

What to See and Do with Children

Sliding Rock. Slide for 150 wet and wild feet on a natural water slide located north of Brevard, off Highway 276, in Pisgah National Forest. Wear old jeans and tennis shoes and bring a towel. *Tel. 704/877–3265. Open 10–6 late-May–Labor Day.*

Off the Beaten Track

Riverside Cemetery (Birch St., off Montford Ave. north of I–240 in Asheville) is the final resting place of Thomas Wolfe, O. Henry (William Sydney Porter), and early founders and settlers of Asheville. *Open daily during daylight hours.*

Shopping

Crafts **The Folk Art Center** (Milepost 382 on the Blue Ridge Parkway) is the best place to find authentic quality mountain crafts. *Tel. 704/298–7928. Open daily except major holidays.*

Qualla Arts and Crafts (U.S. 441 and Drama Rd., in Cherokee) features authentic Cherokee Indian crafts, as well as items from other American tribes. *Tel. 704/497–3103. Open daily 9–5.*

Biltmore Village, built by George Vanderbilt outside the entrance to his magnificent estate, houses more than 20 antique, craft, clothing, and gift shops. Be sure to check out **New Morning Gallery,** which features two new shops—**Blue Spiral I** and **Belagio's.**

Biltmore Homespun Shop, located on the grounds of the Grove Park Inn and established by Mrs. George Vanderbilt, features woven goods made on the premises. *Macon St., tel. 704/253–7651. Open Apr.–Oct., Mon.–Sat. 9–5:30; Nov.–Mar., Mon.–Sat. 9–4:30.*

Participant Sports

Camping For information on state parks, national forests, and designated sites along the Blue Ridge Parkway and in the Great Smoky Mountains National Park, contact the NC Travel & Tourism Division (tel. 800/VISIT–NC).

Canoeing/White-water Rafting The Nolichucky, French Broad, Nantahala, Ocoee, and Green Rivers offer Class I–IV rapids. About 10 outfitters serve the Asheville area, including **Carolina Wilderness** (Box 488, Hot Springs 28743, tel. 704/622–3535 or 800/872–7437) and **Nantahala Outdoor Center** (U.S. 19W, Box 41, Bryson City, 28713, tel. 704/488–2175).

Gem Mining Franklin has at least a dozen mines where you can get up to your elbows in common mud in search of precious rubies, sapphires, garnets, and other stones. There are many gem shops in the area where you can have your "finds" appraised. *Location maps are available from the Franklin Chamber of Commerce (180 Porter St., Franklin 28734, tel. 704/524–3161). Admission: $4–$5 for adults, $1–$2 for children. Most mines are open mid-May–Oct. 8–5 or dusk.*

Golf Western North Carolina offers over 50 challenging courses. Public courses are located in Asheville, Black Mountain, Brevard, Hendersonville, Lake Lure, Old Fort, and Waynesville. *Contact the Asheville Visitor center, tel. 704/258–3858, or Great Smoky Mountain Golf, tel. 704/258–0123.*

Hiking There are hundreds of trails along the Blue Ridge Parkway and in the Great Smoky Mountains National Park. The Appalachian Trail runs along the crest of North Carolina's highest mountains. *For trail maps, contact the Superintendent (Blue Ridge Parkway, BB & T Bank Bldg., 1 Pack Sq., Asheville 28801, tel. 704/259–0779), or the Superintendent (Great Smoky Mountains National Park, Gatlinburg, TN 37738, tel. 615/436–5615).*

Skiing Ski resorts in the Asheville area include **Cataloochee** (Rte. 1, Box 500, Maggie Valley 28751, tel. 704/926–0285), **Fairfield-Sapphire Valley** (Rte. 70, Box 80, Sapphire Valley 28774, tel. 704/743–3441), and **Wolf Laurel** (Rte. 3, Mars Hill, 28754, tel. 704/689–4111).

Dining

As you might expect in a resort city, dining choices are many: upscale gourmet restaurants, middle-of-the-road country fare, and fast-food establishments.

Category	Cost*
Very Expensive	over $25
Expensive	$15–$25
Moderate	$8–$15
Inexpensive	under $8

**per person without tax (6%), service, or drinks*

Very Expensive **Market Place on Wall Street.** Nouvelle cuisine is served in a relaxed atmosphere. Vegetables and herbs are regionally grown, and bread, pasta, and pastries are made on the premises. *20 Wall St., tel. 704/252–4162. Dress: informal. Reservations must be confirmed by 4 PM. No lunch. AE, MC, V. Closed Sun.*

Moderate **Steven's Restaurant.** International cuisine is offered in an elegant Victorian setting. The restaurant is known for its rack of lamb, freshly baked breads and desserts, and extensive wine list. *157 Charlotte St., tel. 704/253–5348. Dress: informal. Reservations recommended. Sun. brunch. AE, MC, V.*

Inexpensive–Moderate **Black Forest Restaurant.** Enjoy traditional German dishes in a Bavarian setting. Specialties include sauerbraten, knockwurst, schnitzel, and Kasseler Rippchen (cured pork ribs). The restaurant celebrates Oktoberfest in the fall. *2155 Hendersonville Hwy., U.S. 25, tel. 704/684–8160. Reservations suggested. AE, MC. V. Closed Mon.*

Rhapsody's Food and Spirits. This restaurant offers chicken, fish, beef, pork, lamb, and seafood dishes, plus pasta and some Mexican fare. There's à la carte brunch on Sunday. The service is quick and attentive, and the setting is surprisingly intimate, though quite spacious. *28 Tunnel Rd., tel. 704/258–2149. Dress: informal. Reservations not accepted. AE, DC, MC, V.*

Inexpensive **Smoky Mountain Barbecue.** Overalls and crinoline skirts are the order at this local establishment known for its clogging, bluegrass music, barbecue, and rustic atmosphere. The locals who hang out here make everyone, including tourists and convention delegates, feel welcome. *20 S. Spruce St., tel. 704/253–4871. Reservations advised on weekends. Cover is $3 on weekends and $2 on weekdays. AE, DC, MC. Closed Sun. and Mon.*

Lodging

Lodging options range from posh resorts to mountain cabins, country inns, and economy chain motels. There's a bed for virtually every pocketbook.

Category	Cost*
Very Expensive	over $100
Expensive	$60–$100
Moderate	$30–$60
Inexpensive	under $30

** double room; add 8% for taxes*

Hotels and Motels
Expensive **Grove Park Inn and Country Club.** This is Asheville's premier resort, and it's just as beautiful and exciting as it was the day it opened in 1913. The guest list has included Henry Ford, Thom-

as Edison, Harvey Firestone, and Warren G. Harding. Novelist F. Scott Fitzgerald stayed here while his wife Zelda was in a nearby sanitorium. His room was no. 441. In the past few years the hotel has been completely renovated. The two new wings are in keeping with the original design. Facilities include five restaurants. *290 Macon Ave., 28804, tel. 704/252–2711 or 800/438–5800. 510 rooms and suites. Facilities: meeting rooms, pool, sauna, whirlpool, putting green, fitness center, golf, tennis, racquetball, parking garage, airport shuttle, children's program, social program. AE, MC, V.*

Quality Inn Biltmore. Built on the grounds of the old Biltmore Dairy, this hotel is especially convenient for Biltmore Estate visitors. It is attached to the **Biltmore Dairy Bar,** a popular restaurant that offers sandwiches and ice cream. *115 Hendersonville Rd., 28803, tel. 704/274–1800. 160 rooms. Facilities: outdoor pool, jogging trail nearby, meeting rooms. AE, DC, MC, V.*

Inns and B&Bs
Very Expensive

Richmond Hill Inn. Once a private residence, this elegant Victorian mansion on the National Register of Historic Places now serves as an inn. **Gabrielle's,** the gourmet restaurant, is named for the former mistress of the house—wife of congressman and ambassador Richmond Pearson. *87 Richmond Hill Dr., 28806, tel. 704/252–7313 or 800/545–9238. 12 rooms. Facilities: meeting rooms. Dress: informal. Lunch, dinner, and Sunday brunch open to the public. Reservations suggested. AE, MC, V.*

Moderate–Expensive

Cedar Crest Victorian Inn. This beautiful cottage was constructed by Biltmore craftsmen as a private residence around the turn of the century. Jack and Barbara McEwan have lovingly restored it as a bed-and-breakfast inn and filled it with Victorian antiques. Guests are treated to afternoon tea, evening coffee or chocolate, and a breakfast of fruits, pastries, and coffee. *674 Biltmore Ave., 28803, tel. 704/252–1389. 13 rooms. AE, MC, V.*

North Carolina High Country

Majestic peaks, meadows, and valleys characterize the North Carolina High Country (Alleghany, Ashe, Avery, Mitchell, and Watauga counties) in the Blue Ridge Mountains. Once remote, the area has boomed in the past 25 years following the introduction of snowmaking equipment. Now North Carolina is both the Southern ski capital and a summertime playground for hiking, bicycling, camping, fishing, and canoeing. Luxury resorts now dot the valleys and mountaintops. The building of a 10-story concrete condo monolith on Sugar Mountain in Banner Elk caused a public outcry and resulted in the passage of a mountain ridge protection law to restrict this type of construction. On the other hand, the Linn Cove Viaduct on Grandfather Mountain, a bridge that circumvents the peaks and valleys without disturbing them, has received rave reviews from virtually everyone, including environmentalists. The bridge, which opened in 1987, is the final link in the Blue Ridge Parkway. Visitors to the hills take advantage of the many crafts shops, music festivals, theater, and special events such as the Grandfather Mountain Highland Games. The passing of each season is a special visual event in the High Country, with autumn's colors being the most spectacular of all.

Getting Around

By Plane **USAir Express** (tel. 800/428–4322) serves the Hickory Airport, about 40 miles from the High Country.

By Car The closest interstate is I–40, which is intersected by U.S. 321 at Hickory, NC 181 at Morganton, and U.S. 221 at Marion, leading to the High Country. U.S. 421 is a major east–west artery. The Blue Ridge Parkway, a slowly winding road, goes from Shenandoah National Park in Virginia to Great Smoky Mountains National Park in North Carolina and Tennessee, and passes over the mountain crests in the High Country.

By Bus Service from Charlotte to Boone is provided by **Greyhound/Trailways** (tel. 704/262–0501), with arrivals and departures from the Appalcart Bus Station on Winklers Creek Road, off U.S. 321 in Boone.

Important Addresses and Numbers

Tourist Information **North Carolina High Country Host** (701 Blowing Rock Rd., Boone 28607, tel. 704/264–1299 or 800/438–7500).

Emergencies Dial 911 for assistance or go to the emergency room at **Watauga County Hospital** in Boone (tel. 704/262–4100), **Cannon Memorial Hospital** in Banner Elk (tel. 704/898–5111), or **Ashe Memorial Hospital** in Jefferson (tel. 919/246–7101).

Exploring North Carolina High Country

Blowing Rock, a tourist mecca since the 1880s, has retained the flavor of a quiet mountain village. Only a few hundred people are permanent residents, but the population swells each summer. The town is named for a large outcropping of rock, considered the state's oldest tourist attraction. The town of Blowing Rock boasts some of the best restaurants in the High Country and offers a variety of accommodations.

The Blowing Rock (off U.S. 321, on the southern outskirts of town) looms 4,000 feet over the Johns River Gorge. If you throw your hat over the sheer precipice, it may come back to you, should the wind gods be playful. The story goes that a Cherokee brave and a Chickasaw maiden fell in love. Torn between returning to his tribe or staying with her, he jumped from the cliff. Her prayer to the Great Spirit resulted in his safe return to her. During the Depression of the '30s, a local family by the name of Robbins who owned the big rock decided to make it a tourist attraction and charge admission to see it. The formula worked. The family also owns the Tweetsie Railroad theme park. Today's visitors to the Blowing Rock enjoy views from an observation tower and a garden landscaped with mountain laurel, rhododendron, and other native plants. *Tel. 704/295–7111. Admission: $3 adults, $1 children 6–11. Open daily Apr.–May 9–6, June–Sept. 8–8, Oct. 8–7, Nov. weather permitting.*

From downtown Blowing Rock, follow U.S. 221 one mile south to the **Blue Ridge Parkway**—a scenic asphalt ribbon that stretches over mountain crests from northern Virginia to the southernmost mountains of North Carolina. Here are quiet vistas, dramatic mountain ranges, and remnants of pioneer life. Mileposts help tourists find the sites. Consider a stop at the **Moses H. Cone Park** (Mileposts 297.7–295) to see the manor house where the textile magnate lived.

If you want to go hiking, canoe on a mountain lake, fish for trout in a rushing stream, or pitch a tent, head for the 4,000 acres of forest in **Julian Price Park** (Mileposts 295.1–298). Keep driving south and you'll come to Grandfather Mountain, Linville Falls, Asheville, and Cherokee; head north from the park and you'll soon be at Doughton Park, the Peaks of Otter, and Roanoke. The Blue Ridge Parkway is open year-round, but it often closes during heavy snows. Maps and information are available at visitor centers along the highway. *For more information, contact the Superintendent (Blue Ridge Pkwy., BB & T Bldg., 1 Pack Sq., Asheville 28801, tel. 704/259–0779).*

From Blowing Rock, head north toward Boone, via U.S. 321, until you come to **Tweetsie Railroad,** a theme park popular with young children. In its heyday, Tweetsie provided passenger service between Johnson City, Tennessee, and Boone, but the tracks were washed away in a flood in the '40s and never rebuilt. In 1956, the train was placed on a three-mile track and opened as an attraction. The park also features a petting zoo, country fair (May–Oct.), rides, gold panning, a saloon show, and concessions. *Tel. 704/264–9061 or 800/526–5740. Admission: $12.95 adults, $10.95 children ages 4–12 and senior citizens 60 years and older. Open late-May–Labor Day daily 9–6; May weekends 9–6, July weekends until 8; Sept.–Oct. weekdays 9–5 and weekends 9–6.*

A short distance north of Tweetsie is **Mystery Hill,** where visitors can defy the laws of gravity through various experiences. The **Appalachian Heritage Museum,** destroyed by fire in 1989, has found a new home in the 1903 Dougherty House, moved to the site from Boone. *U.S. 321/221, tel. 704/264–2792. Mystery Hill admission: $5 adults, $3.50 children; museum admission: $3.50 adults, $2 children. Discounts for AAA members, senior citizens, and military personnel. Open June–Aug. 8–8; Sept.–May 9–5, Sun. 1–5.*

Boone, named for frontiersman Daniel Boone, is a city of several thousand residents at the convergence of three major highways—U.S. 321, U.S. 421, and NC 105. **"Horn in the West,"** a project of the Southern Highlands Historical Association, is an outdoor drama that traces the story of Boone's life. *The amphitheater is located off U.S. 321, tel. 704/264–2120. Admission: $9 adults, $4.50 children under 13 reserved seating; $8 adults, $4 children general admission. Curtain time is 8:30 nightly except Mon. mid-June through mid-Aug.*

Boone's **Appalachian Cultural Museum** showcases the successes of mountain residents. There are exhibits on stock-car racer Junior Johnson, country singers Lula Belle and Scotty Wiseman, and the now defunct Land of Oz, plus a vast collection of antique quilts, fiddles and handcrafted furniture. *University Hall near Greene's Motel, U.S. 321, tel. 704/262–3117. Admission: $2 adults, $1.75 senior citizens, and $1 children 12–18. Open Tues.–Sat. 10–5, Sun. 1–5. Closed Mon.*

To reach **Ashe County (Jefferson-West Jefferson),** travel five miles east on U.S. 421 to the Blue Ridge Parkway, and follow the parkway north for about 15 miles to Milepost 258.6 near

Glendale Springs. The scene quickly changes from commercial strips to mountain vistas and rural landscapes dotted with manicured farms and quiet villages.

The **Blue Ridge Mountain Frescoes** at Glendale Springs and Beaver Creek were painted by North Carolina artist Ben Long, who found the abandoned churches and painted four big-as-life frescoes, applying rich earthy pigments to wet plaster. "The Last Supper" (measuring 17 × 19.5 feet) is in the Glendale Springs Holy Trinity Church. The others are in St. Mary's Episcopal Church at Beaver Creek, including "Mary, Great with Child," which won the Leonardo da Vinci International Award. *Tel. 919/982–3076. Admission free. Open 24 hours a day. Guide service available with prior arrangements.*

North Carolina's only cheese factory, the **Ashe County Cheese Company,** is also in the area. Visitors enjoy free guided tours of the plant and browsing in the cheese shop. *Main and 4th Sts., West Jefferson, tel. 919/246–2501. Open Mon.–Sat. 8–5.*

You can go in another direction from Boone by following NC 105 south (about 14 miles) to NC 184, which leads to **Banner Elk.** This college and ski resort town is surrounded by the lofty peaks of Grandfather, Hanging Rock, Beech, and Sugar. Banner Elk is home to Elk River Club, one of the most prestigious residential developments on the East Coast.

Linville, eight miles from Banner Elk at the intersection of U.S. 221 and NC 105, sits at the base of Grandfather Mountain. This resort town, distinguished by its chestnut bark homes and lodges, has not changed much since it was built in the 1880s.

Grandfather Mountain's Natural History Museum features exhibits on native minerals, the flora and fauna of the region, and pioneer life. Films on nature are also shown. Two big events draw record crowds to the mountain. The annual Singing on the Mountain is an opportunity to hear old-time gospel music and preaching the fourth Sunday in June. Scottish clans from all over North America gather for athletic events and Highland dancing in July. At other times of the year the mountain is a great place for hiking and picnicking. Children of all ages enjoy seeing the deer, mountain lions, and Mildred the Bear in the Environmental Habitat. *Blue Ridge Parkway and US 221, Linville 28646, tel. 704/733–4337. Admission: $8 adults, $4 children ages 4–12. Hiking permits are $4 per day and may be obtained at the gate or at the Scotchman on NC 105. Open Apr.–mid-Nov., 8 until dusk; mid-Nov.–Mar., 9–4, weather permitting.*

Follow U.S. 221 south for about 10 miles to **Linville Caverns,** the only caverns in the Carolinas. The caverns go 2,000 feet underground and have a year-round temperature of 51 degrees. *Tel. 704/756–4171. Admission: $3.50 adults, $2 children 5–12. Open 9–6 June–Labor Day; 9–5 Apr.–May, Sept.–Oct; 9–4:30 Nov.–Mar; weekends only Dec.–Feb.*

What to See and Do with Children

Emerald Village. Grab a bucket of dirt and get muddy while looking for gems at this old mine that was established by the Bon Ami Company years ago. *McKinney Mine Rd. at Blue Ridge Parkway Milepost 334, tel. 704/765–6463. Museum admission: $3.50 adults, $2.50 students, $3 senior citizens, plus* *cost of gem bucket. Open late-May–early Sept. 9–6, early May and Oct. 9–5.*

Another place to go in the same area is the **Blue Ridge Gemstone Mine.** *McKinney Mine Rd., off Blue Ridge Parkway Milepost 334, tel. 704/765–5264. Admission is $5 and up, depending on the size of buckets selected. Open Apr.–May 9–5, June–Aug. 9–6, Sept.–Oct. 9–4, Nov.–Mar. 9–4.*

Off the Beaten Track

You'll find everything from ribbons and calico to brogans and overalls in the **Mast Store,** an authentic general store that has been the center of the Valle Crucis community for over 100 years. (The company operates a similar store in downtown Boone: Old Boone Mercantile, 104 E. King St., Boone, tel. 704/262–0000; open Mon.–Sat. 10–6, Sun. 1–6) *NC 194 in Valle Crucis, tel. 704/963–6511. Open Mon.–Sat. 6:30–6:30, Sun. 1–6.*

Another option is the **Todd General Store** in Ashe County. It features homebaked goods and handicrafts made by community residents. *Off Hwy. 194 in Todd, tel. 919/877–1067. Open summer, Mon.–Sat. 7–7, Sun. 12:30–5; winter, Mon.–Sat. 8–6., Sun. 12:30–5.*

Shopping

Crafts High-quality handmade brooms, quilts, pottery, jewelry, and other items made by members of the Southern Highland Handicraft Guild can be found at the **Parkway Craft Center,** which operates out of the Moses H. Cone mansion. *Moses H. Cone Park, tel. 704/295–7938. Open May–Oct., daily 9–5:30.*

Handwoven Goods The **Goodwin Weavers** create bedspreads, tablecloths, and afghans on Civil War–era looms and then sell them in their shop. *Off U.S. 321 Bypass, Blowing Rock, tel. 704/295–3394. Open Mon.–Sat. 9–5, Sun. 1–5.*

Participant Sports

Canoeing The wild and scenic New River (Class I and II) provides hours of excitement, as do the Watauga River (Class I and II), Wilson Creek, and Toe River (Class II and III). Outfitters include **Edge of the World Outfitters** (Banner Elk, tel. 704/898–9550) and **Wahoo's Adventures** (Boone, tel. 800/444–RAFT).

Golf The High Country has 18 golf courses, including **Boone Golf Club** (tel. 704/264–8760), **Hanging Rock Golf Course** at Seven Devils/Foscoe (tel. 704/963–6565), **Mountain Glen Golf Club** at Newland (tel. 704/733–5804), and **Mountainaire Golf Course** at West Jefferson (tel. 919/877–4716).

Hiking Trails abound in wilderness areas of national forests and near the Blue Ridge Parkway. The Boone Fork Trail in Julian Price Park, near Blowing Rock, is an easy hike for most people; Shanty Springs, on Grandfather Mountain, is more difficult. The Appalachian Trail follows the not-too-distant North Carolina–Tennessee border. Trail maps are available at the entrance gate of Grandfather Mountain (tel. 704/733–4337), at the Scotchman at NC 105; or from the Superintendent (Blue Ridge

Pkwy., 700 BB & T Bldg., 1 Pack Sq., Asheville 28801, tel. 704/259–0779).

Rock Climbing One of the most challenging climbs in the country is the Linville Gorge, off NC 181. Permits are available from the District Forest Ranger's Office in Marion (tel. 704/652–2144) or from the Linville Falls Texaco Station on U.S. 221. **Edge of the World Outfitters** in Banner Elk (tel. 704/898–9550) provides instruction and guided trips.

Skiing The High Country offers six alpine ski areas, plus many cross-country opportunities. For ski conditions, call 800/438–7500. Downhill skiing is available at **Appalachian Ski Mountain** (Box 106, Blowing Rock 28605, tel. 704/295–7828), **Ski Beech** (Box 1118, Beech Mountain 28604, tel. 704/387–2011), **Hound Ears Club** (Box 188, Blowing Rock 28605, tel. 704/963–4321), **Sugar Mountain** (Box 369, Banner Elk 28604, tel. 704/898–4521), and **Ski Mill Ridge** (U.S. 105 at Foscoe, tel. 704/963–4500). Cross-country skiing is offered at **Moses Cone Park** and at **Linville Falls** on the Blue Ridge Parkway (tel. 704/295–7591), and **Roan Mountain** (tel. 615/772–3303). Tours and equipment are available from **Edge of the World Outfitters** in Banner Elk (tel. 704/898–9550).

Dining and Lodging

Dining In the past 25 years the High Country has seen a tremendous increase in restaurants, from upscale gourmet restaurants to fast-food establishments. Beer, wine, and liquor by the drink are permitted in Blowing Rock, Banner, Elk, and Beech Mountain; beer and wine only in Boone.

Category	Cost*
Very Expensive	over $25
Expensive	$15–$25
Moderate	$8–$15
Inexpensive	under $8

**per person without tax (6%), service, or drinks*

Lodging Overnight lodging in the High Country ranges from mom-and-pop motels to luxurious mountaintop condos and chalets. Contact North Carolina High Country Host (tel. 800/438–7500) for complete information.

Category	Cost*
Very Expensive	over $100
Expensive	$60–$100
Moderate	$30–$60
Inexpensive	under $30

**double room; add 8% for taxes*

Banner Elk
Dining

The Louisiana Purchase. This upscale restaurant specializes in French, Creole, and Cajun dishes. *Hwy. 184, tel. 704/898–5656. Casual dinner attire. AE, MC, V. Moderate.*

Stonewalls. This contemporary rustic restaurant enjoys one of the best views of Beech Mountain. Fare includes steak, prime rib, fresh seafood, chicken, and homemade desserts. *Hwy. 184, tel. 704/898–5550. Reservations required for groups of 7 or more. Casual dinner attire. AE, MC, V. No lunch. Moderate.*

Dining and Lodging

Beech Alpen Inn. Guests have a view of the slopes or the Blue Ridge Mountains at this friendly country inn. A continental breakfast is included in the tariff. *700 Beech Mountain Parkway, Banner Elk 28604, tel. 704/387–2252. Open year-round. 25 rooms (4 with fireplaces). AE, MC, V. Expensive.*

Blowing Rock

Dining and Lodging

Hound Ears Club. This Alpine inn, overlooking Grandfather Mountain and a lush golf course, offers comfortable, well-kept rooms dressed in Waverly print fabrics. *Off NC 105, 8 mi from Boone; Box 188, 28605, tel. 704/963–4321. 27 rooms. Facilities: restaurant, pool, golf, tennis. MC, V. Very Expensive (price includes meals).*

Chetola Resort. This small resort of about 70 acres grew out of a turn-of-the-century stone-and-wood lodge that overlooks Chetola Lake. The original building now houses the resort's restaurant and meeting rooms and is adjacent to the 1988 lodge, which contains the accommodations. (The best rooms have balconies facing the lake.) The property adjoins Moses Cone Park, part of the Blue Ridge Parkway system, with hiking trails and riding facilities. *Box 17, Blowing Rock 28605, tel. 704/295–9301 or 800/CHETOLA. 39 rooms, 3 suites. Facilities: restaurant, indoor pool, sauna, racquetball, fitness center, hot tub, tennis, boating, hiking, meeting rooms, whirlpools in suites. AE, D, MC, V. Expensive–Very Expensive.*

Green Park Inn. This 100-year-plus Victorian charmer on the eastern continental divide offers spacious rooms, wide porches with rocking chairs, and large public rooms decorated in bright colors and wicker. The bilevel restaurant has won high ratings and is often the setting for dinner theater productions and murder mystery weekends. *U.S. 321, Box 7, 28605, tel. 704/295–3141. Open year-round; restaurant May–Oct.; golf and tennis available May–Oct. 88 rooms. Facilities: pool, golf, tennis, meeting rooms. MC, V. Expensive–Very Expensive.*

Boone

Lodging

Broyhill Inn. Though primarily a conference center, this contemporary hotel on the ASU campus is attractive to individual travelers who enjoy a university atmosphere. The dining room offers a great view of the mountains. *96 Bodenheimer Dr., 28607, tel. 800/222–8636 or 800/438–6022. 83 rooms. Facilities: meeting rooms, restaurant. AE, MC, V. Moderate.*

Linville

Dining and Lodging

Eseeola Lodge and Restaurant. Built in the 1880s, this lodge is the cornerstone of Linville. Rich chestnut paneling and stonework grace the interior rooms. *U.S. 221, tel. 704/733–4311. 28 rooms. Facilities: restaurant, lounge, golf, tennis, pool. Open June–Labor Day. MC, V. Very Expensive.*

Little Switzerland

Dining and Lodging

Switzerland Inn and Chalet Restaurant. This Swiss-style lodge overlooking the mountains offers lodge rooms, parlor-bedroom suites, and a lovely honeymoon cottage with a fireplace, plus three meals a day. *Milepost 334, off Blue Ridge Parkway, Box 399, Little Switzerland 28749, tel. 800/654–4026. 66 rooms. Facilities: outdoor pool, tennis courts, shuffleboard, shopping. MC, V. Closed Nov.–Apr. Moderate–Expensive.*

Sparta

Dining and Lodging

Mountain Hearth. This B&B and restaurant is built in a log cabin theme, with antiques and quilts as accents. Fresh, homemade bread is served with breakfast, lunch, and dinner.

Overnight guests are treated to a full complimentary breakfast. *Milepost 231.5, Blue Ridge Parkway, Sparta 28675, tel. 919/372–8743. 5 rooms with bath, 1 cabin with fireplace and whirlpool. MC, V. Closed Dec.–Mar., Mon.–Thurs.; Mar.–Nov., Sun.–Thurs. Moderate–Expensive.*

Valle Crucis
Dining and Lodging

Mast Farm Inn. You can turn back the clock and still enjoy modern amenities at this charming pastoral inn. Guests have a choice of rooms in the farmhouse or the log out-buildings. Breakfast and dinner are included in the tariff. *P.O. Box 704, Valle Crucis 28691, tel. 704/963–5857. Open late-Dec.–early Mar., late-Apr.–early Nov. 9 rooms. MC, V. Expensive.*

7 South Carolina

By Edgar and Patricia Cheatham

Updated by Carol Timblin

From its Low Country shoreline, with wide sand beaches, spacious bays, and forests of palmettos and moss-strewn live oaks, South Carolina extends into an undulating interior region rich with fertile farmlands, then reaches toward the Blue Ridge Mountains, studded with scenic lakes, forests, and wilderness hideaways. What this smallest of Southern states lacks in land area it makes up for in diversity.

The historic port city of Charleston, lovingly preserved, links past with present. Many of its treasured double-galleried antebellum homes were built at right angles to the streets to conserve space and catch ocean breezes. Some are now authentically furnished house museums where visitors savor gracious early-era eloquence. Culturally vibrant, the city nurtures theater, dance, music, and visual arts, showcased each spring during the internationally acclaimed Spoleto Festival USA.

Myrtle Beach is the hub of the Grand Strand, a 55-mile stretch of wide golden-sand beaches and countless family entertainment and recreational activities (especially golf, a top attraction throughout the state). To the south, tasteful, low-key Hilton Head—a sea island tucked between the Intracoastal Waterway and the ocean and divided into several sophisticated, self-contained resorts—also offers beautiful beaches and some of the world's best golf and tennis. Nearby is the port city of Beaufort, where the most rewarding activity is wandering the lovely streets dotted with preserved 18th-century homes, live oaks, and palmettos.

Columbia, the state capital, is a lively (and of course historic) city cleaved by a rushing river. In addition to several museums, a good minor-league baseball team, and a library of Movie-to-news film clips, the city has one of the country's top zoos. It is also home to the newly opened State Museum and one of the South's finest new performing arts complexes, Koger Center for Performing Arts. Nearby lakes and state parks offer abundant outdoor recreation and first-rate fishing.

Thoroughbred Country, centered around the town of Aiken, is a peaceful area of rolling pastures where some of the world's top race horses are trained. It is also notable for magnificent mansions built by wealthy Northerners who vacationed here at the turn of the century.

Upcountry South Carolina, at the northwestern tip of the state, is less visited than most of the rest of the state but well repays time spent there with dramatic mountain scenery, excellent hiking, and challenging white-water rafting.

Since 1670, when the British established the first permanent European settlement at Charleston, the history of the Palmetto State has been characterized by periods of great prosperity contrasted with eras of dismal depression. This vibrant past—from the pioneer, Colonial, Revolutionary, and antebellum periods through the bitter Civil War and Reconstruction years and beyond—is preserved in cherished traditions and an enduring belief in family, which give resonance to the optimism and vitality of today's South Carolina.

Charleston

At first glimpse, Charleston resembles an 18th-century etching come to life. Its low-profile skyline is punctuated with the spires and steeples of 181 churches, representing 25 denominations that have sought out Charleston as a haven (it was known for having the most liberal provisions for religious freedom of the 13 original colonies). Parts of the city appear stopped in time. Block after block of old downtown structures have been preserved and restored for both residential and commercial use. After three centuries of epidemics, earthquakes, fires, and hurricanes, Charleston has prevailed, and it is today one of the South's best-preserved cities.

Along the Battery, on the point of a narrow peninsula bounded by the Ashley and Cooper rivers, handsome mansions surrounded by gardens face the harbor. Called the "Charleston style," this distinctive look is reminiscent of the West Indies, and for good reason. Before coming to the Carolinas in the late 17th century, many early British colonists had first settled on Barbados and other Caribbean islands. In that warm and humid climate they had built homes with high ceilings and rooms opening onto broad piazzas at each level to catch welcome sea breezes. In Charleston, the settlers adapted these designs for other practical reasons. One new twist—building narrow two- to four-story houses (called single houses) at right angles to the street—emerged partly because of the British Crown's policy of taxing buildings according to frontage length. To save money (as well as to catch the prevailing winds), shrewd Charlestonians faced their houses to the side.

Each year, from mid-March to mid-April, the city opens its homes to visitors. In addition to conducting tours of private homes, gardens, and churches, the Festival of Houses celebrates Charleston's heritage with symphony galas in stately drawing rooms, plantation oyster roasts, candlelight tours, and more. For more information, write to the Historic Charleston Foundation (51 Meeting St., Charleston 29401, tel. 803/723–1623).

But Charleston is more than a carefully polished and preserved relic of the past. It is a city with a vibrant cultural life, which finds its greatest expression in the renowned Spoleto Festival USA and its companion festival, Piccolo Spoleto, when hundreds of local and international artists, musicians, and other performers fill the city streets and buildings with sound and spectacle (*see* The Arts, *below*).

Arriving and Departing

By Plane

Airports and Airlines

Charleston International Airport (tel. 803/767–1100) in North Charleston on I–26, 12 miles west of downtown Charleston, is served by **American, Delta, United,** and **USAir.**

Between the Airport and Center City

Airport Limousine Service (tel. 803/767–7111 or 800/222–4771) provides service to downtown Charleston by reservation. The charge is $9 per person one-way, $16 round-trip. By **car,** take I–26S to its terminus, at U.S. 17, near the heart of the city.

By Train

Amtrak (4565 Gaynor Ave., N. Charleston, tel. 803/723–6679 or 800/872–7245).

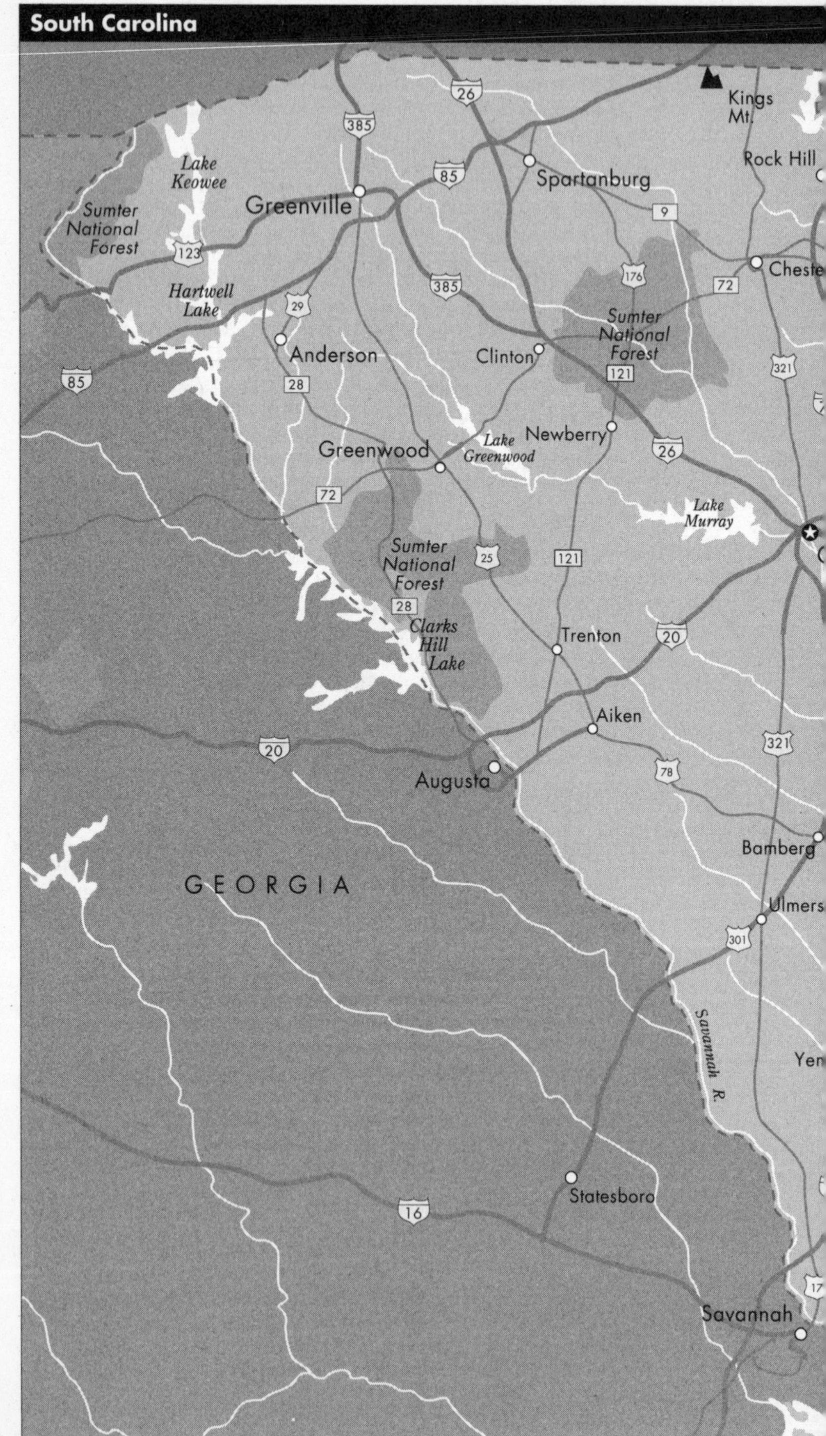
South Carolina
Kings Mt.
Rock Hill
Lake Keowee
Sumter National Forest
Greenville
Spartanburg
Chester
Hartwell Lake
Anderson
Clinton
Sumter National Forest
Newberry
Lake Greenwood
Greenwood
Lake Murray
Sumter National Forest
Clarks Hill Lake
Trenton
Aiken
Augusta
Bamberg
GEORGIA
Ulmers
Savannah R.
Statesboro
Savannah
26
385
85
9
123
176
72
29
385
321
28
121
85
26
72
25
121
28
20
20
321
78
301
16
17

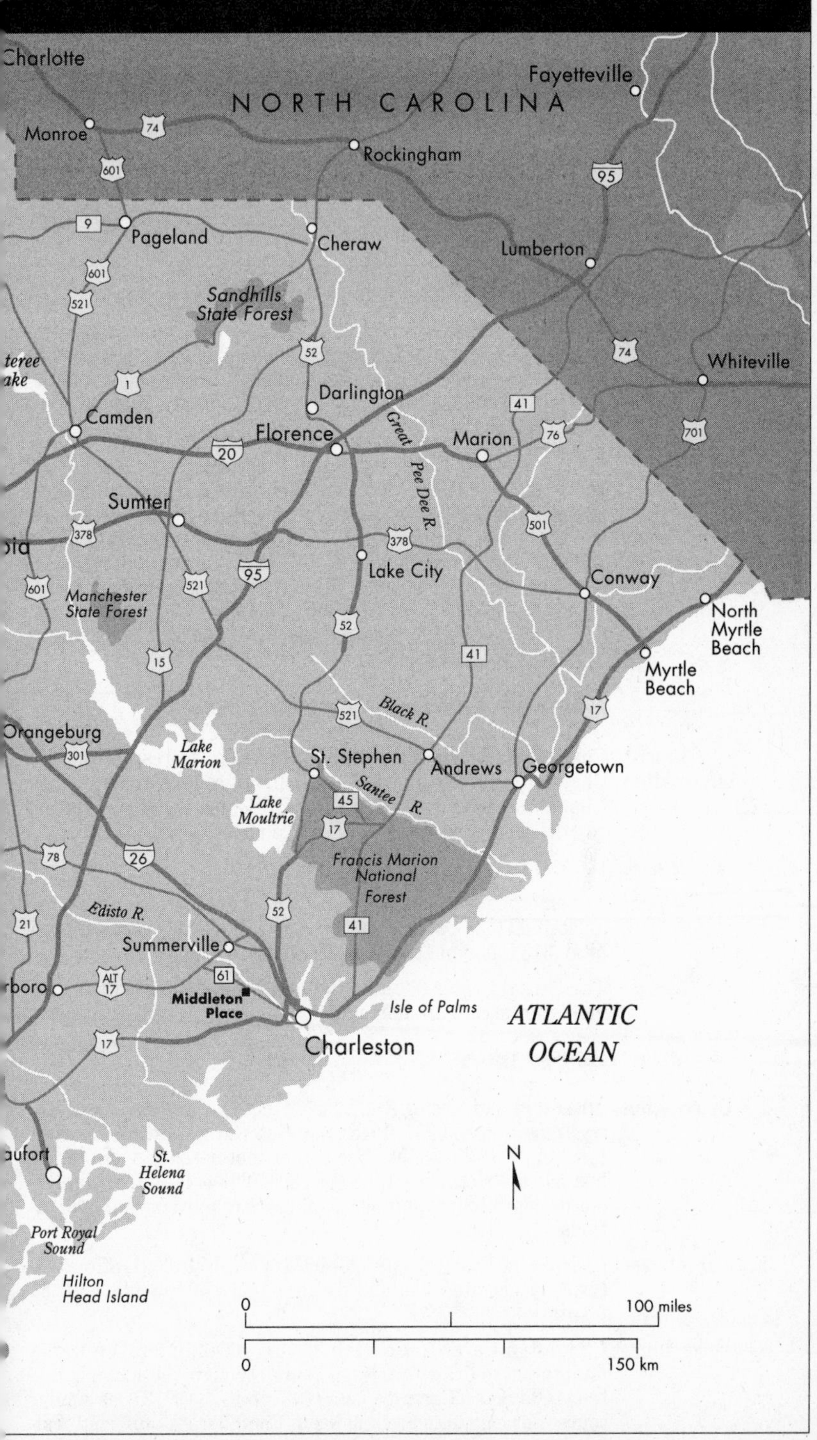

Charlotte
Fayetteville
NORTH CAROLINA
Monroe
74
Rockingham
601
95
9
Pageland
Cheraw
Lumberton
601
521
Sandhills
State Forest
52
74
Whiteville
1
Darlington
Camden
41
Florence
Great
Marion
76
701
20
Pee Dee R.
Sumter
501
378
378
Lake City
95
Conway
521
601
North
Myrtle
Beach
Manchester
State Forest
52
41
15
Myrtle
Beach
Black R.
521
17
Orangeburg
Lake
Marion
301
St. Stephen
Andrews
Georgetown
Santee R.
45
Lake
Moultrie
17
78
26
Francis Marion
National
Forest
Edisto R.
52
21
41
Summerville
61
ALT
17
Middleton
Place
Isle of Palms
ATLANTIC
OCEAN
17
Charleston
St.
Helena
Sound
N
Port Royal
Sound
Hilton
Head Island
0
100 miles
0
150 km

By Bus **Greyhound/Trailways** (3610 Dorchester Rd., N. Charleston, tel. 803/722–7721).

By Car I–26 traverses the state from northwest to southeast and terminates at Charleston. A favorite coastal route for north-south travelers is U.S. 17, which passes through Charleston.

By Boat Boaters traveling the Intracoastal Waterway may dock at the **City Marina** (Lockwood Blvd., tel. 803/724–7357) in the Charleston Harbor or **Wild Dunes Yacht Harbor** (tel. 803/886–5100) on the Isle of Palms.

Getting Around

By Taxi Fares within the city vary from company to company but average $2–$3 per trip. Companies include **Yellow Cab** (tel. 803/577–6565), **Safety Cab** (tel. 803/722–4066), and **Airport Limousine Service** (tel. 803/767–7111 or 800/222–4771).

By Bus Regular bus service within the city is provided by **SCE&G** (South Carolina Electric and Gas Company) between 5:35 AM and 10 PM and to North Charleston until 1 AM. The cost is 50¢; at nonpeak hours (9:30–3:30), senior citizens and disabled persons pay 25¢. Exact change is needed, and free transfers are available. SCE&G also operates the **DASH** (Downtown Area Shuttle) buses, trolley-style vehicles that provide fast service on weekdays in the main downtown areas. The fare is 50¢; $1 for an all-day pass. For schedule information, call 803/724–7420 or 803/747–0922 (regular service).

Important Addresses and Numbers

Tourist Information **Charleston Trident Convention & Visitors Bureau** (Box 975, Charleston 29402, tel. 803/577–2510) offers information on the Charleston area, including Kiawah, Seabrook, Mt. Pleasant, North Charleston, and the Isle of Palms.

Emergencies Dial 911 for emergency assistance.

Hospital The emergency rooms are open all night at **Charleston Memorial Hospital** (326 Calhoun St., tel. 803/577–0600) and **Roper Hospital** (316 Calhoun St., tel. 803/724–2000).

Dentist The **Dental Center** (86 Rutledge Ave., tel. 803/723–7242) provides dental care on short notice.

Guided Tours

Orientation **Adventure Sightseeing** (tel. 803/762–0088), **Carolina Low-country Tours** (tel. 803/797–1045), and **Gateway to Historic Charleston** (tel. 803/722–3969) offer van or motor-coach tours of the historic district. **Gray Line** (tel. 803/722–4444) offers similar motor-coach tours, plus seasonal tours to gardens and plantations.

Special-interest **Livin' in the Past** (tel. 803/723–0933 or 803/871–0891) offers historically oriented van and minibus tours of the city and the plantations.

Carriage Tours **Charleston Carriage Co.** (tel. 803/577–0042) offers 40- to 50-minute horse-drawn-carriage tours through the historic district. **Old South Carriage Tours** (tel. 803/723–9712) has similar tours, but conducted by guides in Confederate uniforms. **Pal-**

©1992 Budget Rent a Car Corporation

Vacation Cars. Vacation Prices. Wherever you travel, Budget offers you a wide selection of quality cars – from economy models to roomy minivans and even convertibles. You'll find them all at competitively low rates that include unlimited mileage. At over 1500 locations in the U.S. and Canada. For information and reservations, call your travel consultant or Budget at **800-527-0700**. In Canada, call **800-268-8900**.

Budget®

THE SMART MONEY IS ON BUDGET.®

We feature Lincoln-Mercury and other fine cars. *A system of corporate and licensee owned locations.*

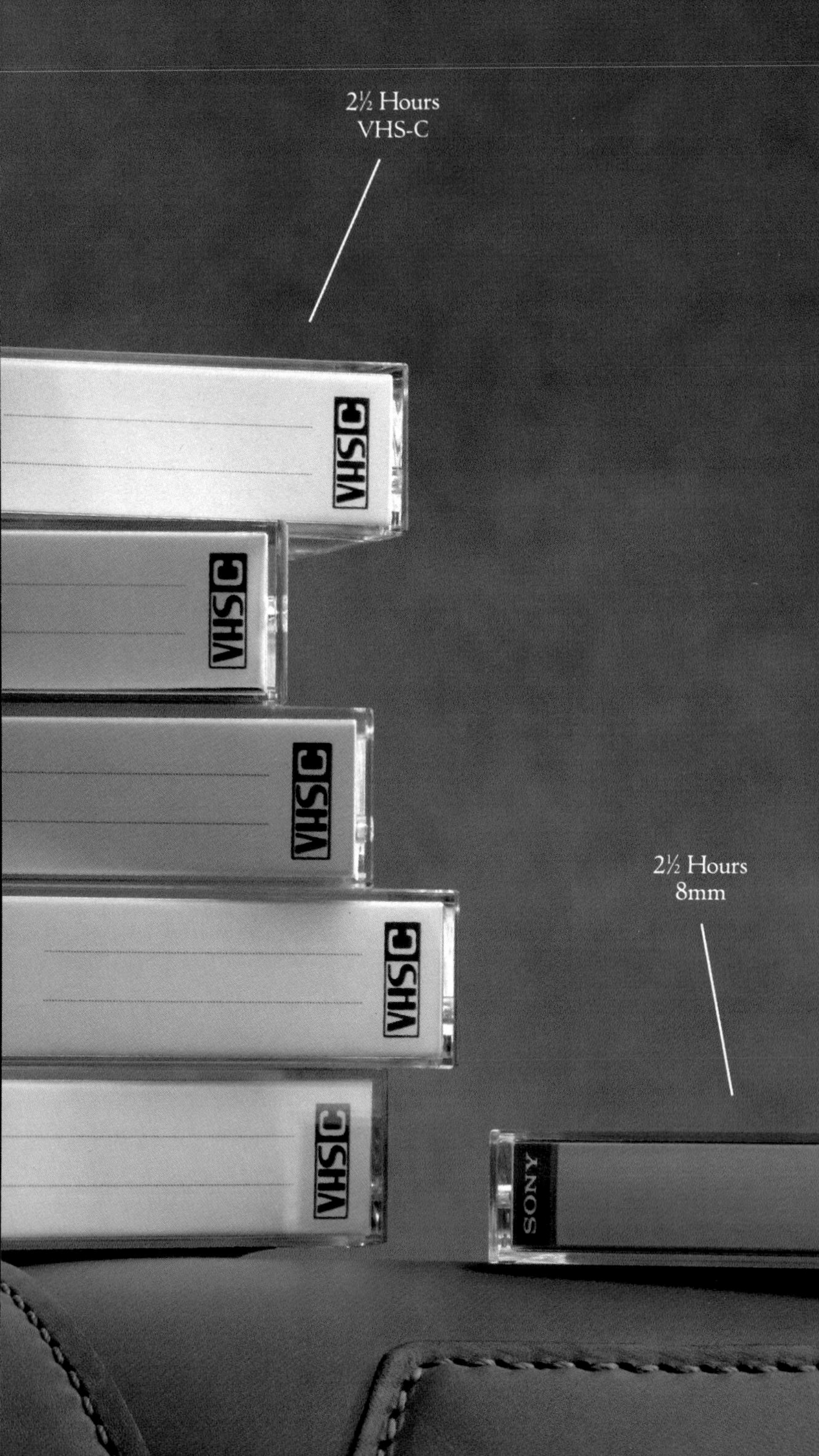
2½ Hours
VHS-C
VHS C
VHS C
VHS C
VHS C
VHS C
2½ Hours
8mm
SONY

SONY

PACK WISELY.

Given a choice, the seasoned traveler always carries less. Case in point: Sony Handycam® camcorders, America's most popular. They record up to 2½ hours on a single tape. VHS-C tapes record only 30 minutes.* And why carry five tapes when you can record everything on one? Which brings us to the first rule of traveling: pack a Sony Handycam camcorder.

*In standard play mode.

© 1992 Sony Corporation of America. All rights reserved. Sony and Handycam are trademarks of Sony.

American Express offers Travelers Cheques built for two.

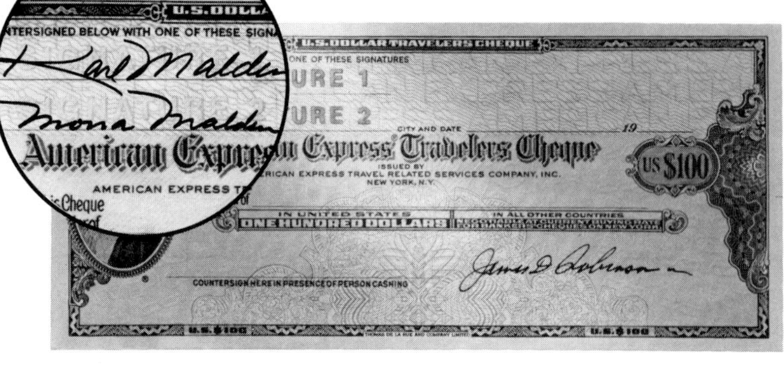

American Express® Travelers Cheques *for Two*. The first Travelers Cheques that allow either of you to use them because both of you have signed them. And only one of you needs to be present to purchase them.

Cheques *for Two* are accepted anywhere regular American Express Travelers Cheques are, which is just about everywhere. So stop by before your next trip and ask for Cheques *for Two*.

©1992 American Express Travel Related Services Company, Inc.

metto Carriage Works (tel. 803/723–8145) offers one-hour horse- and mule-drawn-carriage tours of the historic district.

Cassette Tours **Doin' the Charleston,** St. Helena's Point (tel. 803/763–1233).

Personal Guides Contact **Associated Guides of Historic Charleston** (tel. 803/724–6419); **Charleston Guide Service** (tel. 803/722–8240 or 803/724–5367 for answering service); **Parker Limousine Service** (tel. 803/723–7601), which offers chauffeur-driven luxury limousine tours; or **Tours of Historic Charleston** (tel. 803/722–0026).

Walking Tours Guided tours are given by **Historic Charleston Walking Tours** (tel. 803/722–6460) and **Charleston Tea Party Walking Tour** (tel. 803/577–5896; includes tea in a private garden).

Boat Tours **Charles Towne Princess Gray Line Water Tours** (tel. 803/722–1112 or 800/344–4483) and **Charleston Harbor Tour** (tel. 803/722–1691) offer nonstop harbor tours. **Fort Sumter Tours** (tel. 803/722–1691) includes a stop at Fort Sumter in its harbor tour. It also offers Starlight Dinner Cruises aboard a luxury yacht.

Exploring Charleston

Numbers in the margin correspond to points of interest on the Charleston map.

If you have just a day to spend in Charleston, you might begin with a carriage tour for the tidbits of history and humor that the driver-guides provide as they take you through the main streets of the historic district. This is the best way to decide where to go on your own. Next, browse through the shops of the Old Market area, where most of the carriage tours begin and end. After that, walk south along East Bay Street, past Rainbow Row (a row of pastel-painted houses near Tradd Street), or along any side streets on your way to your choice of the area's four house museums. Spend the rest of the day wandering the cool, palmetto-shaded streets, peeking into private gardens and churches of every stripe, discovering all the little surprises that reveal themselves only to those who seek them out.

If you have more time (and you really should), expand your itinerary by adding more sights within the same area; by adding a shopping excursion at the Shops at Charleston Place or along King Street; by including the Marion Square area, which has an excellent art museum and a house museum; or by adding excursions to magnificent plantations and gardens west of the Ashley River or to major historic sites east of the Cooper. There are also boat excursions and some very nice beaches.

For a good overview of the city before you begin touring, drop
1 by the **Visitor Reception & Transportation Center,** where there's parking (free for two hours; 50¢ per hour thereafter). Take time to see *Forever Charleston*, a multi-media presentation on the city. *375 Meeting St., tel. 803/853–8000. Admission: $2.50 adults, $2 senior citizens, $1.50 children 6–12, under 6 free. Shown daily 9–5 on ½ hour. Center open daily 8:30–5:30; Nov.–Feb., until 5 PM. Closed major holidays.*

Marion Square to the Battery Next you might explore the 1817 **Aiken-Rhett Mansion.** Furnished in a variety of 19th-century styles, with a heavy, ornate
2 look overall, the house was the headquarters of Confederate General P.G.T. Beauregard during the Civil War. *48 Elizabeth St., tel. 803/723–1159. Admission: $5 adults; $3.60 senior citi-*

Aiken-Rhett Mansion, **2**
American Military Museum, **22**
Calhoun Mansion, **26**
Charleston Museum, **3**
Circular Congregational Church, **14**
City Hall, **20**
College of Charleston, **7**
Congregation Beth Elohim, **8**
Dock Street Theatre, **18**
Edmonston-Alston House, **27**
Emanuel African Methodist Episcopal Church, **6**
Exchange Building/Provost Dungeon, **23**
French Huguenot Church, **19**
Gibbes Museum of Art, **11**
Heyward-Washington House and Cabbage Row area, **24**
Joseph Manigault Mansion, **4**
Market Hall, **9**
Nathaniel Russell House, **25**
Old Citadel Building, **5**
Old City Market, **10**
Old Powder Magazine, **15**
St. John's Lutheran Church, **13**
St. Michael's Episcopal Church, **21**
St. Philip's Episcopal Church, **17**
Thomas Elfe Workshop, **16**
Unitarian Church, **12**
Visitor Information Center, **1**
Waterfront Park, **29**
White Point Gardens, **28**

Charleston

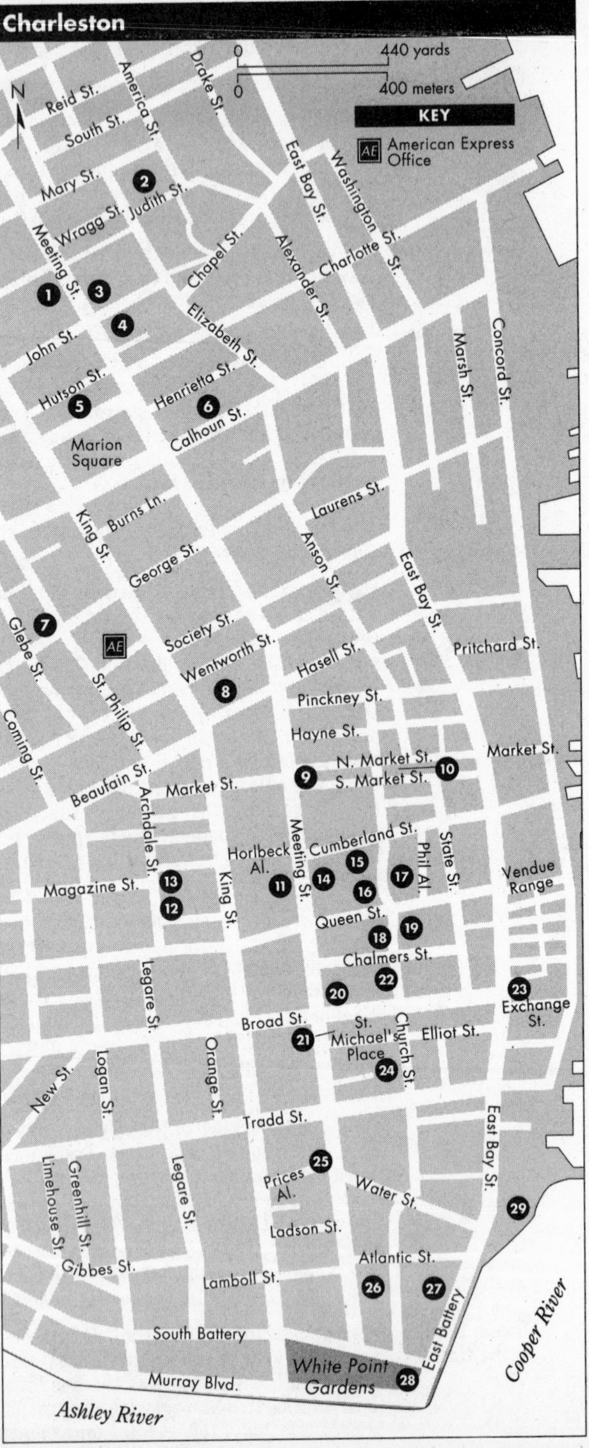

zens; $3 children 3–12, under 3 free. Open Mon.–Sat. 10–5, Sun. 1–5.

Back on Meeting Street, housed in a $6-million contemporary complex, is the oldest city museum in the United States. The
3 **Charleston Museum,** founded in 1773, is especially strong on South Carolina decorative arts. The 500,000 items in the collection—in addition to Charleston silver, fashions, toys, snuff boxes, etc.—include objects relating to natural history, archaeology, and ornithology. *360 Meeting St., tel. 803/722–2996. Admission: $5 adults; $3 children 3–12, under 3 free. Open Mon.–Sat. 9–5, Sun. 1–5. Three historic homes—the Joseph Manigault House, the Aiken-Rhett Mansion, and the Heyward-Washington House—are part of the museum, and a combination ticket can be bought for $15 adults, $9 children.*

Across John Street is one of Charleston's fine house museums,
4 and a National Historic Landmark, the **Joseph Manigault Mansion.** An outstanding example of Adam-style architecture, it was designed by Charleston architect Gabriel Manigault in 1803 and is noted for its carved-wood mantels and elaborate plasterwork. Furnishings are British, French, and Charleston antiques, including rare tricolor Wedgwood pieces. *350 Meeting St., tel. 803/723–2926. Admission: $5 adults; $3 children 3–12, under 3 free (for combination ticket* see *Charleston Museum,* above*). Open Mon.–Sat. 10–5, Sun. 1–5.*

Walk down Meeting Street to Marion Square. Facing the
5 square is the **Old Citadel Building,** built in 1822 to house state troops and arms. Here began the famed South Carolina Military College—The Citadel—now located on the banks of the Ashley River.

Walk down a block, cross Meeting, and turn east to 110 Calhoun
6 Street to visit **Emanuel African Methodist Episcopal Church,** home of the South's oldest AME congregation, which had its beginnings in 1818. The church was closed in 1822 when authorities learned Denmark Vesey used the sanctuary to plan his slave insurrection. It was reopened in 1865 at the present site. *Tel. 803/722–2561 in advance for tour. Open daily 9–4.*

If you've left your car at the visitor center, return now to retrieve it. From here you can either take an excursion to see the
7 lovely **College of Charleston** (founded in 1770 as the nation's first municipal college, with a graceful main building constructed in 1828 after a design by famed Philadelphia architect William Strickland) and/or make a shopping tour of King Street, or you can proceed directly to the market area.

In the market area, head for one of the many parking garages. Now is the time for a carriage tour, many of which leave from here (*see* Guided Tours, *above*). Our tour picks up again at
8 **Congregation Beth Elohim** (90 Hassell St.), considered one of the nation's finest examples of Greek Revival architecture. It was constructed in 1840 to replace an earlier temple—the birthplace of American Reform Judaism in 1824—that was destroyed by fire. *Open daily 10 AM–noon.*

Follow Meeting Street south to Market Street, and at the inter-
9 section on the left you'll see **Market Hall.** Built in 1841 and modeled after the Temple of Nike in Athens, the hall is a National Historic Landmark. Here you'll find the **Confederate Museum,** where the Daughters of the Confederacy preserve and display

flags, uniforms, swords, and other memorabilia. *188 Meeting St., tel. 803/723–1541. Museum admission: $1 adults; 25¢ children 6–12, under 6 free. Hours vary.*

Between Market Hall and East Bay Street is a series of low
10 sheds that once housed produce and fish markets. Called **Old City Market,** the area now features restaurants and shops. There are still vegetable and fruit vendors here, too, along with local "basket ladies" busy weaving and selling distinctive sweet-grass, pine-straw, and palmetto-leaf baskets—a craft inherited from their West African ancestors. *Usually open daily 9 AM–sunset, but hours can vary.*

Time Out This is a great area for some serious time out. Pick up batches of Charleston's famed benne (sesame) seed wafers at **Olde Colony Bakery** (tel. 803/722–2147) in the open-air market. Choose from 13 gourmet food stands in **The Gourmetisserie** (tel. 803/722–4455) in the Market Square shopping complex across South Market Street. Or indulge the urge to munch on oysters on the half-shell, steamed mussels, and clams at **A.W. Shucks** (tel. 803/723–1151) in nearby State Street Market.

Across the street is the **Omni Hotel at Charleston Place** (130 Market St.). You might wander over to peer at the lobby or have cocktails or tea in the intimate Lobby Lounge. The city's only world-class hotel is flanked by a four-story complex of upscale boutiques and specialty shops (*see* Shopping, *below*).

11 Heading south on Meeting Street, see the **Gibbes Museum of Art.** Its collection of American art includes notable 18th- and 19th-century portraits of Carolinians and an outstanding group of more than 300 miniature portraits. Don't miss the miniature rooms—intricately detailed with fabrics and furnishings and nicely displayed in shadow boxes inset in dark-paneled walls—or the Tiffany-style stained-glass dome in the rotunda's 30-foot ceiling. *135 Meeting St., tel. 803/722–2706. Admission: $3 adults, $2 senior citizens and college students, $1 children under 18. Open Tues.–Sat. 10–5, Sun. and Mon. 1–5.*

For a detour, head south on Meeting Street to Queen Street,
12 then west to Archdale. At no. 8 is the **Unitarian Church,** begun in 1772 and completed in 1787. The building was remodeled in the mid-19th century after plans inspired by the Chapel of Henry VII in Westminster Abbey, including the addition of a Gothic fan-tracery ceiling. *No regular visiting hours. Call 803/723–4617 10–noon weekdays in winter, Mon. and Fri. only in summer, to see whether someone can unlock the church.*

At the corner of Clifford and Archdale streets is the Greek Re-
13 vival–style **St. John's Lutheran Church,** built in 1817. Notice the fine craftsmanship in the delicate wrought-iron gates and fence. Organ aficionados may be interested in the 1823 Thomas Hall organ case. The church is open weekdays 9–1 (tel. 803/723–2426 before arrival). Back at Meeting Street, across from
14 the Gibbes is the unusual **Circular Congregational Church.** Legend has it that its corners were rounded off so the devil would have no place to hide. The inside of this Romanesque-style church is simple but pretty, with a beamed, vaulted ceiling. *Tel. 803/577–6400. Open weekdays 9–1.*

On Cumberland Street, one of Charleston's few remaining cob-
15 blestone thoroughfares, is the **Old Powder Magazine,** built in 1713, used as a powder storehouse during the Revolutionary War, and now a museum with costumes, furniture, armor, and other artifacts from 18th-century Charleston. *79 Cumberland St., tel. 803/722–3767. Admission: $1 adults, 50¢ students. Open weekdays 9:30–4.*

16 It's a few steps down Church Street to the **Thomas Elfe Workshop,** the home and workplace of one of the city's famed early furniture makers. Inside this restored miniature "single house," original and replica Elfe furniture is on display. *54 Queen St., tel. 803/722–2130. Admission: $3. Tours weekends, 10, 11, and noon. Closed holidays.*

17 At 146 Church Street is graceful **St. Philip's Episcopal Church** (tel. 803/722–7734). The late-Georgian–style structure, the second on the site, was completed in 1838. In its serene graveyard are buried some legendary native sons, including statesman John C. Calhoun and DuBose Heyward, the author of *Porgy*.

18 The **Dock Street Theatre,** across Queen Street, was built on the site of one of the nation's first playhouses. It combines the reconstructed early Georgian playhouse and the preserved Old Planter's Hotel (ca. 1809). *135 Church St., tel. 803/723–5648. Open weekdays noon–6 for tours ($1).*

19 At 110 Church Street is the Gothic-style **French Huguenot Church,** the only U.S. church still adhering to the original Huguenot liturgy. A French-liturgy service is held each spring. *Tel. 803/722–4385. Donations accepted. Open to visitors weekdays 10–12:30 and 2–4. Closed weekends, holidays, Jan.*

The intersection of Meeting and Broad streets is known as the Four Corners of Law, because structures here represent federal, state, city, and religious jurisdiction. The County Court House and the U.S. Post Office and Federal Court occupy two corners.

20 The Council Chamber of the graceful 1801 **City Hall,** on the northeast corner, has interesting historical displays as well as fine portraits, including John Trumbull's famed 1791 portrait of George Washington and Samuel F. B. Morse's likeness of James Monroe. *Admission free. Open weekdays 9–5. Closed holidays.*

21 On the last corner is **St. Michael's Episcopal Church,** modeled after London's St. Martin's-in-the-Fields. Completed in 1761, this is Charleston's oldest surviving church. Climb the 186-foot steeple for a panoramic view. *Tel. 803/723–0603. Open Mon., Tues., Thurs., Fri. 9–4:30; Wed. 9–3:30; Sat. 9–noon.*

From the Four Corners, head down Broad Street toward the
22 Cooper River. The **American Military Museum** displays hundreds of uniforms and artifacts from all branches of service, dating from the Revolutionary War. *115 Church St., tel. 803/723–9620. Admission: $2 adults, $1 children under 12, military in uniform no charge. Open Mon.–Sat. 10–6, Sun. 1–6.*

23 At the corner of East Bay Street stands the **Exchange Building/Provost Dungeon.** The building itself was originally a customs house. The dungeon was used by the British to confine prisoners during the Revolutionary War; today, a tableau of

lifelike wax figures recalls this era. *East Bay and Broad Sts., tel. 803/792–5020. Admission: $3 adults, $2.50 senior citizens, $1.50 children 6–11, under 6 free. Open daily 9:30–5. Closed major holidays.*

Returning to Church Street and continuing south, you'll come
24 to the **Heyward-Washington House.** Built in 1772 by rice king Daniel Heyward, it was the residence of President George Washington during his 1791 visit. The house is also the setting for Dubose Heyward's *Porgy and Bess*. The mansion is notable for fine period furnishings by such local craftsmen as Thomas Elfe and includes Charleston's only restored 18th-century kitchen open to visitors. This neighborhood is also known as Cabbage Row, the home of Dubose Heyward and an area central to Charleston's African-American history. *87 Church St., tel. 803/722–0354. Admission: $5 adults; $3 children 3–12, under 3 free. Combination ticket with Manigault House, Charleston Museum, and Aiken-Rhett Mansion: $15 adults, $9 children. Open Mon.–Sat. 10–5, Sun. 1–5.*

25 At 51 Meeting Street is the **Nathaniel Russell House,** headquarters of the Historic Charleston Foundation. Built in 1808, it is one of the nation's finest examples of Adam architecture. The interior is notable for its ornate detailing, its lavish period furnishings, and a "flying" circular staircase that spirals three stories with no apparent support. *Tel. 803/723–1623. Admission: $5, children under 6 free. Open Mon.–Sat. 10–5, Sun. 2–5. A combination ticket with the EdmonstonAlston House can be purchased at either location for $8.*

Continuing south, you'll come into an area where somewhat
26 more lavish mansions reflect a later era. The **Calhoun Mansion,** at 16 Meeting Street, is opulent by Charleston standards, an interesting reflection of Victorian taste. Built in 1876, it's notable for ornate plasterwork, fine wood moldings, and a 75-foot domed ceiling. *Tel. 803/722–8205 or 577–9863. Admission: $5 adults; $4.50 senior citizens over 62; $3 children 6–13, under 6 free. Open Wed.–Sun. 10–4, other times by appointment. Closed Jan.*

27 The **Edmonston-Alston House,** at 21 East Battery, is an imposing 1828 Greek Revival structure with a commanding view of Charleston harbor. It is tastefully furnished with antiques, portraits, Piranesi prints, silver, and fine china. *Tel. 803/722–7171 or 803/556–6020. Admission: $5, children under 6 free. A combination ticket with the Nathaniel Russell House can be purchased at either location for $8. Open Mon.–Sat. 10–5, Sun. 1:30–5.*

28 After all this serious sightseeing, relax in **White Point Gardens,** on Battery Point, facing the harbor. It's a tranquil spot, shaded by palmettos and graceful oaks.

29 Another option is **Waterfront Park** in the historic district on the edge of the Cooper River. It offers beautiful river views, fountains, landscaped gardens, and a fishing pier.

East of the Cooper River

Across the Cooper River Bridges, via U.S. 17, is the town of **Mt. Pleasant.** Here, along Shem Creek, where the area's fishing fleet brings in fresh daily catches, seafood restaurants attract visitors and locals alike. Mt. Pleasant is home to **Patriots Point,** the world's largest naval and maritime museum. Berthed here are famed aircraft carrier *Yorktown,* nuclear merchant ship *Savannah,* vintage World War II submarine *Clamagore,* cutter *Ingham,* and destroyer *Laffey.* Tours are offered in all vessels, and the film *The Fighting Lady* is shown regularly aboard the *Yorktown. Tel. 803/884–2727 or 800/327–5723. Admission: $8 adults; $7 senior citizens and military in uniform; $4 children 6–11, under 6 free. Open daily 9–6 Apr.–Oct., 9–5 rest of year.*

From the docks here, Fort Sumter Tours' boats leave for 2¼-hour cruises that include an hour-long stop at **Fort Sumter National Monument.** (The company also has boats leaving from the Municipal Marina, on Charleston's west side.) This is the only way to get there, as the fort is on a manmade island in the harbor. *Tel. 803/722–1691. Cost: $8 adults; $4 children 6–11, under 6 free. Tours depart daily from Charleston at 9:30, noon, and 2:30; from Patriots Point at 10:45, 1:30, and 4; from Mount Pleasant at 1 Easter weekend and June 15–Labor Day. Schedule varies rest of year. Closed Christmas.*

It was at Fort Sumter that the first shot of the Civil War was fired, when Confederate forces at Fort Johnson (now defunct) across the way opened fire on April 12, 1861. After a 34-hour bombardment, Union forces surrendered and Confederate troops occupied Sumter, which became a symbol of Southern resistance. The Confederacy held the fort—despite almost continual bombardment—for nearly four years, and when it was finally evacuated, Fort Sumter was a heap of rubble. Today National Park Service rangers conduct free guided tours of the restored structure, which includes a museum (also free) with historical displays and dioramas. *Tel. 803/883–3123.*

Continuing north out of Mt. Pleasant along U.S. 17, you'll find "basket ladies" at roadside stands. If you have the heart to bargain, you *may* be able to purchase the baskets at somewhat lower costs than in Charleston.

SC 703 will take you to Sullivan's Island and **Fort Moultrie,** completed in 1809 and the third fort on this site. Here Colonel William Moultrie's South Carolinians repelled a British assault in one of the first Patriot victories of the Revolutionary War. The interior has been restored. A film and slide show tell the history of the fort. *W. Middle St., Sullivan's Island, tel. 803/883–3123. Admission free. Open daily 9–6 summer, 9–5 winter. Closed Christmas.*

Back on U.S. 17, about eight miles out of Charleston, is the 1681 **Boone Hall Plantation,** approached via one of the South's most majestic avenues of oaks. The primary attraction is the grounds, with formal azalea and camellia gardens, as well as the original slave quarters—the only "slave street" still intact in the Southeast—and the cotton-gin house used in the film *North and South.* Visitors may also tour the first floor of the classic columned mansion, which was built in 1935 incorporating woodwork and flooring from the original house. *Tel. 803/884–4371. Admission: $6 adults; $5 senior citizens over 55; $2 children 6–12, under 6 free. Open Mon.–Sat. 8:30–6:30, Sun. 1–5 Apr.–Labor Day; Mon.–Sat. 9–5, Sun. 1–4 rest of year. Closed holidays.*

West of the Ashley River

Vestiges of the Old South—and Charleston's beginnings—beckon as you cross the Ashley River Bridge. Take SC 171 north to reach **Charles Towne Landing State Park,** commemorating the site of the original Charleston settlement, begun in

1670. There's a reconstructed village and fortifications, English park gardens with bicycle trails and walkways, and a replica 17th-century vessel moored in the creek. In the animal park roam species native to the region for three centuries. Bicycle and kayak rentals and cassette and tram tours are available. *1500 Old Towne Rd., tel. 803/556–4450. Admission: $5 adults; $2.50 senior citizens over 65 and children 6–14, under 6 free; Open daily 9–6 June–Labor Day; 9–5 rest of year. Closed Dec. 24–25.*

Nine miles west of Charleston via the Ashley River Road (SC 61) is **Drayton Hall,** built between 1738 and 1742. A National Historic Landmark, it is considered the nation's finest example of Georgian Palladian architecture. The mansion is the only plantation house on the Ashley River to have survived the Civil War and serves as an invaluable lesson in history as well as in architecture. It has been left unfurnished to highlight the original plaster moldings, opulent hand-carved woodwork, and other ornamental details. *Tel. 803/766–0188. Admission: $6 adults, $3 children 6–18, under 6 free. Guided tours daily 10–4 Mar.–Oct., 10–3 rest of year. Closed major holidays.*

A mile or so farther on SC 61 is **Magnolia Plantation and Gardens.** The 50-acre informal garden, begun in 1685, boasts one of the continent's largest collections of azaleas and camellias and was proclaimed the "most beautiful garden in the world" by John Galsworthy. Nature lovers may canoe through the 125-acre Waterfowl Refuge, explore the 30-acre **Audubon Swamp Garden** along boardwalks and bridges, or walk or bicycle over 500 acres of wildlife trails. Tours of the manor house, built during the Reconstruction period, depict plantation life. There is also a petting zoo and a mini-horse ranch. *Tel. 803/571–1266. Admission: $7 adults; $6.50 senior citizens; $5 teens; $3 children 4–12, under 4 free. House tours $4 extra. Mar. 15–May 15, all prices $1 additional. Open daily 8–5:30.*

Middleton Place, four miles farther north on SC 61, has the nation's oldest landscaped gardens, dating from 1741. Design highlights of the magnificent gardens—ablaze with camellias, magnolias, azaleas, roses, and flowers of all seasons—are the floral *allées*, terraced lawns, and ornamental lakes. Much of the mansion was destroyed during the Civil War, but the south wing has been restored and houses impressive collections of silver, furniture, paintings, and historic documents. The stableyard is a living outdoor museum: here craftsfolk, using authentic tools and equipment, demonstrate spinning, blacksmithing, and other domestic skills from the plantation era. Farm animals, peacocks, and other creatures roam free. *Tel. 803/556–6020 or 800/782–3608. Gardens and stableyard open daily 9–5. Admission: $8 adults; $4 children 4–12, under 4 free. Prices slightly higher mid-Mar.–mid-June. Open daily 9–5. House tours Tues.–Sun. 10–4:30, Mon. 1:30–4:30; $4 extra.*

The picturesque town of **Summerville,** about 25 miles northwest of Charleston via I–26 (Exit 199), is a pleasant place for a drive or stroll. Built by wealthy planters as an escape from hot-weather malaria, it's a treasure trove of mid-19th-century and Victorian buildings—many of which are listed in the National Register of Historic Places—with colorful gardens of camellias, azaleas, and wisteria. Streets often curve around tall pines, since a local ordinance prohibits cutting them down. This is a good place for a bit of antiquing in attractive shops.

About 24 miles north of Charleston via U.S. 52 is **Cypress Gardens,** a swamp garden created from what was once the freshwater reserve of a vast rice plantation. Explore the inky waters by boat, or walk along paths lined with moss-draped cypress trees, azaleas, camellias, daffodils, wisteria, and dogwood. Peak season is late March into April. *Tel. 803/553–0515. Admission (not including boat ride) Feb. 15–Apr. 30: $6 adults; $5 senior citizens; $2 children 6–16, under 6 free. Rest of year, $1 less and boat ride included in admission cost. Open daily 9–5.*

Charleston for Free

The Citadel Corps of Cadets Dress Parade. Visitors are welcome at the military college's parade at Summerall Field every Friday at 3:45 PM during the school year.

The Citadel Memorial Military Museum. Military documents and relics relating to the Civil War, the college, and its graduates are on display at this on-campus museum. *Tel. 803/792–6846. Open weekdays 2–5, Sat. 9–5, Sun. 10–5.*

Hampton Park Concerts in the Park. These concerts, held often on Sunday afternoons, are free. *For information, call 803/724–7327.*

Monday Night Recital Series. The College of Charleston (tel. 803/792–5737) presents guests and faculty artists in free musical performances during the school year.

What to See and Do with Children

American Military Museum (*see* Marion Square to the Battery in Exploring Charleston, *above*).
Boat Ride to Fort Sumter (*see* East of the Cooper River in Exploring Charleston, *above*).
Charles Towne Landing Animal Forest (*see* West of the Ashley River in Exploring Charleston, *above*). Birds, alligators, bison, pumas, bears, wolves, and many other animals roam in natural environments. Children's Days are held during the last two weeks of December.
Charleston Museum (*see* Marion Square to the Battery in Exploring Charleston, *above*). The Discover Me Room, designed just for children, has computers and other hands-on exhibits.
Herbie's Antique Car Museum. Nearly 100 vehicles are on display. *2140 Van Buren Rd., N. Charleston, tel. 803/747–7207. Admission: $4, children under 12 free. Open daily 11–8.*
Magnolia Plantation and Gardens (*see* West of the Ashley River in Exploring Charleston, *above*). The petting zoo and mini-horse ranch appeal to the young at heart of all ages.
Middleton Place (*see* West of the Ashley River in Exploring Charleston, *above*). At this plantation, youngsters can ride in a horse-drawn wagon, pet farm animals, and watch craftsfolk demonstrate their skills.
Palmetto Islands County Park. This family-oriented nature park has a Big Toy playground, a two-acre pond, a canoe trail, an observation tower, and marsh boardwalks. Bicycles, pedal boats, and canoes can be rented in season. *On U.S. 17N, ½ mi past Snee Farm, turn left onto Long Point Rd., tel. 803/884–*

0832. Admission: $1. Open Apr. and Sept., daily 10–6; May–Aug. and Oct., daily 10–7; Nov.–Mar., daily 10–5. Closed major holidays.

Shelling. Kiawah Island has excellent shelling. If you're not staying at the private resort, you can shell at **Beachwalker Park,** the public beach at the west end of the island. *Tel. 803/762–2172. Parking fee: $3. Open May and Sept., daily 10–6; June–Aug., daily 10–7; Apr., and Oct., weekends 10–6.*

Off the Beaten Track

Angel Oak. Reportedly the oldest living thing east of the Rockies, this 1,500-year-old giant has a 25½-foot circumference and a 151-foot limb spread. *From SC 700 turn left onto Bohicket Rd.; after about 1 mi, turn right at sign and follow dirt road, tel. 803/559–3496. Nominal fee. Visitors welcome daily 10–6.*

Avery Research Center for African American History & Culture. Charleston is steeped in African-American history, and those interested in learning more about this well-documented topic should venture to the Avery Research Center. Here you can tour the center's museum galleries and visit the archives. *125 Bull St., tel. 803/727–2009. Admission free. Reading room/archives open Mon.–Fri. 1–4:30 (or morning by appointment). Group tours of research center given Mon.–Fri. 2–4 by appointment.*

Francis Marion National Forest. About 40 miles north of Charleston via U.S. 52, this site comprises 250,000 acres of swamps, vast oaks and pines, and little lakes thought to have been formed by meteors—a good place for picnicking, camping, boating, and swimming (tel. 803/765–5222). At the park's **Rembert Dennis Wildlife Center** (off U.S. 52 in Bonneau, tel. 803/825–3387), deer, wild turkey, and striped bass are reared and studied.

St. James Church. At Goose Creek, about 19 miles north of Charleston, is this remarkably well preserved church, built between 1708 and 1719. Not in use since 1808, it retains the original box pews, slave gallery, and pulpit. The British royal arms are still visible above the chancel. The sexton's house is nearby, and he will open the church on request. *U.S. 52N to U.S. 78; at junction, turn right at stoplight and bridge and drive to top of hill, tel. 803/553–3117. Donation.*

Shopping

Most downtown Charleston shops and department stores are open from 9 or 10 AM to 5 PM. The malls are open 10–9 and on Sunday, 1–6. The sales tax is 5%. Generally, banks are open Monday through Thursday 8:30–5 and Friday from 8:30 to 6.

Shopping Districts. One of the most interesting shopping experiences awaiting visitors to Charleston is the colorful produce market in the three-block **Old City Market** at East Bay and Market streets. Adjacent to it is the **open-air flea market,** with crafts, antiques, and memorabilia. Here (and at stands along U.S. 17 north of Charleston, near Mt. Pleasant) women weave and sell baskets of grass (*see* Marion Square to the Battery in Exploring Charleston, *above*). A portion of the Old City Market where cotton was once auctioned, now called **The Market,** has been converted into a complex of specialty shops and restaurants. Other such complexes in the area are **Rainbow Market** (in two interconnected 150-year-old buildings), **Market Square,** and **State Street Market.** Also, some of Charleston's oldest and finest shops are on **King Street.**

Antiques King Street is the center. **Coles & Company** (84 Wentworth St., tel. 803/723–2142) is a direct importer of 18th- and 19th-century English antiques. **Livingston & Sons Antiques,** dealers in 18th- and 19th-century English and Continental furniture, clocks, and bric-a-brac, has two locations: a large one west of the Ashley (2137 Savannah Hwy., tel. 803/556–6162) and a smaller one in the historic district (163 King St., tel. 803/723–9697). **Geo. C. Birlant & Co.** (191 King St., tel. 803/727–3842) offers a fine selection from the 18th and 19th century English antiques.

Art Galleries The **Birds I View Gallery** (119-A Church St., tel. 803/723–1276) sells bird paintings and prints by Anne Worsham Richardson. The **Elizabeth O'Neill Verner Studio & Museum** (79 Church St., tel. 803/722–4246) is located in a 17th-century house where the late artist, one of Charleston's most distinguished, had her studio. The studio is now open to the public, as is a gallery of her pastels and etchings. Prints of her work are on sale at adjacent **Tradd Street Press** (38 Tradd St., tel. 803/722–4246). The **Virginia Fouché Bolton Art Gallery** (127 Meeting St., tel. 803/577–9351) has original paintings and limited-edition lithographs of Charleston scenes.

Gift Shops **Charleston Collections** (233 King St., tel. 803/722–7267, the Straw Market, Kiawah Island Resort, tel. 803/768–7487, and Bohicket Marina Village, between Kiawah and Seabrook resorts, tel. 803/768–9101) has Charleston chimes, prints, and candies, T-shirts, and more.

One of a Kind Over two dozen upscale boutiques are clustered in a luxurious complex adjoining the Omni Hotel called **The Shops at Charleston Place** (130 Market St., tel. 803/722–4900). Included are branches of Jaeger, Laura Ashley, Gucci, Banana Republic, Polo/Ralph Lauren, Brookstone, Godiva, and Crabtree & Evelyn. Also here is Charleston's and London's own Ben Silver, premier purveyor of blazer buttons, with over 800 designs struck from hand-engraved dies, including college, monogram, British regimental, and specialty motifs. (Ben Silver also sells British neckties, embroidered polo shirts, and blazers.)

Period Reproductions **Historic Charleston Reproductions** (105 Broad St., tel. 803/723–8292) has superb reproductions of Charleston furniture and accessories, all authorized by the Historic Charleston Foundation. Royalties from sales contribute to restoration projects. At the **Thomas Elfe Workshop** (54 Queen St., tel. 803/722–2130), you'll find excellent 18th-century reproductions and objets d'art, Charleston rice beds, handmade mirrors, and Charleston pieces in silverplate, pewter, or porcelain. At the **Old Charleston Joggling Board Co.** (tel. 803/723–4331), these Low Country oddities can be purchased.

Participant Sports

Beaches South Carolina's climate allows swimming from April through October. There are public beaches at **Beachwalker Park,** on Kiawah Island; **Folly Beach County Park** and **Folly Beach,** on Folly Island; **Isle of Palms;** and **Sullivan's Island.** Resorts with extensive private beaches are **Fairfield Ocean Ridge,** on Edisto Island; **Kiawah Island Resort; Seabrook Island;** and **Wild Dunes Resort,** on the Isle of Palms. This is definitely not a "swingles" area; all public and private beaches are family oriented.

Bicycling The **historic district** is level and compact, ideal for bicycling, and many city parks have biking trails. **Palmetto Islands County Park** also has trails. Bikes can be rented at **The Bicycle Shop** (Meeting St., tel. 803/722–8168, or 2000 Northbrook Blvd., tel. 803/764–4780), which offers a self-guided tour of the district; and at the **Charleston Carriage Co.** (tel. 803/577–0042), which also rents tandem bikes. **Pedal Carriage Co.** (tel. 803/722–3880) rents a sort of pedal "surrey with the fringe on top" for two riders (plus two children) and offers a 40-minute self-guided tour of the historic district; it also rents one-speed balloon-tire bikes.

Boardsailing Instructions are provided by **Sailsports** in Mt. Pleasant (tel. 803/881–4056) and **Time Out, Lockwood** Dr. at the Charleston marina (tel. 803/577–5979).

Fishing Fresh- and saltwater fishing is excellent along 90 miles of coastline. Surf fishing is permitted on many beaches, including Palmetto Islands County Park's. Charter fishing boats offering partial- or full-day sails to individuals include **Blue Water Sportfishing Charter,** Charleston-Awendaw area (tel. 803/884–0868). **Bohicket Yacht Charters** on Kiawah/Seabrook Islands (tel. 803/768–7294) arranges charters for groups of four to six for full- or half-day sportfishing, shark fishing, flat-bottom-boat marsh fishing, shrimping, crabbing, shelling, and nature-observing expeditions.

Golf Public courses include **Charleston Municipal** (tel. 803/795–6517), **Patriots Point** (tel. 803/881–0042), **Plantation Pines** (9 holes; tel. 803/599–2009), and **Shadowmoss** (tel. 803/556–8251). **Kiawah Island** (tel. 803/768–2121 or 800/654–2971) and **Wild Dunes** (tel. 803/886–6000 or 800/845–8880) offer golf to nonguests on a space-available basis.

Jogging Jogging paths wind through **Palmetto Islands County Park,** and **Hampton Park** has a fitness trail.

Miniature Golf There are also three 18-hole **Putt-Putt Golf Courses** (tel. 803/797–7874) in the area and 36 holes of miniature golf at **Classic Golf** (tel. 803/881–9614).

Sailing Boats can be rented and yachts chartered from **Bohicket Yacht Charters** on Kiawah/Seabrook Islands (tel. 803/768–7294).

Tennis Courts are open to the public at **Shadowmoss** (tel. 803/556–8251), **Kiawah Island** (tel. 803/768–2121), and **Wild Dunes** (tel. 803/886–6000).

Spectator Sports

Baseball The **Charleston Rainbows,** the San Diego Padres' minor-league team, play at College Park Stadium (701 Rutledge Ave., tel. 803/723–7241). For other sporting events, see the "Database" column in the sports section of the daily *News and Courier.*

Dining

By Eileen Robinson Smith

Updated by Carol Timblin

Known for its Lowcountry specialties—she-crab soup, sautéed shrimp and grits, and variations on pecan pie—Charleston is also a hotbed of new American cuisine. Its chefs are busy creating marriages of the classical and the contemporary, of down-home cooking and haute cuisine. With the strong national interest in both seafood and Southern cooking, Charleston was chosen as the host city for the American Seafood Challenge. For several years, chefs from more than 30 states have competed in what has been called the "toughest hot food competition in the country." Locally, chefs and restaurateurs took advantage of the learning experience the Challenge provided.

Across the East Cooper Bridge, in the trendy suburb of Mount Pleasant, there are a number of good eateries.

The most highly recommended restaurants in each price category are indicated by a star ★.

Category	Cost*
Expensive	over $30
Moderate	$20–$30
Inexpensive	under $20

**per person without tax (5% in SC), service, or drinks*

Expensive
Continental

Robert's of Charleston Dinner Restaurant. This intimate, elegant dining room, complemented by Broadway and light operatic musical entertainment by Chef Robert Dickson and other singers, has been acclaimed by many as one of the city's most enjoyable dining experiences. China, crystal, silver, and linen are set against peach-and-green decor. The prix-fixe menu ($67 per person, includes tax and tip) features seven courses of Continental fare (lobster pâté and slivers of duck as appetizers, miniature vegetables, a variety of entrées, and two types of wine). *Corner of Market and Meeting Sts. in Planters Inn, tel. 803/577-7465 or 800/729-0094 outside SC. Reservations required. Jacket and tie suggested. One seating at 8 PM with additional seating at 6 PM weekends. AE, MC, V. Closed Sun. and most Mon.*

French

Restaurant Million. This restaurant serves French nouvelle cuisine on Limoges china in a building dating to 1788. The rack of lamb is outstanding. *2 Unity Alley, tel. 803/577-7472. Reservations required. Dress: jacket and tie required. AE, DC, MC, V. Closed Sun.*

Low Country ★

Louis's Charleston Grill. When owner-chef Louis Osteen took over the former Shaftesbury Room in the Omni, he created an elegant low-key ambience, with historic photographs of old Charleston on mahogany-panel walls and wrought-iron chandeliers reflected in gleaming crystal and china. The food is "local, not too fancy," and entrées might include scallops pan-seared with corn sauce; pan-fried littleneck clams with green-onion pasta and garlic sauce; dessert might be buttermilk tart with raspberries. *Omni Hotel at Charleston Place, 130 Market St., tel. 803/577-4522. Reservations advised. Jacket advised. AE, MC, V. No lunch.*

Dining

Athens, **1**
Barbadoes Room, **19**
California Dreaming, **2**
Carolina's, **25**
82 Queen, **17**
Gaulart and Maliclet French Cafe, **21**
Louis's Charleston Grill, **13**
Magnolias, Uptown/ Down South, **22**
Moultrie Tavern, **23**
Restaurant Million, **24**
Robert's of Charleston Dinner Restaurant, **14**
Shem Creek Bar & Grill, **10**

Lodging

Best Western King Charles, **12**
Comfort Inn Riverview, **3**
Days Inn Historic District, **16**
Econo Lodge, **5**
Elliott House Inn, **18**
Hampton Inn Airport, **6**
Hawthorne Suites Hotel Historic Charleston, **15**
Heart of Charleston Quality Inn, **8**
Holiday Inn Mt. Pleasant, **11**
John Rutledge House Inn, **20**
Maison DuPre, **9**
Mills House, **19**
Motel 6, **7**
Omni Hotel at Charleston Place, **13**
Planters Inn, **14**
Sheraton Charleston, **4**
Two Meeting Street, **26**

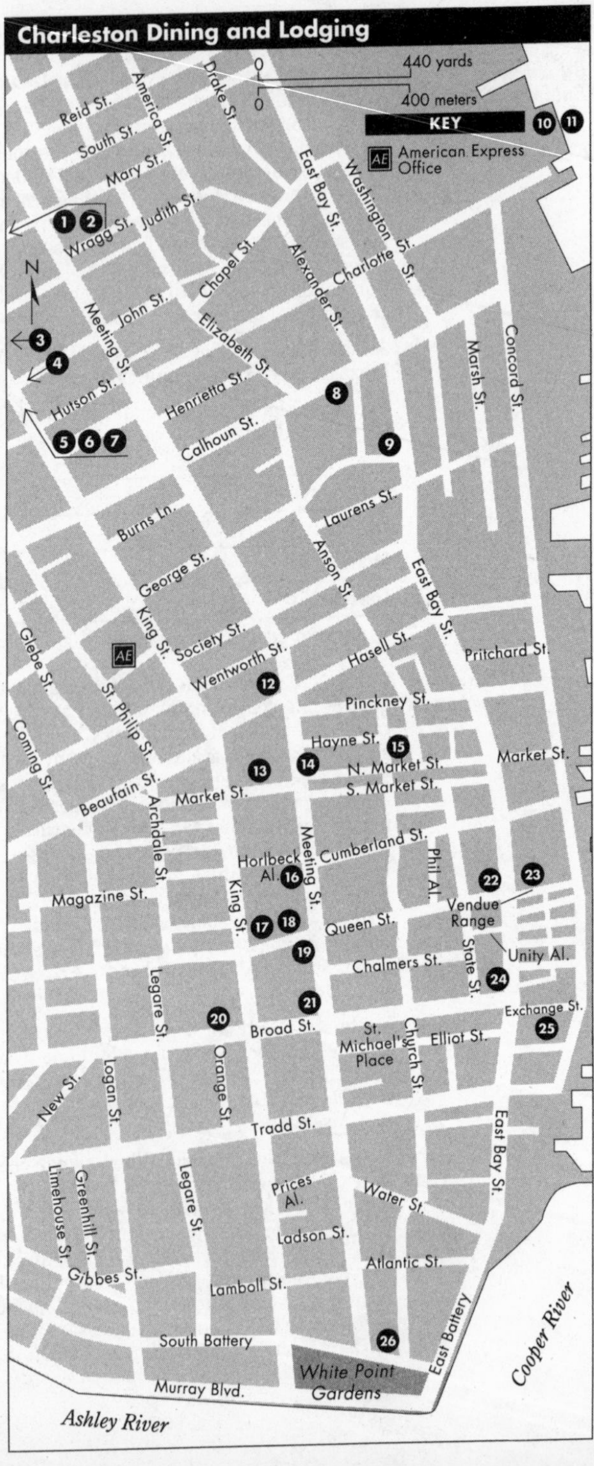

Moderate
American
★

82 Queen. This popular restaurant, part of a complex of pink stucco buildings dating to the mid-1800s, is the unofficial headquarters for many of the city's annual events; during Spoleto, musicians perform in the courtyard garden. Low Country favorites such as crab cakes are served with basil tartar sauce. The traditional commingles with innovations such as scallops simmered in leek sauce over spinach fettuccine, garnished with toasted pine nuts. Ask about the homemade relishes, particularly the garden salsa. For dessert, the Death by Chocolate is exceptional. *82 Queen St., tel. 803/723–7591. Dress: informal. Reservations preferred for dinner. AE, DC, MC, V.*

French

Gaulart and Maliclet French Cafe. This casual, chic eatery serves Continental dishes—breads and pastries, soups, salads, and sandwiches, and evening specials such as coq au vin and paella. Service is prompt. *98 Broad St., tel. 803/577–9797. Reservations not required. Dress: casual. AE, MC, V.*

Low Country

Carolina's. European chic with its black lacquer, white, and peach decor, Carolina's is the brainchild of German restaurateurs Franz Meier and Chris Weihs. Many come here for the "appeteasers" and the late-night (until 1 AM) offerings, which include everything from baby back smoked ribs to pasta with crawfish and tasso (spiced ham) in cream sauce. Dinner entrées are selections from the grill: Carolina quail with goat cheese, sundried tomatoes and basil; salmon with cilantro, ginger, and lime butter; and lamb loin with jalapeño chutney. *10 Exchange St., tel. 803/724–3800. Dress: informal. Reservations suggested. AE, MC, V. Dinner only. Closed Sun.*

Moultrie Tavern. This reconverted brick 1883 warehouse is filled with artifacts and artwork from the Civil War era. Chef/owner Robert Bohrn, who greets guests in a Confederate uniform, is a historian and unearths his own relics. The fife-and-drum music plays continuously and the food and spirits are authentically 1860s. Try an early Southern specialty: baked oyster and sausage pie with puff pastry. *18 Vendue Range, tel. 803/723–1862. Dress: informal. Dinner reservations recommended. AE, MC, V. Closed Sat. lunch and Sun.*

Seafood

Barbadoes Room. This large, airy plant- and light-filled space has a sophisticated island look and a view out to a cheery courtyard garden. Entrées include sautéed jumbo shrimp and scallops served with creamy wild mushroom sauce on a bed of fresh spinach; linguini with an assortment of fresh shellfish in a light saffron sauce; and grilled breast of duck served with tarragon pear sauce. There's an elegant and extensive Southern-style breakfast menu and a popular Sunday brunch. *115 Meeting St., in the Mills House Hotel, tel. 803/577–2400. Jacket and tie suggested at dinner. Reservations required for Sun. and holiday brunch, suggested for dinner in season. AE, DC, MC, V.*

Inexpensive
American

California Dreaming Restaurant & Bar. The floor-to-ceiling windows of this heavy-volume restaurant, in an impressive stone fort on the Ashley River, look out at night on the lights of the harbor. The crowds come for the great view, low prices, and bountiful platters of food, such as Texas smoked ribs, barbecued chicken, prime rib, and catch of the day. To make the wait bearable, take to the bar for a frothy frozen margarita. *1 Ashley Pointe Dr. (5 min from downtown), tel. 803/766–1644. Dress: informal. No reservations. AE, MC, V.*

Greek **Athens.** Located just six minutes from downtown, a sojourn here is like a Greek holiday. The *bouzouki* music is straight from the *Plaka* in Athens. George Koutsogiannaks, one of three owners, is the vocalist on tape. The *kalamari lemonato* (baby squid in lemon) is like that served in the *tavernas* on the isle of Hydra. Traditional dishes moussaka and pasticcio are mainstays, but in keeping with current health trends, the freshest of seafood appears on the special board and a vegetarian plate with eggplant, pita, feta cheese, stuffed grape leaves, and *spanakopita* (spinach pie) has been added. The homemade Greek pizza with 12 different spices is Charleston's best. *325 Folly Rd., Cross Creek Shopping Center, James Island, tel. 803/795–0957. MC, V. Closed Sun. lunch.*

Low Country/ Southern ★ **Magnolias Uptown/Down South.** This popular place, in an 1823 warehouse on the site of the old customs house, is cherished by Charlestonians and visitors alike. The magnolia theme is seen throughout, and a custom-built circular bar overlooks the dining room. Specialties include grilled dolphin fillet topped with creamed crabmeat and fresh herbs. Even a predictable New York strip steak is distinctive, served with sweet local onion chutney and new-potato hash browns. Equally innovative appetizers include seared yellow grits cakes with white chicken gravy and Cajun ham, and cheese ravioli with creamed shrimp, sea scallops, and fresh dill. *185 E. Bay St., tel. 803/577–7771. Dress informal. Reservations advised. AE, MC, V.*

Seafood **Shem Creek Bar & Grill.** This pleasant dockside spot is perennially popular for its oyster bar and light fare (until 10 PM Mon.–Wed., until 1 AM Thurs.–Sun.). There's also a wide variety of seafood entrées, including a steam pot—lobsters, clams, oysters, and sausages with melted lemon butter or hot cocktail sauce—big enough for two. *508 Mill St., Mt. Pleasant, tel. 803/884–8102. Dress: informal. No reservations. AE, D, MC, V.*

Lodging

Hotels and inns on the peninsula are generally more expensive. Also, rates tend to increase during the Spring Festival of Houses (mid-March to mid-April) and the Spoleto Festival USA (late May to early June); at those times, reservations are essential. During Visitors' Appreciation Days, from mid-November to mid-February, discounts of up to 50% may apply. For a Courtesy Discount Card, write to the **Charleston Trident Convention and Visitors Bureau** (Box 975, Charleston 29402, tel. 803/577–2510).

Three organizations offer rooms in homes, cottages, and carriage houses: **Charleston East Bed and Breakfast League** (1031 Tall Pine Rd., Mt. Pleasant 29464, tel. 803/884–8208), **Charleston Society Bed & Breakfast** (84 Murray Blvd., Charleston 29401, tel. 803/723–4948), and **Historic Charleston Bed and Breakfast** (43 Legare St., Charleston 29402, tel. 803/722–6606). Those interested in renting condominiums or houses on the beach on the Isle of Palms—some with private pools and tennis courts—might contact **Island Realty** (Box 157, Isle of Palms 29451, tel. 803/886–8144).

The most highly recommended properties in each price category are indicated by a star ★. For a map pinpointing locations, *see* Dining, *above*.

Category	Cost*
Very Expensive	over $150
Expensive	$90–$150
Moderate	$50–$90
Inexpensive	under $50

**double room; add 7% for taxes*

Hotels and Motels
Very Expensive

Best Western King Charles Inn. This inn in the historic district has spacious rooms furnished with period reproductions. *237 Meeting St., 29401, tel. 803/723–7451 or 800/528–1234. 91 rooms. Facilities: pool, dining room, lounge. AE, DC, MC, V.*

Hawthorn Suites Hotel Historic Charleston. Charleston's newest luxury hotel, its traditionally inspired architecture highlighted by a restored entrance portico from an 1874 bank now a meetings facility. Its three luxuriant gardens, named for 18th-century French botanist André Michaux, are planted with indigenous shrubs, trees, and flowers. The spacious suites, all decorated with 18th-century reproductions and canopied beds, include full kitchens or wet bars with microwave ovens and refrigerators. *181 Church St., 29401, tel. 803/577–2644 or 800/527–1133. 164 suites. Facilities: lounge, restaurant, business services, concierge, fitness center, pool, whirlpool, video library, complimentary full breakfast and afternoon refreshments, 6 meeting rooms, valet parking. AE, DC, MC, V.*

Expensive

★ **Mills House Hotel.** Antique furnishings and period decor give great charm to this luxurious Holiday Inn property, a reconstruction of a historic hostelry on its original site in the historic district. There's a lounge with live entertainment, and excellent dining in the Barbadoes Room (*see* Dining, *above*). *115 Meeting St., 29401, tel. 803/577–2400 or 800/465–4329. 215 rooms. Facilities: restaurant, 2 lounges, pool. AE, DC, MC, V.*

★ **Omni Hotel at Charleston Place.** Among the city's most luxurious hotels, this graceful, low-rise structure in the historic district is flanked by upscale boutiques and specialty shops (*see* Shopping, *above*). The lobby features a magnificent hand-blown Venetian glass chandelier, an Italian marble floor, and antiques from Sotheby's. Rooms are furnished with period reproductions. *130 Market St., 29401, tel. 803/722–4900 or 800/843–6664. 443 units, including 46 suites. Facilities: fitness center with heated pool, sauna, whirlpool, Nautilus; concierge floor with complimentary food and drink service; 2 restaurants including Louis's Charleston Grill (see Dining,* above*), 2 lounges with entertainment. AE, DC, MC, V.*

Sheraton Charleston Hotel. Some rooms and suites in this 13-story hotel outside the historic district overlook the Ashley River. Spacious rooms and suites are highlighted with Queen Anne furnishings, and there's concierge service. Live entertainment and dancing contribute to the lounge's local popularity. *170 Lockwood Dr., 29403, tel. 803/723–3000 or 800/325–3535. 337 rooms. Facilities: 4 lighted tennis courts, pool, jogging track, coffee shop, dining room, lounge, meeting rooms. AE, D, DC, MC, V.*

Moderate–Expensive

Holiday Inn Charleston/Mt. Pleasant. Just over the Cooper River Bridge, a 10-minute drive from the downtown historic district, is this new full-service hotel. Everything has been graciously done: brass lamps, crystal chandeliers, Queen

Anne–style furniture. "High-tech suites" offer PC cable hookups, large working areas, glossy ultramodern furniture, and refrigerators. *250 U.S. 17 Bypass, Mt. Pleasant 29464, tel. 803/884–6000 or 800/465–4329. 158 rooms. Facilities: outdoor pool, sauna, exercise room, cable TV/movies, meeting facilities and ballroom, concierge floor, laundry, restaurant, raw bar, lounge with DJ. AE, DC, MC, V.*

Moderate ★ **Comfort Inn Riverview.** Close to the Ashley River, the historic district, and restaurants, this 7-story contemporary inn offers free parking and complimentary Continental breakfast. *144 Bee St., 29401, tel. 803/577–2224 or 800/228–5150. 123 rooms. Facilities: pool, nonsmoking rooms. AE, MC, V.*

Days Inn Historic District. This inn is well located and attractively furnished. *155 Meeting St., 29401, tel. 803/722–8411 or 800/325–2525. 124 units. Facilities: pool, dining room. AE, DC, MC, V.*

Heart of Charleston Quality Inn. *125 Calhoun St., 29401, tel. 803/722–3391 or 800/221–2222. 126 rooms. Facilities: restaurant, lounge, pool, downtown courtesy van, free parking. AE, D, MC, V.*

Inexpensive **Econo-Lodge Airport.** This budget-chain unit is eight miles from downtown. Contemporary-style rooms are spacious and well maintained. *4725 Arco Ln., N. Charleston 29405, tel. 803/747–3672 or 800/446–6900. 48 rooms. Facilities: cable TV/free movies. Senior citizen, military/government discounts. AE, DC, MC, V.*

Hampton Inn Airport. This economy arm of Holiday Inns offers lower rates with full service amenities. Rooms are decorated in contemporary style. *4701 Arco Ln., N. Charleston 29418, tel. 803/554–7154 or 800/426–7866. 125 rooms. Facilities: pool, cable TV/free movies, suite for small meetings. AE, DC, MC, V.*

Motel 6. This well-maintained motor inn, part of a budget chain, is 10 miles from the downtown historic district. The decor is cheerful, colorful, and contemporary. *2551 Ashley Phosphate Rd., N. Charleston, 29418, tel. 803/572–6590. 126 rooms. Facilities: pool, cable TV/movies. DC, MC, V.*

Inns and Guest Houses

The charms of historic Charleston can be enhanced by a stay at one of its many inns, most housed in restored structures. Some are reminiscent of European inns; one is tastefully contemporary, tucked away on the grounds of a famous estate. For complete listings, consult the "Charleston Area Visitors Guide," published by the Charleston Trident Convention & Visitors Bureau (Box 975, Charleston 29402, tel. 803/577–2510).

Historic District ★ **John Rutledge House Inn.** This 1763 house, built by John Rutledge, one of the signers of the U.S. Constitution, was opened in 1989 as a luxury inn. Ornate ironwork on the facade features a palmetto tree and eagle motif, signifying Rutledge's service to both his state and his nation. Wine and tea are served in the ballroom, and Continental breakfast and newspapers are delivered to your room. Two charming period carriage houses also accommodate guests. *116 Broad St., tel. 803/723–7999 or 800/476–9741. 11 rooms in mansion, 4 in each carriage house. AE, MC, V. Very Expensive.*

Elliott House Inn. Listen to the chimes of St. Michael's Episcopal Church as you sip champagne in the courtyard of this lovely old inn in the heart of the historic district. Then retreat to a cozy room, furnished in period furniture, including canopied four-posters and Oriental carpets. *78 Queen St., 29401, tel. 803/*

723–1855 or 800/729–1855. 26 rooms. Facilities: cable TV, bicycles, Continental breakfast. AE, MC, V. Expensive.

Maison DuPré. A quiet retreat off busy East Bay Street, this 1801-inn, the center of which is the Benjamin DuPres house, was created out of three restored homes and two carriage houses. Enjoy a full Low Country–tea, Continental breakfast, evening turndown, and tickets to the Nathaniel Russell house museum—all complimentary. The inn is filled with antiques and each room features an original painting by Lucille Mullholland, who operates the inn with her husband Robert. *317 E. Bay St., 29401, tel. 803/723–8691 or 800/662–INNS. 12 rooms, 3 suites. AE, MC, V. Expensive.*

Planters Inn. Rooms and suites here are beautifully appointed with opulent furnishings, including mahogany four-poster beds and marble baths. There's a concierge and 24-hour room service. *112 N. Market St., 29401, tel. 803/722–2345 or 800/845–7082. 41 rooms and suites. AE, DC, MC, V. Expensive.*

★ **Two Meeting Street.** As pretty as a wedding cake and just as romantic, this turn-of-the-century inn, located near the Battery, features Tiffany windows, carved English oak paneling, and a chandelier from Czechoslovakia. There are two very private honeymoon suites. Guests are treated to afternoon sherry and Continental breakfast. *2 Meeting St., 29401, tel. 803/723–7322. 9 rooms. No credit cards. Expensive.*

West of the Ashley

★ **Middleton Inn and Conference Center.** This contemporary-style lodge with sumptuously furnished rooms is located on the grounds of Middleton Place Plantation. Floor-to-ceiling windows are hung with wooden shutters, and working fireplaces are serviced by tools forged by the estate's blacksmith. There is a cafe. *Ashley River Rd. (U.S. 61), Middleton Place, 29407, tel. 803/556–0500 or 800/543–4774. 55 rooms. Facilities: pool, tennis courts. AE, MC, V. Expensive.*

Resort Islands

The semitropical islands dotting the South Carolina coast near Charleston are home to some of the nation's finest resorts. A wide variety of packages makes them more affordable than you would imagine. Peak-season rates (during spring and summer vacations) range from \$100 to \$250 per day, double occupancy. Costs often drop considerably off-season.

★ **Kiawah Island Resort.** Choose from 150 inn rooms, 48 suites, and 300 completely equipped one- to four-bedroom villas in two luxurious resort villages on 10,000 wooded acres. There are 10 miles of fine broad beaches, four golf courses, two tennis centers, jeep and water safaris, land sailing, canoeing, surfcasting, fishing, and children's programs. There's also a general store and shops. Dining options are many and varied: Low Country specialties in the Jasmine Porch and Veranda, Indigo House; Continental cuisine in the Charleston Gallery; lagoonside dining at the Park Cafe; casual dining in the Sand Wedge, Sundancers, Jonah's. *On Kiawah Island, 21 mi from Charleston (take U.S. 17S to Main Rd., take left and follow signs), Box 12357, Charleston 29412, tel. 803/768–2121 or 800/654–2924 nationwide; 800/845–2471 in SC). AE, DC, MC, V. Very Expensive.*

Seabrook Island Resort. There are 360 completely equipped one- to three-bedroom villas, cottages, and beach houses. Beach Club and Island Club, open to all guests, are centers for dining and leisure activities. Amenities include championship golf, tennis and equestrian centers, bicycling, water sports, pools, children's programs. *On Seabrook Island, 23 mi from Charleston (take U.S. 17S to SC 171S to SC 700, then follow signs), Box 32099, Charleston 29417, tel. 803/768–1000 or 800/845–5531. AE, DC, MC, V. Very Expensive.*

Wild Dunes. This lavish, 1,500-acre resort has 360 villa accommodations, each with a kitchen and washer and dryer. There are two widely acclaimed golf courses, a racquet club, a yacht harbor on the Intracoastal Waterway, bicycling, nature trails, surfcasting, water sports, and children's programs. Guests enjoy beef specialties at The Club House and seafood at The Island House, where all dishes are created by a French master chef. There's a lounge with live entertainment. *On the Isle of Palms, 12 mi northeast of Charleston (take U.S. 17 to SC 703), Box 1410, Charleston 29402, tel. 803/886–6000 or 800/845–8880 nationwide. AE, DC, MC, V. Very Expensive.*

The Arts

Pick up the Schedule of Events at the Visitors Information Center (85 Calhoun St.) or at area hotels, inns, and restaurants. For an advance copy, contact **Charleston Trident Convention and Visitors Bureau** (Box 975, Charleston 29402, tel. 803/577–2510). Also see "Tips for Tourists" each Saturday in *The News & Courier/The Evening Post.* And the weekend ARTS-line (tel. 803/723–2787) gives information on arts events for the week.

Arts Festivals

Spoleto Festival USA. Founded by renowned maestro Gian Carlo Menotti in 1977, Spoleto has become one of the world's greatest celebrations of the arts. For two weeks, from late May to early June, opera, dance, theater, symphonic and chamber music performances, jazz, and the visual arts are showcased in concert halls, theaters, parks, churches, streets, and gardens throughout the city. For information: Spoleto Festival USA (Box 704, Charleston 29402, tel. 803/577–4500).

Piccolo Spoleto Festival. The spirited companion festival of Spoleto Festival USA showcases the best in local and regional talent from every artistic discipline. There are about 700 events—from jazz performances to puppet shows—held at 60 sites in 17 days, from mid-May through early June, and most performances are free. For a program, available May 1 each year, contact the Office of Cultural Affairs, Piccolo Spoleto Festival (133 Church St., Charleston 29401, tel. 803/724–7305).

Moja Arts Festival. Theater, dance, and music performances, art shows, films, lectures, and tours celebrating the rich heritage of the African continent are held at sites throughout the historic district the first two weeks in October. For information: The Office of Cultural Affairs (133 Church St., Charleston 29401, tel. 803/724–7305).

Southeastern Wildlife Exposition. Held in February, one of Charleston's biggest annual events features art by renowned wildlife artists. *211 Meeting St., 29401, tel. 803/723–1748.*

Concerts

The College of Charleston has a **Monday Night Recital Series** (*see* Charleston for Free, *above*). The **Charleston Symphony Orchestra** (tel. 803/723–7528) presents its Classics Concerts Series at Gaillard Municipal Auditorium (77 Calhoun St., tel. 803/577–4500). Its Brass Quintet plays at the Charleston Museum Auditorium (360 Meeting St., tel. 803/722–2996) and the Garden Theatre (371 King St., tel. 803/722–6230). Its Woodwind Quintet also performs at the Charleston Museum Auditorium, and its chamber music series is held at various locations.

Dance The **Charleston Ballet Theatre** (tel. 803/723–7334) and the **Charleston Civic Ballet** (tel. 803/722–8779 or 577–4502) perform at Gaillard Municipal Auditorium. The **Robert Ivey Ballet Company** (tel. 803/556–1343), a student group at the College of Charleston, gives a fall and spring program of jazz, classical, and modern dance at the Simons Center for the Arts.

Theater The **Footlight Players,** the **East Cooper Theater,** and the **Young Charleston Theatre Co.** stage performances at the Dock Street Theatre. The East Cooper Theatre also stages some performances at the Garden Theatre. Performances by the College of Charleston's drama department and guest theatrical groups are presented during the school year at the **Simons Center for the Arts** (tel. 803/792–5600).

Nightlife

Beach Bar **Windjammer** (tel. 803/886–8596), on the Isle of Palms, is an oceanfront spot featuring live rock music.

Dance Clubs In the market area, there's **Fannigans** (tel. 803/722–6916), where a DJ spins Top-40 hits, and the best of beach music. The "shag," South Carolina's state dance, popularized in the early '60s, is alive and well here. **Juke Box** (tel. 803/723–3431), across from Waterfront Park, with a DJ, '50s and '60s music, and a '50s look (waitresses wear cheerleader outfits); and **Myskyns** (tel. 803/577–5595), with live rock, reggae, R&B, or other bands most nights and an 8-by-10 video screen.

Hotel and Jazz Bars The **Best Friend Lounge** (tel. 803/577–2400), in the Mills House Hotel, has a guitarist playing light tunes Monday–Saturday nights. In the **Lobby Lounge** (tel. 803/722–4900) cocktails and appetizers are accompanied by piano. **Coconut Club,** in the Old Seaman's Chapel (32 N. Market St., tel. 803/723–3614), features jazz Thursday through Saturday night in a quiet atmosphere that actually allows conversation. Light appetizers are served, and there's a 1:30 Gospel brunch on Sunday.

Restaurant/ Lounges **A.W. Shucks** (tel. 803/723–1151) is a popular spot for relaxed evenings set to taped easy-listening. **Cafe 99** (tel. 803/577–4499) has laid-back '60s and '70s music indoors and out by vocalists and guitarists. **East Bay Trading Co.** (tel. 803/722–0722) has a small dance floor in its lively bar and a DJ playing Top 40s Friday and Saturday nights.

Dinner Cruise For an evening of dining and dancing afloat on the luxury yacht *Spirit of Charleston,* call 803/722–2628. *The Pride* operates from the Ripley Light Marina dock and is an 84-foot gaff-topsail schooner available for daily harbor excursions and cruises to Savannah, Georgia. Phone Capt. Bob, 803/795–1180.

Myrtle Beach and the Grand Strand

The Grand Strand, a resort area along the South Carolina coast, is one of the Eastern Seaboard's megafamily-vacation centers, and the state's top tourist area. The main attraction, of course, is the broad, beckoning beach—55 miles of it, stretching from the North Carolina border south to Georgetown, with Myrtle Beach at the hub. But the Strand has something for everyone: 48 championship golf courses, designed by such legends as Arnold Palmer, Robert Trent Jones, and Tom and George Fazio; excellent seafood restaurants; giant shopping malls and factory outlets; amusement parks, water slides, and arcades; a dozen shipwrecks for divers to explore; fine fishing; nine private campgrounds, most on the beach; plus paddle-wheeler cruises, antique-car and wax museums, the world's largest sculpture garden, a version of the Grand Ole Opry, an antique pipe organ and merry-go-round, a minor-league baseball team, and a museum dedicated entirely to rice.

Getting Around

By Plane The Myrtle Beach Jetport is served by **American, American's American Eagle** affiliate; **Delta** and its **Atlantic Southeast Airlines** affiliate; and **USAir.**

By Car Located midway between New York and Miami, the Grand Strand can be reached from all directions via Interstates 20, 26, 40, 77, 85, and 95, which connect with U.S. 17, the major north–south coastal route through the Strand.

By Train **Amtrak** (tel. 800/872–7245) service for the Grand Strand is available through a terminal in Florence. Buses connect with Amtrak there for the 70-mile drive to Myrtle Beach.

By Bus **Greyhound–Trailways Bus Lines** (tel. 803/524–4646) serves Myrtle Beach.

Public transportation is provided by **Coastal Rapid Transit Authority** (tel. 803/248–7277). It operates daily between 6 AM and 1:15 AM. The fare is 75¢, exact change required.

By Taxi Service is provided by **Coastal Cab Service** in Myrtle Beach (tel. 803/448–3360 or 803/448–4444).

By Boat Boaters traveling the Intracoastal Waterway may dock at **Hague Marina** (Hwy. 707, Myrtle Beach, tel. 803/293–2141).

Guided Tours

Palmetto Tour & Travel in Myrtle Beach (tel. 803/626–2660) and **Leisure Time Unlimited** in Myrtle Beach (Gray Line) (tel. 803/448–9483) offer tour packages, guide service, and charter service. At the **Georgetown County Chamber of Commerce and Information Center** (U.S. 17, tel. 803/546–8436), you can pick up free driving- and walking-tour maps or rent cassette walking tours. Also from here (Mar.–Oct.), you can take three different tours of historic areas: by tram, by 1840 horse-drawn carriage, or by boat.

Important Addresses and Numbers

Tourist Information **Georgetown County Chamber of Commerce and Information Center** (Box 1776, U.S. 17, Georgetown 29442, tel. 803/546–8436 or 800/777–7705). **Myrtle Beach Area Chamber of Commerce and Information Center** (1301 N. Kings Hwy., Box 2115, Myrtle Beach, 29578, tel. 803/626–7444 or 800/356–3016).

Emergencies Dial 911 for emergency assistance.

Hospital The emergency room is open 24 hours a day at the **HCA Grand Strand General Hospital** (off U.S. 17 at 809 82nd Ave. Pkwy., Myrtle Beach, tel. 803/449–4411).

Dentist For emergency service, call **Sexton's Dental Clinic** (901 Medical Plaza, 82nd Ave. Pkwy., Myrtle Beach, tel. 803/449–0431).

Exploring the Grand Strand

Myrtle Beach—whose population of 26,000 increases to about 350,000 in summer—is the center of activity in the Grand Strand. It is here that you find the amusement parks and other children's activities that make the area so popular for family vacations, as well as most of the nightlife that keeps parents and teenagers happy after beach hours. North of Myrtle Beach, in the North Strand, there is Little River, with a thriving fishing and charter industry, and the several communities —each with its own small-town flavor—that make up North Myrtle Beach. In the South Strand, Surfside Beach and Garden City are family retreats of year-round and summer homes and condominiums. Farther south are Murrells Inlet, once a pirate's haven and now a popular fishing port, and Pawleys Island, one of the East Coast's oldest resorts. Historic Georgetown, the state's third-oldest city, forms the southern tip.

Our tour begins in **Myrtle Beach.** At the **Myrtle Beach Pavilion and Amusement Park,** you'll find activities for all ages and interests: thrill and kiddie rides, including the Carolinas' largest flume, plus video games, a teen nightclub, specialty shops, antique cars, and sidewalk cafés. *Ninth Ave. N and Ocean Blvd., tel. 803/448–6456. Fees for individual attractions; family discount book available. Open daily 1 PM–midnight late-May–Sept., weekends rest of year.*

More of the unusual awaits at **Ripleys Believe It or Not Museum.** Among the more than 750 exhibits is an eight-foot, 11-inch wax replica of the world's tallest man. *901 N. Ocean Blvd., tel. 803/448–2331. Admission: $5.25 adults; $3.25 children 6–12, under 6 free. Open daily 10 AM–10 PM Apr.–Dec. Closed Jan.–Feb.*

Drama, sound, and animation highlight religious, historical, and entertainment sections in the **Myrtle Beach National Wax Museum.** *1000 N. Ocean Blvd., tel. 803/448–9921. Admission: $4.50 adults; $2 children 6–12, under 6 free. Open daily 9 AM–9 PM Feb.–mid-Oct. Closed rest of year.*

When your family's appetite for more raucous amusements has been sated, it's time to head out of town. Going south on Kings Highway, you'll come to **Murrells Inlet,** a picturesque little fishing village that boasts some of the most popular seafood restaurants on the Grand Strand. It's also a great place for chartering a fishing boat or joining a half- or full-day group excursion.

Three miles south, on the grounds of a Colonial rice plantation, is the largest outdoor collection of American sculpture, with works by such American artists as Frederic Remington and Daniel Chester French. **Brookgreen Gardens** was begun in 1931 by railroad magnate/philanthropist Archer Huntington and his wife, Anna, herself a sculptor. Today, more than 500 works are set amid beautifully landscaped grounds, with avenues of live oaks, reflecting pools, and over 2,000 plant species. Also on the 9,000-acre site is a wildlife park, an aviary, a cypress swamp, nature trails, and an education center. *18 mi south of Myrtle Beach off U.S. 17, tel. 803/237–4218. Admission: $5 adults; $2 children 6–12, under 6 free. Tape tours, $2.50 extra. Open daily 9:30–4:45 except Christmas.*

Across the highway is **Huntington Beach State Park,** the 2,500-acre former estate of the Huntingtons. The park's focal point is the Moorish-style "castle" Atalaya, once the Huntingtons' home, now open to visitors in season. In addition to the splendid beach, there is surf fishing, nature trails, an interpretive center, a salt-marsh boardwalk, picnic areas, a playground, concessions, and a campground. *Tel. 803/237–4440. Admission free; parking fee in peak months; incidentals fees. Open daily during daylight hours.*

Farther south is one of the first summer resorts on the Atlantic coast, **Pawleys Island.** Prior to the Civil War, wealthy planters and their families summered here to avoid malaria and other fevers that infested the swampy coastal region. Four miles long and a half-mile wide, it's made up mostly of weathered old summer cottages nestled in groves of oleander and oak trees. The famed Pawleys Island hammocks have been handmade here since 1880. In several shops, you can watch them being fashioned of rope and cord by local craftsfolk (*see* Shopping, *below*).

Bellefield Nature Center, south on U.S. 17, is at the entrance of Hobcaw Barony, the vast estate of the late Bernard M. Baruch. Here he consulted with such guests as President Franklin D. Roosevelt and Prime Minister Winston Churchill. The nature center, operated by the Belle W. Baruch Foundation, is used for teaching and research in forestry and marine biology. *Tel. 803/546–4623. Admission free. Open weekdays 10–5, Sat. 1–5.*

Georgetown, on the shores of Winyah Bay, was founded in 1729 by a Baptist minister and soon became the center of America's Colonial rice empire. A rich plantation culture took root here and developed on a scale comparable to Charleston's. Today, oceangoing vessels reach Georgetown's busy port through a deepwater channel, and the town's prosperity is based on industry (such as its paper mill and an iron foundry) and tourism.

In the heart of town, the graceful market-meeting building, topped by an 1842 town clock and tower, has been converted into the **Rice Museum,** which traces the history of rice cultivation through maps, tools, and dioramas. *Front and Screven Sts., tel. 803/546–7423. Admission: $2 adults, $1 military, students free. Open weekdays 9:30–4:30, Sat. 10–4:30 (until 1 PM Oct.–Mar.), Sun. 2–4:30 PM. Closed major holidays.*

Nearby, **Prince George Winyah Episcopal Church,** named after King George II, still serves the congregation established in 1721. It was built in 1737 with bricks brought over from Mother England. *Broad and Highmarket Sts., tel. 803/546–4358. Donation suggested. Visitors welcome weekdays 8–4.*

Overlooking the Sampit River from a bluff is the **Harold Kaminski House** (ca. 1760). It's especially notable for its collections of regional antiques and furnishings, and for its Chippendale and Duncan Phyfe furniture, Royal Doulton vases, and silver. *1003 Front St., tel. 803/546-7706. Admission: $4 adults; $3 senior citizens; $2 children 12–16, under 12 free. Open weekdays 10–5, tours hourly. Closed holidays, 2 weeks at Christmas.*

Twelve miles south of Georgetown, **Hopsewee Plantation,** surrounded by moss-draped live oaks, magnolias, and tree-size camellias, overlooks the North Santee River. The mansion is notable for its fine Georgian staircase and hand-carved Adam candlelight moldings. *U.S. 17, tel. 803/546-7891. Admission: $5 adults; $1 children 6–18, under 6 free. Open Tues.–Fri. 10–5 Mar.–Oct., other times by appointment. Grounds only, including nature trail, $1 per car.*

Hampton Plantation State Park, at the edge of the Francis Marion National Forest (*see* Off the Beaten Track in Charleston section, *above*), preserves the home of Archibald Rutledge, poet laureate of South Carolina for 39 years until his death in 1973. The 18th-century plantation house is a fine example of a Low Country mansion. The exterior has been restored; cutaway sections in the finely crafted interior show the changes made through the centuries. The grounds are landscaped, and picnic areas are available. *Off U.S. 17, tel. 803/546-9361. Admission: $1 adults; 50¢ children 6–18, under 6 free. Grounds free; open Thurs.–Mon. 9–6. House open Sat. 10–3, Sun. noon–3.*

What to See and Do with Children

Brookgreen Gardens (*see* Exploring, *above*).

Hawaiian Rumble. One of 45 mini-golf courses in the area, it features a smoking mountain that erupts fire and rumbles at timed intervals. *3210 33rd Ave. S, U.S. 17 S, Myrtle Beach, tel. 803/272-7812. Admission: $4 all day 9–5, $4 per round 5–midnight; children under 5: $2. Closed Jan.–Feb.*

Huntington Beach State Park (*see* Exploring, *above*).

Myrtle Beach Grand Prix. Auto-mania heaven, it offers Formula 1 race cars, go-carts, bumper boats, mini-go-carts, kiddie cars, and mini-bumper boats for adults and children age 3 and up. *Two locations: 3201 S. Kings Hwy., Myrtle Beach, tel. 803/238-4783, and Windy Hill, U.S. 17N, N. Myrtle Beach, tel. 803/272-6010. Rides priced individually, average ride $3.50. Open daily 10 AM–11 PM Mar. 10–Oct. 31.*

Myrtle Beach Pavilion and Amusement Park (*see* Exploring, *above*).

Myrtle Waves Water Park. There's splashy family fun for all ages in 17 rides and activities. *U.S. 17 Bypass and 10th Ave. N, Myrtle Beach, tel. 803/448-1026. Cost: $10.95, $8.45 after 3 PM, $5.95 spectators and over 54, children under 3 free. Open daily 10–6 (Tues.–Thurs. until 8) Memorial Day weekend–Labor Day, weekends only rest of May, after Labor Day–Sept. 30. Closed rest of year.*

Shopping

Malls **Myrtle Square Mall** (2502 N. Kings Hwy., Myrtle Beach, tel. 803/448–2513) is an upscale complex with 71 stores and restaurants, and a 250-seat Food Court. **Barefoot Landing** in North Myrtle Beach (tel. 803/272–8349) is a unique shopping/restaurant complex built over marshland and water. **Briarcliffe Mall** (10177 N. Kings Hwy., Myrtle Beach, tel. 803/272–4040) has 100 specialty shops, JC Penney, and K-mart. Both malls, the area's largest, are open Monday–Saturday 10–9:30 (until 9 in winter), Sunday 1–6.

Discount Outlets Off-price shopping outlets abound in the Grand Strand. **Waccamaw Pottery and Outlet Park** (U.S. 501 at the Waterway, Myrtle Beach, tel. 803/236–0797) is one of the nation's largest. In several buildings, over three miles of shelves are stocked with china, glassware, wicker, brass and pewter, and countless other items. Outlet Park has about 50 factory outlets with clothing, furniture, books, jewelry, and more. Open Monday through Saturday 9–10. The **Hathaway Factory Outlet** (tel. 803/236–4200), across from Waccamaw, offers menswear by Christian Dior, Ralph Lauren, and Jack Nicklaus and women's wear by White Stag and Geoffrey Beene, among others. Open daily 9–6 (until 8 Mon.–Sat. in summer).

Specialty Stores **The Hammock Shops at Pawleys Island** (tel. 803/237–8448) is a handsome complex of 17 boutiques and gift shops built with old brick brought from England as ballast. In one shop, summer visitors can see rope hammocks being made. Other wares include jewelry, toys, antiques, and designer fashions. The shops are open daily 10–5 in winter; Monday–Saturday 9:30–9, Sunday 12:30–6 in summer.

Beaches

All the Grand Strand beaches are family oriented, and almost all are public. The widest expanses are in North Myrtle Beach, where the sand stretches for up to an eighth of a mile from the dunes to the water at low tide. Those who wish to combine their sunning with nightlife and amusement-park activities can enjoy it all at Myrtle Beach. Vacationers seeking a quieter day head for the South Strand communities of Surfside Beach and Garden City, or historic Pawleys Island. All along the Strand, you can enjoy shell hunting, fishing, swimming, sunbathing, sailing, surfing, jogging, or just strolling.

Participant Sports

Fishing Because offshore waters along the Grand Strand are warmed by the Gulf Stream, fishing is usually good from early spring through December. Anglers can walk out over the Atlantic from 10 piers and jetties to try for amberjack, sea trout, and king mackerel. Surfcasters may snare bluefish, whiting, flounder, pompano, and channel bass. In the South Strand, salt marshes, inlets, and tidal creeks yield flounder, blues, croakers, spots, shrimp, clams, oysters, and blue-claw crabs. Some conveniently located marinas that offer both half- and full-day fishing and sightseeing trips are **Capt. Dick's** (U.S. 17 Bus., Murrells Inlet, tel. 803/651–3676), and **Hague Marina** (tel. 803/293–2141).

The annual **Grand Strand Fishing Rodeo** (Apr.–Oct.) features a "fish of the month" contest, with prizes for the largest catch of a designated species. The October **Arthur Smith King Mackerel Tournament** offers more than $350,000 in prizes and attracts nearly 900 boats and 5,000 anglers.

Golf The Grand Strand—known as the World's Golf Capital—has more than 75 public courses. Many are championship layouts by top designers. All share meticulously manicured greens, lush fairways, and challenging hazards. Spring and fall are the busiest seasons because of warm temperatures and off-season rates. An organization called **Golf Holiday** (tel. 803/448–5942), whose members include hotels, motels, condominiums, and golf courses along the Grand Strand, offers many package plans throughout the year.

Popular courses include: in Myrtle Beach, **Arcadian Shores Golf Club** (tel. 803/449–5217) and **Dunes Golf and Beach Club** (tel. 803/449–5236); in North Myrtle Beach, **Gator Hole** (tel. 803/249–3543), **Oyster Bay Golf Links** (tel. 803/272–6399), and **Robbers Roost Golf Club** (tel. 803/249–1471); and at Calabash, **Marsh Harbor Golf Links** (tel. 803/249–3449).

Scuba Diving In summer, a wide variety of warm-water tropical fish finds its way to the area from the Gulf Stream. Off the coast of Little River, rock and coral ledges teem with coral, sea fans, sponges, reef fish, anemones, urchins, arrow crabs, and stone crabs. Several outlying shipwrecks are home to schools of spadefish, amberjack, grouper, and barracuda. Instruction and equipment rentals are available from **The Hurricane Fleet** (Vereen's Marina, U.S. 17N, North Myrtle Beach, tel. 803/249–3571).

Tennis There are over 150 courts on the Grand Strand. Facilities include hotel and resort courts, as well as free municipal courts in Myrtle Beach, North Myrtle Beach, and Surfside Beach. Among tennis clubs offering court time, rental equipment, and instruction are **Myrtle Beach Racquet Club** (tel. 803/449–4031), **Myrtle Beach Tennis and Swim Club** (tel. 803/449–4486), and Surfside Beach's **Grand Strand Tennis Club** (tel. 803/650–3330).

Water Sports Surfboards, Hobie Cats, Jet Skis, Windsurfers, and sailboats are available for rent at **Downwind Sails** (Ocean Blvd. at 29th Ave. S, Myrtle Beach, tel. 803/448–7245).

Spectator Sports

Baseball Between early April and late August, the **Myrtle Beach Blue Jays,** farm club for the Toronto Blue Jays, play about 70 home games at the 3,500-seat Coastal Carolina Stadium (tel. 803/347–3161), off U.S. 501 less than 10 miles from downtown Myrtle Beach.

Dining

A wealth of seafood, fresh from inlets, rivers, and ocean, graces the tables of coastal South Carolina. Enjoy it in lavish portions, garnished with hush puppies, cole slaw, and fresh vegetables, in many family-style restaurants. Or sample Continental or classic American preparations at elegant resorts and upscale restaurants. The most highly recommended restaurants in each price category are indicated by a star ★.

Category	Cost*
Very Expensive	over $25
Expensive	$15–$25
Moderate	$7–$15
Inexpensive	under $7

**per person without tax (5% in South Carolina), service, or drinks*

Georgetown
Seafood
★

Rice Paddy. This cozy restaurant is apt to be crowded at lunch, when local business folk flock in for homemade vegetable soup, garden-fresh salads, and sandwiches. Dinner is more relaxed, and the menu showcases broiled fresh seafood. Crabmeat casserole is a tasty specialty. So is veal scaloppine. *408 Duke St., tel. 803/546–2021. Dress: informal. Reservations not required. AE, MC, V. Closed Sun. Moderate.*

Murrells Inlet
Seafood
★

Planter's Back Porch. Sip cool drinks in the spring house of a turn-of-the-century farmhouse, then have dinner in a garden setting reminiscent of a 19th-century Southern plantation. Black wrought-iron chandeliers are suspended from high white ceiling beams, and hanging baskets of greenery decorate white latticework archways separating the fireplace-centered main dining room and the airy, glass-enclosed porch. You can't go wrong with baked whole flounder, panned lump crabmeat, or the hearty Inlet Dinner showcasing several fresh daily catches. *U.S. 17 and Wachesaw Rd., tel. 803/651–5263 or 803/651–5544. Dress: informal. Reservations not required. AE, MC, V. Closed Dec.–mid-Feb. Moderate.*

Myrtle Beach
Seafood
★

Rice Planter's Restaurant. Dine on fresh seafood, quail, or steaks grilled to order in a homey setting enhanced by Low Country antiques, rice-plantation tools and artifacts, and candlelight. Shrimp Creole is a house specialty; among the appetizers, don't miss the crab fingers! Bread and pecan pie are home-baked. *6707 N. Kings Hwy., tel. 803/449–3456 or 803/449–3457. Dress: informal. Reservations not required. AE, MC, V. Closed Dec. 25 and 26. Moderate.*

Sea Captain's House. At this picturesque restaurant with a nautical decor, the best seats are in the windowed porch room, with its sweeping ocean views. The fireplace in the wood-paneled inside dining room casts a warm glow on cool off-season evenings. Menu highlights include she-crab soup, Low Country crab casserole, and avocado-seafood salad. Breads and desserts are home-baked. *3002 N. Ocean Blvd., tel. 803/448–8082. Also on U.S. 17 Bus., Murrells Inlet, tel. 803/651–2416. Both: Dress: informal. Reservations not required. AE, MC, V. Closed mid-Dec.–mid-Feb. Moderate.*

Southern Suppers. Here's hearty family dining in a cozy farmhouse filled with country primitive art; handmade quilts line the walls. The menu features an all-you-can-eat seafood buffet. You can also order down-home Southern specialties such as fried chicken, country-fried steak, and country ham with redeye gravy and grits. *U.S. 17S, midway between Myrtle Beach and Surfside Beach, tel. 803/238–4557. Dress: informal. Reservations not required. No liquor. MC, V. Closed Oct.–Feb. Moderate.*

Steak

Slug's Rib. A Carolinas institution, this immensely popular restaurant has a welcoming contemporary setting, with outdoor lounge overlooking the Intracoastal Waterway. It features only aged prime rib. There is also a children's menu. *9713 N. Kings Hwy., tel. 803/449-6419. Dress: informal. No reservations. AE, DC, MC, V. Moderate–Expensive.*

North Myrtle Beach
Seafood

Marina Raw Bar. This casual eatery overlooking Vereen's Marina is famous for fresh oysters, clams, and other seafood, served broiled, grilled, or fried. *U.S. 17, tel. 803/249-3972. Dress: casual. Reservations not required. AE, MC, V. Moderate.*

Pawleys Island
American Regional

Scarlett's. Tables decked with white linen, crystal and silver sparkle against green walls in this open, plant-filled room overlooking a lake where swans and ducks drift lazily by. Director Gerald Collins and chef Paul Brown focus on classic Southern cuisine highlighted by South Carolina seafood, poultry, and produce. Specialties include Carolina mountain trout stuffed with lump crabmeat and chopped herbed mushrooms, and chicken breast Rochambeau, sautéed and served over Holland rusk with artichoke hearts, sliced ham, and broiled tomatoes in a *marchand de vin* brown sauce. Desserts are outstanding. *U.S. 17 on mainland 2 miles north of Pawleys Island at Litchfield by the Sea Resort and Country Club, tel. 803/237-3000. Dress: informal. Reservations suggested. AE, MC, V. Moderate–Expensive.*

Low Country

Poogan's Porch. A sister to a Charleston restaurant by the same name, this new restaurant specializes in such unusual Low Country fare as fried Carolina alligator, seasoned with buttermilk batter and tossed in a salad of lettuce, cabbage, and jalapeño honey dressing. *The Hammock Shops, U.S. 17 S, tel. 803/237-4848. Dress: casual. Reservations suggested. AE, MC, V. Closed Sun. Moderate.*

Lodging

Among other lodgings options, condominiums are popular on the Grand Strand, combining spaciousness and modern amenities and appealing especially to families. You can choose among cottages, villas, and hotel-style high-rise units. Maid service is frequently available. For the free directories *Grand Hotel and Motel Accommodations* and *Grand Condominium and Cottage Accommodations*, write the Myrtle Beach Area Convention Bureau (710 21st Ave. N, Ste. J, Myrtle Beach, SC 29577, tel. 803/448-1629 or 800/356-3016).

Attractive package plans are available between Labor Day and spring break. Also, see Golf section in Participant Sports regarding golf packages. The most highly recommended properties in each price category are indicated by a star ★.

Category	Cost*
Very Expensive	over $100
Expensive	$65–$100
Moderate	$45–$65
Inexpensive	under $45

**double room; add 7% for taxes*

Georgetown
Moderate

Five-Thirty Prince Street Bed & Breakfast. Located in the heart of historic Georgetown, this B&B is known for its eclectic decor. Hot-pink walls set off the lemon-color sofas and various antiques in the parlor, and guests dine in the cool green-and-white latticed dining room. Traditional southern hospitality is dished out by innkeeper Nancy Bazemore. *530 Prince St., 29940, tel. 8083/527–1114. 3 rooms. No credit cards.*

Myrtle Beach
Very Expensive
★ **Myrtle Beach Hilton and Golf Club.** This luxurious high-rise oceanfront property—part of the Arcadian Shores Golf Club—is highlighted by a dramatic 14-story atrium. Spacious, airy rooms, all with sea views, are decorated in chic plum, mauve, gray, and rose tones and accented by ultracontemporary lamps and accessories. *701 Hilton Rd., Arcadian Shores, 29577, tel. 803/449–5000 or 800/445–8667. 392 rooms. Facilities: 600-foot private beach, oceanfront pool, tennis, golf, restaurant, lounges, entertainment, shops. AE, DC, MC, V.*

Radisson Resort Hotel. The Grand Strand's newest luxury property, this 20-story glass-sheathed tower is part of the Kingston Plantation complex of shops, restaurants, hotels, and condominiums set amid 145 acres of oceanside woodlands. Guest rooms are highlighted by bleached-wood furnishings and attractive artworks. The balconied one-bedroom suites have kitchenettes. *9800 Lake Dr., 29577, tel. 803/449–0006 or 800/333–3333. 513 suites. Facilities: 2 restaurants and lounge; privileges at sports/fitness complex offering racquetball, tennis, squash, aerobics, exercise equipment, sauna, pools, whirlpool. AE, DC, MC, V.*

Expensive–Very Expensive
Best Western/The Landmark. The rooms in this high-rise oceanfront resort hotel are tastefully decorated in a modern style. Some have balconies and refrigerators. *1501 S. Ocean Blvd., 29577, tel. 803/448–9441 or 800/528–1234. 325 rooms. Facilities: pool, children's activity program, game room, dining rooms, lounges, nightclub, live nightly entertainment (*see *Nightlife*, below*). AE, DC, MC, V.*

Breakers Resort Hotel. The rooms in this oceanfront resort are airy and spacious, with contemporary decor. Many have balconies and refrigerators. *2006 N. Ocean Blvd., Box 485, 29578–0485, tel. 803/626–5000 or 800/845–0688. 247 rooms. Facilities: restaurant, 3 oceanfront pools, indoor and outdoor whirlpools, saunas, exercise room, restaurant, lounge, laundry, children's programs. AE, DC, MC, V.*

Sheraton Myrtle Beach Resort. All rooms and suites have recently been renewed to create a fresh, contemporary effect. Oceanfront Lounge, highlighted by tropical colors and rattan furnishings, is a lively evening gathering spot. *2701 S. Ocean Blvd., 29577, tel. 803/448–2518 or 800/325–2525. 219 units. Facilities: restaurant, seaside dining, deck, lounge, health club, arcade, gift shop, heated outdoor pool, indoor pool. Golf and tennis package plans. AE, DC, MC, V.*

Expensive
Driftwood-on-the-Oceanfront. Under the same ownership for over 50 years, this facility is popular with families. Some rooms are oceanfront; all have recently been redecorated in sea, sky, or earth tones. *1600 N. Ocean Blvd., Box 275, 29578, tel. 803/448–1544. 90 rooms. Facilities: room refrigerators, 2 pools, laundry. AE, DC, MC, V.*

Holiday Inn Oceanfront. This in-town oceanfront inn is right at the heart of the action. The spacious rooms are decorated in cool sea tones. After beach basking, you can prolong the mood in the inn's spacious, plant-bedecked indoor recreation center, which comprises an indoor pool, exercise room, game room, and gift shop. *415 S. Ocean Blvd., 29577, tel. 803/448–4481 or 800/465–4329. 310 rooms. Facilities: oceanfront pool with bar, heated indoor pool, snack bar, sauna, whirlpool, game room, restaurant, 2 lounges (1 with live entertainment). AE, DC, MC, V.*

Moderate–Expensive

Comfort Inn. This new inn, 400 yards from the ocean, is clean, well furnished, and well maintained. *2801 S. Kings Hwy., 29577, tel. 803/626–4444 or 800/228–5150. 153 rooms. Facilities: 8 Jacuzzi suites, 6 kitchen suites, outdoor pool, health club with whirlpool and sauna, cable TV, restaurant, par-3 golf course adjacent. AE, DC, MC, V.*

Moderate

Cherry Tree Inn. This rambling, low-rise oceanfront inn is in a quiet North Strand section and caters to families. It is furnished Scandinavian-style. *5400 N. Ocean Blvd., 29577, tel. 803/449–6425 or 800/845–2036. 57 rooms. Facilities: kitchens, cable TV, Jacuzzi, laundry, video games, heated pool (enclosed in winter). AE, MC, V.*

North Myrtle Beach

Inexpensive

Economy Inn. This hotel, formerly an Econo-Lodge, is across from the airport and near Waccamaw Pottery. *3301 U.S. 17S, 29582, tel. 803/272–6191. 40 rooms. Facilities: pool, cribs, cable TV. AE, DC, MC, V.*

Pawleys Island

Moderate–Expensive

Litchfield by the Sea Resort and Country Club. Contemporary gray-blue wood suite units on stilts, a short walk from the beach, nestle amid 4,500-acre gardenlike grounds, which include three private golf clubs open to guests. *U.S. 17, 2 miles north of Pawleys Island, tel. 803/237–3000 or 800/845–1897. 97 suites. Facilities: restaurant, lounge, exercise room, whirlpool, sauna, racquetball court, indoor-outdoor pools, 17 tennis courts, conference center. AE, MC, V.*

Moderate

Ramada Inn Seagull. This is a very well-maintained inn on a golf course (excellent golf packages are available). The rooms are spacious, bright, and airy. *U.S. 17S, Box 2217, 29585, tel. 803/237–4261 or 800/272–6232. 99 rooms. Facilities: pool, dining room, lounge with entertainment, in-room movies. AE, DC, MC, V.*

The Arts

Theater productions, concerts, art exhibits, and other cultural events are regularly offered at the **Myrtle Beach Convention Center** (21st Ave. N, Myrtle Beach, tel. 803/448–7166). **The Atalaya Arts Festival** at Huntington Beach State Park in the fall is a big draw. **Art in the Park,** featuring arts and crafts, is staged in Myrtle Beach's Chapin Park three times during the summer season. (Call the Myrtle Beach Area Chamber of Commerce, tel. 800/356–3016, ext. 136, for details.)

Nightlife

Clubs offer varying fare, including beach music, the Grand Strand's unique sound '50s-style. During summer, sophisticated live entertainment is featured nightly at some clubs and resorts. Some hotels and resorts also have piano bars or lounges featuring easy-listening music.

In Myrtle Beach: **Sandals,** at the Sands Ocean Club (tel. 803/449–7055) is an intimate lounge with live entertainment. **Coquina Club,** at the Best Western Landmark Resort Hotel (tel.

803/448–9441), features beach-music bands. *Shagging* (the state dance) is popular at **Studebaker's** (tel. 803/626–3855 or 448–9747) and **Duck's** (229 Main St., N. Myrtle Beach, tel. 803/249–3858). At The Breakers Hotel, **Top of the Green Lounge and Sidewalk Cafe** (tel. 803/626–5000) is a popular spot, with nightly dancing and entertainment.

In North Myrtle Beach, the lounge at **Holiday Inn on the Ocean** (tel. 803/272–6153) showcases live bands.

In Murrells Inlet, **Drunken Jack's** (tel. 803/651–2044 or 803/651–3232) is a popular restaurant with a lounge overlooking the docks and fishing fleets.

Country-and-western music shows are popular along the Grand Strand, which is home to five music halls: **the Dixie Jubilee** (U.S. 17 Business, N. Myrtle Beach, tel. 803/238–8888), **The Carolina Opry** (which has recently relocated from Surfside Beach to 82nd Ave. N, Myrtle Beach, tel. 803/238–8888), **Southern Country Nights** (U.S. 17 Business, Surfside Beach, tel. 803/238–8888), the **Myrtle Beach Opry** (1901 N. Kings Hwy., Myrtle Beach, tel. 803/448–6779), and Dolly Parton's **Dixie Stampede** (8500 N. Kings Hwy., Myrtle Beach, tel. 803/497–9700).

Hilton Head and Beyond

Anchoring the southern tip of South Carolina's coastline is 42-square-mile Hilton Head Island, named after English sea captain William Hilton, who claimed it for England in 1663. It was settled by planters in the 1700s and flourished until the Civil War. Thereafter, the economy declined and the island languished until Charles E. Fraser, a visionary South Carolina attorney, began developing the Sea Pines resort in 1956. Other developments followed, and today Hilton Head's casual pace, broad beaches, myriad activities, and genteel good life make it one of the East Coast's most popular vacation getaways.

Beaufort is a gracious antebellum town with a compact historic district preserving lavish 18th- and 19th-century homes. Southward lies Fripp Island, a self-contained resort with controlled access. And midway between Beaufort and Charleston is Edisto ("ED-is-toh") Island, settled in 1690 and once a notable center for cultivation of silky Sea Island cotton. Some of its elaborate mansions have been restored; others brood in disrepair. About the only contemporary touches on the island are a few cottages in a popular state park and modern villas in Fairfield Ocean Ridge Resort.

Getting Around

By Plane **Hilton Head Island Airport** (tel. 803/681–8244), is served by **American Eagle, Delta, Key Air,** and **USAir Express.** Most travelers use the **Savannah International Airport,** about an hour from Hilton Head via transfer bus or limousine, which is served by American, Continental, and United.

By Car The island is 40 miles east of I–95 (Exit 28 off I–95S, Exit 5 off I–95N).

By Taxi **Yellow Cab** (tel. 803/686–6666) and **Taxi World** (tel. 803/681–TAXI) provide service in Hilton Head. Cabs here do not have meters; there is a flat rate of $6, plus a preset fare according to zone. For more than two passengers, an additional charge of $2 per person is levied.

By Boat Hilton Head Island is accessible via the Intracoastal Waterway, with docking available at several marinas, including **Shelter Cove Marina** (tel. 803/842–7001), **Harbour Town Marina** (tel. 803/671–2704), and **Schilling Boathouse** (tel. 803/689–5873).

Guided Tours

Low Country Adventures (tel. 803/681–8212) and **Colonial Historic Tours** (Savannah, GA, tel. 912/233–0083) offer tours as well as transportation from Savannah and Hilton Head Island airports. **Daufuski Seafari** (tel. 803/785–5654) conducts tours of nearby Daufuski Island. **Discover Hilton Head** (tel. 803/842–9217) gives historical tours of the island every day. **Hilton Head Helicopters** (tel. 803/681–9120) offers sightseeing flights as well as shuttle service from Savannah's airport. Hilton Head's **Adventure Cruises** (tel. 803/785–4558) offers dinner, sightseeing, and murder-mystery cruises. Self-guided walking or driving tours are available through the **Greater Beaufort County Chamber of Commerce** (tel. 803/524–3163).

Important Addresses and Numbers

Tourist Information **Beaufort County Chamber of Commerce,** Box 910, 1006 Bay St., Beaufort, 29901–0910, tel. 803/524–3163. Open weekdays 9–4:30, Saturday 10–3. **Hilton Head Island Chamber of Commerce,** Box 5647, Hilton Head Island, 29938, tel. 803/785–3673. Open weekdays 8:30–5:30, Saturday (June–Sept.) 10–4. **Hilton Head Welcome Center,** On Route 278 next to the bridge to Hilton Head Island (open daily 9–6) and at 6 Lagoon Road at the south end of the island (open daily 8 AM–9 PM).

Emergencies Dial 911 for emergency assistance.

Doctor For nonlife-threatening emergencies, no appointment is necessary at **Family Medical Center** (South Island Square, U.S. 278, tel. 803/785–2900); open daily 8–8.

Exploring Hilton Head and Beyond

Lined by towering pines, wind-sculpted live oaks, and palmetto trees, Hilton Head's 12 miles of beaches are a major attraction of this semitropical barrier island. And its oak and pine woodlands, meandering lagoons, and temperate ocean climate provide an incomparable environment for golfing, tennis, water sports, beachcombing, and sea splashing.

Choice stretches of the island are occupied by various resorts, or "plantations," among them Sea Pines, Shipyard, Palmetto Dunes, Port Royal, and Hilton Head. In these, accommodations range from rental vacation villas and lavish private homes to luxury hotels. The resorts are also private residential communities, although many have restaurants, marinas, shopping areas, and/or recreational facilities that are open to the public. All are secured, and visitors cannot tour the residential areas unless arrangements are made at the visitor or security office near the main gate of each plantation.

In the south of the island, at the **Audubon–Newell Preserve,** you'll find unusual native plant life identified and tagged in a pristine 50-acre site. There are trails, a self-guided tour, and plant walks seasonally. *Palmetto Bay Rd., tel. 803/671–2008. Admission free. Open daily during daylight hours.*

Also in the south, and part of the Sea Pines resort, is the **Sea Pines Forest Preserve,** a 605-acre public wilderness tract. There are seven miles of walking trails, a well-stocked fishing pond, a waterfowl pond, and a 3,400-year-old Indian shell ring. Both guided and self-guided tours are available. *Tel. 803/671–6486. $3 per-car fee for nonguests. Open daily 7 AM–9:30 PM. Closed during the Heritage Golf Classic in April.*

On Hilton Head Plantation, you might stop to note the earthwork fortifications that mark the site of **Fort Mitchell,** built in 1812 on a bluff overlooking Skull Creek as part of a large system across the island's northern end.

Beach walks are conducted daily in season by the Environmental Museum of Hilton Head for a nominal fee (tel. 803/842–9197; the museum itself is years away from opening).

Off the island, there's the **James M. Waddell, Jr., Mariculture Research & Development Center,** three miles west. Here methods of raising seafood commercially are studied, and visitors are invited to tour its 24 ponds and the research building to see work in progress. *Sawmill Creek Rd., near U.S. 278–SC 46 intersection, tel. 803/837–3795. Admission free. Tours weekdays at 10 AM and by appointment.*

North of here is the waterfront city of **Beaufort.** Established in 1710, Beaufort achieved immense prosperity toward the close of the 18th century when Sea Island cotton was introduced as a money crop. Many of the lavish houses that the wealthy landowners and merchants built—with wide balconies, high ceilings, and luxurious appointments—today remain, a legacy of an elegant and gracious era.

Across the street from the Beaufort County Chamber of Commerce (where you can pick up maps, tour information, and literature) is the **George Elliott House Museum,** which served as a Union hospital during the Civil War. It was built in 1840 in Greek Revival style, with leaded-glass fanlights, pine floors, and rococo ceilings. The furnishings include some fine early Victorian pieces. *1001 Bay St., tel. 803/524–8450. Admission: $3 adults, $2 children. Open weekdays 11–3, Sun. 1–3.*

Nearby, the **John Mark Verdier House Museum,** an Adam-style structure built around 1790 and headquarters for Union forces during the war, has been restored and furnished as it would have been between 1790 and the visit of Lafayette in 1825. Guided tours are available. *801 Bay St., tel. 803/524–6334. Admission: $3 adults, $2 children under 15. Open Tues.–Sat. 11–4 Feb.–mid-Dec. Closed rest of year and Thanksgiving.*

Built in 1795 and remodeled in 1852, the Gothic-style arsenal was home of the Beaufort Volunteer Artillery. It now houses the **Beaufort Museum,** with prehistoric relics, Indian pottery, and Revolutionary and Civil War exhibits. *713 Craven St., tel. 803/525–7471. Donations requested. Open weekdays 10 AM–noon, 2–5 PM; Sat. 10 AM–noon. Closed Sun., holidays.*

St. Helena's Episcopal Church, dating from 1724, was also touched by the Civil War: It was turned into a hospital and gravestones were brought inside to serve as operating tables. *501 Church St., tel. 803/524–3163. Donations appreciated. Visitors welcome Mon.–Sat. 10–4.*

Part of the 304-acre Historic Beaufort District, **Old Point** includes many private antebellum homes not open to visitors. Some may be open during the annual Fall House Tour, a mid-October weekend, and the Spring Tour of Homes and Gardens, in April or May. The rest of the year, you'll have to content yourself with appreciating the fine exteriors.

Before setting out to explore outlying areas, pause in the **Henry C. Chambers Waterfront Park** to rest and survey the scene. Its seven landscaped acres along the Beaufort River, part of the Intracoastal Waterway, include a seawall promenade, a crafts market, gardens, and a marina. Some events of the popular mid-July Beaufort Water Festival, as well as a seasonal farmers'/crafts market, take place here.

Nine miles southeast of Beaufort via U.S. 21 is **St. Helena Island,** site of the **Penn Center Historic District** and the **York W. Bailey Museum.** The institution was established in the middle of the Civil War as the South's first school for freed slaves. Today, the center provides community services. The museum (formerly Dr. Bailey's clinic) has displays reflecting the heritage of sea island blacks. *Land's End Rd., St. Helena Village, tel. 803/838–2432 or 803/838–2235. Suggested donation: $1 adults, 50¢ children 12 and under. Open weekdays 9–5.*

Nine miles farther east via U.S. 21 is **Hunting Island,** a secluded domain of ocean beaches, semitropical woodlands, and the photogenic 140-foot-high **Hunting Island Lighthouse,** built in 1859 and abandoned in 1933. If you want to make the effort to climb the spiral staircase—all 181 steps—you'll be rewarded with sweeping vistas of the island, ocean, and marshland. The 5,000-acre barrier island is a popular state park offering three miles of broad swimming beach, hiking, nature trails, and surf, inlet, and lagoon fishing. *Nominal admission per car in summer. For cabin reservations, write Hunting Island State Park, St. Helena Island, 29920, tel. 803/838–2011.*

Heading north from Beaufort on U.S. 21 to Gardens Corner, taking Rte. 17N to Rte. 174, and following that road east to the ocean will bring you to **Edisto Island** (80 miles from Beaufort). Here, magnificent stands of age-old oaks festooned with Spanish moss border quiet streams and side roads. Wild turkeys roam freely in open grasslands. Trawlers dock at rickety piers in an antiquated fishing village that looks like a monochromatic etching in early morning mists. Most of the island's inhabitants are descendants of former slaves, and they preserve many aspects of their African heritage, such as painting doorways and windowsills bright blue to ward off evil spirits.

Edisto Beach State Park, one of the state's most popular, offers three miles of beach with excellent shelling. There are cabins by the marsh and campsites by the ocean. The cabins are basic but clean and offer full housekeeping facilities. *For information and reservations, contact: Superintendent, Edisto Beach State Park, 8377 State Cabin Rd., Edisto Island 29438, tel. 803/869–2156 or 869–3396.*

What to See and Do with Children

On Hilton Head Island, each major hotel and resort offers some **summer youth activities** or a full-scale youth program. Every summer hundreds of visiting youngsters join island youth in the weekly camps offered by the Island Recreation Center. **Day camp** activities include tennis lessons, beach trips, arts and crafts, games, contests, and special events. **Sports camps** include basketball, boardsailing, golf, racquetball, sailing, soccer, tennis, and volleyball. *Contact: Hilton Head Island Recreation Association, 21 Wilborn Rd., Box 22593, Hilton Head Island, 29938, tel. 803/681–7273.*

Most hotels and resorts offer **baby-sitting** lists. During daylight hours, some **day-care services** welcome drop-ins on an hourly basis for youngsters six months to six years; check the yellow pages; or ask your hotel's concierge or front-desk staff.

Hunting Island State Park (*see* Exploring Hilton Head and Beyond, *above*) has playgrounds and is a fine picnicking site.

Off the Beaten Track

From Hilton Head Island, you can visit remote **Daufuskie Island** by boat. It was the setting for Pat Conroy's novel *The Water Is Wide,* which was made into the movie *Conrack*. Most inhabitants, descendants of former slaves, live on small farms. Remnants of churches, homes, and schools scattered among the live oaks, pines, palmettos, and semitropical shrubs serve as reminders of antebellum times, when the island was well populated and prosperous. With its unspoiled natural environment, Daufuskie won't remain off the beaten track for very long. Two major developments are under way. Boats offering excursions to the island from various marinas in Hilton Head include *The Adventure* in **Shelter Cove Harbor** (tel. 803/681–8222) and *The Gypsy* in **Harbour Town Marina** (tel. 803/842–4155). **Daufuski Seafari** (tel. 803/785–5654) also gives tours.

South of Beaufort is **Parris Island,** home of the U.S. Marine Corps Recruit Depot, where visitors are welcome to observe recruit training. Guided tours are available. Also on the base, the **Parris Island Museum** features a collection of vintage uniforms, photographs, special exhibits, and weapons. On the grounds is a replica of the Iwo Jima flag-raising monument. *Museum: Tel. 803/525–2951. Admission free. Open daily 10–4:30. Closed major holidays.*

Shopping

Malls Major Hilton Head Island shopping sites include **The Mall at Shelter Cove** (Hwy. 278, ½ mi north of Palmetto Dunes Resort, tel. 803/686–3090), with 55 shops and four restaurants; and **Coligny Plaza** (Coligny Circle, tel. 803/842–6050), with 60-plus shops, restaurants, a movie theater, and a supermarket.

Antiques **Christina's Antiques Et Cetera** (Village at Wexford, Hwy. 278, tel. 803/686–2320) features Oriental and European antiques and New Guinea primitives. **Den of Antiquity** (20 mi north of Hilton Head on U.S. 170, in Beaufort, tel. 803/842–6711), the area's largest antiques shop, carries a wide assortment of Low Country and nautical pieces. **Harbour Town Antiques** (at Harbour Town, Hilton Head, tel. 803/671–5999) has an impressive collection of American and English furniture, plus unusual pieces of Oriental and English porcelain.

Art Galleries In Hilton Head, the **Red Piano Art Gallery** (220 Cordillo Pkwy., tel. 803/785–3737) showcases works by island artists and craftsfolk. In Beaufort, the **Rhett Gallery** (809 Bay St., tel. 803/524–3339) sells Low Country art by Nancy Ricker Rhett, William Means Rhett, Stephen Webb, and James Moore Rhett.

Jewelry On Hilton Head, **The Bird's Nest** (Coligny Plaza, tel. 803/785–3737) sells locally made shell and sand-dollar jewelry. **The Goldsmith Shop** (3 Lagoon Rd., tel. 803/785–2538) features classic jewelry, island charms, custom designs, and repairs. **Touch of Turquoise** (The Mall at Shelter Cove, tel. 803/842–3880, and Beach Market at Coligny Circle, tel. 803/842–8936) sells authentic Indian jewelry, sand-dollar pendants, and more. In Beaufort, **The Craftseller** (210 Scott St., tel. 803/525–6104) showcases jewelry and other items by Southern craftsfolk.

One of a Kind **The Christmas Shop** (Atrium Mall, Hwy. 278, tel. 803/785–6002) sells Christmas ornaments and trees, plus toys, dolls, and gifts for all seasons.

Outlets **Shoppes on the Parkway** (Hwy. 278, tel. 803/686–6233), comprises nearly 30 outlets, including Dansk, Gorham, Aileen, and Van Heusen. **Low Country Factory Outlet** (Hwy. 278 at the island gateway, tel. 803/837–4339), has 40 outlets, offering national brands of clothing, shoes, and housewares.

Beaches

On Hilton Head, the ocean side features wide stretches of gently sloping white sand, extending for the island's entire 12-mile length. Many spots remain secluded and uncrowded. Although resort beaches are reserved for guests and residents, there are about 35 public beach entrances from Folly Field to South Forest Beach near Sea Pines. Two main parking areas are at Coligny Circle, near the Holiday Inn, and on Folly Field Road, off U.S. 278 near the Hilton Head Island Beach and Tennis Resort. Signs along U.S. 278 point the way to Bradley, Burkes, and Singleton beaches, where parking space is limited.

Hunting Island State Park has three miles of broad swimming beaches. **Edisto Beach State Park** on Edisto Island also has nearly three miles of public beach.

Participant Sports

Bicycling There are pathways in several areas of Hilton Head (many in the resorts), and pedaling is popular along the firmly packed beach. Bicycles can be rented at most hotels and resorts. One of the oldest rentals here is **Harbour Town Bicycles** (Graves Plaza, Hwy. 278, tel. 803/785–3546; South Beach Cycles, tel. 803/671–7300) and **Palmetto Dunes Resort** (tel. 803/671–5386).

Fishing On Hilton Head, you can pick oysters, dig for clams, or cast for shrimp; supplies are available at **Shelter Cove Marina** at Palmetto Dunes (tel. 803/842–7001). Local marinas offer in-shore and deep-sea fishing charters. Each year a billfishing tournament and two king mackerel tournaments attract anglers.

Golf Hilton Head has 30 championship courses built by world-renowned golf architects, and 20 are open to the public, including

Palmetto Dunes Plantation (tel. 803/785–1138); **Sea Pines Plantation** (tel. 803/671–2446); and **Port Royal and Shipyard Plantations** (tel. 803/689–5600). New on the scene are **Island West Golf Course** (Hwy. 278, tel. 803/689–6660) and **Old South Golf Links** (Hwy. 278, tel. 803/785–5353). Harbour Town Golf Links at Sea Pines Plantation hosts the MCI Heritage Golf Classic every spring. (For details on the tournament, call 803/671–2448 or outside SC 800/677–2293.)

Horseback Riding Many trails wind through woods and nature preserves. There are five fully equipped stables in the Hilton Head area: **Lawton Stables** in Sea Pines (tel. 803/671–2586), **Moss Creek Plantation Equestrian Center** (tel. 803/837–6117), **Rose Hill Plantation Stables** (tel. 803/757–3082), **Sandy Creek Stables** near Spanish Wells (tel. 803/681–4610), and **Seabrook Farm Stables** in Hilton Head Plantation (tel. 803/681–5415).

Tennis There are more than 300 courts on Hilton Head. Four resorts—**Sea Pines** (tel. 803/671–2494), **Shipyard Plantation** (tel. 803/686–8804), and **Port Royal** (tel. 803/681–3322)—are rated among the top 50 tennis destinations in the United States. Racquet clubs that welcome guest play on clay, composition, hard-surface, synthetic, and even a few grass courts include **Port Royal Tennis Club** (tel. 803/686–8803), **Palmetto Dunes** (tel. 803/785–1152), **Sea Pines Racquet Club** (tel. 803/671–2494), and **Van der Meer Tennis Center** (tel. 803/785–8388 or 800/845–6138). Each April, top professional women's stars participate in the Family Circle Magazine Cup Tennis Tournament at Sea Pines Racquet Club (tel. 803/671–2448 or 800/845–6131).

Windsurfing Lessons and rentals are available from **Windsurfing Hilton Head** at Sea Pines Resort's South Beach Marina (tel. 803/671–2643) and at Shelter Cove Plaza (tel. 803/686–6996).

Spectator Sports

Polo There are matches every other Sunday during spring and fall at **Rose Hill Plantation** (tel. 803/842–2828).

Dining

All along this stretch of South Carolina coastline, fresh seafood is showcased on menus. But Hilton Head Island is a cosmopolitan community, with restaurants to suit every palate. The most highly recommended restaurants in each price category are indicated by a star ★.

Category	Cost*
Very Expensive	over $25
Expensive	$15–$25
Moderate	$7–$15
Inexpensive	under $7

**per person without tax (5% in South Carolina), service, or drinks*

Beaufort *Continental* **Anchorage House.** The ambience of this 1765 structure is enhanced by period furnishings, candlelight, and gleaming silver and crystal. Sherry-laced she-crab soup, crabmeat casserole, and other Low Country specialties share the menu with Continental fare. *1103 Bay St., tel. 803/524–9392. Jackets suggested at dinner. Reservations suggested. AE, DC, MC, V. Closed Sun., major holidays. Moderate–Expensive.*

Hilton Head Island
Continental

Harbourmaster's. With sweeping views of the harbor, this spacious, multilevel dining room offers such dishes as chateaubriand and New Zealand rack of lamb laced with a brandy demiglaze. Service is deft. Prix-fixe early dinners ($16.95) are offered daily except Sunday. *In Shelter Cove Marina, off U.S. 278, across from Palmetto Dunes, tel. 803/785–3030. Jacket required at dinner. Reservations required. AE, DC, MC, V. Closed Sun. and during Jan. Very Expensive.*

★ **Barony.** An intimate series of softly lighted seating areas with "upscale country French" decor range off the main dining room, which is centered with a display of drop-dead desserts, marzipan flowers, and exotic cheeses and breads. There's crystal and silver, and a quartet of tuxedoed waiters for every table. In addition to the regular Low Country and Continental entrées, elegant lowcalorie menus are offered, such as chilled coconut-and-pineapple soup, asparagus salad with quail eggs, sorbet, poached fillet of Dover sole with seafood mousse, and macédoine of fresh fruits with raspberry sauce. *The Westin Resort, Hilton Head Island. 135 S. Port Royal Dr., tel. 803/681–4000. Jacket and tie required. Reservations suggested. AE, DC, MC, V. Closed Mon. Expensive–Very Expensive.*

Low Country

Old Fort Pub. Tucked away in a quiet site overlooking Skull Creek, this rustic restaurant specializes in such dishes as oyster pie, oysters wrapped in Smithfield ham, Savannah chicken-fried steak with onion gravy, and hoppin' john. *In Hilton Head Plantation, tel. 803/681–2386. Dress: informal. No reservations. AE, DC, MC, V. No lunch Sun. Moderate.*

Seafood

Crazy Crab. This casual eatery serves the freshest seafood on the island—steamed, fried, baked, or broiled . . . any way you like it—at two locations overlooking the water. They're famous for their steamed seafood pot and Crazy Crab boil. *Hwy. 278, tel. 803/681–5021 (dinner only); and Harbour Town Yacht Basin, tel. 803/671–9494 (lunch and dinner). Dress: casual. Reservations not accepted. AE, DC, MC, V. Moderate.*

Hemingway's. This oceanfront restaurant serves pompano *en papillote*, trout amandine with herbed lemon-butter sauce, fresh grilled seafoods, and steaks, in a relaxed, Key West–type atmosphere. *Hyatt Regency Hilton Head, in Palmetto Dunes Resort, tel. 803/785–1234. Dress: informal. Reservations suggested. AE, DC, MC, V. Moderate.*

Hudson's Seafood House on the Docks. This huge, airy, family-owned restaurant has its own fishing fleet; catches are rushed straight from the boats to the kitchens. The dining room always seems full, but service is quick and friendly and diners never feel rushed. There's a separate oyster bar, as well as an adjacent family-style restaurant, The Landing. *1 Hudson Rd., on the docks, tel. 803/681–2773. The Landing; 803/681–3363. Dress: informal. No reservations. AE, MC, V. Moderate.*

Lodging

Hilton Head Island is home to some of the nation's finest and most luxurious resort developments. **Sea Pines,** the oldest and best-known, occupies 4,500 choice, thickly wooded acres. Its three championship golf courses include renowned Harbour Town Links, designed by Pete Dye and Jack Nicklaus and one of the top 20 U.S. courses. There's a fine beach, two racquet clubs, riding stables, two shopping plazas, and a 500-acre forest preserve. Accommodations are in luxurious homes and villas fronting the ocean or the golf courses.

Sea Pines's emphasis on preserving the integrity of the island's ecology has set the tone for resorts that have followed. Among them, differences are subtle. In **Shipyard Plantation,** Marriott's Hilton Head Resort caters to groups from 50 to 1,500; its luxuriant garden setting, water sports, and fitness center make it a favorite with family vacationers as well. This plantation also has a wide array of villa condominiums, most overlooking an excellent golf facility with three championship nines. There's a racquet club and a small beach club.

Palmetto Dunes Resort includes the Hyatt Regency Hilton Head, the island's largest resort hotel. It has a concierge floor and extensive meeting space and services, making it especially appealing to groups. A good array of vacation packages attracts families as well. With kitchenettes and all-oceanfront rooms, the Mariner's Inn–A Clarion Hotel (also in Palmetto Dunes) is a great favorite with families and honeymooners. Palmetto Dunes is home of the renowned Rod Laver Tennis Center and has a good stretch of beach and three championship golf courses. In addition to its hotels, there are several luxury rental villa complexes overlooking the ocean.

At **Port Royal Plantation** is the new, super-luxurious Westin Resort, Hilton Head Island. With vast meeting spaces and an emphasis on upscale amenities, it caters to the upscale business traveler and middle-aged to older affluent vacationers. Not that families aren't warmly welcomed, but the atmosphere is a bit more formal than elsewhere on the island. Port Royal has three championship golf courses, which have hosted PGA events, and its racquet club offers play on clay, hard, and grass courts.

Hilton Head Plantation, a private residential community, is on the northern, "quiet side" of the island. It has no rentals, but two of its golf courses are available for public play.

Not all lodgings are located within the resorts. The high-rise Holiday Inn, for example, occupies a choice patch of beach and is very popular with families and smaller groups. It's easily accessible from the main business area.

Hilton Head Central Reservations (Box 5312, Hilton Head Island, 29938, tel. 803/785–9050 or 800/845–7018) is a good source of detailed information about various island resorts and properties. It represents almost every hotel, motel, and condominium-rental agency on the island. Other rental options are available through the **Hilton Head Condo Hotline** (tel. 803/785–2939 or 800/258–5852, ext. 53).

Rates can drop appreciably in the off-season (on Hilton Head Island, Nov.–Mar.), and package plans are available year-round. The most highly recommended properties in each price category are indicated by a star ★.

Category	Cost*
Very Expensive	over $145
Expensive	$95–$145
Moderate	$55–$95
Inexpensive	under $50

**double room; add 7% for taxes*

Beaufort
Expensive

Rhett House Inn. True southern hospitality can be had at this storybook inn in the heart of the historic district. Art and antiques fill the rooms, and guests are served breakfast and afternoon tea. *1009 Craven St., 29902, tel. 803/524–9030. 9 rooms, 1 suite. Facilities: pool table, bicycles. MC, V.*

Two Sons Inn. Guests at this B&B, a restored 1917 Neoclassical home overlooking the Beaufort River, enjoy large rooms, afternoon tea-and-toddy hour, and full breakfast. *1705 Bay St., 29902, tel. 803/522–1122 or 800/552–4244. 5 rooms. MC, V.*

Moderate

Best Western Sea Island Inn. At this well-maintained resort inn in the downtown historic district, rooms feature period decor. *1015 Bay St., Box 532, 29902, tel. 803/524–4121 or 800/528–1234. 43 rooms. Facilities: pool, cable TV, restaurant, lounge. AE, DC, MC, V.*

Holiday Inn of Beaufort. This motor inn is conveniently located for visitors to Parris Island or the Marine Corps Air Station. *U.S. 21 and Lovejoy St., Box 1008, 29902, tel. 803/524–2144 or 800/465–4329. 152 rooms. Facilities: heated pool, tennis, cable TV/movies, restaurant. AE, DC, MC, V.*

Edisto Island
Moderate–Expensive

Fairfield Ocean Ridge Resort. This is a good choice for vacationers seeking to combine all the resort amenities with a get-away-from-it-all setting. There are accommodations in well-furnished two- and three-bedroom villa units tastefully decorated in contemporary style. *1 King Cotton Rd., Box 27, 29438, tel. 803/869–2561 or 800/845–8500. 100 units. Facilities: pool, wading pool, beach, marina, fishing, tennis, golf, miniature golf, social and recreational programs, children's activities, nature trails, restaurant, lounge. AE, DC, MC, V.*

Fripp Island
Moderate–Expensive

Fripp Island Resort. The resort encompasses the entire island, and access is limited to guests only. The two- and three-bedroom villas are contemporary in decor. *19 mi south of Beaufort via U.S. 21, 1 Tarpon Blvd., 29920, tel. 803/838–3535 or 800/845–4100. 133 units. Facilities: pools, tennis courts, championship golf course, full-service marina with rental boats, bicycle and jogging trails, laundry, children's program, 3 restaurants. AE, MC, V.*

Hilton Head Island
Very Expensive

Hyatt Regency Hilton Head. The island's largest resort hotel has completed a $32-million renovation. Rooms are beautifully decorated, and some feature balconies. *U.S. 278, in Palmetto Dunes Resort, Box 6167, 29938, tel. 803/785–1234 or 800/233–1234. 505 rooms. Facilities: swimming pools, health club, sailboats, concierge floor, extensive convention facilities, cable TV/movies, coffee shop, dining rooms, lounges, entertainment, dancing. Guests have privileges at 3 18-hole championship golf courses and 25 hard, grass, and clay tennis courts at Palmetto Dunes, plus 3 mi of private beach. AE, DC, MC, V.*

★ **Westin Resort, Hilton Head Island.** Among the island's newest luxury properties, this horseshoe-shaped hotel sprawls in a lushly landscaped oceanside setting. The expansive guest rooms, most with ocean view, are furnished in a mix of period reproduction and contemporary furnishings. All have comfortable seating areas and desks. Public areas display museum-quality Oriental porcelains, screens, paintings, and furnishings. *At Port Royal Resort, 135 S. Port Royal Dr., 29928, tel. 803/681–4000 or 800/228–3000. 415 rooms, 38 suites. Facilities: pool, water sports, health club, 3 restaurants* (see *The Barony in Dining*, above*), 2 lounges with live entertainment, pianist in elegant lobby lounge. AE, DC, MC, V.*

Expensive–Very Expensive **Hilton Resort.** There's a Caribbean-island feel to this five-story resort hotel set in an enclave. The grounds are beautifully landscaped. All oceanside, the rooms are spacious and colorfully decorated in a modern style. *In Palmetto Dunes Resort, 23 Ocean Ln., Box 6165, 29938, tel. 803/842–8000 or 800/221–2222. 324 rooms. Facilities: pool, health club, sauna, whirlpool, volleyball, canoeing, fishing, biking, sailing, restaurant, full resort privileges of Palmetto Dunes. AE, DC, MC, V.*

Marriott's Hilton Head Resort. This oceanside hotel has spacious rooms with informally elegant tropical decor and ocean, garden, or forest views. The lobby is highlighted by a dramatic five-story atrium. Pathways wind amid lagoons and gardens to a wide, sandy private beach. Marriott Resorts (tel. 803/785–2040 or 800/527–3490) also offers villa rentals. *130 Shipyard Dr., Shipyard Plantation, 29928, tel. 803/842–2400 or 800/334–1881. 313 rooms, 25 suites. Facilities: pool, exercise rooms, sauna, rental catamarans, 3 restaurants, privileges at nearby golf and tennis clubs. AE, DC, MC, V.*

Expensive **Holiday Inn Oceanfront Resort.** This handsome high-rise motor hotel is located on a broad, quiet stretch of beach. The rooms are spacious and well furnished in a contemporary style. *S. Forest Beach Dr., Box 5728, 29938, tel. 803/785–5126 or 800/465–4329. 249 rooms. Facilities: outdoor pool, poolside bar, restaurant, lounge with entertainment, golf, tennis, marina privileges. AE, DC, MC, V.*

Inexpensive–Moderate **Red Roof Inn.** This two-story inn is especially popular with families. It's a short drive to the public beaches. *5 Regency Pkwy. (U.S. 278), 29928, tel. 803/686–6808 or 800/843–7663. 112 units. Facilities: cable TV/movies. AE, DC, MC, V.*

The Arts

Community Playhouse (Arrow Rd., tel. 803/785–4878) presents up to 10 musicals or dramatic productions each year and offers a theater program for youths. During the warmer months, there are free outdoor concerts at **Harbour Town** and **Shelter Cove.** Concerts, plays, films, art shows, theater—along with sporting events, food fairs, and minitournaments—make up Hilton Head Island's **SpringFest,** which runs for the entire month of March. For information, contact SpringFest (Box 5278-D, Hilton Head Island, SC 29938, tel. 803/686–4944).

Nightlife

Dancing At the **Battery** (tel. 803/681–4000), in The Westin Resort, Hilton Head Island, at Port Royal Resort, there's entertainment every night except Monday and dancing nightly to a five-piece band. At **Club Indigo** (tel. 803/785–1234), a large cabaret downstairs at the Hyatt Regency Hilton Head, there is dancing and two shows nightly Monday through Saturday. At the **Mockingbird Lounge** (tel. 803/842–2400), in the Marriott's Hilton Head Resort, Shipyard Plantation, there's a dance band at night Monday through Saturday. **Scarlett's** (tel. 803/842–8000), a sophisticated oceanfront night spot in the Hilton Resort, Palmetto Dunes, features smooth jazz nightly. At **W.G. Shucker's** (tel. 803/785–8050), a lively spot on Palmetto Bay Road, there's dancing nightly on the island's largest dance floor. **Tiki Bar** (tel. 803/785–5126), a locally popular lounge in the Holiday Inn Oceanfront Resort, has nightly entertainment.

Easy Listening

Cafe Europa (tel. 803/671–3399), at the Lighthouse in Harbourtown, has nightly piano entertainment. **The Gazebo** (tel. 803/681–4000), The Westin Resort, Hilton Head Island's opulent lobby lounge overlooking tropical grounds and the ocean, offers classical entertainment at the grand piano afternoons and early evenings every night but Saturday. **Hemingway's Lounge** (tel. 803/785–1234), adjoining Hemingway's at the Hyatt Regency Hilton Head, Palmetto Dunes Resort, has live entertainment in a casually elegant setting. **The Marsh Tacky** (tel. 803/681–4000), an oceanfront lounge at The Westin Resort, Hilton Head Island at Port Royal, has informal entertainment every night but Sunday. **Playful Pelican** (tel. 803/681–4000), the pool bar at the same location, has a live calypso band Tuesday through Sunday from 1 to 4 PM.

Elsewhere in the State

The State Capital

Columbia. Centrally located in South Carolina, Columbia was founded in 1786 as the capital city. The Italian Renaissance style State Capitol dates from 1855, and contains rich appointments of marble, mahogany, art works, and a replica of Houdon's statue of George Washington. *Intersection of Main and Gervais Sts., tel 803/734–2430. Admission free. Guided tours every half hour. Open weekdays 9–noon and 1–4.*

The South Carolina State Museum, Columbia. Located in a refurbished textile mill, the museum interprets in multi-faceted exhibits South Carolina's history, archaeology, fine arts, and scientific and technological accomplishments. A permanent exhibit portrays noted black astronauts (dedicated to South Carolina native Dr. Ronald McNair, who died on the *Challenger*), and another focuses on the cotton industry and slavery. An iron gate made for the museum by Phillip Simmons, the "dean of Charleston blacksmiths," is also on display. *301 Gervais St., tel. 803/737–4921. Admission: $3 adults; $2 senior citizens, college students, and military with I.D.; $1.25 children, 6–17. Open Mon.–Sat. 10–5, Sun. 1–5, closed Christmas.*

Riverbanks Zoological Park, Columbia. Showcase for over 2,000 birds and animals representing over 450 different species, some endangered, in natural habitats, the Zoological Park is among the nation's best. It also offers a cage-free aviary, reptile house, aquarium, and breeding facilities for rare and fragile species. *Junction of I–126 and Greystone Blvd., tel. 803/779–8717. Admission: $3.75 adults; $2.50 senior citizens over 62; $3 children 13–18. Open weekdays 9–4, weekends 9–5 in summer; daily 9–4 rest of year, closed Dec. 25.*

The Greenville County Museum of Art, Greenville. Housed in an innovative modern structure, the museum displays American art dating from the Colonial era. Exhibited are works by Paul Jenkins, Jamie Wyeth, Jasper Johns, and noted Southern artists along with North American sculpture. *420 College St., tel. 803/271–7570. Admission free. Open Tues.–Sat. 10–5, Sun. 1–5, closed major holidays (open Easter).*

Kings Mountain National Military Park. The "turning point" Revolutionary War battle on October 7, 1780, was fought on this site. A contingent of colonial Tories commanded by Major Patrick Ferguson, the only British participant in the engagement, was soundly defeated by rag-tag patriot forces from the Southern Appalachians. Visitor Center exhibits, dioramas, and an orientation film describe the action. A paved 1½-mile self-guided trail leads through the battlefield. *20 mi NE of Gaffney off I–85 via marked side road which is entered in North Carolina then leads back into South Carolina, tel. 803/936–7921. Admission free. Open Memorial Day–Labor Day, daily 9–6; rest of year 9–5; closed Christmas and New Year's Day.*

8 Tennessee

By Patricia and Edgar Cheatham

Updated by John Branston

Mountains and music—these two gifts Tennessee was given in abundance and shares generously with millions of guests each year.

In Memphis, in the southwest corner of the state, on the banks of the Mississippi River, the Blues were born. Beale Street produced or nurtured some of the finest talents of the genre, from W. C. Handy, who became known as the Father of the Blues, to Elvis Presley, the King of Rock and Roll. Today, with live music in Handy Park and in numerous nightclubs, Beale Street is once again alive with the sounds that made it a legend.

Nashville, of course, is Nashville—the country music capital of the world. Here, at the center of the state, there's country on every corner. In addition to stars' homes, recording studios, and country-related museums and other attractions, there's the Grand Ole Opry, the long-running radio-show extravaganza that has launched many a singer's and picker's career and is now part of a theme park built around live country music shows. Even the biggest fan will come away satisfied.

As for mountains, they don't come any more beautiful than the Great Smokies, part of the Appalachian chain, in East Tennessee (and shared by North Carolina). Covered with a dense carpet of wildflowers in spring and ablaze with foliage in autumn, the Smokies—named for the mysterious mantle of blue haze that so often blankets them—are a joy to hike, meander, or drive through. Spend some time in the little mountain towns and villages to sample homegrown bluegrass music and traditional cooking and crafts (such as the making of fine wood dulcimers), along with the natural warmth of the people.

Memphis

Memphis was founded in 1819, but long before that, the Mississippi River on whose banks it was built exerted a powerful influence on the area. An Indian river culture that existed here from the 11th through the 15th century is documented in archaeological excavations, reconstructions, and exhibits at the Chucalissa Indian Village. The river itself is celebrated with a museum dedicated to its history—part of a unique entertainment-oriented park occupying an island in the river.

The other significant influence on the city has been the music that has flowed through it. W. C. Handy moved from Alabama to Memphis in 1902–3, drawn by the long-thriving music scene, and it was here that he produced most of the songs that made him famous. The recent history of legendary Beale Street reflects that of all modern Memphis. Economic decline in the mid-20th century brought the city to its knees, and the unrest following the assassination in 1968 of Dr. Martin Luther King, Jr., at the Lorraine Motel, just south of Beale, dealt a near-fatal blow (*see* Exploring Memphis, *below*). Today, thanks to public improvements and local boosters whose efforts to save their city and their heritage can be seen at every turn, Memphis has been brought back to life and Beale Street bursts with clubs and restaurants, as it did in its heyday.

One young boy influenced by the Blues, who went on to become the King of Rock and Roll, is remembered at Graceland, the estate where he lived, died, and lies buried. The great crowds

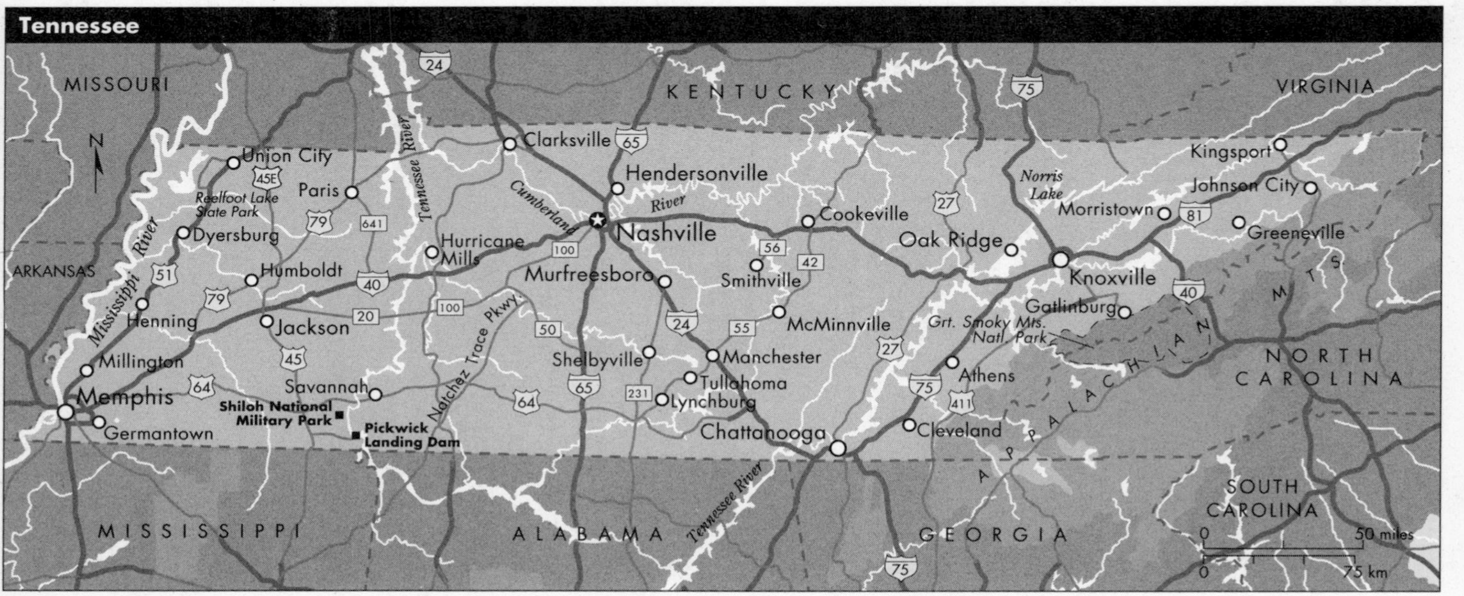
Tennessee
MISSOURI
KENTUCKY
VIRGINIA
ARKANSAS
MISSISSIPPI
ALABAMA
GEORGIA
NORTH CAROLINA
SOUTH CAROLINA
APPALACHIAN MTS
Union City
Paris
Reelfoot Lake State Park
Dyersburg
Humboldt
Henning
Millington
Memphis
Germantown
Jackson
Savannah
Shiloh National Military Park
Pickwick Landing Dam
Hurricane Mills
Clarksville
Hendersonville
Nashville
Murfreesboro
Shelbyville
Lynchburg
Tullahoma
Manchester
Smithville
McMinnville
Cookeville
Chattanooga
Cleveland
Athens
Oak Ridge
Knoxville
Gatlinburg
Grt. Smoky Mts. Natl. Park
Norris Lake
Morristown
Kingsport
Johnson City
Greeneville
Mississippi River
Tennessee River
Cumberland River
Natchez Trace Pkwy.
N
0 50 miles
0 75 km
24
65
75
45E
79
641
51
40
20
100
45
64
50
56
42
24
55
27
231
411
81

that flock to the mansion are testimony to the enduring legacy of Elvis's music.

For true Blues fans, a good time to visit is during Blues Music Week in October, when the art form is celebrated with musical performances and other activities throughout the city. The week culminates in the National Blues Music Awards Show, which is attended by luminaries of the music world. For information on a three-day vacation package that includes admission to the awards show as well as to the jam afterward, contact the Blues Foundation (174 Beale St., 38103, tel. 901/527–2583). Most weekends throughout the year, there's plenty of Blues to be heard on the front porch of the Handy home or in Handy Park (*see* Exploring Memphis, *below*).

Many people plan their visit to coincide with the month-long Memphis in May International Festival, at a time when the summer's heat and humidity have not yet begun to set in. Each year the cuisine, crafts, and other cultural offerings of a different country are saluted over four consecutive weekends. The first of these weekends sees the clubs and sidewalks of Beale Street playing host to a rollicking, Blues-based Music Festival, and the second finds hordes of the hungry flocking to the river for the World Championship Barbecue Cooking Contest. A sports weekend featuring races on land and water follows, succeeded by the grand finale of Sunset Symphony, during which the Memphis Symphony plays on the banks of the Mississippi, and a soloist's powerful rendition of "Old Man River" brings the festival to an end and the crowd to its feet.

Arriving and Departing

By Plane

Airports and Airlines Memphis International Airport is 9½ miles south of downtown. It is served by **American, Delta, Northwest, Northwest Airlink, TWA, United,** and **USAir.**

Between the Airport and Center City There is **taxi** service to downtown hotels. Taxi fare is about $15. Both are operated by Yellow Cab (tel. 901/577–7700). By **car,** take I–240 to downtown.

By Train **Amtrak** (545 S. Main St., tel. 901/526–0052).

By Bus **Greyhound Southeast Lines** (203 Union Ave., tel. 901/523–7676).

By Car From Memphis, I–55 leads north to St. Louis and south to Jackson, Mississippi; I–40, east to Nashville and Knoxville. I–240 loops around the city.

By Boat The paddle-wheel steamers *Delta Queen* and *Mississippi Queen* (tel. 800/543–1949) stop at Memphis on excursions between New Orleans, St. Louis, Cincinnati, and St. Paul.

Getting Around

By Taxi The fare is $1.25 for the first ⅑₁ mile, $1.10 for each additional mile. There are stands at the airport and bus station.

By Bus Memphis Area Transit Authority (tel. 901/274–6282) buses cover the city and immediate suburbs. Weekdays, there is service from 4:30 AM to 11:15 PM; Saturday, 5 AM–6:15 PM; Sunday, 9 AM–6:15 PM. The base fare is 95¢. Transfers cost 5¢. Exact change is required. There is short-hop service on designated buses between Front, Third, and Exchange streets from 9 AM to 3 PM and between downtown and the Medical Center complex from 7 AM to 6 PM (cost: 35¢).

Important Addresses and Numbers

Tourist Information **Visitors Information Center,** 340 Beale Street, 38103, tel. 901/576–8171. Open Monday–Saturday 9–5. **Memphis Convention and Visitors Bureau,** Morgan-Keegan Tower, 50 N. Front Street, Suite 450, 38103, tel. 901/576–8181. Open weekdays 8:30–5.

Emergencies Dial 911 for **police** and **ambulance** in an emergency.

Hospital Near-downtown hospitals with 24-hour emergency service include **Baptist Memorial Hospital** (889 Madison Ave., tel. 901/522–5252) and **Methodist Hospitals of Memphis** (1265 Union Ave., tel. 901/726–7000).

Guided Tours

Orientation Both **Cottonland Tours** (tel. 901/774–5248) and **Gray Line** (tel. 901/948–8687) offer three-hour motor-coach tours that include downtown highlights as well as Graceland.

Special-interest **Cottonland Tours** has gardens-and-galleries, Graceland, "Old Man River," shopping, nightlife, and Southland Greyhound Park excursions. **Gray Line** offers Elvis Memorial, nightlife, and Mud Island tours. **Unique Tours** (tel. 901/527–8876 or 800/235–1984) has three-day, two-night tours of Graceland, the National Civil Rights Museum, Mud Island, and other attractions. **Blues City Tours** (tel. 901/522–9229) offers tours of Memphis and attractions, including Graceland, Mud Island, Beale Street; riverboat rides; and nightly tours that include dinner and a show. The **Center for Southern Folklore** (tel. 901/525–3655) gives tours of Beale Street, a farm on the Delta, and prominent areas of musical interest. **Heritage Tours** (tel. 901/527–3427) explores the area's rich black cultural heritage.

Walking Tours At the **Memphis Convention and Visitors Bureau** (*see* Important Addresses and Numbers, *above*), pick up a free downtown tour map.

Carriage Tours **Bluff City Carriage Co.** (tel. 901/521–9462) and **Carriage Tours of Memphis** (tel. 901/527–7542) have horse-drawn carriage rides through the downtown area.

Boat Tours **Memphis Queen Cruise Line** (tel. 901/527–5694) offers 1½-hour sightseeing and dinner cruises Wednesday through Sunday March through December and daily May through September.

Exploring Memphis

Numbers in the margin correspond to points of interest on the Downtown Memphis and Memphis maps.

Downtown A good place to start is the **Visitors Information Center** on
1 Beale Street (*see* Important Addresses and Numbers, *above*), where you can pick up free maps, brochures, and other literature about Memphis. There's free parking in lots behind the center.

2 At Main Street and Beale is the magnificent 1928 **Orpheum Theatre,** a former vaudeville palace and movie theater, refurbished as a center for the performing arts. Step inside to ad-

A. Schwab's, **4**
The Center for Southern Folkore, **3**
Chucalissa Indian Village, **19**
Dixon Gallery and Gardens, **17**
Mud Island, **8**
Graceland, **18**
Handy Park, **5**
Magevney House, **10**
Mallory-Neeley House, **11**
Memphis Brooks Museum of Art, **15**
Memphis Zoological Gardens and Aquarium, **14**
National Civil Rights Museum, **13**
National Ornamental Metal Museum, **21**
Old Daisy Theatre, **6**
Orpheum Theatre, **2**
Pink Palace Museum and Planetarium, **16**
The Pyramid, **9**
T. O. Fuller State Park, **20**
Visitors Info., **1**
W. C. Handy Memphis Home and Museum, **7**
Woodruff-Fontaine House, **12**

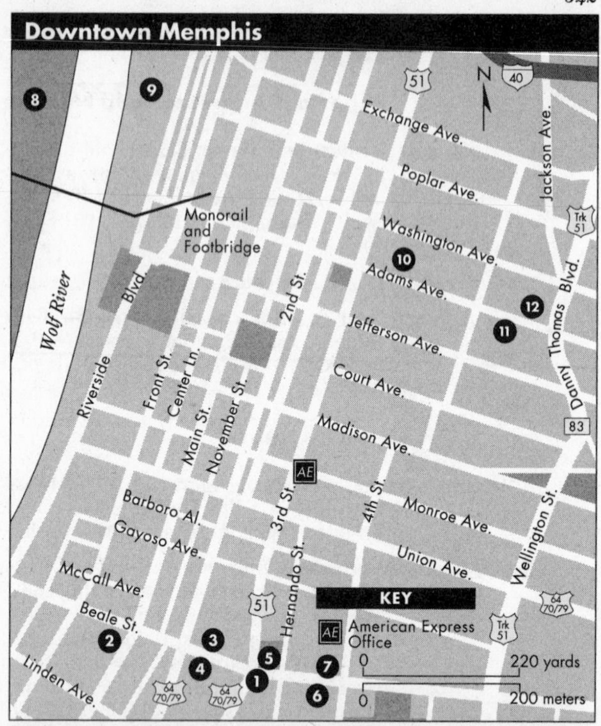

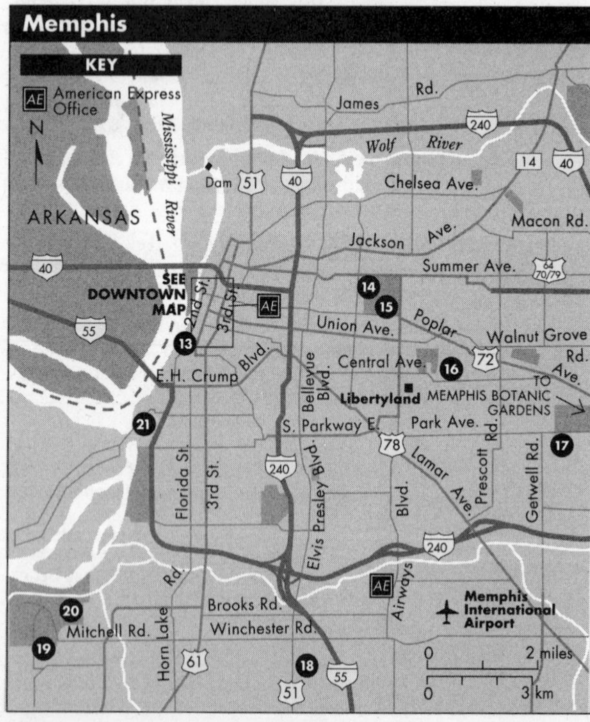

mire its crystal chandeliers, gilt decorations, and ornate tapestries. Proceeding east, you'll pass a bronze statue of Elvis.

3 The **Center for Southern Folklore** features exhibits on the people, music, food, crafts, and traditions of the South, focusing in particular on the Mississippi Delta region. The center will also arrange a walking tour of Beale Street (*see* Guided Tours, *above*). At the gift shop, you can purchase regional folk art, handiwork, cassettes, videos, and books pertaining to the region. *152 Beale St., tel. 901/525–3655. Admission: $2 adults; $1 children, senior citizens, and students. Open Mon.–Sat. 9–5:30, Sun. 1–5:30.*

At 163 Beale Street you can step into the past at the highly ec-
4 centric, 114-year-old **A. Schwab's** dry-goods store, where Elvis
used to buy some of his glitzy threads and where you can pick
5 up a voodoo potion (*see* Shopping, *below*). In **Handy Park,** between Third and Fourth streets, pause to admire the statue of
W. C. Handy clutching his famed trumpet.

6 At 329 Beale Street is the renovated **Old Daisy Theatre,** which
today, as when it was built in 1918, runs silent short films
(shown continuously 10–5 daily, free, tel. 901/525–1161). From
here, you can take a tram tour with guides who will fill you in on
Beale Street's musical past (*see* Guided Tours, *above*). Diago-
7 nally across the street, at 352 Beale, is the **W. C. Handy Memphis Home and Museum** (tel. 901/527–2583; admission: $1; open
10–5 daily). In this house (moved from its original location elsewhere in Memphis), where Handy wrote some of his most famous music, he is remembered through photographs, sheet
music, and other memorabilia.

If you're traveling by car, you might want to retrieve it before setting out on the next part of the tour, or you can continue walking. Parking on Front Street between Poplar and Adams puts you in a good position to explore two very different areas: the Victorian Village Historic District and Mud Island.

Whether you get there by monorail, pedestrian walkway, or
8 car, you should see **Mud Island,** a 52-acre park that explores
Memphis's intimate relationship with the river. There, at the **Mississippi River Museum,** galleries bring the history of the Mississippi to life with exhibits ranging from scale-model boats to life-size, animated river characters (Mark Twain spins his tales anew here) to the Theater of River Disasters. But the most extraordinary exhibit is outside: **River Walk,** a five-block-long scale model of the Mississippi that replicates its every twist, turn, and sandbar from Cairo, Illinois, to New Orleans, ending in a huge swimming pool bordered by a man-made, sandy beach. Other features include shops, river-view restaurants serving regional foods, and a 5,064-seat amphitheater that hosts name entertainment. The famed World War II B-17 bomber *Memphis Belle* is housed in an open pavilion topped by a gleaming white dome. At press time (September 1992), Mud Island's future was uncertain. Call ahead to confirm hours and admission. *The footbridge and monorail are at 125 Front St., tel. 901/576–7241. Grounds-only admission: $1 adults, 50¢ children 4–12; Mississippi River Museum admission: $5 adults, $3.50 children 4–12 and seniors; pool and beach: $2 adults, $1.50 children 4–12 and seniors. Grounds open daily 9–6, Apr. 1–Dec. 31; museum 9–6, last admission 4:30. Pool and beach open 11–6 daily, May 29–Sept. 6.*

To leave the 20th century behind, return to Front Street and walk east on Adams Street through the **Victorian Village Historic District,** comprising some 25 blocks on Adams between Front and Manassas. Here, 18 houses ranging from neoclassical to Gothic Revival have been restored to their appearance in the days when cotton was king. Most are privately owned, but the three that follow are open to the public.

9 The newest Memphis landmark, the **Pyramid,** is at Front and Auction, six blocks north of Adams Street. This 320-foot-tall arena opened in 1991 and is home to the Memphis State University Tigers and a forum for concerts and other events.

10 The charming little white clapboard **Magevney House,** built in the 1830s, is Memphis's oldest dwelling and the former home of a pioneer schoolteacher. It's furnished with some of his original possessions. Magevney was a strong Catholic—the city's first Catholic church service was held in this house, and he later built the church next door. *198 Adams Ave., tel. 901/526–4464. Admission free. Open Tues.–Sat. 10–4. Closed Jan. 1, July 4, Thanksgiving, and Christmas Eve and Christmas Day.*

11 The **Mallory-Neely House** is a 25-room Italianate Victorian home that contains original family furnishings. Note the hand-carved cornices and frescoed ceilings on the first floor, and the double front doors' stained-glass panels. *652 Adams Ave., tel. 901/523–1484. Admission: $4 adults, $3 students and senior citizens. Open Tues.–Sat. 10–4, Sun. 1–4. Closed Thanksgiving, Christmas, and New Year's.*

12 The **Woodruff-Fontaine House** is an exquisite three-story French Victorian mansion. The grand drawing room is graced with the original parquet floors and large mirrors. Antique furnishings include Aubusson carpets, marble mantels, and a Venetian crystal chandelier. From the tower, gaze out at Memphis's skyline, then browse through the formal garden with its 100-year-old gingerbread playhouse and chapel. *680 Adams Ave., tel. 901/526–1469. Admission: $4 adults, $3 senior citizens and military, $2 children 6–18, children under school age free. Open Mon.–Sat. 10–4, Sun. 1–4. Closed July 4, Thanksgiving, and Christmas Eve and Christmas Day.*

The motel on Mulberry Street where Dr. Martin Luther King
13 Jr. was assassinated has been transformed into the **National Civil Rights Museum,** the first in the United States. The $8.8 million complex, opened in the summer of 1991, documents "the sights, sounds, outrage, danger, and emotion of the civil rights movement," in the words of D'Army Bailey, president of the museum foundation. A Montgomery, Alabama bus; scenes of sit-ins; and audiovisual displays are part of the educational program. *450 Mulberry St., tel. 901/521–9699. Admission: $5 adults, $4 senior citizens and students, $3 children 6–12, free Mon. 3–5. Open weekdays and Sat. 10–5, Sun. 1–6 (1–5 Sept.–May). Closed Tues.*

Fanning Out

Two miles east of the Victorian district is **Overton Park,** where
14 the city's zoo and art museum are found. The **Memphis Zoological Gardens and Aquarium** is one of the South's most notable zoos. Here you can view more than 400 species on 36 wooded acres. There's a 10,000-gallon aquarium, a large reptile facility, and a natural African veldt setting for larger creatures. For the youngsters, there's an animal-contact area, a lake, and car-

nival rides. *Tel. 901/726–4775. Admission: $5 adults, $3 senior citizens and children 2–11; free for all Mon. after 3:30 PM. Open daily 9–5. Closed major holidays.*

15 The collections of the **Memphis Brooks Museum of Art,** also in the park, span eight centuries, including a notable collection of Italian Renaissance works, plus English portraiture, Impressionist and American modernist paintings, decorative arts, prints, photographs, and one of the nation's largest displays of Doughty bird figurines. *Tel. 901/722–3500. Admission: $4 adults, $2 senior citizens and students. Open Tues.–Sat. 10–5, Sun. 11:30–5. Closed major holidays.*

16 Southeast of the park is the **Memphis Pink Palace Museum and Planetarium,** adjacent to the rambling 1920s pink marble mansion built by Clarence Saunders, whose Piggly Wiggly self-service stores were predecessors of today's supermarkets. Exhibits are eclectic, including natural and cultural history displays, a hand-carved miniature three-ring circus, and displays of African game. *3050 Central Ave., tel. 901/320–6320. Admission (museum/planetarium): $3/$2.50 adults; $2/$1.75 senior citizens and children 5–13, under 5 free. Combination tickets $5.50 adults, $3.75 senior citizens and children 4–13. Open Mon.–Sat. 9–8, Sun. 9–6, May 1–Aug. 31; Tues.–Sat. 9:30–4, Sun. 1–5 rest of year. Closed Jan. 1, Thanksgiving, and Christmas Eve and Christmas Day. Special exhibit, "The Etruscans," May–Aug.*

17 A very different personal statement is made by the **Dixon Gallery and Gardens,** with 17 acres of formal and informal gardens and woodlands—a welcoming bucolic enclave near the heart of the city. The estate and its superb art collections were given to the community by the late Margaret and Hugo Dixon, philanthropists and cultural leaders. Included in the intimate museum are French and American Impressionist paintings, British portraiture and landscapes, and the Stout collection of 18th-century German porcelain. The gardens display regional flowering plants and statuary. *4339 Park Ave., tel. 901/761–2409. Admission: $4 adults, $3 senior citizens and students, $1 under 12, free for all on Tues. Open Tues.–Sat. 10–5, Sun. 1–5. Closed major holidays.*

Twelve miles southeast of downtown is perhaps the most vis-
18 ited Memphis attraction: **Graceland,** a poignant reminder of the many facets of fame. The tour of the Colonial-style mansion once owned by Elvis Presley reveals the spoils of stardom—from his gold records to his glittering show costumes—and a circuit of the grounds (shuttle service is available) leads inevitably to the tomb where he is buried. Separate tours are available of his car museum and his jet, the *Lisa Marie,* named for his daughter. *3717 Elvis Presley Blvd. (I–55S to exit for Jackson, Miss., then exit for Elvis Presley Blvd.), tel. 901/332–3322 or 800/238–2000 outside TN. Home tour admission: $7.95 adults, $4.75 children 4–12, under 4 free.* Lisa Marie *admission: $3.95 adults, $2.75 children 4–12, under 4 free. "Sincerely Elvis" museum admission: $1.75. Combination tickets are available. Parking: $2. Reservations suggested in summer. Open daily 8–7 June 15–Aug. 10; 8–6 June 1–14, Aug. 11–31; 8–5 May 1–31; 9–5 rest of year. Closed major holidays and Tues. Nov.–Feb.*

19 At the peaceful, thought-provoking **Chucalissa Archeological
Museum, about 10 miles southwest of downtown, you'll catch
glimpses of a simple river culture that existed from AD 1000 to
1500. The four-acre reconstruction is operated by Memphis State
University, and on-site archaeological excavations are often conducted during the summer. In the museum, you'll see prehistoric
tools, pottery, and weapons and a free 15-minute slide presentation describing Chucalissa life and culture. Outside, skilled Choctaw craftsfolk fashion jewelry, weapons, and pottery. An annual
20 August powwow is a highlight. The adjacent **T. O. Fuller State
Park** (tel. 901/543–7581) offers camping, golf, and swimming.
*1987 Indian Village Dr., tel. 901/785–3160. Admission: $3
adults, $1.50 senior citizens and children 4–11, children under
4 free. Open daily 9–5. Closed major holidays.*

On the way back to downtown Memphis (via U.S. 61, following
21 the green Tour Memphis signs) is the **National Ornamental
Metal Museum,** the nation's only museum preserving the art
and the craft of metalworking—from wrought iron to gold.
There's also a working blacksmith shop and special exhibitions
and demonstrations. *374 W. California St., tel. 901/774–6380.
Admission: $2 adults; $1 senior citizens; 75¢ children 5–18,
under 5 free; free to all on Wednesday morning. Open Tues.–
Sat. 10–5, Sun. noon–5. Closed major holidays.*

The Hinterland

From Memphis, you can branch out in various directions to explore quieter, historic byways that seem light-years removed from the busy river city. Driving northward along U.S. 51 through the fertile Mississippi River bottomlands brings you into the heart of King Cotton's domain. About 48 miles along the way, you'll come to **Henning,** a friendly little town remarkably untouched by its world acclaim. This is the boyhood home and burial place of Alex Haley, Pulitzer Prize–winning author of *Roots.* At the **Alex Haley State Historic Site and Museum,** you can visit the comfortable bungalow to see family portraits, mementos, and furnishings. *Haley St., tel. 901/738–2240. Admission: $2.50 adults, $1 children 6–16. Open Tues.–Sat. 10–5, Sun. 1–5.*

Reelfoot Lake—about 55 miles farther on (via U.S. 51N and TN 21W), in Tennessee's northwest corner—gains a peculiar and mysterious beauty from a romantic scattering of cypress trees and charred stumps. The 13,000-acre lake was formed when earthquakes caused the Mississippi River to flood into the sinking land where a luxuriant forest once stood. From late-November through mid-March the lake is a major sanctuary for American bald eagles. At **Reelfoot Lake State Resort Park** (tel. 901/253–7756), the Tennessee Department of Conservation conducts eagle-spotting tours.

From Memphis, you can also follow I–40 85 miles northeast to **Jackson,** a railroad hub that was home to Johnathan Luther (Casey) Jones. Immortalized in the "Ballad of Casey Jones," the famed engineer became a hero by staying aboard his locomotive in a vain attempt to stop his engine from plowing into another train. In Casey Jones Village (at U.S. 45 Bypass), the **Casey Jones Home and Railroad Museum** (tel. 901/668–1223) contains a diverse assortment of railroad memorabilia. On the grounds is a replica of Old No. 382, Casey's steam engine. **Brooks Shaw's Old Country Store** (tel. 901/668–1223), also located in the village, features a restaurant that serves three buffet meals daily; an 1890s-style ice-cream parlor; and gift, souvenir, confectionery, and antiques shops. *Admission: $3 adults, $2 children 6–12. Museum open Mon.–Sat. 8–8, Sun. 1–5 June–Sept.; Mon.–Sat. 9–5, Sun. 1–5 rest of year. Restaurant open daily 6:30–9; store open daily 6–10. Closed Easter, Thanksgiving, and Christmas.*

One hundred miles east of Memphis via U.S. 64, then 10 miles south on TN 22, is **Shiloh National Military Park,** site of one of the Civil War's grimmest and most important battles. At the visitor center, you'll see a film explaining the battle's strategy, along with a display of Civil War relics. A self-guided auto tour leads past markers explaining monuments and battle sites. Almost 4,000 soldiers, many unidentified, are buried here in the national cemetery. *Tel. 901/689–5275. Visitor center open daily 8–6 June–Aug., 8–5 rest of year. Closed Christmas. Admission: $1 adults, children under 17 and senior citizens free.*

Nearby (110 mi east of Memphis on TN 57E) is **Pickwick Landing Dam** (tel. 901/689–3135), one of the TVA's showcase hydroelectric projects. From the top of the dam, which rises high above the Tennessee River to create Pickwick Lake, there are sweeping views. You're welcome to visit the power plant during daylight hours. **Pickwick Landing State Resort Park** (tel. 901/689–3129) offers a resort inn, a restaurant, playgrounds, swimming beaches, picnic areas, and a par 72, 18-hole golf course.

Memphis for Free

Beale Street Substation Police Museum. Come in and browse through 148 years of Memphis police history, including confiscated weapons, photographs dating to the 1800s, and an old-style jail cell. *159 Beale St., tel. 901/528–2370. Open 24 hrs.*

Crystal Shrine Grotto. At this dramatic cavern of natural rock, quartz crystals, and other semiprecious stones, relief sculptures carved by artist Dionicio Rodriguez in the late 1930s depict scenes from the life of Jesus. *Memorial Park Cemetery, 5668 Poplar Ave., tel. 901/767–8930. Open daily 9–4.*

Laurel Hill Vineyard. A surprising find in the heart of town, this small winery offers tours that include a slide presentation and a wine tasting. *1370 Madison Ave., tel. 901/725–9128. Tours weekdays 10–12:30, 1:30–5:30; additional tours Sat. 10–2 Nov.–Dec.*

Memphis Botanic Gardens–Goldsmith Civic Garden Center. The outdoor gardens range over 87 acres and include Japanese, rose, iris, herb, wildflower, perennial, and cactus gardens, and azalea and dogwood trails. The Garden Center showcases tropical plants and hosts horticultural shows. *750 Cherry Rd., tel. 901/685–1566. Botanic Gardens open Tues.–Sat. 9–sunset, Sun. 11–sunset. Garden Center open weekdays 9–4:30 year-round; weekends 1–5. Admission: $2 adults, $1.50 senior citizens, $1 children 6–17.*

What to See and Do with Children

Adventure River. This 25-acre water park has a giant wave pool, water slides, raft and inner-tube rides, a man-made river, a kiddie pool, and more. *6880 Whitten Bend Cove (12 mi east of downtown, off I–40), tel. 901/382–WAVE. Open 10–8, week-*

ends only in May, daily Memorial Day–Labor Day. Admission: $12 adults, $11 children 3–12, $3 senior citizens over 62.

Chucalissa Archeological Museum (*see* Fanning Out in Exploring, *above*).

Libertyland. At this family amusement park, there are 24 rides, ranging from thrillers to leisurely paddleboat excursions and rides for tots. Don't miss the 1909 handcrafted carousel, one of the nation's oldest. There are also three live music shows. *940 Early Maxwell Blvd., tel. 901/274–1776. Admission: $6 adults and children over 4, $2 senior citizens over 55; $3 for all after 4 PM, children under 4 free. Thrill-ride ticket $8 extra. Open Sat. 10–9, Sun. 1–9 May 2–June 7; Wed.–Fri. 12–9, Sat. 10–9 June 10–Aug. 30. Closed rest of year.*

Meeman-Shelby Forest State Park. Get back to nature at this 12,500-acre park bordering the Mississippi, with boat rides, hikes, tours, arts and crafts, campfires, and games. *16 mi north of Memphis, off U.S. 51, tel. 901/876–5215. Admission free; some usage fees. Open daily 7 AM–10 PM.*

Memphis Zoological Gardens and Aquarium (*see* Fanning Out in Exploring, *above*).

Mud Island (*see* Downtown in Exploring, *above*). Younger children will especially like Huck's Backyard, a one-acre river-theme playground.

Off the Beaten Track

Agricenter International. This 1,000-acre complex showcases agricultural technology. Visit the hydroponics center, crop areas, aquaculture farm, forest and nature preserve, orchards, and vineyards. There's also a farmer's market and farm shows. *7777 Walnut Grove Rd., tel. 901/757–7777. Admission free. Open weekdays 8–4:30. Closed major holidays.*

Lichterman Nature Center. Within the city limits is a 65-acre wildlife sanctuary preserving forest, field, pond, and marsh habitats. Walk the banks of a 12-acre lake or follow animal tracks by a woodland stream; visit a greenhouse where native wildflowers are propagated or tour a hospital for wild animals. Youngsters can explore a discovery room with nature games or watch honey being made in observation hives. *5992 Quince Rd., tel. 901/767–7322. Open Tues.–Sat. 9:30–5, Sun. 1–5. Admission: $3 adults; $2 senior citizens, students, children 4 and over; children under 4 free.*

Shopping

Stores are generally open Monday–Saturday 10–6, Sunday 1–5 (in shopping malls, Mon.–Sat. 10–9, Sun. 1–6). Banks are generally open weekdays 8:30–4. First Tennessee Bank is open until 6:30 PM on Fridays.

Shopping Districts

Over a dozen shopping centers and malls are scattered about the city. The **Mid-America Mall,** on Main Street between Beale and Poplar, is one of the nation's longest pedestrian malls. It is being completely overhauled and turned into a trolley mall, scheduled to open by early 1993. **Overton Square** (24 S. Cooper St., tel. 901/274–0671)—a three-block midtown shopping, restaurant, and entertainment complex in artfully restored vintage buildings and newer structures—features upscale boutiques and specialty shops.

Specialty Stores
Children's Clothes **The Woman's Exchange** (88 Racine St., Memphis, tel. 901/327–5681) specializes in children's wear and handcrafted items. There's a Christmas shop in November and December.

Crafts and Collectibles **The Checkerberry Shoppe** (2247 Germantown Rd. S, Germantown, tel. 901/754–3601) has quilted wall hangings, country dolls, salt-glazed stoneware, handmade baskets, stained glass, miniatures, and antique reproductions.

Elvis Presley Memorabilia Six shops at **Graceland** (3717 Elvis Presley Blvd., tel. 901/332–3322 or 800/238–2000) sell every Elvis-related item imaginable, from cookie jars and T-shirts with his face plastered over them to Elvis records and tapes to collectible vintage items.

Off-price Outlet **Belz Factory Outlet Mall** (3536 Canada Rd., Exit 20 off I–40, 20 miles east of downtown Memphis, Lakeland, tel. 901/386–3180) includes 50 stores with apparel, household goods, furniture, recreational items, and more.

One of a Kind **A. Schwab's** (163 Beale St., tel. 901/523–9782) is an old-fashioned dry-goods store whose motto is "If you can't find it at A. Schwab's, you're better off without it!" Elvis shopped here, and you can, too—for top hats, spats, tambourines, bow ties, dresses to size 60, and men's trousers to size 74. And everybody gets a free souvenir.

Participant Sports

Boating and Fishing You'll find boat rentals at **Meeman-Shelby Forest State Park** (16 mi north of Memphis off U.S. 51, tel. 901/876–5215), **Pickwick Landing State Resort Park** (110 mi east of Memphis on TN 57E, tel. 901/689–3129), and **Reelfoot State Resort Park** (Tiptonville, on TN 78 30 mi north of Dyersburg, tel. 901/253–7756). You can fish year-round for bass, crappie, trout, bream, and catfish.

Golf The Memphis Park Commission (tel. 901/454–5740) operates eight public courses, the most central of which are **Overton Park** (9 holes; tel. 901/725–9905) and **Galloway** (18 holes; tel. 901/685–7805).

Hiking There are trails at **Meeman-Shelby Forest State Park** (tel. 901/876–5215), **Shelby Farms Plough Recreation Area** (tel. 901/382–4250), **Lichterman Nature Center** (tel. 901/767–7322), and **T. O. Fuller State Park** (tel. 901/529–7581).

Horseback Riding **Shelby Farms Plough Recreation Area** (tel. 901/572–4278) offers hayrides as well as horses for riding.

Ice Skating The **Ice Capades Chalet,** in the Mall of Memphis (tel. 901/362–8877), is the area's only skating facility.

Jogging There are trails at **Shelby Farms Plough Recreation Area** (tel. 901/382–4250), which also has paddleboats, fishing, picnic areas, and nature walks.

Tennis The Memphis Park Commission (tel. 901/454–5755) operates several facilities that offer lessons, tournaments, and league play. **Leftwich** (tel. 901/685–7907), **Ridgeway** (tel. 901/767–2889), and **Whitehaven** (tel. 901/332–0546) have indoor courts.

Water Sports **Water-skiing** is available at the parks listed under Boating and Fishing, above.

Spectator Sports

Auto Racing The new 600-acre **Memphis Motorsports Park** hosts weekly dirt-track and drag racing. *5500 Taylor Forge Rd., tel. 901/358-7223. Open Mar.–Nov.*

Baseball You can cheer for the **Memphis Chicks,** a class AA team of the Kansas City Royals and member of the Southern League, at Tim McCarver Stadium (tel. 901/272–1687).

Dog Racing Greyhound racing draws hordes of Memphians and visitors into Arkansas, which allows pari-mutuel betting. **Southland Greyhound Park** is a posh facility, with closed-circuit viewing and a restaurant. *1550 N. Ingram Blvd. (via I–40 or I–55 from downtown Memphis), W. Memphis, AR, tel. 501/735–3670. Open early Apr.–early Nov. Under 18 not admitted.*

Football Each December a top Southern collegiate event—the **Liberty Bowl Football Classic**—is held at the Liberty Memorial Stadium (tel. 901/325–5759), which hosts the Memphis State University Tigers and other football teams.

Golf In June the Tournament Players Club at Southwind Country Club hosts the **Federal Express St. Jude Classic,** featuring top pros. The 1993 tournament is July 26–August 1. (tel. 901/748-0534).

Dining

By Tom Martin

Not so long ago, Memphis offered little more than various neighborhood restaurants featuring "home cooking," several Chinese chop-suey houses, a handful of Italian spaghetti-and-lasagna spots, and numerous establishments serving pork barbecue. Even the city's few higher-priced restaurants served only the ordinary.

Happily, the dining choices have not only expanded greatly but dramatically improved in quality during the past 15 years. In addition to a number of restaurants serving imaginative American cuisine, Memphis now boasts many competent and attractive international dining rooms. Hotel dining in Memphis, which used to mean tired menus and lifeless cooking, has been revitalized, and today the city's most inspired dishes are often served in its finer hotels.

Memphis's top culinary attraction, however, remains barbecue, and a visit to one of the 70-odd barbecue restaurants is recommended for anyone wanting to savor local color as well as tasty ribs. True fanciers may want to schedule their visit around the International Pork Barbecue Cooking Contest, which is held during the annual Memphis in May International Festival and draws 300 teams from around the world (as well as more than 100,000 spectators) for its three-day run on the banks of the Mississippi.

The most highly recommended restaurants in each price category are indicated by a star ★.

Category	Cost*
Very Expensive	over $50
Expensive	$40–$50

Moderate	$20–$40
Inexpensive	under $20

**per person without tax (7.75% in Tennessee), service, or drinks*

Very Expensive
Continental

Justine's. Fresh roses from the restaurant's gardens adorn each table, and soothing piano music flows through the six dining rooms of this restored mansion, built in 1843. In operation over 30 years, Justine's is a gracious reminder of the style of the Old South. The New Orleans–influenced menu is hardly innovative, but it is reliable, especially the fresh and well-prepared seafood. Excellent specialties are crabs Justine, a crabmeat casserole with buttery sauce; broiled pompano with chives, parsley, and lemon; and beef tenderloin with artichoke hearts and béarnaise sauce. *919 Coward Pl., tel. 901/527–3815. Jacket and tie recommended. Reservations advised, especially on weekends. AE, DC, MC, V. Closed Sun. and Mon.*

Indian

East India Company. Chef-owner Raji Jallepalli blends nouvelle styles and Indian seasonings in a cuisine as subtle and refined as can be found. Her creations range from fragrant Indian consommé with white peppercorns and coriander to supreme of duck with curry masala sauce or grilled scallops and lobster in lentil pastry with a ginger-flavored beurre blanc. Several intimate dining rooms in a former residence have elegant and refined decor. *712 W. Brookhaven Circle, tel. 901/685–8723. Reservations accepted. AE, MC, V. Closed Sun. and Mon.*

Nouvelle French

★ **Chez Philippe.** The decor—high ceilings, *faux* marble columns, huge murals depicting a masked ball—is wonderfully lavish, and lilting harp music adds a finishing touch of elegance. The service, by waiters in white tie, is impeccable. Most important, the cuisine—Memphis's most innovative and sophisticated—lives up to its regal setting. Chef José Gutierrez is recognized as one of the country's outstanding young chefs, and his talent is evident in a menu that ranges from delicate terrines to lamb tenderloin in puff pastry to hot soufflés. *The Peabody Hotel, 149 Union Ave., tel. 901/529–4188. Jacket and tie recommended. Reservations advised. AE, DC, MC, V. Closed Sun.*

Expensive
French

Cafe Society. Chef David Morrow brings fresh imagination and a surprising range of ingredients to this bright storefront restaurant in midtown. Expect to find treats like coconut fried shrimp with pineapple chutney, sautéed salmon with sun-dried tomato cream, and grouper with *aioli.* The best dessert is the ice cream in puff pastry. *212 N. Evergreen, tel. 901/722–2177. Reservations accepted. AE, MC, V. Closed Sat. lunch.*

La Patisserie Bistro. The storefront setting in an east Memphis shopping center is as unpretentious as the atmosphere inside this bistro and bakery. But make no mistake, the food on the plate is sublime. Prices are reasonable, especially considering the imagination behind dishes such as chicken blanquette served in a hollow baguette, and Senegalese curry soup with fresh apple. *5689 Quince, tel. 901/767–0069. MC, V. Closed Sun.*

★ **La Tourelle.** The quiet setting is reminiscent of a small country restaurant in France, with fine lace curtains and wood floors. Three- and five-course prix fixe meals are served nightly, or you can order à la carte. Chef Erling Jensen brings his Danish heritage to the restaurant with a changing menu that empha-

Dining

Automatic Slim's Tonga Club, **4**
Café Roux, **25**
Cafe Society, **11**
Captain Bilbo's River Restaurant, **5**
Charlie Vergos' Rendezvous, **2**
Chez Philippe, **3**
Doe's Eat Place, **6**
Dux, **3**
East India Company, **21**
Hemmings, **23**
John Wills Barbecue Pit, **15**
Justine's, **9**
La Patisserie Bistro, **24**
La Tourelle, **14**
Marena's, **9**
Paulette's, **12**

Lodging

Days Inn Memphis Airport, **18**
Econo Lodge, **16**
Econo Lodge Airport, **20**
The French Quarter Suites Hotel, **13**
Hampton Inn Airport, **17**
Holiday Inn Crowne Plaza, **1**
La Quinta Motor Inn-Medical Center, **8**
Lowenstein-Long House, **7**
Memphis Airport Hotel, **19**
Omni Memphis, **22**
The Peabody, **3**

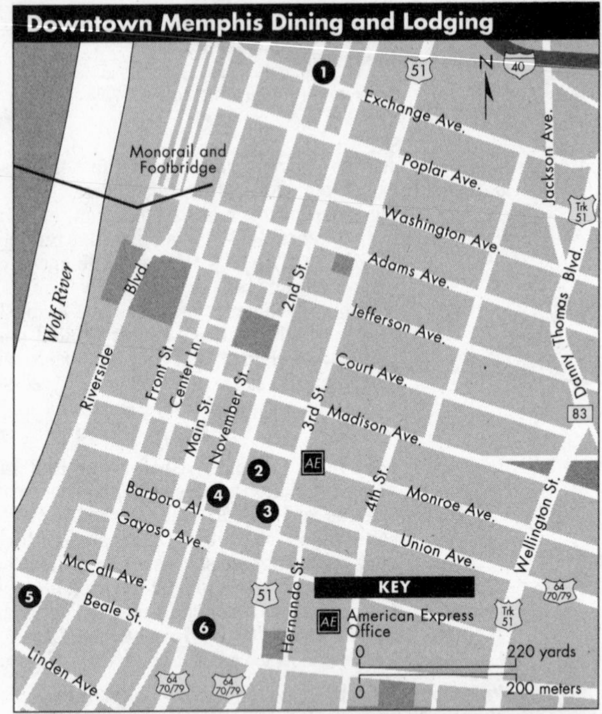

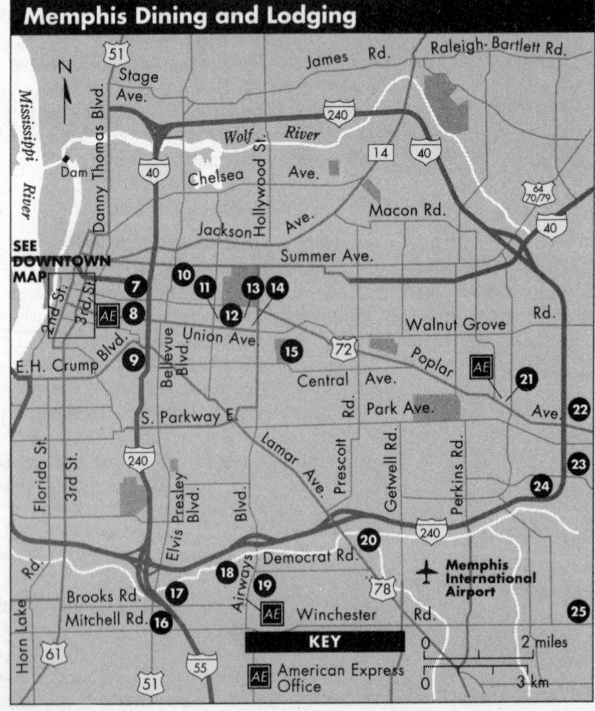

sizes fresh seafood, interesting side dishes, and beautiful presentations. The Queen Mother cake is a triple chocolate knockout. *Overton Sq., 2146 Monroe Ave., tel. 901/726–5771. Jacket and tie recommended. Reservations recommended. MC, V. Closed Mon.*

New American ★

Dux. Stylishly done up in black, white, and maroon, this pleasing hotel restaurant serves such popular specialties as seared tuna with black sesame seeds and ginger-scallion sauce, corn-and-red-pepper polenta with coriander and tomato relish, baked squab in phyllo pastry, and, for dessert, white chocolate charlotte with raspberry *coulis*. The restaurant's entrance is decorated with beautiful glass and ceramic ducks in honor of the real ones you'll see in the hotel's famous lobby. *The Peabody Hotel, 149 Union Ave., tel. 901/529–4199. Dress: informal. Reservations accepted. AE, DC, MC, V.*

Hemmings. An impressive new entry to Memphis dining, this restaurant is set in the distinctive Saddle Creek shopping development of suburban Germantown. The decor is in crisp shades of pale blue and ivory, with high ceilings and huge windows. The menu, inspired by the cooking of California and the American southwest, changes every few weeks. Typical of the creative choices are venison cutlets over grilled corn cakes with tomato salsa, pit-roasted breast of duck with bok choy and papaya chili sauce, and roasted quail with andouille sausage on a bed of grilled corn relish. *7615 West Farmington Rd., Germantown, tel. 901/757–8323. Jacket and tie recommended. Reservations advised. AE, DC, MC, V.*

Moderate

American

Doe's Eat Place. This downtown restaurant specializes in huge steaks, hamburgers, and hot tamales in a diner setting. *138 Beale St., tel. 901/526–3637. Dress: casual. Reservations not necessary. AE, MC, V.*

Continental

Paulette's. This Overton Square restaurant was serving bistro-style cooking before it became popular in Memphis; for more than a decade, Paulette's has retained its vitality. With a crisp, fresh house salad, airy popovers with strawberry butter, and killer desserts, Paulette's packs them in at lunch and dinner. Entrées include several crepe dishes, along with grilled salmon, baked scallops, and brochettes of shrimp or beef. *2110 Madison Ave., tel. 901/726–5128. Reservations accepted. AE, MC, V.*

Mediterranean

Marena's. This midtown restaurant opened in 1991 to rave reviews. The decor features colorful hand-painted furniture and paneling. The food is just as artistic, with Mediterranean specialties from North Africa to the middle east to the south of France. Menus change monthly, but are always full of surprises. *1545 Overton Park, tel. 901/278–9774. Dress: informal. Reservations recommended. AE, DC, MC, V.*

Seafood

Captain Bilbo's River Restaurant. This riverfront place is one of Memphis's busiest restaurants, and though it seats more than 300, the waiting list often exceeds one hour. Fortunately, you can listen to live music in the comfortable bar while you wait. The dishes served are simple but consistently well prepared. Among the better offerings are shrimp in a brown-butter sauce, flounder stuffed with shrimp and crabmeat, and fried oysters and shrimp. *263 Wagner Pl., tel. 901/526–1966. Dress: informal. Reservations accepted. AE, MC, V.*

Southwestern **Automatic Slim's Tonga Club.** This is a popular new restaurant specializing in Southwestern and Caribbean fare served in thick and spicy sauces. Try the cowboy Travis steak. *83 2nd St., tel. 901/525-7948. Dress: casual. Reservations accepted. AE, MC, V.*

Inexpensive
Barbecue
★ **Charlie Vergos' Rendezvous.** Charlie Vergos has become something of a Memphis ambassador of barbecued ribs: Not only does his downtown basement restaurant draw thousands of tourists each year, but he also ships his ribs by air express all over the country. The decor here is museumlike: The walls are filled with memorabilia and bric-a-brac, from old newspaper cartoons to Essolene gas signs. But what packs in the crowds is the delicious pork loin plate and the barbecued pork ribs. *52 S. Second St., tel. 901/523-2746. Dress: informal. No reservations. AE, MC, V. Closed Sun. and Mon.*

★ **John Wills's Memphis Bar & Grill.** John Wills parlayed his two victories in the International Pork Barbecue Cooking Contest into this successful restaurant, open since 1983. Attractive, with green tables, natural-wood booths, and cute photos of pigs adorning the walls, the busy establishment offers a wide selection of well-prepared barbecued meats, including beef and pork ribs, pork shoulder, beef brisket, and sausage. The barbecued beans are nicely spiced, and the coleslaw has a tart mustard seasoning. *5101 Sanderlin St., tel. 901/761-5101. Dress: informal. No reservations. AE, MC, V.*

Cajun
★ **Café Roux.** Chef Michael Cahhal has been one of Memphis's most popular food personalities for close to a decade. He has run as many as four restaurants at a time, but his efforts are now concentrated on two restaurants, both called Cafe Roux. They feature the lively Cajun and Creole cooking of southwestern Louisiana, with prices moderate enough to draw huge crowds. Be prepared for a wait on weekends, as folks line up to taste the *chaurice* sausage, oyster po' boys, and Acadian-style catfish. The crawfish étouffé is a classic. *7209 Winchester Ave., tel. 901/755-7689 and 94 S. Front St., tel. 901/525-7689. Dress: informal. No reservations. AE, DC, MC, V.*

Lodging

Memphis hotels are especially busy during the spring, when the Memphis in May International Festival and June's Cotton Carnival Memphis are in progress, in mid-August, when pilgrims observe Elvis Presley's death, and between Christmas and New Year's during the Liberty Bowl Football Classic. Be sure to reserve well in advance during those times. To find out about B&Bs in Memphis, contact the **Bed & Breakfast in Memphis Reservation Service** (Box 41621, Memphis, 38174, tel. 901/726-5920).

The most highly recommended properties in each price category are indicated by a star ★. For maps pinpointing locations, *see* Dining, *above*.

Category	Cost*
Very Expensive	over $125
Expensive	$70–$125

Moderate	$50–$70
Inexpensive	under $50

**double room; add 11.75% for taxes*

Very Expensive

Omni Memphis. This luxury property, a 27-story circular glass tower, is in the flourishing eastern suburbs near I–240. From your glass-walled aerie, you'll have sweeping vistas of the sprawling metropolis and its outskirts. *939 Ridge Lake Blvd., 38119, tel. 901/684–6664 or 800/843–6664. 380 rooms. Facilities: cable TV/movies, pool, health club, coffee shop, restaurant, lounge with live entertainment; arrangements for golf, spa, tennis privileges. AE, DC, MC, V.*

★ **Peabody.** After languishing in disrepair for two decades, and finally closing, this 12-story landmark downtown hostelry was impeccably restored and reopened in 1981. Guest rooms were enlarged, refurbished, and redecorated with period reproduction furnishings. The lobby preserves its original stained-glass skylights and ornate travertine marble fountain—home to the hotel's famed resident ducks, who come down each morning from their penthouse apartment and parade across a red carpet to the stirring sounds of Sousa's "King Cotton March." Each afternoon, the ceremony is repeated as they return to their rooftop "Duck Palace." *149 Union Ave., 38103, tel. 901/529–4000 or 800/732–2639. 454 rooms. Facilities: indoor pool, health club, 4 dining rooms including Chez Philippe and Dux (*see *Dining*, above*), lounge with live entertainment, lobby bar serving cocktails and afternoon tea. AE, DC, MC, V.*

Expensive

★ **French Quarter Suites Hotel.** With its mellow rose-brick exterior and classic architectural lines, this pleasant New Overton Square hostelry is reminiscent of an older, New Orleans–style inn. All the one-bedroom suites have living rooms and whirlpool tubs, and some are balconied. *2144 Madison Ave., 38104, tel. 901/728–4000. 105 suites. Facilities: cable TV/movies, health club, pool. AE, DC, MC, V.*

Holiday Inn Crowne Plaza. Memphis was the birthplace of Holiday Inns, and this is the flagship of the area's seven-inn fleet. Adjacent to the downtown Convention Center, this sleek high-rise hotel (18 floors) offers a concierge floor and sizable meeting facilities, plus ample work space and lighting in the spacious guest rooms and suites. The lobby lounge, a tasteful, greenery-filled retreat, is a pleasant spot to relax and listen to music from the grand piano. *250 N. Main St., 38103, tel. 901/527–7300 or 800/465–4329. 402 rooms. Facilities: cable TV/movies, indoor pool, health club, whirlpool, sauna, 2 restaurants, lobby lounge. AE, DC, MC, V.*

Memphis Airport Hotel. Guest rooms are ranged around a five-story, skylit, greenery-bedecked atrium lobby. Relax in the well-equipped fitness centers or in a whirlpool-bath suite (with kitchenette). The hotel has attractively priced packages for weekend visitors. *2240 Democrat Rd., 38132, tel. 901/332–1130. 380 rooms. Facilities: cable TV/movies, indoor pool, heated outdoor pool, 2 lighted tennis courts, 2-mi jogging track, separate fitness centers for men and women, restaurant, lobby bar with wide-screen TV and piano, nightclub lounge, video checkout. AE, DC, MC, V.*

Moderate

★ **Hampton Inn Airport.** This is a member of the economy-priced system that was spun off from the Holiday Inn chain. The building is a pleasing contemporary design. Spacious, well-lighted rooms have Scandinavian-style teakwood furnishings. A hospitality suite has comfortable chairs, tables, and an audiovisual unit. *2979 Millbranch Rd., 38116, tel. 901/396–2200 or 800/426–7866. 128 rooms. Facilities: cable TV/movies, pool. AE, DC, MC, V.*

Lowenstein-Long House. If you're on a budget but still want a special lodging experience, this may be for you—especially if you're into Victoriana. This castlelike mansion on an acre of lawn was built at the turn of the century by department-store magnate Abraham Lowenstein and is listed on the National Historic Register. All the rooms are spacious, with high ceilings and large private baths. Some have four-poster beds and fireplaces; none have TVs. *217 N. Waldran Blvd., 38105, tel. 901/527–7174. 8 rooms. Facilities: kitchen and laundry facilities. No credit cards.*

Inexpensive **Days Inn Memphis Airport.** Accommodations at this completely renovated three-story motor inn are light, sunny, well-maintained, and spacious. This is an especially good buy for the economy-minded business traveler and visitor to nearby Graceland. *2949 Airways Blvd., 38116, tel. 901/345–1250 or 800/325–2525. 145 rooms. Facilities: cable TV, meeting rooms, dining room, lounge with dancing and wide-screen TV, oversize pool. AE, DC, MC, V.*

★ **Econo Lodge.** In the Executive section of this two-story inn, rooms are extra-large, with a mini-living room, spacious work table, good lighting, and comfortable overstuffed chairs. All rooms have private patios. The grounds are expansive and well landscaped, in a resortlike setting. *3280 Elvis Presley Blvd., 38116, tel. 901/345–1425 or 800/446–6900. 128 rooms. Facilities: cable TV/movies, outdoor pool, wading pool, playground, restaurant. AE, DC, MC, V.*

Econo Lodge Airport. This well-kept two-story motor inn is conveniently located near the airport and Graceland. King-size beds and suites are available. *3456 Lamar Ave., 38118, tel. 901/365–7335 or 800/446–6900. 100 rooms. Facilities: cable TV, pool, meeting rooms. AE, DC, MC, V.*

La Quinta Motor Inn–Medical Center. This two-story inn near the medical center and midtown attractions offers spacious, well-maintained rooms. King Plus rooms have a full-length mirror, a large working area, and an oversize bed. *42 S. Camilla St., 38104, tel. 901/526–1050 or 800/531–5900. 130 rooms. Facilities: cable TV, outdoor pool. AE, DC, MC, V.*

The Arts

For a complete listing of weekly events, check the Playbook section in the Friday *Memphis Commercial Appeal*, or *The Memphis Flyer*, distributed free at newsstands around the city. The Visitor Information Center will also provide an up-to-date rundown of events.

Concerts During the warmer months, there are free concerts at noon Monday, Wednesday, and Friday at the **Court Square Gazebo** in the Mid-America Mall (tel. 901/526–6840). Big-name entertainers and musical groups appear at the **Mud Island Amphitheatre** (tel. 901/576–7241). Among the offerings at the **Orpheum Theatre** (tel. 901/525–3000) are easy listening and jazz concerts.

Dance The Orpheum Theatre is also the scene of performances by two dance companies: **Memphis Concert Ballet,** featuring professional dancers and celebrity guest artists; and **Tennessee Ballet Company of Memphis,** with local performers.

Opera **Opera Memphis** performs at Vincent de Frank Music Hall, Cook Convention Center (tel. 901/678–2706 for tickets).

Theater **Playhouse on the Square** (tel. 901/725–0776, Sept.–July) features the city's only repertory company. The **Orpheum Theatre** (tel. 901/525–3000 for tickets), an impeccably restored former vaudeville palace, is the site of Broadway shows and other productions. **Center Stage,** at the Jewish Community Center (901/761–0810), and the **Circuit Playhouse** (tel. 901/726–5521, Sept.–June) offer a wide variety of performances. At **Memphis Children's Theatre** (tel. 901/452–3968), performances are directed, designed, and acted entirely by children. Community theaters include **Theatre Memphis** (tel. 901/682–8323), acclaimed as one of the best in the States, and **Germantown Community Theatre** (tel. 901/754–2680), in a restored schoolhouse. Memphis State's **University Theatre** (tel. 901/454–3975) and Rhodes College's **McCoy Theatre** (tel. 901/726–3839, Oct.–May) present dramatic and musical productions starring students, faculty, and guest performers.

Nightlife

Blues **Captain Bilbo's River Restaurant.** This spot overlooking the Mississippi offers floor shows, live entertainment, and dancing nightly in the bar. *263 Wagner Pl., tel. 901/526–1966. Open Sun.–Thurs. 5–10:30, to 11 Fri.–Sat.*

B. B. King's Blues Club. Live Blues nightly is accompanied by southern food specialties. *147 Beale St., tel. 901/524–5464.*

Omni New Daisy Theatre. At this 600-seat nightclub, where B.B. King got his start, Blues, jazz, and (predominantly) rock bands perform. *330 Beale St., tel. 901/525–8981.*

Rum Boogie Cafe. There's live Blues and dancing nightly. *182 Beale St., tel. 901/528–0150. Open Mon.–Thurs. 11:30 AM–1 AM, Fri. 11:30 AM–2 AM, Sat. noon–2 AM, Sun. noon–midnight.*

Nightclubs **Alfred's on Beale.** One of the city's hottest dance clubs also serves food. Rock bands perform every Friday and Saturday night, and a DJ spins popular dance tunes during the week. *197 Beale St., tel. 901/525–3711. Open daily 11 AM–3 AM.*

Bad Bob's Vapors. This airport-area supper club that holds 1,000 people features dancing to live country and rock 'n' roll bands daily. *1743 E. Brooks Rd., tel. 901/345–1761. Open daily 3 PM–3 AM.*

Hotel Lounges **Dad's Place.** Dance to Top 40, country, rock, and big-band sounds nightly. *Ramada Inn SW Airport, 1471 E. Brooks Rd., tel. 901/332–3500. Open daily 4:30 PM–1 AM.*

Lobby Lounge. Enjoy cocktails or late-night pastries in a sumptuous hotel lobby. *The Peabody Hotel, 149 Union Ave., tel. 901/529–4000. Open weekdays 10:30 AM–12:30 AM, weekends until 1 AM.*

Zeiggy's. At this video lounge, there's dancing and complimentary hors d'oeuvres nightly. *Holiday Inn–Memphis E, 5795*

Poplar Ave., tel. 901/682–7881. Open Tues.–Sat. noon–2 AM, Sun. and Mon. noon–midnight.

Overton Square Spots **Paulette's.** Come here for easy-listening piano music. *2110 Madison Ave., tel. 901/726–5128. Open Mon.–Thurs. 11 AM–11 PM, Fri. and Sat. 11 AM–midnight, Sun. 11 AM–9 PM.*

Nashville

Heralded as the Country Music Capital and birthplace of the "Nashville Sound," Tennessee's fast-growing capital city is also a leading center of higher education, appropriately known as the Athens of the South. Both labels fit. Far from developing a case of civic schizophrenia at such contrasting roles, Nashville has prospered from them both, becoming one of the middle South's liveliest and most vibrant cities in the process.

Much of Nashville's role as a cultural leader, enhanced by the presence of the new performing arts center, derives from the many colleges, universities, and technical and trade schools located here. Several, including Vanderbilt University, have national or international reputations, and many have private art galleries. As ancient Athens was the "School of Hellas," so Nashville fills this role in the contemporary South.

As every fan knows, it was Nashville's "Grand Ole Opry" radio program, which began as station WSM's "Barn Dance" in 1925, that launched the amazing country music boom. The Opry now performs in a sleek $15 million Opry House, but it's still as gleeful and down-home informal as it was when it held forth in the old Ryman Auditorium. Joining the Opry in Nashville are dozens of country music attractions—some large, some small, many begun by or memorials to individual stars.

You'll also enjoy forays into the surrounding Tennessee Heartland, a pocket of gently rolling Cumberland Mountain foothills and bluegrass meadows. It's one of the state's richest farming areas.

Arriving and Departing

By Plane

Airports and Airlines Nashville Metropolitan Airport, approximately eight miles from downtown, is served by **American, American Eagle, Comair, Delta, Northwest, Southwest, TWA, United,** and **USAir.**

Between the Airport and Center City Airport **shuttle service** (tel. 615/275–1180) to and from downtown is $8 for the first person and $4 for each additional person. To reach downtown by **car,** take I–40W.

By Train Amtrak does not serve the Nashville area.

By Bus **Southeastern Greyhound Lines** terminal is at 8th Ave. S and McGavock St., tel. 615/256–6141.

By Car From Nashville, I–65 leads north into Kentucky and south into Alabama, and I–24 leads northwest into Kentucky and Illinois and southeast into Georgia. I–40 traverses the state east–west, connecting Knoxville with Nashville and Memphis.

By Boat The **Delta Queen Steamboat Co.** (tel. 504/586–0631) offers four-night paddlewheeler cruises between St. Louis and Nashville, with stops along the way.

Getting Around

By Bus **Metropolitan Transit Authority (MTA)** buses (tel. 615/242–4433) serve the entire county. Service on most routes begins at 4–5 AM and continues until 11:15 PM. The regular adult base fare is $1.15 (exact change required). For disabled persons, a van is available for downtown transport (tel. 615/351–RIDE).

By Trolley **Nashville Trolley Co.** (tel. 615/242–4433) also offers rides in the downtown area. The fare is 75¢ (exact change).

By Taxi The fare is a basic $1.50, plus 10¢ for each quarter-mile. It's best to phone for service: **Checker Cab** (tel. 615/254–5031), **Nashville Cab** (tel. 615/242–7070), **Yellow Cab** (tel. 615/256–0101).

Important Addresses and Numbers

Tourist Information **Nashville Area Chamber of Commerce,** 161 4th Ave. N, tel. 615/259–3900. Open weekdays 8–4:30. **Visitor Information Center,** I–65 and James Robertson Pkwy., Exit 85, tel. 615/242–5606. Open daily 8–5 (until 8 PM Memorial Day–Labor Day).

Emergencies Dial 911 for **police** and **ambulance** in an emergency.

Hospitals Emergency rooms are open all night at centrally located **Baptist Hospital** (2000 Church St., tel. 615/329–5555) and **Vanderbilt University Medical Center** (1211 22nd Ave. S, tel. 615/322–7311).

Dentist For emergency service, contact any of three **American Dental Center** facilities: on Woodland St., tel. 615/256–2321; on Old Harding Pike, tel. 615/662–0035; or on Bransford Ave., tel. 615/292–3301.

24-hour Pharmacy **Farmer's Market Pharmacy** (715 Jefferson St., tel. 615/242–5501).

Guided Tours

Orientation Several companies offer tours that may include drives past stars' homes and visits to the Grand Ole Opry, Music Row, and historic structures. Among them are **American Sightseeing** (tel. 615/256–1200 or 800/826–6456), **Gray Line** (tel. 615/227–2270 or 800/251–1864), **Grand Ole Opry Tours** (tel. 615/889–9490).

Special-interest **Country & Western Gray Line Tours** (tel. 615/883–5555) offers a daily Twitty City/Johnny Cash Special motorcoach tour, which drives past homes of stars and visits Twitty City/Music Village USA and the House of Cash. **Johnny Walker Tours** (tel. 615/834–8585 or 800/722–1524) has an evening Music Village Nightlife Tour, which includes a Southern-style barbecue buffet dinner and top-name country entertainment in Music Village Theater. **Stardust Tours** (tel. 615/244–2335) offers a daily Music Village Sunset Tour, which includes the Music Village Theater entertainment and buffet dinner. **Nissan** (tel. 615/459–1400) offers free tours of its vast, supermodern Smyrna auto plant on Tuesday and Thursday. Call for an appointment; only children in fifth grade or older are allowed on tours.

Walking Tours At the Nashville Area Chamber of Commerce or the Visitor Information Center (*see* Important Addresses and Numbers, *above*), pick up a self-guided tour of downtown.

Excursion-boat Tours **Belle Carol Riverboat Co.** (tel. 615/244–3430 or 800/342–2355) offers Cumberland River sightseeing, luncheon, and dinner cruises from the Nashville Old Steamboat Dock. From its dock, **Opryland USA** (tel. 615/889–6611) offers daytime cruises with Opryland-style entertainment and evening dinner cruises aboard its four-deck *General Jackson* showboat.

Exploring Nashville

Numbers in the margin correspond to points of interest on the Downtown Nashville and Nashville maps.

Nashville sprawls. In getting around, it helps to remember that the river horizontally bisects the central city. Numbered avenues, running north–south, are west of and parallel to the river; numbered streets are east of the river and parallel to it.

Downtown Though considerably smaller, the Cumberland River has been
as important to Nashville as the Mississippi has been to Memphis. That this is still true can be seen by any visitor to
1 **Riverfront Park** at First Avenue and Broadway, a welcoming
green enclave on the west bank of the Cumberland, with an expansive view of the busy barge traffic on the river. The park
serves as a popular venue for summer concerts and picnics, as
well as a docking spot for riverboat excursions (*see* Guided
2 Tours, *above*). North on First Avenue is **Fort Nashborough.**
High on the limestone bluffs overlooking the river that brought settlers here, a crude log fort, built in 1779 for protection and shelter, overlooks Nashville. Today it has been painstakingly re-created to serve as a monument to the city founders' courage, and, in five log cabins, costumed interpreters evoke the indomitable spirit of the American age of settlement. *Tel. 615/255–8192. Admission free. Open daily.*

By the early 19th century, logs had given way to brick and marble. Downtown was thriving, and today it thrives anew, thanks
to an extensive preservation program. From Fort Nashborough, turn left onto Church Street and you'll be in the heart
3 of the **Historic Second Avenue Business District,** where 19th-
century buildings have been handsomely restored to house offices, restaurants, boutiques, and residences.

Continue west on Church Street, which between Fourth and
Eighth avenues is cobblestoned and tree-lined, retaining a picturesque quality reminiscent of a European town. At the cor-
4 ner of Fifth is the **Downtown Presbyterian Church,** an Egyptian
Revival tabernacle (c. 1851) designed by noted Philadelphia architect William Strickland.

Strolling north on Fifth Avenue, you'll come to one of the city's
finest contemporary structures: the James K. Polk Office
5 Building, home to the impressive **Tennessee State Museum.**
Here over 6,000 artifacts are displayed in settings that explore
life in Tennessee. Included are a log cabin, an exhibition of Indian life, and a demonstration of bygone printing techniques.
6 (Also part of the complex is the **Tennessee Performing Arts Center.**) *505 Deaderick St., tel. 615/741–2692. Admission free.
Open Tues.–Sat. 10–5, Sun. 1–5. Closed New Year's Day, Easter, Thanksgiving, Christmas.*

Walking west along Charlotte Avenue, you'll come to the Greek
7 Revival **State Capitol,** also designed by Strickland, who was so
impressed with his creation that he requested—and re-

Barbara Mandrell Country, **12**
Belmont Mansion, **23**
Belle Meade Mansion, **21**
Car Collectors Hall of Fame, **14**
Cars of the Stars, **17**
Cheekwood, **22**
Country Music Hall of Fame, **10**
Country Music Wax Museum and Mall, **15**
Downtown Presbyterian Church, **4**
Fort Nashborough, **2**
Hank Williams Jr. Museum, **13**
The Hermitage, **25**
Historic Second Avenue Business District, **3**
House of Cash, **26**
Jim Reeves Museum, **19**
Music Valley Wax Museum of the Stars, **18**
Opryland USA, **16**
Parthenon, **20**
Riverfront Park, **1**
Ryman Auditorium and Museum, **9**
State Capitol, **7**
Studio B, **11**
Tennessee Performing Arts Center, **6**
Tennessee State Museum, **5**
Travellers' Rest, **24**
Twitty City/Music Village USA, **27**
War Memorial Building, **8**

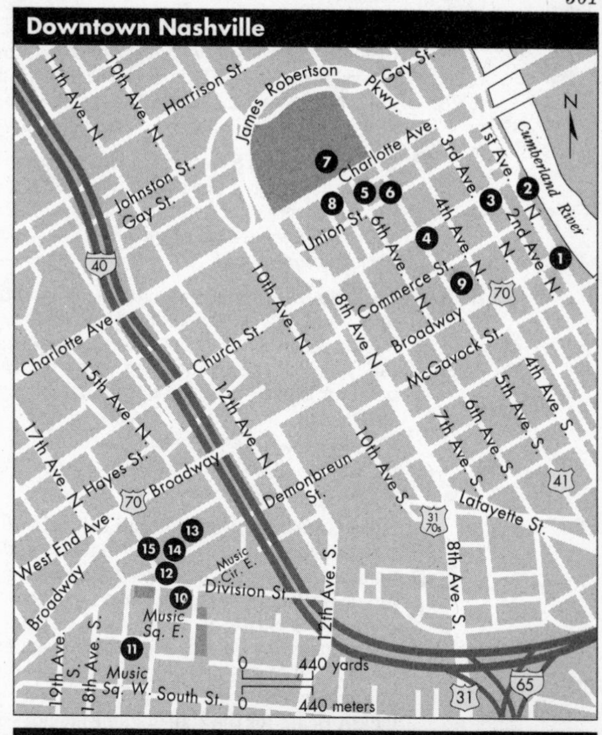

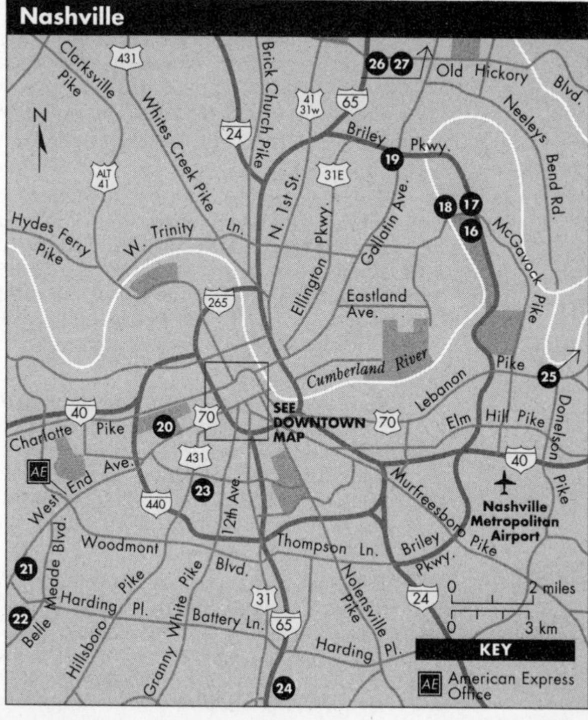

ceived—entombment behind one of the building's walls. On the grounds—guarded by statues of such Tennessee heros as Andrew Jackson—are buried the 11th U.S. president, James K. Polk, and his wife. *Tel. 615/741–1621. Open for free tours weekdays, 9–4, Sat. 10–5, Sun. 1–5. Closed major holidays.*

8 On the corner of Seventh and Union is the **War Memorial Building,** built to honor the state's World War I dead and now housing a collection of military memorabilia. *Tel. 615/726–0518. Admission free. Open Mon.–Sat. 10–5, Sun. 1–5. Closed major holidays.*

Music Row

The leap from state capital to music capital is not as great as it may seem. If you're walking, you might head down Fifth Ave-
9 nue to pass recently renovated **Ryman Auditorium and Museum,** home of the Grand Ole Opry from 1943 to 1974 and now open for tours—a shrine for die-hard Opry fans. *116 Opry Pl. (Fifth Ave. N, between Broadway and Commerce Sts.), tel. 615/254–1445. Admission: $2.50 adults; $1 children 6–12, under 6 free. Open daily 8:30–4:30. Closed Thanksgiving, Christmas.*

By car, take the Demonbreun exit off I–40 to Music Row, the heart of Nashville's recording industry and a center for country
10 music attractions. The ample free parking next to the **Country Music Hall of Fame and Museum** is convenient to all the country attractions clustered nearby and is another reason to begin your Music Row tour at Nashville's premier country music museum. Costumes, instruments, film, photos, insights: the Hall of Fame has it all (including Elvis Presley's "solid gold" Cadillac). A ticket for the Hall of Fame includes admission to the leg-
11 endary RCA **Studio B** a few blocks away. Elvis, Dolly Parton, and countless others once recorded here; now the studio is a hands-on exhibit area showing how records are produced. *4 Music Sq. E, tel. 615/256–1639. Admission: $6.50 adults, $1.75 children 6–11, under 6 free. Open daily 8–8 June–Aug., 9–5 rest of year. Closed New Year's Day, Thanksgiving, Christmas.*

Those inspired by their visit to Studio B might stop by the **Recording Studios of America** (1510 Division St., tel. 615/254–1282) to record, at nominal cost, a demo tape of their own. The
12 studio is part of **Barbara Mandrell Country,** an intimate look at the career and family life of that superstar (including a replica of her bedroom). *Tel. 615/242–7800. Admission: $6 adults, $2.25 children, under 5 free. Open daily 9–5 Sept.–May; 8–8 June–Aug.*

The car seems to be as much a country music icon as the guitar, a fact underlined by two museums on Demonbreun Street. At
13 the **Hank Williams Jr. Museum,** family memorabilia includes Hank Sr.'s '52 Cadillac and Hank Jr.'s '58 pink Cadillac. *1524 Demonbreun St., tel. 615/726–2962. Admission: $4.50 adults, children under 13 free with an adult. Open daily 8 AM–6 PM Mar.–Sept., 8–3 Oct.–Feb.*

14 A few doors away, the **Car Collectors Hall of Fame** displays another of Elvis's Cadillacs (alongside one of George's), Webb Pierce's startling "silver dollar car," and 50 other flashy vehicles with country provenances. *1534 Demonbreun St., tel. 615/255–6804. Admission: $4.95 adults; $3.25 children 6–11, under 6 free. Open daily 9–5 Sept.–May, 8–8 June–Aug.*

15 In the same block, you'll find the guitars: At the **Country Music Wax Museum and Mall** are over 60 figures of country stars, complete with original stage costumes, and musical instruments. *118 16th Ave. S, tel. 615/256–2490. Admission: $4 adults, $3.50 over 55, $1.75 children 5–12, under 5 free.* In the same building is Waylon Jennings's private collection of six automobiles, including the General Lee used in the TV series, "The Dukes of Hazard." *Admission: $3 adults, $2.50 over 55, $1.75 children. Open daily 9–9 May–Aug., 9–5 Sept.–Apr.*

Opryland

16 Country music lovers may continue their pilgrimage at **Opryland USA,** an attraction-filled show park just 15 minutes from downtown via Briley Parkway. The complex was created in part because the enormously popular Grand Ole Opry—66 years old and still going strong—had outgrown its old stomping grounds, the Ryman. Each weekend, top stars perform at the nation's oldest continuous radio show, in the world's largest broadcast studio (it seats 4,424). There are special matinees in summer. *To avoid disappointment, purchase tickets in advance. Request a ticket-order form from Grand Ole Opry, 2808 Opryland Dr., 37214, tel. 615/889–3060. Admission: reserved seats $15.70 evenings, $13.53 matinees; upper balcony $13.53 evenings, $11.37 matinees.*

The show park also offers more than a dozen live shows ranging from bluegrass bands to huge stage productions, and there are 22 thrilling rides, including Chaos, a $7-million indoor thriller combining a roller-coaster ride and spectacular audio-visual effects. The **Roy Acuff Musical Collection and Museum** (tel. 615/889–6700) contains memorabilia, including many guns and fiddles, of the "king of country music." **Minnie Pearl's Museum,** relocated to the same building in 1989, provides a nostalgic tour of the performer's life. Admission to the museums in Opryland Plaza is free; hours vary widely, so it's best to inquire locally. The *General Jackson,* Opryland's new showboat, offers several cruises daily with a musical revue while you dine (tel. 615/889–6611). There's also dining at food stands or full-service restaurants, and shopping for trinkets or treasures. *Tel. 615/889–6700. Admission: $23.76 one-day, $35.67 two-day, $75.72 3-day passport, including Grand Ole Opry matinee, daytime cruise, country concert at Chevrolet Geo Theater. Children under 4 free. Open weekends only late-Mar.–May, Sept., Oct.; daily late-May–Labor Day. Closed Nov.–late-Mar. Hours vary widely but are generally 9–6 weekdays, 9–9 weekends except 9–9 daily in summer; call to be sure.*

17 Just north of Opryland USA is the inevitable **Cars of the Stars,** where classic cars share center stage with those of such country notables as Randy Travis, Dolly Parton, and Roy Acuff (about 45 cars in all). *2611 McGavock Pike, tel. 615/885–7400. Admission $3.50 adults; $3 senior citizens; $2 children 6–12, under 6 free. Open daily 8 AM–9 PM Memorial Day–Labor Day, 9–5 rest of year. Closed Thanksgiving, Christmas.*

18 Next door is **Music Valley Wax Museum of the Stars,** with life-size wax figures of more country stars, and outside is the **Sidewalk of the Stars,** Nashville's version of Graumann's Chinese, with the footprints, handprints, and signatures of over 200 country music performers. *2515 McGavock Pike, tel. 615/883–3612. Admission: $3.50 adults, $3 senior citizens, $1.50 children. Open daily 8 AM–10 PM Memorial Day weekend–Labor Day, 9–5 rest of year.*

Fans of Gentleman Jim Reeves will not want to miss the collec-
19 tion of memorabilia at the **Jim Reeves Museum,** in an attractive 1794 house. This place continues the tradition of up close and personal à la Barbara Mandrell: Jim's bedroom furniture is on display, too. *1023 Joyce Lane (off Briley), tel. 615/226–2062. Admission: $4 adults; $3 over 64, $2 children 6–12, under 6 free. Open daily 9–5. Closed New Year's Day, Thanksgiving, Christmas.*

Farther Afield

Apart from the many educational and cultural institutions that lend credence to Nashville's Athens of the South sobriquet are the gracious estates that form a necklace of emerald green around the city. To get into the spirit, begin your tour at Cen-
20 tennial Park's **Parthenon,** an exact copy of the Athenian original right down to the Elgin Marbles. Newly renovated, including the addition of a huge statue of Athena, the Parthenon houses an art gallery with changing exhibits. *Tel. 615/862–8431. Admission: $2.50 adults, $1.25 senior citizens and children 4–17, under 4 free. Open Tues.–Sat. 9–4:30 (until 8 on Thurs.), Sun. 12:30–4:30.*

21 **Belle Meade Mansion** is a stunning Greek Revival house, the centerpiece of a 5,300-acre estate that was one of the nation's first and finest thoroughbred breeding farms. It was also the site of the famous Iroquois, the oldest amateur steeplechase in America, which is still run each May but in nearby Percy Warner Park. A Victorian carriage museum continues the equine theme. *110 Leake Ave. (from Centennial Park, head west on West End Ave. and follow the signs for Belle Meade—not to be confused with Belle Meade Blvd.), tel. 615/356–0501. Admission: $5 adults, $3.50 children 13–18, $2 ages 7–12; under 6 free. Open Mon.–Sat. 9–5, Sun. 1–5.*

22 The Georgian-style mansion at nearby **Cheekwood** (take Harding Rd. east, turn right on to Belle Meade Blvd., and look for a sign) is now a fine arts center, and the surrounding 55-acre **Tennessee Botanical Gardens** showcases herbs, roses, irises, daffodils, and area wildflowers. Greenhouses, streams, and pools make this a delightful spot for a picnic. *Forrest Park Dr., tel. 615/356–8000. Admission: $5 adults; $4 senior citizens and college students with ID, $2 children 7–18, under 6 free. Open Mon.–Sat. 9–5, Sun. 1–5. Closed New Year's Day, Thanksgiving, Dec. 24–25, 31.*

23 **Belmont Mansion,** now on the campus of Belmont College, was the home of Adelicia Acklen, Nashville's answer to Scarlett O'Hara, who married "once for money, once for love, and once for the hell of it." This outstanding Italianate villa of the 1850s is a Victorian gem right down to its cast-iron gazebos. *Take Belle Meade Blvd. north from Cheekwood. Turn right on to West End Ave., then right on to Blakemore, which becomes Wedgewood. Turn right on to Magnolia Blvd., first left, then follow signs. Corner of Acklen Ave. and Belmont Blvd., tel. 615/269–9537. Admission: $4 adults, $1 children 6–12, under 6 free. Open Tues.–Sat. 10–4, also Mon., Jun–Aug. Closed major holidays.*

From here, take I–65 south to the first of two Harding Place
24 exits to **Travellers' Rest,** the early 19th-century clapboard home of pioneer landowner John Overton. Following the fortunes of Overton, the law partner, mentor, campaign manager, and lifelong friend of Andrew Jackson, whose own home is nearby,

the house metamorphosed from a 1799 four-room cottage to a 12-room mansion with Federal and Greek Revival additions. *636 Farrell Pkwy., tel. 615/832–2962. Admission: $4 adults, $2 children 6–18, under 5 free. Open Mon.–Sat. 9–5, Sun. 1–5 June–Aug.; Mon.–Sat. 9–4, Sun. 1–4 Sept.–May. Closed New Year's Day, Thanksgiving, Christmas.*

Forming the eastern end of this semicircle of homes is the
25 **Hermitage,** 12 miles east of Nashville (I–40E to Old Hickory Blvd. exit), where the life and times of Tennessee's beloved Old Hickory are reflected with great care. Andrew Jackson built this mansion on 600 acres for his wife, Rachel, and both are entombed here. The **Andrew Jackson Center,** a 28,000-square-foot museum, visitor, and education center, opened in 1989, contains many Jackson artifacts never before exhibited. A 16-minute film, "Old Hickory," is shown in its auditorium; the structure also includes Rachel's Garden Cafe and a museum store. Tours take you through the mansion, furnished with many original pieces. Across the road stands **Tulip Grove,** built by Mrs. Jackson's nephew, and **The Hermitage Church,** fondly known as "Rachel's Church." *4580 Rachel's Lane, Hermitage, tel. 615/889–2941. Admission (includes Tulip Grove and church): $7 adults, $6.50 senior citizens, $3.50 children 6–18, under 6 free. Open daily 9–5. Closed Christmas and Thanksgiving.*

In Hendersonville, 20 miles northeast of downtown Nashville (eight miles from The Hermitage), there are yet more shrines
26 to country music notables. The **House of Cash** displays possessions and memorabilia of the "Man in Black," a legend in his own time, including some superb Frederic Remington bronzes. *700 Johnny Cash Pkwy., tel. 615/824–5110. Admission: $6 adults, $4 senior citizens, $1 children 6–12, under 6 free. Open Mon.–Sat. 9–4:30 Apr.–Oct.*

27 **Twitty City/Music Village USA** is not only the home of superstar Conway Twitty but also a 15-acre entertainment complex with live shows, shops, restaurants, and museums highlighting the life and times of such entertainers as Bill Monroe, Ferlin Husky, and Marty Robbins. *Music Village Blvd., Hendersonville, tel. 615/822–6650 or 615/822–1800. Admission: $6 adults; $4.50 children 6–15, under 6 free. Open daily 9–5; Thanksgiving–Dec. Mon.–Fri. 5–9, Sat.–Sun. 5–10. Live music year-round.*

Nashville for Free

TV Tapings. Several shows produced at Opryland USA and other Nashville sites—including *Hee Haw* (June and October only) and TNN cable programs—are open to visitors, and most are free. *Call TNN Viewer Services at 615/883–7000 for schedules and to make reservations.*

U.S. Tobacco Museum. The wide-ranging collections include antique pipes, tobacco jars, cigar-store figures, and snuff boxes. *800 Harrison St., tel. 615/271–2349. Open Mon.–Sat. 9–4.*

Entertainment in the Parks. The Metro Nashville Parks Department (tel. 615/259–6399) presents free summer concerts and outdoor arts shows in some of the area's 70 public parks.

What to See and Do with Children

Children's Discovery House. This is a youngster's dream, with bubble blowers on the front lawn, colored chalk by the sidewalks, dress-up clothes, a play store and play hospital, a nature collection, and more. *503 N. Maple St., Murfreesboro, tel. 615/890–2300. Open Tues.–Sat. 10–5, Sun. 1–5 (closes 1 hr earlier in summer). Admission: $3 adults; $2 children 2 and over, under 2 free.*

Cumberland Museum and Science Center. Children are invited to look, touch, smell, climb, listen, and explore. The planetarium has star and laser shows. *800 Ridley Blvd., Nashville, tel. 615/862–5160. Admission: $5 adults, $4 children 3–12 and senior citizens. Planetarium $1. Open Wed.–Sat. 9:30–5, Sun. 12:30–5.*

Fort Nashborough (*see* Downtown in Exploring Nashville, *above*).

Opryland USA (*see* Opryland in Exploring Nashville, *above*). The petting zoo especially delights the younger ones.

Picnicking. Get away for a day outdoors, picnicking, horseback riding, hiking, and walking through the nature preserves at 14,200-acre **J. Percy Priest Lake** (11 mi east of Nashville off I–40, tel. 615/889–1975) or 22,500-acre **Old Hickory Reservoir** (15 mi northeast of Nashville via U.S. 31E, tel. 615/822–4846).

Tennessee State Museum (*see* Downtown in Exploring Nashville, *above*). The walk-through and Civil War exhibits especially appeal to children.

Wave Country. This water park near Opryland has a large wave pool and a three-flume water slide. *Two Rivers Pkwy., off Briley Pkwy., tel. 615/885–1052. Admission: $4 adults; $3 children 5–12, under 4 free. Open daily 10–8 Memorial Day–Labor Day.*

Off the Beaten Track

Lynchburg is home to the **Jack Daniels Distillery,** where you can observe every step of the sour-mash-whiskey-making art. *¼ mi northeast of town on TN 55, tel. 615/759–4221. Guided tours daily 8–4. Closed major holidays.*

Miss Mary Bobo's Boarding House is a Tennessee institution. Diners flock to the big two-story 1867 white frame house with a white picket fence to feast family-style at tables groaning with fried chicken, roast beef, fried catfish, stuffed vegetables and sliced tomatoes fresh from the gardens out back, corn on the cob, homemade biscuits, cornbread, pecan pie, lemon icebox pie, fruit cobblers, and strawberry shortcake. *½ block from the Public Square, Lynchburg, tel. 615/759–7394. Dress: informal. Reservations required, at least a week in advance in summer. One meal served each day, promptly at 1 PM, Mon.–Sat. Closed major holidays. Fixed price is $9 adults, $4 children under 12, including tax (no tipping permitted). MC, V.*

During July and August, you can tour studios of some of the state's most talented craftsfolk at the **Joe L. Evins Appalachian Center for Crafts.** The sales gallery has crafts from throughout the Appalachian Mountains. *70 mi east of Nashville in Smithville (exit Rte. 273 off I–40, go 6 mi south on 56), tel. 615/*

597–6801. Open daily 9–5. Closed Easter, Thanksgiving, Dec. 25–Jan. 2.

At the **Loretta Lynn Ranch,** in Hurricane Mills, the singer's personal museum is housed in an old restored gristmill. Narrated hayride tours of the 3,500-acre ranch are offered during the summer; you can also tour her stately antebellum home. *West of I–40W to TN 13N, tel. 615/296–7700. Admission: $3 adults; $1 children 6–12, under 6 free. Open daily 8–5 Apr. 15–Oct. 31.*

Try your luck at fishing at the **Bucksnort Trout Ranch.** This working hatchery next to a pretty creek offers family fishing, poles and bait included. *Exit 152 off I–40, 70 mi west of Nashville. No telephone. Admission free, pay for what you catch. Open Fri.–Sun., Apr.–Oct.*

Old Stone Fort State Park, in Manchester (U.S. 41, southeast of Nashville off I–24, tel. 615/728–0751), contains a walled structure believed to have been built at least 2,000 years ago. The scenic 600-acre site, on bluffs overlooking Duck River, is laced with waterfalls and has a visitor center, a nine-hole golf course, and campsites.

Alfred Stieglitz rewarded Fisk University's progressive arts program with a bequest from his collection of 20th-century paintings and his own superb photographs. These are now on display in the **Van Vechten Art Gallery** on the campus. Stieglitz's wife, Georgia O'Keeffe, helped install the collection, highlighted by her own paintings. The gallery also features African sculpture. *Fisk University at 17th Ave. N, tel. 615/329–8543. Admission: $3.50 adults, children free. Open Tues.–Fri. 10–5, weekends 1–5.*

Shopping

Major downtown stores are generally open Monday–Saturday 10–5. The shopping malls are open Monday–Saturday 10 to 9 or 9:30 and Sunday 1–6. Banks are generally open weekdays 8:30–3:30 (until 5 or 6 on Fri.).

Shopping Districts

Church Street is the major downtown shopping area; there you'll find department stores, smaller chain stores, and numerous boutiques. **Fountain Square** (2244 Metro Center Blvd., tel. 615/256–7467) is a complex of 35 shops, a food court, pushcart vendors in season—all ranged round a 48-acre lake. There is free live entertainment nightly, from classical music to mime to dance.

Specialty Stores

Antiques

Murfreesboro, about 30 miles outside Nashville, calls itself the Antique Center of the South. Pick up a free antiques shopping guide at Cannonsburgh Pioneer Village, a living museum of 19th-century life in the South (tel. 615/890–0355). In Nashville, browse for distinctive 18th- and 19th-century English antiques and art objects at **Madison Antique Mall** (320 Gallatin Rd. S, tel. 615/865–4677), **Nashville Antique Mall** (657 Wedgewood Ave., tel. 615/256–1465), and **Smorgasbord Antique Mall** (4144-B Lebanon Rd., tel. 615/883–5789).

Arts and Crafts

You'll find works of major regional artists at **Cumberland Gallery** (4107 Hillsboro Circle, tel. 615/297–0296). For pottery and ceramics, seek out **Forrest Valley Pottery,** a working studio (325 Forest Valley Dr., tel. 615/356–5136).

Country-and-Western Wear Stores geared to the latest look in country clothing include **Boot Country** (2412 Music Valley Dr., tel. 615/883–2661), **Loretta Lynn's Western Stores** (120 16th Ave. S, tel. 615/256–2814; 435 Donelson Pike, tel. 615/889–5582), and the **Nashville Cowboy** (118 16th Ave. S, tel. 615/242–9497; 1516 Demonbreun St., tel. 615/256–2429).

Records and Tapes Fans can find good selections of records and tapes at **Conway's Twitty Bird Record Shop** (1530 Demonbreun St., tel. 615/242–2466), **Ernest Tubb Record Shops** (2414 Music Valley Dr., tel. 615/889–2474; 417 Broadway, tel. 615/255–7503), and **The Great Escape** (1925 Broadway, tel. 615/327–0646; 139 Gallatin Rd. N, Madison, tel. 615/865–8052).

Farmer's Market Every day from late spring through early autumn, farmers and gardeners set up stands in a downtown area bounded by Seventh and Eighth avenues North and Jefferson Street.

Flea Market From treasures to just plain "junque"—you'll find it at the **Nashville Flea Market** at the Tennessee State Fairgrounds. Usually, at least 450 traders, craftsfolk, and dealers will be plying their wares the fourth weekend of every month (except Sept. and Dec.). *Tel. 615/383–7636. Admission free. Open Sat. 9–6, Sun. noon–6.*

Participant Sports

Boating and Fishing You'll find boat rentals at **J. Percy Priest Lake** (11 mi east of Nashville, off I–40, tel. 615/883–2351) and **Old Hickory Reservoir** (15 mi northeast of Nashville via U.S. 31E, tel. 615/824–7766).

Golf Among courses open to the public year-round are **Harpeth Hills** (tel. 615/862–8493), **Hermitage Golf Course** (tel. 615/847–4001), and **Rhodes Golf Course** (9 holes; tel. 615/242–2336). Hermitage is the site each April of the LPGA Sara Lee Classic.

Horseback Riding You can jog or canter on gentle steeds at **Riverwood Recreation Plantation and Riding Academy** (tel. 615/262–1794), and **Ramblin' Breeze Ranch** (tel. 615/876–1029).

Ice Skating From September through April, there's indoor skating at **Sportsplex** (tel. 615/862–8480), in Centennial Park.

Jogging Favorite sites include **Centennial Park,** the **Vanderbilt University running track, J. Percy Priest Lake,** and **Percy Warner Park.** The 1,700-plus-member running club Nashville Striders (tel. 615/833–4124) can recommend choice spots and will provide information on many summer races.

Mini-golf Enjoy this uniquely American family sport at **Grand Old Golf** (tel. 615/871–4701), across the street from the Opryland Hotel.

Tennis Several municipal tennis facilities offer good play. **Centennial Sportsplex Tennis Center** (tel. 615/862–8480) has outdoor courts plus indoor courts.

Spectator Sports

Baseball You can root for the AAA **Nashville Sounds,** an affiliate of the Cincinnati Reds, from April through August at Herschel Greer Stadium (tel. 615/242–4371).

Horse Show For 10 days from late August to early September, Shelbyville hums as visitors, horses, and riders come from all over the land for the **Tennessee Walking Horse National Celebration,** the world's greatest walking horse show. Information: Box 1010, Shelbyville 37160, tel. 615/684–5915.

Stock-car Racing Top drivers compete at the **Nashville Motor Raceway,** State Fairgrounds (tel. 615/726–1818), from April through October.

Dining

By Tom Martin

If you expect Nashville dining to be all cornbread, turnip greens, and grits, you're in for a staggering surprise. You will find some of Tennessee's most sophisticated restaurants, with service that is as polished as any you'll find in cities twice the size. The combination of politics (Nashville is the state capital), country music (the city is home to the Grand Ole Opry), conventions, and business (several major companies are headquartered here) means a lot of entertaining is done in restaurants. That in turn has meant prosperity and longevity for some of the city's best places. It is not unusual to find waiters, captains, and chefs who have worked in the same place for a decade. Such tenure translates into quality dining and the food is anything but country cooking.

The most highly recommended restaurants in each price category are indicated by a star ★.

Category	Cost*
Expensive	over $30
Moderate	$12–$30
Inexpensive	under $12

**per person without tax (7.75% in Tennessee), service, or drinks*

Expensive
American

Belle Meade Brasserie. Mark Rubin and Robert Siegel have created a comfortable suburban restaurant and a menu filled with surprises—corn fritters and pepper jelly, New York strip cowboy-style, San Francisco–style crabcakes, and shrimp and scallops served on a bed of black linguine. Desserts are just as compelling, including a knockout Russian raspberry gratin. *101 Page Rd., tel. 615/356–5450. Dress: casual but neat. AE, DC, MC, V. Closed Sun.*

Merchants. A $3.2 million renovation of a historic property in downtown Nashville, this former hotel provides three levels of dining and an appealing outdoor patio. Specialties include California-style pizzas, the freshest seafoods, and meats grilled over native hardwoods. The menu changes to lighter fare in summer and all rolls, pastas, and pastries are made fresh daily. Save room for the Key lime pie. *401 Broadway, tel. 615/254–1892. Dress: casual but neat. Reservations recommended. AE, DC, MC, V.*

Classic French
★

Julian's Restaurant Français. If you can't travel to the City of Light, dine at Julian's instead, for here, in the intimate rooms of a turn-of-the-century town house, chef Patrice Bouley serves some of the best French cuisine this side of Paris. Her creations include sautéed veal sweetbreads in Sauternes sauce and duck in black-currant sauce. *2412 West End Ave., tel. 615/327–2412. Jacket and tie suggested. Reservations suggested. AE, DC, MC, V. Closed Sun.*

Dining
Arthur's, **7**
Belle Meade Brasserie, **12**
Cakewalk Restaurant, **14**
F. Scott's, **13**
Julian's Restaurant Français, **15**
Loveless Cafe, **10**
Mario's Ristorante Italiano, **2**
Maude's Courtyard, **3**
Merchants, **8**
Mère Bulles, The Wine Bar and Restaurant, **9**
106 Club, **11**
The Wild Boar, **4**

Lodging
Comfort Inn Hermitage, **23**
Courtyard by Marriott-Airport, **22**
Embassy Suites Nashville Hotel, **20**
Hampton Inn Vanderbilt, **1**
Holiday Inn-Briley Parkway, **21**
Howard Johnson at Opryland, **17**
Hyatt Regency Nashville, **5**
La Quinta Motor Inn, **16**
Opryland Hotel, **19**
Ramada Inn Across from Opryland, **18**
Stouffer Nashville Hotel, **6**

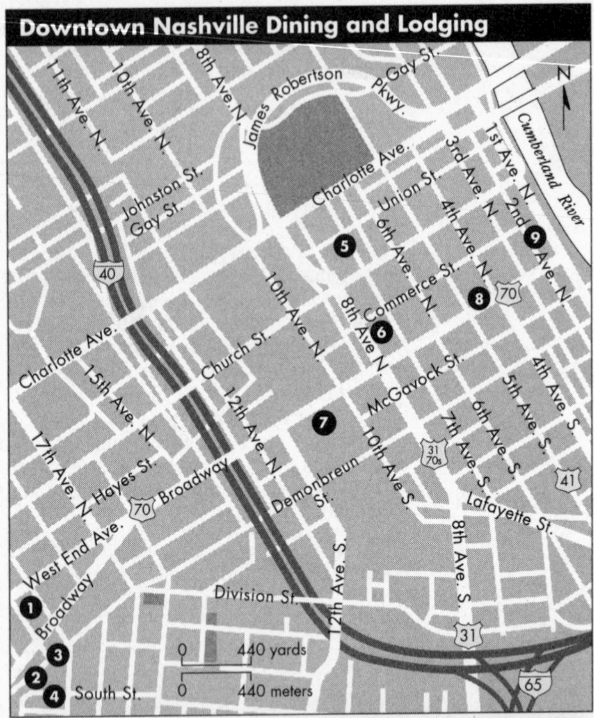

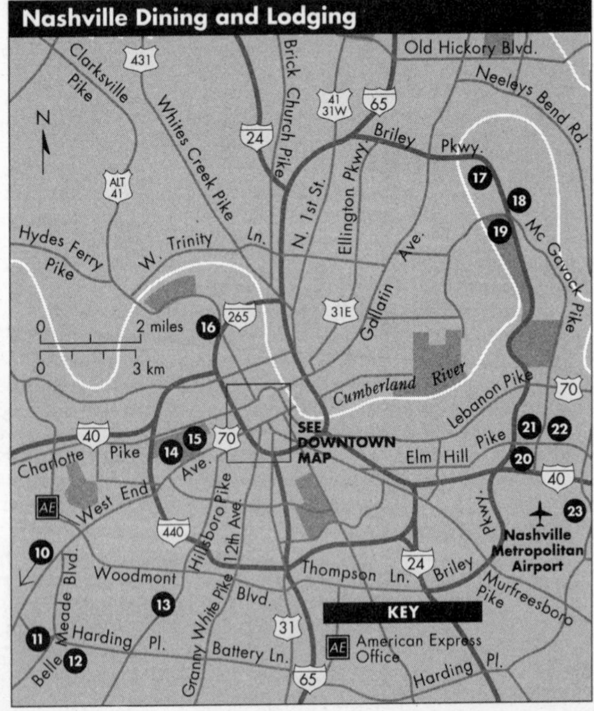

Continental ★ **Arthur's.** This restaurant is located in the renovated Union Station, where an upscale hotel has taken the place of the train terminal. The six-course meals are dazzling, and the ambience is romantic. Be sure to save room for dessert, especially the bananas Foster. The decor is lush, with lace curtains, velveteen-upholstered chairs, white linen, and fine silver service. *In Union Station. 1001 Broadway, tel. 615/255–1494. Jacket and tie suggested. Reservations suggested. AE, DC, MC, V. Dinner only Mon.–Sat.*

Mère Bulles, the Wine Bar and Restaurant. There's an aura of casual elegance in this locally popular restaurant with brass-trimmed mahogany bar and changing artworks decorating mellow, exposed brick walls. Guests can enjoy tapas and drinks in the cozy lounge, then move into one of three intimate dining areas with views of the river. There's live entertainment nightly, usually jazz or folk music. Specialties include Veal Mère Bulles, pesto Mère Bulles—shrimp and scallops with walnut-pesto sauce served on a bed of shell pasta. There are 50 wines by the glass and a stock of over 170 selections by the bottle. *152 2nd Ave. N, tel. 615/256–1946. Jacket and tie suggested. Reservations advised. AE, DC, MC, V.*

Wild Boar. Chef David Poulton and local restaurateur Mario Ferrari have pooled their enormous talents to create The Wild Boar. The restaurant emphasizes game and American cuisine. The menu also features trout, lobster, duck, and beef dishes, with several that are prepared at tableside. The atmosphere is casual. *2014 Broadway, tel. 615/329–1313. Dress: casual but neat. AE, DC, MC, V. Closed Sun. and Mon.*

Northern Italian ★ **Mario's Ristorante Italiano.** Owner Mario Ferrari is the genius behind this Nashville institution. Country music stars, visiting celebrities, and local society come here to see and be seen. The atmosphere is elegant, with lots of brass and an impressive wine collection on view, yet it's never stuffy. Pastas created by Chef Sandro Bozzatto are memorable, the seafood and veal—such as the *saltimbocca*, veal medallions with mozzarella, prosciutto, mushrooms, and fresh sage—are equally palate-pleasing. *2005 Broadway, tel. 615/327–3232. Jacket suggested. Reservations required, 2–3 days ahead on weekends. AE, DC, MC, V. Closed Sun.*

Moderate

American **F. Scott's.** At this elegant café and wine bar patrons enjoy the regularly changing collection of contemporary art. Chef Josh Weekley's creations are contemporary and American-style. F. Scott's has one of the largest wine lists in Nashville, with many fine wines available by the glass. *2220 Bandywood Dr., tel. 615/269–5861. Dress: informal. Reservations accepted. AE, MC, V.*

Continental **Maude's Courtyard.** "Meet me at Maude's" is more than an advertising slogan—it's a way of life in Nashville. Owner Morton Howell III encourages his chefs to add personal flair to every dish. Some examples: swordfish Marseilles, superb seafood gumbo—a true Louisiana recipe, scampi and scallops brochette, and veal florentine. A covered courtyard with a fountain and several fireplaces throughout the restaurant allow guests to choose their own ambience. Sundays, there's live jazz by the Bourbon Street Trio. *1911 Broadway, tel. 615/320–0543. Dress: informal. Reservations recommended. AE, DC, MC, V. No lunch Sat.; Sun., brunch only.*

106 Club. A black baby grand and a bar of shiny black enamel and glass brick set the atmosphere in this intimate, Art Deco dining room in suburban Belle Meade. The cuisine is a mix of California nouvelle and international favorites such as Bahamian sailfish. The pasta primavera is one of the best in town. In the evening, the outdoor patio is a good place to relax with one of 106's rich desserts and listen to old and new melodies on the baby grand. *106 Harding Pl., tel. 615/356–1300. Dress: casual but neat. Reservations suggested. AE, DC, MC, V.*

Mixed Menu **Cakewalk Restaurant.** The first things to catch your eye at this cozy bistro are the intriguing paintings by local artists on the turquoise walls. The eclectic cuisine is equally imaginative, blending the best of nouvelle California, a bit of Southwestern, and a dash of Cajun/Creole, with some down-home American specialties thrown in for fun. Desserts are outstanding—especially the Kahlua cake, a four-layer chocolate cake laced with liqueur. *3001 West End Ave., tel. 615/320–7778. Dress: informal. Reservations recommended for dinner. DC, MC, V.*

Inexpensive *Southern* ★ **Loveless Cafe.** An experience in true down-home Southern cooking. Don't come for the decor—which is also down-home, including red-and-white-checked tablecloths—but, rather, for the feather-light homemade biscuits and preserves, country ham and red-eye gravy, and fried chicken. *8400 Hwy. 100, tel. 615/646–9700. Dress: informal. Reservations suggested, especially on weekends. No credit cards. Closed Mon.*

Lodging

Nashville offers a very impressive selection of hotel, motel, and all-suite accommodations in all price categories and levels of luxury. Although some establishments increase rates slightly during the peak summer travel season, most maintain the same rates year-round. Some downtown luxury hotels offer special weekend rates to attract guests to otherwise vacant rooms.

Bed & Breakfast Host Homes of Tennessee (Box 110227, Nashville, TN 37222, tel. 615/331–5244) has listings for homes here and throughout the state.

The most highly recommended properties in each price category are indicated by a star ★. For maps pinpointing locations, *see* Dining.

Category	Cost*
Very Expensive	over $130
Expensive	$79–$130
Moderate	$50–$79
Inexpensive	under $50

**double room; add 11.75% for taxes*

Very Expensive ★ **Embassy Suites Nashville Hotel.** Near the airport and Opryland is this hotel of all suites, ranged around a nine-story parklike atrium lobby with live plants, meandering watercourses, and tropical birds. Suites are comfortably furnished in tasteful contemporary style; each has a wet bar, a refrigerator, and two color TVs. *10 Century Blvd., 37214, tel. 615/871–0033 or 800/432–7272. 294 suites. Facilities: cable TV/movies, indoor pool,* *whirlpool, sauna, exercise room, free full buffet breakfast, dining room, lounge, live entertainment. AE, DC, MC, V.*

Hyatt Regency Nashville. Downtown near the State Capitol, this 28-story tower has Hyatt's signature vast, skylighted atrium lobby awash with greenery, along with the glassed-in elevators that still seem to fascinate all but the most blasé occupants. Rooms are extra spacious and contemporary in decor. The hotel is topped by Nashville's only revolving rooftop restaurant. *623 Union St., 37219, tel. 615/259–1234 or 800/233–1234. 476 rooms, including 32 suites. Facilities: cable TV/movies, restaurant, coffee shop, cocktail lounge, nightly dancing, live entertainment, recreational privileges at Y. AE, DC, MC, V.*

★ **Opryland Hotel.** This massive hostelry adjacent to Opryland has recently almost doubled in size. Even if you don't stay here, come out to take a look—it's an attraction in its own right. The two-acre glass-walled Conservatory is a lush enclave of tropical vegetation, streams, waterfalls, statuary, and fountains. The Cascade is another skylighted interior space with streams, waterfalls, and a half-acre lake. The hotel claims to have more meeting space than any other in the nation. The culinary staff is directed by a member of the U.S. Culinary Olympics Team. *2800 Opryland Dr., 37214, tel. 615/883–2211. 1,891 rooms, including suites. Facilities: 3 restaurants, coffee shop, 5 lounges with live entertainment, heated pool, wading pool, lighted tennis (fee). AE, DC, MC, V.*

Stouffer Nashville Hotel. This luxurious ultracontemporary high-rise hotel adjoins Nashville Convention Center and is also connected to the new Church Street Centre Mall with fine shops, restaurants, and entertainment. Spacious rooms are highlighted by period reproduction furnishings. Executive Club concierge floors offer extra privacy and personal services. *611 Commerce St., 37203, tel. 615/255–8400 or 800/468–3571. 673 units, including 34 suites, 46 Club level rooms. Facilities: spa, indoor pool, whirlpool, sundeck, sauna, exercise facilities, cable TV, restaurant, coffee shop, cocktail lounge, 24-hr. room service, complimentary coffee and newspaper wake-up, garage, airport transportation. AE, DC, MC, V.*

Expensive

★ **Courtyard by Marriott–Airport.** This handsome new low-rise motor inn with a sunny, gardenlike courtyard offers some amenities you'd expect in higher-priced hotels: spacious rooms, king-size beds, oversize work desks, and hot-water dispensers for in-room coffee. *2508 Elm Hill Pike, 37214, tel. 615/883–9500 or 800/321–2211. 145 rooms, including 12 suites. Facilities: cable TV/movies, restaurant, lounge, heated indoor pool, sauna, whirlpool, exercise room. AE, DC, MC, V.*

Holiday Inn–Briley Parkway. To while away your time between flights or Opryland visits, there's the trademark Holidome Indoor Recreation Center, with pool, sauna, whirlpool, game room, table tennis, pool tables, and putting green. Business travelers will appreciate the conference center and spacious, well-lighted guest rooms. *2200 Elm Hill Pike at Briley Pkwy., 37210, tel. 615/883–9770 or 800/465–4329. 385 rooms, including 4 suites. Facilities: cable TV, restaurant, lounge with live entertainment, coin laundry. AE, DC, MC, V.*

Ramada Inn Across from Opryland. This contemporary-style, well-maintained new low-rise motor inn has the closest location to the theme park other than the Opryland Hotel. *2401 Music Valley Dr., 37214, tel. 615/889–0800 or 800/272–6232. 308* *rooms, including 7 suites. Facilities: cable TV/movies, rental refrigerators, heated indoor pool, sauna, whirlpool, dining room, lounge, live entertainment. AE, DC, MC, V.*

Moderate **Comfort Inn Hermitage.** Near the Hermitage, this inn offers reasonably priced accommodations, some with water beds or whirlpool baths. *5768 Old Hickory Blvd., 37076, tel. 615/889–5060 or 800/228–5150. 106 rooms, including 7 suites. Facilities: pool, cable TV/movies. AE, DC, MC, V.*

★ **Hampton Inn Vanderbilt.** Near the Vanderbilt University campus, this inn is new, clean, and contemporary. The rooms are colorful and spacious. A multipurpose hospitality suite has a conference table, chairs, and an audiovisual unit for meeting and business groups. *1919 West End Ave., 37203, tel. 615/329–1144 or 800/426–7866. 163 rooms. Facilities: cable TV/free movies, pool. AE, DC, MC, V.*

Howard Johnson at Opryland. Conveniently located near Opryland and other attractions, this chain unit offers rooms that are comfortable and bright. *2600 Music Valley Dr., 37214, tel. 615/889–8235 or 800/388–3066. 212 rooms. Facilities: cable TV/movies, pool, restaurant, coffee shop, lounge with live entertainment, band and dancing nightly in season. AE, DC, MC, V.*

La Quinta Motor Inn. The rooms here are especially spacious and well lighted, with a large working area and oversize bed. King Plus rooms have a full-length mirror and an ottoman. *2001 Metrocenter Blvd., 37227-0001 (1 mi north of downtown), tel. 615/259–2130 or 800/531–5900. 121 rooms. Facilities: cable TV, pool, 24-hr restaurant adjacent. AE, DC, MC, V.*

The Arts

For a complete listing of weekly events, consult the Visitor Information Center or the local newspapers. For information on concerts and special events, call WSM Radio's entertainment line (tel. 615/737–9595) or TV Channel 5's hot line (Thurs.; tel. 615/248–5200). Ticketmaster (tel. 615/737–4849) has information on events at various Nashville venues.

Concerts Country music takes center stage at the 4,424-seat **Grand Ole Opry Auditorium** (tel. 615/889–3060). The Nashville Symphony Orchestra's classical and pops series and concerts by out-of-town groups are staged at **Andrew Jackson Hall** (tel. Ticketmaster at 615/741–2787), part of the Tennessee Performing Arts Center (TPAC). Chamber concerts take place at TPAC's **James K. Polk Theater** (tel. 615/741–7975). Some rock and country events are held at the **Nashville Municipal Auditorium** (tel. 615/862–6395). The **Starwood Amphitheatre** (tel. 615/641–7500) is the site of rock, pop, country, and jazz concerts, musicals, and special events; it's also the summer home of the Nashville Symphony. Vanderbilt University stages music, dance, and drama productions (many free) at its **Blair School of Music** (tel. 615/322–7651).

Festivals **Summer Lights.** The last weekend in May, more than half a million visitors attend Nashville's unique music and arts festival, showcasing top names and newcomers in pop, rock, jazz, country, classical, and reggae on five outdoor stages downtown. The work of 50 Tennessee visual artists are exhibited in warehouses and storefronts along First and Second avenues. Local cuisine is available from street vendors or sidewalk cafés, and clowns and other street entertainers fill the Family Arts Arcade. Most events are free. *Contact: Metro Nashville Arts Commission, 111 Fourth Ave. S, 37201, tel. 615/862–6720.*

International Country Music Fan Fair. For six days in early June following Summer Lights, this celebration is staged at the Tennessee State Fairgrounds, Vanderbilt University's Dudley Field, and Opryland USA. There are more than 35 hours of musical events, autograph sessions with country music stars, and the Grand Masters Fiddling championship. Many tour companies offer packages, but call well ahead of time. *Contact: Fan Fair, 2804 Opryland Dr., 37214, tel. 615/889–7503.*

Theater **James K. Polk Theater** hosts touring Broadway shows and local theatrical performances. For theater-in-the-round, there's the **Andrew Johnson Theater.** The **Academy Theatre** (tel. 615/254–9103) hosts children's theater performances. **Chaffin's Barn,** 8204 Hwy. 100 (tel. 615/822–1800), offers dinner theater year-round, and a live country show is staged here daily Memorial Day–Labor Day.

Nightlife

Revues **Ernest Tubb Midnight Jamboree.** Here's a live radio show with performances by new talent as well as Opry stars, sometimes including Justin Tubb, son of the late Ernest Tubb. *2414 Music Valley Dr., tel. 615/889–2474. Show Sat. midnight–1 AM (arrive by 11:30 PM).*

Grand Ole Opry. If you can attend only one event, make it this one (*see* Opryland in Exploring, *above*).

Nightclubs **Ace of Clubs.** This popular club features rock and pop music by such stars as Delbert McClinton. *114 2nd Ave., tel. 615/737–4849. Shows nightly, time and cover charge vary.*

Boots Randolph's. One of the city's landmark night spots, this sophisticated supper club features Boots—"Mr. Yakkety Sax"—at 9:30 (and 11:30 PM, if there's a crowd) in the showroom, and Jimmy Travis at 7:30 (and 10 PM) in the lounge. *209 Printers Alley (between Third and Fourth Aves.), tel. 615/256–5500. Open Mon.–Sat. 9–11 PM (or later).*

McGavocks Place II Nightclub. Here's dancing to live bands or recorded music with a DJ and music videos in a turn-of-the-century atmosphere. *Sheraton Music City Hotel, 777 McGavock Pike, tel. 615/885–2200. Open Mon.–Sat. 4 PM–2 AM, Sun. 6 PM–1 AM.*

Nashville Palace. Here you'll find live country entertainment, highlighted by popular Music City entertainers and rising talent. Throughout the summer, Monday night shows feature Grand Ole Opry stars. *2400 Music Valley Dr., tel. 615/885–1540. Show nightly at 9 PM. Cover charge.*

Stock Yard Bull Pen Lounge. Upstairs is a popular steak-and-seafood restaurant and lounge with live entertainment. Downstairs, the Bull Pen features dancin', pickin', and singin' as many of Nashville's big names show up for performances—both scheduled and unscheduled. *901 Second Ave. N and Stock Yard Blvd., tel. 615/255–6464. Open Mon.–Thurs. 7:30 PM–1 AM, Fri. and Sat. 7:30 PM–2 AM.*

Hotel Lounges **Alberts.** A DJ spins records, and there's a video screen and dance floor. *Marriott Hotel Nashville, I–40 at Briley Pkwy., tel. 615/889–9300. Open Mon.–Sat. 4 PM–1:30 AM. Hungry-hour buffet Mon.–Fri. 5–7 PM.*

Aviator's. Laser lights accent dancing to contemporary and past hits. Complimentary hors d'oeuvres served weeknights 5–8 PM. *Park Suite Hotel, 10 Century Blvd., tel. 615/871–0033. Open Mon.–Sat. 4 PM–1 AM.*

Cascades Lounge. Country-jazz harpist Lloyd Lindroth entertains (6:30–11 Tues.–Sat.) amid the tropical splendor of Opryland Hotel's indoor garden, which features the "Dancing Waters," an intricate fountain electronically synchronized to accompany the harpist's evening performances. *2800 Opryland Dr., tel. 615/883–2211. Open Mon.–Sat. 11 AM–1 AM, Sun. noon–11 PM.*

Jack Daniel's Saloon. There's live entertainment nightly in this lounge adorned with memorabilia from the famed Lynchburg distillery. *Opryland Hotel, 2800 Opryland Dr., tel. 615/883–2211. Open Mon.–Sat. 11 AM–2 AM, Sun. noon–2 AM.*

Reflections Lounge. Live entertainment Friday and Saturday nights features top-name acts from throughout the country. *The Doubletree Inn, 2 Commerce Pl., tel. 615/244–8200. Open Mon.–Thurs. 4 PM–midnight, Fri.–Sat. 4 PM–1 AM. Reservations required.*

Sessions. Enjoy Top-40 hits in a high-tech lounge with video screens. There's live entertainment on Friday and Saturday nights. *Hyatt Regency Nashville Hotel, 623 Union St., tel. 615/259–1234. Open Mon.–Wed. 4 PM–1 AM, Thurs.–Sat. 4 PM–2 AM.*

East Tennessee

Updated by Chris Wohlwend

East Tennessee combines wholesome and savory vacation ingredients much in the way a skilled mountain cook creates a sumptuous down-home feast, with bounty from forests, fields, flowing streams, and the family farm. From the misty heights of the Great Smoky Mountains to the Holston, French Broad, Nolichucky, and Tennessee rivers, it offers a cornucopia of scenic grandeur and recreational offerings.

The highest and most rugged elevations are in the Great Smoky Mountains National Park, a cool and scenic retreat for those seeking relief from the heat of summer. The gateway city to the park is Gatlinburg, not too long ago a remote little place with a few hotels and some mountain crafts shops. Now hordes of visitors are attracted here for outdoor recreation. Neighboring Pigeon Forge—site of Dolly Parton's theme park, Dollywood, and numerous other tourist attractions—has become a favorite with family vacationers.

Mountain folkways often persist in smaller communities, but the major towns and cities—like Knoxville and Chattanooga—are up-to-date and quite diverse. Wherever you travel in East Tennessee, the glory of mountains and meadows, forests and farms, rivers and lakes, inspires you to pause, linger awhile, and refresh the spirit.

Getting Around

By Plane Knoxville Airport is served by **American Eagle, Delta** and its affiliate **Comair, Northwest, Trans World Express, United/United Express,** and **USAir.**

By Car I–75 runs north–south from Kentucky through Knoxville, then to Chattanooga, where it enters Georgia. I–81 enters East Tennessee from Virginia at Bristol and continues southwest until it ends at the junction with I–40 northeast of Knoxville. I–40 enters from North Carolina, traces a northwesterly course to Knoxville, then heads west. U.S. 11 joins Chattanooga with Knoxville.

By Train There is no Amtrak service in East Tennessee.

By Bus There are **Southeastern Greyhound Lines** stations at Chattanooga (tel. 615/267–6531) and Knoxville (tel. 615/522–5141).

Guided Tours

In Knoxville, **Knoxville Tours, Inc.** (tel. 615/688–6232) offers local and area tours, with pickup at Knoxville Quality Inn West, 7621 Kingston Pike. In Pigeon Forge, **Mountain Tours and Pigeon River Bus Line** (tel. 615/453–0864) offers guided tours to Cades Cove, Cherokee (NC), Roaring Fork Motor Nature Trail, and out-of-the-way places in the Great Smoky Mountains. **Smoky Mountain Guide Service** (tel. 615/436–2108) in Gatlinburg has native guides for tours in the Smokies. Self-guided-tour maps and brochures are available at many local visitor information centers.

Important Addresses and Numbers

Tourist Information **Chattanooga Area Convention and Visitors Bureau** (1001 Market St., Chattanooga 37402, tel. 615/756–8687, 800/322–3344 out of state, 800/338–3999 in TN).
Knoxville Convention and Visitors Bureau (500 Henley St., Box 15012, Knoxville 37901, tel. 615/523–7263). **Smoky Mountain Visitors Bureau** (7906 Lamar Alexander Pkwy., Townsend 37882, tel. 615/984–6200). **Northeast Tennessee Tourism Council** (Box 375, Jonesborough 37659, tel. 615/753–5961).

Emergencies Dial 911 for **police** and **ambulance** in an emergency.

Exploring East Tennessee

Numbers in the margin correspond to points of interest on the East Tennessee map.

The tour outlined on the following pages requires about three to five days for leisurely enjoyment. It takes you through cities and towns clustered in comfortable valleys, sprawled on upland plateaus, tucked away in hidden reaches of high mountains. Here and there you'll encounter poverty-ridden hardscrabble places, but many communities boast respectable economies and some have achieved enviable prosperity. Expect the unexpected from East Tennessee.

Knoxville 1 We begin (and end) in **Knoxville.** In 1786, Patriot General James White and a few pioneer settlers built a fort here beside the Tennessee River. A few years later, territorial Governor William Blount selected White's fort as capital of the newly formed Territory of the United States South of the River Ohio and renamed the settlement after his long-time friend, Secretary of War Henry Knox. It flourished from the very beginning, and became the first state capital when Tennessee was admitted to the Union in 1796.

In the 20th century, Knoxville has been synonymous with energy: the headquarters of the TVA, with its vast complex of hydroelectric dams and impounded recreational lakes, is here,

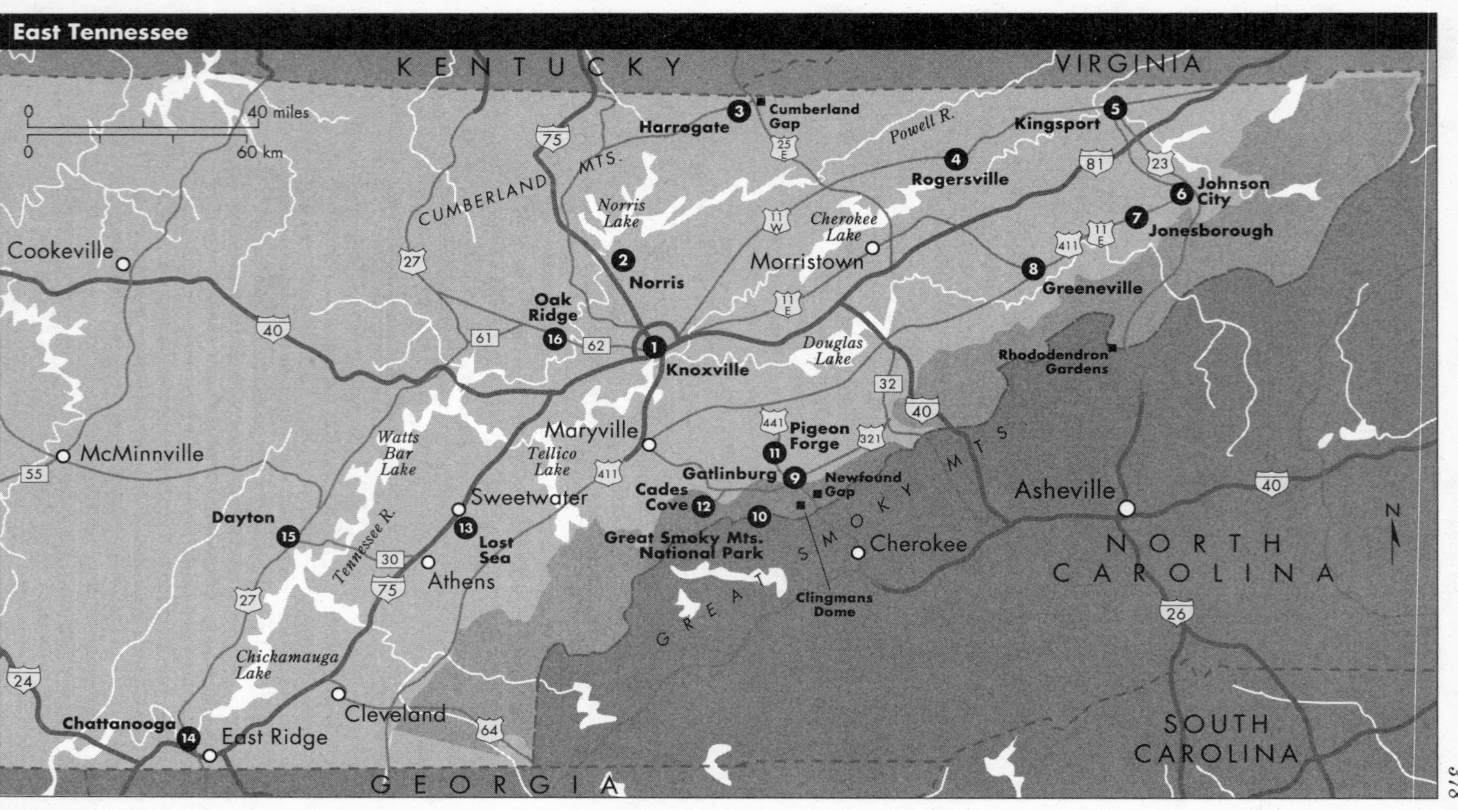
East Tennessee
KENTUCKY
VIRGINIA
NORTH CAROLINA
SOUTH CAROLINA
GEORGIA
0 40 miles
0 60 km
CUMBERLAND MTS.
GREAT SMOKY MTS.
Harrogate
Cumberland Gap
Kingsport
Powell R.
Rogersville
Johnson City
Jonesborough
Norris Lake
Cherokee Lake
Cookeville
Norris
Morristown
Greeneville
Oak Ridge
Knoxville
Douglas Lake
Rhododendron Gardens
Watts Bar Lake
Tellico Lake
Maryville
Pigeon Forge
McMinnville
Gatlinburg
Newfound Gap
Cades Cove
Asheville
Sweetwater
Dayton
Lost Sea
Great Smoky Mts. National Park
Cherokee
Tennessee R.
Athens
Clingmans Dome
Chickamauga Lake
Cleveland
Chattanooga
East Ridge
N
1
2
3
4
5
6
7
8
9
10
11
12
13
14
15
16
75
25 E
81
23
11 W
11 E
411
27
40
61
62
32
441
321
55
30
26
24
64

and during World War II, atomic energy was secretly developed at nearby Oak Ridge. Today the University of Tennessee adds its own energy—intellectual and cultural—to this dynamic city.

Enough of Knoxville's history has been preserved to interest rather than overwhelm visitors. At the **Governor William Blount Mansion,** a modest white frame structure dating from 1792, the governor and his associates planned the admission of Tennessee as the 16th state in the Union. The home is furnished with original and period antiques, along with memorabilia of Blount's checkered career. A visitor center in the adjacent **Craighead-Jackson House,** built in 1818, presents an introductory slide program, museum exhibits, and a glass collection. *200 W. Hill Ave., tel. 615/525–2375. Admission: $3 adults; $2.50 senior citizens; $1.50 children 6–12, under 6 free. Open Tues.–Sat. 9:30–4:30, Sun. 2–4:30 Mar.–Oct.; Tues.–Fri. 9:30–4:30 rest of year. Closed major holidays and Christmas week.*

Other eras of Knoxville's history can be savored at **James White's Fort** (tel. 615/525–6514), a series of seven log cabins with authentic furnishings and pioneer artifacts; the **John Sevier Historical Site** (tel. 615/573–5508), where Tennessee's first governor built his summer home, Marble Springs; and the **Armstrong-Lockett House** (tel. 615/637–3163), an eloquent farm mansion dating from 1834, now a showcase of American and British furniture, silver, and ornate appointments, along with terraces and fountains in Italianate gardens.

The **McClung Museum** (tel. 615/974–2144; free), on the University of Tennessee campus, has diverse collections of anthropology, natural history, geology, science, and fine arts. The **Knoxville Museum of Art** is housed in a handsome $10.5-million, 52,000-square-foot structure in World's Fair Park. Designed by renowned museum architect Edward Larrabee Barnes, the four-level concrete and steel building is faced in Tennessee pink marble. The museum includes four exhibition galleries, an exploratory gallery for children, a great hall, an auditorium, a museum store, and outdoor sculpture and educational program gardens. *410 Tenth St., tel. 615/525–6101. Admission: $2 adults, $1 students and senior citizens, children under 12 free. Open Tues. 4–9, Wed.–Sat. 10–5, Sun. noon–5. Closed major holidays, Christmas Eve, and New Year's Eve.*

The **East Tennessee Discovery Center and Akima Planetarium** contain displays of pioneer tools and clothes, mounted animals, and fresh- and saltwater aquariums. Youngsters especially like the hands-on and audiovisual exhibits. *516 Beaman St., in Chilhowee Park, tel. 615/637–1121. Admission: $3 adults; $2 senior citizens over 65 and students, $1 2–5, under 2 free. Museum open Tues.–Fri. 2–5, Sat. 1–5. Planetarium shows Sat. 2:30 PM. Closed major holidays.*

Plan on a full day at the **Knoxville Zoological Gardens,** famous for breeding large cat species and African elephants. The 1,100 animals include a rare red panda, wild creatures native to the African plains, polar bears, seals, and penguins. There are rides on a miniature steam train or an elephant, as well as a petting zoo. *In Chilhowee Park on Rutledge Pike S, 4½ mi east of I-40 Exit 392, tel. 615/637–5331. Admission: $6 adults; $3.50 children 3–12 and senior citizens; children under 3 free; park-*

ing $1. Open daily 9:30–6 Memorial Day weekend–Labor Day weekend, 10–4:30 rest of year. Closed Christmas.

For relaxed enjoyment and views of an especially scenic portion of the Tennessee River, step aboard the ***Star of Knoxville*** (tel. 615/522–4630 or 800/525–STAR). One-and-a-half-hour sightseeing excursions as well as dinner cruises are offered April–December on Saturdays and Sundays.

To the North and East

From Knoxville, scenic U.S. 441 leads northwest to **Norris,** a distance of about 20 miles. This delightful planned town was
2 built in 1933 as a workers' community during construction of the **Norris Dam,** TVA's first. The dam, which spans the Clinch River and impounds a 72-mile-long lake, has a visitor lobby and two overlooks. Some of the best views, though, are from **Norris Dam State Park** on Route 1 (tel. 615/426–7461). Here also is the **Lenoir Museum,** where Indian, pioneer, Civil War, and regional historical artifacts are displayed. A restored country store and an 18th-century gristmill (where you can purchase stone-ground cornmeal) are on the grounds.

The prime attraction at Norris is the **Museum of Appalachia,** where about 35 log structures—among them a molasses mill powered by mules—have been restored in a mountain-village setting. Period furnishings and implements are found in the buildings, and there are pioneer craft demonstrations and a working farm. Locals sometimes bring their musical instruments for an old-time hoedown. *On TN 61, 1 mi east of I–75 Exit 122, tel. 615/494–7680. Admission: $5 adults; $3.50 senior citizens; $3 children 6–14, under 6 free; family rates also available. Open daily 8 AM–dusk Apr.–Oct., 8–5 rest of year.*

A 50-mile drive northeast of Norris along I–75, U.S. 25W, and
3 TN 63 leads to **Harrogate,** by the Virginia border. Here, at **Lincoln Memorial University,** founded in 1896, the Great Emancipator's principles and philosophies prevail. **Lincoln Memorial Museum** contains the world's third-largest collection of Lincolniana. One of the most poignant exhibits is the ebony-and-silver cane Lincoln carried to Ford's Theatre. *On campus, off U.S. 25E, tel. 615/869–6237. Admission: $2 adults; $1.50 senior citizens; $1 children 6–12, under 6 free. Open weekdays 9–4, Sat. 11–4, Sun. 1–4. Closed major holidays.*

From Harrogate, drive about 50 miles along U.S. 25E and 11W
4 to **Rogersville,** a little hideaway East Tennessee town. Savor its undisturbed atmosphere, pleasant homes, churches, and ancient trees. Then linger a while.

A 28-mile drive along U.S. 11W through rolling hills, meadows,
5 and woodlands brings you to thriving **Kingsport,** founded in 1761. At **Exchange Place,** a restored pioneer homestead, craftspeople demonstrate their skills in commodious log houses. Their handmade quilts, baskets, wood carvings, ceramics, and stuffed dolls are sold in nearby shops. *4812 Orebank Rd., tel. 615/288–6071. Admission free. Open Sat. and Sun. 2–4:30, Thurs.–Fri. 10–2, and for groups by appointment.*

The **Netherland Inn,** built in 1818, was for 150 years a stop on the Great Stage Road. Now restored as a museum, it features period furnishings and accessories, a flatboat, a garden, and a log cabin with displays for children. *2140 Netherland Inn Rd., tel. 615/247–3211. Admission: $3 adults, $1 students, children* *under 6 free. Open Sat.–Mon. 2–4:30 May 1–Sept. 30; by appointment other times.*

Bays Mountain Park on Route 4 (tel. 615/229–9447) is a remarkable sanctuary for native plants and animals. Here you'll find an interpretive center, self-guided nature trails, natural history programs, a small zoo, a planetarium, and (in season) float trips by barge on a large lake.

Heading South

6 A 21-mile drive southeast along U.S. 23 brings you to **Johnson City,** an important center for agriculture, manufacturing, and education—it is home to Washington College, the oldest institution of higher education in the state, and East Tennessee State University, with more than 9,000 students.

At **Tipton-Haynes Historic Site,** the 19th-century main house, granary, horse barn and law office have been authentically restored. *4 mi south of U.S. 23 Exit 31 via University Pkwy. and S. Roan St., tel. 615/926–3631. Admission: $2 adults, $1.50 senior citizens, $1 students with adults. Open weekdays 10–4:30, Sat.–Sun. 2–5 Apr. 1–Oct. 31; weekdays 10–4 Jan. 8–Mar. 31.*

Rocky Mount, a two-story log mansion completed in 1772, was Governor William Blount's territorial capitol from 1790 until he moved to Knoxville two years later. Faithful restoration and careful selection of authentic furnishings testify to a simple yet eloquent pioneer lifestyle. There's also a cookhouse, slave quarters, a blacksmith shop, and a flax house. Exhibits and demonstrations focus upon the role of women in frontier times. Guided tours are available. *4 mi northeast on U.S. 11E at Piney Flats, tel. 615/538–7396. Admission: $5 adults, $2.50 students, children under 6 free. Open Mon.–Sat. 10–5, Sun. 2–6. Closed Thanksgiving, Dec. 21–Jan. 5, weekends Jan.–Feb.*

About eight miles south via U.S. 11E/321, you'll drive into a
7 veritable time warp: **Jonesborough,** the state's oldest town. Visitors admire a trio of antebellum churches, lovely vintage houses, brick and wooden fretwork shops, and the period Court House. Of the many special events held here, the most famous is October's National Storytelling Festival, when professional and amateur storytellers from all around the United States and abroad flock here for a weekend to enchant hordes of curious visitors. At the **Visitor Center and History Museum** (just off U.S. 11E on Boone St., tel. 615/753–5961), a slide show and exhibits describe the town's history.

After a 25-mile drive southwest along U.S. 11E/411, you'll
8 come to the pleasant town of **Greeneville,** founded in 1783. Young Andrew Johnson settled here in 1826 after an arduous trek over the mountains from North Carolina, opened a tailor shop, and married. **Andrew Johnson National Historic Site** preserves his primitive tailor shop, the homestead where he lived from 1851 until his death in 1875, and his hilltop gravesite, marked by an elaborate monument. Displays in the visitor center include notes he made at his impeachment trial. *Depot and College Sts., tel. 615/638–3551. Admission to Homestead: $1 adults, children under 17 and senior citizens with Golden Age Passports free. Open daily 9–5. Closed Christmas.*

9 Sixty-one miles south via U.S. 411/321 is **Gatlinburg,** Tennessee's premier mountain resort town. Set in the narrow valley of the Little Pigeon River (actually a turbulent mountain

stream), it has something for everyone. Family attractions include the **American Historical Wax Museum** (tel. 615/436–4462), the **Gatlinburg Sky Lift** (tel. 615/436–4307) to the top of Crockett Mountain, the **Guinness World Record Museum** (tel. 615/436–9100), and the **Ober Gatlinburg Tramway** (tel. 615/436–5423) to a mountaintop amusement park, ski center, and shopping mall/craft market.

Christus Gardens, in a quiet setting overlooking the river, exhibits life-size dioramas of Christ's ministry with background sacred music. Sculptures, a courtyard garden, biblical-era coins, and other artifacts may also be seen here. *510 River Rd., tel. 615/436–5155. Admission: $7 adults; $3 children 7–11, children under 6 free. Open daily 8 AM–9 PM Apr.–Oct., 9–5 rest of year.*

10 At the **Great Smoky Mountains National Park,** shared by North Carolina and Tennessee, the southern Appalachians reach their ultimate grandeur as 16 peaks soar more than 6,000 feet. From Gatlinburg, the northern gateway to the park, drive south along the scenic Newfound Gap Road (U.S. 441) to the Sugarlands Visitor Center at park headquarters. Here are informative films, exhibits, maps, and brochures about the park. Driving along on the Newfound Gap Road, stop often at scenic overlooks, perhaps taking time to explore one or more of the nature trails that lead off from many of them. The road ascends to **Newfound Gap** on the Tennessee–North Carolina border, a haunting viewpoint. From here, a seven-mile spur road leads to **Clingmans Dome**—at 6,643 feet, the highest point in Tennessee—where you can walk up a spiral pathway to the top of an observation tower for panoramic views of the Smokies. Spring and summer displays of wildflowers, dazzling rhododendron, and mountain laurel invite explorers to experience this most visited of national parks. But autumn is the favorite season for the spectacular foliage. *Tel. 615/436–5615. Open daily 8–6 Apr. 5–May 31, 8–7 June–Aug., 8–6 Sept.–Oct., 8–4:30 rest of year. Closed Christmas Day.*

From Gatlinburg, follow the crowds half a dozen miles or so
11 along U.S. 321/441 and you come to **Pigeon Forge,** with tourism amenities straddling the main thoroughfare for several miles. Popular visitor attractions (many seasonal) have burgeoned here, among them **Magic World** and **Ogle's Water Park** (*see* What to See and Do with Children, *below*), and **Carbo's Police Museum** (tel. 615/453–1358).

A new dinner theater, **Dixie Stampede** (tel. 615/453–4400 or 800/356–1676), offers a hearty chicken and ribs dinner mid-April–Thanksgiving weekend in a 1,000-seat arena; it's accompanied by a colorful, all-new western-themed musical show and rodeo.

The 1830s-era **Old Mill** (tel. 615/453–4628) beside the Little Pigeon River still grinds corn, wheat, and rye on water-powered stone wheels. Here you can purchase flour, meal, grits, and buckwheat. Across the road is **Pigeon Forge Pottery** (*see* Shopping, *below*).

Dollywood, Dolly Parton's popular theme park, brings to life the folklore, fun, food, and music of the Great Smokies. In a re-created 1880 mountain village, scores of talented and friendly craftspeople demonstrate their artistry. Museum exhibits trace Parton's rise to stardom. The many amusement rides include a thrilling river raft trip, and "Thunder Express," a twisting, turning coaster ride through a dense backwoods setting. Live music shows are performed on the park's seven stages. Throughout the season, some of the nation's best known entertainers lead a line-up of over 200 performances in "Showcase of Stars." Occasionally Dolly shows up for a surprise appearance. The season ends with the gala National Crafts Festival in an old-fashioned harvest setting from late September to early November. When hunger strikes, try Aunt Fanny's Dixie Fixin's Restaurant for down-home mountain cookery. *700 Dollywood La., tel. 615/428–9400. Admission: $22.10 adults, $15.45 children 4–11, under 3 free. Free admission next day on tickets purchased after 3. Open last weekend Apr.–first weekend Nov., daily 9–6; extended hours mid-June–Labor Day weekend, most weekends; closed Thurs. May, Sept., Oct. Phone ahead to verify hours.*

To the West From Pigeon Forge, drive west on U.S. 321, a lovely scenic route, for about 20 miles to the junction of TN 73, which be-
12 comes Laurel Creek Road, leading to **Cades Cove** in the Great Smoky Mountains National Park. Here an isolated mountain valley, farmhouses, barns, churches, and an old gristmill still in operation can be seen and visited via a loop road. From spring through autumn, special park ranger programs and demonstrations describe the pioneer agriculture, crafts, and folkways in the Cove. The Visitor Center (tel. 615/436–5615) has exhibits and provides information and literature. At the old gristmill you can take a tour and purchase stone-ground cornmeal. (Open daily Apr. 5–Oct.) For a deep-forest drive, take Parson Branch Road, a quiet, one-way trek out of the park to U.S. 129. The Foothills Parkway will get you back into the park.

Drive southwest for 54 miles along U.S. 321, U.S. 441, and TN
13 68 for a visit to the **Lost Sea,** outside Sweetwater, where you can explore a 4½-acre underground lake by glass-bottom boat. *Tel. 615/337–6616. Admission: $7 adults; $3.50 children 6–12, under 6 free. Open daily 9 AM–dusk. Closed Christmas Day.*

Continue on TN 68 until you reach I–75, then take it south for
14 70 miles to **Chattanooga,** a city of Civil War battlefields, museums of all kinds (art, antiques, history, even knives), the new Tennessee Aquarium, the world's steepest incline railway, and a famous choo-choo. **Point Park** (tel. 615/821–7786), a unit of the Chickamauga and Chattanooga National Military Park, commemorates a Union victory at the bloody Battle of Lookout Mountain. Views of the city and of the Tennessee River are stunning. The ***Southern Belle*** sternwheel steamboat (tel. 615/266–4488) offers sightseeing excursions and brunch, dinner, and moonlight cruises on the scenic river from April through October.

The spectacular new **Tennessee Aquarium** features a three-tiered look at freshwater ecosystems, following the Tennessee River system from its mountain birth through mid-stream foothills to the lowlands. There are seven freshwater tanks and two terrestrial environments. Alligators, sharks, and stingrays are included among the 3,500 living specimens on exhibit. *537 Market St., tel. 615/266–3467. Admission: $8.75 adults, $4.75 children 3–12, under 3 free. Open May 1–Labor Day Fri.–Sun. 10–8, Mon.–Thurs. 10–6; 10–6 rest of year.*

Chattanooga Choo-Choo and Terminal Station commemorate the first major public passenger train service between the North and the South, which began in 1880. An engine and car of the original train are displayed, and you can ride an antique trolley, dine in a choice of restaurants (including one—the Station House—that is a dinner theater), browse through old-style shops, wander among floral displays, and see a fine exhibit of model railroads. The splendid Terminal Building, dating from 1905, is a gem. In its former main lobby, a magnificent, ornate dome rises 85 feet above an area now part of the Transcontinental restaurant. *1400 Market St., tel. 615/266-5000. Trolley rides: 50¢ adults, 25¢ children under 13. Model railroad exhibit: $1.75 adults; 75¢ children 6–12, under 6 free. Terminal open daily 11–10. Model railroad exhibit open Mon.–Sat. 10–10, Sun. noon–9:30. Closed Christmas Day.*

The **Lookout Mountain Incline Railway** is the world's steepest, reaching a gradient of 72.7 percent. The ride is truly sensational: it feels like the cars are moving straight up and down the mountainside. A one-way trip lasts 20 minutes. *Station at base, 3917 St. Elmo Ave.; at the top, 827 E. Brow Rd.; tel. 615/821-4224. Round-trip fare: $6 adults, $4 children; one-way fare: $5 adults, $3 children. Operates daily 8:30 AM–9 PM Memorial Day–Labor Day; daily 9–6 rest of year.*

15 A 36-mile drive north along U.S. 27 will bring you to **Dayton,** where the famous Scopes "Monkey Trial" was held in 1925. At the **Rhea County Courthouse,** the room where the trial took place has been preserved. There is also a small museum with displays about the trial. *301 New Market St., tel. 615/775-7808. Admission free. Open Mon.–Thurs. 8–4; Fri. 8–5:30. Closed weekends and major holidays.*

16 Sixty-two miles north along U.S. 27, I–40E, and TN 58 is **Oak Ridge,** the famous "atomic city," established secretly during World War II. Some of the original installations here include the **Oak Ridge National Laboratory,** still involved in programs of nuclear fission and magnetic fusion energy; the **Graphite Reactor,** 10 miles southwest, now a National Historic Landmark, with a display area open to the public; and the **K-25 Visitors Overlook** for views of the **Oak Ridge Gaseous Diffusion Plant,** where uranium is enriched for use in nuclear reactors.

The **American Museum of Science and Energy** focuses upon uses of nuclear, solar, and geothermal energy, mainly for peaceful purposes. Exhibits include hands-on experiments, demonstrations, and computer games. A slide show furnishes valuable background on Oak Ridge and the museum. *300 Tulane Ave., tel. 615/576-3200. Admission free. Open daily 9–6 June–Aug., 9–5 rest of year. Closed major holidays.*

A drive of 22 miles on TN 62E brings you back to Knoxville, where our tour of East Tennessee concludes.

What to See and Do with Children

American Museum of Science and Energy, Oak Ridge (*see* To the West in Exploring, *above*).
Chattanooga Choo-Choo and Terminal Station (*see* To the West in Exploring, *above*).
Dollywood, Pigeon Forge (*see* Heading South in Exploring, *above*).

Knoxville Zoological Park (*see* Knoxville in Exploring, *above*).

Lost Sea, Sweetwater (*see* To the West and Home in Exploring, *above*).

Magic World. This theme park centered on a magic show also offers rides and a haunted castle. *607 N. Parkway, Pigeon Forge, tel. 615/453–7941. Admission: $10.95, children 2 and under free; season pass $15.95. Open Apr.–Oct. Hours vary widely.*

Ogle's Water Park. This is a family park with a giant wave pool, a kiddie play area, eight water slides, and miniature golf. *1115 N. Parkway, Pigeon Forge, tel. 615/453–8741. Admission: $13.12 adults; $12.02 children 4–11, under 4 free. Open daily 10–8 June and July, 11–6 Aug.; weekends only 11–6 May and first half Sept.*

Students' Museum and Akima Planetarium (*see* Knoxville in Exploring, *above*).

Tennessee Aquarium (*see* To the West in Exploring, *above*).

Off the Beaten Track

Rhododendron Gardens. Atop 6,285-foot Roan Mountain on the border of Tennessee and North Carolina is the world's largest natural display of the multihued flowering shrub. Quiet pathways wend among the 600 acres of plants, which generally reach peak bloom in mid-June. So numerous are the varieties of plants and wildlife that naturalists from throughout the world come to observe and study. At nearby **Roan Mountain State Park,** there's a museum, a picnic area, a campground, a swimming pool, rental cabins, and a restaurant. *U.S. 19E to TN 143, tel. 615/772–3303. Open year-round.*

Shopping

Crafts The mountain towns of East Tennessee are known for Appalachian folk crafts, especially wood carvings, corn-husk dolls, pottery, dulcimers, and beautiful handmade quilts. These crafts can be found in shops throughout the state, but a good central location for all of them is the **Great Smoky Arts and Crafts Community,** a collection of 50 shops and craftsmen's studios along eight miles of rambling country road. Begun in 1937, the community includes workers in leather, pottery, weaving, hand-wrought pewter, stained glass, quiltmaking, handcarving, marquetry, and more. Everything sold here is made on the premises by the 64 members. Also here are two restaurants and the popular Wild Plum Tearoom. *Off U.S. 321, 3 mi east of Gatlinburg, tel. 615/436–3808. For more information on the community and the special crafts shows held at Thanksgiving and Easter, write Box 366, Gatlinburg 37738.*

Other area shops selling mountain crafts are **Pigeon Forge Pottery** (301 Middle Creek Rd., Pigeon Forge, tel. 615/453–3883), where internationally esteemed tableware, vases, and bird and animal figurines are handmade and sold; **Ogle & Son's Broom Shop** (Brookside Village on U.S. 321, Gatlinburg, tel. 615/436–5931); and **Arrowcraft Shop** (576 Parkway, Gatlinburg, tel. 615/436–4604), with regional and other crafts.

Iron Mountain Stoneware plant. Hidden away in the northeastern corner of Tennessee and entirely surrounded by the Cherokee National Forest is the tiny village of Laurel Bloomery, the only place where the high-fired stoneware is made. It is also available through numerous retail outlets in the Appalachian Mountains. *TN 91, about 8 mi north of jct with U.S. 421, tel. 615/727-8888. Open daily 8-5. Closed Christmas Day.*

Participant Sports

Fishing At Norris Lake, there's seasonal angling for striped bass, walleye, white bass, and muskie. There are boat launch ramps (but no rentals) at **Norris Dam State Resort Park** (tel. 615/426-7461) and on Chickamauga Lake, near Chattanooga, at **Booker T. Washington State Recreational Park** (tel. 615/894-4955).

Golf East Tennessee courses open to the public include **Brainerd Golf Course** in Chattanooga (tel. 615/855-9405), **Whittle Springs Municipal Golf Course** in Knoxville (tel. 615/525-1022), **Bent Creek Mountain Inn and Country Club** in Gatlinburg (tel. 615/436-3947), **South Hills Golf Club** in Oak Ridge (tel. 615/483-5747), and **Warrior's Path State Park Golf Course** in Kingsport (tel. 615/323-4990).

Hiking An unusually elevated and scenic portion of the **Appalachian Trail** runs along high ridges in the Great Smoky Mountains National Park. The Trail can be easily reached at Newfound Gap from U.S. 441 (Gatlinburg, tel. 615/436-5615).

Horseback Riding **McCarter's Riding Stables** (tel. 615/436-5354) in Gatlinburg arranges guided horseback riding in the Great Smoky Mountains National Park from April through October.

Ice Skating A rink is open year-round at **Ober Gatlinburg Ski Resort** (tel. 615/436-5423).

Rafting and Canoeing **USA Raft Expeditions, Inc.** (tel. 615/743-7111; Mar.-Oct.), based in Erwin, south of Johnson City, provides guided whitewater ventures. Ocoee's **Cripple Creek Expeditions** (tel. 615/338-8441; Apr.-Oct.) offers canoe rentals and guided raft trips. **Hiwassee Outfitters** in Reliance (tel. 615/338-8115; mid-Mar.-early Nov.) has canoes, rafts, tubes, and funyaks. **Rafting in the Smokies** in Gatlinburg (tel. 615/436-5008; Apr.-Oct.) offers guided white-water raft trips.

Skiing At **Ober Gatlinburg Ski Resort** (tel. 615/436-5423 or, Nov.-mid-Mar. only, 800/251-9202), the slopes of Mount Harrison—reached by double and quad chairlifts—provide dramatic winter skiing. Summer skiing on grass and other surfaces is also available for those who must.

Dining

Mountain cooks have long been noted for preparing fresh ingredients many different ways. Corn remains the old standby, used in the making of grits, luscious muffins, cornbread, and savory spoonbread. At historic water-powered gristmills you can stock up on flour and cornmeal ground between massive antique limestone wheels. The limestone residue blends with the flour and meal, adding nutrients and flavor.

Barbecued ribs, thick pork chops, and generous slices of country ham with red-eye gravy rank as all-time favorites. Freshwater fish, such as varieties of trout, walleye, crappie, muskie, and catfish, will also be found in varied and delicious preparations (but remember to save room for home-baked pies and cobblers).

The most highly recommended restaurants in each price category are indicated by a star ★.

Category	Cost*
Very Expensive	over $25
Expensive	$15–$25
Moderate	$10–$15
Inexpensive	under $10

**per person without tax (7.75% in Tennessee), service, or drinks*

Chattanooga
Expensive–Very Expensive
★

Green Room. A formal Georgian elegance dominates the spacious, columned dining room. Favorites from the basically Continental menu are smoked native duckling with cherry sauce, and rack of lamb with mustard-and-browned-garlic sauce. For dessert, try the popular apple-pecan baklava. The moderately priced Sunday buffet is popular. *The Radisson Read House–A Plaza Hotel, 827 Broad St., tel. 615/266–4121. Jacket and tie required. Reservations suggested during the week, required Sun. and holidays. AE, DC, MC, V. Closed Mon. No lunch Tues.–Sat., no dinner Sun.*

Inexpensive–Moderate

Chatt's. Though located in a Howard Johnson Hotel, this restaurant is privately owned and managed. The shrimp-and-steak combination—jumbo shrimp sautéed in garlic butter and served with a tender rib-eye steak—is a house specialty. Fried cornbread accompanies homemade vegetable, bean, onion, red potato, creamed broccoli, and cauliflower soups. Brass accents, paintings, live greenery, white napery, candlelight, and comfortable armchairs provide a low-key, elegant ambience. *100 W. 21st St., tel. 615/265–3151. Dress: informal. No reservations. AE, DC, MC, V.*

Gatlinburg
Moderate–Expensive
★

Burning Bush Restaurant. Antique-style furnishings and accessories evoke a Colonial atmosphere; the menu is Continental. Broiled Tennessee quail and beef Rossini—an eight-ounce fillet served on an English muffin with Madeira sauce—are house specialties. Bountiful breakfasts are also featured. *1151 Parkway, tel. 615/436–4669. Dress: informal. Reservations recommended. AE, DC, MC, V.*

Smoky Mountain Trout House. Of the eight distinctive trout preparations to choose from at this cozy restaurant, an old favorite is trout Eisenhower: pan-fried, using corn-meal breading and bacon flavorings, and served with bacon-and-butter sauce and a side dish of mushrooms. Prime rib, country ham, and fried chicken are also available. *410 N. Parkway, tel. 615/436–5416. Dress: informal. No reservations. AE, DC, MC, V. Closed Dec.–Mar.*

Inexpensive
★

Ogle's Buffet Restaurant. Indulge in bountiful feasting, either in the soft-green-and-beige dining room or on the patio, which extends over a turbulent mountain river. The buffet tables offer five choices of country-style meat, such as fried chicken, prime rib, country ham; five vegetables fresh from the farm; and 70 fixin's for your salad. Don't overlook the sourwood honey. *On the Parkway near traffic light No. 3, tel. 615/436–4157. Dress: informal. No reservations. MC, V. Closes at 4 PM Sun.*

Pancake Pantry. A house specialty is Austrian apple-walnut pancakes covered with apple cider compote, black walnuts, apple slices, sweet spices, powdered sugar, and whipped cream. Other selections include waffles, omelets, sandwiches, soups, and fresh salads. Century-old brick, polished-oak paneling, rustic copper accessories, and spacious windows create a delightful ambience. Box lunches are available for mountain picnics. *628 Parkway, tel. 615/436–4724. Dress: informal. No reservations. No credit cards. Open daily 7 AM–4 PM June–Aug., 7 AM–3 PM rest of year. Closed Thanksgiving, Christmas Day.*

Knoxville *Moderate–Expensive* ★ **Regas Restaurant.** This cozy Knoxville classic, with fireplaces and original art, has been around for 70 years. The specialty, prime rib, is carefully aged on the premises, baked very slowly all day, then sliced to order and served with creamy horseradish sauce. *318 Gay St., tel. 615/637–9805. Dress: informal. Reservations advised. AE, MC, V. Closed major holidays. No lunch Sat. No dinner Sun.*

Inexpensive–Expensive **Copper Cellar/Cumberland Grill.** A favorite of the college crowd and young professionals, the original downstairs Copper Cellar has an intimate atmosphere with friendly service. Upstairs, the Cumberland Grill features aged Colorado beef, fresh seafood, salads, sandwiches, and award-winning desserts. There's a children's menu and a lavish Sunday brunch. *1807 Cumberland Ave., across from University of Tennessee campus, tel. 615/673–3411. Dress: informal. Reservations suggested. Open daily 11 AM–11 PM. AE, D, DC, MC, V.*

Inexpensive **Bob Evans Farm Restaurant.** At this country-style restaurant, part of a chain, piquantly seasoned fresh country sausages in many varieties and flavors are the specialty. For accompaniment, you can choose from side orders of eggs, pancakes, biscuits, and grits. Though breakfast specialties are always available, there's also a full lunch and dinner menu. *5604 Merchants Center Blvd., tel. 615/689–8555; 208 Bob Evans La., tel. 615/690–3739. Dress: informal. No reservations. Open weekdays 6 AM–11:30 PM, weekends 24 hrs. Closed Christmas, Thanksgiving.*

Pigeon Forge *Moderate* **Green Valley Restaurant.** Here's a place for family-style dining on country ham, homemade biscuits, and gravy for breakfast, sautéed rainbow trout or lobster tail for dinner. The well-lit room has a cathedral ceiling with exposed beams and a two-story fireplace. *4125 S. Parkway, tel. 615/453–3500. Dress: informal. No reservations. AE, MC, V. Closed Christmas.*

Inexpensive ★ **Apple Tree Inn Restaurant.** A traditional East Tennessee menu is offered here, including fried chicken and a special spoonbread: a regal soufflé of cornmeal, flour, eggs, buttermilk, and seasonings, served hot from the baking dish. Order family-style or individually. At the center of the spacious dining room is an apple tree, which grows through an opening in the ceiling. *3215 S. Parkway, tel. 615/453–4961. Dress: informal. No reservations. AE, MC, V. Closed Dec.–Feb.*

Lodging

Some restored historic hotels in larger cities offer lodging in settings reminiscent of earlier times. The major resort areas of Gatlinburg and Pigeon Forge have abundant choices. For reservations at hotels, motels, chalets, and condominiums throughout the area, contact **Smoky Mountain Accommodations Reservation Service** (526 E. Parkway, Suite 1, Gatlinburg 37738, tel. 615/436–9700 or 800/231–2230). For B&B reservations, contact **Bed & Breakfast Host Homes of Tennessee** (Box 110227, Nashville 37222, tel. 615/331–5244).

In the categories below, the high-season summer and autumn rates are given; these drop considerably at other times of the year.

The most highly recommended properties in each price category are indicated by a star ★.

Category	Cost*
Very Expensive	over $100
Expensive	$75–$100
Moderate	$50–$75
Inexpensive	under $50

**double room; add 11.75% for taxes*

Chattanooga
Moderate–Expensive

★ **Chattanooga Choo-Choo Holiday Inn.** The hotel adjoins the showcase 1905 Southern Railway Terminal, with restaurants, lounges, shops, exhibits, gardens, and operating trolley. Guest rooms stress luxurious appointments, especially the restored Victorian-era parlor cars converted to overnight aeries. *1400 Market St., 37402, tel. 615/266–5000 or 800/465–4329. 360 units, including suites and 48 parlor cars. Facilities: cable TV, indoor and outdoor pools, whirlpools, lighted tennis courts, 3 dining rooms, coffee shop, lounge with entertainment. AE, DC, MC, V.*

Howard Johnson Hotel. This five-story hotel, recently renovated, has a warm, contemporary atmosphere with greenery and cheerful accessories in public areas. Guest rooms in various styles feature modern art, wicker and rattan furnishings, and spacious work areas. *100 W. 21st St., 37408, tel. 615/265–3151 or 800/654–2000. 103 rooms. Facilities: cable TV, pool, coin laundry, game room, Executive Club, dining room, cocktail lounge. AE, DC, MC, V.*

★ **Radisson Read House–A Plaza Hotel.** A traditional favorite in the Mid-South, the Georgian-style Read House dates from the 1920s and has been impeccably restored to its original grandeur. The lobby, listed on the National Register of Historic Places, is highlighted by a large archway, stately columns, and panels of polished walnut. Guest rooms in the main hotel continue the Georgian motif; rooms in the annex are more contemporary. *827 Broad St., 37402, tel. 615/266–4121 or 800/333–3333. 250 rooms, including suites and ten 2-bedroom units. Facilities: cable TV, pool, sauna, whirlpool, dining room, restaurant, coffee shop, lounge. AE, DC, MC, V.*

Inexpensive

Econo Lodge East Ridge. Rooms are spacious, contemporary in style, clean, and well-maintained. *1417 St. Thomas St., 37412, tel. 615/894–1417 or 800/446–6900. 89 rooms. Facilities: TV, pool, restaurant. AE, DC, MC, V.*

Gatlinburg
Very Expensive

★ **Buckhorn Inn.** This inn in a remote woodland setting about six miles outside the city has welcomed guests—including seclusion-seeking diplomats, government officials, and celebrities—for more than 40 years. The views of Mt. LeConte and the

Great Smokies are spectacular. Inside, the country-inn atmosphere is reinforced by wicker rockers, paintings by local artists, a huge stone fireplace, and French doors that open onto a large stone porch. Breakfast and dinner are included in the rates and are hearty and warming: home-baked breads, creamed soups, marinated beef tenderloin, fruit tortes. *Off U.S. 321, 2140 Tudor Mountain Rd., 37738, tel. 615/436–4668. 7 rooms with mountain-style furnishings, no phones or TV; 4 cottages with cable TV, cooking equipment, fireplace, screened porch; all units have private baths. Facilities: spring-fed lake for fishing, off-trail hiking in nearby Great Smoky Mountains National Park. No credit cards.*

Expensive ★ **Holiday Inn Resort Complex.** The hotel is near the Convention Center and the aerial tramway, which in winter whisks ski addicts to the snowy slopes at Ober Gatlinburg. The Holidome Indoor Recreation Center is attractive and cheerful, with lavish plantings, a pool, and a spacious atrium. *520 Airport Rd., 37738, tel. 615/436–9201 or 800/465–4329. 402 rooms and suites. Facilities: cable TV, 2 indoor pools, outdoor pool, whirlpool, 2 saunas, putting green, coin laundry, pizza parlor, dining room, coffee shop, cocktail lounge, nightclub, live entertainment in season, meeting areas. AE, DC, MC, V.*

Moderate–Expensive **Best Western Twin Islands Motel.** In the center of Gatlinburg, beside the surging Little Pigeon River, this motel is notable for its low-key contemporary architectural style. All rooms have balconies overlooking the river. *U.S. 441, Box 648, 37738, tel. 615/436–5121 or 800/223–9299. 107 rooms and suites, 5 kitchen units; whirlpool or waterbed units, king rooms with hot tubs, some fireplaces available. Facilities: cable TV, heated pool, fishing on premises, playground, coin laundry, restaurant. AE, DC, MC, V.*

Park Vista Hotel. This large hotel on a mountain ledge has modern, lavishly decorated public areas and large, eloquently appointed guest rooms, each with a balcony overlooking colorful garden grounds, the town of Gatlinburg, the Little Pigeon River, and the mountains beyond. The white, semicircular contemporary tower, though handsome, seems rather out of place here in the Great Smoky Mountains. *Airport Rd. at Cherokee Orchard Rd., Box 30, 37738, tel. 615/436–9211 or 800/421–7275. 304 rooms, 11 parlor suites. Facilities: cable TV, indoor pool, saunas, whirlpool, health spa, coin laundry, restaurant, dining room, cocktail lounges, nightclub, live entertainment, meeting rooms. AE, DC, MC, V.*

Rainbow Motel. Here is a small, neat, well-maintained lodging, a pleasant choice for budget-minded vacationers. *390 E. Parkway (3 blocks east of U.S. 441), Box 1397, 37738, tel. 615/436–5887 or 800/422–8922. 41 rooms, including 1 with whirlpool, 1 efficiency, two 2-bedroom units. Facilities: cable TV, heated pool, refrigerators available. AE, DC, MC, V.*

Knoxville

Very Expensive ★ **Hyatt Regency Knoxville.** This is a handsome, contemporary adaptation of an Aztec pyramid atop a hill overlooking the city and mountainous hinterlands. The nine-story atrium lobby blends modern furnishings and artworks in Mesoamerican motifs with abundant flora and colorful accessories. *500 Hill Ave. SE, Box 88, 37915, tel. 615/637–1234 or 800/233–1234. 386 rooms, including luxury suites, three 2-bedroom units. Facilities: cable TV, pool, playground, exercise room, cocktail lounge, coffee shop, rooftop dining room. AE, DC, MC, V.*

Moderate ★ **La Quinta Motor Inn.** Rooms are spacious and well lighted, with convenient working areas. *258 Peters Rd. N, 37923, tel. 615/690–9777 or 800/531–5900. 130 rooms, including King Plus. Facilities: cable TV, heated pool. AE, D, DC, MC, V.*

Pigeon Forge
Expensive **Best Western Plaza Inn.** Located within easy reach of shops, restaurants, and family attractions, the inn offers amenities for the entire family. Rooms are spacious and well furnished, and some have refrigerators; some overlook mountain scenery, others an indoor swimming pool. *501 S. Parkway, Box 926, 37863, tel. 615/453–5538 or 800/232–5656. 140 rooms, including suites with fireplaces and whirlpool baths, and 2 2-bedroom units; waterbeds available. Facilities: cable TV, indoor and outdoor pools, saunas, game rooms. AE, DC, MC, V.*

Bilmar Motor Inn. This is a clean, basic motel for budget-minded vacationers. *3786 S. Parkway, 37863, tel. 615/453–5593. 52 rooms, 2 with whirlpool. Facilities: cable TV/movies, pool, wading pool. AE, D, MC, V.*

Grand Hotel. Centrally located near major attractions, this five-story inn features some ultramodern rooms with waterbeds and fireplaces. *306 N. Parkway, 37863, tel. 615/453–0056 or 800/247–8282. 120 units, including suites, 27 rooms with whirlpools, 11 efficiencies. Facilities: cable TV. AE, DC, MC, V.*

Holiday Inn. This inn is situated in the middle of the action. The vast Holidome Indoor Recreation Center features lush greenery and activities for the entire family. Especially pleasant rooms and extra services are available on the concierge floor. *3230 N. Parkway, 37863, tel. 615/428–2700 or 800/465–4329. 208 rooms and suites. Facilities: cable TV, restaurant, indoor pool, sauna, whirlpool, health club, coin laundry, game room, specialty shops. AE, DC, MC, V.*

The Arts

Theater **Sweet Fanny Adams Theatre and Music Hall** in Gatlinburg (tel. 615/436–4038) offers original musical comedies, Gay '90s revues, and old-fashioned sing-alongs. **Archie Campbell Memorial Theater** in Pigeon Forge (tel. 615/428–3218) features comedy and music by *Hee Haw* star Phil Campbell and his friends. The **Backstage Playhouse** in Chattanooga (tel. 615/629–1565) is a weekend dinner theater. The **Carousel Theatre,** at the University of Tennessee in Knoxville (tel. 615/974–5161), presents professional and student players at a theater-in-the-round.

Religious Plays ***The Smoky Mountain Passion Play,*** depicting the life of Christ, and ***Damascus Road,*** the story of the Apostle Paul, are staged on alternate evenings at an outdoor theater in Townsend (tel. 615/448–2244 or 984–4111).

Concerts, Opera, and Dance Events at the **Tivoli Theater** in Chattanooga (tel. 615/757–5050) include concerts and operas. The **Knoxville Opera Company** (tel. 615/523–8712) sponsors New York Metropolitan Opera competitions each year, along with two locally produced operatic performances. The **Knoxville Symphony Orchestra** (tel. 615/523–1178) presents seven concerts a year, often with esteemed guest artists. **Lamar House Bijou Theater** in Knoxville (tel. 615/522–0832) offers seasonal ballet, concerts, and plays.

Nightlife

Gatlinburg At Ober Gatlinburg's **Old Heidelberg Restaurant** (take the aerial tramway from downtown; tel. 615/430–3094), there's dancing to DJ-selected rock and roll. The lounge at **Sade and Dora's** (tel. 615/436–9201) at the Holiday Inn Resort Complex features live entertainment and dancing. The **Park Vista Hotel** (tel. 615/436–9211) has upbeat entertainment and a DJ in the high energy Matrix Lounge. Spirits' Lounge at the **Edgewater Hotel** (tel. 615/436–4151) features live country and easy-listening.

Knoxville **Manhattan's** (tel. 615/525–4463), a lively saloon and grill in the "Old City," has Big Band music, entertainment Tues.–Sat., with free hors d'oeuvres 5–7 PM. There's a pianist evenings in an Old World ambience at **The Orangery Restaurant's Lounge** (tel. 615/588–2964).

Oak Ridge The **Reactor Room Lounge** (tel. 615/483–4371) at the Holiday Inn reflects Atomic City right down to dance floor, with lights that pulsate to the beat of the DJ's offerings.

9 Virginia

By Francis X. Rocca

Updated by John Bowen

Virginia does not have something for *everyone*. It does not, for example, have a major-league sports franchise (though the Washington Redskins enjoy a loyal following). No, Virginia is not an essential trip by any means—unless, of course, you wish to understand the United States.

The state ranks second to none as the venue of seminal events in American history. English-speaking North America began at Jamestown. The breach with England was instigated largely in Williamsburg and then confirmed at Yorktown. The tensions latent within the young nation were bloodily released on the soil of the Old Dominion: More than two-thirds of the War Between the States was fought here.

Virginia has been recovering ever since from the ravages of civil war. Finally flourishing, it draws prestige from an antebellum legacy undisturbed by progress. The skyscrapers of Richmond spring out of a 19th-century cityscape. Towns in the Shenandoah Valley look so authentically antebellum that they routinely serve as movie sets. Many important battlefields and historic houses have been restored and opened to the public.

The Commonwealth's prehistory is also well defended, in the vast official wilderness of state and national parks and forests. The natural beauty is abundant and diverse: beaches on one side, mountains on the other. The amount of unspoiled land, both unsettled and un-cultivated, is a wonder in a state so crowded with Civilization—but not, fortunately, with people.

Shenandoah Valley and the Highlands

The Shenandoah Valley is best known for its rugged beauty and rural charm, yet its cities and towns have much to offer in the way of history and culture. Staunton preserves the birthplace of Woodrow Wilson, the 28th president of the United States and the latest of eight from Virginia. Bath County, where the salutary mineral waters flow, has been a fashionable resort for two centuries. Lexington is a town dense with historic sites —including the birthplace of Sam Houston and the last home of Stonewall Jackson—and has remained practically unchanged in its appearance since the 19th century. Roanoke is the only city in the country to have a mountain within its limits; its nickname, the "Star City of the South," derives from the large illuminated star topping the mountain. The name also reflects Roanoke's pride in its long-standing role as the cultural and commercial center of western Virginia.

The Highlands in the southwest have been neglected by travelers, for no good reason. The scenery is too beautiful to ignore, and there is plenty of indoor and outdoor recreation—in this region there are seven state parks, three national parks, and six national forests. The town of Abingdon has a well-preserved collection of 18th- and 19th-century buildings, hosts two renowned regional festivals, and is the home of the state theater of Virginia, the Barter Theatre.

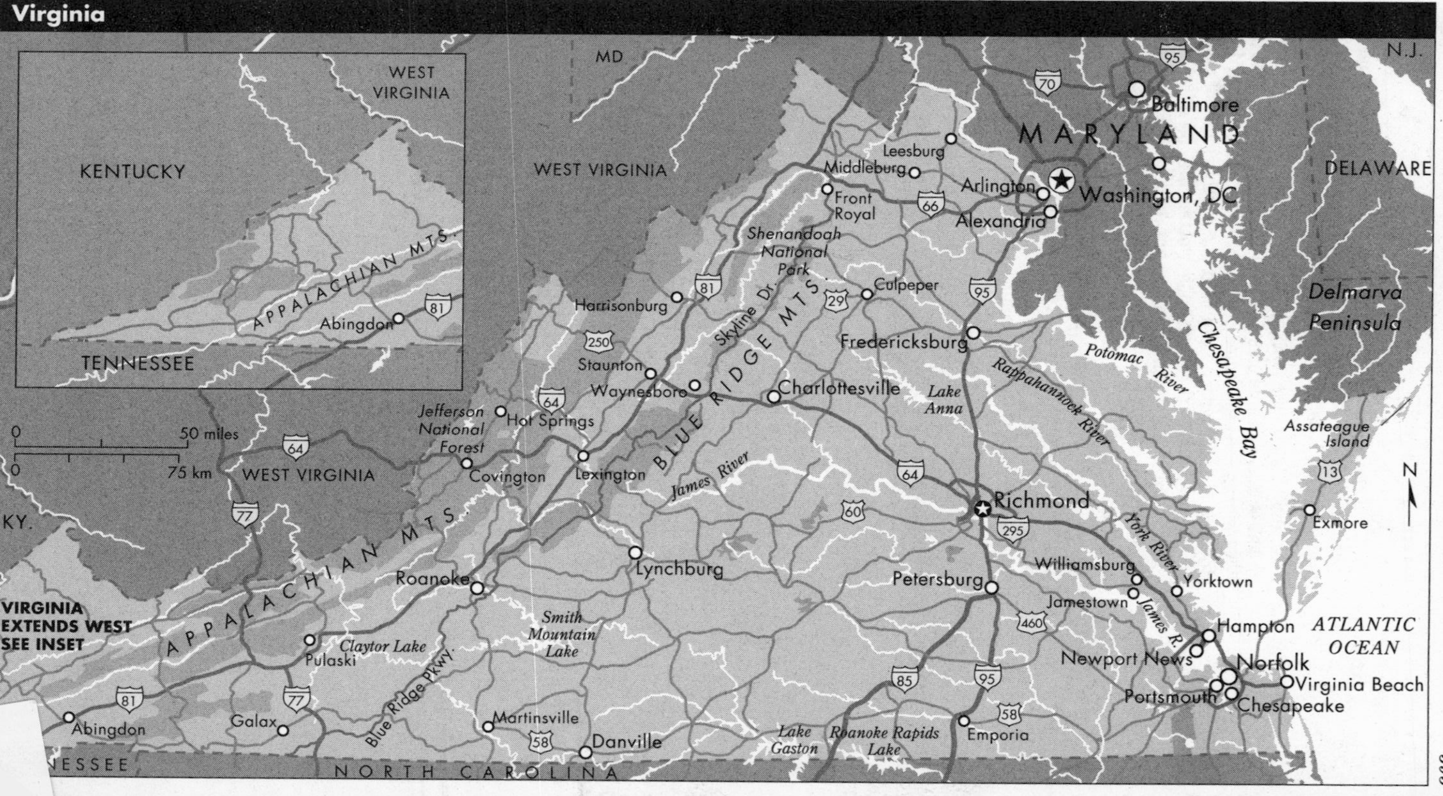

Virginia
WEST VIRGINIA
KENTUCKY
APPALACHIAN MTS.
Abingdon
81
TENNESSEE
MD
WEST VIRGINIA
N.J.
95
70
Baltimore
MARYLAND
DELAWARE
Leesburg
Middleburg
Arlington
Washington, DC
Front Royal
66
Alexandria
Shenandoah National Park
Skyline Dr.
Culpeper
29
81
Harrisonburg
95
Delmarva Peninsula
250
Fredericksburg
Chesapeake Bay
Potomac River
Rappahannock River
Staunton
Waynesboro
BLUE RIDGE MTS.
Charlottesville
Lake Anna
Jefferson National Forest
Hot Springs
64
0 50 miles
0 75 km
64
WEST VIRGINIA
Covington
Lexington
James River
64
Assateague Island
13
N
Richmond
60
295
Exmore
KY.
77
APPALACHIAN MTS.
York River
Lynchburg
Roanoke
Williamsburg
Petersburg
Yorktown
Jamestown
James R.
460
Hampton
ATLANTIC OCEAN
VIRGINIA EXTENDS WEST SEE INSET
Smith Mountain Lake
Claytor Lake
Pulaski
Blue Ridge Pkwy.
Newport News
Norfolk
Virginia Beach
Portsmouth
Chesapeake
85
95
81
77
Abingdon
Galax
Martinsville
58
Danville
58
Emporia
Lake Gaston
Roanoke Rapids Lake
TENNESSEE
NORTH CAROLINA

Getting Around

By Plane Eight carriers, including **USAir,** serve Roanoke Municipal Airport. The Tri-City Regional Airport in Bristol, by the Tennessee state line, is served by **USAir/Allegheny,** and others.

By Car I–81 and U.S. 11 run north–south the length of the Shenandoah Valley and continue on south into Tennessee. I–66 west from Washington, DC (90 miles to the east) passes through Front Royal to connect with 81 and 11 at the northern end of the Valley. I–64 connects them with Charlottesville, 30 miles to the east. Route 39 into Bath County connects with I–81 just north of Lexington. I–77 cuts off the southwest tip of the state, running north–south.

By Train **Amtrak** (tel. 800/872–7245) has service three days a week to Staunton (One Middlebrook Ave.), en route between New York and Chicago. The same train stops at Clifton Forge (Ridgeway St.), for The Homestead resort.

By Bus **Greyhound Trailways Lines:** Abingdon (465 W. Main St., tel. 703/628–6622), Lexington (631 Waddell St., tel. 703/463–2424), Roanoke (26 Salem Ave., tel. 703/342–6761), Staunton (100 S. New St., tel. 703/886–2424).

Guided Tours

The **Historic Staunton Foundation** (tel. 703/885–7676) offers free one-hour guided tours of the town every Saturday morning at 11, Memorial Day through October, departing from the Woodrow Wilson Birthplace (24 N. Coalter St.) A brochure is available for a self-guided tour.

For $6, the **Lexington Carriage Company** (tel. 703/463–3777) will take you around town in a horse-drawn carriage for 35 minutes, April–October. A walking-tour brochure is available at the Lexington Visitor Center (*see* Important Addresses and Numbers, *below*).

Important Addresses and Numbers

Tourist Information **Bath County Chamber of Commerce,** Rte. 220, Box 57, Warm Springs 24484, tel. 703/839–5409. Open weekdays 8:30–4:30. For literature and maps 24 hours a day, stop by their gazebo at the intersection of Rtes. 39 and 220. **Front Royal/Warren County Chamber of Commerce,** 414 E. Main St., Front Royal 22630, tel. 703/635–3185. Open weekdays 9–5, Sat. 9–3 in summer. Closed Sun. **Lexington Visitor Center,** 102 E. Washington St., Lexington 24450, tel. 703/463–3777. Open daily 9–5. **Roanoke Valley Convention and Visitors Bureau,** 114 Market St., 24011, tel. 703/342–6025. Open weekdays 8:30–5. **Roanoke Visitors Information Center,** 1 Market Sq., tel. 703/345–8622. Open daily 9–5. **Shenandoah Valley Tourist Information Center** (off I–81 at Exit 67), Box 1040, New Market 22844, tel. 703/740–3132. Open daily 9–5. **Historic Staunton Welcome Center,** 24 N. Coalter St., Staunton 24401, tel. 703/885–8097. Open daily 9–5, except Sun. in Jan. and Feb.

Emergencies Dial 911 for emergency assistance.

Exploring Shenandoah Valley and the Highlands

Numbers in the margin correspond to points of interest on the Shenandoah Valley and the Highlands map.

1 It must be admitted that the justifiable fame of the **Skyline Drive** has its drawbacks. The holiday and weekend crowds in high season—spring or fall—can slow traffic (already held to a maximum speed of 35 mph) to a crawl and put enormous strain on the few lodges, campsites, and eateries along the way. But for those seeking easily accessible wilderness and stunning views, there are few routes that can compete with this one.

Starting at **Front Royal,** the Drive—easily reached from Interstates 64, 66, and 81—winds 105.4 scenic miles south over the
2 mountains of the **Shenandoah National Park** and affords spectacular vistas of the Shenandoah Valley to the west and the rolling country of the Piedmont to the east. The hundreds of miles of hiking trails (including a section of the Appalachian Trail), the canoeing on the Shenandoah River, and the trout fishing in the rushing streams provide many incentives for the action-minded, and the rangers supervise a variety of activities (outlined in the *Shenandoah Overlook,* a free newspaper you can pick up as you enter the park).

It's better to choose another route in the winter; most facilities are closed from November through April, and parts of the Drive itself can be closed due to treacherous conditions. So come during the fine weather, but bring a sweater—temperatures can be brisk. *For information, contact the Park Superintendent, Box 348, Rte. 4, Luray 22835, tel. 703/999–2229. Admission to the park and the Drive: $5 per car; $2 per person on foot, bicycle, or motorcycle.*

You'll also want to wear a sweater for the not-to-be-missed de-
3 tour: **Luray Caverns,** the largest in the state and only nine miles west of the Drive. For millions of years the water has seeped through the limestone and clay to create a variety of suggestive rock and mineral formations. The world's only "Stalacpipe Organ" is composed of stalactites hanging from the ceiling, which are tuned to concert pitch and tapped by rubber-tipped plungers under the organist's control. A one-hour tour starts every 20 minutes. *West on Rte. 211 from Skyline Dr., tel. 703/743–6551. Admission: $9 adults, $8 senior citizens, $4.50 children. Open daily 9–7 June 15–Labor Day, 9–6 Mar. 15–June 15 and after Labor Day to Nov. 14, 9–4 rest of year.*

The trip south on Skyline Drive ends at **Waynesboro,** which is 28 miles west of "Mr. Jefferson's Country" on I–64 (*see* Charlottesville Area). Those whose thirst for the picturesque is not
4 yet sated might continue south on the 470-mile-long **Blue Ridge Parkway,** a direct continuation of the Drive. It extends through the George Washington National Forest to Great Smoky Mountains National Park in North Carolina and Tennessee. Although the Parkway is less pristine, the higher mountains offer even better views, including a 360-degree panorama at the
5 **Peaks of the Otter Recreation Area,** near Roanoke. Like the Drive, it has a variety of lodges, waysides, and self-guided nature walks and a section of the Appalachian Trail; unlike the Drive, admission to the Parkway and its attractions is free.

Perhaps the point of greatest interest—certainly the most fa-
6 mous—is **Mabry Mill,** just north of Meadows of Dan. This grist-

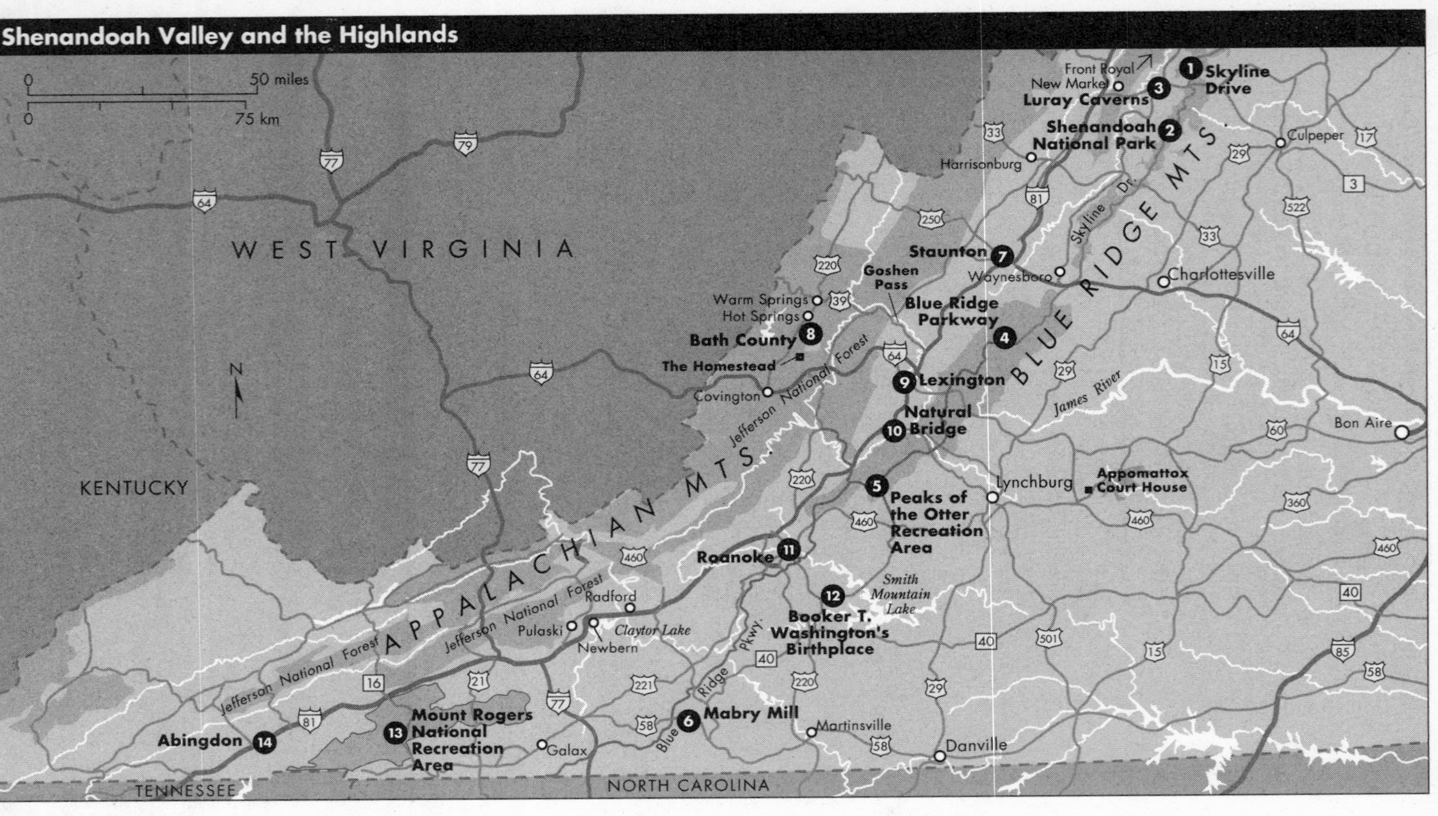
Shenandoah Valley and the Highlands
0 50 miles
0 75 km
N
WEST VIRGINIA
KENTUCKY
TENNESSEE
NORTH CAROLINA
BLUE RIDGE MTS
APPALACHIAN MTS.
1 Skyline Drive
2 Shenandoah National Park
3 Luray Caverns
4 Blue Ridge Parkway
5 Peaks of the Otter Recreation Area
6 Mabry Mill
7 Staunton
8 Bath County
9 Lexington
10 Natural Bridge
11 Roanoke
12 Booker T. Washington's Birthplace
13 Mount Rogers National Recreation Area
14 Abingdon
Front Royal
New Market
Harrisonburg
Culpeper
Charlottesville
Waynesboro
Skyline Dr.
Goshen Pass
Warm Springs
Hot Springs
The Homestead
Covington
Jefferson National Forest
James River
Bon Aire
Lynchburg
Appomattox Court House
Smith Mountain Lake
Radford
Pulaski
Claytor Lake
Newbern
Blue Ridge Pkwy.
Martinsville
Danville
Galax
3
15
16
17
21
29
33
39
40
58
60
64
77
79
81
85
220
221
250
360
460
501
522

mill and sawmill features exhibitions of blacksmithing and other trades. *Blue Ridge Parkway's junction with U.S. 58 at mile 176, tel. 703/952–2947. Admission: free. Open May–Oct., daily 9–5.*

Those who are content to forgo the Parkway and who leave the Drive and the wilderness at Waynesboro will find two interest-
7 ing attractions 11 miles to the west in **Staunton** (pronounced "*Stan*-ton"), a town with a distinguished past. It was once the seat of vast Augusta County—formed in 1738 and encompassing present-day West Virginia, Kentucky, Ohio, and Indiana—and was briefly the capital of Virginia (the general assembly fled here from the British in 1781). It seems a fitting birthplace for a president.

In the **Woodrow Wilson House,** the president was born in 1856. The house has been restored, with period antiques and some original pieces, to reflect its time as the residence of an antebellum Presbyterian minister (which is what Woodrow's father was). Wilson's presidential limousine, a 1919 Pierce-Arrow sedan, is on display in the garage. *24 N. Coalter St., next door to the Welcome Center (I–81 to I–64 at Exit 57), tel. 703/885–0897. Admission: $5 adults, $4 senior citizens, $1 children. Open 9–6 daily Memorial Day–Labor Day, 9–6 Mar.–Memorial Day and Labor Day–Dec., 9–5 Mon.–Sat. rest of the year. Closed Thanksgiving, Christmas, and New Year's Day.*

Just outside town is the new **Museum of American Frontier Culture,** an outdoor living museum that shows the beginnings of agrarian life in America. Four 18th-century farmsteads have been created from original buildings brought from Northern Ireland, England, Germany, and upland Virginia. The attention to authenticity and detail is painstaking. For instance, master craftsmen were brought in from Ulster to thatch the roofs on farm buildings that were transported here from County Tyrone. Livestock have been backbred and ancient seeds germinated in order to create an environment accurate in all respects. *230 Frontier Dr. off I–81 at Exit 222 to Rte. 250W, tel. 703/332–7850. Admission: $4 adults, $3.60 senior citizens, $2 children. Open daily 9–8 Memorial Day–Labor Day, 9–5 rest of year. Closed Christmas and New Year's Day.*

Traveling south again on I–81, a side trip well worth the two-
8 hour detour is bucolic **Bath County.** Take the scenic route: the **Goshen Pass** in Rockbridge County, a three-mile stretch of Route 39 that follows the Maury River through the Allegheny Mountains and is lush with rhododendrons in May. There are no traffic lights in all of Bath County; there are only 10 year-round residents per square mile. But for more than 200 years this peaceful area has been an important resort. Originally, visitors came for the healing thermal springs. Those treatments are no longer much in fashion, but the sulfur waters still flow at Warm Springs, Hot Springs, and Bolar Springs (ranging from 77°F to 106°F.), and many swear by them.

Outdoors enthusiasts will find in Bath County many diversions—public and private, on water and land. *Call or write to the Virginia Division of Parks and Recreation, 203 Governor St., 306, Richmond 23219, tel. 804/786–2132.*

Of the various resorts in the area, the **Homestead** in Hot Springs has evolved into an attraction in its own right. Every imaginable luxury, diversion, and convenience is here for the guests, who at any one time can number 1,000. The golf course was laid out in 1892 and is one of the oldest in continuous use in the States. The first skiing in the South began here in 1959. Tennis, horseback riding, fishing, lawn bowling, skeet shooting, and archery are also available. Staying here is like taking a cruise on a mountain instead of a ship (*see* Lodging, *below*).

9 Returning to I–81, travel 36 miles south to **Lexington,** where two deeply traditional Virginia colleges sit side-by-side, each with a memorial to a soldier who was also a man of peace.

Washington and Lee University is the sixth-oldest college in the United States, founded in 1749 as Augusta Academy. In gratitude for a donation from George Washington, it was renamed Washington College. After Robert E. Lee served as its president following the Civil War, it received its present name. The **Lee Chapel and Museum** on campus contains Washington's christening dress and many relics of the Lee family. Edward Valentine's statue of the recumbent general, behind the altar, is especially moving: The pose is natural and the expression gentle, in contrast to most monumental art, the martial in particular. Here you can appreciate the reverence Lee has inspired. *Tel. 703/463–8768. Admission free. Open Mon.–Sat. 9–4 (9–5 Apr.–Oct.), Sun. 2–5. Closed New Year's Day, Thanksgiving, and the following day, Dec. 24–26 and 31.*

Directly adjacent is the imposing, Gothic-style **Virginia Military Institute,** founded in 1839. Here the **George C. Marshall Museum** preserves the memory of a man who came to this West Point of the South and rose to become chief of staff in World War II and eventually, most famously, the secretary of state who conceived the plan to revive Western Europe after the war. Exhibits trace his brilliant career, which began as aide-de-camp to Black Jack Pershing in World War I. Marshall's Nobel Peace Prize is on display; so is the Oscar won by his aide Frank McCarthy, who produced the 1970 Best Picture, *Patton.* An electronic, narrated map tells the story of World War II in 45 minutes. *Tel. 703/463–7103. Admission free. Open Mon.–Sat. 9–5, Sun. 2–5. Mar.–Oct., Mon.–Sat. 9–4, Sun. 2–4 rest of year. Closed Thanksgiving, Christmas, and New Year's Day.*

The **V.M.I. Museum** is in the lower level of the Institute's Jackson Memorial Hall. Stonewall Jackson's stuffed and mounted horse, Little Sorrel, is on display, as is the general's raincoat, pierced by the confederate bullet that accidentally killed him at Chancellorsville. *Tel. 703/464–7232. Admission free. Open Mon.–Sat. 9–5, Sun. 2–5. Closed Thanksgiving and Christmas Eve through New Year's Day.*

Jackson's private life is on display just a few blocks away at the **Stonewall Jackson House.** He was devoted to physical fitness and the Presbyterian faith, careful with money, and fond of gardening. There is nothing remote about the modest professor you learn of here, in the only house he ever owned. It is furnished with period pieces and a few of the general's belongings. He lived in the house two years, while he taught physics and military science to the cadets at the Institute, until the War Between the States put his tactical genius to bloody use. *8 E. Washington St., tel. 703/463–2552. Admission: $4 adults, $2 children. Open Mon.–Sat. 9–5, Sun. 1–5 Sept.–May; Mon.–Sat. 9–6, Sun. 1–6 June–Aug. Closed Easter, Thanksgiving, Christmas, and New Year's Day.*

10 About 15 miles south of Lexington is the **Natural Bridge,** an impressive arch 215 feet high and 90 feet long that has been gradually carved out of the limestone by the Cedar Creek below. The arch really *is* a bridge, supporting a segment of U.S. 11. The Monocan Indians worshiped it as "The Bridge of God." George Washington surveyed it for Lord Fairfax, and evidently carved his own initials into the rock. Thomas Jefferson bought it and some surrounding acreage because he admired it as a wonder of the world. The sound-and-light show after dark is overkill, but the bridge itself is worth the admission fee. *I–81 to Exit 49 or 50, tel. 703/291–2121. Admission: $7 adults, $6 senior citizens, $3.50 children 6–15. Open daily 7 AM–dusk.*

Next door, the exhibits at **Natural Bridge Wax Museum** are less interesting than its factory tour: a look at the state-of-the-art process by which the realistic biblical and historical figures are assembled. You should not go out of your way, but it is right at the entrance to the bridge. *Tel. 703/291–2426. Admission: $7 adults, $6 senior citizens, $3.50 children. Open daily 9–9 May–Oct., 9–5 Nov.–April.*

11 Fifty-four miles south of Lexington is **Roanoke.** At the heart of this quiet and cheerful city, a hub for the railroad and the arts, is Market Square. A restored warehouse here, called **Center in the Square,** contains three museums and a theater. The **Science Museum of Western Virginia** (tel. 703/342–5700) has displays on Virginia's natural history and computer games that entertain and inform on such topics as energy resources. Many of the exhibits are interactive and therefore especially appealing to youngsters. Shows are held in the planetarium on a varying schedule; call 703/342–5710. The **Roanoke Valley History Museum** (tel. 703/342–5770; admission $2 adults, $1 senior citizens and children) displays a curious collection of regionalia, including prehistoric relics of the local Indians, from whose name for "shell wampum" the name Roanoke is derived. The **Roanoke Museum of Fine Arts** (tel. 703/342–5760; admission free) does not have a big-name collection; the emphasis is regional. The best thing about it is that local artists flock here to work in the studios on the top floor. The **Mill Mountain Theater** presents musicals, Shakespeare, and contemporary drama (*see* The Arts, *below*). *General information for Center in the Square, tel. 703/342–5700. All museums open Tues.–Sat. 10–5, Sun. 1–5; Science and art museums also open until 8 on Fri.*

Just a pleasant stroll away is the **Virginia Museum of Transportation,** devoted almost exclusively to trains. This is not surprising, since Roanoke got its start as a railroad town and is the headquarters of Norfolk and Western Railway Co., part of Norfolk Southern Corp. The dozens of original train cars and engines, many built in town, include a massive "Nickel Plate" locomotive. The museum's collections are unusual, and its unabashed display of civic pride is peculiar to Roanoke. This museum captures the whole spirit of a town. *303 Norfolk Ave., tel. 703/342–5670. Admission: $4 adults, $3 senior citizens, $2 teens, $1.75 children. Open Mon.–Sat. 10–5, Sun. 12–5.*

12 Twenty miles southeast of Roanoke is **Booker T. Washington's Birthplace,** a restored plantation that is now a national monument. Born in slavery, this remarkable educator went on to advise presidents McKinley, Roosevelt, and Taft, and take tea with Queen Victoria. More important, he started Tuskegee Institute in Alabama and was an inspiration to generations of

black Americans. *Rte. 116S to Burnt Chimney, then 6 mi 122N. Tel. 703/721–2094. Admission $1 adults, senior citizens and children free, family rate $3. Open daily 8:30–5. Closed Thanksgiving, Christmas, and New Year's Day.*

Back in Roanoke, you're ready for the long drive out through the rugged Highlands to Abingdon, about 135 miles to the southwest. The main route is I–81, but the longer, more scenic choice would be the Blue Ridge Parkway to I–77 to I–81. (This section of the Parkway includes the previously mentioned Mabry Mill.) Breaks along the route, or destinations in themselves, are the campgrounds, picnic areas, and lakes of the **Jefferson National Forest,** comprising 700,000 acres in patches widely scattered over this section of western Virginia and providing a habitat for bobcat, black bear, and bald eagles. The fo-
13 cal point of this patchwork of parks is the **Mount Rogers National Recreation Area,** east of Abingdon, which contains the highest mountain in Virginia (5,729 feet), as well as an extensive network of trails for riding (for guided tours on horseback, *see* Participant Sports, *below*). The Appalachian Trail crosses the border into Tennessee here. Hunting and fishing are permitted in season. *For information, contact the Forest Supervisor, 210 Franklin Rd. SW, Roanoke 24001, tel. 703/ 982–6270. For information on Mount Rogers only: Rte. 1, Box 303, Marion 24354, tel. 703/783–5196.*

14 **Abingdon** is a cultural crossroads in the wilderness, a town of 5,000 residents that draws tens of thousands of visitors annually with its fine resident theater company and exuberant local celebrations. The most popular attraction by far is the Virginia Highlands Festival in the first two weeks of August, which draws 150,000 people with its wide-ranging musical performances (everything from bluegrass to opera), exhibitions of mountain crafts, and over 100 antiques dealers. This is followed by the Burley Tobacco Festival, where country-music stars perform and prize farm animals are on proud display. *Call the Washington County Chamber of Commerce for information, including dates, which vary widely: tel. 703/ 628–8141.*

Throughout the summer, the prestigious **Barter Theatre** (*see* The Arts, *below*) draws an appreciative crowd. Hume Cronyn, Patricia Neal, Ernest Borgnine, and Gregory Peck are among the actors who began their careers here. The theater was organized by Robert Porterfield in 1932 to give work to penniless thespians and entertainment to cash-poor local farmers, who were welcome to barter for tickets with their surplus crops. They still accept barter, by the way.

What to See and Do with Children

Barter Theatre in Abingdon stages performances especially for kids during their regular season (*see* The Arts, *below*).
Science Museum of Western Virginia (*see* Exploring Shenandoah Valley and the Highlands, *above*).

Off the Beaten Track

The locals in Roanoke will steer you toward more respectable and more expensive establishments, but not because they are ashamed of the **Texas Tavern** (114 Church Ave., tel. 703/342–4825); they just want to keep it to themselves. A sign says We

Serve a Thousand, Ten at a Time, and indeed there are but ten stools. It is often packed, especially late at night, but wait your turn or else answer to one of the tough guys behind the counter. Chili is the specialty.

Participant Sports

Canoeing Canoe rentals are available through **Front Royal Canoe** (Rte. 340, near Front Royal, tel. 703/635–5440), **Downriver Canoe Company** (Rte. 613, near Front Royal, tel. 703/635–5526), and **Shenandoah River Outfitters** (Rte. 684, near Luray, tel. 703/743–4159).

Fishing To take advantage of the trout that abound in **Shenandoah National Park**—in some 50 streams—obtain a five-day Virginia fishing license, which is available in season (early April through mid-October) at concession stands along Skyline Drive.

Golf **Caverns Country Club Resort** (Rte. 211 in Luray, tel. 703/743–6551) has a par-72 18-hole course along the river. **Greene Hills Golf Club** (Rte. 33 in Stanardsville, tel. 804/985–7328) has an 18-hole course open to the public. **The Homestead** in Hot Springs (tel. 703/839–5500 or 800/336–5771) has three. **Wintergreen** (Rte. 664, Nellysford, tel. 804/325–2200 or 800/325–2200) offers 36 holes, half in the mountains, half in the valley.

Hiking There are 500 miles of trails through the **Shenandoah National Park.** The more popular trails are described in the guidebook available at the visitor centers. Other popular trails are on the Blue Ridge Parkway and in Woods Creek Park and Chessie Nature Trail at Lexington.

Horseback Riding Guided tours of Mount Rogers National Recreation Area are offered by **Fairwood Stables** in Troutdale (tel. 703/677–3301). Frequent horse shows and equestrian competitions are held March–Nov. at **The Virginia Horse Center,** Lexington (703/463–2194). Trail riding is offered by **Stoney Run Trails** (703/261–1910) from Rockbridge County near Buena Vista through Blue Ridge Parkway.

Skiing **The Homestead** (Rte. 39, Hot Springs, tel. 703/839–5500 or 800/336–5771) offers cross-country and downhill skiing. **Massanutten Village Ski Resort** (off Rte. 33 in McGaheysville, tel. 703/289–9441) offers equipment rental and snowmaking.

Tennis **The Homestead** in Hot Springs (tel. 703/839–5500 or 800/336–5771) maintains 19 courts, including one all-weather. **Caverns Country Club Resort** (Rte. 211 in Luray, tel. 703/743–6551) has four courts. **Wintergreen** (Rte. 664, Nellysford, tel. 804/325–2200 or 800/325–2200) maintains 25 outdoor tennis courts. Many hotels throughout the region provide courts or have them nearby.

Spectator Sports

Thirty minutes northwest of Front Royal, in West Virginia, is the **Charles Town Race Track** (tel. 304/725–7001), where thoroughbred racing goes on year-round, every day except Tuesday and Thursday.

The **Virginia Horse Center** in Lexington (tel. 703/463–2194) stages competitions—including showjumping, hunter trials, and multibreed shows—several days each week from mid-March through mid-November.

In June and August, **jousting tournaments** are held at the Natural Chimneys area in Mt. Solon, south of Harrisonburg. The day's entertainment also includes a parade and crafts exhibitions. *Tel. 703/350–2510. Park admission: $4 per car.*

Dining

The most highly recommended restaurants in each price category are indicated by a star ★.

Category	Cost*
Very Expensive	over $30
Expensive	$20–$30
Moderate	$10–$20
Inexpensive	under $10

**per person without tax (4.5% sales tax plus local tax), service, or drinks*

Abingdon
American

Tavern. This cozy, comfortable restaurant was a field hospital during the Civil War. Built in 1779, it is the oldest building in town. It has two small dining rooms, a cocktail lounge, and a dart room, all with fireplaces, stone walls, and brick floors. In warm weather, you can dine outdoors on a balcony overlooking historic Court House Hill, or on a brick patio surrounded by trees and flowers. The menu features excellent beef Wellington and rainbow trout from local waters, stuffed with crabmeat and shrimp and cooked in a white wine sauce. For dessert, try the homemade apple crisp. You can enjoy live music at night on Tuesdays, Fridays, and Saturdays. *222 E. Main St., tel. 703/628–1118. Dress: informal. Reservations advised. AE, MC, V. Moderate.*

Lexington
American

Palms. Once a Victorian ice-cream parlor, this is now a full-service restaurant. The tin ceiling is part of the original building, which dates to 1890. Wood booths line the walls of the plant-filled room. Food is prepared and presented with great care. Specialties include broccoli-cheese soup, charbroiled meats, and teriyaki chicken. There is a champagne brunch on weekends. *101 W. Nelson St., tel. 703/463–7911. Dress: informal. Reservations not needed. MC, V. Inexpensive.*

Newbern
Country
★

Valley Pike Inn. This family-owned restaurant midway between Roanoke and Abingdon features fried chicken, country baked ham, roast beef, homemade buttermilk biscuits, and old-fashioned fruit cobblers, all family-style. Wood walls and floor planks give the feeling of eating in a comfortable farmhouse. The inn was built in 1830 at an old stagecoach stop. *I–81 Exit 32, tel. 703/674–1810. Dress: informal. Reservations advised for groups of 5 or more. MC, V. Closed Mon.–Wed. Dinner only. No liquor. Inexpensive.*

Roanoke
American

Billy's Ritz. A fun spot, comfortable and casual, with good soups and salads. *102 Salem Ave., tel. 703/342–3937. Dress: informal. Reservations not needed. AE, MC, V. Moderate.*

French and Continental

Library. This quiet, elegant restaurant decorated with shelves of books specializes in seafood dishes. *3117 Franklin Rd. SW (Piccadilly Square shopping center), tel. 703/985-0811. Jacket required. Reservations required. AE, DC, MC, V. Closed Sun. Very Expensive.*

Staunton
Country

Rowe's Family Restaurant. This homey eatery, with a bright and comfortable dining room filled with booths, has been operated by the same family since 1947. Homemade baked goods are outstanding. Specialties include Virginia ham, steak, and chicken. *I-81 Exit 57, tel. 703/886-1833. Dress: informal. Reservations not needed. D, MC, V. Inexpensive.*

Warm Springs
French and Regional
★

Waterwheel Restaurant. Part of a complex of five restored buildings, this restaurant is in a gristmill that dates back to 1700. A walk-in wine cellar, set among the gears of the original waterwheel, has 100 varieties of wines. The dining area is decorated with Currier and Ives and Audubon prints. Try the salmon steak, broiled and stuffed with smoked salmon, or the Chicken Fantasio, breast of chicken stuffed with wild rice, sausage, apple, and pecans. Desserts feature such old Virginia recipes as Apple Brown Betty, a deep-dish apple pie baked in bourbon. *Grist Mill Sq., tel. 703/839-2231. Dress: informal. Reservations advised. MC, V. No lunch. Closed Sun. and Mon. Expensive.*

Lodging

Lexington and Upcountry Virginia offer charming bed-and-breakfasts and small rural inns. To see about staying in a private home or old, reconverted inn, contact the **Shenandoah Valley Bed & Breakfast Reservations Service** (Box 305, Broadway, VA 22815, tel. 703/896-9702). The most highly recommended properties in each price category are indicated by a star ★.

Category	Cost*
Very Expensive	over $120
Expensive	$90–$120
Moderate	$50–$90
Inexpensive	under $50

**double room, highest rate in peak season; add 4.5% sales tax plus local tax*

Abingdon
★

Martha Washington Inn. Built in 1832 as a private house, turned into a college dormitory in 1860 and then into a field hospital during the Civil War, this spot across from the Barter Theatre has been an inn since 1935. Rooms are furnished with antiques, and some suites have fireplaces. *150 W. Main St., 24210, tel. 703/628-3161 or 800/553-1014. 50 rooms with private bath, 11 suites, some with whirlpool. Facilities: restaurant, lounge. AE, D, DC, MC, V. Very Expensive.*

Alpine Motel. At this remarkably clean motel, with the basic amenities, each room has a beautiful view of Virginia's two highest mountain peaks. *882 E. Main St. (I-81 Exit 9), 24210, tel. 703/628-3178. 19 rooms. Facilities: cable TV. AE, D, MC, V. Inexpensive.*

Blue Ridge Parkway ★

Doe Run Lodge. This resort at Groundhog Mountain, with beautiful vistas, is near golf, skiing, and hunting. *Mile Post 189, Rte. 2, Box 338, Hillsville 24343, tel. 703/398–2212. 38 condominium apartments with 2 or more bedrooms, including 7 villas. Facilities: tennis courts, outdoor pool, stocked fishing pond, restaurant open June–Oct. MC, V. Expensive.*

Rocky Knob Cabins. Rustic cabins with kitchens. No private baths. *Mile Post 174, Box 5, Meadows of Dan 24120, tel. 703/593–3503. DC, MC, V. Closed Labor Day–Memorial Day. Inexpensive.*

Hot Springs ★

The Homestead. Founded in 1891, this is the oldest resort in the United States and one of the most luxurious. It spreads out over 15,000 acres and includes a spa with natural mineral springs, three 18-hole golf courses, 19 tennis courts, 100 miles of riding trails, four ski slopes, four miles of streams stocked with rainbow trout, skeet shooting. All rooms are decorated in Victorian style; many have marble tubs and TV in the bathrooms. *U.S. 220, 24445, tel. 703/839–5500 or 800/336–5771. 592 rooms. Facilities: 7 restaurants, one with orchestra and dancing; indoor/outdoor pools; complete health spa; 3 golf courses; bowling alley. AE, MC, V. Very Expensive.*

Roseloe Motel. A modest and very clean place with some kitchenettes. *Rte. 2, Box 590, 24445, tel. 703/839–5373. 14 rooms. MC, V. Inexpensive.*

Lexington

Maple Hall. This country inn of 1850, located 6 miles north of the Lexington historic district, is a former plantation house set on 56 acres. Rooms are furnished with period antiques and modern amenities. Dinner is served in three ground-floor rooms and on a glassed-in patio of this elegant mid-19th-century farmhouse. Watercolors by local artists adorn the cream-color walls; the main dining room has a large decorative fireplace, and in one of the other rooms the fireplace is used in cold weather. When weather permits, there is dining on an outdoor patio. *Rte. 11, Lexington 24450, tel. 703/463–2044. 21 rooms. Facilities: hiking trails, trout pond, outdoor pool, tennis court. Reservations advised for restaurant; no lunch. MC, V. Expensive.*

Natural Bridge

Natural Bridge Hotel, Inn & Lodge. Within walking distance of the spectacular rock arch (though a shuttle service is offered), all three properties offer a beautiful setting and recreational facilities for the entire family. The hotel and inn have long porches with rocking chairs for enjoying views of the Blue Ridge Mountains; there's ersatz Colonial Virginia decor throughout. *U.S. 11 & Rte. 130, off I-81, Exits 49 or 50; Box 57, 24578, tel. 703/291–2121 or 800/336–5727; in VA 800/533–1410. Hotel: 90 rooms, including 2 honeymoon suites. Inn: 30 rooms. Lodge: 60 rooms. Facilities: restaurant, lounge, cafeteria, snack bar, outdoor pool, 2 tennis courts, walking trails. AE, D, DC, MC, V. Inexpensive–Moderate.*

Radford

Best Western. Rooms are decorated in Colonial Virginia style, and most have views of the Valley and the Blue Ridge Mountains. *1501 Tyler Ave. (Rte. 177, Exit 35 off I–81), Box 1008, 24141, tel. 703/639–3000 or 800/528–1234. 104 rooms. Facilities: room hairdryer and phone, restaurant, lounge, indoor pool, whirlpool, sauna, gym. AE, D, DC, MC, V. Moderate.*

Roanoke

Patrick Henry Hotel. This landmark 1925 building in downtown Roanoke within walking distance of the sights was renovated in 1991. The light-filled lobby has Oriental rugs on its white-marble floors, an eclectic mix of antique furniture, and gilt-touched plasterwork. All of its extra-large rooms have kitchenettes and sitting areas. A nearby YMCA extends health-club privileges to guests, who are transported there by stretch limousine. *617 S. Jefferson St., 24011, tel. 703/345–8811 or 800/833–4567. 100 restored rooms with kitchenette. Facilities: restaurant, pub, lounge, 2 meeting rooms, gift shop, free parking, airport transportation. AE, MC, V. Expensive–Very Expensive.*

Holiday Inn–Civic Center. Convenient downtown location. *501 Orange Ave. (I–581 and Williamson Rd.), 24016, tel. 703/342–8961. 153 rooms. Facilities: restaurant and lounge, exercise room, outdoor pool. AE, D, DC, MC, V. Moderate.*

Smith Mountain Lake

Bernard's Landing. This lakeside resort 45 minutes southeast of Roanoke offers one- to three-bedroom kitchen-equipped accommodations, as well as a wealth of sporting opportunities. *Rte. 940, Box 462, Monita 24121, tel. 703/721–8870 or 800/572–2048. 63 units. Facilities: boating, sailing, fishing, swimming (beach and pool), tennis, racquetball, sauna, Jacuzzi, weight room, playground, restaurant. AE, D, MC, V. Expensive.*

Staunton

Belle Grae Inn. At this restored Victorian mansion, built in 1870, many rooms are furnished with rocking chairs and canopied or brass beds. Free breakfast and afternoon tea are served. *515 W. Frederick St., 24401, tel. 703/886–5151. 12 rooms. Adults only. Facilities: bistro, with live music Wed.–Sat., candlelight dinner in inn, light fare in garden restaurant. AE, DC, MC, V. Moderate.*

★ **Frederick House.** Three restored town houses dating to 1810 make up this inn in the center of the historic district. All the rooms are decorated with antiques. Adjacent is a pub and restaurant. *No smoking on the premises. 18 E. Frederick St., 24401, tel. 703/885–4220. 11 rooms; each with bath, cable TV, phones. AE, D, DC, MC, V. Moderate.*

Warm Springs

Inn at Gristmill Square. In two of five restored buildings, on the same site as the Waterwheel Restaurant (*see* Dining, *above*), the rooms are individually decorated in Colonial Virginia style. In addition to the inn and the restaurant, the complex has a blacksmith's shop and a hardware store. *Rte. 645, Box 359, 24484, tel. 703/839–2231. 14 rooms, including 2 suites and 2 2-bedroom apartments with kitchens. Facilities: restaurant, pub, 3 tennis courts, outdoor pool, sauna. MC, V. Moderate–Expensive.*

The Arts

Dance

The regular company of the **Roanoke Ballet Theatre** (tel. 703/345–6099) is joined by guest artists from around the world for performances in spring and fall at theaters around town.

Music

Garth Newel Music Center in Hot Springs (tel. 703/839–5018) runs a summer weekend chamber-music festival. Plan to picnic on the grounds, and make reservations. There are also special programs at Christmas and the Summer Festival of Arts from mid-June through mid-August.

The **Roanoke Valley Chamber Music Society** (tel. 703/375–2333) hosts distinguished visiting performers from October through May in the Olin Theater on the campus of Roanoke College.

Theater

The **Lime Kiln Arts Theater** in Lexington (tel. 703/463–3074) is just that: the ruins of a lime kiln—an outdoor rock-walled pit.

Here folk and classical concerts are given, in addition to performances of dramatic works both well-known and home-grown, all summer long. The **Mill Mountain Theater** in Roanoke's Center on the Square (Market Sq., tel. 703/342–5740) is a regional theater noted for producing the work of emerging playwrights. **Roanoke Comedy Club** (Williamson Rd., tel. 703/982–8693) combines laughs and dinner nights. The season at Abingdon's **Barter Theatre** (Main St., tel. 703/628–3991) is April through October, with experimental productions from June through August. Call in advance to barter for tickets, or pay the conventional way.

Nightlife

In Roanoke, **Billy's Ritz** (102 Salem Ave., tel. 703/342–3937) has pop music and a young professional crowd. At **The Homestead** in Hot Springs (U.S. 220, tel. 703/839–5500), there's ballroom dancing to live music nightly. In Abingdon, the **Act II Lounge** (150 W. Main St., tel. 703/628–3161) has dancing and entertainment nightly. The lounge is in the basement of the Martha Washington Inn and across from the Barter Theatre.

Charlottesville Area

Charlottesville is at the heart of "Mr. Jefferson's Country," as the locals proudly call it. The influence of the Sage of Monticello is inescapable anywhere in the Commonwealth (and far beyond its borders), but around here, in Albemarle County and in Orange County to the north, it is downright palpable. Also here are sites associated with other giants among his contemporaries and with crucial events in American history.

Since Jefferson founded the University of Virginia in 1819, this area has been a cultural center. The countryside has been discovered by an array of celebrities, including Jessica Lange and Sissy Spacek, who have settled here in recent years. A growing community of writers and artists is making this affluent area the "Santa Fe of the East Coast": a colony of the intellectual and the fashionable in a historic and remote setting.

Getting Around

By Plane Charlottesville-Albemarle Airport is served by **USAir, United Express, Alleghany,** and **T.W. Express.**

By Car Charlottesville is where U.S. 29 (north–south) meets I–64 (east–west), which connects with Interstates 95 and 81.

By Train **Amtrak** trains originating in New York stop at Charlottesville's Union Station (810 W. Main St., tel. 800/872–7245) on the way to Chicago and to New Orleans three times a week and daily, respectively.

By Bus **Greyhound/Trailways Bus Lines** (310 W. Main St., tel. 804/254–5910).

Important Addresses and Numbers

Tourist Information **Charlottesville/Albemarle Convention and Visitors' Bureau** (Rte. 20S, Box 161, Charlottesville, 22902, tel. 804/977–1783).

Emergencies Dial 911 for emergency assistance.

Hospitals Emergency rooms at **Martha Jefferson Hospital** (459 Locust Ave., tel. 804/293–0193) and **Virginia Commonwealth University Hospital** (401 N. 12th St., tel. 804/786–9151) are open 24 hours.

24-hour Pharmacy **People's Drug Store** (2730 W. Broad St., Richmond, tel. 804/359–2497).

Exploring the Charlottesville Area

Start at the **Visitors Center,** where you can get oriented. The people here are glad to answer your questions about attractions and accommodations in the area and the whole state. A free extensive permanent exhibition, "Thomas Jefferson at Monticello," provides background on the house and its legendary occupant. On display are artifacts recovered during recent archaeological excavations. Do not miss it, before or after Monticello; it will make the experience at least twice as rich, since there is so much not explained on the tour. *Rte. 20S from Charlottesville (Monticello exit off I-64), tel. 804/977–1783. Open weekdays 9–5 (until 5:30 Mar.–Oct.). Closed Christmas Day.*

Monticello is the most famous of Jefferson's homes, and his lasting monument to himself—an ingenious masterpiece created over more than 40 years. Not typical of any style, it is characteristic of Jefferson, who made a statement with every detail: the staircases are narrow and hidden because he considered them unsightly and wasteful of space, and contrary to plantation tradition, his outbuildings are in the back, not on the east side, where his guests arrived. In these respects, as in its overall conception, Monticello was a subversive structure, a classical repudiation of the prevalent English Georgian style and the colonial mentality behind it.

As if to reflect this revolutionary aspect, a concave mirror in the entrance hall presents you with your own image upside down. Throughout the house are Jefferson's inventions, including a seven-day clock and a "polygraph," a two-pen contraption with which he could make a copy of his correspondence as he wrote it. The Thomas Jefferson Center for Historic Plants features interpretive gardens, exhibits, and a sales area. The tour guides are happy to answer questions, but they have to move you through quickly since there is always another group waiting. It is impossible to see everything in one visit. *On Rte. 53 (off Rte. 20), 2 mi southeast of Charlottesville, tel. 804/295–8181 or 295–2657. Admission: $7 adults, $6 senior citizens, $3 children 6–11. Open daily 9–4:30 Nov.–Feb., 8–5 rest of year. Closed Christmas.*

Like its grand neighbor, modest **Ash Lawn–Highland** is marked by the personality of its owner. This is no longer the simple farmhouse built for James Monroe, who lived in the small L-shaped single story at the rear. A subsequent owner added the more prominent two-story section. Yet the furnishings are mostly original, and it is not hard to imagine Monroe here at his beloved retreat. The small rooms are crowded with presents from notable contemporaries and with souvenirs from his time as envoy to France. Such coziness befits the fifth president, the first from the middle class. Today Ash Lawn is a working plantation where spectacular peacocks roam the grounds. *On Rte. 795 (off Rte. 53), 2 mi past Monticello, tel. 804/293-9539. Admission: $6 adults, $5.50 senior citizens, $2* *children. Open daily 9–6 Mar.– Oct., 10–5 rest of year. Closed Thanksgiving, Christmas, and New Year's Day.*

Because of its proximity to Monticello and Ash Lawn, **The Historic Michie Tavern** also has become a popular attraction. Most of the complex was constructed in 1784 at Earlysville, 17 miles away, and moved here piece by piece in 1927. Costumed hostesses lead you into a series of rooms, where you hear recorded interpretations of the interiors. A visit here is not as entertaining or educational as the tour of the Rising Sun Tavern in Fredericksburg (*see* Exploring Northern Virginia, *below*): the narration is less informative, and the conditions are too tidy. The restaurant serves mediocre "Colonial" fare (fried chicken) for lunch. The old gristmill has a gift shop. *On Rte. 53 near Monticello, tel. 804/977-1234. Admission: $5 adults; $4.50 senior citizens, students, and the military, $1 children under 12. Open daily 9–5. Closed Christmas and New Year's Day.*

There's not really a whole lot to see in Charlottesville itself, though the visitor center on Route 20 (*see* Important Addresses and Numbers, *above*) does have a walking-tour map of the downtown historic district. The center can provide a complete list of crafts and antiques shops, of which the city has a nice supply. The main shopping area is the Downtown Mall, spread along six blocks of Main Street. Fountains, outdoor restaurants, and restored buildings line the street, which has been bricked over and restricted to pedestrians. Among the area's unique shops is **Paula Lewis** (4th and Jefferson Sts., in Historic Court Square, 2 blocks north of Main St., tel. 804/295–6244), which specializes in handmade quilts from across the country.

At the west end of town is the **University of Virginia,** one of the most distinguished institutions of higher education in the nation. It was founded and designed by Thomas Jefferson, who called himself its "father" in his own epitaph. Experts polled during the U.S. Bicentennial named his campus "the proudest achievement of American architecture in the past 200 years." You will be struck by the innovative beauty of the "academical village": it is subtle—almost delicate—and totally practical. Students vie for rooms in the original pavilions that flank the Lawn, a graduated expanse that flows down from the Rotunda—a half-scale replica of the Pantheon in Rome. Behind the pavilions are gardens and landscaping laced with serpentine walls. To arrange a free one-hour tour, call 804/924–7969.

Time Out Have lunch among UVA students at one of their haunts: **Martha's Café** (11 Elliewood Ave., tel. 804/971–7530). Try the enchiladas or a vegetarian entrée. In warm weather, ask for a table on the patio, where the plantings are lush and appealing.

About an hour north of Charlottesville is another presidential residence, recently opened to the public. Originally the home of James Madison, **Montpelier** in its present condition has more to do with its 20th-century owners, the du Pont family, who enlarged and redecorated it. This dual legacy poses a dilemma in the restoration, since the house only vaguely resembles itself in Madison's day. Markings on walls, floors, and ceilings show the locations of underlying door and window frames, etc., as a preliminary step to future restoration work. The process of restoration is slow, to the credit of the painstaking preservationists of the National Trust. In the meantime, it takes your imagination and your guide's eloquent narration to appreciate the history of this mostly empty house.

The house can be seen only on a 1½- to 2-hour guided tour, which begins with a slide show on the history of the house, then takes you on a shuttle-bus tour of the farm and paddock area, followed by a tour of the mansion and another slide show, free time to wander the delightful grounds and gardens, and a shuttle-bus tour of the cemetery where James, Dolley, and other Madisons are buried. *On Rte. 20, outside the town of Orange, tel. 703/672–2728 or 672–2206. Admission: $6 adults; $5 senior citizens; $1 children 6–12, under 6 free. Open daily 10–4. Closed major holidays.*

Less than two hours south of Charlottesville is an American shrine. The village of **Appomattox Court House** has been restored to its appearance on April 9, 1865, when Lee surrendered the Army of Northern Virginia to Grant. There are 27 structures, including the McLean House, in whose parlor the articles of surrender were signed. The self-guided tour is well mapped out and introduced by exhibits and slide shows in the reconstructed courthouse. First-person interpreters cast as soldiers and villagers answer questions in summer. *U.S. 29S to U.S. 460E to Rte. 24, tel. 804/352–8987. Admission: $1 adults, senior citizens and children free. Open daily 8:30–5 (9–5:30 June–Aug.) Closed Federal holidays.*

What to See and Do with Children

At Charlottesville's **Virginia Discovery Museum,** kids can step inside a giant kaleidoscope or basketball star Ralph Sampson's actual uniform. Plays and musical performances are given, in addition to the permanent hands-on exhibits that are supposed to develop both the imagination and such everyday skills as tying shoes. *400 Ackley La., tel. 804/293–5528. Admission: $3 adults, $2 senior citizens and children. Open Tues.–Sat. 10–5, Sun. 1–5. Closed Mon.*

Participant Sports

Golf **The Crossings** (Junction I–95 and I–295, Glen Allen, tel. 804/266–2254), north of Richmond, has an 18-hole course open to the public.

Spectator Sports

The **University of Virginia** is nationally or regionally ranked in several varsity sports. In season, you can watch the Cavaliers play first-rate ACC basketball in University Hall. There's also football at Scott Stadium, plus baseball, soccer, lacrosse, and more. Check *The Cavalier Daily* for listings.

Dining

All of the restaurants listed are in Charlottesville unless otherwise noted.

The most highly recommended restaurants in each price category are indicated by a star ★.

Category	Cost*
Very Expensive	over $30
Expensive	$20–$30
Moderate	$10–$20
Inexpensive	under $10

**per person without tax (4.5% sales tax plus local tax), service, or drinks*

Very Expensive
French
★

C&O Restaurant. A boarded-up storefront hung with an illuminated Pepsi sign conceals one of the best restaurants in town. Downstairs is a lively bistro serving pâtés, cheeses, and light meals. The stark white formal dining room upstairs features excellent regional French cuisine. Recommended are the coquilles St. Jacques—steamed scallops served in a sauce made of grapefruit juice, cream, and Dijon mustard—and, for an appetizer, the *terrine de campagne*, a pâté of veal, venison, and pork. The wine list includes 300 varieties. *515 E. Water St., tel. 804/971–7044. Upstairs, tie and jacket required; downstairs, informal. Reservations advised. Seatings at 6:30 and 9:30 for dining room. MC, V. Upstairs closed Sun.*

Galerie. Set amid woods and cornfields seven miles from town is an elegant restaurant reminiscent of a French country inn. Specialties include Norwegian salmon with raspberry and lime sauce; duckling braised in port wine and shallot sauce; and rich desserts like *vacherin glacé*—layers of grilled meringue and French vanilla ice cream topped with unsweetened whipped cream and chestnut sauce. The wine list includes 190 varieties. *Rte. 250W, tel. 804/823–5883. Jacket and tie requested. Reservations advised. MC, V. Closed Mon. and Tues.*

Expensive
American

Old Mill Room. In a onetime gristmill (built in 1834), prints and posters of the mill, a fireplace, and wrought-iron chandeliers set the mood as waiters and waitresses in Colonial dress serve such offerings as prime rib and veal Oscar—veal topped with crabmeat, asparagus spears, and béarnaise sauce. Light meals are served in the Tavern downstairs. *In the Boar's Head Inn, U.S. 250W (3 mi from town), tel. 804/296–2181. Dress: casual. Reservations advised. AE, DC, MC, V.*

International
★

Eastern Standard. Here's another restaurant with a formal dining room upstairs and a bistro downstairs. Dining room specialties include rainbow trout stuffed with shiitake mushrooms, wild rice, and fontina cheese; oysters cooked in a champagne and caviar sauce; and loin of lamb with mint pesto. Curries and stirfried Asian dishes are also offered. The bistro is crowded and lively, with taped music, primarily jazz and rock. It serves pastas and light meals. *West End, Downtown Mall, tel. 804/295–8668. Dress: informal. Reservations advised for dining room. AE, MC, V. Dinner only. Upstairs closed Sun.*

Moderate
American

Hardware Store. Deli sandwiches, burgers, salads, seafood, and ice cream from the soda fountain are the specialties in this former Victorian hardware shop. The store was built in 1890, and some of the original wood paneling and brick walls remain. There's outdoor dining in the warm months. *316 E. Main St., tel. 804/977–1518. Dress: informal. Reservations not needed. MC, V. Closed Sun. No dinner Mon.*

Pizza ★ **Crozet Pizza.** Twelve miles west of Charlottesville, you'll find some of Virginia's best pizza. There are 18 different toppings to choose from, including snow peas and asparagus spears. On weekends take-out must be ordered hours in advance. *Rte. 240, Crozet, tel. 804/823–2132. Dress: informal. Reservations not needed. No credit cards. Closed Sun. and Mon.*

Lodging

A B&B service for the area is **Guesthouse Bed & Breakfast, Inc.** (Box 5737, Charlottesville 22905, tel. 804/979–7264 or 804/979–8327). The most highly recommended properties in each price category are indicated by a star ★.

Category	Cost*
Very Expensive	over $120
Expensive	$90–$120
Moderate	$50–$90
Inexpensive	under $50

**double room, highest rate in peak season; add 4.5% sales tax plus local tax*

Downtown Charlottesville *Very Expensive*

Omni Charlottesville. A recent addition to the luxury chain, this attractive hotel looms over the Downtown Mall. The decor is a mixture of modern and Colonial. *235 W. Main St., 22901, tel. 804/971–5500 or 800/843–6664. 208 rooms, 3 suites. Facilities: multilevel restaurant, bilevel lounge with live entertainment, atrium lobby lounge, indoor/outdoor pools, fitness center with saunas, whirlpool, exercise room. AE, DC, MC, V.*

200 South Street Inn. Two historic houses, one of them a former brothel, have been combined and restored to create this old-fashioned inn in the historic district. Furnishings throughout are English and Belgian antiques. Many rooms have private sitting rooms, fireplaces, and whirlpools. *200 South St., 22901, tel. 804/979–0200. 17 rooms, all with private bath and canopy beds, 3 suites. AE, MC, V.*

Near the University *Expensive*

Sheraton Charlottesville. An elegant hotel 7 miles from town. *2350 Seminole Trail (U.S. 29, 3 mi north of jct. Rte. 250 Bypass), 22901, tel. 804/973–2121. 252 rooms. Facilities: indoor/outdoor pools, 2 tennis courts, jogging trails, 2 restaurants, lounge. AE, D, DC, MC, V.*

Moderate

Best Western–Cavalier Inn. Next to the university and an easy drive to Monticello. *105 Emmet St., 22905, tel. 804/296–8111 or 800/528–1234. 118 rooms. Facilities: outdoor pool, restaurant and lounge, cable TV. AE, D, DC, MC, V.*

English Inn. This inn is a motel treatment of the bed-and-breakfast theme on a large but comfortable scale. Continental breakfast is served in a 150-year-old, transplanted Tudor-style dining room with fireplace. There's an attractive three-story atrium lobby with cascading plants. Suites feature king-size beds and reproduction antiques; the other rooms have modern furnishings. *2000 Morton Dr. (jct. U.S. 29 and Rte. 250 Bypass), 22901, tel. 804/971–9900. 67 rooms, 21 king suites with sitting room and wet bar. Facilities: indoor pool, sauna, exercise equipment, restaurant lounge, cable TV. AE, DC, MC, V.*

Inexpensive **Econo Lodge.** This basic chain lodging is next to the university. *400 Emmet St., 22903, tel. 804/296–2104. 60 rooms. Facilities: outdoor pool. AE, D, DC, MC, V.*

Farther Afield
Very Expensive **Boar's Head Inn.** At this luxurious, quiet resort on two small lakes, rooms and suites are simple but elegant, furnished mostly with antiques. Some suites have fireplaces, some are efficiencies, and some rooms have king- or queen-size beds. *U.S. 250 (3 mi from town), Box 5307, Charlottesville 22905, tel. 804/296–2181. 175 rooms, 11 suites. Facilities: 3 restaurants (*see *Old Mill Room in Dining*, above*); complete health club, with 3 pools, squash and racquetball courts, tennis; biking; fishing; hot-air balloon rides. AE, DC, MC, V.*

★ **Mayhurst.** This old Victorian building is a cozy and comfortable B&B about a half-hour northeast of Monticello, surrounded by 36 acres of woods and hiking trails. It was built in 1859 by the grandnephew of James Madison. All the rooms are decorated with early Victorian antiques. Afternoon tea is served. *Box 707 (U.S. 15), Orange 22960, tel. 703/672–5597. 6 rooms with private bath, and a guesthouse. Facilities: pond for fishing and swimming. MC, V.*

The Arts

Dance, music, and theater events of every kind take place all year at the **University of Virginia.** Check *The Cavalier Daily* for details. The **McGuffey Art Center** (201 2nd St. NW, Charlottesville, tel. 804/295–7973), housed in a converted school building, contains the studios of painters and sculptors, and is also the scene of musical and theatrical performances.

Nightlife

Folk **Miller's** (109 W. Main St. Downtown Mall, tel. 804/971–8511) is a large and comfortable bar that also hosts jazz musicians.

Singles **Flood Zone** (18th and Main Sts., Richmond, tel. 804/644–0935), a converted recording studio, has live music for dancing—or for listening while watching from the balcony.

Northern Virginia

Much of this region has been subsumed into the official and residential life of Washington, DC, and has prospered as a result. The affluent and cosmopolitan Northern Virginians are somewhat estranged from the rest of the Commonwealth, yet they are proud of their distinction as Virginians. As their economy grows, they are protecting the historic treasures they hold in trust for the rest of the nation.

Old Town Alexandria remains unsuburbanized; its 2,000 18th- and 19th-century buildings are collectively listed in the National Register of Historic Places. Fairfax and Arlington counties are thriving as satellites of Washington (Tyson's Corner in Fairfax County now has more commercial office space than Miami, Florida) and contain some of America's most precious acreage: Mount Vernon and Arlington Cemetery, respectively. Fredericksburg, only an hour from the nation's capital, seems much farther away: a quiet, well-preserved Southern town, with a 40-block National Historic District. But Fredericksburg was once the bloody scene of conflict, as was Manassas (Bull

Run), 26 miles from Washington—site of some of the most savage battles of the Civil War. The gracious lifestyle of the old South survives in Loudoun County, less than an hour from Washington, where fox hunting and steeplechasing still fill leisure hours.

Getting Around

By Plane **Washington National Airport** (tel. 703/685–8003) in Arlington is served by all major U.S. airlines. **Washington Dulles International Airport** (tel. 703/471–4242) in Loudoun County has departures for most destinations in this country and the world, and **Baltimore–Washington International Airport** (tel. 410/859–7100) also serves the metropolitan Washington area, including Northern Virginia.

By Car I–95 runs north–south along the eastern side of the region. I-66 runs east–west, perpendicular to I–95, cutting off the top third of the region.

By Train There are **Amtrak** (tel. 800/872–7245) stations in Alexandria (110 Callahan Dr.) and Fredericksburg (Caroline St. and Lafayette Blvd.)

By Bus **Greyhound/Trailways Lines:** Fairfax (4103 Rust St., tel. 703/273–7770), Fredericksburg (1400 Jefferson Davis Hwy., tel. 703/373–2103), Springfield (6583 Backlick Rd., tel. 703/451–5800).

Guided Tours

Guided walking tours of Alexandria from April through November begin at the Ramsay House Visitor's Center (221 King St., tel 703/838–4200).

Important Addresses and Numbers

Tourist Information **Alexandria Convention and Visitor's Bureau,** at the Ramsay House Visitor's Center, 221 King St., Alexandria 22314, tel. 703/838–4200. Open daily 9–5. **Arlington Visitor's Center,** 735 S. 18th St., Arlington 22202, tel. 703/521–0772. Open daily 9–5. **Fairfax County Tourism and Convention Bureau,** 8300 Boone Blvd., Suite 450, Vienna 22182, tel. 703/790–3329. Open daily 9–5. **Fredericksburg Visitor's Center,** 706 Caroline St., Fredericksburg 22401, tel. 703/373–1776. Open daily 8:45–7 mid-June through Labor Day; 9–5 rest of year. All closed major holidays.

Emergencies Dial 911 for emergency assistance.

Hospital Emergency Room In Fredericksburg, the **Medic 1 Clinic** is at 3429 Jefferson Davis Highway (tel. 703/371–1664).

Exploring Northern Virginia

Numbers in the margin correspond to points of interest on the Northern Virginia map.

First in war, first in peace, and first on our tour is George
1 Washington, whose **Mount Vernon,** 16 miles south of the city that bears his name, is today the most visited house museum in the United States. About 25% of the furnishings are original; the rest are carefully selected and authenticated antiques.

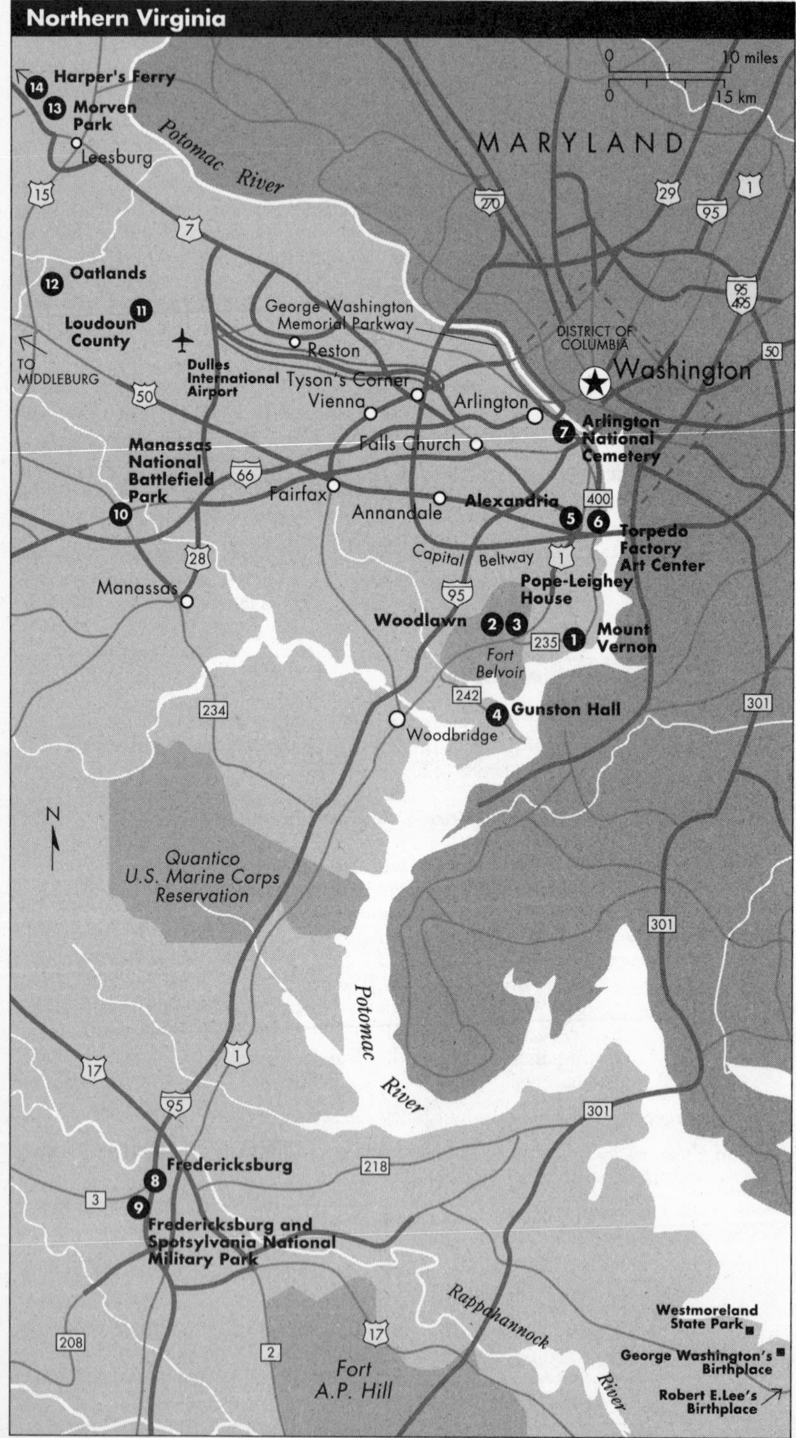
Northern Virginia
0 10 miles
0 15 km
MARYLAND
DISTRICT OF COLUMBIA
Washington
Harper's Ferry
Morven Park
Leesburg
Potomac River
Oatlands
Loudoun County
TO MIDDLEBURG
Dulles International Airport
George Washington Memorial Parkway
Reston
Tyson's Corner
Vienna
Arlington
Arlington National Cemetery
Falls Church
Manassas National Battlefield Park
Fairfax
Annandale
Alexandria
Torpedo Factory Art Center
Capital Beltway
Manassas
Pope-Leighey House
Woodlawn
Mount Vernon
Fort Belvoir
Gunston Hall
Woodbridge
Quantico U.S. Marine Corps Reservation
Potomac River
Fredericksburg
Fredericksburg and Spotsylvania National Military Park
Rappahannock River
Fort A.P. Hill
Westmoreland State Park
George Washington's Birthplace
Robert E.Lee's Birthplace
N

Washington considered himself, first and foremost, a farmer. His farmhouse was a formal one, certainly, but none of the embellishments disguised the noble practicality of its purpose. In the ornate dining room, guests ate at simple trestle tables assembled from boards and sawhorses. More of a sage than an intellectual, he read mostly for practical reference; his enormous library of 900 volumes (now mostly dispersed) was composed largely of presents from the authors. The outbuildings, including kitchen and stable, have been precisely restored. A bit farther on are the graves of George and Martha Washington, laid to rest in the land they loved so well. *From DC, take any Virginia-side bridge to the George Washington Memorial Pkwy. (which becomes Mt. Vernon Memorial Hwy. to the south) and follow signs southward, tel. 703/780–2000. Admission: $7 adults, $6 senior citizens, $3 children under 12. Open daily 9–5 Mar.–Oct., 9–4 rest of year.*

Near Mount Vernon—on land given by Washington to his nephew Lawrence Lewis and step-daughter, Nelly Custis, as a wed-
2 ding gift—is **Woodlawn.** Designed by the architect of the
Capitol, William Thornton, to resemble Lewis's boyhood home, Kenmore, in Fredericksburg, it was begun in 1800, then furnished well, but not lavishly, to accommodate and entertain a family of many children. Today, the formal gardens are well maintained and include a large collection of rare old-fashioned roses. *14 mi south of DC on U.S. 1, and 3 mi from Mount Vernon on the George Washington Memorial Pkwy., tel. 703/780–4000. Admission: $5 adults, $3.50 senior citizens and students. Open daily 9:30–4:30. Closed Thanksgiving, Christmas, and New Year's Day.*

3 Also on the grounds of Woodlawn is the **Pope-Leighey House,** designed by Frank Lloyd Wright and built in 1940. It has no Washington-family connection; it is here because when highway construction augured its destruction on its original site nearby, the National Trust stepped in and moved it to Woodlawn, where it makes a nice contrast to the Federal mansion. The longer you look around and the more that is explained, the more of its peculiar beauty is revealed. It does not appeal to every taste, but it *is* an architectural education. *Tel. 703/780–4000. Admission: $4 adults, $3 senior citizens and students. Open daily 9:30–4:30 Mar.–Dec., weekends only Jan. and Feb. Combined ticket to Woodlawn and Pope-Leighey House: $8 adults, $6 senior citizens and students.*

4 Unlike Mount Vernon, **Gunston Hall,** 15 miles away in Lorton, is rarely crowded with visitors. This was the home of a lesser-known George: George Mason, father of the Bill of Rights. He was one of the framers of the Constitution, then refused to sign it because it did not prohibit slavery, adequately restrain the powers of the federal government, or include a bill of rights. The interior of the house, with its carved woodwork in styles ranging from Chinese to Gothic, has been meticulously restored, using paints made from the original recipes and with carefully carved replacements for the intricate mahogany medallions in the moldings. The grounds—with formal gardens featuring large boxwood hedges—may look familiar, since the last scene in the 1987 movie *Broadcast News* was filmed here, by the gazebo. *U.S. 1S to VA 242S, tel. 703/550–9220. Admission: $5 adults, $4 senior citizens, $1.50 children. Open daily 9:30–5. Closed Christmas.*

5 Nine miles north of Mount Vernon is **Alexandria,** where the Mount Vernon Memorial Highway becomes the George Washington Memorial Parkway. Established in 1749, this city once dwarfed Georgetown, which is just across the Potomac. That was before the Revolution; today Alexandria proudly maintains an identity separate from that of the federal capital. The historic area is Old Town; its main arteries are Washington Street (the parkway as it passes through town) and King Street, which divide the town east–west and north–south, respectively. The shopping (art, antiques, and specialty) is of high quality, as are the sights. Most points of interest are on the east (Potomac) side of Washington Street. Visit them on foot if you are able to walk for 20 blocks or so. Parking is scarce, but the Convention Bureau (*see* Important Addresses and Numbers, *above*) will give you a 72-hour parking permit for the two-hour metered zones, along with a walking tour map. It also offers foreign translations and a video orientation.

Among the town's attractions is the **Boyhood Home of Robert E. Lee,** where he lived off and on for 13 years. The 1795 Georgian town house is furnished in antiques that reflect life in the 1820s. *607 Oronoco St., tel. 703/548–8454. Admission: $3 adults, $1.50 senior citizens, $1 children (under 11 free). Open Mon.–Sat. 10–4, Sun. noon–4. Closed Thanksgiving and Dec. 15–Feb. 1.*

Across the street is the **Lee-Fendall House,** built in 1785 by an in-law and lived in by Lees until 1903. The interior reflects styles from a variety of periods and includes Lee-family furnishings. Labor leader John L. Lewis lived here from 1937 until 1969. *614 Oronoco St., tel. 703/548–1789. Admission: $3 adults, $1 children (under 11 free). Open Tues.–Sat. 10–4, Sun. noon–4. Closed holidays and Mon. The Lee homes sometimes close for private functions; call ahead.*

Christ Church looks much the same as it did when George Washington worshiped here. His pew and that of Robert E. Lee, who was confirmed in the church, are marked by silver commemorative plates. The churchyard contains the graves of several Confederate dead, among others. *118 N. Washington Street at Cameron intersection, tel. 703/549–1450. Admission free. Open Mon.–Sat. 9–4, Sun. noon–4:30. Closed (except for services) major holidays.*

Time Out Take a break for a pint of Guinness or Harp and perhaps a ploughman's lunch (pickles and cheese) at **Murphy's** (713 King St., tel. 703/548–1717). At night this brick-walled pub and restaurant, on two floors of an 18th-century building, resounds with an Irish sing-along.

Gadsby's Tavern Museum comprises two buildings: the tavern and the hotel. The former was built in 1770, 22 years before the latter. General Washington reviewed his troops for the last time from the steps of this building. Lafayette was entertained here during his 1824 visit. The rooms in the tavern have been convincingly restored to their appearance in the 1790s. *134 N. Royal St., tel. 703/838–4242. Admission: $3 adults, $1 children (under 11 free). Open Tues.–Sat. 10–5, Sun. 1–5. Closed major holidays.*

The **Alexandria Black History Resource Center** has two galleries on African-American life in Alexandria. A permanent gallery displays artifacts of local importance, and an art gallery features rotating exhibits by African-American artists. *638 N. Alfred St., tel. 703/838–4356. Admission free. Open Tues.–Sat. 10–4.*

Modern Alexandria is represented by the extremely popular
6 **Torpedo Factory Art Center.** About 180 artists and craftsmen have their studios (with wares for sale) within this renovated waterfront building where torpedo parts were manufactured during the two world wars. The center also houses exhibits of the city's archaeology program (one of the nation's largest and oldest) and laboratories, where you can observe work in progress. *105 N. Union St., tel. 703/838–4565. Admission free. Center: open daily 10–5. Closed Thanksgiving, Christmas, New Year's Day. Archaeology Section: (tel. 703/838–4399) open Tues.–Sat. 10–5 (laboratory open Fri.–Sat. 11–5).*

Visitors will find the grand **Carlyle House** (1753) at the corner of Cameron and Fairfax streets. The Georgian structure was the manor house of a riverside estate, the home of John Carlyle, a Scottish merchant who was one of Alexandria's founders. General Edward Braddock met here with five royal governors in 1755 to plan the strategy and funding of the early campaigns in the French and Indian War. The decor of the house remains 18th-century, with the original woodwork, Chippendale furniture throughout, and decorative items that include Chinese export porcelain. An architectural exhibit on the second floor explains how the house was built. *121 N. Fairfax St., tel. 703/549–2997. Admission: $3 adults, $1.50 senior citizens, $1 children 11–17 (under 11 free). Open Tues.–Sat. 10–5, Sun. 1–5.*

From Alexandria, proceed northward on the Parkway and take in the skyline of Washington, DC across the river. This is a stirring panorama of the famous buildings and monuments in the nation's capital. At Memorial Bridge, cross over into Washington and turn back around. It is worth leaving Virginia for just a moment in order to make this most impressive approach to
7 **Arlington National Cemetery**. Directly behind you, on the Washington side, is the Lincoln Memorial; ahead, high atop a hill, is Robert E. Lee's Arlington House, and a little below it is the eternal flame that marks the grave of John F. Kennedy. All this is aligned with the bridge, and the effect of the arrangement is stunning.

In the cemetery are thousands of veterans buried beneath simple white headstones. The many famous Americans interred here include President Taft, Oliver Wendell Holmes, George C. Marshall, Joe Louis, and John and Robert Kennedy. In and around the Tomb of the Unknown Soldier are the graves of men killed in both world wars, Korea, and Vietnam. It is guarded constantly by members of the Old Guard: 1st Battalion (Reinforced), 3d Infantry. A changing-of-the-guard ceremony takes place every half-hour from 8 to 5 April–September, hourly the rest of the year. *Tel. 703/545–6700. Admission free. Open daily 8–5 Nov.–Mar., 8–7 rest of year.*

Within the cemetery is **Arlington House,** where Robert E. Lee lived for 30 years, until his job obliged him to leave the proximity of the Union capital. The Union confiscated the estate during the Civil War, when Arlington began to function as a cemetery. The massive house is of Greek Revival design, reminiscent of a temple, and is furnished in antiques and reproductions. The view of Washington from the portico is as gorgeous as the sight of the house from the bridge. *Tel. 703/557-0613. Admission free. Open daily 9:30–4:30 Oct.–Mar., 9:30–6 rest of year. Closed Christmas and New Year's.*

A narrated bus tour of Arlington National Cemetery, with stops at Arlington House, the Tomb of the Unknown Soldier, and the Kennedy graves, is given by Tourmobile (tel. 202/554-7020). Tours leave from the visitor center on the site starting at 8 AM. *Cost: $2.75 adults, $1.25 children. Buses operate 8:30–6.*

8 Fifty miles south of Washington on I–95 is **Fredericksburg,** which rivals Alexandria and Mount Vernon for Washington-family associations. The first president lived at nearby Ferry Farm (across the Rappahannock River) between the ages of six and 16 and later bought a house for his mother here, near his sister and brother.

Washington's only sister, Betty, married her cousin Fielding Lewis in 1750, and they built **Kenmore** a few years later. The plain exterior belies the lavish interior; these have been called some of the most beautiful rooms in America. The plaster moldings in the ceilings are even more ornate than Mount Vernon's. Of equal elegance are the furnishings, including a large standing clock that belonged to Betty's mother, Mary. In the reconstructed kitchen next door you can enjoy tea and a fresh facsimile of Mary Washington's gingerbread. *1201 Washington Ave., tel. 703/373-3381. Admission: $5 adults, $2.50 children. Open daily 9–5 Mar.–Nov., 10–4 rest of year. Closed Christmas Eve and Day, and New Year's Eve and Day.*

In 1760, George Washington's brother Charles built as his home what became the **Rising Sun Tavern,** a watering hole for such pre-Revolutionary patriots as the Lee brothers, Patrick Henry, Washington, and Jefferson. A "wench" in period costume leads the tour without stepping out of character. From her perspective you watch the activity—day and night, upstairs and down—at this busy institution. In the tap room, you are served spiced tea. *1306 Caroline St., tel. 703/371-1494. Admission: $3 adults, 75¢ children. Open daily 9–5 Mar.–Nov., 10–4 rest of year. Closed Thanksgiving, Christmas Eve and Day, and New Year's Eve and Day.*

On Charles Street is the modest white **Home of Mary Washington.** George purchased it for her in 1772, and she spent the last 17 years of her life here, tending the charming garden where her boxwood still flourishes and where many a bride and groom now come to exchange their vows. *Charles and Lewis Sts., tel. 703/373-1569. Admission: $3 adults, 75¢ children. Open daily 9–5 Mar.–Nov., 10–4 rest of year. Closed Thanksgiving, Christmas Eve and Day, and New Year's Eve and Day.*

Dr. Mercer might have been more careful than most other Colonial physicians, yet his methods will make you cringe. At the **Hugh Mercer Apothecary Shop,** a costumed hostess will explicitly describe amputations and cataract operations. You will also hear about therapeutic bleeding and see the gruesome devices used in Colonial dentistry. This is an informative if slightly nauseating look at life two centuries ago. *Caroline and Amelia Sts., tel. 703/371-3486. Admission: $3 adults, 75¢ children. Open daily 9–5 Mar.–Nov., 10–4 rest of year. Closed Thanksgiving, Christmas Eve and Day, and New Year's Eve and Day.*

The **James Monroe Museum and Memorial Library** is the tiny one-story building where the future fifth president of the United States practiced law from 1787 to 1789. In this building are many of Monroe's possessions, collected and preserved by his family until this century, including the desk on which Monroe signed the doctrine named for him. *908 Charles St., tel. 703/373–8426. Admission: $3 adults, 75¢ children. Open daily 9–5. Closed Thanksgiving, Christmas Eve and Day, and New Year's Eve and Day.*

Chatham Manor is a fine example of Georgian architecture, built between 1768 and 1771 by William Fitzhugh on a site overlooking the Rappahannock River and the town of Fredericksburg. Fitzhugh, a plantation owner, frequently hosted such luminaries as Washington and Jefferson. At the time of the Civil War, Union forces commandeered the house and converted it into a headquarters and hospital. President Lincoln conferred here with his generals; Clara Barton, founder of the American Red Cross, and the poet Walt Whitman tended the wounded. Later its owners restored the house and gardens and gave the property to the National Park Service. Concerts are often given here in summer. *Chatham La., tel. 703/373–4461. Admission: free. Open daily 9–5. Closed Christmas and New Year's.*

Time Out Stop for a gourmet sandwich or some quiche at the **Made in Virginia Store Deli** (807 Caroline St., tel. 703/371–2030). Do not skip the rich desserts.

Four nearby Civil War battlefields—Fredericksburg, Chancellorsville, the Wilderness, and Spotsylvania Courthouse—con-
9 stitute the **Fredericksburg and Spotsylvania National Military Park.** All are within 17 miles of Fredericksburg. At the in-town visitor's center for the park, there's a slide show about the battles and there are two floors of exhibits. On the fields, signs and exhibits point out moments in the battles. *1013 Lafayette Blvd. (U.S. 1), tel. 703/373–4461. Admission free. Open 8:30–6:30 June 15–Labor Day, weekdays, 9–5 and weekends 9–6 rest of year. Closed Christmas and New Year's.*

Heading west from Washington instead of south brings you to
10 another major Civil War battlefield: **Manassas National Battlefield Park.** The self-guided tour begins at the visitor center, which offers exhibits and audiovisual presentations that greatly enhance the visit. Here the Confederacy won two important victories—and Stonewall Jackson won his famous nickname. It's a 26-mile drive: Take I–66 west to Route 234 (don't be fooled by the earlier Manassas exit for Route 28); the visitor center is half a mile north on the right. *Tel. 703/754–7107. Admission: $1 adults, children under 16 and senior citizens free. The visitor center is open daily 8:30–6 in summer, 8:30–5 rest of year; the park is open until dusk.*

After Manassas, return to I–66, following it west to U.S. 15,
11 the road to horse country. The major towns here, in **Loudoun County,** are Leesburg and Middleburg, where residents claim the living is some of the best in Virginia and prove it with their gracious homes, fox hunts, and steeplechases. Touring the well-tended countryside is a pleasure; its history is detailed in exhibits at the **Loudoun County Museum and Visitors Center** in Leesburg (16 W. Loudoun St., tel. 703/777–7427). This is the place to pick up information on scenic drives and area attrac-

tions. Of the latter, three in particular capture the horsey atmosphere of this fine green county.

12 **Oatlands,** six miles south of Leesburg on U.S. 15, is a former 5,000-acre plantation built by a great-grandson of the famous King Carter. In 1827, a stately portico was added to the original 1803 manor house. The house has been beautifully restored, and the manicured fields that remain host a variety of public and private equestrian events from spring to fall—including April's popular Loudoun Hunt Point-to-Point, a steeplechase that brings out the whole community for picnics on blankets and tailgates, and Draft Horse and Mule Day in late summer, when competing teams flex their muscles in pulling contests and craftspeople spread out their wares for an all-day fair. *Tel. 703/777–3174. Admission: $5 adults, $4 students and senior citizens; children under 12 free weekdays. Other charges apply for special events. Open Mon.–Sat. 10–4:30, Sun. 1–4:30. Closed from just before Christmas until mid-Mar.*

13 A mile north of Leesburg is **Morven Park,** a mansion open to the public, as well as a stronghold of horsedom: The **Westmoreland Davis Equestrian Institute** (a private riding school), the **Winmill Carriage Museum** (boasting over 100 horse-drawn vehicles), and the **Museum of Hounds and Hunting** make their home on this 1,200-acre estate. The price of admission includes entrance to 16 rooms in the mansion and the two museums. *Rte. 7 north from Leesburg, then follow signs, tel. 703/777–2414. Admission: $4 adults, $3.75 senior citizens, $2 children. Open Tues.–Sat. 10–5, Sun. 1–5 Memorial Day–Labor Day. Closed mid-Oct.–first week in May, weekends only at other times (call ahead).*

North of Leesburg, just over the border in West Virginia, is
14 **Harper's Ferry National Historic Park,** where John Brown atempted to free slaves in 1859. Brown, a radical abolitionist, was hanged following his failed uprising. Visitors can explore the park's interpretive center and learn more about Harper's Ferry's tumultuous role in the Civil War. *Take Rte. 7 north to Rte. 9, Harper's Ferry, WV, tel. 304/535–6223. Admission free. Open daily 8–5.*

What to See and Do with Children

The **Pet Farm Park** in Vienna, Fairfax County, is inhabited by ostriches, giant tortoises, baboons, zebras, and other exotica, plus domestic farm animals. The whole family can take a hayride, and there are pony and elephant rides for the children. *Adjacent to Lake Fairfax, on Hunter Mill Rd., at the intersection of Leesburg Pike (Rte. 7) and Rte. 606, tel. 703/759–3636 or 759–3637. Admission: Weekdays $5.25 adults, $4.25 children; weekends $6.25 adults, $5.25 children. Open daily 10–5 May 15–Labor Day; weekdays 10–3, weekends 10–5 rest of year.*

At **Wolf Trap Farm Park,** also in Vienna (Rte. 7, I–495 Exit 10W), performances for children—including mime, puppets, animal shows, music, drama, and storytelling—are held throughout the year. The first Saturday of each month from October through May, there are two shows a day in The Barns ($10–$15; tel. 703/255–1939). From mid-July through August, daily performances take place at the outdoor Theater in the Woods (admission free; tel. 703/255–1823). On Labor Day weekend, a three-day International Children's Festival brings together performers from the States and abroad (admission per day: $6 adults, $4 children; tel. 703/255–1939).

Off the Beaten Track

On display at Alexandria's 333-foot-high **George Washington Masonic National Memorial** is furniture and regalia that Washington used during his stint as Charter Master of the local Masonic Lodge. Exhibits demystify the legendary international organization, explaining its traditions, aims, and activities—unless there is something they are not telling us. Every 45 minutes until 4 PM, an elevator tour takes you to the top for a singular view of the town and of Washington nearby. *A 20-min walk from the river, or ride the DASH bus west on King St. to Shooter's Hill (60¢ exact change, includes transfer for return trip). Admission free. Open daily 9–5. Closed Thanksgiving, Christmas, and New Year's Day.*

Participant Sports

Bicycling The **Mount Vernon Bicycle Trail** (tel. 703/285–2598) is 19 miles of asphalt along the shore of the Potomac and through Alexandria. **Burke Lake Park Bicycle Trail** (tel. 703/323–6600) in Fairfax County is 4.7 miles long. The **Arlington Parks and Recreation Bureau** (tel. 703/358–3317) has a free map of the Arlington County Bikeway System, available on request. The **Washington and Old Dominion Railroad Regional Trail** (better known by hikers) follows the roadbed of the "Virginia Creeper" tracks from Shirlington (near I–95) to Purcelleville, 44 miles away in the Allegheny foothills (tel. 703/941–5000). The **Fredericksburg Visitor's Center** (tel. 703/373–1776) has mapped out rides of 3, 9, and 20 miles that take in the historical and natural beauty of the town.

Golf **Algonkian Park** in Leesburg (tel. 703/450–4655), **Burke Lake Park** in Fairfax (tel. 703/323–1641), in Fredericksburg **Shannon Green Resort** (tel. 703/786–8385) and **Twin Lakes Course** (tel. 703/631–9099) have 18-hole courses.

Horseback Riding **Paper Chase Farms** (off Rte. 50 in Middleburg, tel. 703/687–5255), set in rolling green hills just beneath the Blueridge Mountains, offers riding lessons and stables with close to 50 horses in its two barns.

Ice Skating Indoor rinks include **Fairfax Ice Arena** (tel. 703/323–1131) and **Mount Vernon Recreation Center** (tel. 703/768–3223).

Tennis There are dozens of public courts all over the Virginia suburbs of Washington; many are lighted and some are accessible to the disabled. For a directory of courts in Fairfax county, call **Fairfax County Park Authority** (tel. 703/246–5700).

Spectator Sports

Check the sports pages of the *Washington Post* or the *Fairfax Journal* for events at George Mason University, which run the gamut of intercollegiate athletics. The Fredericksburg *Free-lance Star* lists events at Mary Washington College.

Dining

The most highly recommended restaurants in each price category are indicated by a star ★.

Category	Cost*
Very Expensive	over $30
Expensive	$20–$30
Moderate	$10–$20
Inexpensive	under $10

**per person without tax (4.5% sales tax plus local tax), service, or drinks*

Alexandria
American

View. With three walls of picture windows, this 14th-floor restaurant atop the Key Bridge Marriott Hotel more than fulfills the promise of its name. The Washington Monument and the spires of Georgetown University are among the most prominent landmarks seen across the Potomac. The interior is mostly burgundy—the carpeting, the leather banquettes, the wallpaper, even the ceiling. Prominent entrées include broiled lobster, served out of the shell with an unusual cucumber flan; and medallions of New York strip steak, broiled in Jack Daniels sauce and served with hot peppers. This is a grazing restaurant; all the entrées are also available as appetizers, in one form or another. A salad of seasonal fruit is served warm with chicken and quail. At the popular Sunday brunch buffet, swordfish and oysters are among the more than 50 items offered. *Key Bridge Marriott, 1401 Lee Hwy., tel. 703/243–1745. Reservations advised. Dress: casual but neat. AE, D, DC, MC, V. No lunch. Very Expensive.*

Early American

Old Gadsby's Tavern. Located in Old Town, this tavern will take you back 200 years with its decor, cuisine, and unique entertainment. While you dine, John Douglas Hall, in the costume and character of an 18th-century gentleman, performs on the lute and chats about the latest news and gossip of Colonial Virginia. The tavern, built in 1792, was a favorite of George Washington's, and he is remembered today on the menu, with George Washington's Favorite Duck: cornbread-stuffed roast duck with fruit-and-madeira sauce. Other special offerings are Colonial Game Pye, of lamb, pork, and rabbit; Sally Lunn bread; and rich English trifle. Upstairs is a museum showing authentic table settings and the section of the tavern that was once a hotel. *138 N. Royal St., tel. 703/548–1288. Dress: informal. Reservations advised. AE, DC, MC, V. Moderate.*

Greek
★

Taverna Cretekou. Whitewashed stucco walls and brightly colored macramé tapestries bring the Mediterranean to the center of Old Town. In the warm months, you can dine in the canopied garden. The Lamb Exohikon—lamb baked in a pastry shell—and the swordfish kabob are especially good. All wines served are Greek. *818 King St., tel. 703/548–8688. Dress: informal. Reservations advised. AE, DC, MC, V. Closed Mon. Moderate.*

Arlington
Vietnamese
★

Cafe Dalat. Photos and silkscreens of Vietnamese scenery decorate this restaurant, which caters to the area's large Vietnamese population. Try the Fairy Combination, crispy noodles with chicken, scallops, shrimp, and mixed vegetables; beef wrapped in grape leaves; or any fish dish. Portions are generous. *3143 Wilson Blvd., tel. 703/276–0935. Dress: informal. Reservations not needed. No credit cards. Inexpensive.*

Fredericksburg
French

Le Lafayette. Enjoy well-prepared French cuisine made with fresh Virginia ingredients and served in a colonial setting in a 1771 Georgian-style house. Recommended are both the brook trout and Chesapeake Bay seafood, plus the imaginative Continental dishes such as grilled breast of duck in red currant sauce over fresh, braised red cabbage; poached filet of salmon in saffron broth with mussels, leeks, and tomatoes; and pecan-crusted rack of lamb. *623 Caroline St., tel. 703/373–6895. Dress: casual. Reservations advised. AE, DC, MC, V. Lunch 11:30–3, dinner 5:30–10:30 Tues.–Thurs., 5–11 Fri.–Sat., 5:30–9:30 Sun. Expensive.*

Italian

Ristorante Renato. This unlikely Italian restaurant in the center of a Colonial town has a strong if coventional menu. Romeo and Juliet is a dish of veal and chicken covered with mozzarella and swimming in white-wine sauce; the Shrimp Scampi Napoli has a butter-lemon sauce. *Williams and Prince Edward Sts., tel. 703/371–8228. Dress: informal. Reservations advised on weekends. AE, MC, V. Moderate.*

Great Falls
Country French
★

L'Auberge Chez François. At this spot about 35 minutes northwest of Arlington, Alsatian cuisine is served in a country-inn atmosphere. The building, of white stucco and dark exposed beams, is set on six acres, with a garden that can be seen from the dining room. Inside, two fireplaces, flowered tablecloths, and stained glass set the mood for such specialties as salmon soufflé—fillet of salmon topped with a mousse of scallops and salmon and a white-wine or lobster sauce. *332 Springvale Rd. (Rte. 674), tel. 703/759–3800. Jacket required. Reserve 2 weeks ahead. AE, MC, V. Closed Mon. Dinner only (from 2 PM on Sun.). Very Expensive.*

Tyson's Corner
American

Clyde's. This is a superior branch of the popular Georgetown pub. Its four dining rooms offer a choice of styles—such as the Palm Terrace, with high ceilings and lots of greenery—but all are basically Art Deco; one room is formal. The long, electic menu always includes fresh fish of the season, in such preparations as trout Parmesan. The wine list is equally long. Quality is high, and service is attentive. *8332 Leesburg Pike, tel. 703/734–1901. Dress: informal (except jacket in formal room). Reservations suggested. AE, D, DC, MC, V. Expensive.*

Lodging

The most highly recommended properties in each price category are indicated by a star ★.

Category	Cost*
Very Expensive	over $120
Expensive	$90–$120
Moderate	$50–$90
Inexpensive	under $50

**double room, highest rate in peak season; add 4.5% sales tax plus local tax*

Alexandria ★ **Holiday Inn–Old Town.** This luxury hotel's rooms are decorated in Federal style, with such high-tech touches as "executive phones" with computer-modem capabilities. Bathrooms have marble tubs and floors. *480 King St., 22314, tel. 703/549–6080 or 800/465–4329. 227 rooms. Facilities: indoor pool and sauna, restaurant, disco, barber shop, beauty shop. AE, D, DC, MC, V. Very Expensive.*

★ **Morrison House.** This small, luxurious hotel in Old Town is decorated in Federal style throughout, complete with four-poster beds. Afternoon tea is served as it must have been 200 years ago. *116 S. Alfred St., 22314, tel. 703/838–8000. 42 rooms, 3 suites. Facilities: 24-hr butler and room service, French restaurant. AE, DC, MC, V. Very Expensive.*

Arlington **Holiday Inn–National Airport.** A basic high-rise Holiday Inn off the highway, with modern, cheerful decor and a convenient location a mile from the airport. *1489 Jefferson Davis Hwy., 22202, tel. 703/521–1600 or 800/465–4329. 295 rooms, 11 suites. Facilities: outdoor pool, restaurant bar, racquetball club adjacent. AE, D, DC, MC, V. Very Expensive.*

Marriott Crystal Gateway. This modern, elegant hotel caters to the business traveler and the tourist who wants to be pampered. Its two towers rise 17 stories above the highway. Inside, there's black marble, blond wood, Oriental touches, and lots of greenery. Rooms are modern. *1700 Jefferson Davis Hwy., 22202, tel. 703/920–3230 or 800/228–9290. 592 rooms, 110 suites. Facilities: indoor/outdoor pools; health spa with whirlpool, sauna, and exercise rooms; 4 restaurants and lounges; nightclub. AE, DC, MC, V. Very Expensive.*

Fredericksburg **Best Western–Johnny Appleseed.** This family-oriented two-story motel is five minutes from the battlefields. Rooms are motel basic; queen-size beds are available. *543 Warrenton Rd. (U.S. 17 at Jct. I–95), 22405, tel. 703/373–0000 or 800/528–1234. 85 units, 1 suite, 4 efficiencies. Facilities: outdoor pool, playground, nature trail, volleyball, restaurant, free HBO. AE, D, DC, MC, V. Inexpensive.*

Hampton Inn. A cheerful and comfortable new motel on the interstate, near the historic district. *2310 Plank Rd., 22401, tel. 703/371–0330 or 800/426–7866. 166 rooms, including king suites with whirlpools. Facilities: outdoor pool, Continental breakfast. AE, D, DC, MC, V. Inexpensive.*

Tyson's Corner **Ramada Hotel.** This luxury hotel and convention center has spent $21 million on renovation and additions recently. It is a high-rise property on the highway, about 10 miles west of Arlington. *7801 Leesburg Pike (Rte. 7 and I–495), 22043, tel. 703/893–1340 or 800/228–2828. 391 rooms, 13 suites. Facilities: indoor pool, sauna, whirlpool, exercise room, restaurant, nightclub. AE, D, DC, MC, V. Expensive.*

The Arts

The **Fairfax County Council of the Arts** (tel. 703/642–0862) is a clearinghouse for information on performances and exhibitions all over Northern Virginia.

The **Wolf Trap Farm Park for the Performing Arts,** in Vienna, operates out of a grand outdoor pavilion in the warmer months, and the rest of the year in the Barns (18th-century farm buildings transported from upstate New York). The best performers appear here, in programs that span the whole range of musical entertainment except extreme rock, plus dance. It is one of the major performing-arts venues for the entire area around Washington (*see also* What to See and Do with Children, *above*). *I-495 Exit 11S, tel. 703/255-1860. The Barns: tel. 703/938-2404.*

The **Harris Theater** at George Mason University (tel. 703/323-2075) is the scene of acclaimed student drama. The **Lazy Susan Dinner Theater** (tel. 703/550-7384) has a varied program all year long.

Nightlife

Bluegrass In Arlington, **Whitey's** (tel. 703/525-9825) is a crowded, noisy, and irresistible dive with a loyal following of diverse ages and backgrounds.

Irish and Folk **Murphy's Grand Irish Pub** in Alexandria (tel. 703/548-1717) has a fire blazing in winter and boisterous entertainment all year. **The Old Brogue** (tel. 703/759-2759) has lively music.

Jazz Upstairs at Alexandria's **Two Nineteen** (tel. 703/549-1141) there's jazz, or hang out in the basement sports bar. **Buffalo Roam Restaurant** in Fredericksburg (tel. 703/373-2833) alternates jazz with bluegrass and offers comedy on the upper level.

Singles **Clyde's** in Tyson's Corner (tel. 703/734-1901) is famous all over the DC area as a mecca for unattached professionals.

Richmond

At the fall line of the James River, 71 miles southeast of Charlottesville, is the capital of the Commonwealth: Richmond. Discovered in 1607, it replaced Williamsburg as the capital in 1779 and became the capital of the Confederate States in 1861.

Richmond's historical significance alone makes it an important place to visit; moreover, it is a metropolis surprisingly lively and sophisticated for its size (the population is under a quarter of a million—second in Virginia to the bustling Norfolk–Virginia Beach–Hampton Roads complex. Following years of urban decay, this pinnacle of the Old South is prospering anew. Long a center for shipping and banking, it has fostered high-technology and the heavier industries in order to flourish. The results can be seen in an array of distinctive neighborhoods.

Monument Avenue is a wide thoroughfare lined with stately houses, divided by a verdant median, and punctuated by statues of Civil War heroes. Two of the major streets retain their traditional identifications: Main with banks and Grace with shops. Shockoe Slip is several blocks of warehouses converted into a fashionable shopping-and-entertainment zone on Cary Street, between 12th and 15th streets. The James Center, adjoining Shockoe, is a complex of shops, office buildings, and restaurants. The Fan District—so called because its streets fan out to the west from Laurel Street—is bordered by Monument Avenue on the north, Main Street on the south, and The Boulevard on the west. This treasury of restored turn-of-the-century town houses has been the "hip" neighborhood for several decades. It may, in time, be succeeded as such by venerable Church Hill to the east (the area around St. John's Church, at

25th and Broad Sts.), which is still more fashionable than safe after dark.

Arriving and Departing

By Plane Richmond International Airport (tel. 804/226–3000), recently expanded, is served by 12 airlines, including **American** (tel. 800/433–7300), **Delta** (tel. 800/293–6111), **United** (tel. 800/241–6522), and **USAir,** the major regional carrier. A taxi ride downtown from the airport is $16–$18.

By Train **Amtrak** (tel. 800/872–7245) trains headed north toward New York and south toward Florida or Newport News pass through here daily. The station is at 7519 Staples Mill Road.

By Bus **Greyhound/Trailways Lines** (2910 N. Boulevard, tel. 804/254–5910).

By Car Richmond is at the intersection of Interstates 95 and 64, which run north–south and east–west, respectively. U.S. 1 and U.S. 301 also run north–south by the city.

Getting Around

By Bus and Trolley **Greater Richmond Transit** (101 S. Davis Ave., tel. 804/358–4782) operates a bus and a trolley service. Public buses run from 5 AM to 12:30 AM daily. The fares are 75¢–$1.20, exact change. Free trolley service is available within downtown Richmond Monday through Saturday from 11 AM to 11 PM.

By Taxi Taxis are metered and charge $1.50 the first ⅕ mile, $1.50 for each additional passenger.

Important Addresses and Numbers

Tourist Information The **Virginia Division of Tourism** (1021 E. Cary St., 23219, tel. 800/932–5827) maintains another office in the Old Bell Tower on the grounds of the Capitol (9th St., tel. 804/786–4484). The **Metro Richmond Visitor's Center** is at 1700 Robin Hood Road (Exit 14 off Interstates 95 and 64, tel. 804/358–5511).

Emergencies Dial 911 for emergency assistance.

Minor Emergencies There are 24 walk-in medical-care centers in and around town; check the Yellow Pages for those nearest you.

24-hour Pharmacy **People's Drug Store,** 2730 W. Broad St. (tel. 804/359–2497).

Guided Tours

Orientation On weekends, the **Cultural Link Trolley,** leaving from the Science Museum, makes a continuous 55-minute loop, stopping at 34 cultural and historic landmarks. You can pace yourself, getting on and off when and where you like. *Tel. 804/358–GRTC. Cost: per day: $5 adults, $2.50 children, under 5 free. Runs Sat. 10–5, Sun. 12:30–5:30.*

Guided Tours **Historic Richmond Foundation** (tel. 804/780–0107) gives various bus and walking tours. **Winning Tours** (804/358–6666).

Boat Tours **Historic Richmond Foundation** (tel. 804/780–0107) offers specialized scenic-tour and dining cruises. **Richmond Discoveries** (tel. 804/795–5781) provides special group tours along the James River.

Exploring Richmond

Numbers in the margin correspond to points of interest on the Richmond map.

Start downtown at the **Court End** district, the heart of old Richmond, which includes seven national historic landmarks, three museums, and 11 other buildings on the National Register of Historic Places—all within eight blocks. At any one of the museums you will receive a self-guided walking tour with the purchase of a discount block ticket ($9 adults, $8.50 senior citizens, $4 children 7–12; groups of 10 or more are $6 per person), good for all admission fees.

1 The first museum, the **John Marshall House,** was built in 1790 by the Chief Justice of the Supreme Court, who was also secretary of state and ambassador to France. It is now fully restored and furnished with a convincing mix of period pieces and heirlooms. *9th and Marshall Sts., tel. 804/648–7998. Admission: $3 adults, $2.50 senior citizens, $1.25 children. Open Tues.–Sat. 10–5, Sun. 1–5. Closed major holidays.*

2 The **Valentine Museum,** in the former home of sculptor Edward Valentine, is devoted to the life and history of Richmond. Exhibits include Early American clothing and toys. The building will remain open throughout its current extensive restoration, which is fascinating to observe in progress. *1015 E. Clay St., tel. 804/649–0711. Admission: $3.50 adults, $3 senior citizens, $2.75 students, $1.50 children. Open Memorial Day–Labor Day, Mon.–Thurs. 10–7, Fri.–Sun. 10–5; Labor Day–Memorial Day, Mon.–Sat. 10–5, Sun. noon–5.*

3 The **Jackson Ward Historic District** comprises the region between Broad and Leigh streets, bounded by Belvidere Street
to the west and 2nd Street to the east. Notable for its old homes
and rich history as Richmond's 19th- and early 20th-century
4 African-American community, it's also home to the **Maggie
Lena Walker House.** Maggie Walker was the first African-
American (not to mention female) bank president in nation; she
founded the Saint Luke Penny Savings Bank in 1903. The house
is now a museum containing artifacts relevant to the Jackson
Ward District's history. *110 Leigh St., tel. 804/780–1380. Admission free. Open Tues.–Sun. 9–5.*

5 The **Museum and White House of the Confederacy** are better seen in that order. The former offers elaborate permanent exhibitions on the Civil War era. The "world's largest collection of Confederate memorabilia" features such relics as the sword General Lee wore for the surrender at Appomattox. At the White House, next door, preservationists have painstakingly re-created the interior as it was during the Civil War, when Jefferson Davis lived here. *1201 E. Clay St., tel. 804/649–1861. Admission to both sites (1 site): $7 ($4) adults; $5 ($3.50) senior citizens; $3.50 ($2.25) children 7–12, under 7 free. Open Mon.–Sat. 10–5, Sun. 1–5. Closed holidays.*

6 The **Virginia State Capitol** was designed by Thomas Jefferson in 1785. Inside is a wealth of sculpture, including busts of each of the eight presidents Virginia has given the nation; also the famous life-size, and lifelike, statue of George Washington by Jean-Antoine Houdon. In the old Hall of the House of Delegates, Robert E. Lee accepted the command of the Confederate forces in Virginia. Also on the grounds is the Old Bell

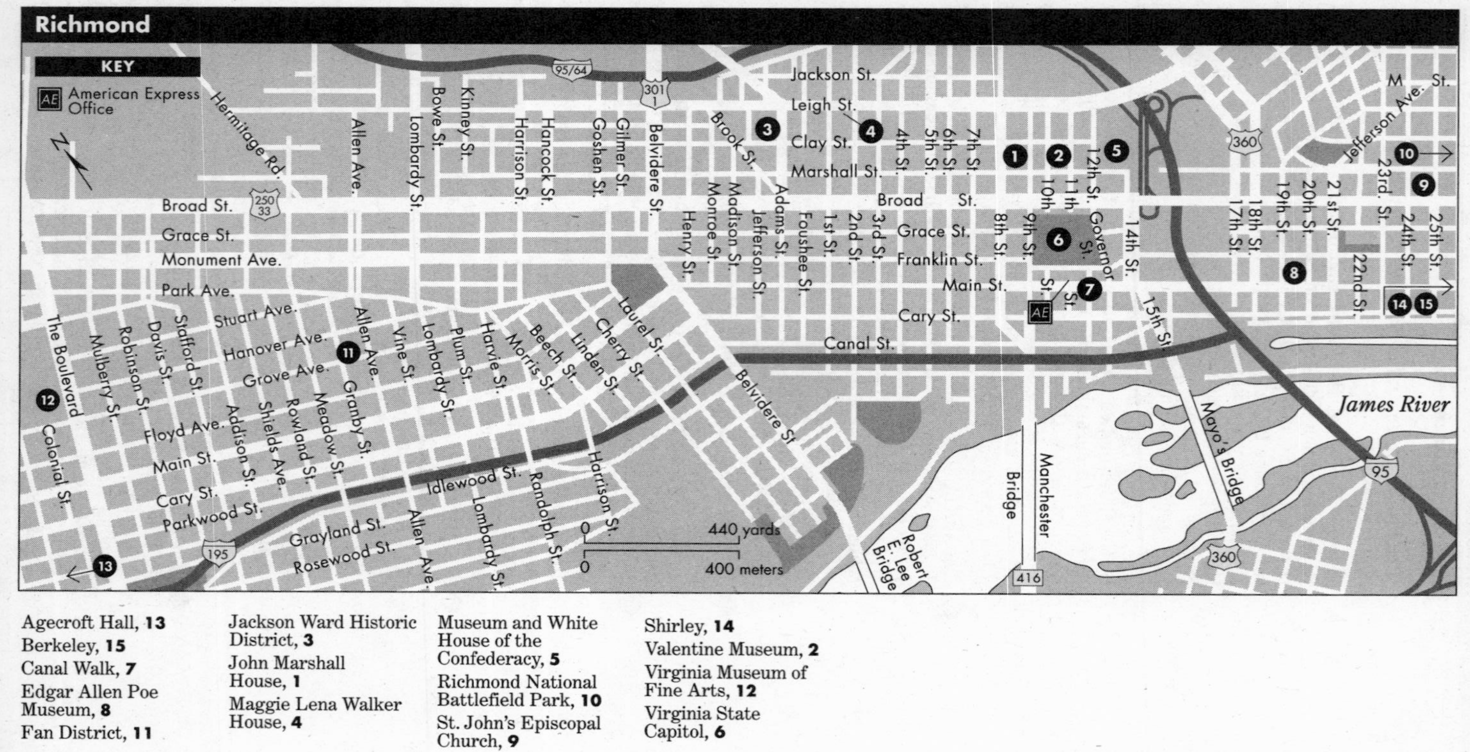

Agecroft Hall, **13**
Berkeley, **15**
Canal Walk, **7**
Edgar Allen Poe Museum, **8**
Fan District, **11**
Jackson Ward Historic District, **3**
John Marshall House, **1**
Maggie Lena Walker House, **4**
Museum and White House of the Confederacy, **5**
Richmond National Battlefield Park, **10**
St. John's Episcopal Church, **9**
Shirley, **14**
Valentine Museum, **2**
Virginia Museum of Fine Arts, **12**
Virginia State Capitol, **6**

Tower, where you can get travel information about the whole state. *Capitol Sq., tel. 804/786–4344. Admission free. Open daily 9–5 Apr.–Nov.; Mon.–Sat. 9–5, Sun. 1–5 rest of year. Closed Thanksgiving, Christmas, and New Year's Day.*

Across 9th Street from Capital Square is **St. Paul's Church,** where Jefferson Davis, president of the Confederacy, was at Sunday worship in 1865 when he received word from Lee that his Confederates could no longer hold Richmond.

7 The **Canal Walk** starts south of the Capitol at 12th and Main and follows the locks of the James River–Kanawha Canal, proposed by George Washington. At 12th and Byrd, under the archway, watch a free slide show (daily 9–5) about the history of the canal. Follow the river to **Brown's Island,** across from the ruins of the Tredegar Iron Works. The island, terminus of the scenic walk, boasts a heliport and some unique sculptures, and hosts concerts in season.

Leaving downtown Richmond, follow Main Street east to the
8 Church Hill Historic District and the **Edgar Allan Poe Museum,** inside the Old Stone House. Poe never lived in the house (built in 1737) that his disciples have turned into a shrine, with some of his possessions on display. The Raven Room is hung with illustrations inspired by his most famous poem. *1914 E. Main St., tel. 804/648–5523. Admission: $5 adults, $4 senior citizens, $3 students. Open Tues.–Sat. 10–4, Sun. and Mon. 1:30–4. Closed Christmas.*

9 Three blocks north is Broad Street, leading east to **St. John's Episcopal Church.** For security reasons, the rebellious Second Virginia Convention met here, instead of at Williamsburg, and on March 23, 1775, Patrick Henry delivered at this church the speech in which he insisted: "Give me liberty or give me death!" *25th and Broad Sts., tel. 804/648–5015. Admission: $2 adults, $1.50 senior citizens, $1 children. Open Mon.–Sat. 10–3:30, Sun. 1–3:30. Closed Easter, Christmas Eve and Day, and New Year's Eve and Day.*

At the eastern end of Broad Street is the visitor center for the
10 **Richmond National Battlefield Park,** the launching point for tours of the Richmond and other Civil War battlefields in the surrounding countryside. Here you can watch a movie about the city during the war and a slide show about the battlefields, then pick up a map to use on your self-guided tour. *3215 E. Broad St., tel. 804/226–1981. Admission free. Open daily 9–5. Closed Christmas and New Year's Day.*

Returning west on Broad Street, turn south on The Boulevard,
11 12 along the edge of the **Fan District,** and you'll come to the **Virginia Museum of Fine Arts,** with major collections from Paul Mellon and Sydney Lewis. The museum's most startling exhibits have to be Duane Hanson's true-to-life wax figures: With their contemporary, unglamorous attire, and provocative poses they fool visitors all the time. But the paintings by Goya, Renoir, Monet, and van Gogh are quite real, and so are the African masks, Roman statuary, Oriental icons, and five Fabergé eggs. *Boulevard and Grove Ave., tel. 804/367–0844. $2 donation suggested. Open Tues.–Sat. 11–5 (Thurs. until 10), Sun. 1–5. Closed July 4, Thanksgiving, Christmas, and New Year's Day.*

Just west of the Fan District, in the Windsor Farms neighbor-
13 hood, is **Agecroft Hall,** built in the 15th century in Lancashire

and transported here in 1925. Set amid gardens, it contains an extensive assortment of Tudor and early Stuart furniture and art plus a few priceless anomalies, such as a Ming vase. *4305 Sulgrave Rd., tel. 804/353–4241. Admission: $3 adults, $2.50 senior citizens, $1.50 students. Open Tues.–Sat. 10–4, Sun. 2–5. Closed major holidays.*

Take VA 5 east toward Williamsburg to see two historic plantation houses less than half an hour from Richmond. The most im-
14 pressive fact about **Shirley** is that the same family, the Carters,
have lived here for 10 generations. Their claim to the land goes back to 1660, when it was settled by a relative, Edward Hill. The house was built in 1723; Robert E. Lee's mother was born here. Your first view of the elegant Georgian manor is a dramatic one: the house stands at the end of an allée lined by towering Lombardy poplars. Inside, the impressive hall staircase rises for three stories without any visible support. *VA 5E to Rte. 608, tel. 804/829–5121. Admission: $6 adults, $5 senior citizens, $4 students under 22, $3 children under 13. Open daily 9–5. Closed Christmas.*

15 Continue east a bit on VA 5 for **Berkeley.** It is said that the first Thanksgiving was celebrated not in Massachusetts but here, on December 4, 1619. The plantation was later the home of U.S. president William Henry Harrison. The Georgian brick house, built in 1726, is furnished with period antiques, not original pieces. The gardens are in excellent condition, particularly the boxwood hedges. There is a restaurant on the premises, with seating indoors and out. *VA 5E, then follow signs, tel. 804/829–6018. Admission: $7 adults, $4 teenagers, $3 children, $6.30 senior citizens. Open daily 8–5. Closed Christmas.*

What to See and Do with Children

Richmond Children's Museum is a hands-on experience with its own cave and make-believe activities. *740 N. 6th St., tel. 804/788–4949. Admission: $3 adults, $2 children 2–12. Open Tues.–Sun. (daily July–Aug.).*

Science Museum of Virginia, in John Russell Pope's erstwhile Union Station, offers many exhibits for children and adults. *2500 W. Broad St., tel. 804/367–1013. Admission: $3.50 adults, $3 children 4–17.*

Maymont House and Garden includes a children's farm and live animals native to Virginia among its gardens. The Victorian house was the turn-of-century home of civic leader James Dooley. *1700 Hampton St., in suburban West End, tel. 804/358–7166. Grounds open daily (admission free), other exhibits on seasonal schedule.*

The **King's Dominion** entertainment complex is strictly for children, but parents may revert to childhood under its influence. The more than 100 rides include simulated white-water rafting and a stand-up roller coaster. There is also a monorail ride through a game preserve and shows by trained dolphins and cartoon characters. *22 mi north on I–95, Doswell exit, tel. 804/876–5000. Admission: $23.95 adults, $15.95 children 3–6, $18.95 senior citizens, free for children under 3. Parking $3. Open June, daily 9:30–8; July–Aug., daily 9:30–10; Apr.–May, Sept.–Oct., weekends 9:30–8. Closed Oct.–Mar.*

Shopping

In general, banks are open weekdays 9–3, Saturdays 9–noon. Shops open at 10 AM Monday–Saturday, noon on Sunday. Malls stay open until 9 PM Monday–Saturday, 6 PM Sunday; downtown stores close at 5:30.

6th Street Marketplace, as you might guess, is between 5th and 7th—also between Grace and Leigh. Here you'll find more than 50 specialty shops, chain stores, and eateries.

Shockoe Slip (E. Cary St., between 12th and 15th Sts.), in the cobblestoned tobacco warehouse district of the 18th and 19th centuries, has boutiques and branches of such upscale stores as **Beecroft & Bull** and **The Toymaker of Williamsburg.**

At the **Farmers Market** (17th and Main Sts.) fresh produce is sold directly by the farmers. Nearby are boutiques, art galleries, and antiques shops, many in converted warehouses and factories.

Participant Sports

Within Richmond and the three suburban counties, there are open to the public—for free or at a nominal charge—405 tennis courts, 45 swimming pools, 20 golf courses, and seven miles of fitness trails. The following are just a few of the facilities available; the Visitor's Center (tel. 804/358–5511) and Division of Tourism (tel. 804/786–4484) have complete listings.

Golf **The Crossings** (tel. 804/266–2254), 20 minutes north of downtown in Glen Allen, at the intersection of I–95 and I–295,has an 18-hole that is course open to the public.

Jogging There is a **running track** in the park around the Randolph pool (on Idlewood St.) and a **fitness track** in Byrd Park (off The Boulevard).

Rafting From April through October, the **Richmond Raft Co.** (tel. 804/222–7238) offers guided white-water rafting through the heart of the city on the James River (Class 3 and 4 rapids), float trips upriver, and overnight camping/rafting trips.

Swimming Among the city-run outdoor pools—open only in summer—are the **Randolph pool** (on Idlewood Ave.), which has a little park with a running track and tennis and basketball courts, and the **Bell Meade pool** (off Jefferson Davis Hwy.); call the City Dept. of Recreation and Parks for more information, 804/780–5930.

Tennis **Byrd Park** (off The Boulevard) has lighted courts.

Spectator Sports

The **Richmond Coliseum** (tel. 804/780–4956), which seats 12,000, hosts ice shows, basketball games, wrestling matches, and tennis tournaments.

Auto Racing Twice a year, in September and February, races are held at the **Richmond Fairgrounds Raceway** (I–64, Exit Laburnum Ave. tel. 804/329–6796).

Baseball The Richmond Braves, a Triple-A farm team for Atlanta, play at **The Diamond** (tel. 804/359–4444), a 12,500-seat stadium.

Basketball Games at Randolph-Macon College, University of Richmond, Virginia Commonwealth University, and Virginia Union University are listed in the *Times-Dispatch* and the *News Leader*.

Dining

The most highly recommended restaurants in each price category are indicated by a star ★.

Category	Cost*
Very Expensive	over $30
Expensive	$20–$30
Moderate	$10–$20
Inexpensive	under $10

**per person without tax (8.5%), service, or drinks*

Very Expensive *Classic French* **La Petite France.** The atmosphere is formal, with emerald green walls and tuxedoed waiters. The traditional food and service set the standard for Richmond's best. Specialties include Dover sole amandine and chateaubriand. *2912 Maywill St., tel. 804/353–8729. Jacket and tie required. Reservations advised. AE, DC, MC, V. Closed Sun. and Mon.*

Expensive *Nouvelle Cuisine* **Mr. Patrick Henry's.** Two 1858 houses were restored and joined to make this restaurant and inn (upstairs there are three suites with kitchenettes and fireplaces). The dining room is Colonial in atmosphere, with antiques and fireplaces; there's also an English-style pub in the basement and a garden café. Especially popular dishes are the crisp roasted duck with crushed-plum sauce, and the crabcakes. *2300 E. Broad St., tel. 804/644–1322. Dress: informal. Reservations advised. AE, DC, MC, V. No dinner Sun.*

Moderate *Italian* **Amici Ristorante.** This restaurant features northern Italian cuisine. Game, including specialties such as stuffed quail and venison sautéed in juniper berry sauce, and duck, is regularly on the menu alongside fresh pasta and veal dishes. *3343 W. Cary St., tel. 804/353–4700. Dress: informal. Reservations advised. MC, V.*

Inexpensive *American* **Joe's Inn.** Spaghetti—especially spaghetti à la Greek, with feta and provolone cheese baked on top—is the specialty, but try the sandwiches, too. The regulars, who predominate at this local hangout in the Fan District, make outsiders feel right at home. *205 N. Shields Ave., tel. 804/355–2282. Dress: informal. Reservations not needed. AE, MC, V.*

Lodging

The most highly recommended properties in each price category are indicated by a star ★. For a map pinpointing locations, *see* Dining, *above*.

Category	Cost*
Very Expensive	over $120
Expensive	$90–$120

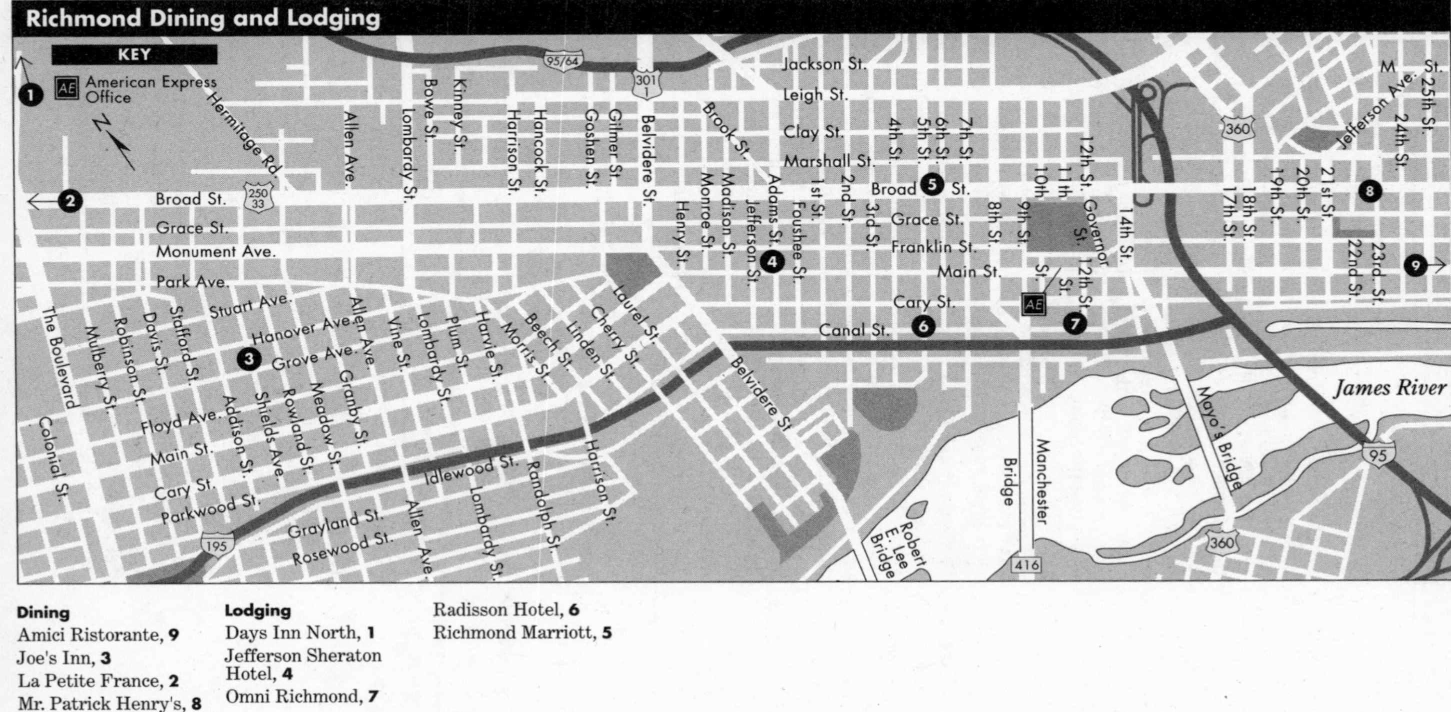
Richmond Dining and Lodging
KEY
American Express Office
James River
Mayo's Bridge
Manchester Bridge
Robert E. Lee Bridge
Jackson St.
Leigh St.
Clay St.
Marshall St.
Broad St.
Grace St.
Franklin St.
Main St.
Cary St.
Canal St.
Monument Ave.
Park Ave.
Stuart Ave.
Hanover Ave.
Grove Ave.
Floyd Ave.
Hermitage Rd.
The Boulevard
Colonial St.
Belvidere St.
Brook St.
Governor St.
Idlewood St.
Jefferson Ave.

Moderate	$50–$90
Inexpensive	under $50

**double room, highest rate in peak season; add 9.5% for taxes*

Very Expensive
★ **Jefferson Sheraton Hotel.** A regal, 26-step staircase reputedly used as a model for the one in the movie *Gone With the Wind* graces the lobby of this famous old downtown hotel. Built in 1895, it is a National Historic Landmark that has been restored to its former glory by Sheraton. Guests are given passes to the YMCA spa across the street. *Franklin and Adams Sts., 23220, tel. 804/788–8000 or 800/343–6320. 273 rooms, including 26 suites. Facilities: 3 restaurants, lounges. AE, D, DC, MC, V.*

Omni Richmond. This luxury hotel in the James Center Complex opened in 1987. Rooms are furnished in contemporary style, and the lobby is homey despite the Italian marble. *100 S. 12th St., 23219, tel. 804/344–7000 or 800/843–6664. 363 rooms, 12 suites. Facilities: indoor/outdoor pool; sun deck; health club with racquetball, squash courts, indoor track, Nautilus, whirlpool, saunas; 3 restaurants; bar. AE, D, DC, MC, V.*

Expensive
Radisson Hotel. Guest rooms in this wedge-shaped hotel in the business district have views of the Richmond skyline or the James River; triangular rooms at the point of the wedge have both views. The wallpaper is uniformly gray, carpeting is brown or pewter, and bedspreads have a paisley pattern whose colors match the carpeting. Guests get free covered parking and free transportation on request to area attractions and the airport. The three-story atrium lobby features an operating waterfall. Two concierge floors have additional amenities. *555 E. Canal St., 23219, tel. 804/788–0900 or 800/333–3333. 300 rooms. Facilities: 2 restaurants, 2 bars, nightclub, indoor pool, health club with Jacuzzi, saunas. AE, D, DC, MC, V.*

Richmond Marriott. The lobby of this luxury hotel near the 6th Street Marketplace has a marble floor and crystal chandeliers; rooms are furnished in a contemporary style. Concierge service is offered. *500 E. Broad St., 23219, tel. 804/643–3400 or 800/228–9290. 400 rooms. Facilities: 3 restaurants, nightclub, indoor pool, exercise room, tanning room. AE, D, DC, MC, V.*

Moderate
Days Inn North. This three-story motel is located 2 miles from downtown. *1600 Robin Hood Rd., 23220, tel. 804/353–1287. 87 rooms. Facilities: restaurant, bar, outdoor pool. AE, D, DC, MC, V.*

The Arts

The campus of Virginia Commonwealth University is usually teeming with artistic activity. Events here and throughout the city are listed in the *Times-Dispatch* and the *News-Leader*.

Theater
Barksdale Theatre, in historic Hanover Tavern (tel. 804/537–5333), built in 1723, was the first dinner theater in the country, founded in 1953. Performances are given Wednesday through Saturday. Touring companies are often featured at the **Carpenter Center** (tel. 804/782–3900), a restored 1928 motion-picture palace. A unique Moorish-style auditorium called **The Mosque** (tel. 804/780–4213), at Main and Laurel streets, is worth a peek even when the stage is dark. The **Swift Mill Creek Playhouse** (tel. 804/748–4411) is a dinner theater set in a 17th-century

gristmill. The Virginia Museum of Fine Arts maintains an equity theater, **Theatre Virginia** (tel. 804/367–0831).

Music The **Richmond Symphony** (tel. 804/788–1212), more than 30 years old, often features internationally known guest performers. Members of the orchestra perform as **The Sinfonia** for concerts of chamber music; and with popular guest artists, the versatile orchestra plays as **The Richmond Pops.**

Dance There are two professional ballet companies in town: the **Richmond Ballet** (tel. 804/359–0906) and the more experimental **Concert Ballet of Virginia** (tel. 804/780–1279).

Nightlife

Comedy The **Richmond Comedy Club** (1218 E. Cary St., tel. 804/745–3166) is modeled on successful establishments in New York and Los Angeles.

Folk At **The Jade Elephant** (909 W. Grace St., tel. 804/353–9674) you can enjoy cheap, well-made drinks while you listen to performers who usually appear solo.

Jazz **Benjamin's** (2053 W. Broad St., tel. 804/355–3667) is a favorite with younger Richmonders.

Bogart's (203 N. Lombardy St., tel. 804/353–9280) is a cozy club.

Rock **The Flood Zone** (18th and Main Sts., tel. 804/644–0935) is a converted recording studio where you can listen and dance to live music, or listen and watch from the balcony.

Tidewater and the Eastern Shore

The Historic Triangle comprises Williamsburg, Jamestown, and Yorktown, sites that figure crucially in the preindependent history of the United States. Williamsburg, once the capital of a colony that extended into present-day Minnesota, is now most famous for its Historic Area, restored to 18th-century perfection. Jamestown is where the English first settled successfully in North America; it is no longer an inhabited town. Yorktown, the site of the last major battle of the War of Independence, remains a living—albeit minuscule—community. The towns are linked by the scenic, 23-mile-long Colonial Parkway.

The enormous port of Hampton Roads—located where the Chesapeake Bay and the James River converge, and comprising Hampton, Newport News, and Norfolk—has been crucial in the discovery and settlement of this nation, the struggle for its independence, and the conflict that nearly dissolved its union. Past violence and hardship are a dramatic background for the busy and prosperous present day.

On the peninsula, Hampton hosts a famous weekend jazz festival in June and the even bigger "Bay Days" extravaganza, including fireworks and boat races, for three days in September. Norfolk is the U.S. headquarters for the North Atlantic Treaty Organization (NATO), which is honored in the annual Azalea Festival during the third week of April, when a queen from the year's honored member nation is chosen amid parades, air shows, dances, and exhibitions. The celebration resumes on the first full weekend in June during Harborfest, when the tall ships and more than one million guests come to town.

Virginia Beach is one of the most popular East Coast resorts. It is not a quiet seaside retreat but an entertainment mecca more likely to be enjoyed by the young. For those who crave natural beauty, largely undisturbed, the nearby Eastern Shore is an exquisite reward.

Arriving and Departing

By Plane Newport News–Williamsburg International in Newport News and Norfolk International are served by **USAir, United Express, Trans World Express, American Eagle, Westates.**

By Car I–64 runs northwest to intersect with I–95 at Richmond and southeast to the peninsula. U.S. 58 and VA 44 connect I–64 to Virginia Beach. U.S. 13 runs north from Virginia Beach over the Chesapeake Bay Bridge-Tunnel to the Eastern Shore.

By Train **Amtrak** (tel. 800/872–7245) trains stop at Williamsburg (468 N. Boundary St.) on their way from New York, Washington, and Richmond to Newport News. There is daily Amtrak service to Newport News (9304 Warwick Blvd.) from Boston and points in between.

By Bus **Greyhound-Trailways Lines:** Hampton (22 S. Armistead Ave., tel. 804/722–9861), Newport News (9702 Jefferson Ave., tel. 804/599–3900), Norfolk (701 Monticello Ave., tel. 804/627–5641), Virginia Beach (2402B Pacific Ave., tel. 804/422–2998), Williamsburg (468 N. Boundary St., tel. 804/229–1460).

Guided Tours

Orientation **Colonial Williamsburg** offers two-hour guided walking tours of the Historic Area every day. **Historic Air Tours** runs flights over the Colonial settlements, James River plantations, and historic battlefields. For information, write to Box 681, Williamsburg, 23187, or call 804/253–8185. The **Norfolk Tour** (tel. 804/441–5266) is a free self-guided driving or walking tour of the city's most popular attractions; at each you can pick up a leaflet with directions to the others, which are marked with blue-and-gold signs. From April through October the **Norfolk Trolley** (tel. 804/623–3222) takes you on a guided tour of the historic downtown area, letting you on and off as you please. Tickets are sold at the TRT kiosk outside the Waterside. Cost: $1.50 adults; 75¢ children, senior citizens, and the disabled.

Boat Tours **American Rover Sailing Tours** (tel. 804/627–7245), which operates a striking 135-foot topsail schooner, cruises Hampton Roads' nautical historical landmarks and the Norfolk naval base. The **Elizabeth River Ferry** (tel. 804/623–3222) from the Waterside in Norfolk to Portsmouth is faster and more fun than the tunnel, and it operates every day year-round. Cost: 75¢ adults; 50¢ children, senior citizens, and the disabled. The ***Carrie B*** (tel. 804/393–4735), a reproduction Mississippi riverboat, cruises Hampton Roads to give you a look at the naval shipyard, as well as the site of the Civil War battle between the *Monitor* and the *Merrimac*. The ***Miss Hampton II*** tour boat in Hampton (tel. 804/722–1102) offers a cruise on the bay that carries you past ships at the world's largest naval base and docks for a guided tour of pre–Civil War Fort Wool, recently opened to tourists. **Wharton's Wharf** (tel. 804/245–1533) in Newport News offers a comprehensive cruise of the harbor, and some special voyages on the James and the Intracoastal Waterway. On the Eastern Shore, you can take a guided tour of the Assateague Channel on a cruise boat or a Wildlife Safari boat ride through the Chincoteague National Wildlife Refuge from **Island Cruises** (tel. 804/336- 5511).

Special-interest Colonial Williamsburg's **Lanthorn Tours** takes visitors on an evening walking tour of selected trade shops where jewelry and other products are made the 18th-century way. A separate ticket is required for this program and may be purchased at the visitors center or Lumber House. Carriage and wagon rides are available daily, weather permitting. General ticket holders may purchase tickets on the day of the ride at the Lumber House (tel. 804/229–1000).

Important Addresses and Numbers

Tourist Information **Chincoteague Chamber of Commerce** (Box 258, Chincoteague 23336, tel. 804/336–6161), **Eastern Virginia Chamber of Commerce** (Drawer R, Melfa 23410, tel. 804/787–2460), **Hampton Tourist Information Center** (710 Settlers Landing Rd., Hampton 23669, tel. 804/727–1102), **Norfolk Convention and Visitors Bureau** (236 E. Plume St., Norfolk 23510, tel. 804/441–1852 or 800/368–3097), **Virginia Peninsula Tourism and Conference Bureau** (8 San Jose Dr., Suite 3B, Newport News 23606, tel. 804/873–0092 or 800/333–7787), **Virginia Beach Visitors Center** (19th St. and Pacific Ave., Virginia Beach 23451, tel. 804/425–7511 or 800/368–6511). **Williamsburg Area Tourism and Conference Bureau** (Drawer GB, 201 Penniman Rd., Williamsburg 23187, tel. 804/253–0192 or 800/368–6511).

Emergencies Dial 911 for emergency assistance.

Minor Emergencies **First Med. of Williamsburg** (tel. 804/229–4141) and **Community Emergency Care Center** (tel. 804/253–6005) in Williamsburg. **Sentara Medical Care Centers** in Hampton (tel. 804/850–4410), Newport News (tel. 804/599–6117 and 838–4288), Norfolk (tel. 804/583–0404), and Virginia Beach (tel. 804/671–1674 or 804/463–7062).

Exploring Tidewater and the Eastern Shore

Numbers in the margin correspond to points of interest on the Tidewater and Eastern Shore map.

1 Begin at **Colonial Williamsburg,** which is a marvel. The Historic Area comprises 173 acres of restored buildings populated by costumed interpreters and craftspeople. In the various shops you can observe coopers, milliners, wigmakers, and other tradesmen at their tasks, and their wares are for sale nearby. The taverns serve period-style food and beverages.

Begin at the visitor center, where you buy your tickets. Here you can watch an introductory movie, starring Jack Lord (of "Hawaii Five-O" fame) as an apocryphal patriot in the early 1770s. *I-64 Exit 56, tel. 804/229–1000. Admission: The Patriot's Pass ($26 adults, $12.50 children) is good for a year and admits the bearer to every Colonial Williamsburg–run site, including Bassett Hall and Carter's Grove Plantation. A range*

Tidewater and Eastern Shore

of less expensive tickets is available for those who haven't the time or inclination to see every site. Tickets are also sold at the courthouse in the Historic Area. In winter, some of the sites close down on a rotating basis; Carter's Grove closes in Jan. and Feb.; otherwise, every attraction except DeWitt Wallace (whose hours change frequently) is open daily. For a Vacation Planner, write Colonial Williamsburg, Box C, Williamsburg, VA 23187 (tel. 800/447–8679).

A good three or four days can be spent in Colonial Williamsburg alone—there's so much to see and do. Be sure to allow enough time, because this place is too good to rush through. You have to tour the Historic Area on foot, but in case you get tired, shuttle buses follow a route along the perimeter of the area and will take you to and from the visitor center. There are some 25 attractions on and off broad, mile-long Duke of Gloucester Street, which serves as the spine of the whole area; you should start at its east end, which is closest to the visitor center and includes the building that made the town so important.

At the east end of Duke of Gloucester is the **Capitol,** where you can take an informative tour that explains the early stages in the development of American democracy from its English parliamentary roots. Here the pre-Revolutionary House of Burgesses, made up of the rising gentry, challenged the bigger landowners who sat on the royally appointed Council, an almost medieval institution. It was the House that eventually arrived at the resolutions that amounted to rebellion. In the courtroom you'll hear the harsh Georgian sentences meted out: for instance, petty theft was a capital crime. Note this official building's ornate interior, characteristic of aristocratic Virginia—a marked contrast to the plain town meeting halls in New England, where other Founding Fathers were governing themselves.

The **Governor's Palace,** at the center of Duke of Gloucester Street, was completed in 1720 for Alexander Spotswood, and after the Revolution it housed the Commonwealth's first two governors, Patrick Henry and Thomas Jefferson. It burned in 1781; a 20th-century reconstruction stands on the original foundation. Little inside is original, but the antiques are matched to an extraordinary inventory of 16,000 items. The lavish decorations include 800 guns and swords arrayed on the walls and ceilings of several rooms.

Anchoring the west end of the street is the **Wren Building,** part of the campus of the College of William and Mary, the second-oldest college in the United States (founded in 1693). This building, erected in 1695, was based on the work of Sir Christopher Wren, the London architect for whom it was named—and who never made it to the Colonies. The professors' Common Room suggests Oxford and Cambridge, which were models for this institution. Jefferson studied and later taught law here—to James Monroe, among others.

Sharing the limelight with the handsome public buildings, restored homes, tidy reconstructed shops, and costumed interpreters are three very personal legacies from some modern-day benefactors of this historic town. The Public Hospital serves as Colonial disguise for the relatively new **DeWitt Wallace Decorative Arts Gallery** on Francis Street, where furniture, textiles, prints, metals, and ceramics from England and

America are on display. The collection includes a full-length portrait of Washington by Charles Willson Peale. The **Abby Aldrich Rockefeller Folk Art Center,** a mile away on South England Street (a good time to take the shuttle bus), is a showcase for American "decorative usefulwares," such as toys, furniture, weathervanes, and quilts, along with folk paintings and sculptures. This is a populist complement to the exquisite DeWitt Wallace. Eclectic and precious furnishings make **Bassett Hall** a most personal house museum. Mr. and Mrs. John D. Rockefeller, Jr., who bankrolled the restoration of Colonial Williamsburg, beginning in the 1920s, lived in this two-story 18th-century house among Chinese, American, and English antiques. The 19th-century Turkish prayer rugs are outstanding.

About six miles east of Williamsburg on U.S. 60 is the palatial
2 **Carter's Grove Plantation.** The house, built in 1750, is more luxurious than others of the period, since it was built as a showcase by Carter Burwell, whose grandfather King Carter had made his fortune elsewhere among the family's vast holdings. Though atypical, it is perfectly authentic and the epitome of Williamsburg in all its educational glamour. *Tel. 804/220–7649. Admission included in Patriots Pass; separately, $10. Open daily 9–5. Closed Jan., Feb., first 2 weeks in Dec.*

3 For sheer contrast, you might stop at **Busch Gardens,** three miles east of Williamsburg on U.S. 60. This 360-acre, razzle-dazzle family entertainment park features water and other rides, shows, and eight European hamlets (*see* What to See and Do with Children, *below*).

Nine miles west of Williamsburg on the Colonial Parkway is
4 **Jamestown Island,** the site, in 1607, of the first permanent English settlement in North America. All that is left of the city is its foundations and the ruins of a 1639 tower—now part of the Memorial Church, built on the site of the original. The island is ringed by a five-mile nature drive. There are guided tours daily during the summer and on spring weekends. *Tel. 804/229–1733. Cost: $5 per car, $2 per pedestrian or cyclist. Open daily 9–6:30 June–Labor Day, 9–5 rest of year. Closed Christmas.*

As you leave the island (which is linked by a small isthmus to the rest of Virginia), stop at **Glass House Point,** at the park entrance, to observe a demonstration of glass-blowing, an unsuccessful business venture of the early colonists.

5 Adjacent to Jamestown Island is **Jamestown Settlement,** a living-history museum formerly known as Jamestown Festival Park. A version of the early fort has been built, and within it "colonists" cook, make armor, and tell of a hard life under thatched roofs and between walls of wattle and daub. In the Indian Village, enter a wigwam and watch a costumed interpreter make tools and pottery. Stroll to the pier and inspect reproductions of the boats in which the settlers arrived. *Between Rte. 31 and Colonial Pkwy., tel. 804/229–1607. Admission: $7 adults, $3.50 children. Open daily 9–7 June 15–Aug. 15, 9–5 rest of year. Closed Christmas and New Year's Day.*

Fourteen miles east of Williamsburg on the Parkway is
6 **Yorktown Battlefield.** In the visitor center here is a museum with George Washington's original field tent, pitched and furnished as it was during the fighting. You can see the battlefield by self-guided auto tour, stopping at the signs. For $2 the gift

shop will rent you a cassette player with a taped tour to hear as you drive around. *Tel. 804/898–3400. Admission free. Visitor center open daily 8:30–5, with extended hours in the spring, summer, and fall. Closed Christmas.*

On the western edge of the battlefield is the **Yorktown Victory Center,** where you will find a Continental Army encampment, with tents and a covered wagon. Costumed soldier-interpreters will try to enlist you and then answer your questions. Indoor sight-and-sound presentations are arranged along a street of an "18th-century town." *Exit Colonial Pkwy. at VA 238, tel. 804/887–1776. Admission: $5.75 adults, $2.75 children. Open daily 9–5. Closed Christmas and New Year's Day.*

7 Follow Route 238 into **Yorktown,** whose Main Street is a picturesque array of preserved 18th-century buildings, many still in use. **Moore House,** where the terms of surrender were negotiated, and **Nelson House,** the residence of a Virginia governor and signer of the Declaration of Independence, are open for tours in summer. On adjacent Church Street is **Grace Church,** built in 1697 and still an active Episcopal congregation.

Thirty miles south of Williamsburg on I–64, near the tip of the
8 Virginia peninsula, is **Hampton,** the oldest existing continuous English-speaking settlement in the United States. Little from the earliest days survives because of repeated shellings and conflagrations over the years. Hampton's **Fort Monroe,** dating to 1834, is the only active-duty fort in the nation that is enclosed by a moat. A federal stronghold in Confederate territory, it was attacked by the *Merrimac* and defended by the *Monitor* in their famous battle near here. After the war, Confederate President Jefferson Davis was imprisoned for two years in a casemate (a chamber for the artillery within a fort's wall), which is now the **Casemate Museum.** Exhibits tell of the fort's history. *Rte. 258 (Mercury Blvd.), tel. 804/727–3391. Admission free. Open daily 10:30–5.*

It is not well known that the U.S. space program began in Hampton, the first headquarters of NASA. The history of the future is on display at the **Langley Research Center,** where astronauts trained for Project Mercury and Apollo missions. The visitor center has exhibitions on both aeronautics and space exploration, with artifacts from the moon landings, including a lunar rock. *Follow signs off I–64, tel. 804/864–6000. Admission free. Open Mon.–Sat. 8:30–4:30, Sun. noon–4:30. Closed Easter, Thanksgiving, Christmas, and New Year's Day.*

Hampton University, the alma mater of Booker T. Washington, is one of the nation's oldest and finest African-American and Native-American universities; it's also been designated a national monument. The **Hampton University Museum** houses an estimable collection of African-American and Native-American art from North America and Africa. *Corner Queen and Tyler streets (take I–64, exit 267, and follow signs to museum), tel. 804/727–5308. Admission free. Open Mon.–Fri. 8–5, Sat. and Sun. noon–4.*

9 Adjacent to Hampton is **Newport News** and the **Mariner's Museum,** whose exhibits cover the history of seafaring in all its aspects. Some of the hand-carved models are so tiny you must look at them through magnifying glasses; all are completely accurate. Full-size vessels are on display in surprising numbers, among them a sailing yacht, a speedboat, an Indian bark canoe,

a gondola, and even a Japanese submarine. A boat is usually under construction in one gallery. $3 million has been spent for renovation. *I–64, Exit 62A, tel. 804/595–0368. Admission: $4 adults, $3.50 senior citizens, $1.50 children. Open Mon.–Sat. 9–5, Sun. noon–5. Closed Christmas.*

The third town in the triumvirate that makes up the port of Hampton Roads, and the only one not on the peninsula, is
10 **Norfolk.** It is reached by way of the Hampton Roads Bridge-Tunnel. There is plenty to see in this old navy town, but it is rather spread out, so you will have to drive.

Norfolk Botanical Gardens, 175 acres close by the airport, is well known for abundant azaleas and camellias. From March into September, boats and trackless trains carry visitors along seasonal routes to different plants and flowers, including 4,000 roses and even a palm tree. *Azalea Garden Rd., off Norview Ave. (Airport exit off I–64), tel. 804/441–5386. Admission: $2. Boat and train tours: $2. Open daily 8:30–dusk.*

The **Hermitage Foundation Museum** is a 16th-century English Tudor–style house reproduced by Gilded Age textile tycoons. Inside is this country's largest private collection of Oriental art, including a 1,400-year-old marble Buddha from China, plus art from the Middle East, India, Europe, and America. You may picnic outside along the Lafayette River. *7637 North Shore Rd., tel. 804/423–2052. Admission: $4 adults, $2 children under 18, military free. Open Mon.–Sat. 10–5, Sun. 1–5. Closed Thanksgiving, Christmas, and New Year's Day.*

By any standards, the **Chrysler Museum** qualifies as a major American art museum; works by such artists as Gainsborough and Roy Lichtenstein suggest the collection's variety and stature. The comfortable exhibition spaces make this an inviting, rather than intimidating, experience. *Olney Rd. and Virginia Beach Blvd., tel. 804/622–2787. Admission free, donation suggested. Open Tues.–Sat. 10–4, Sun. 1–5. Closed July 4, Thanksgiving, Christmas, and New Year's Day. Closed Mon.*

The **Douglas MacArthur Memorial** is the burial place of the controversial war hero. Rooms adjoining the mausoleum house mementos of his career. Next door his staff car is on display and a 24-minute biography is screened continuously. *Bank St. and City Hall Ave., tel. 804/441–2965. Admission free. Open Mon.–Sat. 10–5, Sun. 11–5. Closed Thanksgiving, Christmas, and New Year's Day.*

The **Moses Myers House,** built in 1792, is exceptional not just for its elegance; Norfolk's first Jewish resident lived here. The original furnishings include family portraits by Gilbert Stuart and Thomas Sully. *323 E. Freemason St., tel. 804/622–1211. Admission: $2 adults, $1 students, military free. Jan.–Mar.: open Tues.–Sat. noon–5. Rest of year: open Tues.–Sat. 10–5, Sun. noon–5. Closed July 4, Thanksgiving, Christmas, and New Year's Day.*

The **Waterside,** at 333 Waterside Drive, is a shopping center billed as "Tidewater's festival marketplace." It is decorated in a nautical motif, appropriate to its location on the harbor. This is a comfortable place to eat and shop, and its TRT kiosk (tel. 804/623–3222) is the launching point for several tours (*see* Guided Tours, *above*).

Time Out **Doumar's** (20th St. and Monticello Ave., tel. 804/627–4163) is a drive-in restaurant founded in 1934 by the inventor of the ice-cream cone. Veteran waitresses carry to your car the specialties of the house: barbecue, natural limeade, and ice cream in fresh waffle cones made according to the original recipe.

The **U.S. Norfolk Naval Base** is an impressive sight. This is the home of more than 125 ships of the Atlantic and Mediterranean fleets, including the USS *Theodore Roosevelt*, a nuclear-powered carrier with a crew of 6,300—the second-largest warship in the world. In the winter, call the Naval Base Tour Office to schedule a sailor-guide to ride for free in your car. Tour buses operate year-round, departing from the TRT kiosk at the Waterside and from the Naval Base Tour Office. *Hampton Blvd., tel. 804/623–3222 or 444–7955. Admission: $4 adults; $2 children, senior citizens, and the disabled.*

11 **Virginia Beach** is 18 miles east of Norfolk, on the Atlantic Ocean. Here you will find the exquisite little **Adam Thoroughgood House,** built in 1636 and betraying its medieval English influences with every brick. The farmhouse's 17th-century garden is equally charming. *1636 Parish Rd., tel. 804/460–0007. Admission: $2 adults, $1 children. Open Tues.–Sat. 10–5, Sun. noon–5, Apr.–Dec.; Tues.–Sat. noon–5 rest of year. Closed Thanksgiving, Christmas, and New Year's Day.*

The sea is the subject at the **Virginia Marine Science Museum.** This massive facility, with more than 200 exhibits, became the most visited museum in the state in its first year of operation. You can predict the weather with computers, travel to the bottom of the sea in a simulated submarine, watch fish up close in tanks that re-create different underwater environments, and go birdwatching out back in the salt marsh, on a deck equipped with long-range scopes. *General Booth Blvd., ¼ mi south of the Rudee Bridge, tel. 804/425–3474. Admission: $4.25 adults, $3.85 senior citizens and $3.50 children. Open daily 9–5 (June 15–Sept. 15 Mon.–Sat. 9–9, Sun. 9–5).*

Take U.S. 13 north from Virginia Beach over the 17.5 miles of an engineering marvel: the **Chesapeake Bay Bridge-Tunnel.** This is a rare experience: you're surrounded by the sea while never leaving the comfort of your car. There is an observation pier and restaurant at the midpoint. On the other side is the Eastern Shore, where the wildlife, sea, and sun are abundant and humans, even in fashionable Chincoteague, are not.

Continue north on U.S. 13 for 63 miles to VA 175 to find the
most unspoiled spot on the Eastern Shore: unpopulated
12 **Assateague Island,** a 37-mile-long wildlife refuge and recreational area that extends into Maryland. The beaches and trails for hiking and biking are extensive and uncrowded. In addition to the exquisite scenery, as many as 300 species of birds can be seen here, including migrant geese and swans. The most famous residents are the wild ponies, supposedly descended from Spanish workhorses who survived a shipwreck off these shores. *Admission: $3 per car and $1 per pedestrian or cyclist. Wildlife drive closed to cars before 3 PM. The visitor center (tel. 804/336–6577) is open daily 9–4 (8–6 July–Aug.).*

13 **Chincoteague,** smaller and closer to shore, has a hardy, self-reliant population. On the last Thursday of July the ponies from Assateague are driven across the channel to Chincoteague,

where they are placed at auction; those unsold swim back home. The rest of the year is less exciting, but the proximity to fine beaches and natural beauty make the whole summer here a pleasant and relaxing vacation time. The **Oyster Museum** tells the history of the area. *Main St., tel. 804/336-6117. Admission: $1 adults, 25¢ children. Open daily 11-4:45 June-Aug., weekends 11-4:45 Mar.-May and Sept.-Nov. Closed Dec.-Feb.*

Both the museum and the Oyster Festival on Columbus Day weekend (a food fair with oysters in every form from stew to fritters) celebrate a great local industry. *Tickets to the festival are limited to 2,000 and must be purchased well in advance from the Chamber of Commerce, tel. 804/336-6161.*

14 **NASA's Wallops Visitor Center** is near Chincoteague on Wallops Island, at the site of early rocket launchings. Satellites are sent up from here occasionally, but what goes on mostly is atmospheric research. There is a collection of spacecraft, plus exhibits and videos about the program. *Tel. 804/824-2298 or 804/824-1344. Admission: free. Open July-Aug., daily 10-4; Thurs.-Mon. 10-4 rest of year. Closed major nonsummer holidays.*

What to See and Do with Children

In addition to guided walking tours especially for children (age four and older), **Colonial Williamsburg** often organizes special "Programs for Young People." Inquire at the courthouse.

Busch Gardens—a theme park based on "The Old Country," with environments evoking England, France, Italy, and Germany—is a mecca for the little ones, though not their exclusive preserve. There are rides, including a suspended roller coaster and water rafting; music and dancing; and plenty of food and drink (including Anheuser-Busch beer, for grown-ups). *3 mi east of Colonial Williamsburg on U.S. 60, tel. 804/253-3350. All-day tickets are $22.95, with different rates for longer and shorter visits. Parking $3. Hours vary widely; call to confirm. Open weekends only Apr.-mid-May, daily mid-May-Labor Day, Fri.-Tues. Labor Day-Oct. Closed Nov.-Mar.*

Virginia Zoological Park in Norfolk is the largest in the state, with 350 species living on 55 acres—including rhinos and ostriches as well as such domestic animals as sheep. With the assistance of docents, children may handle some animals. Performing elephants and sea lions, which may not be handled, make scheduled appearances. Next door, Lafayette Park has picnic shelters and facilities for tennis, basketball, football, and softball. *3500 Granby St., Norfolk, tel. 804/441-2706. Admission: $2 adults, $1 children, free before 11 AM. Open daily 10-5.*

Water Country USA, 3 miles east of Williamsburg on Route 199, has a dozen aquatic rides: Among them, the "Amazon" is a trip through tunnels and waterfalls on an inner tube big enough for two, and the "Jet Stream" is a flume the rider can slide down on an inner tube. A wave pool five times Olympic size is quiet for 10 minutes, then produces waves for 13 minutes; it is not suitable for swimming. *Rte. 199, tel. 804/229-9300 or 800/343-7946. Admission: $14.95 adults, $12.95 children, $10 senior citizens. Open Memorial Day-Labor Day, daily 10-7; late May and early Sept., weekends 10-7.*

Beaches

Along Water Street (Rte. 238) in **Yorktown** is a public beach for swimming and fishing. Right over the bridge across the York River, at **Gloucester Point,** is one that also has boat ramps. Beware of sea nettles (jellyfish) in July and August. The 14 miles of beach along the Chesapeake Bay in Norfolk are called **Ocean View Beaches.** The waters are, of course, much calmer than the ocean, and safer for children. There is good fishing here for sea trout and flounder. **Virginia Beach** has 28 miles of oceanfront. Nonetheless, it gets crowded during the summer. The lively boardwalk scene may be more of an attraction at that time of year. On the Eastern Shore, five miles of well-maintained beach, with bathhouses and picnic areas, are on the southern end of Assateague Island, at **Tom's Cove Hook.** Nearby, the ponies roam the 10 miles of **Wild Beach,** which is not supervised.

Participant Sports

Bicycling Colonial Williamsburg ticketholders can rent bicycles at the Lodge on South England Street; everyone else can try **Bikesmith** (tel. 804/229–9858) on York Street. A 20-mile route is mapped out in the pamphlet "Biking through America's Historic Triangle," available at bike shops.

Canoeing **Northwest River Park** in Chesapeake (tel. 804/421–3145) and **Munden Point Park** in Virginia Beach (tel. 804/426–5296) rent canoes for use on park property.

Fishing Charters are offered in season (Apr. or May through Oct.) by **Al Hartz Poquoson Charter Boats** (tel. 804/868–6821) and **Chesapeake Charter Service** (tel. 804/723–0998). For angling, try **Airfield Lake,** six miles east of Wakefield on Route 628. On Chincoteague Island, boat rentals, bait, and tackle are available through **Barnacle Bill's** (tel. 804/336–5188), **Captain Bob's** (tel. 804/336–6654), and **R&R Boats** (tel. 804/336–5465).

Golf **Colonial Williamsburg** (tel. 804/220–7696). operates two courses, nine- and 18-hole. **Kingsmill Resort** (tel. 804/253–3906), near Busch Gardens, has two courses. **Hampton Golf and Tennis** (tel. 804/727–1195) has an 18-hole course. **The Hamptons Golf Course** (tel. 804/766–9148) offers 27 holes. **Newport News Park** (tel. 804/886–2848) offers two 18-hole courses. **Lake Wright** (tel. 804/461–2246) in Norfolk and **Cypress Point** (tel. 804/490–8822) in Virginia Beach have 18-hole courses.

Tennis In Williamsburg, **Colonial Williamsburg** (tel. 804/220–7794) has six courts, **Kingsmill** (tel. 804/253–3945) has 10 clay and two hard courts open to the public, and there are public courts at **Kiwanis Park** on Longhill Road and at Quarterpath Park on Pocahontas Street. **Hampton Golf and Tennis** (tel. 804/727–1194) offers seven courts, and there are 14 at **Owl Creek** (804/422–4716) in Virginia Beach.

Water Sports In Virginia Beach, **Chick's Beach Sailing Center** (tel. 804/481–3067) has Windsurfer rentals and lessons; they also rent Hobie Cats. **Lynnhaven Dive Center** (tel. 804/481–7949) and **Scuba Ventures** (tel. 804/481–3132) offer scuba lessons, gear, and trips.

Spectator Sports

The **College of William and Mary** in Williamsburg fields varsity or club teams in football, basketball, baseball, track, wrestling, field hockey, soccer, swimming, tennis, and gymnastics. Check the weekly listings in the *Virginia Gazette* for specifics.

Auto Racing **Langley Speedway** (tel. 804/865–1992) in Newport News features late-model stock cars, grand stock, All-American stock, and ministock. Races are run March through September.

Baseball The **Peninsula Pilots** play at the Darling Stadium in Hampton (tel. 804/244–2255) April through August. The **Tidewater Tides** play at Metropolitan Park in Norfolk (tel. 804/461–5600) April through August.

Golf Kingsmill in Williamsburg hosts the **Anheuser-Busch Classic** every July.

Tennis The **Wightman Cup** women's tennis tournament is held at Williamsburg in October.

Dining

The most highly recommended restaurants in each price category are indicated by a star ★.

Category	Cost*
Very Expensive	over $30
Expensive	$20–$30
Moderate	$10–$20
Inexpensive	under $10

**per person without tax (4.5% sales tax plus local tax), service, or drinks*

Hampton
American

Buckroe's Island Grill. Architecturally and culturally, this is a two-level restaurant. At night, the second level of the Chesapeake Bay, lighthouse-style building features a large bar surrounded by a few tables. Outside the porch reverberates noisily with the voices of young adults and those who wish they were. The ground-level is more sedate. So is lunchtime. A limited but choice menu is offered. *1 Ivory Gull Crescent, Hampton 23664, tel. 804/850–5757. Dress: casual. Reservations suggested. AE, MC, V. Moderate.*

Seafood
★

Victor's. The rich soups set the standard for a superior meal. Specialties are veal scalloppine sauté, with Riesling sauce and chanterelle mushrooms, and venison with Zinfandel sauce and mushrooms. There's a long wine list and a wide choice of desserts. The place has a contemporary look, with mauve and green decor. Service is enthusiastic and polite. *700 Settlers Landing Rd., in the Radisson Hotel, tel. 804/727–9700. Dress: informal. Reservations advised. AE, D, DC, MC, V. Expensive.*

Norfolk
American

Kelley's. This sports bar offers the best cheeseburgers in town, as well as delicious homemade soups. There's musical entertainment on Sunday nights. *1408 Colly Ave., tel. 804/623–3216. Dress: informal. Reservations not needed. AE, MC, V. Inexpensive.*

Italian **Il Porto.** Plenteous portions of pasta, seafood, and veal are served in a dining room with a river view, and on the terrace in the warm months. The bar is bright and commodious, and there's a piano player to entertain most nights. *The Waterside, tel. 804/627–4400. Dress: informal. Reservations advised. AE, MC, V. Moderate.*

Seafood ★ **Ship's Cabin.** The steaks are as good as the fish—the filet-mignon-and-crabcake combination is perfect if you're really hungry—and there's a variety of fresh breads, including blueberry bread that's almost a dessert in itself. *4110 E. Ocean Ave., tel. 804/583–4659. Dress: informal. Reservations advised. AE, DC, MC, V. Expensive.*

Virginia Beach *Seafood* **Lighthouse.** There may be no better place in town for fresh seafood, especially shrimp and lobster. The six dining rooms all overlook the ocean or the inlet. *1st St. and Atlantic Ave., tel. 804/428–7974. Dress: informal. Reservations advised. AE, D, DC, MC, V. Expensive.*

Williamsburg *Continental* ★ **Regency Room.** This restaurant in the Williamsburg Inn is the place to dine if you're looking for an elegant atmosphere, attentive service, and excellent cuisine. Crystal chandeliers, oriental silkscreen prints, and full silver service set the tone. Specialties include rack of lamb, carved at the table; lobster bisque; and rich ice cream desserts. *S. Francis St., tel. 804/229–1000. Tie and jacket required for dinner and Sun. brunch; informal for breakfast and lunch. Reservations advised. AE, MC, V. Very Expensive.*

International ★ **Trellis.** Although it's in an old Colonial building, the hardwood floors, ceramic tiles, and green plants evoke the feeling of being in a country inn in the Napa Valley. There are five small, cozy dining rooms, one overlooking historic Duke of Gloucester Street. The wine vault has 8,000 bottles, most from California vineyards, a few from Virginia. Try the grilled swordfish served with crispy fried leeks and sautéed onions, and Death by Chocolate dessert, seven layers of chocolate topped with cream sauce. *Merchant Sq., tel. 804/229–8610. Dress: informal. Reservations advised. AE, MC, V. Expensive.*

Yorktown *Seafood* **Nick's Seafood Pavilion.** This riverside eatery has a wide selection of fresh seafood—including seafood shish kebab (lobster, shrimp, scallops, tomatoes, peppers, mushrooms, and onion, served with pilaf and topped with brown butter) and a buttery lobster pilaf—along with Chinese dishes and a fine baklava. *Water St., tel. 804/887–5269. Dress: informal. Reservations advised. AE, DC, MC, V. Expensive.*

Lodging

Cottages on Chincoteague Island are available for rental through **Vacation Cottages** (Rte. 1, Box 547, East Side Dr., Chincoteague 23336, tel. 804/336–3720). The most highly recommended properties in each price category are indicated by a star ★.

Category	Cost*
Very Expensive	over $120
Expensive	$90–$120

Moderate	$50–$90
Inexpensive	under $50

**double room, highest rate in peak season; add 4.5% sales tax plus local tax*

Hampton
Expensive

Radisson Hotel Hampton. Located on the downtown waterfront, this hotel offers a spectacular view, with floor-to-ceiling bay windows in every room. Next door is Carousel Park and the new Virginia Air & Space Center. *700 Settlers Landing Rd., 23669, tel. 804/727–9700 or 800/333–3333. 172 rooms. Facilities: roof-top pool, health club, bar, restaurant, lounge. AE, D, DC, MC, V.*

Moderate

Holiday Inn Hampton. Halfway between Colonial Williamsburg and Virginia Beach is this complex of buildings set on 13 beautifully landscaped acres. A recent addition is a four-story atrium with plants and fountains. *1815 W. Mercury Blvd., 23666, tel. 804/838–0200 or 800/465–4329. 324 rooms. Facilities: indoor/outdoor pools, spa, fitness course, exercise and game rooms, restaurant, lounge. AE, D, DC, MC, V.*

Norfolk
Expensive
★

Hilton–Airport. Don't let the gray cement exterior scare you away. Inside, this 2½-year-old highway-side Hilton is very pleasant. The six-story hotel has a concierge floor, an atrium, some king-size beds and free shuttle service to the airport. *1500 N. Military Hwy., 23502, tel. 804/466–8000 or 800/445–8667. 246 rooms, 4 suites. Facilities: outdoor pool, tennis, health club, 2 restaurants, 2 lounges with live jazz weekends, coffee shop. AE, D, DC, MC, V.*

Moderate

Holiday Inn–Waterside. Some rooms in this 12-story downtown inn have king-size beds and recliners. *700 Monticello Ave., Norfolk, 23501, tel. 804/627–5555 or 800/465–4329. 347 rooms. Facilities: outdoor pool, restaurant, nightclub. AE, D, DC, MC, V.*

Inexpensive

YMCA of Tidewater. An amazing bargain. This is a co-ed Y, with daily maid service, private baths. *312 W. Bute St., 23510, tel. 804/622–6328. 68 single rooms, 4 family rooms, 4 doubles. Facilities: health club, with indoor pool, indoor track, racquetball court, Nautilus. MC, V.*

Virginia Beach
Very Expensive

Cavalier Hotels. This resort complex combines the original Cavalier hotel—a 1920s six-story building on a hill, with traditional decor—and a modern, oceanfront high rise across the street. *Atlantic Ave. and 42nd St., 23451, tel. 804/425–8555 or 800/446–8199. 400 rooms. Facilities: private beach, indoor/outdoor pools, tennis and platform tennis, children's wading pool, playground, children's activities, baby-sitting service, 4 restaurants, 2 lounges with nightly entertainment in season. AE, D, DC, MC, V.*

Moderate

Idlewhyle Motel. This motel right on the beach usually caters to families, who can choose either efficiencies or guest rooms. *Atlantic Ave. and 27th St., 23451, tel. 804/428–9341. 23 rooms, 23 efficiencies. Facilities: coffee shop, indoor pool, sundeck. AE, MC, V.*

Williamsburg
Very Expensive
★

The Williamsburg Inn. Adjacent to the Historic Area, and owned and operated by Colonial Williamsburg, the inn is the grand hotel of Williamsburg. Built in 1932, it is decorated in luxurious English Regency style throughout. The surrounding

Colonial houses, also part of the inn, are decorated in Federalist style but with modern kitchens and baths. The Tazewell Club—a $5-million facility with full fitness offerings as well as conference rooms and executive suites—is available to guests of any of the Colonial Williamsburg operated properties. *136 E. Francis St., 23185, tel. 804/229–1000 or 800/447–8679. 235 rooms, 150 in inn, 82 in Colonial houses. Facilities: outdoor pool, golf, tennis, health club, restaurant, lounge, tavern. AE, MC, V.*

Expensive **Williamsburg Woodlands.** This newly renovated motel—another official Colonial Williamsburg hostelry—is on the grounds of the visitor center. Rooms are in separate buildings set in a pine grove. All inn facilities are open to motel guests. *Information Center Dr., 23187, tel. 804/229–1000 or 800/447–8679. 315 rooms. Facilities: 3 pools, miniature golf, putting green, tennis, playground, cafeteria, restaurant. AE, MC, V.*

Moderate **Heritage Inn.** This is a charming and comfortable inn one mile from the Historic Area. The three-story building is about 25 years old and decorated inside and out in Colonial style. *1324 Richmond Rd., 23185, tel. 804/229–6220 or 800/782–3800. 54 rooms. Facilities: outdoor pool with patio, restaurant. AE, DC, MC, V.*

Inexpensive **Bassett Motel.** Three blocks from the Historic Area, this single-story brick property is quiet, well run, and family oriented. *800 York St. (U.S. 60), Williamsburg, 23185, tel. 804/229–5175. 18 rooms. MC, V.*

The Arts

Music A variety of popular song and dance shows (country, gospel, opera, German folk) are held in several theaters at **Busch Gardens,** and the 5,000-seat Royal Palace Theater there features famous pop stars of every kind. The 10,000-seat W&M Hall at the **College of William and Mary** is also the scene of concerts by well-known artists on tour. The **Virginia Opera,** at Norfolk Center Theater (tel. 804/623–1223), is widely acclaimed for its regular company, and international stars have performed as guests. The season (Oct.–Mar.) often features world and American premieres. Concerts of all kinds are held year-round at the **Scope Center** (tel. 804/441–2161) in Norfolk.

Theater Student drama at the **College of William and Mary** (tel. 804/221–4000) goes on during the school year. In Norfolk, the **Virginia Stage Company** (tel. 804/627–1234) performs at Wells Theatre, Broadway shows on tour appear at **Chrysler Hall** (tel. 804/441–2161), and the **Tidewater Dinner Theater** (tel. 804/461–2933) performs Thursday through Sunday.

Nightlife

Rock **J.B.'s Lounge** at the Fort Magruder Inn near Williamsburg (tel. 804/220–2250) has a bar with some music and a transient crowd. **Frisbee's** (tel. 804/599–4488) is the most popular spot for rock in Newport News.

Jazz **Artifacts** is a piano bar in the lobby of the Norfolk Airport Hilton (tel. 804/466–8000).

Dance At the **Orient Express,** in the Norfolk Airport Hilton (tel. 804/466–8000), the latest dance tunes are performed live. **2000 West**

in the Interstate Inn Hampton (tel. 804/722–2000) has DJ and full band. **Gino's Restaurant & Lounge** in Hampton (tel. 804/722–0077) offers a DJ nightly and live band on weekends. **David's** in Portsmouth (tel. 804/393–6071) has dancing to top 40 and "progressive" music, a raw bar, and game room.

Index

Personal Itinerary

Departure *Date*

Time

Transportation

Arrival *Date* *Time*

Departure *Date* *Time*

Transportation

Accommodations

Arrival *Date* *Time*

Departure *Date* *Time*

Transportation

Accommodations

Arrival *Date* *Time*

Departure *Date* *Time*

Transportation

Accommodations

Addresses

Name

Address

Telephone

Name

Address

Telephone

Name

Address

Telephone

Name

Address

Telephone

Name

Address

Telephone

Name

Address

Telephone

Name

Address

Telephone

Name

Address

Telephone

Name

Address

Telephone

Name

Address

Telephone

Name

Address

Telephone

Name

Address

Telephone

Name

Address

Telephone

Name

Address

Telephone

Name

Address

Telephone

Name

Address

Telephone

Over 1500 Great Weekend Escapes...

in Six Fabulous Fodor's Guides to Bed & Breakfasts, Country Inns, Cottages, and Other Weekend Pleasures!

The Mid-Atlantic Region

The South

New England

The West Coast

England and Wales

Canada

Fodor's

Where the best memories begin

Fodor's Travel Guides

U.S. Guides

Alaska
Arizona
Boston
California
Cape Cod, Martha's Vineyard, Nantucket
The Carolinas & the Georgia Coast
Chicago
Disney World & the Orlando Area
Florida
Hawaii
Las Vegas, Reno, Tahoe
Los Angeles
Maine, Vermont, New Hampshire
Maui
Miami & the Keys
New England
New Orleans
New York City
Pacific North Coast
Philadelphia & the Pennsylvania Dutch Country
San Diego
San Francisco
Santa Fe, Taos, Albuquerque
Seattle & Vancouver
The South
The U.S. & British Virgin Islands
The Upper Great Lakes Region
USA
Vacations in New York State
Vacations on the Jersey Shore
Virginia & Maryland
Waikiki
Washington, D.C.

Foreign Guides

Acapulco, Ixtapa, Zihuatanejo
Australia & New Zealand
Austria
The Bahamas
Baja & Mexico's Pacific Coast Resorts
Barbados
Berlin
Bermuda
Brazil
Budapest
Budget Europe
Canada
Cancun, Cozumel, Yucatan Penisula
Caribbean
Central America
China
Costa Rica, Belize, Guatemala
Czechoslovakia
Eastern Europe
Egypt
Euro Disney
Europe
Europe's Great Cities
France
Germany
Great Britain
Greece
The Himalayan Countries
Hong Kong
India
Ireland
Israel
Italy
Italy's Great Cities
Japan
Kenya & Tanzania
Korea
London
Madrid & Barcelona
Mexico
Montreal & Quebec City
Morocco
The Netherlands Belgium & Luxembourg
New Zealand
Norway
Nova Scotia, Prince Edward Island & New Brunswick
Paris
Portugal
Rome
Russia & the Baltic Countries
Scandinavia
Scotland
Singapore
South America
Southeast Asia
South Pacific
Spain
Sweden
Switzerland
Thailand
Tokyo
Toronto
Turkey
Vienna & the Danube Valley
Yugoslavia

Special Series

Fodor's Affordables

Affordable Europe

Affordable France

Affordable Germany

Affordable Great Britain

Affordable Italy

Fodor's Bed & Breakfast and Country Inns Guides

California

Mid-Atlantic Region

New England

The Pacific Northwest

The South

The West Coast

The Upper Great Lakes Region

Canada's Great Country Inns

Cottages, B&Bs and Country Inns of England and Wales

The Berkeley Guides

On the Loose in California

On the Loose in Eastern Europe

On the Loose in Mexico

On the Loose in the Pacific Northwest & Alaska

Fodor's Exploring Guides

Exploring California

Exploring Florida

Exploring France

Exploring Germany

Exploring Paris

Exploring Rome

Exploring Spain

Exploring Thailand

Fodor's Flashmaps

New York

Washington, D.C.

Fodor's Pocket Guides

Pocket Bahamas

Pocket Jamaica

Pocket London

Pocket New York City

Pocket Paris

Pocket Puerto Rico

Pocket San Francisco

Pocket Washington, D.C.

Fodor's Sports

Cycling

Hiking

Running

Sailing

The Insider's Guide to the Best Canadian Skiing

Fodor's Three-In-Ones (guidebook, language cassette, and phrase book)

France

Germany

Italy

Mexico

Spain

Fodor's Special-Interest Guides

Cruises and Ports of Call

Disney World & the Orlando Area

Euro Disney

Healthy Escapes

London Companion

Skiing in the USA & Canada

Sunday in New York

Fodor's Touring Guides

Touring Europe

Touring USA: Eastern Edition

Touring USA: Western Edition

Fodor's Vacation Planners

Great American Vacations

National Parks of the West

The Wall Street Journal Guides to Business Travel

Europe

International Cities

Pacific Rim

USA & Canada

WHEREVER YOU TRAVEL, HELP IS NEVER FAR AWAY.

From planning your trip to providing travel assistance along the way, American Express® Travel Service Offices* are always there to help.

For the office nearest you, call

1-800-YES-AMEX

American Express Travel Service Offices are found in central locations throughout the South.

*Comprises Travel Service locations of American Express Travel Related Services Company, Inc., its affiliates and Representatives worldwide. © 1992 American Express Travel Related Services Company, Inc.